OXFORD WORLD'S CLASSICS

THE OXFORD SHAKESPEARE

General Editor · Stanley Wells

The Oxford Shakespeare offers new and authoritative editions of Shakespeare's plays in which the early printings have been scrupulously re-examined and interpreted. An introductory essay provides all relevant background information together with an appraisal of critical views and of the play's effects in performance. The detailed commentaries pay particular attention to language and staging. Reprints of sources, music for songs, genealogical tables, maps, etc. are included where necessary; many of the volumes are illustrated, and all contain an index.

JILL L. LEVENSON, the editor of *Romeo and Juliet* in the Oxford Shakespeare, is Professor of English, Trinity College, University of Toronto.

THE OXFORD SHAKESPEARE

Currently available in paperback

All's Well that Ends Well
Anthony and Cleopatra
As You Like It
The Comedy of Errors
The Complete Sonnets and Poems
Coriolanus
Cymbeline
Hamlet
Henry V
Henry IV, Part 1
Henry IV, Part 2
Henry VI, Part One
Henry VI, Part Two
Henry VI, Part Three
Julius Caesar
King Henry VIII
King John
King Lear
Love's Labour's Lost
Macbeth
Measure for Measure
The Merchant of Venice
The Merry Wives of Windsor
A Midsummer Night's Dream
Much Ado About Nothing
Richard III
Pericles
Romeo and Juliet
The Taming of the Shrew
The Tempest
Timon of Athens
Titus Andronicus
Troilus and Cressida
Twelfth Night
The Two Noble Kinsmen
The Winter's Tale

The rest of the plays are forthcoming.

OXFORD WORLD'S CLASSICS

WILLIAM SHAKESPEARE

Romeo and Juliet

Edited by

JILL L. LEVENSON

OXFORD
UNIVERSITY PRESS
Great Clarendon Street, Oxford OX2 6DP

Oxford University Press is a department of the University of Oxford. It furthers the University's objective of excellence in research, scholarship, and education by publishing worldwide in

Oxford New York

Athens Auckland Bangkok Bogotá Buenos Aires Cape Town Chennai Dar es Salaam Delhi Florence Hong Kong Istanbul Karachi Kolkata Kuala Lumpur Madrid Melbourne Mexico City Mumbai Nairobi Paris São Paulo Shanghai Singapore Taipei Tokyo Toronto Warsaw

with associated companies in Berlin Ibadan

Oxford is a registered trade mark of Oxford University Press in the UK and in certain other countries

Published in the United States by Oxford University Press Inc., New York

First published by the Clarendon Press and as an Oxford World's Classics paperback 2000
Reissued 2008

British Library Cataloguing in Publication Data
Data available

Library of Congress Cataloging in Publication Data
Shakespeare, William, 1564–1616.
Romeo and Juliet / edited by Jill L. Levenson.
(Oxford world's classics)
Includes index.
1. Vendetta—Italy—Verona—Drama. 2. Youth—Italy—Verona—Drama. I. Levenson, Jill L. II. Title. III. Series: Shakespeare, William, 1564–1616. Works. 1982.
PR2831.A2L48 2000 822.3′3—dc21 99–41084

ISBN 978–0–19–953589–7

4

Typeset by Jayvee, Trivandrum, India
Printed in Great Britain by
Clays Ltd, St Ives plc

PREFACE

My appreciation of *Romeo and Juliet* grew when I first had to teach it to undergraduates who wanted no part of its sentiment. As a result I began to explore other dimensions of the play, most of them contributing to its witty experimentation not only with a familiar story but also with various styles: verse and rhetoric, tragedy and comedy. In the 1980s I had the opportunity to write a small book about its theatre history; it turned into another fascinating pursuit. Assembling this edition has been a labour of love, the culmination of work on many aspects of a brilliant text.

I owe a great deal to the play's most recent editors for their scholarship: Brian Gibbons, G. Blakemore Evans, and John Jowett. Thanks to the co-operation of Oxford University Press, I also had access to R. B. McKerrow's unpublished notes for the Oxford Shakespeare. Many colleagues have made significant additions to my research. Until the edition went to press both Shakespearians and non-Shakespearians sent information they thought would be useful, sometimes their own still unpublished material: the latest items came from Katherine Duncan-Jones, Barbara Hodgdon, M. J. Kidnie, and Hersh Zeifman. Others, like Patricia Brückmann, continued to check documentation or evaluate data until the last minute. My colleagues in Ontario have shown exceptional patience as I've imposed on their good natures with endless questions and theories. In particular Brian Parker has been, as always, a generous mentor; Randall McLeod and Paul Werstine have also raised important issues which I've attempted to address; Ian Lancashire helped me to interpret scholarship on database. Lawrence Kerslake facilitated correspondence about a French production, making telephone calls and translating letters.

The Commentary to this edition incorporates details from 170 or so prompt books. That theatre history is now publicly available as a database, the concept of my former student and valued colleague David Galbraith. As he implemented this idea—transferring paper and microfilm data to a Web site at the Centre for Reformation and Renaissance Studies at the University of Toronto—he was assisted especially by Margaret McGeachy and William Bowen. I had a

Standard Research Grant (1992–5) from the Social Sciences and Humanities Research Council of Canada to defray the cost of the database and textual research for the edition.

In collating early texts and studying prompt books I depended upon many libraries and special collections. For their interest and exceptional service I want to single out Marian J. Pringle, Senior Librarian, and her staff at the Shakespeare Centre, Stratford-upon-Avon; Niky Rathbone, Shakespeare Librarian, and her staff at the Shakespeare Library in the Birmingham Reference Library; Dorothy L. Swerdlove and the staff at the Theatre Collection of the New York Public Library; and the staffs at the British Library, the Huntington Library, and the Theatre Museum, London. Without the library resources at the University of Toronto—Rare Books, the Robarts Library, and Trinity Library—with their very fine staffs, I would not have been able to complete this book: I wrote most of it in my carrel at the main library while Elsie Del Bianco, skilled and always courteous, persevered with various searches at Trinity Library until the volume was ready to be printed.

It has been a great pleasure belonging to the team that produces the Oxford Shakespeare, not least because Stanley Wells, the General Editor, is himself a model editor who graciously offered his expertise and time whenever they were needed to keep the volume on track. In his openness to new approaches and his tolerance of my painstaking research methods he has been reinforced by Frances Whistler at Oxford University Press. Christine Buckley was the excellent copy-editor of this book, not only dealing with the mechanics of production, but also raising significant questions about content from type-setting to friars' garb. Janet MacLellan was typically smart and conscientious in preparing the index. If any flaws remain, they are my responsibility.

Finally, I want to thank the generations of students who have shared this play with me, among them the Trinity College Drama Society who performed my text of Quarto 2 in 1997. I am most grateful to my friends and family, who have had to compete with this project for my attention. My mother has seen it through from the beginning to final proofs. Whatever inconveniences I may have caused her, she has remained my most loyal and enthusiastic fan.

JILL L. LEVENSON

CONTENTS

Aerosmith

Guns and Roses

The cure

Jaded

The Killers

LIST OF ILLUSTRATIONS

INTRODUCTION

The Romeo and Juliet Narrative before Shakespeare

IN an age of virtual realities Shakespeare's *Romeo and Juliet* can seem like a hologram. From one angle it appears to dramatize a love-story which transcends time and place. The youthful passion it enacts may cease like lightning, but it reflects an absolute, an ideal of sexual love expressed in the play's most lyrical verse. From another angle the tragedy enacts a love-story shaped by the social and literary conventions of late sixteenth-century England. These give the narrative a political edge and historicity, moderating its idealism. Since the advent of modern psychology a third angle allows for a different construction formulated on change rather than absolutes. From this point of view Shakespeare traces a paradigm of adolescent behaviour.

These perspectives, one by one or in combination, reveal a complex and even contradictory play. With little adjustment they reveal similar complexities in the popular fiction enacted by the play. Pre-existing novellas which transmitted the Romeo and Juliet story incorporate elements of myth and romance into narratives of a different kind. A new genre, they depended on a rhetorical tradition that promoted not only invention and variety but verisimilitude.[1] Shakespeare's well-known alterations—telescoping events and coincidence, elaborating characters, heightening rhetoric—enhance the heterogeneous design, calling attention to the inconsistencies which form the narrative, the coexistence of the timeless and the timely.

As a result, the design of the fiction has determined the play's effect in different periods and cultures. It originated in archetypes which probably account for the emotional impact of Shakespeare's tragedy and its derivatives in media such as music and drama. It adapted to changing historical circumstances—sixteenth-century Italian city states, Elizabethan England, America in the 1950s—and mirrored the world of each audience with varying degrees of realism. Its literature was at first self-consciously rhetorical,

[1] Robert J. Clements and Joseph Gibaldi, *Anatomy of the Novella: The European Tale Collection from Boccaccio and Chaucer to Cervantes* (New York, 1977), pp. 8–18.

attempting to win readers and achieve credibility. Once it became familiar in the sixteenth century, any artist could play on expectation by altering its prototypes. Shakespeare was the first to modify not only events and characters but style, creating a version which would become the model for those to follow. In the process he left traces of his strategy. Recovering the fiction will therefore permit a glimpse of the artist at work.

Myth. The primary source of the Romeo and Juliet fiction is myth, the early narratives 'obscure in origin, protean in form and ambiguous in meaning'.[1] Despite this amorphousness, mythical narratives share certain features which help to define them. They are simple, bold, and symbolical, epitomizing a vast number of analogous stories.[2] They deal in ideas or desires which are timeless, 'ordering . . . human experience at a level . . . wider, deeper, and more permanent than the rationalized scene and the literal facts of the moment'.[3] According to Northrop Frye, 'myth is the imitation of actions near or at the conceivable limits of desire', in a space where the human encounters the divine.[4] There may have been half a dozen myths that governed all the rest, narratives concerned with rites of passage in this world and upheavals among the gods. Whatever shape they took, these stories became the matrix of literature.[5]

Wagner gave the name *Liebestod* to the myth which informs the fiction of Romeo and Juliet. Although the meaning of this term shifts—love-in-death, death-in-love, love's death—it refers to a specific narrative format and psychological event. Two young lovers face insurmountable obstacles; they encounter the obstacles with defiance and secret plans, but their resistance fails because of accident or misjudgement; finally both die for love.[6] By linking passion with death the *Liebestod* myth sets the limits of desire at the highly charged point where lovers feel they have transcended

[1] K. K. Ruthven, *Myth*, The Critical Idiom, 31 (1976), p. 1.

[2] Denis de Rougemont, *Love in the Western World*, trans. Montgomery Belgion, rev. edn. (Princeton, 1983), p. 18.

[3] Francis Fergusson, *The Idea of a Theater: A Study of Ten Plays: The Art of Drama in Changing Perspective* (Princeton, 1949), p. 72.

[4] *Anatomy of Criticism: Four Essays* (Princeton, 1957), p. 136.

[5] See Ruthven, *Myth*, p. 58.

[6] Maya C. Bijvoet, *Liebestod: The Function and Meaning of the Double Love-Death* (New York and London, 1988), pp. 2–3.

ordinary human experience, driven to union which means dissolution of self, a permanent metamorphosis. Paradox dominates a narrative in which the compulsion to love is a compulsion to die, and death is the price for an absolute. In this psychological configuration suffering becomes aphrodisiac and passion is brief.

Between antiquity and the Middle Ages the *Liebestod* myth took shape not only in folklore but in literature. A range of storytellers from the anonymous to Ovid and Malory related the misadventures of Hero and Leander, Pyramus and Thisbe, Tristan and Isolde. In their variety the stories qualify Denis de Rougemont's view that the myth descended into 'profane' life from the thirteenth century:[1] they quickly became particularized through their settings and obstacles;[2] the medieval versions immediately absorbed the conventions of chivalry. During the early Christian era components of the myth circulated through Greek romance, notably the separation plots and character types such as young lovers and opposing parents. Romance included other elements which would attach themselves to the Romeo and Juliet legend, specifically the sleeping potion and premature burial. Whether they transmitted the myth whole or piecemeal, all of the literary versions were rhetorical to different degrees of sophistication.

If *Liebestod* is the keynote, other myths resonate with the Romeo and Juliet legend. For instance, Marjorie Garber has identified correspondences with the story of Cupid and Psyche, which also connects marriage and death: the love-relationship takes place in a surround of darkness; a young woman becomes free of paternal control; she undergoes a series of trials which mark her progress to maturity.[3] Typically both of these myths centre on rites of passage, those crucial advances in an individual life from one biological or social condition to another. The most widely accepted description of such rites enumerates three phases: separation from the old state, transition between old and new, incorporation into the new. During the middle phase initiates hover in liminality, a period of suspension or ambiguity which is both dangerous and liberating.[4]

[1] *Love in the Western World*, p. 170.

[2] Bijvoet, *Liebestod*, pp. 9–10.

[3] *Coming of Age in Shakespeare* (London and New York, 1981), pp. 165–70.

[4] Garber, *Coming of Age in Shakespeare*, pp. 5–12, summarizes the work of Arnold van Gennep and Victor Turner. See also Rush Rehm, *Marriage to Death: The Conflation of Wedding and Funeral Rituals in Greek Tragedy* (Princeton, 1994), p. 5.

In fact and fiction young lovers exist in this liminal phase on the verge of adult commitment to both a sexual partner and society. The *Liebestod* myth and its literary versions catch them at that moment of change, failing to make a transition into the community, alone at the turning-point. The story of Cupid and Psyche focuses on the initiation of the young woman. In both cases the rituals which normally accompany such rites of passage become part of the narrative, incomplete in various ways or conspicuous by their absence. Marriage is the most striking of these rituals: Pyramus and Thisbe never reach this state; Hero and Leander take a private vow; initially Psyche weds Cupid without seeing him; Tristan and Isolde marry other partners and consummate their own relationship in adultery. By the sixteenth century the Romeo and Juliet story would incorporate night visits and funeral in addition to marriage. Decades before the sixteenth century, however, the combination of traditional myth and contemporary ritual manifested disturbance not only in the private sphere of the lovers but in the public sphere represented by their social world.[1]

Novella. The Romeo and Juliet story familiar to Shakespeare's audience originated in Italy during the fifteenth century. Masuccio Salernitano included most of the plot in the thirty-third tale of his *Novellino* (1476), the story of Mariotto and Ganozza. During the fifty-odd years between this version and Luigi da Porto's *Historia novellamente ritrovata di due nobili amanti . . .* (*c.*1530), a legend which corresponds with the Romeo and Juliet narrative seems to have grown very popular, especially in northern Italy. Stories extant in manuscripts from the fifteenth and early sixteenth centuries preserve the topos of love and death, combining it with details from romance. When da Porto assembled the full-scale narrative, he probably drew not only on Masuccio, but on the legendary material, an anonymous fifteenth-century novella ('Ippolito e Lionora'), Ovid's account of Pyramus and Thisbe (*Metamorphoses* 4.67–201), and Boccaccio's *Decameron*. Da Porto showed originality less through inventiveness than through conflation of the various models.[2] As motive for the secret marriage he incorporated a feud

[1] Rehm, *Marriage to Death*, pp. 7–9 and 136–40, draws a similar conclusion about Greek tragedy.

[2] For da Porto's sources, see George H. Bumgardner, Jr., 'An Antecedent of *Romeo and Juliet*', *Yale University Library Gazette*, 49 (1975), 268–76; Barry Jones,

analogous to civil disturbances in late medieval Italy; and he attributed this state of affairs to the Montecchi and Cappelletti, names of political factions which first appeared in Dante's *Purgatorio* 6.106–8.

Da Porto's formulation proved highly successful, and it determined the course of the narrative in at least two ways. At the most basic level it established a sequence of twelve incidents which would remain fundamentally unchanged through the sixteenth century: Romeo's initial, abortive love affair; the Capulet feast, where Romeo and Juliet first encounter each other and immediately become enamoured; the meeting at Juliet's house,[1] when they plan to marry; the carrying out of these plans with the assistance of a friar; the brawl between Montagues and Capulets which leads to Romeo's banishment; Romeo and Juliet's leave-taking of each other; the Capulets' arrangement for Juliet to marry a man of their choice; Juliet's appeal to the friar for help, resulting in the potion scheme; Juliet's false death, reported to the exiled Romeo as true; the scene in the tomb, where both lovers die; the governor's distribution of justice; and the reconciliation of the two families.

More significantly, da Porto's version constructed the story as a novella, a recent genre; and the four derivatives which transmitted the narrative from Italy to France and England borrowed its form as well as its content. The lineage of Shakespeare's *Romeo and Juliet*, beginning with da Porto's novella, continues through Matteo Bandello's version in his *Novelle* (1554); Pierre Boaistuau's translation of Bandello in his *Histoires tragiques, extraictes des oeuures italiennes de Bandel, & mises en nostre langue françoise. Les six premieres, par Pierre Boisteau* . . . (1559); Arthur Brooke's verse translation of Boaistuau, *The Tragicall Historye of Romeus and Juliet written first in Italian by Bandell, and nowe in Englishe by Ar. Br.* (1562; generally accepted as Shakespeare's immediate source); and William Painter's prose translation of Boaistuau, 'The goodly Hystory of the true, and constant Loue between Rhomeo and Ivlietta . . .', in *The Palace of Pleasure* (1567).[2]

'Romeo and Juliet: Boccaccio and the Novella Tradition', *Stanford Italian Review*, 1 (1979), 75–99; and Luigi Monga, 'Romeo and Juliet Revisited: More *novelle* from the Italian Renaissance', *Manuscripta*, 33 (1989), 47–53.

[1] Da Porto gives only passing attention to Romeo's first infatuation, and creates two meetings at Juliet's house when the lovers plan marriage.

[2] Da Porto and Bandello inspired the other three extant versions of the tale: Adrian Sevin's brief fictional version (1541–2), another novella; Clizia's *Giulia e*

These five novellas do not qualify as masterpieces, but few novellas did after Boccaccio's. Starting with Roger Ascham's complaints in *The Scholemaster* (1570), many critics of early Renaissance fiction have expressed impatience with the genre, which they repeatedly describe as philistine: eventful, prolix, and wanting intellectual content. Whatever its literary value, however, the novella established a cultural background for the events it related. In this instance, it helps to account for the peculiar complexity of the Romeo and Juliet sequence. Each of the novellas in the main line of descent reflects contemporary social, economic, and political realities with subtle differences, and each conveys its historicized plot through rhetorical devices which argue its authenticity.

Only Bandello's novella has received extended analysis in historical terms. Barry Jones demonstrates how social and economic conditions during the Italian Renaissance affected attitudes towards marriage, and how the conditions and attitudes shaped the literary material.[1] In particular, standards for consolidating the city state, and prosperous families, influenced characterization. All of Bandello's male figures try to curb disruptive elements in their society; no one challenges men of authority in church or government. Even Romeo speaks at length as a reasonable pacifist, notably in the episode where Tebaldo's assault on him provokes the fatal counter-attack. By comparison Giulietta loses self-control and drives the action more forcefully towards catastrophe; she embodies various threats to a masculine ideal of social order. At the same time she represents the position of women as capitalism altered the exchange pattern in the economy and therefore in marriage. According to this system, women could earn interest—like a bill of exchange rather than an item of intrinsic worth—and their transfer implied the creation of surplus value. Giulietta, already commodified by da Porto's formal marriage arrangements, becomes a 'kind of goods' ('è mercadanzia') with Bandello's.[2]

Romeo (1553), a long poetic version of a novella in ottava rima; and Luigi Groto's *La Hadriana* (1578), a novella masquerading as a tragic drama.

[1] '*Romeo and Juliet*: The Genesis of a Classic', in *Italian Storytellers: Essays on Italian Narrative Literature*, ed. Eric Haywood and Cormac Ó Cuilleanáian (Dublin, 1989), pp. 150–81. The following interpretation of Bandello is based on this essay. See also Jones's 'Romeo and Juliet: Boccaccio and the Novella Tradition', 75–99.

[2] *Novelle*, ed. Giuseppe Guido Ferrero (Turin, 1974), p. 458.

In such a context the love affair itself turns into an obstacle. Since Bandello was a Dominican friar, it comes as no surprise that his dedication promises an exemplary tale urging temperance.[1] Yet the tragic course of events in this novella and the tentative reconciliation at the end do more than illustrate the virtues of moderation in an abstract sense. On another level, they promote the interests of the ruling oligarchies in a world where social pursuits and commerce secured a mercantilist economy. Jones explains that Renaissance city states now emphasized extended families and family alliances. As church and state became reconciled, they reasserted prohibitions against clandestine marriages. The *Decameron*, both an indirect and immediate source for Bandello, announced this phase of Europe's economic and social history. When it uses its legacy, Bandello's version approves patriarchy, discredits women, and argues its points of view.[2] It filters myth through ideology, not only acting out the new commercialism through events, but recording its idiom. At the Capelletti ball Romeo examines the young women critically, as if he were in the market to buy a doublet or a horse; at Fra Lorenzo's monastery, in a rare moment of wordplay, Giulietta describes Count Paris of Lodrone as a thief ('ladrone') who steals another's property.[3]

Of course the novella changed as it crossed national borders, a point made by H. B. Charlton in 1939,[4] and modifications to the narrative's content or style locate the Romeo and Juliet story at different cultural sites. In Boaistuau's version, the ominous premonitions, deadlier feud, and final distribution of punishments cast Bandello's Verona and its ideology in a less flattering light. Boaistuau reflects a more negative view of contemporary values, pessimism which he expressed in his 1558 treatise with its inclusive title: *Le Theatre du monde, où il faict un ample discours de toutes les*

[1] *Novelle*, p. 439.

[2] Jones, '*Romeo and Juliet*: The Genesis of a Classic', pp. 158–60, and 'Romeo and Juliet: Boccaccio and the Novella Tradition', 76–8. Appropriately Bandello makes Romeo's first love hard-hearted (*Novelle*, pp. 440–1); Boaistuau and his English translators would attribute her resistance to a virtuous upbringing.

[3] *Novelle*, pp. 443, 461.

[4] 'France as Chaperone of Romeo and Juliet', in *Studies in French Language and Mediaeval Literature Presented to Professor Mildred K. Pope* (Manchester, 1939), pp. 43–59. Charlton bases his argument on differences in literary techniques, which he judges according to his own preference for naturalism: he concludes that Bandello was a genius, Boaistuau a bore.

miseres de l'homme, ensemble de plusieurs vices qui regnent pour le jourd'huy en tous les estats de la terre. A humanist who practised science, Boaistuau was writing at a time when political and religious crises in France threatened almost all systems of community. Nevertheless, one social institution remained constant, in economic and other ways, as Natalie Zemon Davis defines the historical moment:

> Despite all this slippage of life, the image of the patriarchal family stayed firmly in place. Marriage customs varied considerably from province to province and from class to class, and rules of succession were even more diverse, but everywhere the family was conceived as a unit from which one took identity, dowry, or inheritance and then passed these on, enhanced if possible, to the next generation.[1]

With his translation of Bandello, Boaistuau portrays a world so disordered that even the image of the patriarchal family barely withstands the stress: his rival houses dismember and tear each other in the central fight, covering the ground with arms, legs, thighs, and blood.[2] The French writer idealizes both lovers as representatives of 'parfaicte et acomplie amitié', making them sacrifices to social disorder; and he turns the sequence of events into a manifestation of the arbitrary fortune which becomes prominent in his account. If signs of a mercantile economy remain in Julliette's role and Capellet's marriage arrangements, they are less pervasive in characterization and idiom. New signs create negative impressions: Boaistuau invents the apothecary, for example, whose extreme poverty impels his consent to the sale of poison.[3] In this novella a dysfunctional society upsets domestic structure, the last unit of stability in a turbulent world. Boaistuau conceives myth in terms of moral exemplum, or *le théâtre du monde*. When Julliette appears dead, the republic seems imperilled, 'et non sans cause'; and when both lovers have committed suicide, grief leads to peace between the families as pity overcomes those who had not been controlled by prudence or counsel.[4]

Brooke and Painter adapted Boaistuau's vision of a chaotic

[1] 'Boundaries and the Sense of Self in Sixteenth-Century France', in *Reconstructing Individualism*, p. 53.

[2] *Histoires tragiques*, ed. Richard A. Carr (Paris, 1977), p. 83.

[3] *Histoires tragiques*, pp. 119, 108.

[4] *Histoires tragiques*, pp. 106, 119.

France to Elizabethan England in its first decade, a nation managing to contain political and religious conflict. With their translations, the deployment of rhetoric and plain diction rationalizes the story; style makes social disorder seem controllable and less urgent. Despite such modulations Brooke and Painter, sympathetic to the lovers, share Boaistuau's interest in a bigger picture: both attribute events to fortune, a concept which Brooke inflates with more than a dozen references, a few of them set pieces; and both impart Boaistuau's conception of a violent society that disrupts the patriarchal norm. In these versions, however, fate seems a reminder of potential threats rather than a cause of real ones, and Verona a sensational warning against irrationality and loss of control. Moreover the English translations differ from each other, the young gentleman-poet fixing the narrative in a perspective not identical with that of the young civil servant. Brooke tends to expand the French version, heightening features which mirror economic—and ethical—conditions in a local setting. For instance, he fills out Boaistuau's sketch of Julliette's nurse and, in the process, shows her accepting payment of six crowns from Romeus for delivering a message: 'In seven years twice told she had not bowed so low, | Her crooked knees, as now they bow . . .' (669–70). The incident leads Brooke to advise lovers, 'thy purse thou must not spare' (706). Generally Painter's translation stays closer to Boaistuau's text, an almost literal rendering of the moral exemplum. Nevertheless, at the start it reduces the appeal to authority and adds a promise of romantic adventures and devices, slightly diffusing the political implications of the original.

Another variation distinguishes the two English versions. Whereas Painter follows the French novella in depicting the 'entire and perfect amity' of Rhomeo and Julietta (124), Brooke creates uncertainty about his narrator's point of view. Finally Brooke preserves '[t]he memory of so perfect, sound, and so approvèd love' (3012), but his prose address 'To the Reader' tells a different story even more sternly than Bandello's dedication:

> And to this end (good Reader) is this tragical matter written, to describe unto thee a couple of unfortunate lovers, thralling themselves to unhonest desire, neglecting the authority and advice of parents and friends, . . . abusing the honourable name of lawful marriage, the cloak the shame of stol'n contracts, finally, by all means of unhonest life, hasting to meet most unhappy death. (pp. 284–5)

Moralizing and sententiae punctuate Brooke's text here and there, reminders of this purpose; they testify to the strong Protestant bias evident in his other translation, an anonymous Huguenot tract known as *The agreemente of sondry places of scripture* (published after Brooke's death in 1563). Perhaps Brooke reproduces, more distinctively than Painter and even unintentionally, the conflicting ideas about sex and marriage which shifted the social position of women during the Elizabethan period. On the one hand, economic and demographic factors continued to diminish women as commodities; on the other, the Reformation began to advocate companionate marriage strengthened by love and shared sexual pleasure.[1] Brooke's fiction, the work of a new writer, may register inconsistencies both in his own thinking and in that of his age.

Obviously sixteenth-century experience—socio-economic and cultural—influenced the ways in which novelists told the Romeo and Juliet story and readers understood it. As the English translations show most clearly, it affected not only content but style. Bandello's version established the mode of expression, which invited the audience to judge the story as if they were participating in a rhetorical occasion.[2] Typical of the period, this fiction depends on the forms of oration and dispute. Figures of repetition ornament the narrative while securing each event firmly in place.

While rhetoric flourished, 'polymorphous and ubiquitous',[3] the novellas took shape as rhetorical compositions based on the story as da Porto had arranged it. They used each of the dozen plot elements as a *res* or subject matter, amplifying episodes through the larger processes of rhetoric and, more specifically, through a limited number of figures. Similar in tone, they advance through the narrative–speech–narrative–speech pattern which Richard A. Lanham defines as a staple of Western literary composition:

[1] See Carol Thomas Neely's Introduction to *Broken Nuptials in Shakespeare's Plays* (New Haven and London, 1985), especially pp. 7–19.

[2] Arthur F. Kinney gives this description for the writing of Renaissance fiction generally in 'Rhetoric and Fiction in Elizabethan England', in *Renaissance Eloquence: Studies in the Theory and Practice of Renaissance Rhetoric*, ed. James J. Murphy (Berkeley, Los Angeles, and London, 1983), p. 388. For studies of the narrative's style see my 'Romeo and Juliet before Shakespeare', *SP* 81 (1984), 325–47, and 'Shakespeare's *Romeo and Juliet*: The Places of Invention', *SSu* 49 (1996), 45–55.

[3] Wayne A. Rebhorn, *The Emperor of Men's Minds: Literature and the Renaissance Discourse of Rhetoric* (Ithaca, NY, 1995), p. 6.

narrators argue their interpretations of events; 'lovers orate spontaneously', engaging in debate with themselves and others; and rhetorical figures decorate each fiction from beginning to end.[1] In Brooke's *Tragical History*, the narrator occasionally evaluates the suasion in rhetorical terms:

> Oh how we can persuade, our self to what we like,
> And how we can dissuade our mind, if aught our mind mislike.
> (429–30)

These novellas, like other Renaissance literature, adapted rhetorical discourse for use in their fictions. Among the borrowings, they incorporated features from the three kinds of orations: demonstrative or epideictic, when the narrator praises Verona or attributes of the characters, or when the characters praise or dispraise one another or their circumstances; judicial or forensic, when Friar Laurence defends himself in open assembly before a judge; and, most frequently, deliberative, 'whereby we do persuade, or dissuade, entreat, or rebuke, exhort, or dehort, commend, or comfort any man'.[2] When Juliet discovers who Romeo is, she sounds like this in Bandello:

> Now let us assume that he really loves me, as I am ready to believe he does, and that he wants me as his legitimate wife: should I not be reasonable and consider the fact that my father will never agree to it? And yet, is it just possible that this union could bring the two families together again in peace and harmony? I have heard it said many times that such marriages have brought about peace not only between private citizens and gentlemen, but that often times true peace and amity ensued between the greatest princes and kings engaged in the cruelest wars. Perhaps I shall be the one to bring peace to these two households by such means.[3]

Boaistuau and Painter shorten this argument; Brooke lengthens it, particularly with allusions to 'sage writers' (409), and condemns it outright (429–32). Yet the discussion remains essentially

[1] Lanham defines the pattern and describes the lovers in *The Motives of Eloquence: Literary Rhetoric in the Renaissance* (New Haven and London, 1976), p. 9.

[2] Thomas Wilson, *The Arte of Rhetorique* (1553, repr. Amsterdam and New York, 1969), D4. Kinney quotes this passage in his *Humanist Poetics: Thought, Rhetoric, and Fiction in Sixteenth-Century England* (Amherst, Mass., 1986), p. 10.

[3] *Novelle*, p. 447. I am grateful to Professor Anne Paolucci for translations from the Italian.

logical in each version, a deliberation which finally calms Juliet and supplies her with an objective. It is typical of these fictions where everyone deliberates, resolves, and argues, from Juliet herself to Juliet's nurse.

If the novellas seem copious, oratory supplies the abundance: the details which crowd the narrative constitute evidence for the many arguments. If the novellas generated emotion for their original audiences, rhetorical figures of pathos must have heightened the story's mythological and romantic elements. These figures are especially prominent in the complaints which punctuate the sequence, in the lovers' exchanges, and in the narrators' appeals for empathy:

> [Juliet] in so wondrous wise began her sorrows to renew
> That sure no heart so hard (but it of flint had been)
> But would have rued the piteous plaint that she did languish in.
> (Brooke 1092–4)[1]

But figures of pathos make up only about ten per cent of the two hundred or so devices catalogued by Sister Miriam Joseph; and those cited in her larger grammatical category, the orthographic/syntactical schemes, play a modest role in Bandello, Boaistuau, and Painter.[2] Yet the figures of grammar also provide a source of emotional power in rhetorical speech. According to Brian Vickers, who identifies these figures and three kinds of wordplay (figures of logos) as the most important group, they serve as 'representations of human emotional and psychological states', or 'little reservoirs of energy'.[3] Bandello and his translators, depending on the simplest devices of repetition, often produce stylistic languor.

Sixteenth-century readers seem not to have noticed any failure of rhetoric or contradictions in the narrative's presentation, its measured account of boundless passion. Yet the lovers' story assumed the inconsistencies of its genre, which imitated both history

[1] For the corresponding passage in Painter's version, see 97.

[2] For this description of the novellas' rhetoric I have adopted Sister Miriam Joseph's organization of the figures into four groups (grammar, logos, pathos, ethos) and the names which she has assigned to the schemes.

[3] *Classical Rhetoric in English Poetry* (1970), Chapters 3 and 4 (quotations from pp. 121, 122). See also Vickers's essay on 'Shakespeare's Use of Rhetoric' in *A New Companion to Shakespeare Studies*, ed. Kenneth Muir and S. Schoenbaum (Cambridge, 1971), pp. 83–98.

and romantic literature. Aspirations to history account for the circumstantiality of the novellas which, like most Renaissance fiction, strain towards verisimilitude.[1] As details fill out each *res*, slowing the tempo, they explain everything: Friar Laurence's education; the use of rope ladders in Italy; Romeo's living arrangements in Mantua. Each act has a specific motive; each event, a distinct cause and inevitable results. At irregular intervals, however, the stock gestures of romantic love or anguish—the tears, moans, groans, and faints—interrupt reasoned discourse. Often stock language accompanies the gestures. Romeo and Juliet show their devotion primarily through apostrophes, hyperbolic words and acts, and conceits which are feudal, military, or physiological; they express their pain in similar fashion, with fewer conceits. When other characters suffer, they react in the same fashion. The response of Capulet's wife to Juliet's apparent death, for example, corresponds to Juliet's behaviour at Romeo's suicide.

Frequently the narrators heighten the inconsistencies. With the authority assumed by the Renaissance historian, they comment on the action, instructing the reader how to understand the story.[2] In their asides, they underline the reasonableness of reason and the intensity of passion. The narrators in Bandello, Boaistuau, and Painter gloss examples of sensible behaviour with brief remarks.[3] By comparison, Brooke's narrator intervenes more emphatically, in particular to commend the sagacity of Friar Laurence. Making this trait conspicuous, Brooke has added to the story the friar's harangue to Romeo when the young lover is distraught over his banishment (1352–480). The action halts completely for this sermon and the narrator's observations:

> So wisely did the friar unto his tale reply,
> That he straight carèd for his life, that erst had care to die.
> (1351–2)

When they annotate moments of ardour, all of the narrators encourage the reader to appreciate the remarkable strength of feeling

[1] On this tendency in Renaissance fiction, see William Nelson, *Fact or Fiction: The Dilemma of the Renaissance Storyteller* (Cambridge, Mass., 1973).

[2] See Robert Scholes and Robert Kellogg, *The Nature of Narrative* (New York, 1966), pp. 250–6.

[3] See, for instance, Bandello, *Novelle*, p. 442, and Boaistuau, *Histoires tragiques*, p. 67.

displayed, as in passages where Verona mourns the apparent death of Juliet:

> . . . even from the hoary head unto the witless child,
> She won the hearts of all, so that there was not one,
> Ne great, ne small, but did that day her wretched state bemoan.
> (Brooke 2470–2)

Some of the features which produced inconsistency in Renaissance novellas also served as standards of excellence. At least since the sixteenth century, verisimilitude and circumstantiality measured narrative success; Belleforest, translating Bandello's stories, praised them especially for 'la verité de l'histoire'.[1] When this authenticity and its supporting rhetoric encountered sentiment, they generated the peculiar tone which typifies the genre. George B. Parks refers to this phenomenon in a study of early fiction. While charting the tradition of the psychological novel which ended with John Lyly's *Euphues* (1578)—stories which emphasized 'the rhetoric of sentiment'—he describes how narrative before Shakespeare treats psychological or subjective material concerning the predicaments or motivations of characters. He defines the incongruity of the Romeo and Juliet novellas when he analyses *Euphues*, illustrating how Lyly's work unfolds 'mainly in dialogue and soliloquy, and even though the style of the speeches is frequently impersonal and argumentative or "rhetorical", yet they are regularly fraught with emotion'.[2]

Nevertheless, the allusions of contemporary writers to the Romeo and Juliet story indicate only that Renaissance audiences took from the novellas a straightforward, melancholy tale of young love.[3] Apparently readers perceived what the authors explicitly directed them to see: 'The unfortunate death of two unhappy lovers, one of whom died of poison, the other of grief, with a

[1] Quoted by Madeleine Doran, *Endeavors of Art: A Study of Form in Elizabethan Drama* (Madison, Wis., 1964), p. 136.

[2] 'Before *Euphues*', in *Joseph Quincy Adams Memorial Studies*, ed. James G. McManaway, Giles E. Dawson, and Edwin E. Willoughby (Washington, DC, 1948), pp. 475, 477.

[3] See, for example, allusions quoted in René Pruvost, *Matteo Bandello and Elizabethan Fiction* (Paris, 1937), pp. 70, 76, 84. Barnaby Rich's reference is typical in his *A RIGHT EXCELENT and pleasaunt Dialogue, betwene MERCVRY AND AN ENGLISH Souldier* . . . (1574), M1v, linking Romeo and Juliet with 'many other loving wights, who in regard of Venus' law, had endured many bitter torments, and yielded themselves to martyrdom'.

number of unforeseen events'.[1] The circumstantial, sensible accounts of the tragedy must have proved to their satisfaction that Romeo and Juliet faced obstacles which reasonableness itself could not surmount, odds which made their advance towards death inevitable and therefore pitiful. The rhetoric must have moved them; and they responded to the constants in the narrative—the characters and sequence of events—rather than the changing cultural accretions.

Travelling through Europe for two generations before Shakespeare wrote his play, the sixteenth-century literary formulation prospered. In Italy and France five extant versions appeared within thirty years and generated numerous imitations and borrowings.[2] In England, too, there is ample proof of the narrative's currency: reprintings of the translations made by Brooke and Painter, and an abundance of references to Romeo and Juliet in contemporary literature.[3] Clearly Shakespeare dramatized a story familiar to his audience through popular sources for at least thirty years. Despite accommodations to various cultures, the fiction reached the end of the century as a narrative best known for its emotional intensity in a genre belonging to an earlier time.

'Romeo and Juliet': The Play

Shakespeare's *Romeo and Juliet* was, and still is, famous for its affect. In his essay on feeling and early modern theatre, Gary Taylor cites allusions from the seventeenth and eighteenth centuries, notably to the tragedy's last couplet, indicating that audiences

[1] Bandello, *Novelle*, p. 439.

[2] For the story's history in Italy, see Reginald Anthony Saner, 'Romeo and Juliet in Sixteenth Century Drama', unpublished Ph.D. thesis, University of Illinois, 1962. Henri Hauvette, *La 'Morte Vivante'*, Bibliothèque de la Revue des Cours et Conférences (Paris, 1933), pp. 160, 185, supports this conclusion with reference to the success of Italian and French editions, imitations, and adaptations of da Porto and Bandello. See also René Sturel, *Bandello en France au XVIe siècle* (Geneva, 1970), repr. of 1918 edition, pp. 2–3, and Alessandro Torri, *Bibliografia della Novella 'Giulietta e Romeo' di Luigi Da Porto* (Florence, 1961), pp. 9–11.

[3] According to the STC, Brooke's version was printed in 1562, 1567, 1587; Painter's, in 1567, [1580?]. For allusions to the story, see Bullough, *Narrative and Dramatic Sources of Shakespeare*, i. 275; Emil Koeppel, *Studien zur geschichte der italienischen novelle in der englischen Litteratur des sechzehnten jahrhunderts* (1892), *passim*; Pruvost, *Matteo Bandello*, pp. 19–94; and Mary Augusta Scott, *Elizabethan Translations from the Italian* (Boston and New York, 1916), pp. 225–6.

appreciated this play as 'the ultimate in woe'.[1] However the text has been adapted since the Restoration, woe and love have remained keynotes of successful performance; and *Romeo and Juliet* has enjoyed a number of highly successful periods in production, from the second half of the eighteenth century to the end of the twentieth, from staging by David Garrick to cinema by Franco Zeffirelli and Baz Luhrmann (see the discussion of theatre history below, 'Restoration to Late Twentieth Century'). Theatre tends to pitch emotion for adult audiences; recent films, keying sentiment for more than one generation, have moved record numbers of teenagers with the incomparable 'story of more woe'.

Love, Death, and Adolescence. One source of affect in *Romeo and Juliet* must be the mythical component of the narrative, potential which the dramatic version exploits to a far greater degree than the novellas. Again and again Shakespeare reinforces *Liebestod* and resonant myths, not only with references to Cupid and Venus but with allusions to unrelated Ovidian stories connecting disaster and transformation: Phaëton, the most prominent (2.2.4, 2.4.9, 3.2.1–4, 5.3.306), as well as Danaë (1.1.210), Echo (2.1.207–9), Julius Caesar (3.2.22–5), Philomel (3.5.4), and Proserpina (5.3.105). At times citations of supporting myth and legend appear in unlikely places, such as Mercutio's catalogue of five tragic heroines in his mockery of Romeo as lover (2.3.40–2). Despite comic distractions like this, promises of woe to come occur everywhere in the play. The motif of death as Juliet's bridegroom, identified by M. M. Mahood and T. J. B. Spencer,[2] is introduced at the end of the fourth scene (ll. 247–8) and repeated until its enactment in 5.3. Wordplay and irony also anticipate the tragic close. On seeing Juliet at the dance, Romeo observes 'Beauty too rich for use, for earth too dear' (see 1.4.160 n.). In their first private conversation Juliet confesses, as she compares Romeo to a pet bird, 'Yet I should kill thee with much cherishing' (2.1.229). The familiar version of the wedding scene concentrates foreboding in the exchange between Friar Laurence and Romeo (2.5.1–15).[3]

[1] 'Feeling Bodies', in *Shakespeare and the Twentieth Century: The Selected Proceedings of the International Shakespeare Association Congress, Los Angeles, 1996*, ed. Jonathan Bate, Jill L. Levenson, and Dieter Mehl (Newark, Del., and London, 1998), p. 264. (See also p. 259.)

[2] Mahood, p. 57, and Spencer's edition, 1.5.135 n.

[3] The impression of imminent disaster is less intense in the 1597 version of

The play also enhances the rite of passage which the myth represents. While the novellas emphasize the lovers' failure to make the social transition symbolized by marriage, they present little psychological complexity. Literary conventions which stylize thought and emotion allow the protagonists almost no individuality: Romeo and Juliet are patterns of young love, his age unspecified, hers noted (during her father's marriage negotiations) as sixteen in Brooke, eighteen or so in the others. By contrast, the dramatic version catches the lovers specifically in the early and middle phases of adolescence. Its portrayal of these phases, remarkable for its accuracy and thoroughness, is animated by sexual energy. When wordplay imitates sexual play, it expresses thoughts and sensations typical of this often chaotic period of transition.[1] The staging itself, readily adaptable to film, charges events:

> Visually, the play remains memorable for a number of repeated images—street brawls, swords flashing to the hand, torches rushing on and off, crowds gathering. The upper stage is used frequently, with many opportunities for leaping or scrambling or stretching up and down and much play between upper and lower areas. The dominant feelings we get as an audience are oppressive heat, sexual desire, a frequent whiz-bang exhilarating kinesthesia of speed and clash, and above all a feeling of the keeping-down and separation of highly charged bodies, whose pressure toward release and whose sudden discharge determine the rhythm of the play.[2]

Perhaps the sexually charged enactment of adolescence explains the emotional appeal of *Romeo and Juliet* to modern teenagers and to adults still in touch with their earlier selves.

In its portrayal of adolescent phases, *Romeo and Juliet* uses the sequence of the well-known story as a point of departure. It adds scenes and shorter passages to the fictional narrative which enlarge the social worlds of the lovers before reducing them, and which therefore complicate relationships with families or friends. Consequently the changes of adolescence, part of a larger dynamic, set off repercussions at every level of the action: the protagonists verbalize them and act them out; Romeo's friends mirror or

Romeo and Juliet, which has fewer lines to anticipate its ending and a different wedding scene. (See below, 'The Mobile Text'.)

[1] On the eroticism of verbal wit, see Stephen Greenblatt, 'Fiction and Friction', in *Reconstructing Individualism*, pp. 48–50.

[2] Michael Goldman, *Shakespeare and the Energies of Drama* (Princeton, 1972), p. 33.

disagree with his behaviour; and the older generation, misconstruing almost all of the signs, hasten events towards calamity.

In the opening scene, for example, more than half of the dialogue elaborates on Romeo's state of mind. When the prototype failed to rationalize his initial lovesickness in the novellas, an anonymous friend lectured him on the wastefulness of unrequited love, and Romeo immediately accepted his advice to find a more compassionate mistress. Revising this episode, the play makes Romeo's behaviour the subject of conversation between his father and his cousin Benvolio: Romeo isolates himself, restless and uncommunicative, seeking an ambience that suits his mood. Benvolio not only shares some of Romeo's feelings (ll. 114–26), but recognizes the correspondence:

> I, measuring his affections by my own . . .
> Pursued my humour, not pursuing his,
> And gladly shunned who gladly fled from me.
> (ll. 122–6)

Yet neither relative can identify Romeo's problem, an obvious case of unsettled hormones, and Benvolio determines to help Montague find the cause. During the eighty-line exchange between Romeo and Benvolio which follows, play on words and on conventions of love-poetry replaces the anonymous lecture, establishing the distinctive language of the young male peer group that will include Mercutio. With his ripostes to Benvolio's speeches, Romeo scores points in a contest of wits that displays self-conscious masculinity in adolescent patter:

> ROMEO
> In sadness, cousin, I do love a woman.
> BENVOLIO
> I aimed so near when I supposed you loved.
> ROMEO
> A right good markman, and she's fair I love.
> BENVOLIO
> A right fair mark, fair coz, is soonest hit.
> ROMEO
> Well, in that hit you miss: she'll not be hit
> With Cupid's arrow, she hath Dian's wit; . . .
> (ll. 200–5)

The fourth scene introduces Mercutio, the character invented from a few sentences in the original narratives; and it adds at the start an episode of more than one hundred lines where he interacts with Romeo, almost engulfing him with the power of his imagination in the Queen Mab speech, expressing his anger and his sexual fantasies. Often Mercutio's banter, witty and combative, escalates to rough bawdy; it voices preoccupations which the other young men disguise with more propriety. Between this episode and the beginning of the third act, Romeo's two close friends appear where the audience could not have expected them from precedents, leaving Capulet's party (1.4.232–7), serving as prelude to the moonlit balcony scene (2.1.3–43), filling time until the Nurse delivers her first message to Romeo (2.3.1–134). Intruding on the love-story, they accentuate Romeo's growing distance from their social life. The opening scene of the third act centres on them, especially Mercutio, who provokes the fight which leads to Romeo's exile. After the explosion of violence which kills Mercutio, Benvolio too disappears from the play, and Romeo's isolation becomes different in kind. As his social world disintegrates, the drama returns to its source-narrative and Romeo engages with characters who expedite his fate: Friar Laurence, the Nurse, his man Balthazar, the Apothecary. The fifth act contains a different kind of invention, Romeo's dream and recollections of the Apothecary's shop in 5.1, and his encounter with Paris in 5.3. Late in the play these discrete moments again focus his state of mind, his brief escape into wish-fulfilment and his suicidal despair.

Like the novellas, the play introduces Juliet after the exposition which dissociates Romeo from the feud; but it immediately adds two scenes which position the character within her family and add up to a biographical sketch. The fictions present a stereotypical beauty at her father's celebration, 'a maid, right fair of perfect shape', who attracts Romeo's eye (Brooke 197). Anticipating the party, the second and third scenes of the drama portray the young Juliet as she is viewed through the eyes of others: her father, a potential suitor, her mother, and her nurse. When she appears in the third scene, Juliet has little to say, barely hinting the complexities to come, but she is well-defined in social terms. If the play conceals her state of mind, it announces her age, her status as an only child and heir, her suitability for betrothal, and her condition of total dependency on her parents. She belongs to an affluent early modern household run by her father. In addition to the immediate family there are servants for everything from delivering messages to serving food.[1] Later scenes will show them moving furniture, providing torches, gathering provisions for the cook, and collecting logs for a fire. Interpolations, these episodes portray an establishment bustling with male and female servants, some more experienced and responsible than others. The household includes Samson and Gregory, the serving-men inclined towards sex and violence: Shakespeare created them to open the play.

Certainly the Nurse holds a privileged position among the rest; she shares the counsel of Juliet and her mother during 1.3. A nurse in every sense of the word, she breast-fed the infant Juliet and cared for the growing child. She delivers the history of Juliet's brief life, allowing the audience to imagine a toddler being weaned, taking her first steps, going through the initial stage of separation from a mother-figure with its attendant hazards: Juliet fell out with the breast, and she toppled over as she ran. When the Nurse repeats her husband's joke about Juliet losing her balance—'Thou wilt fall backward when thou hast more wit' (1.3.44, 58)—unknowingly she not only mocks the narrative in progress, but calls attention to the second stage of development now under way. Whatever the age of puberty for girls in Elizabethan England, Juliet has apparently reached it in Shakespeare's Italy.[2] 'Well, think of marriage now' (l. 71), her mother advises Juliet, who is almost fourteen. Younger girls have become mothers, and Capulet's Wife herself gave birth to Juliet when she was about Juliet's age (ll. 71–5).

After the first act, the play invents little narrative around the character of Juliet. Instead, it makes adjustments to the Capulet family of the novellas, in particular to Capulet himself, which strengthen initial impressions of Juliet's place in the household.

[1] Peter Laslett discusses this configuration of family and servants in *Family Life and Illicit Love in Earlier Generations: Essays in Historical Sociology* (Cambridge, 1977), Chapter 1.

[2] In *The World We Have Lost—Further Explored*, 3rd edn. (1983), Peter Laslett gives a summary of data about the age of sexual maturity in the late sixteenth century; and he suggests that '[Shakespeare] was deliberately writing a play about love and marriage amongst boys and girls without any recognition of the facts about the age of women at their weddings or at sexual maturity' (p. 85). Nevertheless, the play accurately observes the stages of what psychoanalysts now call individuation. Meredith Skura, *The Literary Use of the Psychoanalytic Process* (New Haven and London, 1984), pp. 182–6, offers a helpful overview of theoretical work on child development; important studies of the adolescent phase have been done by Erik Homburger Erikson, Heinz Kohut, and Peter Blos.

From the beginning this father busily engages in his daughter's marriage arrangements, rushing them along from 3.4. His interference generates irony and suspense in the third act; his negotiations with Paris continue while Juliet consummates her marriage with Romeo. Significantly, his efforts call attention to the conflict which results when Juliet attempts to escape his authority. In 3.5 this confrontation, which starts with Capulet's Wife, occupies most of the long scene: nearly two hundred lines of dialogue follow the sixty-five-line parting of Romeo and Juliet. The family episode, in its sheer bulk, represents the obduracy which the lovers face. Here social and economic considerations are primary; and the adolescent girl who tries to assert independence hears, in blunt terms, that she is her father's property. Many of Capulet's insults—'green-sickness carrion' (l. 155), 'wretched puling fool' (l. 183), 'whining maumet' (l. 184)—emphasize Juliet's youth. In 4.2 he will stress her intractableness: 'A peevish self-willed harlotry it is', 'How now, my headstrong' (ll. 13, 15); but he will express approval when she seems to concede:

> I have learned me to repent the sin
> Of disobedient opposition
> To you and your behests; . . .
> (ll. 16–18)

In effect, the play simulates what Anna Freud calls 'the atmosphere in which the adolescent lives':

> . . . [the] anxieties, the height of elation or depth of despair, the quickly rising enthusiasms, the utter hopelessness, the burning—or at other times sterile—intellectual and philosophical preoccupations, the yearning for freedom, the sense of loneliness, the feeling of oppression by the parents, the impotent rages or active hates directed against the adult world, the erotic crushes—whether homosexually or heterosexually directed—the suicidal fantasies, etc.[1]

Although writers since antiquity had recognized and recorded the experience of adolescence, none had dramatized it so comprehensively.[2]

[1] 'Adolescence', *Psychoanalytic Study of the Child*, 13 (1958), 260.

[2] Often writers describe this stage as part of their own inner landscapes. Norman Kiell cites a variety of early examples throughout *The Universal Experience of Adolescence* (New York, 1964). At the beginning of *The Adolescent Passage: Developmental Issues* (New York, 1979), Peter Blos quotes a passage from Aristotle's *Rhetoric*

The play observes the transitional phase from an adult's point of view as the younger generation assume the attitudes typical of the process; it also adopts the adolescent's point of view as the developing personality responds to family and other social values and beliefs. Consequently it presents adolescence in Verona not only as it is perceived by those who have survived it, usually in a distant or vanished past, but also as it is felt by those who are growing through it until violence abruptly stops their progress. Finally the play totalizes this experience, which psychoanalytic theory and recent data continue to link with emotional turmoil: the whole adolescent population, including the most stable personalities, feel the pressures of new sexual impulses and socialization as adults.[1] The dramatic action displays a range of adolescent behaviours from Benvolio to Tybalt, less disturbed to more disturbed, showing these figures in relation to one another and to adults, especially father-figures.[2] But only spectators, and perhaps actors, have access to the entire prospect. None of the characters fully apprehends the decisive changes in the younger generation which will profoundly disrupt their society, ending the Capulet and Montague lines and killing Mercutio and Paris, two of the Prince's kinsmen.

Clearly Shakespeare's additions and adjustments contribute to the narrative's inclusiveness as well as its various ironies. One modern study of adolescence begins with *Romeo and Juliet* 2.2, the exchange between Romeo and Friar Laurence about Romeo's inconstancy. Original to the play, this dialogue sets adolescent intensity and impatience against adult perplexity and rationalization; its tension is diverted rather than resolved. Friar Laurence may joke about Romeo's passions—tears, sighs, and groans over

which gives a circumstantial account of male adolescence (pp. 12–13). On ideas characteristic of Shakespeare's period, see Ilana Krausman Ben-Amos, *Adolescence and Youth in Early Modern England* (New Haven and London, 1994), especially Chapters 1 and 8.

[1] See, for example, Harvey Golombek and Peter Marton, 'Adolescents over Time: A Longitudinal Study of Personality Development', *Adolescent Psychiatry*, 18 (1992), 213–84.

[2] On Tybalt see, for instance, 1.4.202–3 n. Two essays regard Tybalt as a troubled adolescent who compensates for his insecure masculinity with hostile aggressiveness: Marjorie Kolb Cox, 'Adolescent Processes in *Romeo and Juliet*', *Psychoanalytic Review*, 63 (1976), 386, and Sara Munson Deats, 'The Conspiracy of Silence in Shakespeare's Verona: *Romeo and Juliet*', in *Youth Suicide Prevention: Lessons from Literature*, ed. Deats and Lagretta Tallent Lenker (New York and London, 1989), p. 81.

changing objects of love—but he never acknowledges their sources, and at last he will indulge them in an attempt to end the feud (ll. 90–2).[1] Through the rest of the play this pattern continues: Friar Laurence redirects not only Juliet's suicidal inclinations (4.1), as his prototypes had, but also Romeo's (3.3), both efforts to reconcile the families. In a few days the repressed feelings overwhelm both the protagonists and Friar Laurence. They also overwhelm the other adults in the play, from Montague to the Nurse, who misunderstand the younger generation in their charge. Again and again the drama focuses on this kind of misunderstanding which is probably, in Peter Blos's summation, 'as old as generations themselves'.[2] The lovers and parent-figures never confront their growing distance from one another; and the parent-figures, from one angle, represent adults in adolescent fantasy and perception.[3]

The peer group which centres on Mercutio, the leader of high social status who takes the greatest risks, represents a constant of adolescent experience observed by Aristotle in his *Rhetoric*: '[Young men] are fonder of their friends, intimates, and companions than older men are, because they like spending their days in the company of others'.[4] In Western cultures the male peer group provides space for transition from childhood dependencies to adult relationships: the adolescent experiments with social conventions—dress, gesture, vocabulary—as he establishes his sexual identity according to the group's standard; he may also experiment with fantasy and introspection.[5] Nevertheless, the family remains a source of shelter and security: Romeo, still a ward, will follow Mercutio and Benvolio to dinner at his father's house (2.3.130–2).[6]

[1] Henry P. Coppolillo, 'The Tides of Change in Adolescence', in *The Course of Life*, vol. 4, *Adolescence*, ed. Stanley I. Greenspan and George H. Pollock (Madison, Conn., 1991), pp. 235–6.

[2] *Adolescent Passage*, p. 14.

[3] See Hyman L. Muslin, 'Romeo and Juliet: The Tragic Self in Adolescence', *Adolescent Psychiatry*, 10 (1982), 112, and Katherine Dalsimer, *Female Adolescence: Psychoanalytic Reflections on Works of Literature* (New Haven and London, 1986), p. 81. Dalsimer adds that the match with Paris is the same type of representation.

[4] Quoted in Blos, *Adolescent Passage*, p. 13.

[5] Both Blos, *Adolescent Passage*, and Kiell, *Universal Experience*, devote chapters to the subject of peer groups. See also Erik Homburger Erikson, 'The Problem of Ego Identity', *Journal of the American Psychoanalytic Association*, 4 (1956), 72–3.

[6] On Romeo's status see Bruce W. Young, 'Haste, Consent, and Age at Marriage: Some Implications of Social History for *Romeo and Juliet*', *Iowa State Journal of Research*, 62 (1988), 465.

Like the signs of dissonance between generations, those of interaction within the peer group are obvious in the play. From the approach to Capulet's party, the three named members show concern with style and decorum, sometimes pointedly dismissing what others think. When Romeo asks if they will enter with a formal speech, for example, Benvolio responds, 'The date is out of such prolixity', and he concludes:

> But let them measure us by what they will,
> We'll measure them a measure and be gone.
> (1.4.3–8)

Mercutio, putting on a mask required by the occasion, asks, 'What care I | What curious eye doth quote deformities?' (ll. 28–9). Since they plan to present themselves in a uniform way, Mercutio attempts to talk Romeo out of the loverlike attitude that sets him apart. His idiom of choice is the pun, unsubtle and ribald, characteristic of the language these young men share. Although not unique to them—Samson and Gregory introduce bawdy wordplay as contest when the play opens—the pun combines with other rhetorical figures to produce a distinct mode of expression, what Erik Homburger Erikson would call a 'strange code'.[1] Mercutio is aware of this distinction and what it means. After the long match of wits with Romeo in 2.3, which ultimately becomes more and more obscene until it stops, he is convinced that Romeo has returned to the fold: 'Now art thou sociable, now art thou Romeo, now art thou what thou art by art as well as by nature' (ll. 84–5).

As Romeo begins to remove himself from the group, testing sexual partnership, Mercutio seems to consolidate his own position. Mercutio remains witty to the end, a trait Aristotle calls 'well-bred insolence'; and he argues to the end, another acceptable way to release feelings he may not understand.[2] Moreover, he stereotypes everyone he encounters, including that person in the group or, more often, excluding a misfit.[3] Sometimes he plays with the stereotypes, describing the peacemaker Benvolio as a quarrelsome gallant (3.1.5–29). But his portrayal of Tybalt as totally

[1] 'Ego Identity', 73.

[2] Aristotle's *Rhetoric*, quoted in Blos, *Adolescent Passage*, p. 13. Kiell, *Universal Experience*, pp. 428–9, makes the point about arguing. Wit as well as argument 'enables the individual to search out his self through verbal pyrotechnics' (Kiell, p. 429).

[3] On this sort of stereotyping see Kiell, *Universal Experience*, p. 397.

Fig. 1. Mercutio (Bernard Lloyd), with a life-size female doll, on his way to the Capulet party in Terry Hands's 1973 RSC production.

unfashionable—in his duelling style, his affected speech, and his other social habits—distinguishes the young Capulet as an outsider (2.3.18–34); and the differences emphasize what Mercutio promotes as the values of his own group. Among the other simplifications, Mercutio stereotypes women, from the elusive Rosaline to the down-to-earth Nurse, always in demeaning them. From Mercutio's point of view women debilitate men, reducing them to impotence and effeminacy: infatuated Romeo appears to him '[w]ithout his roe, like a dried herring' (2.3.36), that is, sexually depleted. All women objectify sex, even the Nurse ('A bawd, a bawd, a bawd!', 2.3.122). At a stage of psychological development which may be slightly earlier than Romeo's, Mercutio expresses more interest in his friend's sex life than in his own: Romeo's body supplies images for his phallic wordplay, most strikingly in a series of puns at 1.4.20–6 and 2.1.35–9. With their friendship, typifying the androgynous world of male adolescents, the play enacts not only male bonding but Mercutio's unacknowledged homoerotic desire.[1]

Romeo and Juliet meet in this incoherent world of shifting identities and relationships, each at a different phase of adolescent development. According to 1.2 and 1.3, Juliet has just entered adolescence from latency, its juncture with childhood. When she first appears she reveals no consciousness of her sexuality, behaviour characteristic of girls her age, despite the subject of the conversation: 'How stands your dispositions to be married?' (1.3.67). 'It is an honour that I dream not of' (l. 68), Juliet responds, and she is just as abstract when her mother asks, 'can you like of Paris' love?' (l. 98):

> I'll look to like, if looking liking move.
> But no more deep will I indart mine eye
> Than your consent gives strength to make it fly.
> (ll. 99–101)

At this point Juliet accommodates herself to social conventions which take no account of the transitional period she has begun: her mother and nurse expect the child to turn into a woman without delay.[2]

By comparison Romeo has advanced farther, both in becoming autonomous and in directing his sexual feelings towards an object. Shakespeare makes this object Rosaline, a Capulet, identifying the anonymous lady of the sources with the enemy house. As a result Romeo's first love anticipates his second, and both externalize the emotional conflict which he attempts to articulate in formal, poetic terms; they represent not only unattainable but forbidden desire,

[1] A number of critics have commented on Mercutio's sexual attraction to Romeo. See, for example, Joseph A. Porter, *Shakespeare's Mercutio: His History and Drama* (Chapel Hill, NC, and London, 1988), pp. 145–63; Bruce R. Smith, *Homosexual Desire in Shakespeare's England: A Cultural Poetics* (Chicago and London, 1994), p. 64; Jonathan Goldberg, '*Romeo and Juliet*'s Open Rs', in *Queering the Renaissance*, ed. Goldberg (Durham, NC, and London, 1994), repr. in Porter, *Critical Essays*, pp. 91–4. Mercutio's phallic wordplay illustrates Freud's interpretation of the joke, summarized by Skura, as 'a displaced version of a sexual or aggressive wish, allowing the teller to express his forbidden wish in an acceptable way' (*Literary Use*, p. 180). Obviously jokes cannot work without an audience, and Mercutio's puns generally demand of his peer group 'complicity, sanction, and reassurance' (p. 181).

[2] Both Cox, 'Adolescent Processes', 383–4, and Dalsimer, *Female Adolescence*, pp. 84–90, discuss the psychological implications of this scene.

sexual impulses which may revive his earliest, Oedipal sensations.[1] In isolation or company Romeo seeks the 'sharp, intense affective states' which compensate for the losses of adolescence, especially detachment from parental figures.[2] He uses Petrarchan language to describe the anxiety of a self-conscious personality loosed from its moorings: 'Tut, I have lost myself, I am not here; | This is not Romeo, he's some other where' (see 1.1.193–4 n. and 'Tragedy, Comedy, Sonnet' below).

The meeting of Romeo and Juliet in 1.4 initiates a series of events which both deepen and particularize their story. If the broad outline of young love reappears—instant attraction and complementarity—the play fills it in with shades of meaning. Instead of the first conversation which Romeo dominates in the sources, the lovers share verse as sensitive children might share a game: each 'not only enters the other's imaginative world but also transforms that world by his or her presence'. They take part in a dialogue through which they begin to perceive each other, not narcissistically as mirror images, but mutually as distinct personalities.[3] Through the course of their dramatic narrative, continuing transformations allow them the full interplay of male and female roles which C. L. Barber and Richard P. Wheeler noticed in Shakespeare's plays to 1595, an exchange developed in *Romeo and Juliet* from suggestions in the novellas.[4] On the stage Romeo condemns his own effeminacy at Mercutio's death (3.1.113–15), as Friar Laurence will condemn it later (3.3.108–12, 125–6, 142–3), but he will act until his suicide with the emotion and impulsiveness Friar Laurence assigns to women; Juliet accepts the sleeping potion and in the end kills herself with manly resolve, admitting 'no inconstant toy nor womanish fear' (4.1.119).[5] The intensity of the

[1] See Cox, 'Adolescent Processes', 381, and Dalsimer, *Female Adolescence*, p. 93.

[2] Blos, *Adolescent Passage*, p. 159, defines these states.

[3] Compare Brooke 275–316, and Painter, 85–6. My terminology is adapted from Carol Gilligan's description of identity formation in female adolescents: 'Remapping the Moral Domain: New Images of the Self in Relationship', in *Reconstructing Individualism*, pp. 237–52; the quotation comes from p. 243.

[4] Barber and Wheeler, *The Whole Journey: Shakespeare's Power of Development* (Berkeley, Los Angeles, and London, 1986), p. 14. The suggestions occur in the sources when, for instance, Friar Lawrence berates Romeus's effeminate behaviour on hearing the sentence of banishment (Brooke 1353–8), and when he advises Juliet to follow his instructions in using the potion '[w]ith manly courage' (Brooke 2146; compare Painter, 109).

[5] Critics have repeatedly pointed out the reversal of gender roles: for instance,

passion which recasts gender roles changes Romeo and Juliet in other ways: it is audible in the constant modulations of their speech; and it is palpable in the urgent rhythms of their actions, as the play compresses time from months in Brooke and Painter to less than a week.[1] Always it collaborates with the conditions which rush the lovers through adolescence to the edge of adulthood, a paradoxical state of independence and relatedness. Together passion and contingencies accelerate the irregular phases of progress or regression for both protagonists.

Yet each lover remains singular.[2] As Edward Snow argues persuasively, their voices express their differences. Romeo and Juliet articulate little of their experience as conscious thought; rather, they expose facets of their personalities in idiosyncrasies of diction.[3] Characteristically Romeo's figurative language, dominated by eyesight, gives material forms to his desire which rationalize and contain it; Juliet's, generated by all the senses, allows hers a formlessness which slips through boundaries. He frames images to reduce their immediacy; she releases them to take the measure of emotion. 'Thus where Romeo tells [Juliet] to "look" out her window at the "envious streaks" that "lace the severing clouds in yonder east", she in turn tries to convince him it is the nightingale

Goldberg, '*Romeo and Juliet*'s Open Rs', pp. 87–8; Sudhir Kakar and John M. Ross, *Tales of Love, Sex and Danger* (Delhi, 1986), pp. 28–32; and Gayle Whittier, 'The sublime androgyne motif in three Shakespearean works', *Journal of Medieval and Renaissance Studies*, 19 (1989), 187–96. According to anthropologists, the inversion can be ritualized in some cultures as part of adolescent rites of passage, 'either to suggest the marginality of the transitional state . . . or to allow each sex to obtain something of the other's power'. In hierarchical societies, if not in the play, they can provide healthy outlets for conflicts within the system. (See Natalie Zemon Davis, 'Women on Top', in *Society and Culture in Early Modern France: Eight Essays* (Stanford, 1975), p. 130.)

[1] On the subjectivity represented by the time-scheme, see Dalsimer, *Female Adolescence*, pp. 79–81, and Julia Kristeva, *Tales of Love*, trans. Leon S. Roudiez (New York, 1987), p. 213.

[2] The two earliest versions of *Romeo and Juliet* present this singularity with a disparateness. Because the 1597 text is shorter (see below, 'The Mobile Text'), the protagonists speak less and therefore reveal less of themselves. Juliet's soliloquies in 3.2 and 4.3 are especially brief.

[3] The next paragraphs are indebted to Snow's essay, 'Language and Sexual Difference in *Romeo and Juliet*', in *Shakespeare's 'Rough Magic': Renaissance Essays in Honor of C. L. Barber*, ed. Peter Erickson and Coppélia Kahn (Newark, Del., London, and Toronto, 1985), repr. in Andrews, *Critical Essays*, pp. 371–401. Michael Rustin makes the point about 'Thinking in *Romeo and Juliet*' in Chapter 9 of his book *The Good Society and the Inner World: Psychoanalysis, Politics and Culture* (London and New York, 1991), pp. 231–53.

that "pierc'd the fearful hollow" of his ear (3.5.1–10)'.[1] When they share an image cluster, these divergences become particularly noticeable. In their first private conversation, for example, just over a dozen speeches produce two distinctive marine conceits. Both figures are attempts to define love, his conceivable and hers difficult to imagine:

> I am no pilot, yet wert thou as far
> As that vast shore washed with the farthest sea,
> I should adventure for such merchandise.
> (2.1.125–7)

> My bounty is as boundless as the sea,
> My love as deep; the more I give to thee,
> The more I have, for both are infinite.
> (2.1.176–8)

The signs of masculine and feminine sensibilities, his restraint contrasts with her self-abandonment, his distancing of experience with her absorption in it.

Often Romeo links desire with death, a vein of morbidity pronounced in his speeches from 1.1, his devotion to Rosaline a living death (l. 220), to 5.3, his perception of himself as 'a dead man' interring Paris (l. 87).[2] After marrying Juliet he associates desire with guilt as well, first about the death of Mercutio, then about his own sexual initiation. At the beginning of 5.1 the soliloquy which conveys his dream reflects not only an adolescent wish to create a new self through the beloved person (his lady's kiss makes Romeo an emperor, ll. 8–9), but also fear of a dreadful price for sexual manhood ('I dreamt my lady came and found me dead', l. 6).[3] Momentarily Romeo's dream suppresses his guilt as the dreamer takes control, reviving as a powerful man of authority; but Romeo's other speeches in this act emphasize his implication in the destructiveness which perpetuates the feud. His last dialogue and soliloquies—addressing the Apothecary, Paris, Tybalt, and Juliet—define injustice and futility as he perceives them in the

[1] Snow, 'Language and Sexual Difference', p. 377.

[2] See Marilyn L. Williamson, 'Romeo and Death', *SSt* 14 (1981), 129–37.

[3] Norman N. Holland analyses the soliloquy in 'Romeo's Dream and the Paradox of Literary Realism', *Literature and Psychology*, 13 (1963), repr. in *The Design Within: Psychoanalytic Approaches to Shakespeare*, ed. M. D. Faber (New York, 1970), pp. 41–54.

world of the play. Since adult Verona is oblivious to crises like this and affords no means to defuse them, Romeo is forced to extemporize a ritual of escape. The dramatic catastrophe elaborates the fictional ones: he kills himself after confronting Paris, who re-enacts his earlier role as lover, a fragmented character to the end.[1]

For Juliet sexuality is a pleasure and an affirmation that satisfy her need for connectedness.[2] After 1.3 she acts on these feelings, a personality who insists on their fulfilment and imagines it vividly in the doomed hours before her wedding night (3.2.1–31). Until the last scene she overcomes morbidity or, as Friar Laurence puts it, 'cop'st with death himself to scape from it' (4.1.75). Beginning with the first dialogue on the balcony she faces danger with strategies, actively seeking to avoid the consequences of union with Romeo. Unlike him, she quickly suppresses guilt. When it surfaces in 4.3, for example, in her soliloquy on the vial of potion—she envisions herself mad in her forefathers' vault and Romeo threatened by Tybalt's ghost—she stops the fantasy by taking the drug: 'Romeo, Romeo, Romeo! Here's drink—I drink to thee' (l. 57). She says little about injustice in the world and she dies with few words, leaving an impression more consistent and focused than that of her lover. By the end of the play her character may be more firmly centred as well, an integrity aware of itself just before it disappears. Her prototypes wake from deathlike sleep confused by light in the tomb: 'She wist not if she saw a dream, or sprite that walked by night' (Brooke 2708; cf. Painter, 118). But Shakespeare's Juliet tells Friar Laurence: 'I do remember well where I should be, | And there I am' (5.3.149–50). '"[R]emembering well" . . . enables her to venture over the threshold between life and death, consciousness and unconsciousness, the self and the non-self, and find herself where she "should be" when she returns.'[3]

[1] Kiell, *Universal Experience*, p. 715, refers to the rituals and ceremonies in cultures which acknowledge in adolescence the death of an earlier personality with the emergence of an adult. On the relationship between Romeo and Paris, see Paula Newman and George Walton Williams, 'Paris: The Mirror of Romeo', *Renaissance Papers 1981* (1982), 13–19.

[2] In her article 'The Relational Self: Implications for Adolescent Development', *Adolescent Psychiatry*, 19 (1993), 228–39, Judith V. Jordan speculates that even now 'boys are socialized toward a power/dominance experience of self while girls are socialized toward a love/empathy mode of self' (234). Snow, 'Language and Sexual Difference', pp. 387–9, suggests that Juliet may have been socialized towards connectedness by the Nurse.

[3] Snow, 'Language and Sexual Difference', p. 387.

Patriarchy. Where Brooke and Painter deleted cultural history from the Romeo and Juliet narrative, Shakespeare restores it with late Elizabethan background. Once again the lovers come together in what Jacques Derrida terms 'contretemps', 'produced at the intersection between interior experience . . . and its chronological or topographical marks'.[1] The feud, more complex in the play than in the fictions, surrounds the protagonists with an ideology which affects the way they think and act. As Susan Snyder has shown, the feud represents how ideology works: beliefs, assumptions, and especially practices which reduce everything and everyone to sameness. Enemy Montagues and Capulets share this social terrain, where even the peacemaking Benvolio fights with Tybalt as if by reflex. At the same time this feud enacts a particular ideology which inscribes the play with its chronological or topographical marks.[2] Patriarchy, the system which licenses individual men of power to transfer their authority to other individual men, had already added historical dimensions to the novellas.[3] In the drama it is more of a presence, filling all the public space and intruding on privacy as well, not only in the family but in the subjective experience of individuals. Some of its most prominent features match current realities more exactly than they do in the sources, making the play immediate and critical.[4]

Extended in these ways, the feud allows the narrative to draw correspondences between patriarchal state and patriarchal family, political and social order. Prince Escalus attempts to regulate his city, Capulet his family, and both fail because of conflicts within the system. In the early modern era, this juxtaposition contributed more to the play than symmetry. It set unpredictable state against predictable family; eruptive Verona against an established household; forms subject to change—political, economic, cultural—against 'old-accustomed' forms (1.2.20).[5] Finally the most stable

[1] 'Aphorism Countertime', in *Acts of Literature*, ed. Derek Attridge (New York and London, 1992), p. 421.

[2] 'Ideology and the Feud in *Romeo and Juliet*', *SSu* 49 (1996), 87–96.

[3] This definition of patriarchy is adapted from Derek Cohen, *Shakespeare's Culture of Violence* (New York, 1993), p. 3.

[4] Coppélia Kahn discusses the feud as an expression of patriarchy in a seminal essay which has been published in more than one form: see 'Coming of Age in Verona', in *The Woman's Part: Feminist Criticism of Shakespeare*, ed. Carolyn Ruth Swift Lenz, Gayle Greene, and Carol Thomas Neely (Urbana, Chicago, and London, 1980), pp. 171–93.

[5] Davis, 'Women on Top', pp. 142–3, describes this contrast in historical terms.

unit of the larger community cannot avoid the stresses inherent in the ideology, but it endures, and Verona endures. Only the younger generation, who internalize imperatives of the feud in the process of becoming adults, pay the ultimate price for its unreasonable demands. The play depicts their crisis in contemporary terms, heightening correspondences in the fiction with analogies from Elizabethan life.

In the earliest texts of *Romeo and Juliet*, unlawful violence is the most obvious sign of pressure within the system as a whole. As Derek Cohen says, writing about other Shakespearian plays, '[a]cts of violence belong to patriarchy as surely as fathers do'.

> They appear . . . to issue directly from that system, indeed, are often logical, rational products of it. . . . Violence, both criminal and legitimate, is an essential form of cultural expression though it is always the dominant culture within society which gets to define criminality and legitimacy. For this reason acts of violence are all political in that they are absorbed by and conform to and, additionally, are produced by a social code which valorizes order as a social value.[1]

Violence in *Romeo and Juliet*, generally unauthorized, not only facilitates the mechanics of plot but adds political implications. At the centre of each novella one dangerous confrontation had occurred: the brawl between Montagues and Capulets that leads to Romeo's banishment. Shakespeare invents two more conflicts, the row in 1.1 and the duel in 5.3, producing a narrative driven by social disorder through violence.[2] Like the ideology in which they originate, the signs are pervasive.

Always ready for armed conflict, weapons appear everywhere in *Romeo and Juliet*. They range from current to obsolete—the rapiers of young gentlemen to the long sword of old Capulet—giving the familiar story new menace as well as concrete signifiers.[3]

[1] *Shakespeare's Culture of Violence*, p. 1.

[2] Joan Ozark Holmer considers the three fight scenes, focusing on 3.1, in '"Myself Condemned and Myself Excus'd": Tragic Effects in *Romeo and Juliet*', *SP* 88 (1991), 345–62; I interpret the violence as less static in '"*Alla stoccado* carries it away": Codes of Violence in *Romeo and Juliet*', in *Shakespeare's 'Romeo and Juliet'*, ed. Halio, pp. 83–96. In addition, Sergio Rossi analyses 'Duelling in the Italian Manner: The Case of *Romeo and Juliet*', in *Shakespeare's Italy: Functions of Italian Locations in Renaissance Drama*, ed. Michele Marrapodi, A. J. Hoenselaars, Marcello Cappuzzo, and L. Falzon Santucci (Manchester and New York, 1993), pp. 112–24.

[3] A. Forbes Sieveking's early description of 'Fencing and Duelling' in *Shakespeare's England: An Account of the Life and Manners of his Age*, ed. Sir Walter

Repeatedly the text calls for weapons as props; often the props make emblematic comments on the action.[1] In the first scene Prince Escalus commands, 'Throw your mistempered weapons to the ground' (1.1.83), and they lie on the stage in disarray for Romeo to notice soon after he enters (l. 169). In the last scene Friar Laurence finds the 'masterless and gory swords' dropped by Paris and Romeo (5.3.142), and Capulet discovers Romeo's dagger 'mis-sheathèd in my daughter's bosom' (l. 205). The text seems to require all of the male characters, except Friar Laurence, to wear weapons or have ready access to them; it reflects Elizabethan practice. At the Capulet ball Tybalt, outraged by Romeo's presence, orders his page, 'Fetch me my rapier, boy' (1.4.168); on the day after the feast Peter neglects to defend the Nurse with the weapon he carries (2.3.146–9). Friar Laurence, like the Apothecary, has poison at hand (2.2.23–4); Capulet's Wife plans to order some (3.5.88–91).

Weapons and fighting occur not only in the play's action but in the dialogue. As a topic of conversation they open the exchange between Samson and Gregory, a conversation that will be echoed later by Peter and the Musicians at the end of 4.4. They distinguish Mercutio's speeches: his fantasy of Queen Mab includes the soldier who dreams 'of cutting foreign throats, | Of breaches, ambuscados, Spanish blades' (1.4.81–2); his characterization of Tybalt portrays a duellist in the Spanish style:[2]

> O, he's the courageous captain of compliments. He fights as you sing prick-song, keeps time, distance, and proportion; he rests his minim rests, one, two, and the third in your bosom—the very butcher of a silk button—a duellist, a duellist, a gentleman of the very first house of the first and second cause. Ah, the immortal *passado*, the *punto riverso*, the *hay*! (2.3.18–25)

Mercutio's caricature of Benvolio as a quarreller trivializes the causes for which gentlemen fight: 'Thou hast quarrelled with a

Alexander Raleigh, Sir Sidney Lee, and C. T. Onions, 2 vols. (Oxford, 1916), ii. 394, rightly identifies in *Romeo and Juliet* 'a perfect epitome of the cause and materials for fighting, of the quarrels that arose, and of the weapons used in their liquidation in Shakespeare's days'.

[1] The props are enumerated below, in 'Initial Staging'. Although illustrations in these paragraphs are drawn from the 1599 version of *Romeo and Juliet*, examples are also prolific in the 1597 text.

[2] See Adolph L. Soens, 'Tybalt's Spanish Fencing in *Romeo and Juliet*', *SQ* 20 (1969), 121–7.

man for coughing in the street, because he hath wakened thy dog that hath lain asleep in the sun' (3.1.23–6).

While furnishing content, implements and acts of combat also provide the dialogue with metaphors. These figures blend with standard topoi of the Petrarchan idiom through which all of the dramatis personae express themselves; a social code animates a literary one.[1] As Leonard Forster explains, the play enacts a conventional stereotype of amatory poetry: 'The enmity of Montague and Capulet makes the cliché of the "dear enemy" into a concrete predicament; the whole drama is devoted to bringing this cliché to life'.[2] Among the tropes connected with this stereotype are military equipment and assault.[3]

The fusion of metaphors begins crudely in the conversation of Samson and Gregory: 'I will push Montague's men from the wall, and thrust his maids to the wall', 'when I have fought with the men, I will be civil with the maids, I will cut off their heads' (1.1.15–17, 20–2). With Romeo's description of Rosaline the conflated tropes, though still extreme, become more refined:

> . . . she'll not be hit
> With Cupid's arrow, she hath Dian's wit;
> And in strong proof of chastity well armed,
> From love's weak childish bow she lives uncharmed.
> She will not stay the siege of loving terms,
> Nor bide th'encounter of assailing eyes . . .
> (1.1.204–9)

The conceits often assume this second form through the rest of the play. In the orchard scene, for instance, Romeo finds more peril in Juliet's eye than in twenty of her kinsmen's swords: 'Look thou but sweet, | And I am proof against their enmity' (2.1.115–16). Immediately he reports to Friar Laurence that he has been feasting with his enemy, 'Where on a sudden one hath wounded me | That's by me wounded' (2.2.50–1). Mercutio describes the lovelorn Romeo as unfit to answer Tybalt's challenge: 'he is already dead, stabbed with a white wench's black eye, run through the ear with a love-song, the very pin of his heart cleft

[1] On the literary and social codes see below, 'Tragedy, Comedy, Sonnet'.

[2] *The Icy Fire: Five Studies in European Petrarchism* (Cambridge, 1969), p. 51.

[3] I have dealt extensively with the play's use of the Petrarchan idiom in 'The Definition of Love: Shakespeare's Phrasing in *Romeo and Juliet*', *SSt* 15 (1982), 21–36.

with the blind bow-boy's butt-shaft' (2.3.12–15). Before the wedding, in a famous passage Friar Laurence imagines the ends of violent delights as the igniting of gunpowder by fire (2.5.9–10). When the lovers part the lark, whose sound pierced their ears, serves as herald to the morning; streaks of light seem envious and clouds severing (3.5.3–8). Finally Romeo defies the stars, determined to end his grief with poison so potent

> that the trunk may be discharged of breath
> As violently as hasty powder fired
> Doth hurry from the fatal cannon's womb.
> (5.1.63–5)

Charged with its ideology, violence determines all forms of expression in Verona, from public conversations to dress to the vocabulary of desire. It spans generations, and it infiltrates the love-story through both incident and verbal style. In the late sixteenth century it gained immediacy from the current events it reflected: violence was an intransigent reality in early modern England. Proclamations against fighting in public had been issued by Henry VII, Henry VIII, and Elizabeth.[1] Despite these and other measures, civil disorder erupted in town and countryside until the turn of the century: brawls disturbed Fleet Street and the Strand; dangerous feuds threatened the peace of whole counties.[2] As the Tudors attempted to contain the capacity for violence, and therefore the power, of the aristocracy, infractions continued to escape them. By the 1590s Queen Elizabeth's policies were beginning to take hold, defusing violence through litigation or limiting it to private confrontation in duels, but street outbreaks persisted and the number of recorded duels and challenges jumped from five in the 1580s to nearly twenty in this decade.[3] With its feud, street fight, duelling, casualties, and deployment of combat imagery,

[1] See Charles Edelman, *Brawl Ridiculous: Swordfighting in Shakespeare's Plays* (Manchester, 1992), pp. 17, 174–5.

[2] Lawrence Stone, *The Crisis of the Aristocracy, 1558–1641* (Oxford, 1965), pp. 229–32.

[3] Stone, *Crisis of the Aristocracy*, p. 245. Christopher Fitter argues that the Crown and its agents ignored aristocratic infractions but imposed severe punishments on lower-class Londoners, causing riots. In his view the play reflects the kinds of class tensions such inequity exacerbated ('"The quarrel is between our masters and us their men": *Romeo and Juliet*, Dearth, and the London Riots', *ELR* 30 (2000)).

Romeo and Juliet offers a panoramic view of violence in Elizabethan England. In the midst of its chaos and death Prince Escalus seems to mirror Elizabeth's conduct towards the élite: temporizing procrastination, 'studied neutrality'.[1]

More specifically, the play's most striking outbursts of violence reflect a contemporary preoccupation with duelling. According to Diane Bornstein, Elizabethan gentlemen not actively engaged in duels constantly read about them, trained for them by learning to fence, and discussed them.[2] By the time *Romeo and Juliet* was composed in the mid-1590s, three manuals dealt with both the art and its ethical code: Sir William Segar's *The Book of Honor and Armes* (1590), Giacomo di Grassi's *His True Arte of Defence* (1594), and Vincentio Saviolo's *Practise* (1595).[3] Like members of his audience, Shakespeare was familiar with the material in these publications, and he may even have known Segar and Saviolo.[4] Certainly he parodied the more absurd fine points throughout his dramatic career, from *Love's Labour's Lost* to *Cymbeline*.[5] With *Hamlet* he would explore a contradiction most noticeable in Saviolo but present in di Grassi and Segar: both skill and moral self-consciousness determine victory in a duel; both decorum and providential justice govern the outcome. With *Romeo and Juliet* he examines this contradiction less than he diminishes its moral terms and, by extension, the violence they rationalize. In the fight scenes moralizing and its paradoxes, central to the duelling code, remain conspicuous by their virtual absence: all of the duellists finally ignore not only the procedures but also the ethics of fighting. Three times the play shows a visually stunning match ending in chaos or death. It follows the issuing of a challenge to its conclusion in two fatal duels and exile. Throughout it echoes instruction published by Saviolo—from appropriate behaviour at great feasts to

[1] Stone, *Crisis of the Aristocracy*, pp. 233–4.

[2] Introduction to Sir William Segar, *The Book of Honor and Armes (1590) and Honor Military and Civil (1602)* (Delmar, NY, 1975), [p. 4].

[3] The manuals of Segar and Saviolo are related to each other: both borrow from Girolamo Muzio's *Il Duello* (1550), and Segar's treatment of honour abridges Saviolo's. For the complicated connections, see Ruth Kelso, 'Saviolo and his *Practise*', *MLN* 39 (1924), 33–5. Di Grassi's volume was originally published in Italian in 1570.

[4] See Bornstein, Introduction, *The Book of Honor and Armes*, [p. 5], and S. P. Zitner, 'Hamlet, Duellist', *University of Toronto Quarterly*, 39 (1969), pp. 17–18 n. 16.

[5] Edelman, *Brawl Ridiculous*, pp. 20–1.

Fig. 2 and 3. Two sixteenth-century expressions of violence showing the contradictions between theory and practice: fighters with rapiers and daggers ready for *stoccadoes* and *imbroccatas*—thrusts over and under the dagger—in Vincentio Saviolo's *Practise* (1595), sig. device 2[v]; and the second duel in *Romeo and Juliet*, Franco Zeffirelli's stage version at the Old Vic, 1960.

strategies for avoiding conflict with a 'friend'[1]—demonstrating over and over again that it does not work.

Violence in all of its manifestations urgently signals disruptions in the patriarchal state of Verona: 'civil blood makes civil hands unclean' (Prologue 4); unlawful outbreaks betray a faltering system which cannot enforce regulations distinguishing criminality from legitimacy. With less force it makes a similar point about the patriarchal family, bound to the state in the play and in fact. What Natalie Zemon Davis writes about the patriarchal family from the sixteenth century to the eighteenth applies to Capulet's situation: 'In the little world of the family, with its conspicuous tension between intimacy and power, the larger matters of political and social order could find ready symbolization'.[2]

From the first scene violence intrudes on Capulet's household, calling him from it on a Sunday morning as he responds to Montague, armed and also drawn from his home, by demanding his long sword.[3] Soon violence will intrude on Capulet's marriage negotiations with Paris: their first exchange about Paris's suit in 1.2 follows Capulet's allusion to the feud and the Prince's efforts to suppress it; the festivities for viewing Juliet in 1.4 are threatened by Tybalt's fury over Romeo's appearance; and the wedding plans in 3.4 and the fourth act go awry, as far as Capulet knows, with the death of Tybalt. Of course these disturbances are superficial, little tremors from a deep cataclysm. With Juliet's defection and its terrible consequences Capulet loses his grip, more visibly than Montague, on his authority as a patriarch.

By the second scene it becomes clear that Capulet has in sight the main objective for marriage arrangements in the Elizabethan age:

> Although children were theoretically able to negotiate their own marriages, parents, especially upper-class parents, continued to regulate spousals in order to achieve or maintain status, cement alliances, gain economic advantage, and ensure continuity of family and property. Indeed, parental pressures may have been especially strong in the period

[1] Saviolo's *Practise*, in *Three Elizabethan Fencing Manuals*, comp., introd. James L. Jackson (Delmar, NY, 1972), pp. 322, 217–18.

[2] 'Women on Top', p. 127.

[3] In the shorter 1597 version of *Romeo and Juliet* a stage direction alone gives the impression of intrusive violence: it calls for entrances by '*old Montague*' and '*old Capulet*', with their wives, into the middle of a street fight (1.1.49.1–3).

(as they certainly are in the plays) due to economic and demographic factors that tended to increase competition for suitable matches.[1]

The dialogue with Paris, which Shakespeare invented, reveals that old Capulet feels his mortality; later episodes, in particular an exchange with his relative at the party (1.4.143–53), will reinforce the effect. At this point the scene positions Capulet to begin transacting his succession. According to the first stage direction Paris is a count, a titled suitor whose status Capulet's Wife will soon confirm (1.3.106). Capulet describes Juliet as his only heir, young and vulnerable (ll. 8–11, 14–15). In his longest speech he sets his terms and observes Elizabethan protocols for arranging a marriage, consent by child and parent.[2]

> Earth hath swallowed all my hopes but she;
> She's the hopeful lady of my earth.
> But woo her, gentle Paris, get her heart,
> My will to her consent is but a part;
> And she agreed, within her scope of choice
> Lies my consent and fair according voice.
> (1.2.14–19)

The correctness of these proceedings contrasts not only Capulet's behaviour in 3.4 and 3.5, but also the unplanned encounter of Romeo and Juliet about to happen in 1.4. Meantime the next scene modifies this decorous picture with its portrayal of the women in Capulet's home: his Wife serves as the agent for his plans, yet the three women form a domestic circle with a life of its own. They generate an impression of female autonomy which the Nurse brings to life in half the lines with her frank sexuality, her anecdotes about nurture and falling backward.[3]

Within a few minutes of stage time Juliet starts to enact that autonomy, choosing her own candidate for husband (1.4.247–8), and later she makes her own marriage arrangements (2.1.186–91). She corresponds in several ways to Bandello's Giulietta, more responsible than Romeo for the course of events and more

[1] Neely, *Broken Nuptials*, p. 10.

[2] See Young, 'Haste, Consent, and Age at Marriage', 466–7.

[3] For other comments on this all-female scene, see Dympna C. Callaghan, 'The Ideology of Romantic Love: The Case of *Romeo and Juliet*', in Callaghan, Lorraine Helms, and Jyotsna Singh, *The Weyward Sisters: Shakespeare and Feminist Politics* (Oxford and Cambridge, Mass., 1994), pp. 84–6, and Snow, 'Language and Sexual Difference', pp. 387–91.

threatening to the patriarchal scheme than her other prototypes. In the play capitalism again becomes an active principle still identified with consolidation of the state and prosperous families.[1] Marriage continues to mean, in the first place, establishment of a new economic unit, a permanent association between two families, and membership of the husband in the community.[2] Ignoring most of these requirements, Juliet too obstructs economic and social progress as much of early modern Europe understood it. Yet she also corresponds to Boaistuau's Julliette, victimized by a system that in the end reveals its own weaknesses and idealizes her.

Similarly, the love Juliet shares with Romeo is a threat to the patriarchal system of family and state. The play makes it sympathetic, a means by which the protagonists discover both themselves and a transcendent mutuality. With more artfulness than Brooke's narrative, it supports the idea of companionate marriage which gained currency during the Elizabethan period; it acknowledges the views advocated by church and state which encouraged marital sexuality.[3] Nevertheless, the love which the play endorses is not only transformative but 'death-marked' (Prologue 9), the product of mythical and literary tradition. Having a predetermined outcome, it cannot transgress very far. Although it disappoints patriarchy and exposes it, ultimately it does not effect significant change in the ideology.

Act 3, Scene 5 illustrates the play's treatment of its central conflict, an opposition without victory; here the little world of the family symbolizes larger matters. By this time the lovers have consummated a marriage performed without parental consent, an offence against the authority of the feuding families. Grieving and fearful after Romeo's departure, Juliet can barely defend herself against her father's emotional assault. Capulet, secure in his paternal rights, has violated accepted Elizabethan practices in his

[1] Callaghan, 'The Ideology of Romantic Love', pp. 71–2, and Diane Elizabeth Dreher, *Domination and Defiance: Fathers and Daughters in Shakespeare* (Lexington, Ky., 1986), p. 40.

[2] Laslett describes these connections between marriage and the social structure of pre-industrial England in *The World We Have Lost—Further Explored*, p. 101.

[3] See Thomas Moisan, '"O Any Thing, of Nothing First Create!": Gender and Patriarchy and the Tragedy of *Romeo and Juliet*', in *In Another Country: Feminist Perspectives on Renaissance Drama*, ed. Dorothea Kehler and Susan Baker (Metuchen, NJ, and London, 1991), p. 116, and Callaghan, 'The Ideology of Romantic Love', pp. 79–80.

rush to complete arrangements with Paris; he has allowed no time for wedding preparations, reading of banns, or proper courtship.[1] In both cases the violations imply strength of will, but Capulet has an ideology to excuse his breach of custom. When the confrontation happens Capulet, unaware that he has already lost control of his daughter, tries to force her into submission. His last words in the scene threaten disinheritance and death:

> An you be mine, I'll give you to my friend;
> An you be not, hang, beg, starve, die in the streets!
> For, by my soul, I'll ne'er acknowledge thee,
> Nor what is mine shall never do thee good.
>
> (ll. 191–4)

Finally Capulet only hastens the inevitable with this speech, and he will not know Juliet's real transgression until the inevitable occurs.

The lovers cannot change or break their social constraints because they have so completely internalized them. However far they escape from gender norms—Juliet in manly risk-taking, Romeo in conciliatory gestures—circumstances force them to return: Juliet reaches a hallucinatory state verging on hysteria before she takes the sleeping potion; Romeo commits murder once in revenge, twice in fury. Nor can they escape their identities as members of rival houses. Everything's in a name, a genealogical marker of an individual's public and private history.[2] Perhaps the most transparent sign of ideology in the lovers' characterization is their appropriating of its language, especially the idiom of finance and quantification.[3] The economic terms which Bandello introduced to the

[1] Young, 'Haste, Consent, and Age at Marriage', 467–8. See also Ann Jennalie Cook, *Making a Match: Courtship in Shakespeare and his Society* (Princeton, 1991), pp. 211, 100–1.

[2] On this subject, see especially Derrida, 'Aphorism Countertime', pp. 416–33, and Catherine Belsey, 'The Name of the Rose in *Romeo and Juliet*', *Yearbook of English Studies*, 23 (1993), repr. in Porter, *Critical Essays*, pp. 70–2.

[3] Greg Bentley writes about 'Poetics of Power: Money as Sign and Substance in *Romeo and Juliet*', *Explorations in Renaissance Culture*, 17 (1991), 145–66. Other critics who analyse the connections between the love-story and its cultural setting include Kirby Farrell, *Play, Death, and Heroism in Shakespeare* (Chapel Hill, NC, and London, 1989), Chapter 8, repr. with variations as 'Love, Death, and Patriarchy in *Romeo and Juliet*', in *Shakespeare's Personality*, ed. Norman N. Holland (Berkeley, Los Angeles, and London, 1989), pp. 86–102; Moisan, 'Gender and Patriarchy', pp. 113–36; and Nathaniel Wallace, 'Cultural Tropology in *Romeo and Juliet*', *SP* 88 (1991), 329–44. In the longest of these essays, Callaghan's 'The Ideology of

novella become even more prominent in the play; and both lovers use them, even to convey their feelings for each other. Particularly noticeable in the wedding scene, this determinate language communicates passion in the distinct voices of the two lovers. When Romeo challenges Juliet to express joy equalling his ('if the measure of thy joy | Be heaped like mine', ll. 24–5), she answers:

> They are but beggars that can count their worth;
> But my true love is grown to such excess,
> I cannot sum up sum of half my wealth.
> (2.5.32–4)

Dympna C. Callaghan describes *Romeo and Juliet* as a 'lyrical document of universal love' which stands within history 'doing the work of culture, instigating and perpetuating the production of socially necessary formations of desire'.[1] Whether or not the play accomplishes such work, it certainly records its own cultural era with its contradictions and defaults. In this sense it shows adult society trying to ward off anomie while a young generation invites it, adapting a compromised ideology in the fervour to become individuals. Adolescent impatience and unreasonableness, keynotes of Mercutio and Tybalt in particular, encapsulate the feud, from its rivalries for power to its allegiances and poignancy. If Romeo and Juliet resist their socialization and for several fleeting days create a private world apart from Verona, they nevertheless continue to incorporate the familiar in the new, and they struggle to reconcile the new with the familiar. The play depicts them as vulnerable young lovers, fragile embodiments of ideas and values that test the status quo. In the coda to their deaths it qualifies their achievement. Their fathers celebrate the marriage with equally valuable gold-plated figures; Capulet regards the lovers as '[p]oor sacrifices of our enmity' (5.3.304). A melancholy spectacle, the tragedy brings '[a] glooming peace' (l.305)—hardly new in Verona—but no signs of lasting change.

Style and Genre. The first audiences of *Romeo and Juliet*, whatever their social and economic distribution,[2] must have been surprised

Romantic Love', pp. 59–101, '[t]he goal . . . is to examine the role of *Romeo and Juliet* in the cultural construction of desire' (p. 59).

[1] Callaghan, 'The Ideology of Romantic Love', p. 88.

[2] On the composition of Elizabethan audiences, see Andrew Gurr, *Playgoing in Shakespeare's London*, 2nd edn. (Cambridge, 1996), *passim*.

by this rendering of the famous story. Shakespeare changed traditions as he used them in this play, continuously and often radically. With the opening sonnet, literary and dramatic customs appear just long enough to be identified: the work presents itself as a tragedy based on a familiar narrative and expressed through love-poetry. But once the action starts, Shakespeare immediately modifies these customs and they begin to seem unfamiliar, slightly eccentric. As the dramatic narrative takes its course, anomalous variations repeatedly jar established patterns. Their frequency and placement again and again strike the note of wit that prevents *Romeo and Juliet* from becoming an intense two-hour dirge for young love.

As this discussion of the play has already noticed, Shakespeare reworked the widely known sixteenth-century fiction with substantive changes. He retained two basic features, the sequence of events and the characters' roles, but he adjusted even these. In an important essay on *Romeo and Juliet*, Harry Levin describes how the dramatist patterned this material by imposing symmetry on much of it. Symmetry affects the formulation of the narrative, where scenes of violence alternate at regular intervals with domestic scenes set in Capulet's house; it affects the arrangement of characters, who appear in counterpoised sets from Montagues and Capulets to Benvolio and Tybalt to the Friar and the Nurse; and it affects the rhetoric of the verse, which more than a hundred times balances lines by repeating words in them: 'These violent delights have violent ends' (2.5.9). In its order and balance it contributes to the strong impression of design in the play. If *Romeo and Juliet* transmits a compound of volatile materials—romance at its limits, adolescent turmoil, patriarchy under stress—it contains these potentially explosive components by stylizing them. According to T. J. B. Spencer in the New Penguin edition, 'Nothing in European drama had hitherto achieved the organisation of so much human experience' (p. 7).

But stylization of form and language accomplishes more than containment. It becomes a commentary on the action, a reminder of controls which are absent in both public and private life. At the same time its formalities parallel rituals in Verona—from organization of marriages to organization of funerals—and frequently they too disappoint expectation. In the process they not only complicate the narrative, but call attention to its aesthetic. They critique the novellas which had become fixed in their idiom and rhetoric; and they critique themselves, the rhetorical, dramatic, and poetic conventions adapted to this version of the narrative. Stylizing the fiction as a play, Shakespeare took the Romeo and Juliet plot out of its well-known frame of reference, the particular conflation of rhetoric, realistic details, and stock literary devices which produced a uniformly serious ambience for the lovers' story. With his alterations the tone of the dramatic narrative, self-reflective and variable, is far more expressive than the sobering voices of the novellas. It is also ironic. By means of standard devices—repeated references to fate, the stars, premonitions, dreams, and chance—the play insists, as the fictional narrators had insisted, upon its own coherence and the reasonableness of its fable. It gives broad hints towards its own interpretation, but invariably it contradicts them, especially with allusions to the concept of fortune which Brooke had made so prominent. In the drama the impression of coincidence, emphatic in the course of the action, competes with the impression of cosmic fate, a motif in the language. At last the competition itself proves more important than either contestant.

(*a*) *Rhetoric*. Through its treatment of rhetoric *Romeo and Juliet* breaks with the tradition of the novellas, which had used the art primarily to decorate and rationalize the sequence of events. Shakespeare worked at rhetoric in this play: there is evidence of revision in extravagant passages (such as 3.2.73–85),[1] and schemes appear everywhere until the end. He deliberately reinvented the medium which had conveyed the Romeo and Juliet story, a project which allowed him to engage with it in new ways. As scholarship demonstrates, he employed a number of strategies in the encounter.[2]

For example, Shakespeare cuts and reallocates deliberative argument, assigning most of what remains to characters other than the protagonists. Their counsel, which frequently halts rash action, more often accelerates disaster and gives rise to irony. At the centre of the play Friar Laurence has the most extensive speech

[1] See Pearlman, pp. 107–11, for the connection between rhetoric and revision in the 1599 quarto.

[2] For a guide to rhetorical studies of the play, see my article 'Shakespeare's *Romeo and Juliet*: The Places of Invention', 45–55. The Commentary to this edition pays particular attention to rhetorical devices. In the following paragraphs the illustrations come from the longer 1599 quarto; most have parallels in the 1597 quarto.

of disputation. This passage of fifty-one lines, 3.3.107–57, illustrates one of Shakespeare's straightforward techniques for calling rhetoric into question: setting an accomplished performance into a context which reduces its effect. Attempting to calm Romeo, distraught at news of his banishment, Friar Laurence delivers a rhetorical tour de force based on Brooke's less accomplished original (1353–480). Brooke's version leaves no doubt that the Friar's rhetoric has the desired effect on Romeus; Shakespeare's is ambivalent. Unlike his receptive prototype, Romeo damns philosophy before Friar Laurence begins (ll. 57–60), and he provokes the speech with a desperate question (itself rhetorical):

> O tell me, Friar, tell me,
> In what vile part of this anatomy
> Doth my name lodge? Tell me, that I may sack
> The hateful mansion.
>
> (ll. 104–7)

After Friar Laurence concludes we hear not Romeo but the Nurse, who exclaims, 'O, what learning is!' (l. 159); and Romeo reacts in response not to the argument but to the promise of seeing Juliet.

Ambivalence, which accompanies disputation and some of the pathos in *Romeo and Juliet*—the laments over the sleeping Juliet in 4.4 are a striking instance (see ll. 67–90 n.)—assumes most importance in the figures of ambiguity which permeate the narrative. As Mahood has shown in the second chapter of her seminal book, wordplay begins with the Prologue and never disappears from the text. Like other rhetorical devices, it interacts with different kinds of figures: Friar Laurence's staid arguments in 3.3 and 4.4 include wordplay. Often it destabilizes equilibrium, disrupts order, or baffles predictability. It opens a familiar story to new interpretations while making the familiar devices seem inadequate, in themselves, to the demands of narration. In this edition the Commentary tracks wordplay, which proliferates and varies, from the pun on *civil* in the fourth line of the opening sonnet to the equivocation *poor sacrifices of* at the very end of the text (5.3.304).

Frequently Shakespeare organizes wordplay as a contest which may postpone the love-story even though it involves the protagonists. This format, wordplay as contest, transcribes in rhetorical figures a competitive element in the social exchange of Verona. Many times it correlates with invention of another kind: new characters, episodes, or speeches. Mercutio and Romeo share a series of puns on their way to the Capulet party (1.4.12–26) and at a meeting on the street (2.3.43–82). In 2.3.83–7, lines noted above, Mercutio makes it clear that he views the second exchange, a concentrated display of rhetorical figures, as the most proficient kind of social discourse, the language of his peer group. Yet this conversation spins words so fast and automatically that it threatens to empty them of meaning:

MERCUTIO Sure wit, follow me this jest now till thou hast worn out thy pump, that when the single sole of it is worn, the jest may remain, after the wearing, solely singular.

ROMEO O single-soled jest, solely singular for the singleness!

(ll. 59–63)

In this episode wordplay and other figures, agents of sociability, flirt with nonsense. They also create an interlude in the sequence of the love-story.

As a medium of social exchange in *Romeo and Juliet*, this combination of figures resembles other kinds of play: it has a precarious edge where a speaker may lose control of the game; it licenses players to court disaster or mask deception. During the new episode in 3.1 Mercutio challenges Tybalt in rhetorical terms: 'Will you pluck your sword out of his pilcher by the ears? Make haste, lest mine be about your ears ere it be out' (ll. 78–80). Tybalt, who never responds to Mercutio's verbal sparring, takes this dare literally. Mercutio dies in character, famously, with a series of puns and other figures. No longer part of a competition, the devices now communicate disbelief and outrage. In the aftermath of this scene wordplay will fuse with various schemes to negotiate risky situations through subterfuge. Juliet in particular depends on equivocation to communicate with her family and with Paris.

Clearly rhetorical figures in *Romeo and Juliet* not only amplify the narrative but also call attention to the processes of amplification. Several well-known passages labour devices as if they were inviting a critical assessment of both the schemes and their effects. What strikes modern sensibility as sheer flamboyance is probably a figure stretched beyond its usual range, performing a more complex function. At 3.2.45–50, Juliet's frenzied series of puns on aye/i/I/eye produces three effects (see ll. 45–50 n.). In this scene, ll. 73–85, and at 1.1.172–7, extended passages of synoeciosis, condensed paradox or oxymoron, project confused emotions and points of view: Romeo's about Rosaline; Juliet's about Romeo, who has just killed Tybalt. The formal, imprecise figures express what the speakers feel but fit their subjects awkwardly.

Perhaps Mercutio's Queen Mab speech at 1.4.51–93 offers the most elaborate array of rhetorical devices in a passage invented for the text. It stands far enough apart from the sequence that Pearlman considers it an interpolation: 'Mercutio's excursus is not articulated with the remainder of *Romeo and Juliet* in terms of plot, content, language, or intellection. There is no overlap between the realist, materialist Mercutio and the Mercutio who celebrates Queen Mab in elaborate, imaginative, and romantic terms.'[1] His conclusions about Mercutio notwithstanding, Pearlman raises an important issue by emphasizing the singularity of the speech: Mercutio takes up the subject of dreams, introduced by Romeo but absent from the other narratives at this point, and amplifies it for forty lines. R. O. Evans calls Mercutio's performance 'a demonstration of rhetorical fireworks', and he claims that no Elizabethan writer would employ so many figures without intending to make the passage conspicuous.[2] From the start Shakespeare extends the use of anaphora (repetition at the beginnings of clauses) and zeugma (one verb serving more than one clause), outdoing the illustrations in contemporary textbooks. These grammatical devices frame other kinds of schemes from apostrophe to figures of ambiguity and ominatio, or prognostication of evil.

Scattered through the text, a number of other passages seem to reflect explicitly on the play's use of rhetoric. The first and most obvious follows Romeo's apostrophe to love in a burst of contradictions. 'Dost thou not laugh?', he asks Benvolio. The answer, 'No, coz, I rather weep', compounds the deflation even as it directs the exchange towards more derivative paradoxes (1.1.179). In the wedding scene Juliet makes a comment about decorum which applies not only to Romeo's language but also to the play's:

> Conceit, more rich in matter than in words,
> Brags of his substance, not of ornament.
>
> (2.5.30–1)

[1] 'Shakespeare at Work', p. 119. See n. 20 on pp. 129–30 for a summary of criticism which argues that the speech is relevant.

[2] See pp. 81, 86. My summary of devices in Mercutio's Queen Mab speech condenses Evans's detailed analysis, pp. 73–86.

However the audience interprets *conceit* (see l. 30 n.), Juliet refuses to compete with Romeo in formal terms.[1] Of course she does so rhetorically, in a speech which elaborates its subject through wordplay, polyptoton (words from the same root with different endings), and an epigram. At the end of 4.4 Peter and the musicians provide a more extensive commentary. As Thomas Moisan explains the episode, these characters subject the operations of rhetoric to common sense, take amplification literally, and deconstruct a phrase from Richard Edwards's *Paradise of Dainty Devices* (1576), 'a compendium of the lachrymose rhetoric we have heard *fortissime* throughout the mourners' speeches'.[2]

Juliet's vexed question in 2.1 may also refer to the medium she speaks:

> What's in a name? That which we call a rose
> By any other word would smell as sweet; . . .
> (ll. 86–7)

In *Shakespeare and the Rhetoricians*, Marion Trousdale makes a distinction which states what these lines imply:

> Shape is something absolute and suggests parts whose functions, once determined, are irrevocably fixed. A rose in that sense is a rose. But one cannot say the same thing about its name, which, like language itself, is artificial. A name can, at will, both define and embellish, and, unlike the rose, it can divide 'one thing entire to many objects' (*Richard II*, 2.2.17).[3]

Romeo and Juliet allows its audience to measure the advantages of such embellishment against its limitations.

That kind of engagement animates other literary works of the late sixteenth century, as critics have demonstrated.[4] It informs Shakespeare's Sonnets and narrative verse as well as his early plays: Lanham shows how it affects *Venus and Adonis*, *Lucrece*, and

[1] On this passage and the use of conceits in the play, see Edgar Mertner, '"Conceit Brags of His Substance, Not of Ornament": Some Notes on Style in *Romeo and Juliet*', in *Shakespeare: Text, Language, Criticism: Essays in Honour of Marvin Spevack*, ed. Bernhard Fabian and Kurt Tetzeli von Rosador (Hildesheim, Zurich, and New York, 1987), pp. 180–92.

[2] 'Rhetoric and the Rehearsal of Death: The "Lamentations" Scene in *Romeo and Juliet*', *SQ* 34 (1983), 402.

[3] Chapel Hill, NC, 1982, p. 157.

[4] See Joel B. Altman, *The Tudor Play of Mind: Rhetorical Inquiry and the Development of Elizabethan Drama* (Berkeley, Los Angeles, and London, 1978), and the books cited above by Kinney and Rebhorn.

the Sonnets; Trousdale analyses *Love's Labour's Lost*.[1] In most of these texts rhetoric, vigorous and accomplished, comes up against barriers of its own making, rigidities inherent in language. Its processes expose the sources of intractableness: the inability of words to express for their speakers the real conditions of their lives; the potential for amplification to grow out of control.[2] According to Joel B. Altman, Renaissance tragedy takes a particularly dim view of rhetoric: '. . . invention fails, as in comedy, because it cannot transcend man's epistemological condition and attain to truth—and it fails because it deals with a world in which will, not reason, determines human actions'.[3] All of these texts exploit and doubt rhetoric at the same time, raising questions not only about the art itself but also about rhetoricians and the culture that fosters them.[4]

In this vein *Romeo and Juliet* explores the capacity of rhetoric to rationalize human conduct in moving terms. It pursues this investigation with the ambivalence that Kenneth Muir has recognized in Shakespeare's early works.[5] Argument inevitably leads to error, accident, and death, as it did in the Romeo and Juliet fictions. Rhetorical schemes may interrupt the sequence but they fail to change it in any substantive way. While figures amplify events, da Porto's plot and characters move inexorably towards their tragic conclusion. Rhetoric cannot overcome necessity or describe it with precision. Yet it can present the full range of ambiguities that surround every human act. Despite its limitations, rhetorical virtuosity in *Romeo and Juliet* allows more than one interpretation of both events and the verbal medium through which they travel.

(*b*) *Tragedy, Comedy, Sonnet*. In addition to reinventing the medium of the Romeo and Juliet narrative, Shakespeare created a new genre for it, a unique arrangement of tragedy, comedy, and sonnet sequence. H. B. Charlton first addressed the unorthodox treatment of genre in an influential lecture delivered in 1939, '*Romeo and Juliet* as an Experimental Tragedy'.[6] By now others

[1] Lanham, *The Motives of Eloquence*, Chapters 4 and 5; Trousdale, *Shakespeare and the Rhetoricians*, pp. 95–113.

[2] Rebhorn makes these points in *The Emperor of Men's Minds*, p. 235.

[3] *The Tudor Play of Mind*, p. 230.

[4] See Rebhorn, *The Emperor of Men's Minds*, especially Chapter 2.

[5] 'Shakespeare and Rhetoric', *SJ* 90 (1954), 49–68.

[6] *Proceedings of the British Academy*, 1939, 25 (1940), pp. 143–85.

have described the novel disposition of generic features. For example, Levin explains how Shakespeare introduced the subject of romantic love to the genre of English Renaissance tragedy.

> Legend, it had been heretofore taken for granted, was the proper matter for serious drama; romance was the stuff of the comic stage. Romantic tragedy—'*an excellent conceited Tragedie of Romeo and Juliet*', to cite the title-page of the First Quarto—was one of those contradictions in terms which Shakespeare seems to have delighted in resolving. His innovation might be described as transcending the usages of romantic comedy, which are therefore very much in evidence, particularly at the beginning.[1]

When he alludes to 'the usages of romantic comedy', Levin indicates another novelty in Shakespeare's treatment of dramatic genre. With *Romeo and Juliet* tragedy entertains not only new subject matter, but also conventions of plot, character, and style from a totally different theatrical mode which flourished during the 1590s. A number of critics have explored this comic dimension of the play, trying to understand how it functions and what it signifies. In *The Comic Matrix of Shakespeare's Tragedies*, Susan Snyder finds the comic element prominent enough to support her argument that *Romeo and Juliet* goes through genre transformation: 'Action and characters begin in the familiar comic mold and are then transformed or discarded, to compose the shape of tragedy'.[2] No matter how the results are interpreted, Shakespeare's counterpointing of genres affects the play's structure and tone from moment to moment; and it provides means to emphasize the complex bonds between art and social life intrinsic to the dramatic content.[3]

Its earliest title-pages call *Romeo and Juliet* 'An Excellent Conceited Tragedy', 'The Most Excellent and Lamentable Tragedy', and 'The Tragedy'; Francis Meres lists it among Shakespeare's tragedies in his *Palladis Tamia; Wit's Treasury* (1598);[4] and the Folio places it among the tragedies between *Titus Andronicus* and *Timon of Athens*. In short, external evidence insists that the tragic genre governs this work, serving as host to other kinds and modes.

[1] 'Form and Formality in *Romeo and Juliet*', p. 45.

[2] Princeton, 1979, p. 57.

[3] The analysis which follows has been adapted from my essay '*Romeo and Juliet*: Tragical-Comical-Lyrical History', in *Proceedings of the PMR* [Patristic, Mediaeval, and Renaissance] *Conference*, vol. 12/13 (Villanova, Pa., 1990 for 1987/8), pp. 31–46.

[4] Preface by Arthur Freeman (New York and London, 1973), p. 282r.

But external evidence proves somewhat misleading because the dramatic narrative so frequently shifts into comedy, an effect hinted by 'Conceited', which could mean 'witty' (*OED ppl. a.* 1c). Like many other English Renaissance plays, *Romeo and Juliet* contains more than one generic repertoire: tragedy and comedy coexist, overlap, and produce a hybrid form. In some episodes, especially those of lamentation, the two kinds have become difficult to distinguish. Neither scholars nor directors can agree which genre predominates in a tragic–comic passage like 4.4.67–90 (see ll. 67–90 n.).

Renaissance critical theory does little to explain this generic phenomenon, but twentieth-century genre theory helps to account for it by discovering likenesses between early modern tragedy and comedy. According to Alastair Fowler, a genre or 'kind' is a 'type of literary work of a definite size, marked by a complex of substantive and formal features that always include a distinctive (though not usually unique) external structure'.[1] Significantly, Elizabethan tragedy and comedy share the same 'external structure', a formula derived from Latin comedies as the later age perceived them. In both types of dramatic representations the narrative advances in three phases whose proportions may vary: exposition and beginning of the action; complication of incidents; and catastrophe or resolution. Of course, tragedy resolves the complications in death; comedy, in a happy ending.[2] Moreover both genres are, on a scale of epigram to epic, middle-sized but capacious. Within their frames they can accommodate elements not only from each other but also from a wide range of other forms literary and non-literary, small and medium in length. Sometimes they share incidental features, novella sources, protagonists of lesser rank, private situations, a theme of love. In effect, Elizabethan tragedy and comedy had so much in common that a stroke of the pen could change one into the other.[3] With minimum disruption each could admit the other's character types, plot devices, incidents, and tonalities. It was primarily the conclusion that made the difference.

[1] *Kinds of Literature: An Introduction to the Theory of Genres and Modes* (Cambridge, Mass., 1982), p. 74.

[2] On Renaissance concepts of tragic and comic formats, see T. W. Baldwin, *Shakespere's Five-Act Structure* (Urbana, 1947).

[3] See Snyder, *Comic Matrix*, p. 56, and M. C. Bradbrook, *Themes and Conventions of Elizabethan Tragedy* (Cambridge, 1935), p. 37.

Romeo and Juliet emphasizes the points of congruence in its strikingly balanced configuration of tragedy and comedy. Like a metaphysical conceit, it deliberately yokes unlikely partners to illuminate the similarity in difference. As the dramatic sequence progresses, one form literally metamorphoses into the other, sometimes merging at the moment of connection. The play begins with such a transformation. First the audience hear the Chorus promise a tragic ending (Prologue 5–8); then they watch two servants burlesque the Chorus's themes—feud and romantic love—with visual as well as verbal puns (1.1.1–36). At the centre of the action, the scene of Romeo and Juliet's marriage (2.5) fades into Mercutio's banter and Mercutio's death (3.1).

On one level, then, *Romeo and Juliet* dramatizes generic observations; it sums up a development in English Renaissance theatre, offering a representation of practice rather than abstract systems of thought. When the play originally made these observations, both genres already belonged to the public domain and both had already been combined. John Lyly's Prologue to his comedy *Midas* (*c.*1589) indicates the circumstances which called forth the interrelated kinds: a new audience of mixed character and taste demanding the extension of generic limits:

> At our exercises, soldiers call for tragedies, their object is blood; courtiers for comedies, their subject is love; countrymen for pastorals, shepherds are their saints. Traffic and travel hath woven the nature of all nations into ours, and made this land like arras, full of device . . . (iii. 115)

Although Lyly wrote for the private theatre, he describes here the large and varied audiences of the public playhouse, the patrons of drama. With *Romeo and Juliet*, Shakespeare aimed to satisfy these patrons with the blended essences of two favourite genres.

These two popular genres bear the impress of a third kind, the sonnet sequence. From the opening sonnet to the closing sestet, short lyrics in *Romeo and Juliet* form a heterogeneous series. The amatory verse includes not only sonnets but quatrains, octaves, an aubade, an epithalamium, a duet, a quartet, and some straightforward rhymed passages.[1] In its variety, such verse belongs to the tradition of sequences conceived 'as something more than a collection of imploring sonnets'. While the Elizabethan

[1] See my article 'The Definition of Love', 25–6.

sequences frequently end with a longer poetic narrative, the dramatic version conveniently makes the sustained narrative its plot. Lyrics and narrative illuminate each other in both the sequences and the play.[1]

Traced by lyric continuity, the outline of a sonnet sequence extends the length of *Romeo and Juliet*. In addition, the conventions of love-poetry fill the dialogue and inform many situations. All of the dramatis personae express themselves in some variation of the Petrarchan idiom; they speak the standard topoi and rhetoric. Moreover, the feud central to the Romeo and Juliet story allowed Shakespeare to enlarge the oppositions of Petrarchan rhetoric into plot 'as well as into the emotional and social structure of the play'. In Rosalie L. Colie's phrase, the playwright 'unmetaphors' familiar literary devices.[2] Characters enact the verbal conventions: the lover's anguish, the unattainable lady, the equating of love and war.

If genre is 'the place where the individual work enters into a complex network of relations with other works',[3] what does this unusual juxtaposition mean, the adapting of sonnet sequence to tragedy and comedy? In the first and most obvious place, the arrangement once more draws attention to points of likeness among different genres. Like literary criticism, the play indicates that contemporary drama and poetry share the theme of love with its conventional topoi, its changing visage. Shakespeare displays the variety, inclusiveness, and balance which theatrical and lyric genres have in common. By making romantic comedy and amatory verse prominent, he acknowledges the current vogue of each form. Meanwhile, he conspicuously links two genres that take an outsider's view of court life and court values.

In the second place, Shakespeare's juxtaposition reveals differences among the genres which point beyond the aesthetic sphere. They lead us from the work of art to its social context and to dimensions of meaning hidden from view. As the historian Lauro

[1] On the heterogeneity of the sequences, see, for example, John Kerrigan's Introduction to his edition of *The Sonnets* and *A Lover's Complaint* (Harmondsworth, 1986), pp. 7–18, and Thomas P. Roche, Jr., 'Shakespeare and the Sonnet Sequence', in *English Poetry and Prose 1540–1674*, ed. Christopher Ricks (1970; rev. edn. 1986), pp. 73–89. The quotation is from Roche, p. 78.

[2] *Shakespeare's 'Living Art'* (Princeton, 1974), p. 145.

[3] Maria Corti, *An Introduction to Literary Semiotics*, trans. Margherita Bogat and Allen Mandelbaum (Bloomington and London, 1978), p. 115.

Martines might say, they take us 'from poem to world'.[1] The verse-form especially builds such a bridge. Unlike Tudor drama, the sonnet sequences had a well-defined genealogy, set of conventions, milieu, and audience. They derived, of course, from Petrarch; and by the time the sonnet itself reached England through Wyatt (1503–42), it had become the most exacting test of a poet's skill. After the publication of Sidney's *Astrophil and Stella* in 1591, the series occupied a privileged rung on the hierarchy of kinds. Poets from diverse social ranks soon attempted the genre, hoping to improve their status by mastering the aristocratic verse.

The link between status and verse had been forged in the 1580s, when sonnet sequences took their lofty place among the aristocracy. At the highest reaches of Elizabethan social life, courtly love had become a complex mode of play. Courtiers addressed the Queen in the Petrarchan style; they expressed their aspirations to power in the conventional language of love. With its amatory theme, suppliant's posture, and literary credentials, the sonnet sequence could adapt easily to the game. Sidney first exploited this potential, using the politically encoded language as the idiom for his sequence. In Arthur F. Marotti's view, Sidney 'made sonnet sequences the occasion for socially, economically and politically importunate Englishmen to express their unhappy condition in the context of a display of literary mastery'.[2]

As a result, every feature of the Petrarchan situation became a metaphor for something else: the unreachable lady stood for impossible goals; flattery of her charms disguised supplication for patronage; and desire itself represented ambition for advancement, its range benign to wilful. Again and again the English sonneteers tried to profit from this language: Daniel, Spenser, Greville. In the 1590s sonnets 'darkened the air; they emerged by the thousands'.[3] According to Meres, Shakespeare's own 'sugared' versions circulated 'among his private friends' by 1598.[4]

[1] See Chapter 2 of *Society and History in English Renaissance Verse* (Oxford and New York, 1985).

[2] My information about the political background of the sonnet sequences comes from Martines, *Society and History*, *passim*, and Marotti, '"Love is not love": Elizabethan Sonnet Sequences and the Social Order', *English Literary History*, 49 (1982), 396–428. The quotation is from p. 408.

[3] Patrick Cruttwell, *The Shakespearean Moment and Its Place in the Poetry of the Seventeenth Century* (1954), p. 16.

[4] *Palladis Tamia; Wits Treasury*, pp. 281^{v}–282^{r}.

As the genre peaked, attracting both emulation and parody, Shakespeare explored its possibilities as a kind. His sequence uses the conventions not only to appeal for patronage, but to record the struggles of a working poet within the system. Mingling epigram with sonnets and making verbal postures literal, Shakespeare also expresses doubts about this medium directly through the poet-narrator:

> Why write I still all one, ever the same,
> And keep invention in a noted weed,
> That every word doth almost tell my name,
> Showing their birth and where they did proceed?
> O know, sweet love, I always write of you,
> And you and love are still my argument;
> So all my best is dressing old words new,
> Spending again what is already spent; . . .
>
> (Sonnet 76.5–12)

Throughout the sequence, passages of disenchantment and frustration express doubts about the system which the medium promotes.

At about the same time, Shakespeare appropriated these very conventions for *Romeo and Juliet*. He transferred them from the aristocratic milieu to the public theatre, from an élite to a popular venue. Perhaps he meant to dignify his theatrical craft by fusing it with the art of lyric. With allusions to the sonnet sequence, he may have appealed to members of the audience who could appreciate the references: young men from the Inns of Court, courtiers and gentry. He may even have wanted to rethink the genre from a different point of view. Whatever his purpose, Shakespeare has deconstructed the poetic form and distributed it throughout the tragic–comic structure. The narrator's voice becomes many voices as the sonnet monologue is absorbed by the multivocal text. Anatomized in this way and distanced, the lyric form loses some of its affect. It becomes a more tractable subject for appraisal; and its politics change.[1]

[1] Recently three other critics have considered Shakespeare's appropriation of the sonnet in *Romeo and Juliet*: Gayle Whittier, 'The Sonnet's Body and the Body Sonnetized in *Romeo and Juliet*', *SQ* 40 (1989), repr. in Porter, *Critical Essays*, pp. 47–63; Heather Dubrow, *Echoes of Desire: English Petrarchism and Its Counterdiscourses* (Ithaca, NY, and London, 1995), pp. 262–7; and Diane E. Henderson, *Passion Made Public: Elizabethan Lyric, Gender, and Performance* (Urbana and Chicago, 1995), pp. 1–6. The first scholar to emphasize the play's connection with the sonnet was N. Brooke, pp. 80–106.

In the Verona of *Romeo and Juliet*, Shakespeare releases sonnet conventions from their traditional frame of reference in more ways than one. First, he imagines a city where everyone speaks or enacts the Petrarchan idiom. Even the servants who open the play act out the topos of 'dear enemy', reducing it to the absurd. As quarrelling and quibbling intensify in this first scene—as the stage fills with Veronese society—familiar Petrarchan conceits and devices punctuate the dialogue: images of beasts, fish, canker [worms], fire; antitheses and rhetorical questions, sometimes combined ('What, drawn and talk of peace?', l. 66).

The sonnet idiom crosses not only social ranks but generations. With the first descriptions of Romeo's love-melancholy, for example, Benvolio and Montague speak passages of almost equal length (1.1.114–38). Both adopt the topoi of Petrarchism, verbalizing a portrait of the sonnet lover: the pre-dawn secret wanderings, the restlessness, solitude, sleeplessness, tears, and sighs; and they do so through the familiar conceits of locale, prison, sun/clouds, day/night, and through the customary devices of hyperbole and antithesis. Much later in the play, after Romeo's departure for Mantua, Capulet describes his weeping daughter, to her face, by imitating a Wyatt translation of Petrarch (see 3.5.126–36 and n.). No one writes poetry in Verona, but everyone speaks it for better or worse. The Elizabethan language fraught with political metaphor belongs to the city's regular discourse on love and rivalry, its two major themes. Delicately, that language complements more obvious signs of social ambition, the Capulets' wedding arrangements in particular.

With this first adjustment, then, the sonnet idiom becomes a universal language in *Romeo and Juliet*, a subtle indicator of cultural values. With the second, it remains detached from any specific object of power or patronage, a general sign of aspiration. Romeo comes closest to playing the courtly game in the usual way during the first act, when he languishes for Rosaline. Confessing his infatuation to Benvolio, he idealizes the lady in terms associated with Queen Elizabeth as 'lover's mistress, lay Madonna, and medieval Lady of the tourney'[1] (1.1.204–12); he creates a personification of chastity with mythological allusions as well as military

[1] Cruttwell, *Shakespearean Moment*, p. 29.

and religious conceits. At the same time, like the poet-narrator of Shakespeare's early sonnets, he speaks to aristocratic values of marriage and procreation. But the abstraction never materializes; and it loses its force as a vision through Benvolio's sceptical remarks. Consequently, the play's one potential symbol for sociopolitical goals evaporates by the end of the second scene: Rosaline is notable primarily for her absence.

During the fourth scene Romeo finds Juliet, a real and powerless object of love. From that point on the sonnet idiom takes a third liberty: it becomes a private language of desire as its terms and conventions undergo significant change. The courtly metaphor weakens, vehicle separating from tenor. In the speeches of Romeo and Juliet, the sonnet idiom loses much of its political signification. It expresses their desire for each other: the joy of its fulfilment and grief of its frustration. Gradually it acquires variety and resonance, even in the formal setting of Capulet's party. At the lovers' first encounter—the sonnet with quatrain—Romeo introduces religious conceits which he had just used to idolize Rosaline, but now he and Juliet act out the tropes, giving them new meaning. Instead of celebrating an abstraction, the pilgrim/shrine metaphors permit desire its initial, tentative expression as the lovers touch and kiss.

In the passages leading to their marriage, Romeo and Juliet continue to adapt the public language of amatory verse to their secret love. As they find voices to articulate their feelings, Juliet in particular discards pointless words and conventions. She ignores Romeo's conceits early in their garden scene, intent on learning his identity and access. 'What man art thou[?]', she asks, and Romeo elaborates:

> My name, dear saint, is hateful to myself,
> Because it is an enemy to thee.
> (2.1.95, 98–9)

Disregarding the metaphors, Juliet finds her answer elsewhere: 'I know the sound. | Art thou not Romeo, and a Montague?' (ll. 102–3). When she questions, 'How camest thou hither, tell me, and wherefore?', he responds that the power of Cupid gave him means and immunity: 'With love's light wings did I o'erperch these walls', and 'Therefore thy kinsmen are no stop to me' (ll. 105, 109, 112). The conceit fails to reassure her: 'If they do see thee, they will murder thee' (l. 113). In his next attempt, Romeo draws on another Petrarchan cliché:

> Alack, there lies more peril in thine eye
> Than twenty of their swords. Look thou but sweet,
> And I am proof against their enmity.
> (ll. 114–16)

Again Juliet does not hear him: 'I would not for the world they saw thee here' (l. 117). Later she asks Romeo to refrain from swearing lovers' vows. Yet she draws on amatory verse in the same lines for an image to express her hope (ll. 164–5), and she uses hyperbole to describe the intensity of her feelings (ll. 176–8). When dawn approaches the lovers share a figure, 'a wanton's bird' (ll. 222–9), which captures both the tenderness and the fragility of the moment.

During 2.1 Juliet's plain diction seems to refine the courtly mode; it makes the public style not only more personal but more exact. Later in the action—after the death of Mercutio, when events move from crisis to crisis—the higher style frequently modulates abruptly into the lower, or absorbs it in a new poetry. As the play inclines towards tragedy, this dynamic verse registers the lovers' volatile emotions.

When 3.2 begins, for instance, Juliet speaks an epithalamium (ll. 1–31)—a song to celebrate forthcoming nuptials—anticipating the consummation of her marriage. Her poetry overflows with the conventions of Petrarchan verse, their abundance contributing to the vitality of the lines. At this point, amatory verse provides her with a vocabulary to express breathless anticipation and ardency. Yet the verse rings with her voice: much of its diction is plain; it conveys excitement through repetition; and its pitch heightens with intensity. Once the Nurse interrupts with news of calamity, the poetic vocabulary of love suddenly fails Juliet. In the laboured wordplay (ll. 45–50) her diction shrinks to commonplace puns and sound effects. Here the modulation indicates how swiftly Juliet's grief has arrested her imagination. Shortly, as she begins to recover and learns the truth, her verse expands again with typical Petrarchan devices: she describes Romeo in a catalogue of oxymora which obviously do not fit him:

> O serpent heart, hid with a flow'ring face!
> Did ever dragon keep so fair a cave?

> Beautiful tyrant, fiend angelical,
> Dove-feathered raven, wolvish-ravening lamb, . . .
> A damnèd saint, an honourable villain.
>
> (ll. 73–9)

At this moment, the formal, imprecise figures of speech indicate Juliet's unreadiness for this first encounter with sorrow and disillusion. Her lexicon for making distinctions—the conventions of amatory verse—cannot verbalize the true nature of either her husband or her experience. Within a few minutes, however, her diction changes again, and as it does, it communicates that her vision is clearing. Less figurative, more prosaic, it simply analyses the bleak reality just disclosed:

> Some word there was, worser than Tybalt's death,
> That murdered me. I would forget it fain,
> But O, it presses to my memory,
> Like damnèd guilty deeds to sinners' minds:
> 'Tybalt is dead and Romeo banishèd'.
>
> (ll. 108–12)

In effect, variations in the poetry reveal variations in the protagonists: the lovers' changing moods, perceptions, intensities. In later tragedies, Shakespeare would employ less contrived means for portraying character. But here, changes in the verse from moment to moment convey the shifting contours of personality. As the play closes, such changes produce the impression of a more complex but still impetuous Romeo.

In his soliloquy at the beginning of Act 5, Romeo continues to use the familiar language of love-poetry: love sits enthroned in his heart; he has dreamt about his beloved's wondrous lips; and love savours of its customary sweetness. Moreover, the concept of dream in the opening lines, among other things, varies two well-known Petrarchan topoi, 'the reunion with the dead beloved in a dream', and dreaming of the beloved only to awaken to disappointment.[1] Romeo's images and dream belong to a conventional pattern, yet his formulation of his experience is new. In plain but elegant terms, this speech testifies to reflection: Romeo has been

[1] See Forster, *The Icy Fire*, p. 59; Lisle Cecil John, *The Elizabethan Sonnet Sequences: Studies in Conventional Conceits* (New York, 1938), p. 82. A. J. Earl, '*Romeo and Juliet* and the Elizabethan Sonnets', *English*, 27 (1978), 111–12, cites this variation on Petrarchan topoi.

thinking about the dream and his 'unaccustomed spirit' (l. 4) all day, conscious that the dream may be deceptive, and that it contains contradictions. He makes the second observation in a monosyllabic aside: 'Strange dream that gives a dead man leave to think!' (l. 7). When Balthazar interrupts this reverie with mistaken news of Juliet's death, Romeo immediately thinks of suicide. He conveys his despair in a monologue about the Apothecary, transforming Petrarchan images to decorate the squalid shop (ll. 42–8). As he sketches the Apothecary himself, he produces a grotesque image of the unrequited lover (see 5.1.68–71 n.).

While the play takes its course, modulations like these—as well as the more striking poetic changes that occur between scenes, early and late—distinguish the voices of Romeo and Juliet. Our sense that their passion for each other is genuine, and that it sets them apart from the rest of Verona, derives especially from the way they speak. Their soliloquies do not analyse these developments, nor do the assessments of other characters. Nothing in the text explicitly remarks how the lovers have changed. But the variations in their poetry signify both transformation and, finally, uniqueness. Like some of Shakespeare's other plays from this period, *Romeo and Juliet* makes a connection between qualities of love and qualities of imagination. Sexual passion sparks imagination and vice versa; the more sensuous or genuine the feelings, the more original or lyric their expression. In the end Romeo and Juliet not only belong to Verona but rise above it, however briefly. If they engage in its social discourse, using its rhetoric and vocabulary, they also create from that idiom a language which distinguishes them both as lovers and as individuals.

Like Spenser and Donne in the 1590s, Shakespeare has created an amatory drama of two voices, private and public, singular and communal. Ultimately, both voices in *Romeo and Juliet* owe much of their sound and impact to the Elizabethan sonnet sequences; and the private derives from the public. The public voice uses amatory conventions as a matter of course in daily social life. With little imagination, the citizens of Verona understand one another in terms of sonnet conceits and postures, Petrarchan and anti-Petrarchan. Their medium brings with it—and enhances—a political attitude, a disposition towards competition and advancement. As a result, the play's setting corresponds with that of its audience. They share the values that Mercutio satirizes in his

Queen Mab speech, and that Romeo disparages in his exchange with the Apothecary. By contrast, the private voice—a voice expressing mutual love—revitalizes poetic conventions by using them as a medium of desire and self-expression. Articulating passion, the familiar motifs lose some of their customary political implications. They help to create a sphere of amorous reciprocity in a world of marriage transactions; they produce 'a compelling cultural fantasy'[1] in conditions that reflect Elizabethan life.

Finally, the poetic genre allowed Shakespeare to add political import to the melancholy legend. The verse reinforces the opposition between romantic love and marriage, an emotion and an institution, the individual and the social structure. At the same time, the stage gave the poet-dramatist an opportunity to explore thematic and auditory possibilities of the verse beyond his own narratives or sonnets. Moreover, the dramatic genres—with similar forms but different points of view—permitted him to consider all sides of the public–private antithesis. While the known outcome of the famous story tilts the play towards tragedy, the vision of reciprocal love inclines it towards comedy. The conclusion, poising the lovers' death with their fathers' survival, presents a complex metaphoric version of Elizabethan realities.

Performance History

Initial Staging. In its composition *Romeo and Juliet* works striking variations not only on a familiar story but also on the dramatic and literary conventions which recast it. Evidence suggests that its first productions displayed its full range of narrative and stylistic complexities, enhancing the most innovative qualities of the text. Admittedly, that evidence is sparse: the data collected by theatre historians, stage directions and related dialogue from the first two quartos (Q1[2] and Q2), and a few other pertinent bits of information. As Evans points out in his edition, 'No other records exist, not even the date of a performance before the Restoration' (p. 28).[3]

[1] Marotti's phrase, '"Love is not love"', 416.

[2] This edition treats the first quarto as a script in print, whether it represents a version composed for performance or reflects a version already performed.

[3] Evans sums up in a paragraph what is known of the play's early theatre history abroad (pp. 28–9). At this time the story of Romeo and Juliet also appeared in *commedia dell'arte:* see, e.g., 'The Tragic Events' (1611) in *Scenarios of the*

Nevertheless, enough remains to indicate that the circumstances of production were dynamic and flexible, ideally suited to the multifarious play enacting myth, rites of passage, and politics.

Shakespeare may have written the tragedy during a period of theatrical disorganization in England (see below, 'Date(s)'), but the uncertainties caused by the plague and patronage—the closing of the London theatres in 1592–3 and the rearrangement of established companies—had passed before the first performances.[1] Consequently, *Romeo and Juliet* premiered in the extraordinary theatrical scene taking shape during the last years of the sixteenth century: a particular company, sharing a particular style of performance, mounted the play for audiences in Elizabethan public theatres. It is likely that the Chamberlain's Men acted it first at the Theatre and then at the Curtain.

Since Shakespeare probably began to write *Romeo and Juliet* before the Chamberlain's Men incorporated (see below, 'Date (s)), he did not know precisely which actors would perform his script. It follows that he must have prepared it simply for an adult company of twelve actors and a few extras. According to scholarly conjecture, Burbage (in his middle-to-late twenties) may have played Romeo to the Juliet of Master Robert Goffe, a trained boy actor and apprentice in the company (see Evans's edition, p. 28). Whoever they were, male actors performed both leading roles. As their presence gave the characters physicality, their deliveries of the lines conferred more individual traits: imagination, sensuality, youth, impulse, and gender. Other roles were distributed among the remaining members of the troupe; some of them required doubling.[2]

Andrew Gurr emphasizes the heavy demands that *Romeo and Juliet* made on contemporary theatrical venues, especially for its closing scene. In particular it required means to represent balcony, bed, and tomb, all the symbolic enclosures which help to define the

'Commedia dell'Arte': Flaminio Scala's 'Il Teatro delle favole rappresentative', trans. Henry F. Salerno (New York and London, 1967), pp. 128–33.

[1] See Giorgio Melchiori, 'Peter, Balthasar, and Shakespeare's Art of Doubling', *MLR* 78 (1983), 781, 789.

[2] On doubling in *Romeo and Juliet*, see Melchiori, 'Peter, Balthasar, and Shakespeare's Art of Doubling', 777–92, and also John C. Meagher, 'Economy and Recognition: Thirteen Shakespearean Puzzles', *SQ* 35 (1984), 7–14. Scholarship on casting estimates that between thirteen and sixteen actors could have performed the longer version of the play, a distribution of parts not unusual for the 1590s.

world and 'architectonics' of the play.[1] The first two quartos both call for these features in the scenes where a lover is alone or the lovers are alone together. As the Commentary to this edition shows, Elizabethan staging offered a number of solutions: a stage structure, a substantial property, or both. For example, the bed on which Juliet falls in 4.3 must have been some combination of bed, curtain, and space either on the main stage or in the discovery area; the tomb, if not evoked strictly by dialogue, could have materialized as a trapdoor, the rear stage, or a structure.[2] These resources would have permitted removal of the bodies at the end of 5.3, without a procession, by use of a trapdoor or curtain. Various arrangements could have disposed theatrical space metaphorically to mark the lovers' descent from balcony and nuptial bed to the tomb they occupy in the last scene.[3]

Other demands on theatrical venues and companies required less ingenuity. For instance, the first two quartos both call for a variety of modest but emblematic hand-held properties. *Romeo and Juliet* depends on many such items and uses them in a particularly 'controlled' way:[4] their symbolism not only deepens but often connects individual events, enhancing semiotic patterns in the narrative. Again and again the small properties signal violence. Most of them are weapons: swords and bucklers, rapiers, clubs, and partisans in 1.1 (only the second quarto specifies weapons in this scene); rapiers and apparently daggers in 3.1; Romeo's dagger in 3.3; Juliet's knife in 4.1 and 4.3; Peter's dagger in 4.4; rapiers and a dagger in 5.3. At the end of the play the Apothecary's vial of poison (5.1) and Romeo's container for it (5.3) effect violence of another kind; Romeo and Friar Laurence furnish themselves with crowbars, spade, and mattock to break into the Capulet tomb.

In contrast, a number of other properties fill in the domestic

[1] 'The Date and the Expected Venue of *Romeo and Juliet*', *SSu* 49 (1996), 15–25. The quoted term comes from Michael Mullin, 'Motley and *Romeo*: The Designers and the Text', *TJ* 43 (1991), 469.

[2] See Commentary, 4.3.57.1 n. and 5.3.44.2 n.

[3] On this symbolism, see Leslie Thomson, '"With patient ears attend": *Romeo and Juliet* on the Elizabethan Stage', *SP* 92 (1995), 234–7, and David Bevington, *Action Is Eloquence: Shakespeare's Language of Gesture* (Cambridge, Mass., and London, 1984), pp. 111–13.

[4] Ann Pasternak Slater, *Shakespeare the Director* (Brighton and Totowa, NJ, 1982), p. 182.

tableau of Capulet's hospitality, from napkins, platters, trestle-tables, and seats in 1.4 to spits, logs, baskets, and other kitchen supplies in 4.4 (variously specified by the first two quartos). Several items are stage images of verbal motifs central to the play: the torches appearing in 1.4 and 5.3; the flowers and other plant-life analysed by Friar Laurence in 2.2 and strewn to memorialize Juliet in 4.4 and 5.3; the money exchanged by Romeo in 2.3 and 5.1; the rope ladder carried by the Nurse in 3.2 and used by Romeo in 3.5; the ring sent by Juliet in 3.2 and received by Romeo in 3.3. Finally, the early texts call for a few odds and ends: the invitation list in 1.2, a material sign of coincidence; whatever instruments the musicians need in 1.4 and 4.4; the Nurse's fan in 2.3, an item which allows for stage business; and Romeo's letter(s) in 5.3, a device to expedite closure of the narrative.[1]

As J. L. Styan recognized several decades ago, 'Shakespeare takes the conventional equipment of property and costume and uses them as a way of speaking to the audience'. Another 'dramatic opportunity', costumes indicated by the two early texts are also symbolic and not out of the ordinary; the degree of richness would have been determined by a character's social status.[2] On Shakespeare's stage, apparel always represented order and degree even as it identified a festive or liminal sphere which minimized such differences.[3] In *Romeo and Juliet* it creates ironies and fulfils both roles by the way it distinguishes the everyday world of Verona from the world of the lovers. The two quartos require distinctive but uncomplicated items among the stock of Elizabethan costumes: a black cloak for the Chorus; a dressing gown for Capulet in the first scene (only Q2); appropriate garments for the masquers, including masks for Mercutio and Romeo, and (according to the

[1] Both early quartos require the same staging features and properties except for occasional details: for example, Q2 arms the Capulet servants in 1.1 with swords and bucklers (A3[r]), where Q1 says only '*They draw*' (A4[v]); Q1 provides the Nurse with herbs at the beginning of 4.4 (I1[r]), where Q2 calls for an exchange of keys with Capulet's Wife and perhaps some spices (K1[v]). They also differ slightly in their calls for music: Q2 introduces music at Capulet's festivities in 1.4 (C3[r]) and with the arrival of Paris in 4.4 (K1[v]); Q1 implies that music accompanies dancing at the party (C2[v]) and the arrival of Paris (I1[v]). (Citations of the quartos in this note and the following paragraphs can be found in *Shakespeare's Plays in Quarto*, ed. Michael J. B. Allen and Kenneth Muir (Berkeley and Los Angeles, 1981).)

[2] The two quotations are from Styan, *Shakespeare's Stagecraft* (Cambridge, 1967), pp. 36, 32.

[3] See Bevington, *Action Is Eloquence*, pp. 36–8.

dialogue in 2.3) baggy trousers and dancing shoes for Romeo; bridegroom's apparel for Paris in 4.4; rags for the Apothecary in 5.1; and 'best array' for Juliet in 5.3, where she may appear for the last time in the same party dress she wore first in 1.4.

Instructions for the actors, like those for properties and costumes, allowed for changing circumstances of production. As scripts both quartos are flexible, characteristic of Shakespeare's practice with its 'multiplicity which defies categorisation'.[1] Comparable to many other playbooks, for instance, both quartos of *Romeo and Juliet* left the specifics of deploying supernumeraries and other minor parts to the company. Although Q1 may have fewer party-goers (1.4), servants (1.4, 4.2, 4.4), and watchmen (5.3) than Q2, it is equally permissive in the allocation of small roles. During the first scene Q1 calls for '*other Citizens*' (A4^{v}) and Q2 for '*three or foure Citizens*' (A4^{r}); in 3.1 both have the stage direction '*Enter Citizens.*' (F2^{r}, F4^{v}). The two quartos can be similarly ambiguous: '*Enter watch.*', which occurs twice in the last scene of Q1 (K2^{v}), corresponds with '*Enter Boy and Watch.*' in Q2 (L4^{r}). Now and then Q1 reduces the minor roles to a single actor, avoiding the permissiveness of Q2: only one servant engages Capulet in 4.2 and 4.4 (H3^{v}, I1^{r}) where Q2 brings '*two or three*' and '*three or foure*' on stage (I4^{r}, K1^{v}); only '*one*' accompanies Balthazar in 5.3 (K3^{r}) where Q2 has no instructions about watchmen at all (L4^{r}). Yet once Q1 is more permissive than Q2. In the later text the Prince enters 5.3 alone (L4^{v}); in the earlier he arrives '*with others*' (K3^{r}).

The same adaptability is evident in the quartos' directions to performers. While each quarto has a distinct style of address, they both permitted the actors to exercise their skills in the representation of characters and events. They give directions unsystematically, leaving room for improvisation and presupposing actors who know what to do. Q1 is the more explicit text: it spells out cues in its own dialogue and that of Q2; it over-advises in the manner of an inexperienced playwright.[2] Despite its attention to these signals, however, Q1 only sketches the actors' stage business.

In both early quartos the dialogue contains many cues. During the first scene it marks the entrances of the Montague servants and

[1] Slater, *Shakespeare the Director*, p. 49.

[2] On the correlation between experience and instruction in the preparing of early scripts, see William B. Long, 'Stage-Directions: A Misinterpreted Factor in Determining Textual Provenance', *TEXT*, 2 (1985), 127.

Tybalt; at the end of the play it indicates Friar Laurence's arrival at the tomb, and it tells various watchmen when to enter and exit. More frequently it asks for particular motions or gestures: handling of properties like swords and torches, touching or kissing, kneeling and rising, stepping forward from a group. Its Shakespearian vocabulary has been itemized as 'automatic demonstratives [as well as] every form of retrospective description, concurrent description, question, and command'. As Ann Pasternak Slater concludes, 'Actions vary with the character and the moment'.[1] A Capulet servant bites his thumb in 1.1; Capulet's cousin sits in 1.4; Juliet leans her cheek on her hand in 2.1 and rubs the Nurse's back in 2.4; Romeo conveys Paris into the tomb in 5.3. Often the dialogue indicates how an actor might represent an emotional state. At the ball, Capulet asks Tybalt 'wherefore storm you so?' and insists that he 'put off these frowns' (1.4.173, 186). On news of his banishment in 3.3 the desperate Romeo directs himself to tear his hair and fall on the floor of Friar Laurence's cell. When Romeo prepares to return from Mantua to Verona in 5.1, Balthazar describes his appearance as 'pale and wilde' (Q2, K4r), 'dangerous and full of feare' (Q1, I3v). The last speeches of Romeo and Juliet guide the performances of their suicides, the gestures leading to death and the posture of death itself.

Q1 adds stage directions to the dialogue at more than twenty points. A dozen times or so it supplements what the characters say and in the process makes timing more precise. At a climactic moment in 3.1 it describes Mercutio's death blow several lines before he does: '*Tibalt under Romeos arme thrusts Mercutio, in and flyes.*' (F1v). Later it tells Romeo when to rise from the floor in 3.3 (G1r), when to descend in 3.5 (G3v), when to open the tomb and fight with Paris in 5.3 (K1r, K1v); it tells Juliet when to kneel in 3.5 (H1r) and 4.2 (H4r). Plainly it directs the Nurse to address Peter in 2.3 (E3r) and to exit at the end of 3.5 (H2r). As 5.3 begins, before Paris describes his act of remembrance, Q1 offers the stage direction '*Paris strewes the Tomb with flowers.*' (I4v). Soon Friar Laurence '*stoops and lookes on the blood and weapons*' before he asks what blood stains the monument's entrance, and he will observe 'The Lady sturres' immediately after the stage direction '*Iuliet rises.*' (K2r). In one notable instance, however, Q1 lacks dialogue to supplement,

[1] *Shakespeare the Director*, p. 20.

the passage in the first scene of Q2 between Benvolio's entrance and the Prince's. It has a stage direction instead: '*They draw, to them enters* Tybalt, *they fight, to them the Prince, old* Mountague, *and his wife, old* Capulet *and his wife, and other Citizens and part them.*' (A4^{v}).

If the first quarto makes cues prominent, it still leaves a great deal to the actors' judgement. This openness distinguishes the stage directions which elaborate on dialogue rather than repeating it. Often reprinted by editors, many of these stage directions have become familiar. They add details to moments which are vaguer in Q2. In the Q1 version of 1.4, for example, Romeo's party make their farewells to Capulet with a particular signal: '*They whisper in his eare.*' (C4^{r}). Mercutio adds a fillip of impudence to his exchange with the Nurse in 2.3: '*He walkes by them, and sings.*' (E2^{v}). When Romeo threatens suicide in 3.3, it is specifically the Nurse who intervenes: '*He offers to stab himselfe, and Nurse snatches the dagger away.*' (G1^{v}). Stage directions in 4.4 give a choric effect to the lamentations for Juliet and ritualize the mourners' exit: '*All at once cry out and wring their hands*', '*They all but the Nurse go foorth, casting Rosemary on her and shutting the Curtens.*' (I2^{r}, I2^{v}). Twice characters hesitate before leaving the stage: the Nurse at the end of 3.3 (G2^{r}), Paris during 3.4 (G2^{v}). At times they move '*somewhat fast*' (Juliet in 2.5, when she '*embraceth Romeo*' (E4^{r})) or '*hastely*' (the Nurse in 3.5 (G3^{v})).

As the illustrations show, stage directions in the first quarto are more descriptive than cues in the second, but they are hardly more prescriptive.[1] In Styan's terms, the instructions are rich and precise in both texts but never indispensable except for entrances and exits.[2] John Russell Brown is probably right to conclude that nothing subtle or elaborate in the actors' business, movement, gesture, pause, or inflexion could have been fixed.[3] Moreover, it cannot be assumed that all printed stage directions were enacted or that all enacted stage directions were written down.

The permissiveness of both quartos can baffle attempts to imagine the staging of scenes, particularly those requiring balcony, bed, and tomb. In a few of these episodes the locale changes during continuous action, perhaps moving to or from a subsidiary portion

[1] Greg lists the Q1 stage directions in *First Folio*, pp. 226–8; Jay L. Halio gives a helpful summary of the stage directions in both quartos in 'Handy-Dandy: Q1/Q2 *Romeo and Juliet*', in *Shakespeare's 'Romeo and Juliet'*, ed. Halio, pp. 142–4.

[2] *Shakespeare's Stagecraft*, pp. 198, 53.

[3] *Free Shakespeare* (1974), p. 52.

of the main stage. For instance, the famous parting of the lovers in 3.5 begins above '*at the window*' (Q1, G3^{r}), or '*aloft*' on an upper acting level (Q2, H2^{v}). Dialogue and a stage direction in Q1 indicate that Romeo descends by his rope ladder from here to the Capulet orchard, represented by the main stage. When Capulet's Wife enters, however, the main stage apparently turns into Juliet's bedchamber, and a Q1 stage direction suggests that Juliet or the Nurse, after a short speech above, enters below: '*She goeth downe from the window.*' (G3^{v}).[1] In 5.3 neither early text specifies how Romeo opens the tomb, what he opens, or why he says 'I descend into this bed of death' (K1^{r}, L2^{r}). When various characters withdraw from the action at the beginning of that scene, neither quarto indicates where or how far.

The same permissiveness blurs the transitions between scenes in three instances, and it raises questions about the blocking of action in each sequence. When the masquers arrive at Capulet's house, for example, neither quarto clears the stage. After Romeo urges his friends 'on lustie Gentlemen', Q1 has '*Enter old* Capulet *with the Ladies.*' (C2^{v}) and Q2 says '*They march about the Stage, and Seruingmen come forth with Napkins.*' (C2^{v}). In Q2, after an exchange among the servants, '*Enter all the guests and gentlewomen to the Maskers.*' (C3^{r}). Both early texts appear to shift locales, from outside to inside the house, without a scene-break. Neither specifies where the masquers move or stand as other actors enter the stage. With the second example, the first forty-odd lines of the second act, the scene remains fixed in Capulet's orchard: Mercutio and Benvolio enter and exit, but no stage direction clarifies Romeo's movements. Romeo's response at his friends' exit, rhyming with Benvolio's last speech ('found'/'wound'), suggests that he has positioned himself somewhere on stage during their dialogue. He may have left the platform, but neither quarto signals a scene-break. At the beginning of 4.4, both texts imply continuous action as the locale changes from an unspecified room in Capulet's house to Juliet's bedchamber: Capulet exits, but presumably the Nurse stays on stage and moves from the place of her conversation with Capulet to Juliet's bed (an object apparently visible to the audience since the end of 4.3).[2]

[1] See Commentary, 3.5.67.1 n.

[2] As the Commentary, 1.4.112–13 n. explains, this edition omits scene-breaks in these three instances to emphasize the original fluidity of performance. See also the notes to 2.1.2.1 and 4.4.26 '*Exit*'.

When the first two quartos are viewed in a contemporary frame of reference, it appears that *Romeo and Juliet* may have been staged and performed somewhat differently each time the Chamberlain's Men revived it. Obviously all plays change in the theatre, influenced by the responses of actors and audiences to the text, but since the Restoration staging has become more or less set for a series of performances. Like other dramatic works of its era, *Romeo and Juliet* may have changed more radically in its original productions than it would in later runs. It probably appeared in both long and short versions;[1] it certainly left performance decisions for each revival to the acting company.

> The actor reminds us that behind the clothes and the role there remains an unexhausted capacity for new inventions. Shakespearian parts encourage the actor to remain in touch with this ambiguity or 'third dimension' and to continue to give us his sense of freedom, even though the inexorables are closing in around him.[2]

At some performances the company may have emphasized a single dimension of the play, but the extant texts and early modern theatre always permitted the actors to explore more than one level. That exceptional freedom would be curtailed during the Restoration and eighteenth century, not only by performance texts but also by theatrical conventions and political events.

Restoration to the Late Twentieth Century. *Romeo and Juliet* has had a remarkable career on the stage since the Restoration, almost always in production while its fortunes ebbed and flowed. Charting the flow, theatre historians have compiled statistics for the most successful phases of its progress. Charles Beecher Hogan counts 399 performances in London between 1751 and 1800; Felicia Hardison Londré cites 352 revivals internationally in less than four decades after World War II.[3] During the late eighteenth century

[1] Donald W. Foster draws this conclusion in his linguistic study 'The Webbing of *Romeo and Juliet*', in Porter, *Critical Essays*, pp. 131–49.

[2] G. K. Hunter, 'Flatcaps and Bluecoats: Visual Signals on the Elizabethan Stage', *E&S* 33 (1980), 47.

[3] Hogan's data appear in *Shakespeare in the Theatre 1701–1800* (Oxford, 1952 and 1957), i. 461 and ii. 716; Londré makes the point in her contribution on *Romeo and Juliet* to *Shakespeare Around the Globe: A Guide to Notable Postwar Revivals*, ed. Samuel Leiter (New York, Westport, Conn., and London, 1986), pp. 625–59, statistics on p. 630.

Romeo and Juliet outran *Hamlet*; during the twentieth century only *Hamlet* has outrun *Romeo and Juliet*. A measure of these fluctuations, several stage histories and surveys for *Romeo and Juliet* prove helpful guides through its continuous but uneven series of revivals.[1] Not surprisingly, they reveal a variety of departures from the original quartos and the text familiar in modern editions. If Shakespeare wrote his script in a particular climate of theatre, playwrights, managers, actors, and directors since the Restoration have rewritten it as the climate changed. The success of *Romeo and Juliet* in the theatre has depended on adaptation, often at the cost of Elizabethan complexity and nuance. In his 'Prefatory Remarks' to Oxberry's edition (1819), William Hazlitt unwittingly characterized the exchange: 'Of all Shakspeare's plays, this is perhaps the one that is acted, if not the oftenest, with most pleasure to the spectator'. Pleasure has resulted from many adjustments to attract and entertain paying customers over more than three centuries. Usually the adjustments, large and small, isolate one or two components of the play: the love-story, the rite of passage, or politics.

Shortly after the playhouses reopened in the reign of Charles II, a version of *Romeo and Juliet* appeared on 1 March 1662 at the first theatre (a small remodelled tennis court) in Lincoln's Inn Fields. The tragedy's appeal lapsed at that moment for Samuel Pepys, who saw the production by the Duke's Company, Sir William Davenant's organization, and noted it in his *Diary*:

> . . . and thence to the Opera and there saw *Romeo and Julett*, the first time it was ever acted. But it is the play of itself the worst that ever I heard in my

[1] On the eighteenth-century competition, see Hogan, *Shakespeare in the Theatre 1701–1800*, ii. 716–17; for the twentieth-century reversal, see Peter Holding, *'Romeo and Juliet': Text and Performance* (Houndmills and London, 1992), p. 42. Among the guides, three offer theatre history: Holding's book on *Text and Performance*; Katherine L. Wright, *Shakespeare's 'Romeo and Juliet' in Performance: Traditions and Departures* (Lewiston, NY, Queenston, Ont., and Lampeter, 1997); and my *Shakespeare in Performance: 'Romeo and Juliet'* (Manchester, 1987). Two books give brief descriptive listings of twentieth-century productions: William Babula, *Shakespeare in Production, 1935–1978: A Selective Catalogue* (New York and London, 1981), pp. 280–92, and Leiter, ed., *Shakespeare Around the Globe*, pp. 625–59. See also Charles H. Shattuck, *The Shakespeare Promptbooks: A Descriptive Catalogue* (Urbana and London, 1965), pp. 411–32; William P. Halstead, *Shakespeare as Spoken: A Collation of 5000 Acting Editions and Promptbooks of Shakespeare* (Ann Arbor, 1978), ix. 711c–711nn; and Bryan N. S. Gooch and David Thatcher, eds., *A Shakespeare Music Catalogue* (Oxford, 1991), ii. 1341–89.

life, and the worst acted that ever I saw these people do; and I am resolved to go no more to see the first time of acting, for they were all of them out more or less.[1]

The actors had not learned their lines for this first recorded performance of *Romeo and Juliet*, which was probably an adaptation of Shakespeare's text overseen by Davenant.

Although Davenant's version was not published, Christopher Spencer traces its provenance from two kinds of evidence: Davenant's stated intention, when he received exclusive rights to nine Shakespeare plays, of 'reforming' them and 'making them fit', and an anecdote by John Downes, the company's prompter, in *Roscius Anglicanus* (1708).[2]

The anecdote, known for its risqué conclusion, implies that Montague became Count Paris in one Restoration form of the tragedy that evidently retained the original's social context:

Note, There being a Fight and Scuffle in this Play, between the House of *Capulet*, and House of *Paris*; Mrs. *Holden* Acting his Wife, enter'd in a *Hurry*, Crying, O my Dear *Count*! She Inadvertently left out, O, in the pronunciation of the Word *Count*! giving it a Vehement Accent, put the House into such a Laughter, that *London* Bridge at low-water was silence to it.[3]

Probably for the first time an actress, Mrs Mary Saunderson (later Mrs Mary Betterton), played Juliet. Downes gives other information about the original cast, identifying Thomas Betterton as Mercutio and Henry Harris as Romeo. In the same passage he also mentions another adaptation soon after Davenant's, James Howard's tragicomic version which preserved Romeo and Juliet alive: '. . . so that when the Tragedy was Reviv'd again, 'twas Play'd Alternately, Tragical one Day, and Tragicomical another; for several Days together'. With only this brief reference the background of the tragicomic *Romeo and Juliet* remains obscure. Howard may have adapted a Shakespearian text under the influence of Davenant's version.[4]

[1] Ed. Robert Latham and William Matthews (Berkeley and Los Angeles, 1970), iii. 39.

[2] '"Count Paris's Wife": *Romeo and Juliet* on the Early Restoration Stage', *TSLL* 7 (1966), 309–16; quotations from p. 311.

[3] Ed. Montague Summers (1929, repr. New York and London, 1968), p. 22.

[4] See Spencer, '"Count Paris's Wife"', 315–16.

Records of performances after the reopening of the theatres in 1660 are scarce, but the earliest allusions to *Romeo and Juliet* on the Restoration stage suggest that it already fitted a pattern which would last through most of the eighteenth century. For more than a hundred years writers for the stage reconstructed Shakespeare's plays, making cuts and additions, introducing new characters, scenes, endings, and words; these adaptations appeared both on the stage and in print.[1] Thomas Otway's *History and Fall of Caius Marius* (published in 1680) is the first version of *Romeo and Juliet* to illustrate the pattern, initially with more than one distinguished cast.[2] Otway, who may have been influenced by Lucan, adapted the love-story to a Roman setting drawn from North's Plutarch.[3] According to one set of calculations, 750 lines of a total 2,850 derive from Shakespeare.[4] Otway seems to have used a Shakespearian text, perhaps the second or third Folio (1632 or 1663).[5] Like other Restoration dramatists who aimed to refine Shakespeare's diction, he rewrote the derivative lines in prosaic blank verse, part of the hybridization which has distracted later critics from the significance of his work. The most striking feature of *Caius Marius* is

[1] Jean I. Marsden summarizes the process in *The Re-Imagined Text: Shakespeare, Adaptation, & Eighteenth-Century Literary Theory* (Lexington, Ky., 1995), p. 1.

[2] In the first production Thomas Betterton had the title role, Mrs Elizabeth Barry and William Smith played the lovers, James Nokes became famous as the Nurse, and Cave Underhill acted the Mercutio-figure, Sulpitius. Betterton played Caius Marius again in a benefit performance at the Haymarket on 18 February 1707. The supporting cast included Robert Wilks and Mrs Anne Bracegirdle as the lovers, William Bullock as the Nurse, and Benjamin Johnson as Sulpitius. (See Hazleton Spencer, *Shakespeare Improved: The Restoration Versions in Quarto and on the Stage* (Cambridge, Mass., 1927), p. 100.)

[3] For the Lucan connection, see Barbara A. Murray, 'Otway and Lucan: Source of the Sources for *The History and Fall of Caius Marius* (1680)?', *N&Q*, NS 42 (1995), 38–40; for echoes of Shakespeare's Roman plays, Jessica Munns, '"The Dark Disorders of a Divided State": Otway and Shakespeare's *Romeo and Juliet*', *Comparative Drama*, 19 (1985–6), 348 and 361 n. 4.

[4] Roswell G. Ham, *Otway and Lee: Biography from a Baroque Age* (New Haven, 1931), p. 135. Citations of the play come from *The Works of Thomas Otway: Plays, Poems, and Love-Letters*, ed. J. C. Ghosh, vol. 1 (Oxford, 1932).

[5] Otway gives Marius junior two lines about dawn (2.387–8) at the end of a scene corresponding to *Romeo and Juliet* 2.1; there is no dawn reference at the beginning of the next scene, which is completely different from Shakespeare's 2.2. The assignment of the lines may reflect F2 or F3, which eliminate the redundancy of Q2 and Q3 by having Romeo speak the passage; F1 preserves the repetition and Q4 gives the speech to Friar Laurence. (Randall McLeod called my attention to this data about the Shakespearian texts in a paper which is part of his book *Material Shakespeare* (Cambridge, forthcoming). See also Commentary, 2.1.233–4 n.)

its political bias. In this first extant adaptation a single aspect of Shakespeare's play becomes the entire point: the psychological and social experiences of the lovers fade into the turbulent struggles of republican Rome.

Otway's *Caius Marius* was one of ten Shakespeare plays staged between December 1677 and March 1682, a time of ominous political instability in England. When it premiered in the latter half of 1679 at the Duke's Playhouse, Charles II, who had recently been ill, was engaged with Parliament in having his brother, James, excluded from the succession. Otway's version of *Romeo and Juliet*, comparable to other Shakespeare productions of the period, advances a conservative agenda. Warning against civil unrest and rebellion, even in unsettled times, it draws analogies between the narrative, the Exclusion crisis, and events in the 1640s that led to civil war.[1] The feud between Capulets and Montagues becomes a vicious contest between equally depraved factions; the lovers, Marius junior and Lavinia, are types of natural virtue who act out their story in the public domain. Although a few quiet moments interrupt the civil disorder—the first balcony scene, the farewell (in a garden), Lavinia's drinking of the potion—they disappear quickly in the enveloping turmoil. The tomb scene becomes typically crowded and violent. In Otway's arrangement, like that of some early novellas, Lavinia awakens before Marius junior dies, and the doomed lovers interpret events:

> Ill Fate no more, *Lavinia*, now shall part us,
> Nor cruel Parents, nor oppressing Laws.
>
> (5.382–3)

With the death of Marius junior the public sphere invades the private as his father and guards enter the tomb '*driving in* Metellus' (5.410.1), Lavinia's father, who dies within moments at their hands. Lavinia's suicide, with her father-in-law's sword, is a

[1] Recent criticism of Otway's play has emphasized its political implications: Munns, '"The Dark Disorders of a Divided State"', 347–62, and the third chapter of *Restoration Politics and Drama: The Plays of Thomas Otway, 1675–1683* (Newark, Del., and London, 1995), pp. 95–128; Matthew H. Wikander, 'The Spitted Infant: Scenic Emblem and Exclusionist Politics in Restoration Adaptations of Shakespeare', *SQ* 37 (1986), 340–58; John M. Wallace, 'Otway's *Caius Marius* and the Exclusion Crisis', *MP* 85 (1988), 363–72; and Susan J. Owen, *Restoration Theatre and Crisis* (Oxford, 1996), *passim*. In her book, Munns extends her investigation beyond the Exclusion crisis to other historical events and theoretical issues.

public act of defiance, and the tragedy ends without any sign of reconciliation.

The Restoration thrust stage made the horrors of civil war immediate, and its apparatus for scenic effects made them visible. As Marius junior approaches the tomb, '*Scene draws off, and shows the Temple and Monument*' (5.312.1). Soon he '*Pulls down the side of the Tomb*' (5.349.1), making it accessible for the bloody onslaught to follow. Otway forced the audience to gaze at the atrocities of civil war, from massacres to murder and suicide; and the audience must have found the experience salutary, because *Caius Marius* was revived in the 1690s and performed twenty-nine times in the first four decades of the eighteenth century.[1] As a stock piece, this adaptation inaugurated the long-run versions of *Romeo and Juliet* which occupied English-speaking theatres until the twentieth century. Between 1680 and 1735 it displaced Shakespeare's play from the public stage,[2] and it became the version everyone knew: Henry Fielding cites Otway, not Shakespeare, in his burlesque *Tragedy of Tragedies* when Huncamunca cries, 'O, *Tom Thumb*! *Tom Thumb*! wherefore art thou *Tom Thumb*?' (2.3.10).[3] Yet *Caius Marius* did not displace *Romeo and Juliet* in the study. During the first four decades of the eighteenth century Jacob Tonson brought out Shakespeare editions for readers by Rowe, Pope, and Theobald. In a sense Pope's *Romeo and Juliet* is an adaptation of another kind, crafted with care from Rowe's third edition (1714) and Q1.[4] It represents Shakespeare's text to suit eighteenth-century taste, omitting 'mean conceits and ribaldries' which his Preface attributes to the actors (vol. i p. xvi). It would not be used in the theatre until mid-century, when dramatists found it conveniently adjustable for performance. By that time adaptations reflect historical events far less than theatrical history, and theatrical history reflects moral and aesthetic values as well as economic conditions.

Evidently Theophilus Cibber was the first actor-dramatist to

[1] Wikander writes about the effect of violence on the Restoration stage ('The Spitted Infant', 340–58). Hogan provides statistics about performances of *Caius Marius* (*Shakespeare in the Theatre 1701–1800*, i. 461).

[2] In his edition Evans points out that an acting text was prepared in 1694 at the English College at Douai, and that there may have been a performance in 1730 at the Revenge Meeting-house in New York (p. 34 n. 4).

[3] Ed. L. J. Morrissey (Edinburgh, 1970).

[4] See A. D. J. Brown, 'The Little Fellow has done Wonders', *Cambridge Quarterly*, 21 (1992), 120–49.

adopt one of Pope's editions of *Romeo and Juliet* for a production which premiered at the Little Theatre in Haymarket on 11 September 1744.[1] The advertisement promised Shakespeare's play, 'not acted once these 100 years', but Cibber's version combines Shakespeare's tragedy, Otway's, *The Two Gentlemen of Verona*, and his own additions in a format never before performed. While Cibber took passages from Otway and allowed the lovers their conversation in the tomb, he narrowed the focus of his adaptation from political to domestic calamity, the conflict between Romeo and Juliet and their families. Here the feud arises from the anger of mothers: the wives of Capulet and Montague oppose Montague's proposal that the lovers marry. Mid-century decorum and limited financial resources may have contributed to the reduced scope of the play, which lacks quarrelsome servants and a party scene in the first act alone, and gives Mercutio an audience of one for his Queen Mab speech. Nevertheless, Cibber complicated the narrative in performance by playing Romeo to the Juliet of his fourteen-year-old daughter, Jennie. Beginning with the Prologue he invites the audience to see both actors as sympathetic figures from sentimental drama, unfortunate father and loving daughter. The imposition of these stereotypes on his obedient lovers must have given his emotional family drama a unique sexual edge.

A popular success, Cibber's *Romeo and Juliet* closed after ten performances because his theatre was shut down for alleged violations of the Licensing Act of 1737. Two seasons later Thomas Sheridan modified the tragedy for a well-received production at Smock Alley, Dublin. His adaptation, never published, also had a short run. Although neither of these revisions became stock pieces, together they probably inspired the longest-running version in the theatre history of *Romeo and Juliet*: David Garrick's revival, which opened at Drury Lane on 29 November 1748; played over 329 times at Drury Lane and Covent Garden between 1748 and 1776; held the stage for ninety-seven years; and was not finally displaced until the late nineteenth century.[2] Garrick had seen

[1] Marsden gives the background and a reading of Cibber's version in *The Re-Imagined Text*, pp. 87–9 and 100.

[2] Statistics come from George Winchester Stone, Jr., '*Romeo and Juliet*: The Source of its Modern Stage Career', in *Shakespeare 400: Essays by American Scholars on the Anniversary of the Poet's Birth*, ed. James G. McManaway (New York, 1964), pp. 191–2.

Cibber's revival, which he described in a letter to Somerset Draper, 16 September 1744, as 'tolerable enough';[1] and he knew of Sheridan's success. As George C. Branam argues, the two productions '. . . clearly suggested the play's potential in his own theatre when Garrick became manager of Drury Lane in 1747', and '[t]he presence in the company of Spranger Barry and Susanna Cibber to take the principal parts made the prospect well nigh irresistible'.[2]

When Garrick revised *Romeo and Juliet* between 1748 and 1750, he reduced the play's scope even further than Cibber had, from social turmoil to the relationship between the protagonists. Nancy Copeland shows how changes to the plot aligned the tragedy with affective drama, 'relentlessly focusing the action on these sympathy-inspiring lovers and their private emotional world'.[3] Garrick adapted Pope's text (or Hanmer's, reliant on Pope's), which had accomplished the first stages of revision for him: it elevated diction and shortened the play.[4] On the one hand, he retained scenes important to the love-plot without alteration but abbreviated many others and generally decreased the public dimension of the narrative. On the other, he added two spectacles, widely advertised, which enhanced the theatricality of the production: a splendid masque in the ball scene at Capulet's home and a funeral procession for Juliet. In making adjustments, he adapted Shakespeare's text to mid eighteenth-century standards and taste, the entrepreneur bowing to his audience's wishes. He turned *Romeo and Juliet* into pathetic drama, the contemporary blend of romantic love and tragedy, and changes to the plot were only the beginning of the transformation.

As Garrick cut Pope's text for staging, he also produced the kind of lucid narrative format—consistent, didactic, and meaningful—which corresponded with pathetic drama and centred on the trials of its victimized protagonists. Within that format he idealized both lovers: Romeo, unwavering in his devotion to Juliet, never mentions Rosaline; Juliet, perfectly innocent, expresses herself without sexual innuendo or other subtleties. The refinement of language

[1] *The Letters of David Garrick*, ed. David M. Little and George M. Kahrl (Cambridge, Mass., 1963), i. 43.

[2] 'The Genesis of David Garrick's *Romeo and Juliet*', *SQ* 35 (1984), 173.

[3] 'The Sentimentality of Garrick's *Romeo and Juliet*', *Restoration and 18th Century Theatre Research*, 2nd ser., 4 (1989), 5.

[4] Nancy Copeland, 'The Sources of Garrick's *Romeo and Juliet* Text', *ELN* 24 (1987), 27–33.

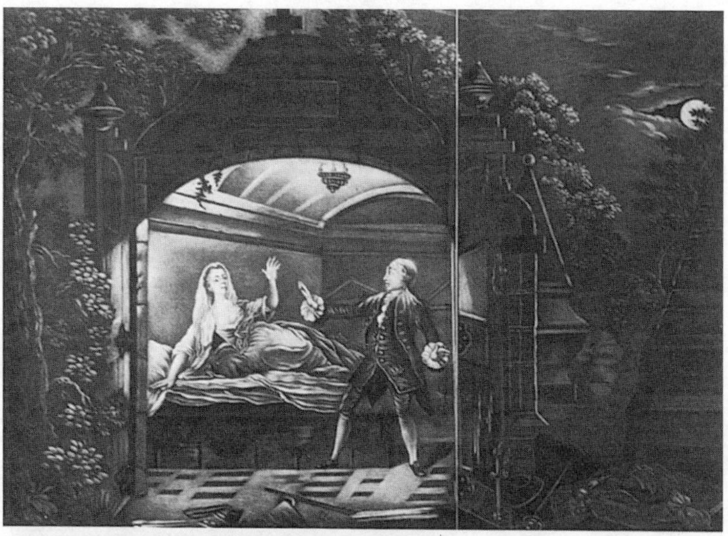

Fig. 4 and 5. A famous production and a painting in the same tradition: David Garrick and Miss Bellamy as Romeo and Juliet, from an engraving by R. S. Ravenet (1753) after a painting by Benjamin Wilson; and Anthony Walker's *Death of Juliet* (1754).

and prosody heightens these impressions; the infusion of pathos enhances them to the limits of good taste. Modifying the death scene, a well-known revision, Garrick followed Otway and Cibber in having Juliet awaken before Romeo expires. In addition, he created a seventy-five-line dialogue for the lovers immediately after Romeo takes the poison. The trials of Garrick's protagonists bring them to the verge of madness: as she becomes conscious, the disoriented Juliet mistakes Romeo for someone forcing her to marry Paris; as he fades, the distracted Romeo believes that enemies are bearing down on his heart and Juliet's:

> Capulet, forbear! Paris loose your hold!
> Pull not our heartstrings thus; they crack, they break.
> O! Juliet! Juliet! (*Dies*).[1]

During the interim, Romeo's joy at Juliet's revival makes him forget that he has already swallowed poison; and they share a minute of blissful ignorance which intensifies their poignancy as fate completes its design.

For spectators who came to see principal actors, Garrick arranged the script as a vehicle for two performers by several means: the late entrances of the protagonists, the abbreviation of events after the catastrophe, and the reductions in the lengths of minor roles.[2] Little on the mid eighteenth-century stage distracted attention from the performances of the featured actors. These productions suffered the usual painted scenes recycled from other plays; they used limited and specific props; and the actors, like their Elizabethan counterparts, wore contemporary dress. Since eighteenth-century theatre focused on the actor's individual style, the projection of character through formal elocution and stylized gestures, the theatrical experience of Garrick's *Romeo and Juliet* must have increased the script's concentration on the protagonists. Reviews make it clear that the leading actors interpreted their roles moment by moment, through the conventional modulations of voice, facial expression, and posture. They constantly restated the lovers' passion, in both senses of the word. During the

[1] Quoted from Garrick's text in *The Plays of David Garrick*, ed. Harry William Pedicord and Fredrick Louis Bergmann (Carbondale, Ill., 1981), iii. 144.

[2] Nancy Copeland, 'Spranger Barry, Garrick's "Great Rival": His Contribution to Eighteenth-Century Acting', unpublished Ph.D. thesis, University of Toronto, 1984, pp. 202–9.

well-documented competition in the autumn of 1750 between Garrick at Drury Lane and Spranger Barry at Covent Garden, numerous printed comparisons illustrate how viewers judged the performances according to the quantity and quality of emotion they stirred. In this context, an anonymous female spectator made an often quoted comment about the balcony scene, more evidence of this revival's concentration on the enactment of the lovers:

> Had I been Juliet to Garrick's Romeo—so impassioned was he, I should have expected that he would have *come up* to me in the balcony; but had I been Juliet to Barry's Romeo—so tender and so seductive was he, I should certainly have *jumped down* to him![1]

Garrick's script entered the nineteenth century slightly altered (*c*.1803) by John Philip Kemble and otherwise resisting most tides of change in Shakespearian performance. As realism gained a following and the narrative arts grew increasingly pictorial, actor-managers from Kemble on attempted to stage Shakespeare with some degree of historical accuracy. This trend coexisted with two others singled out in George C. D. Odell's pioneering theatre history: 'operatising' Shakespeare's comedy and restoring his original texts. With the approach of mid-century, however, Garrick's version of Shakespeare's early tragedy still held the stage. In 1843, according to Odell, *Romeo and Juliet* (along with *The Taming of the Shrew* and *Richard III*) '[w]as still in bondage to Sycorax'; he means adapters in general and Garrick in particular.[2] Moreover, the first nineteenth-century experiments in Germany and England to produce Shakespeare on reconstructed Elizabethan stages disregarded *Romeo and Juliet* in favour of the comedies. Operas and ballets influenced by Garrick's version must have reinforced it; burlesques seem to have made no impression on revivals of the tragedy.

In consequence, an adaptation designed to reflect an eighteenth-century aesthetic and values lasted until the middle of the nineteenth century, not disappearing for good until the end. Whatever their cultural surround, productions of *Romeo and Juliet* continued to centre on the lovers and the performers who played them. Actors of note attempted Romeo, and many well-known

[1] See John Doran, *'Their Majesties' Servants', or Annals of the English Stage* (1897), pp. 187–8.

[2] *Shakespeare from Betterton to Irving*, 2 vols. (New York, 1920), ii. 127–8 and 191.

actresses made their debuts as Juliet. If nineteenth-century revivals varied from eighteenth-century productions and one another, the differences failed to upset the balance of Garrick's *Romeo and Juliet*, a tragedy uniform and decorous at every level of its composition. Most variation resulted from individual acting styles, especially as they affected the representation of youthfulness and the assuming of correct histrionic attitudes. While polite conformity held sway, the tragedy enjoyed no strikingly innovative productions: Kemble and Edmund Kean each offered an uninspiring revival of Garrick's text; William Charles Macready produced an engaging one. Occasionally an actress left a memorable stamp on performances of Juliet: Adelaide Neilson gave her characterization temperamental consistency and a Mediterranean aura; Helen Faucit, responding to Victorian ideals of womanhood, made Juliet less a distinct personality than the type of a victimized lover.[1]

As the decades passed, the character of Romeo became an acknowledged problem for actors. A reviewer in *The Dispatch*, 13 January 1846, connects the problem with recent theatre history: 'The tragedy is seldom performed, for there is no part more difficult to sustain efficiently than *Romeo*. At one time we have seen it a lifeless, sickly, and repulsive conception; at another a rough, indelicate, animal picture.' As Charles H. Shattuck elaborates, Romeo's part did not appeal to mature actors during this period, a plausible explanation for the play's decline in the first half of the nineteenth century:

> The old New Orleans manager Noah Ludlow pretty well expressed the nineteenth-century male actors' attitude toward Romeo when he declared that it requires a boy, not a man, to express Romeo's passion. . . . The regular actor of Macbeth and Othello would find embarrassingly womanish that passage in Friar Lawrence's cell where Romeo is called upon to tear his hair in grief and throw himself upon the ground.[2]

In the event, a woman restored the tragedy: Charlotte Cushman, now regarded by scholars like Shattuck as the greatest American actress of the nineteenth century, created a sensation in London during the 1845/6 season with her portrayal of Romeo.

[1] On Neilson, see Wright, *Shakespeare's 'Romeo and Juliet' in Performance*, pp. 170–82; on Faucit, see Carol J. Carlisle, 'Passion Framed by Art: Helen Faucit's Juliet', *Theatre Survey*, 25 (1984), 177–92.

[2] *Shakespeare on the American Stage* (Washington, DC, 1976), i. 93.

Fig.6. Charlotte Cushman as Romeo, with her sister, Susan, as Juliet, from an 1858 engraving published by Johnson, Fry & Co., New York.

Arousing curiosity and attracting crowds, her interpretation excited more response than the breeches role itself. There had already been a number of female Romeos: Ellen Tree had acted the part in London, and at least sixteen actresses, including Cushman, performed it in the United States during the mid nineteenth century. Bellini's operatic version in 1830 was composed for the mezzo-soprano Giulietta Grisi.[1] More novel than the transvestite role, the ideas informing this production made it exceptional. Cushman reinstated both Shakespeare's text and Romeo's passion in the most narrowly focused version of the play to date, and her

[1] See James Willis Yeater's citation of an undated clipping, 'Women as Romeo', from a Boston newspaper, in his Ph.D. thesis, 'Charlotte Cushman, American Actress', University of Illinois, 1959, p. 117. The opera is mentioned below, pp. 91–2 and p. 92 n. 1.

performance made the new configuration a great success. This *Romeo and Juliet* became part of her repertoire until 1860, occupying its place for twenty-three years and breaking Garrick's hold on Shakespeare's play.

Cushman tried out Shakespeare's text in Southampton on 20 December 1845 before presenting it in London nine days later. Despite her reputed wish to discard the 'flummery' of Garrick's version,[1] her motives for testing the original script remain as obscure as the edition she used. In the dark, contemporary reviewers could not determine who deserved more credit for the Shakespearian text: the actress, or the manager of the Haymarket, Benjamin Webster, who had produced a restored *Taming of the Shrew* in March 1844. Whoever initiated the idea, the production reproduced the Shakespearian plot. At the same time it cut the original text substantially. Many omissions simply abridge the play to accelerate its performance. Some, influenced by Thomas Bowdler's immaculate *Family Shakespeare* (1818), reduce the Elizabethan bawdy and made the production completely inoffensive to 'modern delicacy' (*The Glasgow*, 16 May 1846).[2] All in all, however, Cushman's text, like Garrick's, remains a decorous star vehicle which forgoes the subtleties of Petrarchan games and wordplay. The later entrepreneur, suiting the tragedy and her performance style to audiences at the large new theatres of the period, centred only her own leading role.

Although Cushman nowhere explains her interpretation of *Romeo and Juliet*, or relates it to the Shakespearian script she used, her acting text itself suggests what she found in the original play: the character study of a passionate young man. Altogether, this production reduced or eliminated most passages which failed to connect in some way with the evolution of Romeo. In the process, of course, it changed the structure of Shakespeare's play as radically as the eighteenth century had. Whereas Garrick made both lovers central and uniformly pathetic, however, Cushman elicited

[1] This phrase is quoted in Joseph Leach, *Bright Particular Star* (New Haven and London, 1970), p. 175.

[2] The first edition of *The Family Shakespeare*, published anonymously in 1807, is now assigned to Thomas Bowdler's sister, Henrietta Maria; the second and complete edition, ascribed to Thomas Bowdler, was published in 1818. Since *Romeo and Juliet* did not appear among the twenty plays chosen for the first edition, it appears that Thomas is responsible for bowdlerizing it.

from Shakespeare's contrarieties the vision of one protagonist who experiences passion so intensely that he finally dies of it. With her performance, refinements of that concept—characters who deflate it with their bawdy, events that undercut it with irony—disappear from the script. The remaining verse projects a Romeo either approaching or reaching emotional heights or depths; the remaining plot and characters frame his rising fall. By presenting Shakespeare's text in this way, Cushman both isolated and heightened those features which she could enact for the pleasure of nineteenth-century audiences, emotional extremes as these are revealed in the modulations of Romeo's poetry. She may have unbalanced the tragedy as a whole, but she drew from it the full-scale portrayal of Romeo that Shakespeare created: the temperamental adolescent whose brief and extreme vicissitudes as a lover make him a pattern of tragic experience.

Reviews and other accounts indicate that Cushman impersonated Romeo with all the professional resources she had acquired by 1845, an unusually eclectic style. Describing his response, the playwright James Sheridan Knowles expressed himself in representative terms which Cushman's biographers, critics, and reviewers would later quote. He emphasizes Cushman's intensity in 3.3, the difficult scene where Romeo hears the news of his banishment in Friar Laurence's cell:

> It was a scene of topmost passion; not simulated passion—no such thing; real, palpably real; the genuine heart-storm was on—on in wildest fitfulness of fury; . . . I am sure it must have been the case with every one in the house; but I was all absorbed in Romeo, till a thunder of applause recalled me to myself.[1]

Knowles's panegyric, like most of the reviews in Cushman's scrapbook,[2] reveals more than admiration: it shows how the entire production revolved around the actress's portrayal of Romeo. Certainly her performance raised to the level of brilliance an otherwise humdrum (or worse) production. In the T. H. Lacy acting edition (*c.*1855), the prompt book appears run-of-the-mill. Several reviewers complained about the atrocious scenery, inelegant

[1] Emma Stebbins, *Charlotte Cushman: Her Letters and Memories of her Life* (Boston, 1879), p. 63.

[2] The scrapbook and most records of Cushman's life are housed at the Library of Congress. *The Dispatch*'s place of publication is unknown.

blocking, and shabby costumes for all but the protagonists. More revealing, they made it clear that the supporting cast were at first less than inspiring. Cushman, who focused all of her histrionic strategies on the characterization of Romeo, rose above the unspectacular conditions of performance. Ultimately she carried the whole production with her, projecting through her concept of Romeo an interpretation of the entire tragedy.

In the decades after Charlotte Cushman's performances, *Romeo and Juliet* enjoyed several major revivals based on Shakespeare's text: Edwin Booth's in 1868, Henry Irving's in 1882, Mary Anderson's in 1884, and Maude Adams's in 1899.[1] With these productions, nineteenth-century conventions gradually reduced Shakespeare's text to a series of cues for tableaux. T. S. Eliot would voice another complaint about these conventions: 'strained through the nineteenth century', Shakespeare 'has been dwarfed to the dimension of a part for this or that actor'.[2] Yet even as Irving and Herbert Beerbohm Tree devised their spectacles, another trend in producing Shakespeare steadily pursued its course. In England William Poel led the Elizabethan revival, a movement concerned with the re-creation of Elizabethan staging for Shakespeare's plays. Although Poel's *Romeo and Juliet* at the Royalty Theatre in 1905 closed after four performances, his concept would have a profound influence on subsequent productions. Those who followed him into the twentieth century—Harley Granville-Barker at the Savoy, Barry Jackson at the Birmingham Repertory Theatre, W. Bridges-Adams at the Stratford-upon-Avon Shakespeare Festival, Lewis Casson with his wife Sybil Thorndike, Robert Atkins at the Old Vic, Harcourt Williams at the Old Vic—fostered what J. L. Styan calls 'the Shakespeare revolution', that is, '[t]he search . . . for the theatrical effect and experience of the original performance . . .'.[3] They prepared the way for John Gielgud's Shakespeare productions, in particular his immensely successful *Romeo and Juliet*, which opened at the New Theatre (now the Albery) on 17 October 1935 and became an exemplar for later revivals.

[1] See Evans's edition, p. 41.

[2] 'London Letter: May, 1921', *Dial*, 70 (June 1921), 687, quoted in Gary Taylor, *Reinventing Shakespeare: A Cultural History, from the Restoration to the Present* (New York, 1989), p. 267.

[3] *The Shakespeare Revolution: Criticism and Performance in the Twentieth Century* (Cambridge, 1977), pp. 105–6, 9.

As the two trends followed their courses, the editions of choice were both non-academic and academic, from the Cumberland edition and French's Standard Drama to Furness and the Temple edition. Gielgud adopted the latter for his production, which filled an empty space in more ways than one: it answered the needs not only of contemporary audiences, but also of the commercial stage in London. For a long time *Romeo and Juliet* had not enjoyed a prosperous run in this venue; for more than a dozen years it had enjoyed no run at all. The critic for *The Bystander*, 6 November 1935, describes the kinds of productions which held this stage before Gielgud's:

> We have seen *Romeo and Juliet* presented in the Regal-Arboreal manner of His Majesty's Theatre when Sir Herbert [Beerbohm Tree] was setting an example in florid magnificence which served as a model to the film-producers of a later day, and we have seen the play done in the ultra-modern manner, with Romeo in a gent.'s natty bowler and lavender spats and the balcony represented by a pair of kitchen steps with a potted geranium on the top.

The pictorial method had lasted well into the twentieth century, although Shattuck's Riverside theatre history indicates that 'the Regal-Arboreal manner' in the theatre hardly survived World War I (p. 1917). Meanwhile, naturalism had distorted *Romeo and Juliet*; it suited the picture-frame stage, but not Shakespeare's poetic drama.

Gielgud presented the complete text in a revival which imitated Elizabethan conventions most directly through its staging: a continuous performance on a permanent set, a central tower with acting areas on either side. Despite its innovations, however, this theatrical version focused on the protagonists, whom the director viewed as 'symbolic, immortal types of lovers of all time'.[1] Laurence Olivier, who exchanged the roles of Romeo and Mercutio with Gielgud during the run, thought he was selling 'realism in Shakespeare';[2] the cast, including Peggy Ashcroft as Juliet, worked as an ensemble; and the action shifted between public and private, large and small spaces, according to the rhythms of the text. At the same time Gielgud encouraged the actors to draw their

[1] Quoted in *The Evening Standard*, 10 October 1935.
[2] See Hal Burton, ed., *Great Acting* (1967), p. 17.

Fig. 7. Laurence Olivier as Romeo and Peggy Ashcroft as Juliet in the 1935 New Theatre production.

characters from the dialogue, particularly the verse, and the result was romantic. He enhanced this impression by envisioning the play's events during the Italian Renaissance: his design team, Motley, turned to the art of that period for inspiration.

Although subsequent revivals cut the script, they usually imitated the New Theatre version in most ways, especially costuming. Margaret 'Percy' Harris, one of the Motley designers, suggests a reasonable explanation for this phenomenon: most leading actors—and at least one producer—associated with the tragedy after 1935 had performed for Gielgud.[1] Viewed in retrospect, Gielgud's version had two important effects on later twentieth-century productions of *Romeo and Juliet*: it vitalized them after a slack

[1] Percy Harris made this suggestion during interviews for my book *Shakespeare in Performance: 'Romeo and Juliet'*, which contains detailed studies of the productions by Garrick, Cushman, and Gielgud, as well as those by Peter Brook and Franco Zeffirelli (the two directors next considered here).

period, becoming the first in a sequence of revivals that expanded to a multitude after World War II; and it served as a model for a number of these productions until the late 1950s, when other readings challenged its romanticism.[1]

Two later revivals can be singled out from the crowd for their originality and influence: Peter Brook's for the Royal Shakespeare Company in 1947 and Franco Zeffirelli's for the Old Vic in 1960, a version reworked in his popular film of 1968. Both reflected other genres, Brook's inclining towards film and ballet, Zeffirelli's towards film and opera. Each director purposely used these borrowed conventions to give the old play a new and distinctive slant. In the process they cut the Temple edition in striking ways: Brook, who continued to shape his text during the run, consistently left out the reconciliation of Montagues and Capulets; Zeffirelli omitted one third of the lines as he revised the text. Their styles differed—Brook's sets and costumes were emblematic, Zeffirelli's displayed verismo—but their conceptions of the play had much in common. In these revivals the protagonists lost their mythic dimension: both directors emphasized the failed rite of passage. Brook (in his early twenties) cast young actors, Daphne Slater and Laurence Payne, and gave attention to the public scenes; he created the impression of youth, energy, vitality crowded out of their living space by society, or the deadening customs and organization of an established community. Zeffirelli urged Judi Dench and John Stride to deliver Shakespeare's lines naturalistically, stressing their characters' adolescence and passion. According to his view the subject matter of *Romeo and Juliet*, 'the twin themes of love and the total breakdown of understanding between two generations',[2] had contemporary relevance.

In its cinematic form, Zeffirelli's *Romeo and Juliet* has had a far more lasting effect than Brook's. Many productions since the 1960s have either imitated or reacted against it;[3] the film version has influenced the public's expectations about staging. Nevertheless, both post-war revivals are landmarks in what has become a boundless field. Evans throws up his hands when he contemplates

[1] See Mullin, 'Motley and *Romeo*', 464, 469.

[2] *The Times*, 19 September 1960.

[3] This influence has affected even amateur productions: see Ken Davis and William Hutchings, 'Playing a New Role: The English Professor as Dramaturg', *College English*, 46 (1984), 560–9.

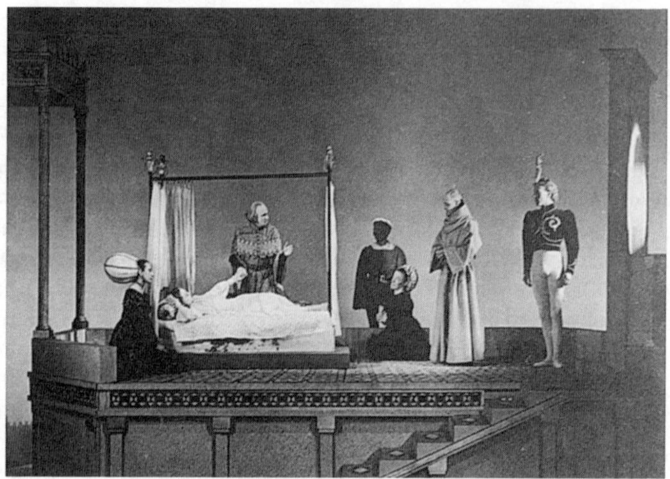

Fig. 8. The discovery of the 'dead' Juliet (Daphne Slater) in Peter Brook's 1947 production at the Shakespeare Memorial Theatre.

in his edition 'the many and often idiosyncratic revivals of *Romeo and Juliet* staged over the past sixty years' (p. 44); he takes his survey in under three pages. Gary Taylor remarks the frequency with which popular plays like *Romeo and Juliet* have been repeated by the Royal Shakespeare Company. From his perspective the tragedy belongs to an unruly multitude of revivals which have populated the stage during the second half of the twentieth century: 'Accelerated productivity and magnified exposure build instant obsolescence into every new production'.[1] But the reviews are not all impatient or bad. Theatre historians and critics regularly cite a few Royal Shakespeare Company revivals—Terry Hands's in 1973 and 1989/90, Barry Kyle and Trevor Nunn's in 1976/7, Michael Bogdanov's in 1986/7—to illustrate notable experimentation with the play, for better or worse.[2] Recently they have documented

[1] *Reinventing Shakespeare*, pp. 295–6, quotation from p. 306. The RSC has mounted *Romeo and Juliet* thirteen times in the fifty years beginning with Brook's 1947 production. By comparison, the Stratford Festival in Canada has produced it slightly less often, seven times between 1960 and 1997.

[2] For example, see Anthony B. Dawson, *Watching Shakespeare: A Playgoer's Guide* (Basingstoke and London, 1988), pp. 129–40; Thomas Clayton, '"Balancing at Work": (R)evoking the Script in Performance and Criticism', in *Shakespeare and the Sense of Performance: Essays in the Tradition of Performance Criticism in Honor*

performances in non-English-speaking countries, where Shakespeare production has increased tremendously since the end of World War II.[1] As Londré reports, *Romeo and Juliet* remained continuously popular in Europe, especially in France, between 1948 and 1985 (the chronological limits of her review).[2] She describes significant performances in eleven non-English-speaking countries ranging from France to Tibet.

The productions isolated for consideration focus more often on rites of passage or socio-political tensions than on the lovers as mythological types. In 1973, for example, Hands's better-known revival—perhaps influenced by Zeffirelli's subtext—emphasized homoerotic elements in the tragedy: Bernard Lloyd's Mercutio carried and then dismembered a life-size female doll, expressing his hostility towards Romeo's seeming disaffection.[3] Later, Bogdanov would give the play a 'quasi-Marxist' interpretation, making the feud a capitalist disaster in late twentieth-century terms: the lovers' tragedy became, in the closing scene, a stunning media event.[4] This kind of appropriation has grown widespread in Europe, where Shakespeare's language sets up fewer constraints and theatrical experiments with his plays face less resistance. According to Dennis Kennedy's overview in *Foreign Shakespeare*, populist directors after 1950 began to superimpose social texts on

of Bernard Beckerman, ed. Marvin and Ruth Thompson (Newark, Del., London, and Toronto, 1989), pp. 229–33; Barbara Hodgdon, 'Absent Bodies, Present Voices: Performance Work and the Close of Romeo and Juliet's Golden Story', *TJ* 41 (1989), repr. in Andrews, *Critical Essays*, pp. 243–65; and Holding, 'Part Two: Performance', in *'Romeo and Juliet': Text and Performance*, pp. 42–75.

[1] On the global spread of Shakespeare productions during this period, see Stanley Wells's lecture 'Shakespeare Around the Globe', originally delivered at the First International Conference of the Shakespeare Association of Pakistan, Karachi, 14 June 1997, International Shakespeare Occasional Paper 6 (Stratford-upon-Avon, 1998), p. 3. There had been important foreign experiments before the War, however, such as Alexander Tairov's at the Moscow Kamerny (or Chamber) Theatre in 1921 (cited by Dennis Kennedy, *Looking at Shakespeare: A Visual History of Twentieth-Century Performance* (Cambridge, 1993), pp. 93–6).

[2] *Shakespeare Around the Globe*, pp. 625, 630–1.

[3] Peter S. Donaldson, interpreting the film, gives the most detailed analysis of Zeffirelli's subtext in the sixth chapter of *Shakespearean Films/Shakespearean Directors* (Boston, 1990), pp. 145–88. In other productions, the failure of the rite in the protagonists' deaths has been viewed as central in one way or another: for example, Michael Kahn's *Romeo and Juliet* at the Folger in 1986 was co-ordinated with school workshops and materials in a campaign to prevent youth suicide (Jay L. Halio, *Understanding Shakespeare's Plays in Performance* (Manchester, 1988), pp. 78–9).

[4] See Clayton, '"Balancing at Work"', pp. 229–33.

Shakespeare's, and by the mid-1970s many of them engaged in self-consciously innovative productions, a trend far less controlled in Europe and Asia than in Great Britain and North America. These productions, often labelled postmodern, stress what Kennedy describes as 'the strangeness of Shakespeare's texts and their interrelationship with other aspects of contemporary culture'.[1]

Occasionally such a performance concentrates on the myth, but not in the way Gielgud did. For instance, Daniel Mesguich's 1985 production at Théâtre de l'Athénée in Paris approached the play through current French literary and psychoanalytic theory: the set was an enormous library, and protagonists from other related narratives of frustrated desire—Cyrano and Quasimodo, lovers

Fig. 9. The ball scene in Daniel Mesguich's production, Théâtre de l'Athénée, Paris, 1985. The director incorporates an episode from *Richard III* to anticipate the deaths of Mercutio, Tybalt, and Romeo. On the floor in the foreground, the dead King Henry VI/Mercutio (Jérôme Angé), Lady Anne (Clotilde de Bayser), and, on his knees, Richard III (Philippe Buquet); in the background, Tybalt (Gervais Robin) and a Capulet servant.

[1] 'Introduction: Shakespeare without his language', *Foreign Shakespeare: Contemporary Performance*, ed. Dennis Kennedy (Cambridge, 1993), pp. 1–18. The quotation comes from Kennedy's transition between essays, 'Postmodern Shakespeare', p. 211.

from later Shakespeare tragedies and from the works of Chekhov, Marivaux, and Racine—appeared on stage, moving in and out of the action.[1] More often foreign revivals reinforce public themes, as Josef Svoboda did in Prague (1963), Peter Schroth and Peter Kleinert in East Berlin (1981), Yves Goulais in Nantes, France (1982), and Robert LePage in his bilingual *Roméo et Juliette* (1991), a Canadian production with Francophone Capulets and Anglophone Montagues.[2] They reflect their immediate social and political conditions, accomplishing what Barbara Hodgdon regards as 'cultural work', participating in historical processes.[3]

When he takes account of Shakespeare abroad, Kennedy concludes that '[Shakespeare's] work has become the closest thing we have to a common cultural inheritance, but it is an inheritance that is thoroughly redefined by each culture that receives it'.[4] Released from its Afterword, this conclusion extends without limits of time or venue. If the performance history of *Romeo and Juliet* is measured along its far-reaching axes, it becomes clear that new definition has meant, since the eighteenth century, adapting the play to different media. It has been pointed out more than once that the tragedy has generated the most, and the most varied, adaptations of all Shakespeare's works.[5] In Stanley Wells's catalogue, a record for the play as well as the story, these add up to 'prose narratives, verse narratives, drama, opera, orchestral and choral music, ballet, film, television and painting', as well as burlesque and parody. A complex dynamic exists between the stage and other media. As Wells indicates, the adaptations have affected theatre history, interacting with it, imposing on it diverse images and expectations.[6] Like the theatrical versions, they tend to isolate one or two components of the narrative. They also interact among themselves.

For instance, Bellini's opera *I Capuleti e i Montecchi* (1830), derived from early Italian fiction, centres on the factionalism of the

[1] Marvin Carlson, 'Daniel Mesguich and intertextual Shakespeare', in *Foreign Shakespeare*, ed. Kennedy, pp. 217–20.

[2] For notices about the first three of these productions, see Kennedy, *Looking at Shakespeare*, pp. 221–3; Londré, *Shakespeare Around the Globe*, p. 630; and Jean-Marie Maguin's review in *Cahiers élisabéthains*, 24 (1983), 77–8.

[3] 'Absent Bodies, Present Voices', p. 259. Compare Dympna C. Callaghan on the cultural work of the play itself, in the discussion of 'Patriarchy' above.

[4] *Foreign Shakespeare*, p. 301.

[5] For example, see Dawson, *Watching Shakespeare*, p. 129.

[6] 'The Challenges of *Romeo and Juliet*', *SSu* 49 (1996), 1 (quotation), 4.

story; Berlioz's dramatic symphony *Roméo et Juliette* (1839), reacting to Bellini's opera, combines symphony, opera, and oratorio in a rendering of Shakespeare's poetry which raises political and aesthetic issues; Gounod's opera *Roméo et Juliette* (1867), influenced more by Garrick than by Berlioz, heightens the passion of the love-story by closing with a duet in which the protagonists invoke God.[1] There are examples from other musical arts. Typically nineteenth-century ballet, romantic and sentimental, reflected nineteenth-century theatrical versions not only in its pictorial style but in its emphasis on the lovers. By the late twentieth century ballet, like postmodern theatre, became engaged in politics.[2] The history of Prokofiev's ballet music aligns this score with other experimental versions of the narrative. Commissioned in 1934 and rejected at first as undanceable, the music finally turned the ballet into a political statement about betrayal and misuse of power.[3] In 1957 the music and choreography of *West Side Story* adapted the lovers' myth to American theatre, centring on the private relationship and the public discord which ends it. This musical became a film in 1961.[4]

By then *Romeo and Juliet* had established a life in cinema. Numerous silent versions (1902–26) and a variety of films with sound preceded the two attempts which anticipated Zeffirelli's: Irving Thalberg and George Cukor's (1936), a Hollywood production of an abridged text with older actors, Norma Shearer and Leslie Howard, in the nineteenth-century mode; and Renato Castellani's (1954), an experiment in cinematography which combined Italian realism with spectacle, also cut the text, and subordinated the young actors Susan Shentall and Laurence Harvey to a generalized vision of social conflict.[5] Aware of both theatrical and cinematic

[1] On the operas, see Peter Conrad, 'Romeos, Juliets, and Music', in *To Be Continued: Four Stories and Their Survival* (Oxford, 1995), pp. 47–93; and Cécile Bonnaventure, '*Romeo and Juliet*: Gounod's Operatic Adaptation of Shakespeare's Tragedy', *Shakespeare Yearbook*, 4 (1994), 229–50.

[2] Camille Cole Howard surveys this art-form in *The Staging of Shakespeare's 'Romeo and Juliet' as a Ballet* (San Francisco, 1992).

[3] Conrad, 'Romeos, Juliets, and Music', pp. 83–9.

[4] Robert Hapgood discusses its fortunes until 1972 in '*West Side Story* and the Modern Appeal of *Romeo and Juliet*', *SJH* 8 (1972), repr. in Andrews, *Critical Essays*, pp. 229–41.

[5] On the early film versions, see Roy Walker, 'In Fair Verona', *The Twentieth Century*, 156 (1954), and Paul A. Jorgensen, 'Castellani's *Romeo and Juliet*: Intention and Response', *Film Quarterly*, 10 (1955), both repr. in *Focus on Shakespearean*

precedent, Zeffirelli absorbed key events and characters from the play, with only one-third of the dialogue, into a new composition. He deliberately contextualized the narrative in the anxieties of the late 1960s, reflecting on issues from sexual identity and generational conflict to Vietnam, omitting passages which interfered with the impression of contemporaneity. In his film version there are few traces of lyricism. He distinguishes the protagonists from other characters by allowing them to speak less—and less articulately—than the others, even while they look beautiful and very young: they were played by the teenage Olivia Hussey and Leonard Whiting, and they had turned into victims of the twentieth-century *Zeitgeist*.

Zeffirelli's film carries the methods of his 1960 theatrical production to their logical conclusions. In the process it became the most popular and lucrative rendition of the tragedy for a period of almost thirty years. Peter S. Donaldson's important study of Zeffirelli's cinematic version, published in 1990, announces that '*Romeo and Juliet* has been the most commercially successful Shakespeare film to date, returning over $50 million on an initial investment of $1.5 million'.[1] According to Hodgdon, this film became institutionalized within the American secondary-school curriculum by the late 1980s; and Joan Ozark Holmer, in a 1996 publication, says that it continues to be the 'most popular filmic afterlife' of the Romeo and Juliet story.[2] Holmer wrote that opinion before the release of Baz Luhrmann's *Romeo + Juliet*, a film made accessible in several other media within months of its appearance: videocassette; a CD-ROM version of the soundtrack with visual images from the film; and a book with both the screenplay and the Shakespeare text.

Luhrmann's film poses a serious challenge to Zeffirelli's, but it remains to be seen whether the contender has displaced the long-time champion. Although Zeffirelli's version of *Romeo and Juliet* obviously reflects its era, it also anticipated concerns of the next few

Films, ed. Charles W. Ekert (Englewood Cliffs, NJ, 1972), pp. 115–24 and 108–15; Kenneth S. Rothwell, 'Hollywood and Some Versions of *Romeo and Juliet*: Toward a "Substantial Pageant"', *Literature/Film Quarterly*, 1 (1973), 343–51; and Anthony Davies, 'The Film Versions of *Romeo and Juliet*', *SSu* 49 (1996), 153–7.

[1] *Shakespearean Films/Shakespearean Directors*, p. 145.

[2] Hodgdon, 'Absent Bodies, Present Voices', pp. 264–5 n. 47; Joan Ozark Holmer, 'The Poetics of Paradox: Shakespeare's Versus Zeffirelli's Cultures of Violence', *SSu* 49 (1996), 163.

Fig. 10 and 11. The lovers at Capulet's party in two popular cinematic versions: Leonard Whiting and Olivia Hussey as Romeo and Juliet in Franco Zeffirelli's 1968 film; Leonardo DiCaprio and Claire Danes in Baz Luhrmann's 1996 film *Romeo + Juliet*.

decades (as Donaldson shows). Luhrmann's revision also reflects its era, perhaps more specifically, in its postmodern style: it echoes key figures in cinematic history, from Busby Berkeley to Federico Fellini to Ken Russell; it uses techniques and images familiar from television networks (MTV) and genres (evening news, *Miami Vice*). At times it even looks back to strategies originating with Garrick, such as the encounter of Romeo and Juliet in the tomb. Like Zeffirelli's, this film adapts the plot, characters, and about one-third of the dialogue to a medium which allows the play a radically new ambience. In this instance, many reviewers agree, the medium results from 'a camp aesthetic pitched at a melodramatic level'.[1] It projects sympathetic lovers, the young Claire Danes and Leonardo DiCaprio, in an urban setting of anarchic gang violence and disintegrating social structures, a political tableau. By the mid-1980s theatrical productions like Bogdanov's had begun to incorporate elements of this aesthetic. Luhrmann's articulation of these elements, described more than once as 'hyperkinetic', has certainly spoken to the very late twentieth century: North American teenagers rushed to see the film more than once, and adults have given it a generally positive, sometimes enthusiastic response. Its millennial vernacular may well last into the twenty-first century.[2]

Versions of the Romeo and Juliet narrative continue to proliferate, and there is no reason to expect a slackening of momentum at any time soon. From Brazilian chapbook to Bosnian documentary, from comic strip to soft-pornographic video, the story dramatized by Shakespeare is reshaped to fit the preoccupations and tastes of modern cultures.[3] Its multiple levels, personal and public, admit frequent change, in particular change which consolidates multiplicity into one dimension, or perhaps two. In its Shakespearian form, stylization usually demands adjustment as well: Elizabethan

[1] José Arroyo, 'Kiss Kiss Bang Bang', *Sight and Sound*, March 1997, 9. For a thorough and objective critical assessment, see Hodgdon's essay in *SSu* 52 (1999).

[2] Another film is in progress as this edition goes to press, a cinematic version of the very successful all-male *Shakespeare's 'R&J'*, performed entirely by four actors, which began playing in New York in September 1997 and by June 1998 had become the longest-running *Romeo and Juliet* either on or off Broadway.

[3] Some of these reworkings have received serious critical attention: for example, the Brazilian chapbook (Candace Slater, 'Romeo and Juliet in the Brazilian Backlands', *Journal of Folklore Research*, 20 (1983), 35–53), and the comic-strip (Stephen Orgel, 'Shakespeare in stunning full colour', *Word & Image*, 1 (1985), 273–7).

conventions of rhetoric and verse make the characters' parts 'almost impossible', as George Bernard Shaw wrote, 'except to actors of positive genius'.[1] English-language performances may cut many lines, as much as two-thirds of the text, to communicate the narrative through contemporary actors to contemporary audiences. Whatever the medium, however, adaptation allows the familiar narrative to proceed with its cultural work. Peter Brook's judgement about the place of innovation in theatre applies as well to most formulations of the Romeo and Juliet story:

> When Garrick played *Romeo and Juliet* in knee-breeches, he was *right*; when Kean staged *The Winter's Tale* with a hundred Persian pot-carriers, he was *right*; when Tree staged Shakespeare with all the resources of the His Majesty's, he was *right*; when Craig staged his reaction to this he was *right* too. Each was justified in its own time; each would be outrageous out of it. A production is only correct at the moment of its correctness, and only good at the moment of its success. In its beginning is its beginning, and in its end is its end.[2]

Date(s)

The dates proposed for the original *Romeo and Juliet* range from 1591 to 1596. For several reasons it is difficult to fix the time more precisely. First, two extant versions of the play represent different phases of its composition; these printed texts correspond with each other and lost manuscripts in largely unknowable ways (see below, 'The Mobile Text'). As a result they allow the possibility that composition occurred over a number of years, by Shakespeare alone, in collaboration with performers, or through redaction by one or more writers. Assigning a year to composition under these circumstances risks isolating one part of the process and simplifying the whole. Second, Shakespeare's situation and that of the theatres remained uncertain during the earlier years of this period, until 1594 when he joined the newly created Lord Chamberlain's Men. Speculation based on theatre history must be tentative, most of it permitting arguments which span the whole six years. Other kinds of evidence, such as topical allusions, seem just as equivocal.

[1] From a review of Forbes-Robertson's production, *The Saturday Review*, 28 September 1895, quoted in Wells, 'The Challenges of *Romeo and Juliet*', 7–8.

[2] 'Style in Shakespearean Production', *Orpheus*, 1 (1948), repr. in *The Modern Theatre: Readings and Documents*, ed. Daniel Seltzer (Boston, 1967), p. 256.

Only language provides less ambiguous clues about the process: linguistic connections with other literary works of the period suggest that composition began in 1593, the tragedy appeared on stage in some form by late 1594 or 1595, and revisions may have continued at least until publication of the second quarto (Q2) in 1599.

The title-page of the first quarto (Q1) establishes that a version of *Romeo and Juliet* reached print by 1597. Although it names a company, information about auspices is not definitive: 'As it hath been often (with great applause) | plaid publiquely, by the right Ho-|nourable the L. of *Hunsdon* | his Seruants'. Malone noted in Boswell (1821) that the company was known as Lord Hunsdon's Men during the period 22 July 1596 to 17 April 1597; it was known as the Lord Chamberlain's Men before and after those years.[1] As Evans points out in his edition, however, the reference could have originated with the publisher as a promotional device, and the company may have acted *Romeo and Juliet* before it became Lord Hunsdon's (p. 1). Certainly Shakespeare could have written the play earlier for the Lord Chamberlain's Men.

Following publication of Q1, a spate of allusions to *Romeo and Juliet* appeared in 1598. E. A. J. Honigmann identifies this year as 'a breakthrough', when the title-pages of Shakespeare's plays acknowledged his reputation by printing his name and writers more frequently paid tribute to works other than *Venus and Adonis* or *The Rape of Lucrece*.[2] At this point non-Shakespearian dramas began to echo *Romeo and Juliet* (among other Shakespearian texts); Francis Meres listed it in *Palladis Tamia; Wit's Treasury* as evidence that '*Shakespeare* among the English is the most excellent . . . for Tragedy' (p. 282[r]); and Marston referred to its popularity in *The Scourge of Villanie*.[3] Marston directs attention to a performance at

[1] I am grateful to Chiaki Hanabusa for informing me that the latter date has been repeatedly mistaken as 17 March 1597 in scholarship on Q1. Greg caught the error, which originated with E. K. Chambers, in *First Folio*, pp. 225 and 232 n. A. (See Hanabusa, 'A Neglected Misdate and *Romeo and Juliet* Q1 (1597)', *N&Q*, NS 46 (1999), 229–30.)

[2] *Shakespeare's Impact on His Contemporaries* (London and Basingstoke, 1982), pp. 26, 28–9.

[3] Evans notes echoes in four plays written in 1598: Porter's *Two Angry Women of Abingdon*, Haughton's *Englishmen for My Money*, and Munday and Chettle's *Downfall of Robert Earl of Huntingdon* and *Death of Robert Earl of Huntingdon* (p. 1 n. 3). See also *The Shakspere Allusion-Book: A Collection of Allusions to Shakspere from*

the Curtain; 'Satire X' mocks Luscus, a playgoer there who seasons his conversation with dramatic lines kept in his commonplace-book, among them 'pure *Juliat* and *Romio*' (l. 39).[1] Clearly allusions register the play's currency in 1598, but they indicate little about its date(s) of composition: writers may have been responding to a relatively new play, a revival, or publication.[2]

Both quartos contain recollections of the comedian Will Kemp, who joined the Lord Chamberlain's Company in 1594: Q1 preserves the name in dialogue, 'Will will tell thee where thou shalt fetch them' (I1r); Q2 prints it for the character name 'Peter' in a stage direction, '*Enter Will Kemp.*' (K3v). Although the published versions must date from 1594 or later, their allusions to Kemp shed almost no light on the time of composition. As two conflicting arguments show, the references can be used to support totally different theories. Giorgio Melchiori speculates that Shakespeare began to write *Romeo and Juliet* in 1592–3, when his position in the theatre was unsure and he had no actor in mind for the various comic roles; the episode in 4.4 with Peter and the musicians was added later, specifically as a vehicle for Kemp.[3] Taking issue with Melchiori, David Wiles accepts a 1594–6 date for composition: he thinks Shakespeare expected Kemp, from the beginning, to play all the comic roles. The roles changed during composition because the dramatist wrote *Romeo and Juliet* in stages. Drafting 5.3 first, he was influenced by Brooke and gave Romeo's servant a comic edge. When he began at the beginning, however, he made revisions which relocated the clown as Peter, the principal Capulet servant.[4]

Information about venue turns out to be equally indeterminate, as Andrew Gurr demonstrates by gathering it into an essay.[5] Gurr

1591 to 1700, ed. C. M. Ingleby *et al.*, 2 vols. (London and Oxford, 1932), i. 46 and *passim*.

[1] 'Satire X' ('Satire XI' in the 1599 edition) in *The Poems of John Marston*, ed. Arnold Davenport (Liverpool, 1961), p. 168. Roslyn Lander Knutson finds another possible satiric allusion to the play in Everard Guilpin's 'Satire V' (ll. 75, 77–8), in *Skialetheia* (1598); see *The Repertory of Shakespeare's Company 1594–1613* (Fayetteville, Ark., 1991), p. 218 n. 7.

[2] See Evans, ed., pp. 1–2, and Knutson, *Repertory*, pp. 167, 202.

[3] 'Peter, Balthasar, and Shakespeare's Art of Doubling', 780–2.

[4] *Shakespeare's Clown: Actor and Text in the Elizabethan Playhouse* (Cambridge, 1987), pp. 83–94. In the last scene, where he reads lines attributed to 'Peter' in Q2 as part of a first draft, Wiles finds 'ample opportunities in performance for the clown' (p. 90).

[5] 'Date and Expected Venue', 15–25.

emphasizes the heavy demands that both texts of *Romeo and Juliet* made on the resources of Elizabethan theatres, especially in their staging of the balcony or window, curtained bed, and monument (see above, 'Initial Staging'); he raises questions about the performance space Shakespeare imagined as he composed the play. Finally these questions remain unresolved, because Shakespeare's affiliations before 1594 are unknown: theatre historians have linked him with a number of companies—Queen's, Pembroke's, Strange's, Sussex's—but he may have been entirely dissociated from the theatres when they were closed during the plague years of 1592–4.[1] Nevertheless, when he joined the Lord Chamberlain's Men in 1594, evidently he brought a large stock of old plays with him;[2] and whatever his previous affiliation, he may have been writing *Romeo and Juliet* with Burbage's Theatre in mind any time between 1592 and 1596.[3] According to Gurr, a pre-1594 date would place *Romeo and Juliet* appropriately with what he calls the 'large plays' of the late 1580s and early 1590s, texts that had extensive staging requirements; a post-1594 date would place it somewhat incongruously among plays that made lighter demands. 'But there is nothing conclusive in any of the evidence . . .'[4]

The apparent topicalities of *Romeo and Juliet* simply confirm a range of dates between 1591 and 1596. Among these the most debated and widely known is the Nurse's memory of a seismic event: ''Tis since the earthquake now eleven years' (1.3.25). In the eighteenth century Thomas Tyrwhitt first proposed as referent a specific earthquake in England, on 6 April 1580, and calculated the play's date as 1591 (see Furness's edition, 1.3.23 n.). As recently as 1982 Honigmann discounted arguments against that calculation.[5] Earlier Sidney Thomas had cited a reference in William Covell's *Polimanteia* (1595) to a terrible earthquake on the Continent, on 1 March 1584, which makes it possible to date the play 1595;[6] and Sarah Dodson added two references to landslips in

[1] See Gurr, 'Three Reluctant Patrons and Early Shakespeare', *SQ* 44 (1993), 169–72, and Melchiori, 'Peter, Balthasar, and Shakespeare's Art of Doubling', 780.

[2] Gurr, *The Shakespearian Playing Companies* (Oxford, 1996), p. 281.

[3] Gurr, 'Date and Expected Venue', 19.

[4] Gurr, 'Date and Expected Venue', 18, quotation from 20.

[5] *Shakespeare's Impact on His Contemporaries*, pp. 67–8.

[6] 'The Earthquake in *Romeo and Juliet*', *MLN* 64 (1949), 417–19. Thomas speculates that Shakespeare may have read *Polimanteia*, because it praises 'Lucrecia Sweet Shakspeare', and borrowed its allusion to the earthquake.

England cited by chroniclers—Blackmoor, Dorsetshire, 13 January 1583 and Motingham, Kent, 4 August 1585—that would allow other dates.[1] Of course, the Nurse's earthquake may have no specific referent. Various tremors during the 1580s (and perhaps even later) made it possible for Shakespeare to rely on his audience's knowledge or memory to give the Nurse's claim verisimilitude (see Gibbons's edition, p. 27). By 1988 Thomas would offer the useful reminder that real references must have become meaningless with revivals or publication. He quotes E. K. Chambers's conclusion that this instance of finding a real calendar in *Romeo and Juliet* 'is pressing the Nurse's interest in chronology—and Shakespeare's—rather hard'.[2]

Chambers's proviso applies to two other theories that would situate the extant versions of *Romeo and Juliet* in 1596. John W. Draper, who fixes the plot by year and day according to the play's internal chronology—astrological references to days of the week and month and phases of the moon—thinks it was written or extensively revised in 1596. E. P. Kuhl, elaborating the implications of a note by Robert Weston Babcock, comes to the same conclusion on the basis of Spanish nuance in the text (for example, the 'ambuscados' and 'Spanish blades' in Mercutio's Queen Mab speech, 1.4.82) which may derive from the capture of Cadiz in June 1596.[3]

Suggesting a date before 1596, M. C. Bradbrook notices correspondences between *Romeo and Juliet* and events during autumn 1594 in the life of the Earl of Southampton, Shakespeare's patron around 1593 to 4: the fight in 3.1 and Romeo's exile may allude to Southampton's protection of Sir Charles and Sir Henry Danvers, who had killed Sir Henry Long in a family feud. Bradbrook also points out that the Southampton family had previously shown interest in the conflict between Montagues and Capulets; George Gascoigne wrote a masque in 1575, *A Hundred Sundry Flowers*, celebrating a double wedding in the Montague family, that of Southampton's mother, and featuring eight Montague gentlemen

[1] 'Notes on the Earthquake in *Romeo and Juliet*', *MLN* 65 (1950), 144. Dodson suggests that there may be still undiscovered phenomena like these, from 1580 to 1585, in England, Italy, and regions adjacent to Italy.

[2] 'On the Dating of Shakespeare's Early Plays', *SQ* 39 (1988), 191; E. K. Chambers, *William Shakespeare: A Study of Facts and Problems* (Oxford, 1930), i. 345.

[3] Draper, 'The Date of *Romeo and Juliet*', *RES* 25 (1949), 55–7; Kuhl, '*Romeo and Juliet*, I, IV, 84 F.', *PQ* 9 (1930), 307–8; Babcock, '*Romeo and Juliet*, I, iv, 86: An Emendation', *PQ* 8 (1929), 407–8.

victorious in battle.[1] On consideration, this evidence too can be read in more than one way. If the printed versions of *Romeo and Juliet* do reflect the dramatic events of 1594, they may have added correspondences to an earlier form of the play. Certainly emphasis on the feud reveals nothing specific about date.

Literary echoes may offer guidance to the history of *Romeo and Juliet* in composition and on the stage, although they require careful handling: circulation of works in manuscript, performance of unpublished play-texts, and other factors sometimes make it problematic to determine the direction of influence. For example, Gibbons and Evans in their editions draw attention to correspondences with Samuel Daniel's *Complaint of Rosamond* (1592). J. W. Lever discovered parallels between the opening of *Romeo and Juliet* 3.5 and verse by Du Bartas in John Eliot's *Ortho-epia Gallica, or Eliot's First Fruits for the French* (1593).[2] With this evidence a starting-point in the early 1590s seems feasible but inexact; it depends on whether Shakespeare read these texts in manuscript or print.

Since 1980, J. J. M. Tobin and Joan Ozark Holmer have stressed correspondences between Thomas Nashe's prose and *Romeo and Juliet* which they use to argue for a date in the mid-1590s. Tobin concentrates on parallels with *Have with You to Saffron-walden* (1596) in themes, phrasing, and a dozen instances of diction; Holmer, trawling more widely through Nashe's life and works, finds connections which supplement Tobin's.[3] While she favours a date in the latter half of 1596, Holmer proposes a *terminus a quo* of 1595 based on links with Saviolo's *Practise*, his fencing manual published that year. She claims that *Romeo and Juliet* enacts the manual's diction and theory, particularly its Italian fencing terms.[4] In a review of Evans's edition, MacDonald P. Jackson expresses scepticism about Nashe's influence and a 1596 date of composition. He summarizes key reservations about the evidence: it

[1] *Shakespeare: The Poet in His World* (New York, 1978), pp. 100–2.

[2] Gibbons, p. 27; Evans, p. 3; Lever, 'Shakespeare's French Fruits', *SSu* 6 (1953), 82–3.

[3] Tobin, 'Nashe and *Romeo and Juliet*', *N&Q*, NS 27 (1980), 161–2, and 'Nashe and the Texture of *Romeo and Juliet*', *Aligarh Journal of English Studies*, 5 (1980), 162–74; Joan Ozark Holmer, 'No "Vain Fantasy": Shakespeare's Refashioning of Nashe for Dreams and Queen Mab', in *Shakespeare's 'Romeo and Juliet'*, ed. Halio, pp. 49–82, and 'Nashe as "Monarch of Witt" and Shakespeare's *Romeo and Juliet*', *TSLL* 37 (1995), 314–43.

[4] '"Draw, if you be men": Saviolo's Significance for *Romeo and Juliet*', *SQ* 45 (1994), 163–89.

cannot be dated accurately because *Saffron-walden* may have circulated in manuscript before publication; it generates parallels with plays accepted as earlier than *Romeo and Juliet*, such as *The Two Gentlemen of Verona*; and shared vocabulary may result from shared speech.[1]

The Shaxicon database on World Wide Web should help to refine the study of linguistic evidence for purposes of dating Shakespeare's plays: it charts the interrelation of rare words in Shakespeare's texts with contemporary works from around 1591 to 1616. According to Donald W. Foster, who created the database, Q1 and the text it has in common with Q2 draw on works published in 1592–3; Q2 variants echo those from 1594–7; and both quartos may have been revised after 1593–4.[2] When he addresses the arguments of Tobin and Holmer, Foster concludes that Nashe borrowed from the underlying manuscript of Q1 in *Saffron-walden*, Shakespeare could have seen Nashe's *Terrors of the Night* (SR 1593, 1594) in manuscript, and Shakespeare had not read Saviolo's *Practise*, although the manual may respond with the motto 'worm's meat' to *Romeo and Juliet* Q1. Foster dates the composition of Q1 1593 and that of Q2 1594; he thinks a version of the tragedy was staged by late 1594 (the SR entry for Book II of Saviolo's *Practise*) or 1595.[3]

Linguistic evidence suggests that *Romeo and Juliet* evolved, in composition and performance, between about 1593 and the end of the century. Shakespeare may have begun writing it during the period of the 'large plays', and the changing text perhaps records or reflects events of the middle and late 1590s: Kemp's (and Shakespeare's) joining the Lord Chamberlain's Men; Southampton's harbouring of a feuding duellist; the impact of various publications and manuscripts. If *Romeo and Juliet* originated in about 1593 and

[1] 'The Year's Contributions to Shakespearian Study: 3. Editions and Textual Studies', *SSu* 38 (1985), 242.

[2] A few obvious caveats should accompany the use of this (or any) linguistic database. In the first place, the lexical cross-sample is not exhaustive and lacks texts. In the second, Foster's choice of editions for the electronic texts may pose problems, and his criteria for inclusion of texts can seem vague. Further, he omits consideration of words which occur more than twelve times in Shakespeare's canon or twenty-five times in the cross-sample; some of these may register a change in Shakespeare's language.

[3] See 'The Webbing of *Romeo and Juliet*', in Porter, *Critical Essays*, pp. 131–49.

reached the stage by 1595, it takes its place in the canon with Shakespeare's early poetry and plays, in particular the romance-centred comedies *Love's Labour's Lost* and *A Midsummer Night's Dream*.

The close relation between *Romeo and Juliet* and *A Midsummer Night's Dream* in content and style has generated much discussion over priority: is *Romeo and Juliet* a serious treatment of the romantic dilemmas in *A Midsummer Night's Dream*, or is *A Midsummer Night's Dream* a parody of the romantic tragedy? The Oxford editors give a linguistic test which makes *Romeo and Juliet* precede *A Midsummer Night's Dream*; Amy J. Riess and George Walton Williams draw the same conclusion from internal evidence; and Foster's linguistic data corroborate these results, indicating that from 1595 on *Romeo and Juliet* and *A Midsummer Night's Dream* track closely together, like scripts performed as companion plays. The two texts probably influenced not only each other and Shakespeare's later plays, but the whole contemporary network of written language and speech.[1]

The Mobile Text[2]

There are two early substantive texts of *Romeo and Juliet*, both quartos published at the end of the sixteenth century with differing title-pages: '*AN* | EXCELLENT | conceited Tragedie | *OF* | Romeo and Iuliet' (1597), and 'THE | MOST EX- | cellent and lamentable | Tragedie, of Romeo | and *Iuliet*.' (1599). All seventeenth-century editions derived from the second of these, which has become the familiar version for modern audiences and readers. Less well-known generally, the first quarto has interested scholars because of its differences from Q2. It is more than one-fifth shorter; and many details—linguistic and theatrical—vary between the two

[1] *Textual Companion*, p. 118; Riess and Williams, '"Tragical Mirth": From *Romeo* to *Dream*', *SQ* 43 (1992), repr. in Porter, *Critical Essays*, pp. 100–6; Foster, 'The Webbing of *Romeo and Juliet*', pp. 135, 133.

[2] I have borrowed this phrase from Philip Brockbank's forward-looking essay 'Towards a mobile text', in *The Theory and Practice of Text-Editing: Essays in Honour of James T. Boulton*, ed. Ian Small and Marcus Walsh (Cambridge, 1991), pp. 90–106. As the following discussion will show, the text of *Romeo and Juliet* has, from the beginning, undergone striking change. 'Mobile text' refers to its indeterminacy, and the section below on 'Editorial Procedures' explains how I have attempted to convey through a book the impression of process.

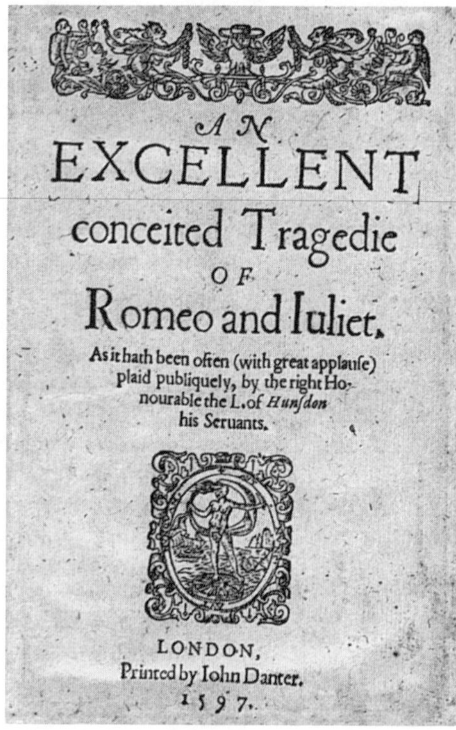
AN
EXCELLENT
conceited Tragedie
OF
Romeo and Iuliet.
As it hath been often (with great applause)
plaid publiquely, by the right Ho-
nourable the L. of Hunsdon
his Seruants.

LONDON,
Printed by Iohn Danter.
1597.

Fig. 12. The title-page of Quarto 1 (1597). See also Fig. 13, p. 135.

quartos. In effect, there are two extant versions of *Romeo and Juliet* which represent the Elizabethan play, two witnesses to distinct phases of its career in the sixteenth century.

Critics since Pope, focusing attention on the textual differences, have attempted to identify the phases and evaluate the quartos. As a result, *Romeo and Juliet* has actively registered changing editorial styles and bibliographic theories, from eighteenth-century eclecticism to twentieth-century New Bibliography. Like its predecessors, this edition will show the impress of the culture that produced it, in particular the millennial postmodern theory which has influenced the way critics view texts. Coincidentally, the scepticism which calls most things in doubt also revitalizes a sense of these early theatrical texts as part of a multivalent and dynamic process.

In the first place that scepticism determines the use of evidence for the study of all texts. According to D. C. Greetham, fluctuating rules for the definition and admissibility of evidence call into question, with renewed urgency, '[t]he relations between substance and accidence, whole and part, truth and accuracy, cause and effect'.[1] The original question, long-standing for English Renaissance dramatic texts, has lately unsettled their bibliographic history. It is becoming a commonplace that the most influential bibliographers of the subject in the twentieth century—W. W. Greg, R. B. McKerrow, Fredson Bowers—at various points recognized the core of uncertainty at the heart of their projects.[2] Yet they and their followers continued to build narratives of filiation about early plays with meagre evidence; and their method, a set procedure adapted from Enlightenment thinking to a more scientific age, has frequently misconstrued the randomness which characterizes the extant documents.[3] Some bibliographers persist in seeking authority for fluid theatrical texts in static concepts: what Jerome J. McGann calls 'the autonomy of the isolated author', or, more recently, what Janette Dillon terms a 'unitary conception of performance'.[4] Under fresh scrutiny, however, their narratives are breaking down, and with them the binaries that have defined the study of early modern play-texts: author versus stage, good quartos versus bad quartos, memorial reconstruction versus foul papers, prompt books versus foul papers, touring versions versus London versions.[5] As the century turns, the vocabulary and

[1] 'Textual Forensics', *PMLA* 111 (1996), 47.

[2] See, for example, Greg, *Editorial Problem*, pp. iv, 156; McKerrow, *Prolegomena for the Oxford Shakespeare: A Study in Editorial Method* (Oxford, 1939), p. 6; and Bowers, 'Established Texts and Definitive Editions', *PQ* 41 (1962), 1–17, or 'Authority, Copy, and Transmission in Shakespeare's Texts', in *Shakespeare Study Today: The Horace Howard Furness Memorial Lectures*, ed. Georgianna Ziegler (New York, 1986), pp. 24–5.

[3] Marion Trousdale explores the 'inherent contradiction between the means of investigation and the matter to be investigated' in 'Diachronic and Synchronic: Critical Bibliography and the Acting of Plays', in *Shakespeare: Text, Language, Criticism: Essays in Honour of Marvin Spevack*, ed. Bernhard Fabian and Kurt Tetzeli von Rosador (Hildesheim, Zurich, and New York, 1987), pp. 304–14 (quotation from p. 306), and 'A Second Look at Critical Bibliography and the Acting of Plays', *SQ* 41 (1990), 87–96.

[4] McGann, *A Critique of Modern Textual Criticism* (Chicago and London, 1983), p. 8. For an analysis of theatrical production as a criterion, see Dillon, 'Is There a Performance in this Text?', *SQ* 45 (1994), 74–86, quotation from 77.

[5] Paul Werstine's studies of the narratives began to appear in 1988; they include the seminal essay 'Narratives about Printed Shakespeare Texts: "Foul

grammar for historicizing such texts are undergoing significant adjustment.

Without the narratives, dualism, authority, and other constructions, early drama-texts look different, unstable and shifting. When there are multiple versions of the same play, the relation between them establishes a field of energy for the viewer's imagination and perhaps an analogue for the play's origins in changing theatrical or other socio-economic factors. McKerrow understood this complexity: 'it is very doubtful whether, especially in the case of the earlier plays, there ever existed any written "final form" . . . We must not expect to find a definitive text'.[1] Over the past two decades this kind of insight has altered the direction of textual studies, including editions. It informs D. F. McKenzie's ideal of creative editing, the means for producing a version which transcends all others but remains true to the intention of the work:

> In this sense, the work may be the form traditionally imputed to an archetype; it may be a form seen as immanent in each of the versions but not fully realized in any one of them; or it may be conceived of as always potential, like that of a play, where the text is open and generates new meanings according to new needs in a perpetual deferral of closure.[2]

McKenzie's simile describes most plays, especially multiple texts like *Romeo and Juliet*: Jacques Derrida has called the tragedy a 'still living palimpsest'.[3] Like a more conventional palimpsest, the first quartos record two of the play's earliest manifestations. In Stephen Orgel's opinion, Elizabethan theatrical companies may have resisted such publications of their plays because transforming a play into a book fixes it, stabilizes the indeterminate.[4] Whatever caused the actors' resistance—if they did resist—it is obvious that physical books, solid and finite, not only mediate but contain variable

Papers" and "Bad" Quartos', *SQ* 41 (1990), 65–86. The list of binaries is based on Dillon's survey in 'Is There a Performance in this Text?', 76–7 and 76 n. 5.

[1] *Prolegomena*, p. 6. See also David Bradley, *From Text to Performance in the Elizabethan Theatre: Preparing the Play for the Stage* (Cambridge, 1992), p. 11.

[2] *Bibliography and the Sociology of Texts* (1986), p. 29.

[3] Jonathan Goldberg translates the phrase in '"What? in a names that which we call a Rose", The Desired Texts of *Romeo and Juliet*', in *Crisis in Editing: Texts of the English Renaissance*, ed. Randall McLeod (New York, 1994), p. 191.

[4] 'Shakespeare Imagines a Theater', in *Shakespeare, Man of the Theater: The Selected Proceedings of the International Shakespeare Association World Congress, Stratford-upon-Avon, 1981*, ed. Kenneth Muir, Jay L. Halio, and D. J. Palmer (Newark, Del., London, and Toronto, 1983), p. 43.

texts. They probably perform these functions with more authority for modern readers than for their early-modern counterparts, because print culture has turned the book into an almost perfect and timeless object preserving stable and permanent works.[1]

The important distinction between vehicle and text—material container and content—will govern the following analysis of publication. In the study of books transmitting *Romeo and Juliet*, bibliographic tools have uncovered precise data along with negative and inconclusive evidence. They help to delineate the extant forms which both store the text and provide a set of instructions for reconstituting the work.[2] In the inquiry about subjects related to the play's text—the manuscript copy for the first two quartos, the connections between these printed books—bibliographic tools have unearthed little information to support more or less elaborate theories. This examination of textual history will consider the publications of *Romeo and Juliet* in the chronological order of their printing. Initially setting out the known, it will then review the speculations which indicate how much remains unknowable.

Quarto 1 (1597). The title-page of Q1 situates both book and text in more than one way. It describes *Romeo and Juliet* as '*AN* EXCELLENT conceited Tragedie', the word *conceited* emphasizing the play's wittiness in a formula used at the end of the sixteenth century primarily to advertise comedies (see pp. 50–1 above). In another bid to attract purchasers, the title-page refers to performances 'with great applause' by Lord Hunsdon's company. Here it identifies the Lord Chamberlain's Men by the title they held for a brief period in 1596–7 (see above, 'Date(s)'). Finally it names the printer John Danter, reproduces one of his ornaments,[3] and specifies the date 1597.

Neither this quarto nor the second was entered in the Stationers'

[1] See Trousdale, 'Diachronic and Synchronic', p. 313, and 'A Second Look at Critical Bibliography and the Acting of Plays', 94.

[2] The phrasing of this distinction borrows terminology from three essays: Leah S. Marcus, 'Renaissance/Early Modern Studies', in *Redrawing the Boundaries: The Transformation of English and American Literary Studies*, ed. Stephen Greenblatt and Giles Gunn (New York, 1992), p. 55; Peter L. Shillingsburg, 'Text as Matter, Concept, and Action', *SB* 44 (1991), 54; and G. Thomas Tanselle, 'Editing without a Copy-Text', *SB* 47 (1994), 5.

[3] See Ronald B. McKerrow, *Printers' & Publishers' Devices in England & Scotland 1485–1640* (1913), device 281.

Register.[1] Although Alfred W. Pollard thought lack of entry made Q1 suspect, non-entrance is negative evidence. It says nothing about copyright or the way Danter acquired this version of the play.[2]

Collation of the five surviving copies has produced no variants.[3] In view of the small sample, these results hardly seem anomalous, and Q1 is not unique among the short quartos: collation has uncovered no variants in the three copies of *2 Henry VI* (*The First Part of the Contention*) (1594) or the five copies of *The Merry Wives of Windsor* (1602).[4] As a result, evidence in these three cases fails to show whether compositors opened the formes to make corrections. The mistakes remaining in all five copies of Q1 are unremarkable in kind and number, proportionately fewer than in the second quarto, which most bibliographers consider authoritative (see below, 'Quarto 1 and Quarto 2: Provenance').[5]

[1] There are only two entries for *Romeo and Juliet* in the Stationers' Register, both recording rights to transfers of the play in its longer version: the first transfer, from Cuthbert Burby to Nicholas Ling, 22 January 1607, includes *Love's Labour's Lost* and *The Taming of A Shrew*; the second, from Nicholas Ling to John Smethwick, 19 November 1607, includes *Hamlet*, *The Taming of A Shrew*, *Love's Labour's Lost*, and twelve other books. Facsimiles of these entries can be found in S. Schoenbaum, *William Shakespeare: Records and Images* (1981), p. 216, plate 124, and p. 217, plate 126.

[2] Pollard, *Shakespeare Folios and Quartos: A Study in the Bibliography of Shakespeare's Plays 1594–1685* (1909), pp. 65, 69. Both Leo Kirschbaum, *Shakespeare and the Stationers* (Columbus, O., 1955), pp. 89–91, and Schoenbaum, *William Shakespeare: Records and Images*, p. 205, discuss the connection between entrance in the Stationers' Register and copyright; Maureen Bell gives recent statistics for 'Entrance in the Stationers' Register', *The Library*, 6th ser., 16 (1994), 50–4. Regarding the copyright of *Romeo and Juliet* in particular, more than one scholar has suggested that Burby, publisher of Q2, may have been involved in the publication of Q1 or acquired copyright later from Danter's widow. (See, for example, Frank G. Hubbard's edition of Q1, University of Wisconsin Studies in Language and Literature, 19 (Madison, 1924), p. 9; Harry R. Hoppe, *The Bad Quarto of 'Romeo and Juliet': A Bibliographical and Textual Study*, Cornell Studies in English, 36 (Ithaca, NY, 1948), pp. 13–15; and Kirschbaum, *Shakespeare and the Stationers*, pp. 263–4.) The absence of Burby's name from any documentation strongly argues against this hypothesis.

[3] The five copies are at the British Library, the Bodleian Library, Trinity College Cambridge, the Folger Shakespeare Library, and the Henry E. Huntington Library; W. W. Greg lists all of them in *A Bibliography of the English Printed Drama to the Restoration* (1939–59), i. 234 (No. 143). Barry Gaines and the editor independently collated the five extant copies, and George Walton Williams collated 1.2.53B–1.3.34 for his edition (see p. 151).

[4] This information appears in Thomas L. Berger, 'Press Variants in Substantive Shakespearian Dramatic Quartos', *The Library*, 6th ser., 10 (1988), 235.

[5] Mechanical errors have been itemized and evaluated by Hubbard in his edition of Q1, pp. 4–7, and by Hoppe, *Bad Quarto*, pp. 8–9; Cedric Watts lists examples of

Types, setting, running-titles, and printing conventions show that two houses divided the printing of Q1: Danter's completed forty per cent of the book, Edward Allde's sixty per cent.[1] As Harry R. Hoppe calculates, signatures A–D generally contain thirty-two lines of text to a page in roman type measuring about ninety-five millimetres in a twenty-line count; signatures E–K generally contain thirty-six lines of text to a page in roman type measuring about eighty-two millimetres in a twenty-line count. The first four gatherings end neatly at the bottom of D4^{v}, without crowding or spacing to fit. In comparison the next six gatherings, which also end neatly on the last page, are noticeably spread out by spaces (between stage directions and text, at tops and bottoms of pages) or rows of ornaments across the pages (beginning on G2^{v}). McKerrow first remarked that the spacing makes signatures E–K fill as many sheets as these gatherings would have occupied if the larger type of A–D had been used. In addition, the running-titles change at E from *The most excellent Tragedie,* | *of Romeo and Iuliet.* to *The excellent Tragedie* | *of Romeo and Iuliet.*; and features of house style, such as the treatment of proper names in stage directions, differ in the two parts.[2]

Hoppe theorized that the two printers worked consecutively and seriatim, the second finishing the project after a raid on Danter's shop during Lent 1596/7.[3] But internal and external evidence, the

textual errors in his edition of Q1 (1995), pp. 27–8. Hoppe ends his survey with an important qualification: 'Since a considerable amount of subjective judgment is involved even in deciding what are printer's errors and what are not, we should not dwell too much on the quantitative difference between the two texts; nevertheless, it reveals the composition and press-work of Q1 as certainly no worse and possibly somewhat better than Q2'.

[1] Hoppe, *Bad Quarto*, p. 3 n. 2, tentatively identified the second printer as Allde; Standish Henning supported the attribution with more type-evidence in 'The Printer of "Romeo and Juliet", Q1', *PBSA* 60 (1966), 363–4; but his data were questioned and reduced by Frank E. Haggard, 'Type-Recurrence Evidence and the Printing of *Romeo and Juliet* Q1 (1597)', *PBSA* 71 (1977), p. 67 n. 5. Most recently, Chiaki Hanabusa has conclusively demonstrated Allde's collaboration by reexamining damaged types in 'Edward Allde's Types in Sheets E–K of *Romeo and Juliet* Q1 (1597)', *PBSA* 91 (1997), 423–8.

[2] See Hoppe's first chapter, 'The Printing of the First Quarto', in *Bad Quarto*, especially pp. 1–4, 41–4; R. B. McKerrow, *The Treatment of Shakespeare's Text by His Earlier Editors, 1709–1768*, Annual Shakespeare Lecture of the British Academy (1933), p. 33 n. 6.

[3] Hoppe, *Bad Quarto*, pp. 38–52. Hoppe first published this theory as 'An Approximate Printing Date for the First Quarto of *Romeo and Juliet*', *The Library*, 4th ser., 18 (1938), 447–55.

former advanced by new techniques, undermines his logic. Type shortage, recurrence, and distribution, as well as spelling and use of spacing materials, indicate that the whole book was cast off and set by formes:[1] a typical shared printing job by two London houses. Initial casting-off in Danter's printing-house would explain not only the completion of D but also the spacing of E–K.[2] In studies since Hoppe's, bibliographers have supported his conclusion that two compositors set E–K; and Frank E. Haggard has shown that outer B, C, and D probably went through the press before the inner formes.[3]

Danter must have split the book with Allde for two of the usual reasons, speed and the productive capacities of the individual printing-houses.[4] The date on the title-page indicates that the quarto was printed at some time during the calendar (rather than the legal) year 1597. In an attempt to make this time-frame more specific, scholars have argued for early 1597 from two pieces of data: a raid on Danter's shop during Lent, 9 February to 26 March;[5] and the title-page reference to 'the L. of *Hunsdon* his Seruants', the name of Shakespeare's company from 22 July 1596 to 17 April 1597 (see above, 'Date(s)).[6]

While this information provides strong circumstantial evidence, it falls short of proof. According to the arguments, a raid closed down Danter's printing-house and Allde finished setting Q1. In fact, both Danter and Allde got into trouble with the Stationers'

[1] Several studies use this kind of evidence to establish how Q1 was printed: George Walton Williams, 'Setting by Formes in Quarto Printing', *SB* 11 (1958), 52–3; W. Craig Ferguson, 'Compositor Identification in *Romeo* Q1 and *Troilus*', *SB* 42 (1989), 212–14; and the three articles cited in p. 109 n. 1 above.

[2] J. A. Lavin notes the implications of casting-off for this shared project in 'John Danter's Ornament Stock', *SB* 23 (1970), 33–4.

[3] Hoppe, *Bad Quarto*, pp. 46–56, assembled evidence for Compositors X and Y; Williams, 'Setting by Formes in Quarto Printing', and Ferguson, 'Compositor Identification in *Romeo* Q1 and *Troilus*', provide corroboration (Williams suggesting that X set outer formes first). Haggard, 'Type-Recurrence Evidence and the Printing of *Romeo and Juliet* Q1 (1597)', 66–73, analyses the composition of the whole quarto.

[4] Philip Gaskell offers three possible reasons in *A New Introduction to Bibliography* (Oxford, 1972, rev. edn. 1978), p. 168; the third involves members of a partnership or owners of copyright and seems not to apply here. For a wider range of possibilities, see Peter W. M. Blayney, *The Texts of 'King Lear' and their Origins* (Cambridge, 1982), i. 49–52.

[5] Greg, *First Folio*, p. 225, corrects this date from 27 March.

[6] See Hoppe, *Bad Quarto*, pp. 45–6, and Lavin, 'John Danter's Ornament Stock', 34.

Company at the same time for similar misdemeanours: the *Records* cite Allde immediately after Danter ('Whereas alsoe latelie') for printing a Catholic volume, and they note defacement of the offending 'peece of presse, wth said letters'.[1] Although Danter might have printed all three of his (known) books of 1597 before mid-March, *STC* 17916 was entered on 22 August (entrance usually preceded printing); and he printed at least one book, *STC* 14691.1, in 1598, before Simon Stafford bought his equipment. Allde remained busy throughout 1597. Further, the printed reference to the company may represent out-of-date information: the person who wrote it could have had inaccurate data, or the reference may have been up-to-date as written but printed some months later. It is therefore likely but not certain that the first quarto edition of *Romeo and Juliet* was printed early in the calendar year 1597.[2]

Quarto 2 (1599) and its Derivatives. The title-page of Q2 differs significantly from that of Q1. While the tragedy remains excellent, it is no longer conceited, and it has been '*Newly corrected, augmented, | and amended*'. The authoritative formula refers to major distinctions between the two substantive quartos: Q2 is more than twenty per cent longer than Q1; it contains over 800 lines which are in some ways variants of corresponding lines; and it includes passages which differ completely from their equivalents (for example, 2.5, 3.2.57–60, 5.3.12–21).[3] Although scholars have assumed that Q2 replaces and/or repudiates Q1, it may simply be

[1] *Records of the Stationers' Company, 1576 to 1602, from Register B*, ed. W. W. Greg and E. Boswell (1930), pp. 56–7.

[2] In written comments on the draft of this material about Q1, Peter W. M. Blayney summarized the printers' output during the relevant period and concluded that 'neither the fact of the raid nor the description of the company constitutes proof that the book was actually printed before the raid'.

[3] Hoppe made less than 'a half-hearted conjecture' that Chettle wrote these passages (*Bad Quarto*, p. 220); Sidney Thomas later argued more confidently for attribution to Chettle on the basis of internal and external evidence ('Henry Chettle and the First Quarto of *Romeo and Juliet*', *RES*, NS 1 (1950), 8–16). Only a few scholars have entertained this possibility. Since the publication of his textual notes for *Romeo and Juliet* in 1987, when he thought the assignment probable, John Jowett has made a case for Chettle's authorship in an appendix to 'Johannes Factotum: Henry Chettle and *Greene's Groatsworth of Wit*', *PBSA* 87 (1993), 486, and in 'Notes on Henry Chettle', *RES*, NS 45 (1994), 518–19. See also Jeffrey Kahan, 'Henry Chettle's *Romeo* Q1 and *The Death of Robert Earl of Huntingdon*', *N&Q*, NS 43 (1996), 155–6. Viewed differently, circumstantial and stylistic evidence has been used to support the candidacy of an anonymous redactor or Shakespeare himself (see below, 'Quarto 1 and Quarto 2: Provenance').

acknowledging a connection with a version of the play authorized by Shakespeare's company. This title-page identifies the performers as the Lord Chamberlain's Men, who have now acted the play publicly 'sundry times'. It names the printer Thomas Creede, reproduces one of his ornaments,[1] and specifies the date 1599.

George Walton Williams collated twelve of the thirteen extant copies for his edition (pp. 150–1), the Bodmer copy being unavailable at that time. Paul Werstine collated the Bodmer copy once it had become accessible, finding 'what Williams identified as the second state of the outer forme of Sheet C, . . . the first states of both the variants in the inner forme of Sheet I, . . . and the first state of the outer forme of Sheet M'; and Barry Gaines has corroborated Werstine's findings.[2] As Evans notes in his edition (p. 208), the few variants listed by Williams indicate a lack of significant press correction. Williams concludes from his study of Q2 that the printers were 'conscientious artisans' (edition, p. xi), yet this book of the play seems to contain many errors, from omitted speech-prefixes to omitted tildes.[3] Apparently the compositors worked from difficult copy.

Until Paul L. Cantrell and Williams investigated the printing of Q2, it had been assumed that one compositor set its type. Their thorough study collects bibliographical evidence to prove that two compositors produced the book: A set most of the text; B assisted him briefly near the conclusion (that is, parts of 4.4 and 5.3).[4] In this account A and B exhibit distinguishable habits of composition. Cantrell and Williams profile these habits from four kinds of evidence based on typographical practices, in particular the setting of stage directions, speech-prefixes, and catchwords. Spelling differences combine with typographical evidence to identify the hand of B in K3^{v}, L3^{v}, L4, L4^{v}, and M1; spelling data alone assign him L3.

Cantrell and Williams use running-titles to establish that the compositors set Q2 with two skeleton formes which recur in regular

[1] McKerrow, *Printers' & Publishers' Devices*, device 299.

[2] Williams locates the copies with his collation; Werstine and Gaines communicated their findings in correspondence with Thomas L. Berger, who cites it in 'Press Variants in Substantive Shakespearian Dramatic Quartos', p. 235 n. 22.

[3] Hoppe, *Bad Quarto*, calculates these errors on pp. 8–9 (see pp. 108–9 n. 5 above); Williams lists what he considers errors on pp. xii–xiii of his edition.

[4] 'The Printing of the Second Quarto of *Romeo and Juliet* (1599)', *SB* 9 (1957), 107–28. The first part of this study deals with compositors and press-work (107–16); the second addresses the problem of the copy (116–28).

sequence from sheet B to the end of sheet K: one skeleton was used for the inner forme, one for the outer, and they alternated seriatim on the press until Sheet L broke the pattern. Consequently presswork corroborates typographical and spelling data, placing a second compositor at a second press to set Sheet L. On the basis of this evidence, Cantrell and Williams set up a conjectural timetable for sheets K, L, and M, assigning pages to the two compositors and indicating the passage of formes through the press. With this information, they attempt to recreate the schedule in the shop when Q2 was printed. Their schedule lacks a chronological frame of reference; scholarship on Creede's shop has not yet considered when in 1599 Q2 was produced. Since the number of lines to the page is a curious feature of this quarto, Cantrell and Williams conclude their study of composition by summarizing its variations in the work of each compositor.

Three other quartos descended from Q2: Q3 reprinted it in 1609; Q4 reprinted Q3 in 1622; and Q5 reprinted Q4 in 1637. Although the Q4 title-page has no date, Williams has used typographical evidence to show that this book was printed by William Stansby before November 1622, when the Folio (F) was imminent: F *Romeo and Juliet* would be set in late spring 1623. Apparently Q4 consulted Q1 to correct some errors; Q3 and Q5 made only compositorial changes.[1]

In the early 1980s, S. W. Reid confirmed and refined the traditional view that F *Romeo and Juliet* was set from Q3 alone.[2] Q3 had inherited many of Q2's errors, both from the printing-house and from the text;[3] F sometimes reproduces these and sometimes attempts to correct them independently of Q1 and Q4. Concentrating on the errors and corrections, Reid argues not only that Q3 was sole copy, but also that it had an intelligent editor who prepared it for publication. Earlier Charlton Hinman, followed by T. H. Howard-Hill, had created a profile of Compositor E who set F *Romeo and Juliet* (ee3–Gg1) except for its first and last

[1] 'The Printer and Date of *Romeo and Juliet* Q4', *SB* 18 (1965), 253–4. See also Williams's edition, pp. xi–xii.

[2] 'The Editing of Folio *Romeo and Juliet*', *SB* 35 (1982), 43–66, and 'McKerrow, Greg, and Quarto Copy for Folio *Romeo and Juliet*', *The Library*, 6th ser., 5 (1983), 118–25. Reid's point of departure is Greg, *First Folio*, pp. 231–2, 235.

[3] See J. K. Walton, *The Quarto Copy for the First Folio of Shakespeare* (Dublin, 1971), p. 233.

pages.[1] This workman was the least competent in Isaac Jaggard's shop: initially he set from printed copy; his pages received more frequent and thorough proof-reading than those of the other compositors; and his work on *Romeo and Juliet*, like most of his other efforts, was intermittent. According to Reid, F's changes were beyond E's capabilities. They include addition of stage directions, regularizing of some speech-prefixes, and even corrections within the dialogue, alterations which generate resemblances to the Q1 version. Although they may have originated in a theatrical manuscript, Reid thinks it more likely that someone connected with the playhouse and familiar with *Romeo and Juliet* in performance carefully annotated printer's copy for the first Folio.[2] Each of the three later Folio editions reprints its immediate predecessor.

Quarto 1 and Quarto 2: Provenance. As a bibliographic survey shows, there is nothing particularly unusual or different about the physical properties of the two books which contain early texts of *Romeo and Juliet*; both quartos display the typographic and linguistic peculiarities—from irregular speech-prefixes to irregular spelling—familiar in printed Elizabethan play-books. Among the facts there is no hard evidence of illicit publication. Nevertheless, the difference in content between the quartos has led editors and critics since J. P. Collier (1842) to give Q1 a bad press. Leo Kirschbaum concludes that scholars have used their knowledge of Danter's problems with the law to rationalize their disappointment with the two short dramatic quartos he printed.[3] That disappointment, which extends to other dramatic quartos of the early

[1] Hinman, *The Printing and Proof-Reading of the First Folio of Shakespeare*, 2 vols. (Oxford, 1963), i. 200–26; Howard-Hill, 'New Light on Compositor E of the Shakespeare First Folio', *The Library*, 6th ser., 2 (1980), 156–78. Compositor B set the first page and reset the last, the latter printed when *Troilus and Cressida* was withdrawn from the Tragedies section and *Timon of Athens* substituted. The original setting of the last page, prepared by E and signed gg3, is extant in a Folger copy (reproduced in Hinman's edition of the Folio (New York, 1996), pp. 916–17). Differences between this cancelled gg3 and reset Gg (see Collation) may imply that B consulted annotated Q3; E tended to be careless in dealing with annotations.

[2] Because of its importance as copy for F *Romeo and Juliet*, the editor collated the seven extant copies at the British Library, the Bodleian Library, Trinity College Cambridge, the Folger Shakespeare Library, the Henry E. Huntington Library (two copies), and the Zentralbibliothek Zürich; collation of this sample produced no variants.

[3] *Shakespeare and the Stationers*, p. 298. The other short quarto of a play was Robert Greene's *Orlando Furioso* (SR entry and title-page date 1594).

modern period, comes from the impression that these texts fall below accepted standards of literary value.[1] In this instance the resulting arguments have raised questions about both the quarto's authenticity and its presswork. Pollard, who first categorized Shakespeare's quartos as 'good' and 'bad', identified Q1 as bad not only because it had no entry in the Stationers' Register, but also because it disagreed with the Folio text. More than once he called Q1 a 'piracy', surreptitiously published.[2] H. R. Plomer and McKerrow have described this quarto as very badly printed.[3] When bibliographers condemn mechanical errors in Q1, they often excuse similar irregularities in Q2; anomalies in the longer quarto become signs of authorial presence, residue of the creative process. Greg recognized the contradiction: '*Romeo and Juliet* is remarkable in that the bad text seems a good deal better, and the good text a good deal worse, than we are accustomed to find'.[4]

Examining discrimination between quartos of Shakespeare plays, Margreta de Grazia finds a deeper and more complex cause underlying disappointment in literary value. New Bibliographers, looking for manuscript copy behind printed texts, deliberately seek traces of Shakespeare's work and attempt to isolate them from other influences; they encounter other influences which seem especially obvious and dense in the short quartos. Yet the objects of this quest are totally hypothetical in any quarto. Even as hypotheses they remain elusive, because plays are what J. Dover Wilson called 'standing copy' or 'continuous copy' which undergo change in the theatre. As he and others enumerate them, many people could have 'rehandled' the manuscript of a Shakespeare play, from Shakespeare and his fellow actors to adapters, revisers, bookkeepers and censors to compositors and proof-readers. This thicket obscures the playwright and his holograph in all printed

[1] See J. K. Walton, *Quarto Copy*, pp. 16–17.

[2] *Shakespeare Folios and Quartos*, pp. 65, 69. The notion of clandestine publishing derives from Heminge and Condell's address in the Folio '*To the great Variety of Readers*', where they say that they have replaced 'diuerse stolne, and surreptitious copies, maimed, and deformed by the frauds and stealthes of iniurious impostors'.

[3] Plomer, 'The Printers of Shakespeare's Plays and Poems', *The Library*, 2nd ser., 7 (1906), 153, and R. B. McKerrow, *A Dictionary of Printers and Booksellers . . . 1557–1640* (1910; repr. Oxford, 1968), p. 84. Plomer makes the more specific and therefore misleading allegations: 'The compositors' work was of the worst description, reversed letters and mis-readings being sprinkled on every page'.

[4] 'Principles of Emendation in Shakespeare', in *Aspects of Shakespeare: Being British Academy Lectures* (Oxford, 1933), p. 147.

texts, although bibliographers rarely conduct their search in the short quartos.[1]

Typically, the pursuit of hypothetical manuscripts for *Romeo and Juliet* continues around and through such obstacles. By the 1980s conjectures about the two substantive versions formed a received narrative about the play's textual history. This account, related in Pollard's idiom, resembles several contemporary with it which were also generated by the New Bibliography and dealt with other multiple-text Elizabethan plays. It began to take shape in the mid twentieth century, when Hoppe determined the fate of the 1597 quarto with the title of his monograph, *The Bad Quarto of 'Romeo and Juliet': A Bibliographical and Textual Study*. He argued that Q1 printed a manuscript reconstructed by the memories of two actors. During the 1940s and 1950s, Greg endorsed the legitimacy of the 1599 quarto, giving his distinguished imprimatur to a view first advanced in 1879. He claimed that most of the second quarto derived from Shakespeare's holograph; only one reprinted passage and occasional bits depended on the first quarto.[2] Once the substantive texts had been characterized, scholars who followed Hoppe and Greg concentrated on figuring out the relationship of the quartos to each other and their common original. John Jowett's Lachmann-like genealogy in *A Textual Companion* to the Oxford Shakespeare (p. 288) illustrates the trend.

Evidence for these speculations is scarce. It consists of three disparate kinds of facts: the dates on the title-pages which indicate that Q2 was printed after Q1; differences between the two texts in length and expression (see above, 'Quarto 2 (1599) and its Derivatives'); and one long segment, as well as a number of short ones, virtually identical in composition. Significantly, Q1 served as copy for Q2 at least once, for a passage of more than eighty lines.[3] Q2 follows this passage in wording, capitals, punctuation, spelling, and typography, in particular the odd use of italics for the speeches

[1] See de Grazia, 'The Essential Shakespeare and the Material Book', *Textual Practice*, 2 (1988), 69–86. De Grazia cites J. Dover Wilson on 79–80.

[2] See *Editorial Problem*, pp. 61–2, and *First Folio*, pp. 229–31. For the original version, see Robert Gericke, '*Romeo and Juliet* nach Shakespeare's Manuscript', *SJ* 14 (1879), 207–73.

[3] It is difficult to set limits for the passage. This edition follows George Walton Williams's, p. 105, which fixes them as 1.2.53B–1.3.34 in his text, therefore 1.2.53–1.3.36 here. See Commentary 1.2.52–1.3.36 n.

of the Nurse.[1] It appears that the Q2 printers may have consulted Q1 elsewhere besides (for instance, 2.1.14, 2.3.95.1, 3.5.27–31).[2] As a result bibliographers generally agree, in an uncommon consensus with serious implications, that the first quarto influenced the second to an extent which cannot be measured with accuracy. The scarce evidence therefore leads to an impasse which blocks the search for copy and a stemma.

Consequently, two critical unknowns interfere whenever bibliographers attempt to historicize the text of *Romeo and Juliet*: the variety of non-authorial interventions possible in early play manuscripts and, more specifically, the influence of Q1 on Q2. Other questions surface with particular theories. Perhaps the theory which raises most of these secondary questions is the one which has become a modern orthodoxy: memorial reconstruction of the first quarto. This concept of transmission originated with Tycho Mommsen in 1857, and it has received wide acceptance since Hoppe's book applied it in 1948. Greg supported it with varying degrees of confidence over more than four decades; recent scholarship has endorsed it.[3]

The theory holds that an actor or actors, probably disaffected, reproduced the play from memory either for production (possibly by Pembroke's company or on provincial tour) or for publication as Q1.[4] The original, a form of *Romeo and Juliet* represented by Q2,

[1] Greg summarizes both quartos' use of italics in 'Principles of Emendation in Shakespeare', pp. 175–6. Among others, he has suggested that the Q1 compositor may have worked from manuscript or an actor's part in Italian hand. See, for example, his *First Folio*, p. 226. Jay L. Halio proposes that Danter may have been short of type in 'Handy-Dandy: Q1/Q2 *Romeo and Juliet*', p. 150 n. 47.

[2] See Brian Gibbons's edition, pp. 21–3, for an overview of scholarship on these bibliographic links.

[3] Mommsen first published his version of the theory in '"Hamlet", 1603; and "Romeo and Juliet", 1597', *The Athenaeum*, 29 (1857), 182. Greg's references to memorial reconstruction include his edition *Shakespeare's 'Merry Wives of Windsor' 1602* (Oxford, 1910), pp. xxvi–xli; *Two Elizabethan Stage Abridgements: 'The Battle of Alcazar' & 'Orlando Furioso'* (Oxford, 1922), pp. 256–60; 'Principles of Emendation in Shakespeare', p. 141; *Editorial Problem*, pp. xxiv, 9, 62–4; and *First Folio*, pp. 225–6. For a recent endorsement, see Kathleen O. Irace, *Reforming the 'Bad' Quartos: Performance and Provenance of Six Shakespearean First Editions* (Newark, Del., London, and Toronto, 1994), *passim*.

[4] This synopsis is based on the whole body of scholarship which spans 140 years. In addition to works already cited, important contributions were made during the middle decades by J. Dover Wilson and A. W. Pollard, 'The "Stolne and Surreptitious" Shakespearian Texts. *Romeo and Juliet*, 1597', *TLS*, 14 August 1919; Leo Kirschbaum, 'A Census of Bad Quartos', *RES* 14 (1938), 20–43, and 'An

may have been a variant abridged or otherwise adapted for provincial performance by Shakespeare's company; the official acting version; or both shortened and full-length renderings in combination. The actor(s) would have remembered this original from taking part in performance or reading the copy. Memory, perhaps assisted by actors' parts or bits of manuscript, may have faltered, a lapse explaining the shortness of the text. For most proponents of this theory, other failures account for other differences between Q1 and Q2. Such critics evaluate the quality of reporting by the coincidence of the two texts, and they often nominate reporters who might have produced the largest numbers of matching lines: the possibilities range from Capulet, the Nurse, and Benvolio to Romeo, Paris, and Mercutio.[1]

In 1987 *A Textual Companion* to the Oxford Shakespeare supported arguments for memorial reconstruction as a means of transmitting play-texts, yet the case for this method has been challenged on several grounds since the 1970s and repeatedly in the 1990s. Uncertainty persists about both external and internal evidence, in particular that connected with theatrical performance, publication of dramatic quartos, and textual criteria for identifying plays recreated from memory.[2]

First, no contemporary evidence survives to verify that any actor(s) ever reconstructed a play memorially; and it seems unlikely that reporters would have forgotten their own lines and cues.

Hypothesis Concerning the Origin of the Bad Quartos', *PMLA* 40 (1945), 697–715; and Alfred Hart, *Stolne and Surreptitious Copies: A Comparative Study of Shakespeare's Bad Quartos* (Melbourne and London, 1942), pp. 341–51.

[1] Another theory based on reporting maintains that either a stenographer in the audience took the play down in shorthand or a hack writer made longhand notes of a performance. Robert E. Burkhart summarizes the brief, unsuccessful history of the former idea in *Shakespeare's Bad Quartos: Deliberate Abridgments Designed for Performance by a Reduced Cast* (The Hague and Paris, 1975), pp. 10–11; Adele Davidson argues that the moribund issue of shorthand needs review in '"Some by Stenography"? Stationers, Shorthand, and the Early Shakespearean Quartos', *PBSA* 90 (1996), 417–49.

[2] See Gary Taylor's General Introduction to *Textual Companion*, pp. 23–8. The contesting views represented here come from Burkhart, *Shakespeare's Bad Quartos*, pp. 19–22; Werstine, 'Narratives about Printed Shakespeare Texts', 65–86; Bradley, *From Text to Performance*, pp. 9–11; Halio, 'Handy-Dandy: Q1/Q2 *Romeo and Juliet*', pp. 123–50; Laurie E. Maguire, *Shakespearean Suspect Texts: The 'Bad' Quartos and Their Contexts* (Cambridge, 1996); David Farley-Hills, 'The "Bad" Quarto of *Romeo and Juliet*', *SSu* 49 (1996), 27–44; and Peter W. M. Blayney, 'The Publication of Playbooks', in *A New History of Early English Drama*, ed. John D. Cox and David Scott Kastan (New York, 1997), pp. 383–422.

As Jay L. Halio emphasizes, an actor's memory was and is a chief professional asset.[1] In discussing Q1 of *Romeo and Juliet*, critical arguments twist and turn when they explain why their candidates, reproducing their own scenes, failed to match the versions in Q2. Kathleen O. Irace finds the pattern of 'fluctuating correlation' between the two quartos so complex that her rationalization of it outdoes the ingenuity of Hoppe's. It involves three actor-reporters who knew both long and short versions of the play.[2]

Second, a few assumptions about Elizabethan publishing which support the theory have no basis in fact. For example, advocates of memorial reconstruction generally consider the play in question corrupt, its state a sign of an illegitimate and therefore pirated manuscript. They presume that a stationer would have manufactured it as a book; and they take for granted that such a procedure would have continued over many years, allowed by the companies and ignored by the purchasers.[3] But no evidence confirms that any play was ever stolen from Shakespeare's company. Moreover, not only the actor(s) but also the stationer and printer would have taken a big risk for a small return, because play-books did not earn high profits under the most legitimate circumstances.[4]

Third, many of the textual features used to identify memorial reconstructions—items ranging from various forms of repetition to descriptive stage directions and vestigial characters—prove ambiguous under examination. Laurie E. Maguire's book *Shakespeare's Suspect Texts:* The *'Bad' Quartos and Their Contexts* thoroughly analyses these features and finds only two or three (such as length of speeches) relevant to the theory. In the process Maguire demonstrates how malleable most of these criteria are: almost all can apply to texts considered authoritative. According to the pertinent features, she concludes that Q1 of *Romeo and Juliet* is not a memorial reconstruction or, in her terms 'the reproduction of a playtext in whole or in part by someone who had at some

[1] 'Handy-Dandy : Q1/Q2 *Romeo and Juliet*', p. 128.

[2] See Irace, *Reforming the 'Bad' Quartos*, pp. 126–31, and Hoppe, *Bad Quarto*, pp. 195–208.

[3] According to *Textual Companion*, p. 26, during Shakespeare's lifetime playtexts different from those now considered authoritative were not published after 1609.

[4] See Blayney, 'The Publication of Playbooks', pp. 383–422; and Werstine, 'Narratives about Printed Shakespeare Texts', 83–5.

stage substantial knowledge of the original playtext as written or performed' (pp. 224–5).

Despite these serious challenges to the theory of memorial reconstruction, it might apply to the first quarto of *Romeo and Juliet*, and even the second, if definition of the concept were broadened and non-pejorative. Recent scholarship by critics of the New Bibliography would allow memory to include Shakespeare's recollection of the original play as he revised it; or an actor's attempt, as he copied an allowed manuscript, to supply it with missing lines from his observation of performance(s); or actors' recreation of scripts from their individual parts or 'sides'. After reviewing Humphrey Moseley's address to readers of the Beaumont and Fletcher Folio (1647), Peter W. M. Blayney proposes a 'commonplace and innocent origin' for anomalous play-texts. Apparently actors made copies of plays for their friends from versions usually abridged for performance, writing down what had been spoken on stage; the quality of such texts would vary according to the actors' source and procedures.[1] A more flexible definition would blur the distinction between the orthodox theory and two minority views about the nature of Q1 copy and the relationship between the quartos. Nevertheless, both minority views raise questions of their own.

Pope introduced the idea that Shakespeare revised and enlarged early versions of his plays, a concept prevalent during the nineteenth century and supported by a small but growing number of scholars since the 1980s.[2] According to this theory, Q1 serves as a first draft for Q2. By contrast, a few scholars have argued recently that Q1 is a deliberate abridgement of Q2, made by a redactor or Shakespeare himself from a holograph basically the same as the copy for Q2.[3] They emphasize the efficiency of the cuts which

[1] 'The Publication of Playbooks', pp. 393–4.

[2] For Pope's remarks, see the Preface to his first edition, vol. i, p. viii. (On pp. xvi–xvii Pope implies that he has seen a playhouse copy where actors made inferior additions to early versions of the texts.) Hoppe, *Bad Quarto*, pp. 58–64, gives a history of the concept to 1948; Irace, *Reforming the 'Bad' Quartos*, pp. 95–114, devotes a chapter to the general topic of revision and the return to this hypothesis in recent years by scholars such as Steven Urkowitz. Working from linguistic evidence, Foster, 'The Webbing of *Romeo and Juliet*', pp. 131–49, argues that Shakespeare wrote both Q1 and Q2, one after the other. Now and then since the nineteenth century critics have assumed that Q1 derives from another playwright's work, or from Shakespeare's revision of someone else's play.

[3] The most extensive studies of this kind are by Burkhart, *Shakespeare's Bad Quartos*, in his chapter on *Romeo and Juliet*, pp. 55–67; Halio, 'Handy-Dandy:

reduce poetry and rhetoric but accelerate the action: abbreviation results in a quickly paced, popular version of the play for performance on a provincial tour or in London. This version may include Shakespearian revisions among the redactor's or vice versa; it may also witness a production of the full play seen by the redactor before he began to modify the text. Whatever course revision may have taken according to these theories, the first quarto acquires legitimacy. Both minority rationales accept as intentional most of the differences between the first quarto and the second, hundreds of variations which make the extant texts seem like two forms of the same play.

Critics unconvinced by Pope's idea argue against it from the orthodox position. Sometimes they use textual criteria for uncovering memorial reconstruction—omissions, errors, transpositions, unevenness—to show that Shakespeare could not have composed such a text. Irace thinks that the second quarto of *Romeo and Juliet* must come from a manuscript unrelated to the first quarto for more than one reason: the compositor of Q2 consulted Q1 when his manuscript became difficult to read; Q2 derives from foul papers; Q2 contains duplications which Q1 has eliminated. The editors of the Oxford Shakespeare find untenable the methodology of recent scholarship which has elaborated on Pope. In their opinion these studies ignore historical evidence for memorial reconstruction, isolate individual passages for discussion rather than taking an overview, and fail to notice differences from genuine cases of authorial revision.[1] None of these objections sabotages the theory of authorial revision or a redactor's work, because all of them rest on hypotheses or taste. With slight adjustment of perspective, some permit both quartos to represent the same original manuscript. The question that does remain is whether a playwright or redactor would have made more than fifteen hundred changes—cuts or additions and other modifications—some of the variants quite minor and not all of them obvious improvements. Without firm or external evidence, that question can have no definitive answer.

According to Paul Werstine, the early theatrical history of *Romeo and Juliet* may be embedded somewhere in the enigmas of

Q1/Q2 *Romeo and Juliet*', pp. 123–50; and Farley-Hills, 'The "Bad" Quarto of *Romeo and Juliet*', 27–44.

[1] See Irace, *Reforming the 'Bad' Quartos*, pp. 95–114, and *Textual Companion*, p. 27.

the first quarto: 'It is relatively easy to distinguish the possible stages of such a history in abstract terms. . . . Yet it seems quite optimistic to believe that such raw stuff as this quarto . . . will readily yield up to rational analysis the record of theatrical process it contains'.[1] Beyond its physical properties this quarto is not forthcoming. It has attracted bibliographers and other critics like a puzzle, engaging them to write a monograph as well as numerous shorter studies. As de Grazia says of all the Shakespeare quartos not used by the Folio, it has invited speculation 'as the produc[t] of highly diversified and heterogeneous activities involving multitudinous minds, purposes, memories, and hands'.[2]

By comparison, Q2 has attracted far less attention. Evidence of revision, first and second thoughts preserved in the printed book, has convinced most textual scholars that Q2 text independent of Q1 derives ultimately from Shakespeare's own manuscript. Scattered through Q2, well-known duplications occur between and within speeches: they appear at the end of 2.1 and the beginning of 2.2, where Romeo and Friar Laurence greet the dawn in very similar four-line passages (D4^{v}); they mark Romeo's complaint in Friar Laurence's cell during 3.3 (G4^{r}) and his farewell to Juliet in the tomb during 5.3 (L3^{r}). In his analysis of Q2 Pearlman finds evidence of revision, both 'verbal tinkering [and] major structural reform'.[3]

Although there is now consensus among editors and other bibliographers about the copy for Q2, there had been a debate which grew increasingly elaborate until the 1950s. In 1879 Robert Gericke originated the theory that Q2 printers depended on Shakespeare's manuscript but consulted Q1 (see p. 116 n. 2 above); almost fifty years later G. Hjort first contended the opposite, that Q2 was printed from Q1 collated with a manuscript.[4] Hjort's

[1] 'The First Quarto of *Romeo and Juliet* and the Limits of Authority', typescript of a paper delivered at the 1985 meeting of the Society for Textual Scholarship, pp. 10–11. In this paper Werstine demonstrates why Gary Taylor's method fails to produce evidence of revisions approved by the playwright and introduced during rehearsal by the company who performed the longer text.

[2] 'The Essential Shakespeare and the Material Book', p. 78.

[3] See the Commentary for these passages (2.1.233–4 n., 3.3.40–3 n., 5.3.102 n.) and Pearlman, pp. 107–30, quotation from p. 125. Evans gives a convenient list of duplications in his edition (p. 208).

[4] 'The Good and Bad Quartos of "Romeo and Juliet" and "Love's Labour's Lost"', *MLR* 21 (1926), 140–6.

theory, influential enough to serve as basis for the Wilson–Duthie edition, was badly weakened by Cantrell and Williams's analysis of printing. With evidence from speech-prefixes—variant forms and compositors' habits in setting them—the study concludes that an independent manuscript was copy for Q2.[1]

Evidence from printing argues that Q2 derives from a manuscript and that its compositors occasionally consulted Q1; evidence from the duplications indicates that the manuscript was probably the playwright's. As William B. Long has demonstrated with regard to stage directions in particular, Elizabethan theatrical personnel interfered with authorial manuscripts (when they interfered at all) mainly to solve problems.[2] The striking duplications seem to qualify as problems which need correcting: they point away from playhouse copy. At the same time, other evidence usually cited to identify Shakespeare's holograph proves less secure: some of it—stage directions vague about the number of actors in a scene or specific about props, minor inconsistencies in the naming of characters—occurs in playhouse copy.[3] Even the striking duplications raise questions: they may have taken place during the original composition, *currente calamo*, or over time; they may record different versions in different performances.[4]

In view of such questions and contingencies, what can we conclude about the manuscripts behind the quartos and the relation between the printed books? Q1 may look like playhouse copy, but if we abandon accepted theories about the origins and features of quartos labelled 'bad', we have no grounds for associating these books with the stage.[5] Q2 may look like the author's holograph,

[1] 'The Printing of the Second Quarto of *Romeo and Juliet* (1599)', 116–28.

[2] 'Stage-Directions: A Misinterpreted Factor in Determining Textual Provenance', 121–37. See also Long's '"A bed/for woodstock": A Warning for the Unwary', *MARDE* 2 (1985), 91–118.

[3] Werstine deals with this kind of ambiguity in '"Foul Papers" and "Prompt-Books": Printer's Copy for Shakespeare's *Comedy of Errors*', *SB* 41 (1988), 232–46. Long considers it as well in the articles cited by the preceding note.

[4] Goldberg suggests a variety of ways and means for revision in '"What? in a names that which we call a Rose"', pp. 186–7.

[5] Two recent studies bear on this point: John Jowett, 'Henry Chettle and the First Quarto of *Romeo and Juliet*', *PBSA* 92 (1998), 53–74, argues that the stage directions in Q1 derive from the printing process rather than the theatre or the playwright; Paul Werstine, 'Touring and the Construction of Shakespeare Textual Criticism', in *Textual Formations and Reformations*, ed. Thomas L. Berger and Laurie E. Maguire (Newark, Del. and London, 1998), pp. 45–66, analyses the connection between 'bad quartos' and performance to show that it has no basis in fact.

but E. K. Chambers thought that a transcriber might have preserved its false starts: it may not be based on authorial working papers although ultimately it derives from them.[1] If Q2 gives only a glimpse of its origins, Q1 offers no certainty. Lack of firm evidence baffles attempts to identify copy for Q1 or to make a connection between the substantive texts. Each hypothetical stemma collapses under the weight of possibilities.

During the 1980s textual critics began to appreciate the volume of these possibilities, and the received narrative of *Romeo and Juliet* started to come apart with reviews of the Arden edition by some of the 'new revisionists'.[2] Randall McLeod (writing as Random Cloud) disconnected the sequence quarto by quarto:

> At odds with the judgment of the First Quarto as Bad is the repeated acknowledgment in the pages of textual introduction that Q1 is a substantive edition . . . There is another substantive edition, however, Q2 the Good, which the editor adopts as his copy-text. . . . His formulation . . . ignores or forgets that whatever the truth about reports and production behind Q1, there must have been a manuscript that initiated it all, and that this manuscript must bear some relation—of identity or difference—to the manuscript that underlies most of Q2.

McLeod proposed a new formulation: the two substantive quartos witness the multiplicity of what Shakespeare wrote; the playwright may have created *Romeo and Juliet* over time and through different phases, 'perhaps in several different manuscripts, each perhaps with its own characteristic aesthetic, offering together several finalities'.[3]

By 1988 Jonathan Goldberg extended his own review of the Arden *Romeo and Juliet* into a full-length paper on the play's text. Whatever their provenance, he argued, both substantive quartos vest their authority in theatrical performances. This fact considered, what is the relationship of the two witnesses? 'Q2 is a different version—or, rather, different versions—of the play. It is a

[1] In correspondence Paul Werstine reminded the editor of these qualifications, citing Dillon, 'Is There a Performance in this Text?', 74–86, and Chambers, *William Shakespeare: A Study of Facts and Problems*, i. 344. Dillon questions five types of criteria which have been used to connect Shakespeare's early quartos with the stage: length, title-pages, memorial reconstruction/pirating, performability, and 'badness'.

[2] The phrase 'new revisionists' is adapted from D. C. Greetham's *Textual Scholarship: An Introduction* (New York and London, 1992), p. 353.

[3] 'The Marriage of Good and Bad Quartos', *SQ* 33 (1982), 423, 429.

selection from or an anthology of a number of productions of *Romeo and Juliets*, one of which was close to the performance represented by Q1 . . .'[1]

Of course these two hypotheses are as impossible to prove as those which supported the narrative of good and bad quartos, but linguistic evidence (see above, 'Date(s)') and data about Elizabethan theatre practice make them seem more persuasive. Of greater consequence, the arguments behind these speculations—raising questions and expressing doubts—release the quartos from limiting categories. Since the 1980s dialogue to revise the categories has continued. One fruitful occasion was a seminar on 'The Language of the So-Called "Bad" Quartos' held at the 1996 International Shakespeare Conference. In discussion Scott McMillin raised the possibility that English Renaissance play-books may have been produced after rehearsal, for both 'good' and 'bad' quartos, with actors slowly running through their lines for a scribe; Nicholas Brooke proposed that these texts may be working papers which the actors left behind for the printer. To paraphrase Brooke, the subject of provenance for such texts is full of 'imponderables'. With their invitation to ponder, both early quartos of *Romeo and Juliet* can be viewed as important records of a tragedy that underwent many changes when first written and performed, beginning a process still vital after four centuries.

[1] Goldberg's review appears in *SSt* 16 (1983), 343–8; his paper, '"What? in a names that which we call a Rose"', was delivered at the twenty-fourth annual Conference on Editorial Problems, University of Toronto, 4–5 November 1988, and published in the proceedings (see p. 106 n. 3 above). The quotation comes from p. 186.

EDITORIAL PROCEDURES

As the Introduction has indicated, the two earliest quartos of *Romeo and Juliet* represent two different and legitimate kinds of witnesses to two different stages of an ongoing theatrical event. This edition treats the quartos as two versions of the play: it includes Q1 as well as Q2 in modern spelling. Q2 takes its traditional position at the front of the volume with Collation and Commentary; it offers the fuller version which was reprinted by Shakespeare's company. Because space is limited, Q1 appears with minimum apparatus. It is present in the Q2 Collation only when its readings bear significantly on the later text. Although I have reduced potentially confusing duplications in Q2 (like the 'dawn speech' assigned to Romeo at the end of 2.1 and to Friar Laurence at the beginning of 2.2), I have interfered as little as possible with either version. The texts themselves furnish evidence for speculation about the relationship between the quartos; the Commentary equips the reader with detailed notes—on text, language, rhetorical devices, and staging cues—to assist such speculation.

In this book of the play, as in all of its predecessors, it is difficult to convey the ongoing theatrical event without hypostatizing it as one text or even two. The theatre history of *Romeo and Juliet* provides a useful reminder of its instability, its condition as a 'mobile text' which has undergone many variations.[1] To animate that history I have compiled a database for productions which is now available at a World Wide Web site (CITD.SCAR.UTORONTO.CA/CRRS/ROMMAIN.HTML). Thus far it has collected profiles of 170 or so prompt books, beginning with those listed by Charles H. Shattuck,[2] recording their cuts and stage directions. Anyone interested can explore the text of *Romeo and Juliet*—speech and actions—through its permutations from the seventeenth century to the late twentieth century.

The modernization of both quarto texts has been governed by the general principles set out by Stanley Wells in the essay he contributed on spelling to Wells and Gary Taylor, *Modernizing Shakespeare's*

[1] My vocabulary and ideas here derive from Brockbank, 'Towards a mobile text', p. 96.

[2] *Shakespeare Promptbooks*, pp. 411–32.

Spelling with Three Studies in the Text of 'Henry V' (Oxford, 1979). Such modernization extends to quotations from other early texts cited in the Introduction and Commentary. According to the conventions of the series, unstressed past participle endings are indicated as *ed* and stressed endings as *èd*. Punctuation is as close to the original as possible, but adjusted to make sense in a modernized text. For instance, when Q2 becomes breathless with commas, the edition avoids full stops and uses semicolons between clauses. Individual decisions about modernization that affects meaning and about textual anomalies are all explained in the Commentary with reference to the Collation. The Q2 Collation also accounts for stage directions in that text, indicating their provenance. Broken brackets signal stage directions that are in any way controversial; and the Commentary discusses, whenever it can, theatrical approaches to staging ambiguities in the text. (Stage directions are also discussed under 'Initial Staging' in the Introduction.) The Commentary deals as well with passages where lineation or scene division is in dispute. Speech-prefixes have been silently normalized. When the text has been unspecific about the speaker, they have been identified by broken brackets (⌈ ⌉) and recorded in the Collation and Commentary.

References to other Shakespeare plays and poems come from *The Complete Works*, ed. Stanley Wells, Gary Taylor, *et al.* (Oxford, 1986); the organization of 'The Persons of the Play' duplicates John Jowett's elegant arrangement for *Romeo and Juliet* in that volume. The edition quotes from the Geneva Bible (1560), since Shakespeare alluded to it more than any other version.

Abbreviations and References

The following abbreviations represent editions consulted and works frequently cited. The place of publication is London unless otherwise specified.

EDITIONS OF SHAKESPEARE

Q1	*An Excellent conceited Tragedie of Romeo and Iuliet*, 1597
Q2	*The Most Excellent and lamentable Tragedie, of Romeo and Iuliet*, 1599
Q3	Reprint of Q2, 1609
Q4	Reprint of Q3, 1622

Q5	Reprint of Q4, 1637
F, F1	The First Folio, 1623
F2	The Second Folio, 1632
F3	The Third Folio, 1663
F4	The Fourth Folio, 1685
Alexander	Peter Alexander, *Complete Works* (1951)
Bevington	David Bevington, *Complete Works*, 4th edn. (New York, 1997)
Boswell	James Boswell, *Plays and Poems*, 21 vols. (1821)
Bryant	J. A. Bryant, Jr., *Romeo and Juliet*, The Signet Classic Shakespeare (New York and Toronto, 1964)
Cambridge	W. G. Clark and W. A. Wright, *Works*, The Cambridge Shakespeare, 9 vols. (Cambridge, 1863–6)
Capell	Edward Capell, *Mr. William Shakespeare his Comedies, Histories, and Tragedies* . . . , 10 vols. (1767–8)
Collier	John Payne Collier, *Works*, 8 vols. (1842–4)
Collier 1858	John Payne Collier, *Shakespeare's Comedies, Histories, Tragedies and Poems*, 6 vols. (1858)
Crofts	J. E. Crofts, *Romeo and Juliet*, The Warwick Shakespeare (1936)
Daniel	P. A. Daniel, *'Romeo and Juliet': Parallel Texts of the First Two Quartos*, The New Shakspere Society (1874)
Deighton	K. Deighton, *Romeo and Juliet* (1893)
Dowden	Edward Dowden, *Romeo and Juliet*, The Arden Shakespeare (1900)
Durham	W. H. Durham, *Romeo and Juliet*, The Yale Shakespeare (New Haven, 1917)
Dyce	Alexander Dyce, *Works*, 6 vols. (1857)
Evans	G. Blakemore Evans, *Romeo and Juliet*, The New Cambridge Shakespeare (Cambridge, 1984)
Furness	Horace Howard Furness, *Romeo and Juliet*, A New Variorum Edition (Philadelphia, 1871)
Gibbons	Brian Gibbons, *Romeo and Juliet*, The Arden Shakespeare (1980)
Globe	W. G. Clark and W. A. Wright, *Works* (Cambridge, 1864)
Hankins	John E. Hankins, *Romeo and Juliet*, The Pelican Shakespeare (Baltimore, 1960)
Hanmer	Thomas Hanmer, *Works*, 6 vols. (Oxford, 1743–4)

Hoppe	H. R. Hoppe, *Romeo and Juliet*, Crofts Classics (New York, 1947)
Hosley	Richard Hosley, *Romeo and Juliet*, The Yale Shakespeare (New Haven, 1954)
Houghton	Ralph E. C. Houghton, *Romeo and Juliet*, The New Clarendon Shakespeare (Oxford, 1947)
Hudson	Henry N. Hudson, *Works*, 11 vols. (Boston, 1851–6)
Johnson	Samuel Johnson, *Plays*, 8 vols. (1765)
Jowett	John Jowett, *Romeo and Juliet*, in *William Shakespeare: The Complete Works* (Oxford, 1986); notes in *Textual Companion* (see entry below)
Keightley	Thomas Keightley, *Plays*, 6 vols. (1864)
Kittredge	George Lyman Kittredge, *The Complete Works of Shakespeare* (Boston, 1936); rev. Irving Ribner (Waltham, Mass., and Toronto, 1971)
Knight	Charles Knight, *Works*, Pictorial Edition, 8 vols. (1838–43)
Malone	Edmond Malone, *Plays and Poems*, 10 vols. (1790)
McKerrow	Ronald B. McKerrow, unpublished papers for the Oxford Shakespeare (in the archives of Oxford University Press)
Mowat–Werstine	Barbara A. Mowat and Paul Werstine, *Romeo and Juliet*, The New Folger Library (New York, 1992)
Munro	John Munro, *The London Shakespeare*, 6 vols. (1958)
Pope	Alexander Pope, *Works*, 6 vols. (1723–5)
Pope 1728	Alexander Pope, *Works*, 10 vols. (1728)
Rann	Joseph Rann, *Dramatic Works*, 6 vols. (Oxford, 1786–94)
Ridley	M. R. Ridley, *Romeo and Juliet*, The New Temple Shakespeare (1935)
Riverside	G. B. Evans (textual editor), *The Riverside Shakespeare*, 2nd edn. (Boston, 1997)
Rolfe	William J. Rolfe, *Romeo and Juliet*, English Classics (New York, 1879)
Rowe	Nicholas Rowe, *Works*, 6 vols. (1709)
Rowe 1714	Nicholas Rowe, *Works*, 8 vols. (1714)
Singer	Samuel Weller Singer, *Dramatic Works*, 10 vols. (Chiswick, 1826)
Singer 1856	Samuel Weller Singer, *Dramatic Works*, 10 vols. (1856)
Sisson	Charles J. Sisson, *Complete Works* (1954)

Spencer — T. J. B. Spencer, *Romeo and Juliet*, The New Penguin Shakespeare (Harmondsworth, 1967)

Staunton — Howard Staunton, *Plays*, 3 vols. (1858–60)

Steevens — Samuel Johnson and George Steevens, *Plays*, 10 vols. (1773)

Steevens 1778 — Samuel Johnson and George Steevens, *Plays*, 10 vols. (1778)

Theobald — Lewis Theobald, *Works*, 7 vols. (1733)

Theobald 1740 — Lewis Theobald, *Works*, 8 vols. (1740)

Warburton — William Warburton, *Works*, 8 vols. (1747)

White — Richard Grant White, *Works*, 12 vols. (Boston, 1857–66)

Williams — George Walton Williams, *The Most Excellent and Lamentable Tragedie of Romeo and Juliet* (Durham, NC, 1964)

Wilson–Duthie — John Dover Wilson and George Ian Duthie, *Romeo and Juliet*, The New Shakespeare (Cambridge, 1955)

OTHER ABBREVIATIONS

Abbott — E. A. Abbott, *A Shakespearian Grammar*, 3rd edn. (1870)

Andrews, *Critical Essays* — *'Romeo and Juliet': Critical Essays*, ed. John F. Andrews (New York, 1993)

Bartenschlager — Klaus Bartenschlager, 'Three Notes on *Romeo and Juliet*', *Anglia*, 100 (1982), 422–5

Booth — Stephen Booth, *Shakespeare's Sonnets* (New Haven, 1977)

Brooke — Arthur Brooke, *The Tragicall Historye of Romeus and Juliet written first in Italian by Bandell, and nowe in Englishe by Ar. Br.*, in Bullough, i. 269–363 (see Bullough, below); cited by line numbers unless otherwise indicated

Brooke, N. — Nicholas Brooke, *Shakespeare's Early Tragedies* (1968)

Bullough — Geoffrey Bullough, *Narrative and Dramatic Sources of Shakespeare*, 8 vols. (1957–75)

Cirlot — J. E. Cirlot, *A Dictionary of Symbols*, 2nd edn. (New York, 1971)

Cotgrave — Randle Cotgrave, *A Dictionarie of the French and English Tongues* (1611)

Daniel — Samuel Daniel, *The Complaint of Rosamond*, in *Poems and 'A Defence of Ryme'*, ed. Arthur Colby Sprague (Cambridge, Mass., 1930)

Dent — R. W. Dent, *Shakespeare's Proverbial Language: An Index* (Berkeley, 1981)

ELN	*English Language Notes*
ELR	*English Literary Renaissance*
E&S	*Essays and Studies*
Evans, R. O.	Robert O. Evans, *The Osier Cage: Rhetorical Devices in 'Romeo and Juliet'* (Lexington, Ky., 1966)
Greg, *Editorial Problem*	W. W. Greg, *The Editorial Problem in Shakespeare* (Oxford, 1942)
Greg, *First Folio*	W. W. Greg, *The Shakespeare First Folio: Its Bibliographical and Textual History* (Oxford, 1955)
Jonson	Ben Jonson, *Works*, ed. C. H. Herford and P. and E. Simpson, 11 vols. (Oxford, 1925–52)
Joseph, Sister Miriam	Sister Miriam Joseph, *Shakespeare's Use of the Arts of Language* (New York, 1947)
Laroque	François Laroque, *Shakespeare's Festive World* (Cambridge, 1991)
Levin	Harry Levin, 'Form and Formality in *Romeo and Juliet*', *SQ* 11 (1960), repr. in Andrews, *Critical Essays*, pp. 41–53
Lyly	*The Complete Works of John Lyly*, ed. R. W. Bond, 3 vols. (Oxford, 1902)
Mahood	M. M. Mahood, *Shakespeare's Wordplay* (1957; repr. 1968)
MARDE	*Medieval & Renaissance Drama in England*
Marlowe	*The Complete Works of Christopher Marlowe*, ed. Fredson Bowers, 2 vols. (Cambridge, 1973)
MLN	*Modern Language Notes*
MLR	*Modern Language Review*
MP	*Modern Philology*
Nashe	*The Works of Thomas Nashe*, ed. Ronald B. McKerrow, repr. with corrections and supplementary notes by F. P. Wilson, 5 vols. (Oxford, 1958)
N&Q	*Notes and Queries*
OED	*Oxford English Dictionary*, 2nd edn. (1989)
Onions	C. T. Onions, *A Shakespeare Glossary*, rev. Robert D. Eagleson (Oxford, 1986)
Ovid	*Ovid's 'Metamorphoses': The Arthur Golding Translation, 1567*, ed. John Frederick Nims (New York, 1965); cited by book and line numbers
Painter	William Painter, 'The goodly Hystory of the true, and constant Loue between Rhomeo and Ivlietta . . .' in

	The Palace of Pleasure, ed. Joseph Jacobs (1890), iii. 80–124; cited by page numbers
Partridge	Eric Partridge, *Shakespeare's Bawdy*, 3rd edn. (1968)
PBSA	*Papers of the Bibliographical Society of America*
Pearlman	E. Pearlman, 'Shakespeare at Work: *Romeo and Juliet*', *ELR* 24 (1994), repr. in Porter, *Critical Essays*, pp. 107–30
Porter, *Critical Essays*	*Critical Essays on Shakespeare's 'Romeo and Juliet'*, ed. Joseph A. Porter (New York, 1997)
PQ	*Philological Quarterly*
Reconstructing Individualism	*Reconstructing Individualism: Autonomy, Individuality, and the Self in Western Thought*, ed. Thomas C. Heller, Morton Sosna, and David E. Wellbery (Stanford, 1986)
RES	*Review of English Studies*
SAB	*Shakespeare Association Bulletin*
SB	*Studies in Bibliography*
SEL	*Studies in English Literature*
Shaheen	Naseeb Shaheen, *Biblical References in Shakespeare's Tragedies* (Newark, Del., 1987)
Shakespeare's 'Romeo and Juliet', ed. Halio	*Shakespeare's 'Romeo and Juliet': Texts, Contexts, and Interpretation*, ed. Jay L. Halio (Newark, Del., 1995)
Sidney	*The Poems of Sir Philip Sidney*, ed. William A. Ringler, Jr. (Oxford, 1962)
SJ, *SJH*	*Shakespeare Jahrbuch, Deutsche Shakespeare-Gesellschaft West*
SP	*Studies in Philology*
Spenser	*The Works of Edmund Spenser: A Variorum Edition*, ed. Edwin Greenlaw, Charles Grosvenor Osgood, and Frederick Morgan Padelford (Baltimore, 1932)
SQ	*Shakespeare Quarterly*
SR	Stationers' Register
SSt	*Shakespeare Studies*
SSu	*Shakespeare Survey*
STC	*A Short-Title Catalogue of Books Printed in England, Scotland, & Ireland, and of English Books Printed Abroad, 1475–1640*, first comp. A. W. Pollard and G. R. Redgrave; 2nd edn., rev. and enl., begun by W. A. Jackson

	and F. S. Ferguson, completed by Katharine F. Pantzer, 3 vols. (1976–91)
Textual Companion	*William Shakespeare: A Textual Companion*, ed. Stanley Wells and Gary Taylor with John Jowett and William Montgomery (Oxford, 1987)
Tilley	M. P. Tilley, *A Dictionary of Proverbs in England in the Sixteenth and Seventeenth Centuries* (Ann Arbor, Mich., 1950)
TJ	*Theatre Journal*
TLS	*The Times Literary Supplement*
TSLL	*Texas Studies in Language and Literature*

THE
MOST EX-
cellent and lamentable
Tragedie, of Romeo
and *Iuliet.*

*Newly corrected, augmented, and
amended:*

As it hath bene ſundry times publiquely acted, by the
right Honourable the Lord Chamberlaine
his Seruants.

LONDON
Printed by Thomas Creede, for Cuthbert Burby, and are to
be ſold at his ſhop neare the Exchange.
1599.

Fig. 13. The title-page of Quarto 2 (1599).

The Most Excellent and Lamentable Tragedy of Romeo and Juliet

THE PERSONS OF THE PLAY

CHORUS

ROMEO
MONTAGUE, his father
MONTAGUE'S WIFE
BENVOLIO, Montague's nephew
ABRAHAM, Montague's serving-man
BALTHAZAR, Romeo's man

JULIET
CAPULET, her father
CAPULET'S WIFE
TYBALT, their nephew
Page to Tybalt
PETRUCCIO
CAPULET'S COUSIN
NURSE to Juliet
PETER
SAMSON } serving-men of the Capulets
GREGORY
CHIEF SERVING-MAN
Other SERVING-MEN
MUSICIANS

Escalus, PRINCE of Verona
MERCUTIO } his kinsmen
County PARIS
Page to Mercutio
Page to Paris

OFFICER
CITIZENS

FRIAR LAURENCE

FRIAR JOHN

An APOTHECARY

CHIEF WATCHMAN

Other CITIZENS OF THE WATCH

Masquers, guests, gentlewomen, followers of the Montague and Capulet factions, attendants

The Most Excellent and Lamentable Tragedy of Romeo and Juliet

Prologue *Enter Chorus*

CHORUS

Two households both alike in dignity,
In fair Verona, where we lay our scene,
From ancient grudge break to new mutiny,
Where civil blood makes civil hands unclean.
From forth the fatal loins of these two foes

Title *The . . . Juliet*| Q2 (*title-page and head title above* 1.1); *The most lamentable Tragedie of Romeo and Iuliet*. Q2 (*running title*); *AN* | EXCELLENT | conceited Tragedie | *OF* | Romeo and Iuliet Q1 (*title-page*); The most excellent Tragedie of | *Romeo and Iuliet*. Q1 (*head title above* 1.1; *similarly running title, sigs.* A4^{v}–D); *The excellent Tragedie of Romeo and Iuliet*. Q1 (*running title, sigs.* E–K); THE TRAGEDIE OF | ROMEO and IVLIET. F (*head title; similarly running title*)

Prologue 0.1–14 **Prologue** . . . mend.| Q (*var.* Q1); *not in* F   0.1 *Enter Chorus*| CAPELL; Corus. Q2

Prologue In Q2 '*The Prologue*', centred in large type, appears above 'Corus', centred in smaller type. '*The Prologue*' probably refers to the introductory sonnet, whereas 'Corus' identifies the speaker, conventionally dressed in a black cloak, who delivers both this prologue and the sonnet between the fourth and fifth scenes. In performance the Chorus has been frequently doubled and sometimes cut. G. B. Shand suggests (in correspondence) that the closing couplet permits identification of the Chorus, as company spokesman, with the bookkeeper or even the author. In l. 14 'here' might refer to what the writer has done, i.e. the book of the play (perhaps carried by the Chorus); and 'our toil'—like 'strive'/'strife' in the epilogues to *Twelfth Night* (l. 404) and *All's Well* (l. 4)—to the efforts through which the actors realize the text in performance. (See notes to ll. 13–14 and cf. Q1's simpler version of l. 14.)

1–14 **Two . . . mend** The Prologue both imitates a common practice of contemporary tragedies written for the public stage and follows Brooke's 'Argument', in sonnet form, for his poem. It also generates anomalies, as Pearlman makes plain (pp. 112–15). First, this chorus and the second one in Q2 establish a pattern which Shakespeare then abandons; they may indicate that he changed his mind about the format of the tragedy as he wrote it. Second, the Prologue appears (somewhat altered) in Q1, suggesting that it was performed in the theatre; however, Q1 lacks the second chorus. Third, F omits the Prologue, perhaps through an error in casting off copy (see Jowett), and begins '*Actus Primus. Scoena Prima*'.

1 **dignity** (a) social rank, (b) nobleness of character; cf. Brooke 25–6, which also describes both families as equal in social advancement, 'endued with wealth, and nobler, of their race'.

2 **Verona** The city represents two traditions, one literary, one theatrical. It provides the setting for novella versions of the story beginning with Luigi da Porto's; and it is one of the Italian cities which served as the main or occasional background for many English Renaissance comedies, including half of Shakespeare's.

3 **ancient grudge . . . new mutiny** The first of many antitheses in the play. Shakespeare follows Brooke 34, 36 in describing the long-standing enmity as a *grudge*, i.e. 'ill-will or resentment due to some

A pair of star-crossed lovers take their life,
Whose misadventured piteous overthrows
Doth with their death bury their parents' strife.
The fearful passage of their death-marked love,
And the continuance of their parents' rage—
Which but their children's end naught could remove—
Is now the two hours' traffic of our stage;
The which if you with patient ears attend,
What here shall miss, our toil shall strive to mend.

Exit

14.1 *Exit*] CAPELL; *not in* Q

special cause, as a personal injury, the superiority of an opponent or rival, or the like' (*OED sb.* 3a). Ill-will bursts into *mutiny*, which means not only 'revolt against authority' but also 'contention' or 'quarrel' (*sb.* 2). (Cf. Capulet's use of *mutiny* at 1.4.193.)

4 **Where** i.e. in Verona

civil . . . unclean The Prologue introduces a rhetorical feature which Levin identifies as a component of the play's symmetry and which occurs more than 100 times: duplication of a word within a line (a form of diacope or ploce) which stresses the word and balances the verse (pp. 47–8). Here the repeated term emphasizes contradictions in Verona. *Civil* applies to citizens living together in a community (*OED a.* 1, first illustration), refers to sharing the advantages of that social condition, and may also mean 'non-military' (*a.* 14a; *OED*'s first example is 1612). The rest of the line subverts these definitions, the literal and figurative senses of the words denoting violence, disorder, absence of civility.

5 **fatal** means both 'fateful' and 'deadly'. This key word introduces the idea of destiny, linking it simultaneously with the lovers' experience and the disastrous anger of their fathers.

6 **star-crossed** 'thwarted by a malign star' (*OED*). The expression redefines *fatal* in terms of astrology and applies it solely to Romeo and Juliet.

take their life A double-edged phrase meaning either 'derive their life' or 'deprive themselves of life', fusing the opening of the story with its conclusion; it also forms a skewed antithesis with 'fatal loins'.

7 **misadventured** unfortunate (*OED*'s only instance)

8 **Doth** The southern form of third person plural in *th* (Abbott 334) heightens the stress on *death* through consonance.

parents' in context, allows three definitions at once, referring to the immediate families, other relatives (*OED sb.* 2), and ancestors.

9 **fearful . . . love** Mahood points out six puns in this line which 'pose the play's fundamental question at the outset: is its ending frustration or fulfilment?' (pp. 56–7). *Fearful* can mean 'frightened', applying to the lovers' helpless responses, or 'fearsome', indicating the spectators' awed reactions. *Passage* denotes both 'course of events' and 'voyage', its second definition anticipating *traffic* in l. 12 and the Petrarchan motif of sea-journey which runs through Romeo's speeches. In addition *passage* means 'death' and enhances the wordplay in *death-marked*, which signifies not only 'marked out for (or by) death; foredoomed', but 'having death as their objective'.

12 **Is** The inflection in *s* with two singular nouns as subject was common (Abbott 336).

two hours' According to contemporary evidence early modern plays lasted between two and three hours (see E. K. Chambers, *The Elizabethan Stage* (Oxford, 1923), ii. 543); but variance in the length of texts indicates there was no standard duration.

traffic *OED* cites *traffic* in this line as an illustration for 'business' (*sb.* 3 *fig.*), but it retains its more literal associations of trade, merchandise (*sb.* 4a), and journey.

13–14 **The which . . . mend** Bartenschlager, comparing the prologues in *Henry V* and

I.I *Enter Samson and Gregory, with swords and bucklers, of the house of Capulet*

SAMSON Gregory, on my word we'll not carry coals.
GREGORY No, for then we should be colliers.
SAMSON I mean, an we be in choler we'll draw.
GREGORY Ay, while you live, draw your neck out of collar.
SAMSON I strike quickly being moved.
GREGORY But thou art not quickly moved to strike.
SAMSON A dog of the house of Montague moves me.

Henry VIII, interprets as an appeal to the audience's imagination. In his reading, *here* represents the Elizabethan theatre; *miss* acknowledges the incompatibility of this stage and 'fair Verona'; and the Chorus invites the audience to complete the theatrical illusion (422–3). His explanation makes sense, but the couplet allows more than one interpretation (see notes to Prologue and l. 14).

13 **The which** This phrase, a definite pronoun, singles out *traffic* as its antecedent (see Abbott 270).

attend (a) listen to, (b) consider (*OED* v. 2a)

14 **What . . . mend** This economical line permits more than one reading, although its general sense remains clear: whatever the audience wants in the performance, the actors will endeavour to provide. But the first term of the antithesis *miss/mend* introduces subtle ambiguity, hinting that any fault may lie with the spectators as well as the play. *OED* defines *miss* in l. 14 as an intransitive verb meaning 'to be unsuccessful' (*v.*[1] 21). With this reading, *mend* denotes 'improve' (*v.* 2a; cf. 3, 5, 9). Line 14 may contain an ellipsis, however, the nominative *you* from l. 13 (see Abbott 401). Taking *you* as its subject, *miss* becomes a transitive verb signifying not only 'to lack' (*v.*[1] 14a; cf. 6, 15, 16), but also 'to fail to "catch" or hear (some part of what one is listening to)' (*v.*[1] 10). In that case, the actors' efforts would 'make up the deficiency' (*v.* 9c). The imperfect rhyme on *ears/here* seems to play on the homonym 'hear' and the auditory implications of the couplet.

I.I H. Granville-Barker describes the modulations of tone and activity in this largely invented scene as 'a change from wood-wind, brass and tympani to an andante on the strings' (*Prefaces to Shakespeare* (1930, repr. 1982), i. 49).

0.1–2 ***Enter . . . bucklers*** Parts of the Chorus's narrative materialize in a comic mode. The *swords and bucklers*—heavy weapons and small round shields usually carried by a handle—indicate the social positions of the two men and caricature the violence of the ancient feud. In addition, they help to establish the play's time-scheme. As Edelman shows, the servants are making their way on a Sunday morning to a Veronese equivalent of Smithfield, where Londoners met for fencing contests and the odd duel (*Brawl Ridiculous*, pp. 34–5).

0.2 ***house of Capulet*** Malone, in a note to l. 30, cites George Gascoigne's 'Devise of a Masque' (1575), which states that partisans of the Montague family wore a token in their hats to distinguish themselves (see Furness).

1 **SAMSON Gregory** The names may enhance the servants' mock-heroic postures, *Samson* referring to the great Hebrew warrior (Judges 13–16) and *Gregory* to the warrior Pope Gregory VII (J. J. M. Tobin, *American Notes and Queries*, 17 (1979), 154). But the audience hears only the name of *Gregory* here and at l. 58.

carry coals (a) do dirty work, (b) put up with insults (proverbial, Dent C464)

2 **colliers** those who carry coal for sale (*OED* 2a). This word often alluded to the dirtiness of the trade or the collier's reputation for cheating (3). Gregory's obvious pun therefore plays on both the literal and figurative senses of *carry coals*.

3 **I mean . . . draw** Samson dismisses Gregory's pun but unintentionally sets off more wordplay with *choler*, which sounds like 'collier'. Clearly he means 'anger'; however, he uses an exact homonym for 'collar'. As a result *draw*

GREGORY To move is to stir, and to be valiant is to stand: therefore if thou art moved thou runn'st away.

SAMSON A dog of that house shall move me to stand. I will take the wall of any man or maid of Montague's.

GREGORY That shows thee a weak slave, for the weakest goes to the wall.

SAMSON 'Tis true, and therefore women being the weaker vessels are ever thrust to the wall: therefore I will push Montague's men from the wall, and thrust his maids to the wall.

GREGORY The quarrel is between our masters and us their men.

SAMSON 'Tis all one, I will show myself a tyrant: when I

quibbles on pulling out swords and hauling a load.

3 **an** if (Abbott 101; not noted later)

4 **while . . . collar** Now Gregory quibbles on *choler/collar*; he takes the latter to mean 'hangman's noose', the ultimate punishment for *choler*. At the same time his gallows-joke introduces the legal and retributive components of the plot. Using a proverbial expression (cf. Dent N69, C513) and blunt paradox, he advises Samson to avoid capital punishment as long as he lives.

5–6 **I strike . . . moved . . . moved to strike** Samson seems to ignore Gregory's wordplay while his own language prompts bawdy puns: *strike* refers not only to aggressive behaviour but also to copulation (see Partridge); *move* alludes to various kinds of provocation, sexual among them. With Gregory's neat reversal (the rhetorical figure antimetabole), the servants introduce a burlesque of Petrarchan conceits linking warfare and sex.

8 **To move . . . to stand** Gregory continues to play on the verb *to move*, now including its intransitive senses and probably one military definition: 'to quit a position' (*OED v.* 16c). He matches it with the synonym *to stir*, which shares its associations of disturbance (*v.* 14c), arousal, and motion (11a, b). In contrast he sets *to stand*, which has obviously different military and sexual implications; and *valiant*, which refers not only to courage in battle but to things which are firm.

10 **move . . . stand** These double entendres finally wrench the contradictory terms together.

11 **take the wall of** refuse the courtesy of a position away from the gutter to

12–13 **weak slave . . . weakest . . . wall** Gregory mocks Samson's position by quoting a proverb, 'The weakest goes to the wall' (Dent W185); he means, 'The coward gives way in a conflict'. Adding to the insult, *slave*, or 'fellow' (*OED sb.*[1] 1c), has connotations of submissiveness; and the rhetorical device polyptoton (repetition of words from the same root) emphasizes *weak/weakest*.

14–15 **women . . . weaker vessels** Samson reinterprets the proverb by means of another (Dent W655) and attempts to recover his inside position; he construes *weakest* as *women*, citing the New Testament (1 Peter 3: 7: 'ye husbands, dwell with them . . . giving honour unto the woman, as unto the weaker vessel'). The biblical metaphor represents the human body primarily as a receptacle of the soul (*OED sb.*[1] 3b), whereas Samson more literally represents the female's body in particular as a receptacle for the male's. The repetition of *therefore* imposes logic on illogic.

15 **thrust . . . wall** *OED sb.*[1] 14 quotes to illustrate the definition 'thrust aside into a position of neglect', but the expression in this context is coarse and sexual ('unfastidious courtship and summary copulation' (Partridge)).

18–19 **quarrel . . . men** i.e. maids have no part in this contention

20 **tyrant** Samson intends 'despot', but *tyrant* also means 'ruffian' (*OED sb.* 4b).

have fought with the men, I will be civil with the maids, I will cut off their heads.

GREGORY The heads of the maids?

SAMSON Ay, the heads of the maids, or their maidenheads, take it in what sense thou wilt.

GREGORY They must take it in sense that feel it.

SAMSON Me they shall feel while I am able to stand, and 'tis known I am a pretty piece of flesh.

GREGORY 'Tis well thou art not fish; if thou hadst, thou hadst been Poor John. Draw thy tool, here comes of the house of Montagues.

Enter two other Serving-men

1.1.21 civil] Q2; cruel Q4 26 in] Q1; *not in* Q2 30 of the] Q2; two of the Q1

21 **civil** Often emended to 'cruel', following Q4, but since Dowden *civil* has been defended because it adds irony, paradox, and antithesis to Samson's speech. Forms of these devices have marked the servants' exchange thus far, and *civil* echoes the Prologue (l. 4) and anticipates the Prince (l. 85, 'civil brawls'); it contributes to the burlesque of Samson's lines while drawing attention to the disarray of civility in Verona.

25 **take it . . . wilt** Proverbial (cf. Dent T27 and ll. 37–8).

25–6 **sense . . . in sense** The servants pun broadly on *sense* as (a) meaning, (b) sensation or organ of sense. In l. 26 Q2's omission of *in* can be rationalized by construing *it* as a genitive or assuming an ellipsis (Abbott 228, 382). But the reading in l. 25 suggests that the printer made 'an easy error' (Jowett) after setting *it*.

26–7 **feel . . . stand** Bawdy wordplay continues with *feel*, which refers to perception by a variety of means (especially touch); repetition of the pun on *stand* from l. 8; and *it*, a still familiar term for sexual intercourse.

28 **pretty . . . flesh** fine fellow, emphasizing physical attributes and appetites

29 **thou . . . fish** Inspired by the phrase 'neither flesh nor fish: neither one thing nor the other' (*OED*, *flesh*, *sb.* 4c; cf. *fish sb.* 4c); punning on the sexual connotations of *fish* (see Partridge), it also introduces a typical Petrarchan image (the *fish* representing the desolate lover).

hadst hadst been (Abbott 387)

30 **Poor John** 'A name for hake (or? other fish) salted and dried for food; often a type of poor fare' (*OED* 1a); implies weak sexual performance, since *Poor John* would hardly 'stand' (i.e. last).

tool i.e. sword (with a bawdy quibble)

30–1 **comes . . . house** Gregory uses a partitive genitive (which indicates a whole divided into parts, the Montague household represented by some of its members), but omits the partitive word (probably 'two' or 'some'). This grammatical construction 'is rare in Shakespeare, but possible' (Williams). In both quartos Gregory employs the common third person plural form of the verb in *s* (Abbott 333; not noted later).

31.1 ***Enter . . . Serving-men*** This direction, common to Q2 and Q1, does not name the Montague servants. Later in Q2 a speech-prefix calls one of the men *Abram*. (abbreviated *Abra.*), the original form of 'Abraham', which means 'father is exalted' (see Genesis 17: 5); the dialogue does not name him. Like 'Samson' and 'Gregory', 'Abram' has grand associations, representing the patriarch and ancestor of the Hebrews. The full text of Q2 suggests that Shakespeare chose the names for comic effect; but the dialogue indicates the loss of this effect between page and stage. (Despite editorial practice, textual evidence does not support naming the second Montague servant 'Balthazar'; the possibility that one actor played both parts does not prove the two characters identical.)

SAMSON My naked weapon is out. Quarrel, I will back thee.

GREGORY How, turn thy back and run?

SAMSON Fear me not.

GREGORY No, marry, I fear thee!

SAMSON Let us take the law of our sides; let them begin.

GREGORY I will frown as I pass by, and let them take it as they list.

SAMSON Nay, as they dare: I will bite my thumb at them, which is disgrace to them if they bear it.

ABRAHAM Do you bite your thumb at us, sir?

SAMSON I do bite my thumb, sir.

ABRAHAM Do you bite your thumb at us, sir?

SAMSON (*to Gregory*) Is the law of our side if I say 'Ay'?

GREGORY No.

SAMSON (*to Abraham*) No sir, I do not bite my thumb at you, sir, but I bite my thumb, sir.

GREGORY Do you quarrel, sir?

ABRAHAM Quarrel, sir? No, sir.

SAMSON But if you do, sir, I am for you; I serve as good a man as you.

40 disgrace] Q2, Q1; a disgrace Q3 41 ABRAHAM] Q (*Abram.*). *The same throughout this scene.* 44 (*to Gregory*)] CAPELL; *not in* Q 46 (*to Abraham*)] CAPELL; *not in* Q

32 **naked weapon** unsheathed sword (with a bawdy quibble)

32–3 **I will back . . . back** Gregory claims to understand *I will back thee* as an offer to retreat backward.

34–5 **Fear . . . fear** Samson uses the obsolete sense 'doubt' (*OED* v. 9); Gregory plays on the still current definition. With the interjection *marry*, Gregory expresses indignation which may be genuine, mock, or both.

36 **of our sides** i.e. on our sides (Abbott 175). Samson indicates that Veronese law does not permit instigation of 'quarrels'.

37 **frown** sneer (*OED* v. 1a)

37–8 **let . . . list** Proverbial (see l. 25 n.).

39 **bite my thumb** *OED* quotes Cotgrave, *Nique*, to define this rude gesture: 'to threaten or defy by putting the thumbnail into the mouth, and with a jerk (from the upper teeth) make it to knack' (*bite*, v. 16). The exchange which results parodies the duelling code which will become central to the play. Abraham's next line indicates that Samson bites his thumb after speaking.

41 **sir** adds contemptuous force to the rhetorical question. In the dialogue which follows, the servants will repeat *sir* ten more times.

42 **I . . . thumb** Samson, aware of legalities (cf. l. 36 and n.), does not acknowledge the object of his insult; he hesitates to make biting his thumb an official challenge, a position that keeps Abraham from giving the lie.

43 **at us** Abraham persists in attempting to confirm the insult, which would qualify as both a defiant challenge and an illegal act.

44 **Is . . . 'Ay'?** Addressed to Gregory. Many editors indicate asides here, but the servants could speak in open defiance.

46–7 **No sir . . . thumb, sir** Quibbling now keeps Samson (briefly) on the right side of the law.

48–9 **Do . . . sir? . . . No, sir** Gregory sets the legal trap for Abraham, who neatly avoids it.

50 **for** i.e. ready for (Abbott 155). Samson attempts to provoke Abraham with a hypothetical situation, a sign perhaps of his diminishing resources.

ABRAHAM No better.
SAMSON Well, sir.

Enter Benvolio

GREGORY Say 'better'—here comes one of my master's kinsmen.
SAMSON Yes, better, sir.
ABRAHAM You lie.
SAMSON Draw if you be men. Gregory, remember thy washing blow.

They fight

BENVOLIO (*drawing*) Part fools, put up your swords; you know not what you do.

Enter Tybalt with his sword drawn

TYBALT
What, art thou drawn among these heartless hinds?
Turn thee, Benvolio, look upon thy death.

59 washing] Q2; swashing Q4 59.1–76 *They fight . . .* foe.] Q2; *They draw, to them enters* Tybalt, *they fight, to them the Prince, old* Mountague, *and his wife, old* Capulet *and his wife, and other Citizens and part them.* Q1 (*with no dialogue*) 60 (*drawing*)] JOWETT; *not in* Q 61.1 *with his sword drawn*] This edition; *not in* Q

52 **No better.** F punctuates l. 52 as a taunting question, but this line works equally well as a statement: Abraham rephrases Samson's comparison (with a slightly negative edge) and avoids starting a quarrel.

53 **Well** Feints and ambiguities have led the servants to an impasse; their exchange illustrates what Vincentio Saviolo defines in his duelling manual as 'foolish lies' (*His Practise* (1595), in *Three Elizabethan Fencing Manuals*, pp. 353–8).

54–5 **one . . . kinsmen** i.e. Tybalt. Q2 places his entrance at l. 61, but his appearance at l. 55—counterpointed with Benvolio's, noticed by Gregory, allowing him time to approach the scene—makes theatrical sense. Meantime, Gregory's willingness to fight with Tybalt's support implies that the law in itself has not restrained the servants until now. As Gregory sees Tybalt, presumably Abraham sees the Montague kinsman Benvolio. In any case, Abraham too prepares to fight.

59 **washing** swashing (*OED ppl. a.* 2). 'Swashing' applies 'to a particular stroke in fencing' and more generally to 'a weapon slashing with great force' (*ppl. a.* 2 cites Q4).

60 **BENVOLIO** Benvolio's conduct here and later suits his name, invented by Shakespeare, which means 'well-wishing'.

60–1 **Part . . . do** Shaheen hears biblical echoes of forgiveness and pacification in this speech and l. 64: Luke 23: 34, Matthew 26: 52, and John 18: 11. Yet Tybalt's next line indicates that Benvolio draws his own sword and joins the fray, initiating a sequence of action which anticipates the crisis of 3.1. His opening lines, originally printed as prose, have been versified by Capell and others. In this edition they appear as prose with verse rhythms, making the transition to blank verse.

62 **art . . . hinds?** Tybalt's insult reformulates wordplay ('heart'/'hart') popular from Renaissance love-poetry: *heartless hinds* are (a) cowardly or foolish servants or boors (see *OED a.* 3, *sb.*[2] 1), and (b) female deer without males ('hartless'). His version charges the servants, and Benvolio, with cowardice to the point of effeminacy. As the stage picture begins to expand, Tybalt sneers at Benvolio for drawing his sword among servants.

63–4 **Turn . . . sword** These lines make it clear that Tybalt approaches the fight

BENVOLIO

I do but keep the peace. Put up thy sword,
Or manage it to part these men with me.

TYBALT

What, drawn and talk of peace? I hate the word
As I hate hell, all Montagues, and thee.
Have at thee, coward.

They fight.

Enter three or four Citizens with clubs or partisans

OFFICER

Clubs, bills, and partisans! Strike, beat them down!
Down with the Capulets, down with the Montagues!

Enter old Capulet in his gown, and his Wife

68.1 *They fight*] Q1 (*see note to ll.* 59.1–76), F (*Fight.*); *not in* Q2

with his sword drawn. In the theatrical context Benvolio's name sounds ironic (cf. l. 66, where Tybalt describes Benvolio's position in terms of an oxymoron).

65 **manage** wield or make use of (*OED v.* 2a)

68 **Have . . . coward** Tybalt simultaneously challenges Benvolio to fight, announces his own intent to attack, and engages Benvolio in sword-play. Later Benvolio will describe to Montague what the original audience would have seen in this encounter (ll. 104–11). As Soens explicates Benvolio's speech, Tybalt's cutting of the winds identifies his Spanish style of fencing, since the favoured Italian school in England disapproved of the cut ('Tybalt's Spanish Fencing in *Romeo and Juliet*', 123–5). The Spanish style, controlled and elegant, contrasts not only with Tybalt's unruly temperament, but also with Benvolio's Italian mode, which places the duellist in a crouch as he thrusts at his opponent. The play will continue to refer to both styles of fencing, not always distinguishing clearly between them.

68.2 ***Enter . . . partisans*** Q2's direction avoids decisions about the number of supernumeraries and the distribution of their props. The *partisan*, a military weapon used by foot-soldiers, consisted 'of a long-handled spear, the blade having one or more lateral cutting projections, variously shaped' (*OED sb.*[2] 1a).

69 **OFFICER** Q2 prints *Offi.* OFFICER seems a plausible expansion, since the term has broad application: anyone 'who performs a duty, service, or function' (*OED sb.* 1), 'holds an office, post, or place' (2), or serves as 'a petty officer of justice or of the peace' (3a). As some editors have suggested, *Offi.* may represent a member (or members) of the watch and belong to the three or four citizens who have just entered. A single officer could lead the rallying cry which follows; more than one could share it.

Clubs . . . partisans This rallying cry echoes that for calling London apprentices to arms, 'prentices and clubs' (*OED*, *club*, *sb.*, 1c), as well as that for summoning the watch to halt a street fight (used figuratively in *Titus* 2.1.37). Thus, it has associations with both creating and trying to end a disturbance. For a moment both associations fit as the citizens enter the fray with their sturdy weapons: *bills* refer to military weapons used especially by the infantry, 'varying in form from a simple concave blade with a long wooden handle, to a kind of concave axe with a spike at the back and its shaft terminating in a spear-head' (*sb.*[1] 2a); 'a similar weapon used by constables of the watch' (2b). But this confrontation immediately becomes a brawl corresponding to an Elizabethan street fight.

70.1 ***gown*** dressing gown

CAPULET

What noise is this? Give me my long sword, ho!

CAPULET'S WIFE

A crutch, a crutch—why call you for a sword?

CAPULET

My sword, I say. Old Montague is come,
And flourishes his blade in spite of me.

Enter old Montague and his Wife

MONTAGUE

Thou villain Capulet! (*To his Wife*) Hold me not, let me
go.

MONTAGUE'S WIFE

Thou shalt not stir one foot to seek a foe.

Enter Prince Escalus with his train

PRINCE

Rebellious subjects, enemies to peace,
Profaners of this neighbour-stainèd steel—
Will they not hear? What ho! You men, you beasts,
That quench the fire of your pernicious rage
With purple fountains issuing from your veins:
On pain of torture, from those bloody hands
Throw your mistempered weapons to the ground,

72 CAPULET'S WIFE] Q2 (*Wife.*). *The same throughout the play.* 75 (*To his Wife*)] JOWETT ([*His Wife holds him back*]); *not in* Q

71 **long sword** An old-fashioned, heavy sword with a long cutting blade.

73 **is come** has come (Abbott 295)

74 **flourishes . . . spite** Capulet indicates that Montague makes his entrance waving his sword in 'spite'.

76 **stir** echoes Gregory's earlier wordplay (see l. 8 n.).

76.1 ***Prince Escalus*** As only this direction in Q2 identifies him by name, a theatre audience never hears him called *Escalus* (as in Brooke), a version of the family name 'della Scala', representing the famous rulers of Verona. Both da Porto and Bandello set the love-story in the era of Bartolommeo della Scala, the early fourteenth century; and Painter calls this authority figure 'Lord Bartholmew of Escala' (81).

train followers (unspecified in number and composition)

77–8 **Rebellious . . . steel** The Prince's opening terms of address amount to oxymora or condensed paradoxes.

79 **Will . . . hear?** Presumably the audience hears Escalus's words; but the citizens have missed the weighty opening of his speech.

80–1 **That quench . . . veins** Dent compares 'Only blood can quench the fire' (B465.1). The elaborate conceit for violence originates in Brooke 49–50 and shares some of its imagery—the fire and fountains—with all Renaissance love-poetry and with pastoral. In context *pernicious* seems to convey its rare or obsolete sense, 'wicked, villainous' (*OED a.*[1] b), as well as its still current meanings, 'destructive, ruinous, fatal'. *Purple*, the poetic colour of blood, contributes to the alliteration.

83–4 **Throw . . . Prince** These lines allow a pause while those assembled obey the order.

83 **mistempered** At the most obvious level, the Prince refers to the process which

And hear the sentence of your movèd Prince.
Three civil brawls bred of an airy word,
By thee old Capulet and Montague,
Have thrice disturbed the quiet of our streets,
And made Verona's ancient citizens
Cast by their grave beseeming ornaments,
To wield old partisans in hands as old,
Cankered with peace to part your cankered hate.
If ever you disturb our streets again,
Your lives shall pay the forfeit of the peace.
For this time all the rest depart away.
You, Capulet, shall go along with me;
And Montague, come you this afternoon,
To know our farther pleasure in this case,
To old Freetown, our common judgement place.

makes steel hard by heating it and then immersing it in a liquid: his subjects have *mistempered* their weapons in one another's blood. 'Tempered' also means 'controlled' in various senses which the citizens have violated. Metonymy (the weapons standing for their owners) or transferred epithet permits one more reading of 'tempered' as 'brought to a desired quality' or 'endowed with a specific temper or disposition' (*OED a.* 1a, 2a). In this case, too, the process has malfunctioned.

84 **movèd** *OED ppl. a.*, first illustration of attributive use in various senses of the verb.

85 **Three** Unlike Brooke or Painter, Shakespeare assigns a number to recent outbreaks of the feud and repeats it at l. 87. The number makes 'new mutiny' (Prologue 3) more specific; and reiteration, as Gibbons suggests, adds an element of formality to the narrative.

airy i.e. empty (cf. Brooke 37, 'first hatched of trifling strife')

88 **ancient** aged, and possibly venerable, long-established

89 **Cast by** throw aside (*OED v.* 75, first illustration)

grave beseeming ornaments Either dignified and seemly attire (*grave*, *beseeming*), or attire suitable to their dignity (*grave-beseeming*), with wordplay on *grave* as place of burial, death (see *OED*, *ornament*, *sb.* 1a).

90 **old partisans . . . hands as old** By this point Q2 has repeated *old* six times in twenty lines of dialogue and two directions. Escalus's use of *ancient*, l. 88, and his pun on *grave*, l. 89, also focus images of old age, adding a dimension to the source narratives. (Q1 gives a different impression because it lacks equivalents for ll. 88–90.) At the same time, Q2 makes its third reference to hands engaged in warfare (cf. Prologue 4 and l. 82), beginning to define a motif.

91 **Cankered** 'rusted', indicating partisans long out of use (*OED ppl. a.* 2), as well as 'evil and malignant'

92–3 **If . . . peace** As Hosley notes, Machiavelli recommends against clemency in dealing with opposing factions, and Prince Escalus will acknowledge the failure of leniency at 3.1.197 and 5.3.294–5. According to Machiavelli, a civil governor may sentence the leaders to death, banish them, or reconcile them, the latter course being the least effective (*Discourses on the First Ten Books of Titus Livius*, 3.27).

93 **forfeit . . . peace** i.e. penalty for breaching the peace

96 **come . . . afternoon** Another indication that the action just witnessed has taken place early in the day.

98 **old Freetown . . . judgement place** Malone first pointed out that Brooke mentions *Freetown* (1974 and 2258) as a castle belonging to Capulet apart from his domicile. Since the play gives Capulet only one residence, it releases the name

Once more, on pain of death, all men depart.
Exeunt all but Montague, his Wife, and Benvolio

MONTAGUE
Who set this ancient quarrel new abroach?
Speak, nephew, were you by when it began?

BENVOLIO
Here were the servants of your adversary
And yours, close fighting ere I did approach;
I drew to part them; in the instant came
The fiery Tybalt, with his sword prepared,
Which as he breathed defiance to my ears,
He swung about his head and cut the winds,
Who, nothing hurt withal, hissed him in scorn.
While we were interchanging thrusts and blows,
Came more and more, and fought on part and part,
Till the Prince came, who parted either part.

MONTAGUE'S WIFE
O where is Romeo—saw you him today?
Right glad I am he was not at this fray.

99.1 *Exeunt . . . Benvolio*] HUDSON (*following* Rowe); *Exeunt*. Q2 100 MONTAGUE] Q2 (*Mounta.*); *M<ountagues>:wife*. Q1

for use elsewhere. According to Evans, Shakespeare's reference to *Freetown* as *old* and *our common judgement place* may have resulted from confusion with 'the old castle of Verona' mentioned by Painter (94). It may also have arisen from *The Tragicall Historye* itself. In the first of Brooke's passages *Freetown* serves as a judgement place, the site where Juliet must assent to marry Paris or face Capulet's sentence of repudiation. Whatever its source, Prince Escalus's description of *old Freetown* supports the impression created by his speech of long-established people and institutions.

100 **set . . . new abroach** i.e. revived. Literally, *set abroach* means 'pierce and set running'; it usually refers to a cask of liquor (or gunpowder), a figure implicit here.

102–11 **Here . . . part** Benvolio narrates events which the audience has just seen, giving the first of three such accounts in the play (the others appear in 3.1 and 5.3). As J. Black points out, these summary narratives counterpoise strong, contradictory visual impressions ('The Visual Artistry of *Romeo and Juliet*', *SEL* 15 (1975), repr. in *Critical Essays*, ed. Andrews, pp. 149–61).

105 **fiery Tybalt** The audience hears *Tybalt*'s name for the first time, as well as a succinct character note.

prepared i.e. drawn (see ll. 63–4 n.)

107 **swung** brandished (*OED* *v.*[1] 4)

cut the winds Benvolio plays on two still familiar definitions of *cut*: the sword slashed the winds, and passed through them sharply. He also refers specifically to the *cut* in fencing, 'a slashing blow or stroke given with the edge of the weapon' (*OED* *sb.*[2] 2b). (On Tybalt's style of duelling, see l. 68 n.) At the beginning of 2.3, Mercutio will elaborate the mockery in prose.

108 **Who** which (Abbott 264)

110–11 **on part and part . . . either part** i.e. on both sides of the fight . . . the two sides. Benvolio describes the most chaotic phase of the action so far in the most carefully proportioned lines of this speech: a heroic couplet balanced by rhetorical devices of repetition (diacope and polyptoton).

112 **saw** Simple past tense for complete present (Abbott 347).

BENVOLIO

Madam, an hour before the worshipped sun
Peered forth the golden window of the east,
A troubled mind drive me to walk abroad,
Where underneath the grove of sycamore
That westward rooteth from this city side,
So early walking did I see your son.
Towards him I made, but he was ware of me,
And stole into the covert of the wood.
I, measuring his affections by my own,
Which then most sought where most might not be
found,
Being one too many by my weary self,
Pursued my humour, not pursuing his,
And gladly shunned who gladly fled from me.

MONTAGUE

Many a morning hath he there been seen,
With tears augmenting the fresh morning's dew,
Adding to clouds more clouds with his deep sighs;
But all so soon as the all-cheering sun

116 drive] Q2; drew Q1; draue Q3 118 this city] Q2; the Citties Q1; the City THEOBALD; this city's WILSON–DUTHIE

114–15 **worshipped sun . . . east** The play's first mythological reference, a personification of the sun as godlike. The words 'peer' and 'pear' (= 'appear') seem to have blended in the sixteenth century: i.e. the sun not only looks out of an opening in the firmament, but becomes visible through it (see *OED v.*[2] etymology and 2, first illustration).

116 **troubled . . . abroad** Benvolio describes himself as suffering wakefulness, a classical symptom of melancholy in general and love melancholy in particular. (Q1 has a different line: 'A troubled thought drew me from companie'.) As a result, he prefigures Romeo.

drive A common archaic form of the past tense, pronounced 'driv' (cf. 'writ' for 'wrote').

117 **sycamore** This tree, sometimes associated with melancholy lovers, appears also in *L.L.L.* 5.2.89 and *Othello* 4.3.38.

118 **westward rooteth . . . city side** i.e. grows toward the west from this side of the city. In the phrase *city side*, *city* assumes the position of an adjective and the effect of a genitive (see Abbott 22 on 'the licence of converting one part of speech into another').

120 **ware** (a) aware, (b) wary

121 **covert** hiding-place

123 **Which then most . . . most . . . found** i.e. Benvolio's feelings, which he had recognized in Romeo, led him at the time to guard his solitude. The second half of this line seems to engage in wordplay: *most* can be read both as a substantive (meaning, e.g., 'most people') and as an adverb (modifying the predicate, analogous to *most sought*). A. S. Cairncross points out that the corresponding paradox in Q1, 'That most are busied when th'are most alone', can be identified as a grammar-school commonplace from Cicero, *De Officiis*, III, f.1 (*SQ* 7 (1956), 449–50).

124 **Being . . . many** Proverbial (Dent O62.1; cf. 3.5.165).

126 **who** him who (Abbott 251)

127–30 **Many . . . sun** Montague elaborates Benvolio's impressions of Romeo, portraying his son as a melancholy lover with the conventional images (*tears*, *dew*,

Should in the farthest east begin to draw
The shady curtains from Aurora's bed,
Away from light steals home my heavy son,
And private in his chamber pens himself,
Shuts up his windows, locks fair daylight out,
And makes himself an artificial night.
Black and portentous must this humour prove,
Unless good counsel may the cause remove.

BENVOLIO

My noble uncle, do you know the cause?

MONTAGUE

I neither know it, nor can learn of him.

BENVOLIO

Have you importuned him by any means?

MONTAGUE

Both by myself and many other friends,
But he his own affection's counsellor

143 his] Q3; is Q2

sighs, *clouds*) and hyperbole of Renaissance love-poetry.

130 **all so** just as. *All* gives emphasis to the adverb of degree (*OED adv*. 7, Abbott 28).

130–2 **all-cheering sun . . . Aurora's bed** A variation on Benvolio's conceit for dawn, creating another tableau both mythological and domestic. In Montague's version the sun waits on Aurora, the Roman goddess of dawn, as she rises from the bed of Tithonus, her mortal lover.

133 **Away from light . . . heavy son** Montague plays obviously on words and antitheses as he echoes Benvolio's description of Romeo at l. 121: *light* (= illumination + the opposite of weighty); *heavy* (= gloomy + weighty); *son*/sun. The *light*/dark opposition, familiar from Petrarchan verse and introduced in this dialogue, will become a central motif in both the tragedy's language and its events.

134–6 **private . . . night** The description suggests that Romeo may deliberately court sleep as a 'balm of woe', as the speaker in Sidney's *Astrophil and Stella* 39 offers 'A chamber deaf to noise, and blind to light'.

135–6 **Shuts . . . night** The window imagery connects Montague's response with Benvolio's previous speech, ll. 114–15, making the two passages an extended conceit with wordplay: i.e. as the sun brings light, Montague's son creates gloom.

135 **windows** i.e. shutters (Wilson–Duthie)

137 **Black . . . humour** *Black* still denotes 'gloomy' in two senses, 'dark' and 'melancholy'. Since it also means 'malignant' or 'deadly', it combines with *portentous* to foreshadow the tragic conclusion. Finally, *black* identifies one of the four humours (the body fluids which pre-modern physiology held to determine physical health and temperament): i.e. *black* bile, thought to produce melancholy. Certainly Montague implies that Romeo suffers from melancholy, although *humour* here also refers more generally to mental disposition, mood, and perhaps whim (cf. *L.L.L.* 1.1.227–9).

138 **may** can (Abbott 307)

140 **learn of** i.e. learn it of (Abbott 404)

141 **importuned** (accented on second syllable)

142 **friends** Perhaps 'relatives' as well as 'non-relations'.

143 **affection's** Q2 prints 'affections', which could be either plural (as in l. 122) or singular. If 'affections' is construed in the singular as 'mental state', 'passion' (*OED sb*. 3), 'disposition' (4), even 'malady', it corresponds to the potentially dangerous 'humour' of l. 137.

Is to himself—I will not say how true—
But to himself so secret and so close,
So far from sounding and discovery,
As is the bud bit with an envious worm
Ere he can spread his sweet leaves to the air
Or dedicate his beauty to the same.
Could we but learn from whence his sorrows grow,
We would as willingly give cure as know.

Enter Romeo

BENVOLIO

See where he comes. So please you step aside,
I'll know his grievance or be much denied.

MONTAGUE

I would thou wert so happy by thy stay

149 same] Q2; sun POPE 1728 (*conj.* Theobald)

144 **true** Playing on familiar definitions of *true* as 'honest', 'reasonable', and 'constant'.

145 **close** Montague means 'secret', but *close* has other denotations appropriate to his description of Romeo's state and also to Romeo's self-portrayal in this act: i.e. 'shut in', 'enclosed with darkness' (*OED a.* 5), 'having no part left open' (cf. ll. 146–9), and 'shut up in prison', 'strictly confined' (cf. 1.2.55).

146 **sounding and discovery** *OED vbl. sb.*[2] 1b quotes as its first example for 'investigation'; *sounding* probably means 'vocal utterance' as well. Both *sounding* and *discovery* refer to the process of 'finding out', although *sounding* alludes to the agent of the search and *discovery*—which signifies 'disclosure' (2a) or 'making known'—to the object. Both words also have still familiar nautical associations connecting them with a central Petrarchan motif in the play: the lover as a navigator who has lost his bearings at sea (ll. 193–4 and 1.4.110–11 introduce the motif).

146–8 **discovery . . . leaves** Although Evans, like Johnson, has found the bud simile introduced without transition, the word *discovery* probably informs the conceit. *OED* 1 cites only Sir Thomas Browne's *Garden of Cyrus* (1658) as first using the term to mean the opening of a bud, but evidence suggests a sixteenth-century connection between disclosure and blossoming: in particular, definitions of the verb 'aperio' in Thomas Cooper's *Thesaurus Linguae & Britannicae* (1565), and also possibly definitions of 'patefacio'.

147 **bud . . . worm** A variation of 'The canker soonest eats the fairest rose' (Dent C56; cf. Sonnet 35.4). The next lines call another proverb into play, 'Beauty is but a blossom' (B169).

envious malicious (*OED a.* 2)

149 **same** Most editors find Theobald's emendation 'sun' more effective poetically, and consider *same* an easy minim misreading of 'sunne'. In the mean time, they admit that *same* makes sense; and sixteenth-century herbals repeatedly refer to wholesome air as a key component in successful gardening.

151 **give cure** (a) restore to health, (b) pay heed (*OED sb.*[1] 1a)

153 **grievance** *OED* 2 cites to illustrate 'distress', but other appropriate definitions are 'cause or source of injury' (1); 'oppressive circumstance' (3); 'disease, ailment, hurt' (4).

154 **stay** refers not only to Benvolio's remaining on stage, but also to the 'staying power' he has just expressed (*OED sb.*[3] 6d), and possibly to his interception of Romeo.

To hear true shrift. Come, madam, let's away.
Exeunt Montague and his Wife

BENVOLIO
Good morrow, cousin.

ROMEO
Is the day so young?

BENVOLIO
But new struck nine.

ROMEO
Ay me, sad hours seem long.
Was that my father that went hence so fast?

BENVOLIO
It was. What sadness lengthens Romeo's hours?

ROMEO
Not having that which, having, makes them short.

BENVOLIO In love.

ROMEO Out.

BENVOLIO Of love.

ROMEO
Out of her favour where I am in love.

BENVOLIO
Alas that love, so gentle in his view,
Should be so tyrannous and rough in proof!

ROMEO
Alas that love, whose view is muffled still,
Should without eyes see pathways to his will.

155.1 *Exeunt Montague . . . Wife*] CAPELL; *Exeunt.* Q2

155 **shrift** revelation of a secret

155.1 ***Exeunt*** l. 158 suggests that the actors should depart quickly.

156 **Good morrow** The first explicit indication that it is morning.

156–7 **Is . . . long** Romeo seems to revise the proverb 'Hours of pleasure are short' (Dent H747; see also H747.1), suiting it to his condition as a melancholy lover. Like Benvolio, he awoke before dawn; but he has apparently lost track of time.

165–6 **Alas . . . proof** After imitating Romeo's melancholy interjection (at l. 157), Benvolio describes *love* as *gentle* in appearance but overbearing and severe in *proof* or effect (*OED sb.* 7, and see 5). In addition *proof*, also associated with armour and arms, may suggest an image of *love* prepared for battle. The definitions of *tyrannous* and *rough* overlap, although *rough* primarily determines the antithesis with *gentle*.

167–8 **Alas . . . will** Variations on Benvolio's figures of speech and verse, a trick of style that occurs in most dialogue—prose as well as poetry—involving Romeo, Benvolio, or Mercutio. Here Romeo answers Benvolio with a couplet in perfect rhyme; repeats the interjection; puns on *view* as 'faculty of vision'; replaces antithesis with paradox; and alludes to the well-known image of blind Cupid (*muffled still* = always blindfolded, *OED v.*[1] 2). According to Romeo, the figure of *love* impossibly finds ways to effect his purposes and domination. Dent suggests a correspondence with 'Love will find a way' (L531).

Where shall we dine? O me! What fray was here?
Yet tell me not, for I have heard it all:
Here's much to do with hate, but more with love.
Why then, O brawling love, O loving hate,
O anything of nothing first created;
O heavy lightness, serious vanity,
Mis-shapen chaos of well-seeming forms,
Feather of lead, bright smoke, cold fire, sick health,
Still-waking sleep that is not what it is:
This love feel I, that feel no love in this.
Dost thou not laugh?

BENVOLIO No, coz, I rather weep.

ROMEO
Good heart, at what?

BENVOLIO At thy good heart's oppression.

173 created] Q2; create Q1   175 well-seeming] Q4; welseeing Q2; best seeming Q1

169 **Where . . . dine?** Romeo seems to use *dine* in its earliest sense: 'Where shall we eat the first meal of the day?' (see *OED* etymology). His question shows his interest in food, which concerns almost everyone from the Capulet household in the first act to the musicians in the fourth. But Romeo, as an unrequited lover, should have lost his appetite. This question abruptly reveals the pose in his melancholy posture.
What . . . here? Implying signs of the recent brawling.

171 **Here's . . . love** For a moment Romeo interprets the theatrical scene as an antithesis, viewing himself as one term. Meantime he quibbles on *to do* as the infinitive of the verb and the substantive 'to-do'.

172 **Why then** This list of contradictions is introduced as if it followed logically and inevitably from the observation in l. 171; but the number of apostrophes and oxymora produce instead a rhetorical expression of confused feelings (see Mahood, p. 70). Many of the conventional figures of speech derive from sixteenth-century love-poetry.

173 **O anything . . . created** Romeo recomposes the proverb 'Nothing can come of nothing' (Dent N285), and perhaps offers his own version of Genesis 1: 1, 2.
created Many editors, citing Abbott 342, adopt Q1's 'create', forming a perfectly rhymed couplet between blank verse lines. Yet Q2 prints an effective alternative: the past participle in *ed* results in a slightly awkward couplet—with imperfect rhyme and a feminine ending—well suited to Romeo's strained poetizing and a passage with few rhymes.

175 **Mis-shapen chaos . . . forms** This inconceivable image of forms confounded in formlessness, or shapes perceptible in a shapeless void, echoes l. 173 and recasts Genesis 1: 1, 2 in totally negative terms.
well-seeming Q2's 'welseeing' apparently omits a tilde through compositor misreading or an omission in the manuscript. This error recurs at e.g. 2.1.108, 2.3.6, 3.1.145, 148, 176.

176 **Feather . . . health** In these oxymora, *cold fire* represents the most commonplace Petrarchan antithesis; *bright smoke* is a version of light/dark, another familiar contradiction (cf. l. 133 and n., l. 174). Dent suggests that *feather of lead* conflates 'As light as a feather' (F150) and 'As heavy as lead' (L134).

177 **Still-waking sleep . . . is** i.e. ever-wakeful sleep that denies the attributes of sleep (presumably as a healing power)

178 **This love . . . in this** The meaning is ambiguous: Romeo either returns to his opening antithesis (l. 171), or makes himself an epitome of unsettled love.

179 **coz** Familiar abbreviation of 'cousin'.

180 **oppression** (a) distress, (b) cruel subjugation (by love, cf. l. 166)

ROMEO

Why, such is love's transgression.
Griefs of mine own lie heavy in my breast,
Which thou wilt propagate to have it pressed
With more of thine; this love that thou hast shown
Doth add more grief to too much of mine own.
Love is a smoke made with the fume of sighs,
Being purged, a fire sparkling in lovers' eyes,
Being vexed, a sea nourished with loving tears.
What is it else? A madness most discreet,
A choking gall and a preserving sweet.
Farewell, my coz.

188 loving] Q2; a louers Q1; lovers POPE

181 **such . . . transgression** Evans compares 'Love is lawless' (Dent L508). In the following lines Romeo makes Benvolio's empathy the example of such a violation.

183 **propagate . . . pressed** Alliteration emphasizes these verbs, which state that Benvolio will cause Romeo's sorrows to increase (*OED*, *propagate*, *v.* 2a, first illustration). But *pressed* allows several readings: (a) thrust, (b) oppressed, as by a tyrant (*v.*[1] 6b), (c) crowded. The first definition produces a sexual pun with *propagate* and *breast*. As Gibbons explains, it also contributes to a botanical image of propagation by layering, a system through which weights placed on trailing plants force them to put down roots and thus form new plants.

186–7 **a smoke . . . a fire** Romeo begins to repeat metaphors in new configurations: these two appeared in l. 176. In l. 186, sibilance makes the point emphatic while diction makes it tautological.

187 **Being purged, a fire** i.e. love purified becomes fire, the highest and brightest of the elements (earth, water, air, fire) once believed to constitute all material bodies. McKerrow suggests that love *purged* may mean love burnt clear of the smoke of sighs, i.e. known to be reciprocated.

188–9 **Being . . . else?** Romeo adds water, a third element, to his conceits of air and fire. Although he omits earth, the least rarefied element, he seems to run out of comparisons at the beginning of l. 189.

188 **loving tears** Editors frequently adopt Q1's 'a louers teares', because it corresponds with 'lovers' eyes'. Most assume that the compositor slipped here, influenced by the number of present participles in ll. 187 and 188. But the author may be responsible for this phrase, slightly incongruous at a point when the verse changes direction: Romeo temporarily exhausts his conceits; antitheses will take over in ll. 189 and 190; and the rhyming couplets stop for this one line.

189 **A madness most discreet** Romeo turns a proverbial phrase, 'Love is a madness' (Dent L505.2), into an oxymoron accentuated by consonance. (Dent compares this proverb with Tilley L517, 'Love is without reason', and Whiting L546, 'Mad love lasteth but a while' (*c.*1520).)

190 **choking gall . . . preserving sweet** This common antithesis appears in many proverbs (e.g. see Tilley S1035, 1038, and Dent G11.1, S1037.1), among other forms of expression. In connection with Romeo and Juliet, Brooke uses it (1464), and Shakespeare returns to it later (2.4.22–3). The modifiers—*choking* and *preserving*—suggest a specific contrast between *gall* as a bitter or poisonous substance (*OED sb.*[1] 5) and *sweet* as the sugar, herb, or other substance which prolongs life. At 2.2.24 Friar Laurence will repeat this particular contrast, making it a central emblem of the tragedy.

BENVOLIO Soft, I will go along.
An if you leave me so, you do me wrong.

ROMEO
Tut, I have lost myself, I am not here;
This is not Romeo, he's some other where.

BENVOLIO
Tell me in sadness, who is that you love?

ROMEO
What, shall I groan and tell thee?

BENVOLIO
Groan? Why no; but sadly tell me who.

ROMEO
A sick man in sadness makes his will:
A word ill-urged to one that is so ill.
In sadness, cousin, I do love a woman.

BENVOLIO
I aimed so near when I supposed you loved.

193 ROMEO Tut] Q2 (*text*), Q1; But Q2 (*c.w.*); *Rom<eo>*. But F3 lost] Q; left DANIEL (*conj.* Allen) 198 A . . . makes] Q2; Bid a . . . make Q1; A . . . good sadnesse makes F2

192 **An if** A strong form of *if* to emphasize the subjunctive (see Abbott 103).

193–4 **Tut . . . other where** Romeo describes himself in Petrarchan terms as a lover whose disappointments have robbed him of his self-possession (literally) and therefore of his individuality. Dent compares 'The lover is not where he lives but where he loves' (L565).

193 **Tut** Although *Tut* appears on the first line of B2[r], the catchword on B1[v] reads 'But'. Williams explains how the erroneous catchword might have resulted from a compositorial slip.

lost Daniel and others have emended *lost* to 'left', arguing that the compositor misread *o* for *e*; and they cite the correspondence with Benvolio's 'leave' in l. 192, as well as parallels of phrasing in *Romeo* and other Shakespeare plays. In its Petrarchan context, however, *lost* seems precisely right.

195 **in sadness** seriously (*OED* 2b). Romeo will play on this phrase in his next lines.

is that is it that. A common ellipsis (Abbott 404).

197–8 **Groan . . . will** Each line may seem to lack a metrical beat, yet both allow several possibilities for lengthening words which would make the verse pentameter (see Abbott 481, 484, 487). In addition, the first part of l. 197, *Groan? Why no*, conforms to Abbott's definition of 'the amphibious section' (513): it completes l. 196 as well as its own verse.

198–9 **A sick man . . . so ill** Modern editors, singling out l. 198 as metrically and otherwise defective, frequently emend it according to the reading in either Q1 or F2. As the previous note indicates, however, this line displays no particular metrical anomaly. Moreover, the Q2 text makes sense. Romeo continues to play on *sadness* and *sadly*, locating the pun at the centre of his analogy in these lines: a sick man, foreseeing death, draws up his will in earnest; Romeo also suffers extreme illness; Benvolio shows himself insensitive by forcing the morbid word *sadness* on Romeo. Finally, Romeo ends this couplet with a fillip of rhetoric—antistasis and diacope—on the term *ill*.

200 **In sadness** A triple pun: he loves in earnest, with steadfastness (*OED* 4), and mournfully.

201 **aimed so near** i.e. guessed as much (*OED v.* 3). The verb *aim* usually denotes projection of a missile towards a target,

ROMEO
A right good markman, and she's fair I love.
BENVOLIO
A right fair mark, fair coz, is soonest hit.
ROMEO
Well, in that hit you miss: she'll not be hit
With Cupid's arrow, she hath Dian's wit;
And in strong proof of chastity well armed,
From love's weak childish bow she lives uncharmed.
She will not stay the siege of loving terms,
Nor bide th'encounter of assailing eyes,
Nor ope her lap to saint-seducing gold.
O she is rich, in beauty only poor,
That when she dies, with beauty dies her store.

207 uncharmed| Q2; vnharm'd Q1 211 rich, in beauty‸| Q2; ~‸ ~, Q1, Q3

the meaning which prompts Romeo's subsequent wordplay.

202 **markman** marksman

203 **fair mark . . . hit** This triplet begins with a bawdy pun (*mark* = vulva, *hit* = copulated with; cf. *L.L.L.* 4.1.117–31) phrased in rhetorical terms (*fair mark, fair coz* = diacope).

204 **in that hit . . . not be hit** Quibbling with the proverb 'To miss his mark (aim)' (Tilley M669).

204–9 **she'll not be hit . . . assailing eyes** In *Dream* 2.1.155–64, Oberon delivers a more elaborate version of the contention between Cupid and 'a fair vestal', a conceit usually held to compliment Queen Elizabeth.

205 **Dian's wit** The goddess Diana, patroness of virginity and hunting, has not only the prudence and acumen but also the skill (*OED sb.* 5b) to avoid the arrows of love.

206 **proof** armour of tried strength. The conceit seems to change from hunting to battle, referring to the commonplace equation of love and war (cf. ll. 165–6 and n.).

207 **weak childish bow** Romeo deflates Cupid's well-known attributes as a beautiful young boy and transfers them to his bow, which nevertheless remains threatening.

uncharmed Many editors since Pope have adopted Q1's 'unharmed', although some defend *uncharmed* as appropriate to Cupid's powers of enchantment and the lady's resistance to his spells. In addition, *uncharmed* means 'unsubdued' and 'unenthralled', suiting the military conceit which continues until l. 209.

208–9 **stay the siege . . . bide th'encounter** *Stay* and *bide* both mean 'abide' in the obsolete sense of 'endure' or 'bear' (*OED*, *abide*, *v.* 16); *encounter* carries not only its negative sense of meeting in conflict but also its neutral one of meeting face to face.

209 **assailing eyes** The metaphor turns the eyes, traditionally a source of love, into a hostile, attacking force.

210 **ope her lap . . . gold** Glancing at the myth of Danaë, confined in a bronze tower by her father, Alcestis, King of Argos, to prevent her from bearing a child prophesied to kill him. Despite these precautions, Jove visited her as or in a shower of gold, impregnating her with Perseus. Clearly Romeo means to enhance the description of his beloved, but unwittingly his diction emphasizes the myth's political content in unflattering terms: he begins the allusion with a bawdy image (*lap* = vulva or vagina) and ends it with a commercial one.

211–12 **she is rich . . . dies her store** The couplet incorporates rhetoric (antitheses, diacope) to express a theme which occupies Shakespeare's first seventeen sonnets: the beautiful person who does not produce offspring forfeits immortality.

BENVOLIO

Then she hath sworn that she will still live chaste?

ROMEO

She hath, and in that sparing makes huge waste:
For beauty, starved with her severity,
Cuts beauty off from all posterity.
She is too fair, too wise, wisely too fair,
To merit bliss by making me despair.
She hath forsworn to love, and in that vow
Do I live dead, that live to tell it now.

BENVOLIO

Be ruled by me; forget to think of her.

ROMEO

O, teach me how I should forget to think!

BENVOLIO

By giving liberty unto thine eyes;
Examine other beauties.

214 makes] Q4; make Q2

211 **rich, . . . poor,** Q2's punctuation emphasizes the pun *beauty*/booty; editors usually place the comma after *beauty* and do not punctuate after *poor*.

212 **store** stock for future use, as well as abundance and treasure (*OED sb.* 1a, 6a). Consequently it fits the theme of procreation, the praise of beauty, and the material subtext of these lines.

213 **still** always

214 **in that sparing . . . waste** i.e. in her economy she proves enormously wasteful (cf. Sonnet 1.12). Antitheses and paradox in this reply contradict the adage that 'Sparing is the first gaining (getting)' (Tilley S712); wordplay (*waste*/waist) adds an image of pregnancy which blurs the meaning.

215–16 **For beauty, starved . . . posterity** Another rhetorical couplet (with a feminine rhyme) expresses the sonnet theme which appeared in ll. 211–12.

215 **starved . . . severity** This alliterative phrase suits the motif of ruinous housewifery ('dies her store', 'in that sparing makes huge waste'), suggesting that the lady deprives beauty of nourishment with her rigour. At the same time it belongs to the Petrarchan lexicon of this passage as it describes the lady's intractability and its disastrous effects ('starve' also means 'cause to die', 'destroy', *OED v.* 6a).

217 **too fair . . . too fair** Romeo opens a new couplet with wordplay on *fair* (punning on the familiar denotations of beauty and justice) and with rhetorical flourish in the manner of l. 178.

218 **merit bliss . . . despair** Alliteration, consonance, and assonance emphasize the antithesis: the beloved earns her salvation (with her vow of chastity) even as she causes Romeo to commit the deadliest sin and to risk losing his. This description of the lady in religious terms had become a convention of Elizabethan amatory verse; and Romeo's despair originated with disappointment in this world rather than loss of faith in the next.

221–2 **forget to think . . . forget to think** The latest series of couplets ended at l. 220; these lines connect through what Booth calls 'rhetorically unclassified word plays' (p. 203).

223 **giving liberty . . . thine eyes** Benvolio directs Romeo to free his eyes in particular, because they were held to engender love (as in l. 209). He imitates Romeo's figures of speech with the word *liberty*, which has a religious usage: 'freedom from the bondage of sin' (*OED sb.*[1] 1b; cf. l. 218 and n.).

ROMEO 'Tis the way
To call hers, exquisite, in question more;
These happy masks that kiss fair ladies' brows,
Being black, puts us in mind they hide the fair.
He that is strucken blind cannot forget
The precious treasure of his eyesight lost;
Show me a mistress that is passing fair,
What doth her beauty serve but as a note
Where I may read who passed that passing fair?
Farewell, thou canst not teach me to forget.

BENVOLIO
I'll pay that doctrine, or else die in debt. *Exeunt*

1.2 *Enter Capulet, the County Paris, and a Serving-man*

CAPULET
But Montague is bound as well as I,
In penalty alike, and 'tis not hard, I think,
For men so old as we to keep the peace.

229 The] Q2 (*text and corrected c. w.*); (*Ie* Q2 (*uncorrected c. w.*)
1.2.0.1 *a Serving-man*] ROWE (*a Servant.*); *the Clowne.* Q2; *not in* Q1

225 **call . . . question** By telling Romeo that he should 'forget to think of her' and 'examine other beauties', Benvolio suggests rational means for controlling love. Romeo answers in the same terms: to *call in question* means 'to examine'.

226–32 **happy masks . . . passing fair** Romeo supports the rather simple contention in ll. 224–5 with three rather simple analogies, the third in essence a restatement of his general point. Dent compares the rhetorically phrased idea in ll. 226–7 with 'Black best sets forth white' (B435); and he questions whether the next lines may be connected with another adage, 'The worth of a thing is best known by the want' (W924).

228 **strucken** struck. Abbott calls this form irregular (344); nevertheless, Shakespeare used it nine times in various works (e.g. *Errors* 1.2.45, *L.L.L.* 4.3.222, *Lucrece* 217).

230 **passing** surpassingly

231 **What** i.e. for what (Abbott 253)
note Since a note assists the memory, Romeo continues to argue that he cannot forget his lady.

234 **pay . . . debt** As *doctrine* means 'lesson' or 'instruction' here, *pay* denotes 'give' in the sense of 'teach'. With the second part of the line Benvolio quibbles on the more familiar definition, 'satisfy a creditor'; he also plays on *debt*, pronounced like 'death' in Elizabethan English (Dent compares 'I will not die in your debt' (D165)). His vow may derive from a proverb, 'He that means to pay gives good security' (Tilley S199), although the first citation appears in Cotgrave. In any case, Benvolio offers his life as security for his promise to teach Romeo this lesson.

1.2 This scene transfers an event from the last third of the source narrative—negotiations for Juliet's marriage to Paris—to the beginning of the play. It adds a substantial amount of new material, some comic; and it makes a transition, along with the next scene, to a more low-key and domestic world than the complex public setting where the action began.

0.1 **County** Count, a title of nobility in some European countries, equivalent to the English 'Earl' (cf. 3.4.12 and 21; not noted later).
Serving-man Q2's direction identifies

PARIS

Of honourable reckoning are you both,
And pity 'tis you lived at odds so long.
But now, my lord, what say you to my suit?

CAPULET

But saying o'er what I have said before:
My child is yet a stranger in the world,
She hath not seen the change of fourteen years;
Let two more summers wither in their pride
Ere we may think her ripe to be a bride.

PARIS

Younger than she are happy mothers made.

CAPULET

And too soon marred are those so early made.

him as '*the Clowne*'; speech-prefixes from l. 38 distinguish him as a serving-man. *Clown* indicates not only his position in Capulet's household but also his lack of education, anticipating his illiteracy later in the scene. It may also suggest that a comic actor was to perform this part. Melchiori assumes that one man played the clown in various 'reincarnations' as Samson, this serving-man, a serving-man who appears later (1.3, 1.4, 4.2, and 4.4), and the Nurse's man Peter ('Peter, Balthasar, and Shakespeare's Art of Doubling', 782). Since the mid nineteenth century, many productions have identified this serving-man as Peter.

1 **bound** under legal obligation (to keep the peace)

2 **In penalty alike** with the same liability for punishment if stated conditions are violated (*OED*, *penalty*, 2d). Since 1.1 the Prince has stipulated equivalent terms for Capulet and Montague.

4 **reckoning** 'estimation' or 'repute' (*OED vbl. sb.* 8); but *reckoning* in the first place denotes estimating in a broader sense of calculation. As Gibbons points out, *at odds* in l. 5 reinforces the wordplay: it signifies 'in dissension' on one level and 'unequal' (*sb.* 2a) on another. In Paris's compliment, therefore, *reckoning* may apply to the ages and ranks of both elderly men, and perhaps to their financial positions as well.

6 **my lord** Paris addresses Capulet as if the householder were a nobleman below the rank of a duke.

9 **change** passage (usually associated with phases of the moon)

fourteen years Shakespeare makes Juliet two years younger and even more vulnerable than her youngest predecessor in Brooke ('Scarce saw she yet full sixteen years: too young to be a bride' (1860)), alterations emphasized by the next two lines.

10 **summers . . . pride** Capulet describes *summers* (= years) as if they were the crops that ripen during that season, and in the next line transfers the imagery to Juliet. The figure works especially well because *pride* means not only 'prime' or 'flower', but 'sexual desire', '"heat"', particularly in females (*OED sb.*[1] 11). At the same time Capulet suggests that events are taking place during the warmest part of the year, corroborated when the Nurse establishes Juliet's birthday, in 'A fortnight and odd days', as 31 July (1.3.15–19). His line begins a series of couplets.

12 **Younger . . . made** Capulet's Wife will echo both content and syntax at 1.3.71–3.

13 **soon marred . . . made** Playing on a familiar proverb, 'Marrying is marring' (Dent M701). (Dent also compares 'To make or (and) mar' (M48).) As well, Capulet seems to pun on the familiar jingle *marred* ('married')/*made* ('maid').

Earth hath swallowed all my hopes but she;
She's the hopeful lady of my earth.
But woo her, gentle Paris, get her heart,
My will to her consent is but a part;
And she agreed, within her scope of choice
Lies my consent and fair according voice.
This night I hold an old-accustomed feast,
Whereto I have invited many a guest,
Such as I love; and you among the store,
One more, most welcome, makes my number more.
At my poor house look to behold this night
Earth-treading stars that make dark heaven light.

18 agreed | Q2; agree Q3

14–15 **Earth . . . earth** Among editors Williams argues most persuasively for omitting these redundant, unrhymed verses of nine beats each. He believes they represent two versions of a line which Shakespeare finally rejected and marked inadequately for deletion. Prompt books show no consensus on the treatment of these lines in production, but a case can be made for retaining them. Capulet will continue to speak repetitive and metrically irregular passages; he does not rhyme consistently in this scene. Here his repetition has the rhetorical authority of antimetabole, a device of conversion which reiterates words in converse order to emphasize and sharpen their meaning (Sister Miriam Joseph, p. 305). Moreover, the repeated terms contribute to wordplay: *earth* = ground, place of burial (*OED sb.*[1] 3), soil suited for cultivation, and the body; *hopes* = persons in whom hopes are centred (presumably Capulet's other offspring) and pieces of enclosed land (*sb.*[2] 1); *hopeful* = promising; and *lady of my earth* = *fille de terre* or heiress (Steevens). The language of property and inheritance, subjects at the heart of this conversation, also fits the metaphoric context of the passage with its allusions to the cycles of seasons, plants, and human life.

17 **will** This line may suggest *will* as both disposition and document.

to her consent i.e. in relation *to her consent* (Onions; see also *OED*, *to*, *prep.* 8c). The next two lines suggest that Capulet views Juliet's *consent* or decision as a whole of which his *consent* is only a part or contributing element.

18 **agreed** agreeing (Abbott 374)

scope Referring to Juliet's opportunity for exercising choice, but with connotations of literal space or land (*OED sb.*[2] 10) which suit Capulet's imagery.

20 **This night . . . feast** Only this version of the Romeo and Juliet story places the Capulet feast in high summer close to Lammas (see 1.3.16 and n.): the earliest novellas make no seasonal references; Brooke and Painter set the festivities at Christmas. According to Laroque, the Lammas festival was not rich in festive tradition: it was secular, 'a temporal landmark' (pp. 141–2); but see 1.3.16 n. The playwright's new arrangement of the calendar recasts all parts of the narrative.

old-accustomed *OED old*, E. 1c cites *old-accustomed* here as an example of *old* functioning adverbially (= of old, long) with a past participle.

22 **the store** i.e. this treasured group of people (*OED sb.* 3, 6a)

24 **my poor house** Understatement of his household becomes one of Capulet's character notes (cf. ll. 32–3, 1.4.235, 3.4.23).

25 **Earth-treading stars . . . light** Capulet's flattering conceit combines the earth imagery that he has just used with conventions of Elizabethan love-poetry: antithesis, hyperbole, and celestial images.

Such comfort as do lusty young men feel
When well-apparelled April on the heel
Of limping winter treads, even such delight
Among fresh fennel buds shall you this night
Inherit at my house. Hear all, all see,
And like her most whose merit most shall be;
Which one more view, of many, mine being one,
May stand in number, though in reck'ning none.
Come, go with me.
(*To Serving-man*) Go, sirrah, trudge about,
Through fair Verona, find those persons out

28 limping] Q2; lumping Q1 29 fennel] Q2; female Q1 32 Which one more] Q2; Which on more Q4; Such amongst Q1; On which more CAPELL 34 (*To Serving-man*)] STAUNTON (*following* Capell); *not in* Q

26 **comfort** means not only 'delight' (*OED sb.* 3) but 'physical refreshment' (2); it enhances the sensuality of the comparison which follows between the pleasure of lusty young men in spring and that of Paris at this night's festivities.

27–8 **When well-apparelled April . . . treads** Editors often compare Shakespeare's Sonnet 98.2–3: 'When proud-pied April, dressed in all his trim, | Hath put a spirit of youth in everything'. Like the Sonnet, Capulet personifies April, adding to his seasonal references with this picture of a dapper spring as it hustles out a faltering winter. The two vivid allusions to 'treading' within four lines suggest that he anticipates with pleasure the dancing of his young guests.

29 **fennel** Many editors prefer Q1's 'female', Gibbons and Jowett noting that a compositor could have misread the minims in the spelling 'femelle'. A minority defend *fennel*, citing literary parallels which connect the plant with love, weddings, and brides (e.g. Lyly's *Sapho and Phao* (1584) 2.4.61, Drayton's *Poly-Olbion* (1613), Song 15.191–8). As a metaphor for young women, *fennel* suits a character and a play that frequently combine lyrical with domestic images. *Fennel* is a fragrant, perennial herb with yellow flowers grown for use in cooking sauces; the bulb may be eaten. It provides the ideal seasoning for a speech preoccupied by cycles of nature, the loveliness of youth, and a celebratory feast.

30 **Inherit** *Inherit* here means 'have' or 'receive' (*OED v.* 3), but probably retains connotations of 'inheritance' and 'heir'. Capulet seems to have marriage arrangements on his mind.

32–3 **Which . . . none** This couplet, which baffled even Johnson, has been cut in many productions (some omitting the whole passage from ll. 24 to 33). To make it intelligible, recent editors have adopted Q4's 'on more view', and they identify the proverb 'One is no number' (Dent O54), which informs the lines and appears as well in Sonnet 136.8. The resulting paraphrase interprets the passage to mean that Paris, on a more thorough inspection of the group that includes Capulet's daughter, will be able to judge her among the rest; and he may or may not find that she holds her own (cf. Brooke 195–6). With the Q2 reading—and on the assumption that *one* is not an alternative spelling of 'on'—the text preserves the effect of diacope which Capulet has been using in the speech. The lines permit a similar paraphrase, perhaps with more emphasis on Paris's impressions (*one more view*) and his decision (*reck'ning* means not only the 'result of counting' but also the 'mode of regarding a matter' (*OED vbl. sb.* 7a)). However the couplet is understood, it seems that rhetoric and wordplay have confounded meaning: the lines may not represent the author's final thoughts.

33 **none** In Q1 and some productions, the Serving-man enters the scene now.

34 **sirrah** Term of address to a social inferior. **trudge** 'an undignified equivalent of "walk"' (*OED v.*[1] 1a)

Whose names are written there, and to them say,
My house and welcome on their pleasure stay.
Exeunt Capulet and Paris

SERVING-MAN Find them out whose names are written here. It is written that the shoemaker should meddle with his yard and the tailor with his last, the fisher with his pencil and the painter with his nets. But I am sent to find those persons whose names are here writ, and can never find what names the writing person hath here writ—I must to the learned—in good time.

Enter Benvolio and Romeo

BENVOLIO
Tut, man, one fire burns out another's burning,
One pain is lessened by another's anguish;
Turn giddy and be holp by backward turning;
One desperate grief cures with another's languish.
Take thou some new infection to thy eye,
And the rank poison of the old will die.

36 there] Q2; here Q1   37.1 *Exeunt . . . Paris*] ROWE; *Exit.* Q2   38–9 written‸ here.] Q1 (~‸ ~, *adding* 'and yet I knowe not who are written here'); written. Here‸ Q2   48 One] Q2 (On)

36 **Whose names . . . there** This may be a cue for Capulet to hand the Serving-man the invitation list which Romeo will read at 64.1, although the gesture can occur as early as l. 34.

37 **on . . . stay** attend on (*OED v.*[1] 16a)

39–42 **It . . . writ** The Serving-man's prose parodies high-flown elements of the play's style through its figures of repetition and its recasting of Lyly's euphuism: 'The shoemaker must not go above his latchet, nor the hedger meddle with anything but his bill. It is unseemly for the painter to feather a shaft, or the fletcher to handle the pencil. All which things make most against me, in that a fool hath intruded himself to discourse of wit' (*Euphues. The Anatomy of Wit* (1578), i. 180). According to M. P. Tilley, the speech may also parody *Euphues* itself (*MLN* 41 (1926), 1–8). In addition, the bawdy quibbles on *meddle*, *yard*, and *pencil* echo the indecent puns of Samson and Gregory as they deflate fancier wordplay in the verse: *meddle* = masturbate and/or copulate; *yard* = penis (usually implying an erection); *pencil* = penis.

39 **meddle** busy himself (*OED v.* 8a)

41 **pencil** paint-brush (*OED sb.* 1a)

44 **in good time** (a) quickly, (b) in the nick of time (*OED sb.* 46c). As Benvolio and Romeo approach, the Serving-man sums up his problem and recognizes its solution in the same phrase.

45–50 **Tut . . . die** Still discussing Romeo's love-melancholy, Benvolio speaks a sestet of aphorisms inspired by Brooke's narrator (203–10; see also 219, 221–2), who stresses that new love drives out old; Benvolio emphasizes that new pain or discomfort expels earlier versions (Dent F277, G446; cf. P457, P456.1). During their exchanges Romeo and Benvolio express impatience (*Tut*) with each other's point of view (cf. 1.1.193, 1.2.97).

46 **another's anguish** i.e. the suffering of another pain (Abbott 88)

47 **holp** helped (Abbott 343)
backward turning i.e. turning in the reverse direction

48 **another's languish** i.e. the languishing for another grief (cf. l. 46 and n.)

49–50 **Take . . . die** Benvolio's sestet has consistently used the conventional poetic terms for a lover's suffering: the quatrain refers to burning passion, anguish, and

ROMEO
Your plantain leaf is excellent for that.
BENVOLIO For what, I pray thee?
ROMEO For your broken shin.
BENVOLIO Why, Romeo, art thou mad?
ROMEO
Not mad, but bound more than a madman is:
Shut up in prison, kept without my food,
Whipped and tormented, and—Good e'en, good fellow.
SERVING-MAN
God gi' good e'en. I pray, sir, can you read?
ROMEO
Ay, mine own fortune in my misery.
SERVING-MAN Perhaps you have learned it without book.
But I pray, can you read anything you see?

disorientation; the couplet focuses on the sensation of noxious disease. In closing Benvolio applies the latter metaphor to the eyes, a traditional source of love, making them a source of pain (cf. Romeo at 1.1.209).

51 **plantain leaf . . . that** Romeo refers to the leaf of a herb used to treat minor injuries. As Benvolio's response indicates, the antecedent of *that* is not yet clear.

52–1.3.36 **For . . . trudge** Hereabout Q2 begins to reprint Q1 for over eighty lines. The exact limits of the passage may be impossible to fix. This edition follows Williams, p. 105. (See Introduction, p. 116 and n.)

53 **For . . . shin** The reply probably carries more than its literal sense. In a note on *L.L.L.* 3.1.67 (Oxford, 1990)—part of another dialogue connecting plantain leaves and a broken shin—G. R. Hibbard explains that '"to break one's shins" was a common expression (Dent S342.1)' which may have meant 'to suffer a disappointment in love'. Romeo seems to dismiss Benvolio's list of love-cures with mocking wit: Benvolio has prescribed common remedies for Romeo's uncommon distress. As the next line shows, Benvolio misses—or pretends to miss—the point.

55–7 **Not mad . . . good fellow** Romeo makes a hasty distinction between literal and literary madness, then devotes a few lines to the second kind. Elaborating a conceit of love as madness (cf. 1.1.189), he describes himself as a victim suffering in the Petrarchan mode—a sense of entrapment and isolation, lack of appetite, intense emotional pain—with terms borrowed from the treatment of madness in the Elizabethan period. At the same time he starts to build a rhetorical construction. When he greets the Serving-man in l. 57, he quits the project abruptly.

57 **Good e'en** A salutation used any time after noon (*OED*).

58 **God gi' good e'en** Another form of the salutation 'good even' in a version of the phrase 'God give you good even' (Q2 reads 'Godgigoden').

59 **Ay . . . misery** Romeo makes his first (ironic) reference to his unhappy fate in an obvious pun, as he answers the Serving-man through the idiom of the unrequited lover.

60 **without book** Literally, 'without the aid of a book, from memory, by rote, by ear'; Dent cites 'To speak without book' (B532). This is the first of several direct and figurative references to books.

61 **can you read . . . see?** The Serving-man defines *read* precisely as 'construing words from a written document', and the pun in l. 59 prompts him to ask if Romeo has mastered this process. (Early texts may have printed ll. 60–1 as verse because these lines are surrounded by verse. Even the Serving-man's greeting at l. 58 scans as a blank verse line.)

ROMEO
Ay, if I know the letters and the language.

SERVING-MAN Ye say honestly, rest you merry.

ROMEO Stay, fellow, I can read.

He reads the letter

'Signor Martino and his wife and daughters;
County Anselme and his beauteous sisters;
The lady widow of Utruvio;
Signor Placentio and his lovely nieces;
Mercutio and his brother Valentine;
Mine uncle Capulet, his wife and daughters;
My fair niece Rosaline, and Livia;
Signor Valentio and his cousin Tybalt;
Lucio and the lively Helena.'
A fair assembly. Whither should they come?

66 County Anselme] Q; Countie Anselmo DYCE 1864–7 (*conj.* Capell); *The Countie* Anselme WILLIAMS 67 Utruvio] Q; Vitruuio F3 71 and Livia] Q1; Liuia Q2

63 **Ye . . . merry** Apparently the trace of a condition ('if') in the previous statement persuades the Serving-man that Romeo cannot read. As the Serving-man starts to leave (see l. 64), his farewell creates the effect of an oxymoron: he wishes the melancholy lover continued mirth. (He will repeat this farewell when he leaves for good at l. 84.)

64.1 ***letter*** This direction calls for the property which represents 'something written' (*OED sb.*[1] 3a), i.e. Capulet's invitation list (l. 36).

65–73 **Signor . . . Helena** Early texts print these lines as prose, but many editors since Dyce (conj. Capell) treat them as verse because they scan and because their authority is Q1. Perhaps the Q1 compositor erred to save space on signatures B3[r] and B3[v]; possibly the playwright had not made up his mind. In any case, this is one of those passages which can be heard as either verse or prose. This edition prefers the rhythms of blank verse.

66 **Anselme** Some editors who print the letter as verse emend this line to make it scan as iambic rather than trochaic pentameter. All but one read *Anselme* as trisyllabic: 'Anselmo'. (As Wilson–Duthie point out, *Anselme* is the name Bandello and Painter give Friar John, a fact which seems to justify Italian pronunciation.) Williams adds 'The' before *County*, a construction found ten times later in the play.

67 **Utruvio** The name in the quartos is evidently as uncommon as that printed in F3. Williams reports that Hosley found *Utruvio* in two plays by Davenant for the King's Men (1627, 1629); McKerrow's unsuccessful search for 'Vitruvio' turned up only the Italian form of 'Vitruvius', the classical architect. Lacking reliable authority, this edition opts for the unemended form.

69 **Mercutio** The first reference to *Mercutio*, in Capulet's list of 'Such as I love'.

70 **Mine uncle Capulet** Probably anticipates cousin (= kinsman) Capulet in 1.4.

71 **My fair niece Rosaline** At l. 86 Benvolio will identify *Rosaline* as Romeo's beloved, a Capulet whom her cousin Juliet will soon displace.

and The Q2 compositor seems to have missed this word in Q1, where it is the last word of signature B3[r].

72 **his cousin Tybalt** i.e. 'The fiery *Tybalt*' first named by Benvolio at 1.1.105. Later, dialogue between Capulet and *Tybalt* (1.4.173–4) will reveal *Tybalt* as Capulet's nephew.

74 **A fair assembly** The list indicates approximately two dozen guests, an illusion created through staging (see 1.4.112–13 n.).

74–5 **Whither . . . come? . . . Up.** The Serving-man responds more to Romeo's

SERVING-MAN Up.

ROMEO Whither to supper?

SERVING-MAN To our house.

ROMEO Whose house?

SERVING-MAN My master's.

ROMEO

Indeed, I should have asked you that before.

SERVING-MAN Now I'll tell you without asking. My master is the great rich Capulet, and if you be not of the house of Montagues, I pray come and crush a cup of wine. Rest you merry. *Exit*

BENVOLIO

At this same ancient feast of Capulet's
Sups the fair Rosaline, whom thou so loves,
With all the admirèd beauties of Verona.

76–7 Whither . . . To] Q2, Q1 (Whether); Whither? to supper? | *Ser*. To F; Whither? | *Ser<vant>*. To Supper, to THEOBALD (*conj*. Warburton); Whither? | *Ser<vant>*. To CAPELL 80 you] Q2; thee Q1 84 *Exit*] F; *not in* Q

phrasing than to his question. The resulting expression, *come up*, may refer to Capulet's house not simply as a location but as an indicator of social rank (see *OED v*. 74a, f, and cf. ll. 81–2). Gibbons finds different wordplay in *come up*, as in 'marry come up' or 'hoity-toity' (cf. 2.4.61 and n.); but this Serving-man does not seem capable of deliberate puns.

75–9 **Up . . . master's** The stichomythic exchange in fourteen beats is cadenced, but does not make up a conventional verse line.

76–7 **Whither . . . house** Editors have rearranged these lines, changing words and punctuation. Most follow F, adding a question mark after *Whither*. Among those who emend, Theobald (conj. Warburton) transfers *to supper* to the Serving-man at l. 77; Williams, following Capell, omits *to supper* as a corruption in Q1 anticipating Benvolio's 'Sups the fair Rosaline' (l. 86). This edition follows Q2 because the lines make sense in this form. Since the Serving-man's response has not answered Romeo's query, Romeo rephrases the question: 'To what place for supper?', i.e. 'for the meal which occasions this social gathering?' (see *OED*, *supper*, *sb*.[1] 1a). Moreover, the dialogue neatly reverses the pattern of exchange between the Serving-man and Romeo before the latter's reading of the invitation list: now Romeo asks the questions, still not grasping the Serving-man's particular kind of literalism.

80 **you** Some recent editors adopt Q1's 'thee' appropriate for addressing a servant, but the pronouns were used inconsistently (Abbott 231, 232). Since *you* could indicate a speaker's dissatisfaction with an inferior, it might hint Romeo's impatience.

82 **great rich Capulet** The word *great* works as both adjective and adverb (see *OED adv*. 1).

83 **crush** drink, quaff (*OED v*. 7 compares 'crack', *v*. 10)

85 **ancient** i.e. long-established (cf. 'old-accustomed' in l. 20)

86 **the fair Rosaline** In the earlier narratives this object of Romeo's infatuation remains anonymous. Shakespeare, inventing the list of guests and Benvolio's use of it, provides a euphonious name with floral and romantic associations. In *L.L.L.* and *As You Like It* the name *Rosaline/Rosalind* is attached to witty heroines.

loves loveth. Evans, citing Franz 152, identifies this syncopated form of the second person singular, present tense.

Go thither, and with unattainted eye
Compare her face with some that I shall show,
And I will make thee think thy swan a crow.

ROMEO

When the devout religion of mine eye
　　Maintains such falsehood, then turn tears to fire;
And these who, often drowned, could never die,
　　Transparent heretics be burnt for liars.
One fairer than my love, the all-seeing sun
Ne'er saw her match since first the world begun.

92 fire] Q; fires POPE　　95 love,] Q2, Q1; ~? Q3; ~: F

88 **unattainted** i.e. uninfected (*OED ppl. a.*, first illustration). Benvolio reworks his metaphor from ll. 49–50, the cured eye representing objectivity.

90 **make . . . crow** Dent compares 'To make a swan a crow' (S1028.1).

91 **devout religion . . . eye** Romeo picks up Benvolio's metaphoric *eye* from l. 88, making it part of the rhyme scheme in the following sestet and recasting it in a different set of conventional Petrarchan terms which describe amatory as religious devotion. In 1.1. Romeo portrayed his lady through religious phrases incidentally (e.g. 'saint-seducing gold', l. 210). At this point his quatrain, full of hyperbole, elaborates a full-blown conceit expressing his adoration of a woman as worship of a divinity. *OED* 6a cites as the first example of *religion* in its transferred sense, meaning 'strict fidelity or faithfulness; conscientiousness; pious affection or attachment'.

92 **Maintains such falsehood** The verb functions in its obsolete 'bad sense' (*OED v.* 12b), meaning 'supports' or 'countenances' an object (*falsehood*) connected with wrongdoing or wickedness. In keeping with the religious conceit, there seems to be wordplay on *falsehood* as 'faithlessness' (1) and 'untrue doctrine', as well as 'deception' (3) and its still familiar definitions.

turn tears to fire i.e. let tears turn to fire (see Abbott 364 for the subjunctive used imperatively). The verb of transformation echoes Benvolio's phrasing in l. 47. When his eyes commit such blasphemy, Romeo claims, his tears (the element of water and sign of his grief) should change to fire (the element of combustion and emblem of passion). Many editors emend *fire* to 'fires', following Pope and creating a perfect rhyme with *liars* in l. 94. As Williams (citing Munro) admits, however, Elizabethan poetry contains many rhymes between words with and without a final *s*.

93 **these . . . die** A paradox sketched emphatically (with alliteration): *these* refers to Romeo's eyes, literally as the organs of tears, figuratively as religious traitors; and each verb relates to both of these senses. At the literal level, his eyes do not fail though often overwhelmed with tears of sorrow. At the figurative level, the religious traitors keep resurfacing like unsuccessful candidates in the submersion test for heresy. Spencer, who first identified this allusion, explains that staying afloat confirmed the suspected person's league with the devil.

94 **Transparent . . . liars** The conceit ends, shifting focus to its figurative level (the proven traitors suffer death by fire) and playing on *transparent*: (a) transmitting light (the eyes), (b) easily seen through (the traitors; *OED* 2b cites as first illustration and compares 'apparent' 3).

95–6 **One . . . begun** The Q2/Q1 comma after *love* allows more than one interpretation: editors read *One fairer than my love* as a rhetorical question or exclamation, but it also works as another object of the verb. As subject, the personified *sun* returns (cf. 1.1.114–15, 130–2) to authorize Romeo's estimation of his mistress's beauty.

96 **begun** began (Abbott 339)

BENVOLIO

Tut, you saw her fair, none else being by,
Herself poised with herself in either eye;
But in that crystal scales let there be weighed
Your lady's love against some other maid
That I will show you shining at this feast,
And she shall scant show well that now seems best.

ROMEO

I'll go along no such sight to be shown,
But to rejoice in splendour of mine own. *Exeunt*

1.3 *Enter Capulet's Wife and the Nurse*

CAPULET'S WIFE

Nurse, where's my daughter? Call her forth to me.

NURSE

Now by my maidenhead at twelve year old,

104 *Exeunt*] POPE; *not in* Q

97–102 **Tut . . . best** Benvolio answers with couplets deflating Romeo's hyperbole by ignoring his reference to the sun; he produces yet another conceit from eye imagery.

98 **Herself poised . . . eye** The conceit of eyes as weighing-instruments begins here.

99 **that crystal scales** *OED* cites as a rare sixteenth-century example of plural *scales* construed as singular (*sb.*[1] 3a). Since the demonstrative adjective *that* was still used with plural substantives (1c), the phrase would have sounded correct however *scales* was understood. *Crystal*, an emblem of transparency associated with water and eyes, echoes Romeo's image in l. 94.

100 **Your lady's love . . . maid** This line allows more than one reading, although Benvolio's point is clear: Romeo should take a balanced view of Rosaline by comparing her with other beautiful young women. Theobald changed *lady's love* to 'lady-love' in order to make both terms of the comparison alike; however, *OED* cites his emendation as the first instance of this compound word. As Evans suggests, ellipsis of the possessive inflexion (i.e. 'maid's') would also permit equalizing of terms.

101 **shining** Cf. Capulet's expectations of 'Earth-treading stars' at l. 25.

1.3 This invented scene derives from two passages in Brooke connected with different events: in one the narrator describes and quotes the 'prating nurse' as she tells Romeus about Juliet's childhood (651–66) and exemplifies the proverb 'A nurse's tongue is privileged to talk' (Dent N355); in the other Capulet's wife commends Paris to Juliet after Romeo's banishment (1893–8). Q1 sets as prose except for l. 1, the equivalents of ll. 95–6 (which rhyme), and a few single lines that may be read as verse or prose. Q2, which has a longer version, prints it similarly until l. 64, after which it clearly indicates verse passages. Although the distinction between prose and verse is difficult, most editors since Capell have arranged the women's lines as verse. This edition presents them as verse to emphasize the rhythmic experimentation in the scene, particularly in the Nurse's speeches where 'prose rhythms are counterpointed against a verse structure' (S. Wells, 'Juliet's Nurse: The Uses of Inconsequentiality', *Shakespeare's Styles*, ed. P. Edwards, I.-S. Ewbank, and G. K. Hunter (Cambridge, 1980), repr. in *Critical Essays*, ed. Andrews, pp. 204–5).

2–80 **Now . . . flower** Q2 sets the Nurse's speeches in italics; Q1 uses italics in this scene and in 1.4. For information on the anomaly, see the Introduction, pp. 116–17.

2 **by my maidenhead . . . old** The Nurse swears by her virginity at the age when

I bade her come. What lamb, what ladybird,
God forbid! Where's this girl? What Juliet!

Enter Juliet

JULIET How now, who calls?

NURSE Your mother.

JULIET
Madam, I am here, what is your will?

CAPULET'S WIFE
This is the matter.—Nurse, give leave a while,
We must talk in secret.—Nurse, come back again,
I have remembered me, thou's hear our counsel.
Thou knowest my daughter's of a pretty age.

NURSE
Faith, I can tell her age unto an hour.

CAPULET'S WIFE She's not fourteen.

NURSE I'll lay fourteen of my teeth, and yet to my teen be it spoken, I have but four, she's not fourteen. How long is it now to Lammas-tide?

she remembers it was still intact. (Dent M45.1 indicates that the expletive was commonplace.) In her oath *year* = years, the flexionless plural still represented in dialectal use (see *OED* Forms).

3–4 **ladybird, | God forbid!** *Ladybird* means not only 'sweetheart' (*OED* 2, first illustration) but also, in a slang sense, 'wanton' (Partridge). With *God forbid!* the Nurse may be excusing her faux pas or, in some editors' opinions, making a sudden appeal that no harm delays Juliet. *What* in both lines, an exclamatory word used to summon a person, may also express impatience (Abbott 73a).

8 **give leave** A common expression (Dent L167.1) as a request for privacy.

10 **remembered me** reflected (*OED v.*[1] 5 *refl.* a)

thou's thou shalt (see *OED*, *shall*, *v.* 5 and Abbott 315, 461 for this contraction)

counsel In addition to its still current definitions (e.g. 'deliberation', 'purpose'), *counsel* means 'matter of confidence' and 'conversation' (*OED sb.* 5b, 1b).

11 **of a pretty age** *Pretty* may denote 'fine' in its most general sense or 'good', 'fair', with reference to the degree of Juliet's maturity.

13 **She's not fourteen** Capulet's Wife echoes his reference to Juliet's age (1.2.9). Both scenes emphasize Juliet's youth and the 'matter' of her readiness for serious courtship.

14 **fourteen . . . teen** The Nurse, punning broadly on the suffix of *fourteen* (*teen* = grief), makes a wager that shows her self-confidence. (The next line completes both the wordplay and the bet.) Wells points out that a performer may choose to interpret this 'self-interruption' as 'a conscious playing with "four" and "teen", or rather the subconscious struggle to clear her mind of verbal entanglements' (p. 199).

16 **Lammas-tide** i.e. the time of the harvest festival, observed on 1 August in the early English church, when loaves of bread made from the first crops (of corn or wheat) were consecrated at Mass. B. Everett notes that Lammas retained symbolic associations with both Midsummer Eve and the harvest festival. For an Elizabethan audience it may have suggested the fall that follows the midsummer equinox, as well as 'sacrificial offerings of first-fruits' ('*Romeo and Juliet*: The Nurse's Story', *Critical Quarterly* 14 (1972), 132–3). A. Crunelle-Vanrigh

CAPULET'S WIFE A fortnight and odd days.

NURSE

Even or odd, of all days in the year,
Come Lammas Eve at night shall she be fourteen.
Susan and she—God rest all Christian souls—
Were of an age. Well, Susan is with God;
She was too good for me. But as I said,
On Lammas Eve at night shall she be fourteen,
That shall she, marry, I remember it well.
'Tis since the earthquake now eleven years,
And she was weaned—I never shall forget it—
Of all the days of the year upon that day;
For I had then laid wormwood to my dug,

finds additional symbolism in the season ('"Too Hot, Too Hot": La foudre et le sablier poétique de l'instant dans *Roméo et Juliette*', in *'Roméo et Juliette': Nouvelles perspectives critiques*, ed. J.-M. Maguin and C. Whitworth (Montpellier, 1993), pp. 147–8). See also 1.2.20 n.

17 **A fortnight . . . days** This sets the events of the play in July.

18 **Even or odd** The expression strikes a few of the Nurse's character notes. It indicates that she misinterprets the *odd days* of Capulet's Wife, which meant 'some additional days'. In the Nurse's ambiguous terms, the days may be *even or odd* in number. It implies a slightly impatient generalization because it sounds like 'even and odd', the obsolete expression signifying 'all included, without exception' (*OED*, *even*, *a.* 15c, *odd*, *a.* 2c). And it repeats the notion of wager, since it refers to a game of chance (*even*, *a.* 15d, *odd*, *a.* 2d).

19 **Come Lammas Eve . . . fourteen** i.e. Juliet was born at night on 31 July, and her fourteenth birthday will take place in just over two weeks. (A few editors suggest that Shakespeare chose this month for its etymological link with Juliet's name.) According to Laroque, an Elizabethan audience would have calculated immediately that the likely date of conception was Hallowe'en (the night of 31 October–1 November). Ambivalent traditions associated with Hallowe'en might have led to a connection with Juliet's tragic destiny (p. 205). However fateful its implications, the Nurse's diction is colloquial.

20–2 **Susan . . . me** In its lack of detail this passing reference to *Susan* conveys several impressions at once. It implies that the Capulets already know the Nurse's past. It suggests that the Nurse had a daughter, born at about the same time as Juliet, who has died. With its three pious commonplaces—*God rest all Christian souls*, *Susan is with God*, *She was too good for me*—it may be interpreted as sincere or not. (Dent compares 'Those that God loves . . . do not live long (The good die young)', G251.) Nevertheless it strikes a poignant note, echoing Capulet's reference to his lost hopes at 1.2.14. Finally it emphasizes the strong element of surrogation in the Nurse's bond with Juliet.

22–4 **But . . . well** The Nurse returns to the point with repetition and emphasis, perhaps avoiding interruption to her train of thought by the others—or even by herself. The interjection *marry* (= Mary) is an intensive.

25–6 **since the earthquake . . . weaned** The Nurse's memory travels from one milestone in her life (Juliet's birth on Lammas Eve) to another (her weaning on the day of an *earthquake*). Since Tyrwhitt, some scholars have tried to date the play from earthquakes in England and Italy during the late sixteenth century (see Introduction, 'Date(s)', pp. 99–100).

28–9 **For . . . wall** The sequence of nouns 'helps to create a vivid picture of peaceful normality' which anticipated the violent disruption (Wells, p. 202).

28 **laid wormwood . . . dug** i.e. the Nurse had prepared to wean Juliet that day by applying the plant *wormwood* (*Artemisia*

Sitting in the sun under the dovehouse wall.
My lord and you were then at Mantua—
Nay, I do bear a brain. But as I said,
When it did taste the wormwood on the nipple
Of my dug and felt it bitter, pretty fool,
To see it tetchy and fall out with the dug!
'Shake', quoth the dovehouse; 'twas no need, I trow,
To bid me trudge.
And since that time it is eleven years,
For then she could stand high-lone—nay, by th' rood,

1.3.34 the] Q2; *not in* Q1   37, 48 years] Q2; *yeare* Q1   38 she could] Q2; *could* Iuliet Q1 by th'] Q2 (*byth*); *by the* Q1

absinthium), proverbial for its bitter taste, to her breast. *Dug(s)* occurs only nine times in Shakespeare's works, three in this speech, and is usually connected with animals or women past child-bearing. (On Juliet's late weaning, see Gail Kern Paster's chapter 'Quarreling with the Dug', in *The Body Embarrassed* (Ithaca, NY, 1993).)

29 **dovehouse** dovecote (an image which is auditory as well as visual and harmonizes with the soft sound effects of the line)

30 **My lord and you . . . Mantua** i.e. Juliet's parents were away at this crucial stage of her development. Spencer explains that *Mantua*, where Romeo will go in exile, is the closest town of any size to Verona (about twenty miles away), as Shakespeare could have known from books and travellers (3.3.149n.). In this line the Nurse pronounces the name with three syllables (cf. 3.3.148), although it may also have two (see 3.5.88, 4.1.124).

31 **Nay . . . brain** *Nay* emphasizes the proverbial phrase (Dent B596), which means 'I have brains' (*OED sb.* 4b), and expresses satisfaction with her memory. Nevertheless, the line has inspired interpretations that also find signs of uncertainty in the Nurse's statement about her mental faculties (see Wells, p. 213 n. 4).

But . . . said Cf. ll. 22–4 and n.

33 **felt it bitter** i.e. perceived its bitter taste (*OED v.* 7)

pretty fool A phrase of endearment and perhaps pity (*OED sb.*[1] 1c) repeated at l. 50.

35 **'Shake', quoth the dovehouse** Literally, 'The dovehouse said "Shake" ', but it is not clear what either verb signifies. The personified dovecote, trembling in the earthquake, may be telling the Nurse to move by imperative or example; or the phrase represents words of comfort that might have been spoken to the baby during the upheaval: 'it allows the unfluttered dovecote to satirise the earthquake, as in a comical baby mock-heroic—to be aloof and detached from what is happening to it' (Everett, 135).

35–6 **'twas . . . trudge** The Nurse says emphatically (*I trow*), with alliteration, that she did not have to be told to leave. (*OED*'s definition of *trudge v.*[1] 1a seems to apply: 'Sometimes merely an undignified equivalent of "walk" '.) Again her speech allows more than one interpretation: (a) she required no encouragement to take shelter, (b) the frustrated child Juliet had no call to send the Nurse away (see Spencer; Everett, 135–6; and Paul Fatout, 'A Note on *Romeo and Juliet*', *SAB* 9 (1934), 107–8). The shortness of l. 36 has been attributed to memorial copy for its text (Williams), as well as to Shakespeare's experimentation with the rhythms of blank verse (Wells, pp. 203–5). The passage which Q2 reprinted from Q1 ends here.

38 **high-lone** by herself, without support. *OED* quotes as the first instance of the adverb, 'An alteration of *alone*, of obscure origin. *High* prob. expresses degree or intensity'; Dent refers to 'To go (stand) (a) high-lone' (G157). M. Mack cites evidence that Juliet's learning of motor skills at the age of nearly three would not have struck an Elizabethan audience as unusually late ('Rescuing Shakespeare', International Shakespeare Association Occasional Paper 1 (Oxford, 1979), 10–11).

She could have run and waddled all about;
For even the day before she broke her brow,
And then my husband—God be with his soul,
A was a merry man—took up the child.
'Yea', quoth he, 'dost thou fall upon thy face?
Thou wilt fall backward when thou hast more wit,
Wilt thou not, Jule?' And by my holidam,
The pretty wretch left crying and said 'Ay'.
To see now how a jest shall come about!
I warrant, an I should live a thousand years,
I never should forget it. 'Wilt thou not, Jule?' quoth he,
And pretty fool, it stinted and said 'Ay'.

CAPULET'S WIFE
Enough of this, I pray thee, hold thy peace.

NURSE
Yes, madam, yet I cannot choose but laugh,
To think it should leave crying and say 'Ay';
And yet I warrant it had upon it brow

39 run and] Q2; *not in* Q1 49 Jule] Q2; Iuliet Q1; *Iulet* F

38 **by th' rood** This archaic expression, emphatic and asseverative, means 'by Christ's cross'; it is rare in Shakespeare. The Q2 spelling 'byth' suggests clipped pronunciation.

39 **run and waddled** The Nurse's memory of her own trudging may have reminded her of Juliet's earliest locomotion.

40 **broke her brow** i.e. hurt her forehead. These recollections make it appear that Juliet's weaning was thoroughly traumatic: a fall just the day before and an earthquake during the event.

41 **my husband . . . soul** The Nurse introduces another member of her family with a pious commonplace signifying that he has died.

42 **A** The unemphatic colloquial form of 'he' (Abbott 402).

43–5 **'Yea' . . . 'Wilt thou not, Jule?'** The Nurse quotes her late husband in an idiom that sounds like hers.

44 **fall backward** 'fall, and then lie, on [your] back' (Partridge), i.e. assume the usual female posture for sexual intercourse. The repeated prediction directs attention to the adolescent Juliet, poised at the boundary between innocence and experience.

45 **holidam** holiness. The Nurse uses an early form of 'halidom', which meant 'Our Lady' according to popular etymology (*OED*, *halidom*).

46 **pretty wretch** A playful term of endearment (*wretch* = little creature) which may express pity (cf. 'pretty fool' in l. 33).

47 **how a jest . . . about** how a joke turns out to be true (*OED*, *come*, *v.* 52e, only illustration); i.e. Juliet has now reached the age of 'more wit' and sexual desire.

50 **stinted** stopped (i.e. 'left crying')

51 **Enough . . . peace** This line expresses impatience, yet a performer can play it against its sense to show Capulet's Wife enjoying the comedy (see Wells, p. 203). Dent hears a proverbial echo (P145).

52 **Yes . . . laugh** Coleridge quotes to illustrate the Nurse's 'childlike fondness of repetition in her childish age—and that happy, humble ducking under, yet resurgence against the check' (*Coleridge on Shakespeare*, ed. Terence Hawkes (Harmondsworth, 1969), p. 135).

54 **it brow** its brow. *Its* was not in common use during Shakespeare's time, when *his* still represented the genitive of *it*. 'Occasionally *it*, an early provincial form of the old genitive, is found for *its*, especially

A bump as big as a young cock'rel's stone;
A perilous knock, and it cried bitterly.
'Yea', quoth my husband, 'fall'st upon thy face?
Thou wilt fall backward when thou comest to age,
Wilt thou not, Jule?' It stinted and said 'Ay'.

JULIET

And stint thou too, I pray thee, Nurse, say I.

NURSE

Peace, I have done. God mark thee to his grace,
Thou wast the prettiest babe that e'er I nursed.
An I might live to see thee married once,
I have my wish.

CAPULET'S WIFE

Marry, that marry is the very theme
I came to talk of. Tell me, daughter Juliet,
How stands your dispositions to be married?

JULIET

It is an honour that I dream not of.

NURSE

An honour! Were not I thine only nurse,

68 honour] Q1; houre Q2   69 honour] Q1; *houre* Q2

when a child is mentioned' (Abbott 228; cf. the nurse describing Juliet's chatter in Brooke: 'Lord how it could full prettily have prated with it tongue' (654)).

55 **a young cock'rel's stone** the testicle of a young cock. This phrase compounds bawdiness, since *cock* means 'penis', and *cockerel* not only denotes a young cock, but also applies figuratively to a young man.

56 **perilous** terrible (*OED a.* 2). The unaccented *i* may have been dropped (Abbott 467), so that *perilous* was pronounced 'parlous', its syncopated form.

60 **say I** Juliet plays (inevitably) on 'say "Ay"', the punch line which the Nurse has just delivered four times.

61 **God . . . grace** may God single you out as one of his chosen (*OED v.* 6a)

63–4 **An . . . wish** The irregularity in this conditional syntax—a consequent verb in the present tense which does not match its antecedent—may be purposeful, a device to enhance the vividness of the lines (Abbott 371). On the shortness of l. 64, see ll. 35–6 n.

63 **once** seems to combine still current definitions (e.g. 'one time only', 'even for the first time') with the now rare meaning 'one day' (*OED* 5).

65 **Marry . . . marry** For a moment Capulet's Wife echoes the Nurse's style with an obvious pun and figure of repetition.

67 **How . . . dispositions** how do your feelings incline (see *OED, disposition*, 7a for a sense of the plural form and Abbott 335 for the singular inflexion preceding a plural subject)

68, 69 **honour** Pope emended Q2 'houre' to Q1 *honour*, but Johnson (among few others) printed 'hour': 'I have restored the genuine word, which is more seemly from a girl to her mother'. Although 'hour' makes sense in l. 68, where it reflects 'married once' (l. 63), it hardly accounts for the Nurse's enthusiasm in the next two lines. Editors repeatedly point out that a compositor's error (misreading a tilde or minim, mistaking *no* for *w*) would easily explain 'hour', and Spencer notes that *honour* allows the Nurse another bawdy pun, perhaps unintentional ('on her', see Partridge).

I would say thou hadst sucked wisdom from thy teat.

CAPULET'S WIFE

Well, think of marriage now; younger than you
Here in Verona, ladies of esteem,
Are made already mothers—by my count—
I was your mother much upon these years
That you are now a maid. Thus, then, in brief:
The valiant Paris seeks you for his love.

NURSE

A man, young lady, lady, such a man
As all the world—why, he's a man of wax.

CAPULET'S WIFE

Verona's summer hath not such a flower.

NURSE

Nay, he's a flower, in faith, a very flower.

CAPULET'S WIFE

What say you, can you love the gentleman?

73 mothers—by my count—] This edition; ~‸ by ~ ~. Q2; ~. By ~ ~‸ F   78 world—] F4; *world.* Q2

70 **sucked . . . teat** Again the Nurse refers to her own breast, here in a modified proverbial expression (cf. Dent E198, 'He sucked evil from the dug'). *Teat* appears only one other time in Shakespeare, *Titus* 2.3.145, even more rarely than the homely word *dug* (see l. 28 n.).

71–3 **younger . . . mothers** Capulet's Wife reiterates Paris's observation (1.2.12), adding that these very young *mothers* are ladies of worth in every sense (see *OED*, *esteem*, *sb.* 4).

73 **—by my count—** Q2 comes to a full stop after *count*, and F (followed by most editors) moves the period back to follow *mothers*. Since the expression *by my count* could apply to the lady's estimate of either the young mothers or her own age at Juliet's birth, the present edition punctuates to allow for ambiguity.

74 **much . . . years** at about the same age (see *OED prep.* 6b, c and Abbott 191). This passage, which makes Capulet's Wife approximately twenty-eight years old, is contradicted by the speech-prefix *Old La<dy>.* which introduces it (and appears six times in the Q2 scene), as well as by a later reference to her 'old age' (5.3.207). Similarly the Nurse, who weaned Juliet only eleven years ago, will be described as 'ancient lady' (2.3.133) and 'old folks' (2.4.15). Although the text never resolves these discrepancies, performers can deal with them by playing for one effect or the other.

78 **world—** Q2 has a full stop, but this edition prints a dash (following F4 and most editors) because the Nurse seems typically to interrupt rather than complete a thought.

a man of wax Literally, 'a waxen image of a man' (*OED*, *wax*, *sb.*[1] 2d). *OED* cites as the first instance of the phrase used for 'emphatic commendation' and explains: 'The origin of this expression is not clear. It may have meant "as faultless as if modelled in wax"' (3c). According to Spencer, the phrase allows yet another bawdy quibble, this time on a penis becoming erect (see *wax sb.*[2], mentioned by *OED* as possibly synonymous with *sb.*[1] 3c, which refers to the process or size of something growing). Dent suggests that the expression was proverbial (cf. D453).

81–96 **What . . . less** Whereas Brooke only mentions that Capulet's wife 'paints' an impression of Paris 'with curious words' (1893–6), Shakespeare elaborates a conceit through which she compares the young suitor to a manuscript book. Pope

This night you shall behold him at our feast;
Read o'er the volume of young Paris' face,
And find delight writ there with beauty's pen;
Examine every married lineament,
And see how one another lends content;
And what obscured in this fair volume lies,
Find written in the margent of his eyes.
This precious book of love, this unbound lover,
To beautify him only lacks a cover.
The fish lives in the sea, and 'tis much pride
For fair without the fair within to hide.
That book in many's eyes doth share the glory

omits this passage, which is not in Q1, calling it 'a ridiculous speech'. A number of later poets and editors concur; many productions have cut the lines in whole or part.

83 **volume** There may be wordplay on (a) book, (b) dimensions (*OED sb.* 6a).

85–6 **Examine . . . content** Capulet's Wife begins to engage in wordplay on both terms of her conceit (handsome suitor/book) as she initiates a series of couplets: *married* = (a) harmonized (*OED ppl. a.* 1b, first illustration of the figurative usage), (b) wedded; *lineament* = (a) feature, (b) illustration (see 1a); *content* (accented on second syllable) = (a) pleasure, (b) subject-matter.

87 **obscured** (a) hidden, (b) not easily understood

88 **margent . . . eyes** Paris's eyes, like the margins of early books, provide commentary on obscure portions of the text: i.e. they reveal whatever remains concealed or doubtful in his face.

89 **book of love** 'Paris is likened to a kind of Ovidian *Ars Amatoria*' (Evans).

unbound i.e. without either (a) matrimonial bonds, or (b) a binding. Gibbons suggests additional play on imagery of embracing in this line and the next, a pun which certainly appears with 'gold clasps' (l. 94).

90 **cover** Mason first pointed out a quibble on (a) binding, and (b) wife (from the legal phrase *feme covert* = married woman; see Furness).

91 **fish . . . sea** This commonplace describes the fish in its natural element and therefore its most congenial (unhooked) state (cf. the proverb 'To love it no more than (as well as) a fish loves water' (Dent F327)). With a simple remark Capulet's Wife introduces her next pronouncement as not only sensible but obvious.

91 **much pride** the very best condition. Besides this primary and still current definition, *pride* has two others which fit the context: (a) fresh-water lamprey (*OED sb.*[2]), (b) sexual desire (*sb.*[1] 11). These produce a fleeting subtext which may help to connect the ideas of Capulet's Wife about fish and marriage. There may also be an allusion to splendid display (*sb.*[1] 6a).

92 **fair . . . hide** The Neoplatonic concept of *fair* outside reflecting *fair* inside applies here to both the metaphoric book (admirable cover suiting excellent contents) and the anticipated betrothal (beautiful wife suiting handsome husband); it may also apply to Paris himself as an ideal man. T. Culbert suggests another reading in light of Q2 punctuation ('For faire without the faire, within to hide:'): the first *fair* refers to Juliet, the second to Paris, and ll. 91–2 mean that Juliet would show false pride to seclude herself from Paris, avoiding her proper role as wife ('A Note on *Romeo and Juliet* I.iii.89–90', *SQ* 10 (1959), 129–32).

93 **share the glory** The ambiguity of each familiar key word in this phrase produces various readings: *share* = (a) apportion, (b) enjoy, possess (with another or others); *glory* = (a) admiration, (b) outstanding beauty. The expression suggests that the book's component parts (binding and narrative) contribute to the praise it enjoys and the beauty it possesses as a whole.

That in gold clasps locks in the golden story.
So shall you share all that he doth possess,
By having him, making yourself no less.

NURSE

No less, nay, bigger—women grow by men.

CAPULET'S WIFE

Speak briefly, can you like of Paris' love?

JULIET

I'll look to like, if looking liking move.
But no more deep will I indart mine eye
Than your consent gives strength to make it fly.

Enter a Serving-man

SERVING-MAN Madam, the guests are come, supper served up, you called, my young lady asked for, the Nurse cursed in the pantry, and everything in extremity. I must hence to wait; I beseech you follow straight.

Exit

CAPULET'S WIFE

We follow thee; Juliet, the County stays.

NURSE

Go, girl, seek happy nights to happy days. *Exeunt*

97 bigger—women] This edition; ~‸~ Q2; ~: ~ F   101 it] Q1; *not in* Q2   105.1 *Exit*] F; *not in* Q

94 **gold clasps . . . golden story** The finished book, down to the fastening of its covers, is described in terms of the precious metal which represents value in several abstract senses (e.g. brilliance, beauty, importance) and as a commodity. This volume of great worth, a metaphor signifying the union of Paris with Juliet, indicates that Capulet's Wife views the match as a social and economic *coup* as well as a fulfilling romance.

97 **bigger—women** Although editors generally follow F—adding a decisive stop, emphasizing the contrast with *less*, and increasing the stress on *grow*—this edition punctuates more lightly. After the elaborate speech of Capulet's Wife the Nurse, eager to interject her own opinion, might well hurry through a pause. She means, of course, that women grow large with child.

98 **like of** find pleasing (*OED v.*[1] 5, Abbott 177)

99 **look to like . . . looking liking** Wordplay on still current definitions of the verb *look* (= (a) expect, (b) direct the sight).

100 **indart mine eye** i.e. cast my glance as if it were a dart. *OED* cites as the first example of *indart*; the prefix adds the sense 'in', intensifies the verb, and fills out the verse (see *en-*, *prefix*[1] 3, Abbott 440).

101 **it** The emendation seems justified by the regular metre at this point.

102 **are come** See Abbott 295 on this passive construction with intransitive verbs.

103–4 **Nurse cursed . . . pantry** i.e. by the other servants who expect her to help with preparations for the feast

106–7 **We . . . days** S. Urkowitz suggests that Juliet's mother and the Nurse repeat the Serving-man's urging because she hangs back for a moment ('"I am not made of stone": Theatrical Revision of Gesture in Shakespeare's Plays', *Renaissance and Reformation*, NS 10 (1986), 91–2).

1.4 *Enter Romeo, Mercutio, Benvolio, with five or six other masquers, torch-bearers*

ROMEO

What, shall this speech be spoke for our excuse?
Or shall we on without apology?

BENVOLIO

The date is out of such prolixity;
We'll have no Cupid, hoodwinked with a scarf,
Bearing a Tartar's painted bow of lath,
Scaring the ladies like a crow-keeper.
But let them measure us by what they will,
We'll measure them a measure and be gone.

1.4.1–112 An invented episode with no precedent in any earlier Romeo and Juliet narratives.

0.1 ***Mercutio*** Listed among Capulet's guests (1.2.69), he now appears for the first time but remains anonymous until l. 93. In effect Shakespeare created this role from a very minor character invented by Bandello and adopted by his French and English imitators (see Brooke 253–90, Painter, 85–6). Mercutio's name connects him with both the complex god and the volatile metal. In *Shakespeare's Mercutio*, Porter analyses the link with the mythological Mercury and suggests another with the historical Marlowe.

0.1–2 ***five . . . torch-bearers*** As McKerrow notes, this permissive Q2 direction does not require *torch-bearers* as well as *masquers*. One of these performers may carry a drum (see l. 112). The conventions of the masque, here and in the sources, solve the practical difficulty of getting Romeo into the Capulet household.

1 **ROMEO** Capell attributes this speech to Benvolio and the next to Mercutio. Although later editors have not borrowed these emendations, some find them plausible, conjecturing that Q1 may have influenced Q2, and that the lines seem stylistically inappropriate to their Q2 speakers.

this speech be spoke Lines 1–2 refer to a convention of English Renaissance masquerading, a formal speech delivered by a presenter to salute the host, compliment the ladies, or apologize for coming uninvited (cf. *L.L.L.* 5.2.155.1–173.1). Romeo uses the short form of the past participle (Abbott 343) in a rhetorical construction (polyptoton).

3 **date . . . prolixity** i.e. tedious formal speeches are no longer current, a view which the Princess and her ladies in *L.L.L.* seem to share (5.2.172). Dent cites 'The date is out' (D42.1).

4 **Cupid . . . scarf** Benvolio describes blindfolded Cupid as a typical presenter (see *Timon* 1.2.118.1–126 for an illustration). Gibbons finds two quibbles on *hoodwinked* which contribute to the play's irony: (a) hooded (as a hawk is subdued), (b) engaged in blind man's buff (see *OED sb.* 1).

5 **Tartar's . . . lath** i.e. a version of the weapon usually associated with Cupid, probably because of the oriental bow's form and strength. This masquer's property, decorated to look like the exotic and powerful lip-shaped bow (distinct from a curved English one), is made of thin strips of wood, like the Vice's dagger in morality plays (see *OED*, *dagger*, *sb.*[1] 1b).

6 **crow-keeper** Either a crow-herd (person hired to protect cornfields from crows) or a scarecrow (*OED*, *crow*, *sb.*[1] 11).

6–7 **crow-keeper. | But** Between these lines editors since Pope have included two found only in Q1 at this point: 'Nor no withoutbooke Prologue faintly spoke | After the Prompter, for our entrance'. Despite various conjectures, from deliberate cut to compositor's error, the omission is unexplained. As a result, this edition of Q2 does not print the lines in its text. Dent compares the first Q1 line with 'To speak (etc.) without book' (B532), an expression found earlier in a Q2 passage printed from Q1 (1.2.60).

7–8 **measure** Playing on the verb (= (a) judge, (b) share, (c) tread) and the noun (= dance).

ROMEO

Give me a torch, I am not for this ambling;
Being but heavy I will bear the light.

MERCUTIO

Nay, gentle Romeo, we must have you dance.

ROMEO

Not I, believe me. You have dancing-shoes
With nimble soles; I have a soul of lead
So stakes me to the ground I cannot move.

MERCUTIO

You are a lover; borrow Cupid's wings,
And soar with them above a common bound.

ROMEO

I am too sore empiercèd with his shaft
To soar with his light feathers, and so bound,
I cannot bound a pitch above dull woe;
Under love's heavy burden do I sink.

MERCUTIO

And to sink in it should you burden love,
Too great oppression for a tender thing.

1.4.21 MERCUTIO] Q4; *Horatio*. Q2

9 **Give . . . torch** Romeo identifies himself with those torch-bearers who did not participate in the masquerades they attended. His request invites stage business.
ambling dancing in an amble, i.e. with the motion or pace of an ambling horse (*OED vbl. sb.* 2, first illustration). The tone seems mildly contemptuous.

13–14 **nimble soles . . . move** Romeo pursues the antithesis and wordplay of heavy/light (*nimble soles/soul of lead*) with a triple pun on *sole/soul*/sowel (= a stake with the end sharpened). The third term distinguishes this quibble from the *sole/soul* version found in other Shakespeare plays (*Merchant* 4.1.122, *Caesar* 1.1.14) which has a separate entry in *OED* (*sole, sb.*[1] 2b).

16 **bound** (a) limit, (b) leap

17 **sore empiercèd** Romeo puns on the adverb *sore* in a hyperbolic description of his pain: *empiercèd* = transfixed.

18 **bound** (a) fastened down, (b) held in bonds or prison (*OED ppl. a.*[2] 2; cf. l. 14 and 1.2.55–6)

19 **cannot bound . . . woe** Recent editors assume that Romeo, playing on the expression 'fly a pitch', means that he cannot attain the height to which a falcon soars. Yet the dejection of the line and its phrase *above dull woe* suggest that *pitch* signifies 'degree' or 'level'. *Dull* belongs to the wordplay on 'heavy', completing the antithesis with 'light' in l. 18; the whole conceit depends on the constrained lover's inability to get off the ground (cf. l. 20).

20 **burden . . . sink** Both terms have bawdy potential which Mercutio immediately exploits.

21 **MERCUTIO** Wilson–Duthie consider the Q2 speech-prefix *Horatio* 'presumably Sh.'s slip'.
should you you would. *Should* denotes contingent futurity after the infinitive used indefinitely (Abbott 322, 356).

21–2 **it . . . thing** Bawdy puns: *it* = sexual organ or intercourse; *thing* = penis or vagina.

22 **oppression** Along with 'weight' and 'distress', *oppression* may carry its now obsolete sense 'forcible violation of a woman, rape' (*OED* 4).

ROMEO
Is love a tender thing? It is too rough,
Too rude, too boist'rous, and it pricks like thorn.

MERCUTIO
If love be rough with you, be rough with love;
Prick love for pricking, and you beat love down.
Give me a case to put my visage in,
A visor for a visor. What care I
What curious eye doth quote deformities?
Here are the beetle brows shall blush for me.

BENVOLIO
Come, knock and enter, and no sooner in,
But every man betake him to his legs.

ROMEO
A torch for me. Let wantons light of heart
Tickle the senseless rushes with their heels;

29 quote] Q2 (cote) 32 betake] Q2, F; betakes Q3

23–4 **Is . . . thorn** Romeo continues to play lovelorn straight man to Mercutio; the text allows an actor to decide whether or not the role is intentional. While the diction is on one level decorous, some of the words have bawdy possibilities: e.g. *boist'rous* = (a) stiff (*OED a.* 2), (b) harsh to the feelings (4, first illustration), (c) violent (7); *pricks* and *thorn* can both be ribald puns (see Partridge). Dent suggests a comparison of ll. 24 ff. with 'It early pricks (It pricks betimes) that will be a thorn' (T232).

25–6 **If . . . down** Mercutio repeats Romeo's very words with rhetorical strategies that thoroughly expose their latent bawdiness; he caps the display with another indecent quibble, *beat love down*, i.e. cause detumescence.

26 **Prick** (a) wound, (b) grieve, (c) stimulate **for** (a) in requital, (b) for purposes of (Wilson–Duthie)

27–9 **Give . . . deformities** These lines require stage business, as Mercutio calls for a mask.

28 **A visor for a visor** A mask for a face (*OED sb.* 4). Mercutio introduces play on the proverb 'A well-favored visor will hide her ill-favored face' (Dent V92; cf. Rosaline's jesting in *L.L.L.* 5.2.388–9). In the following lines he may be mocking either himself or prying socialites.

29 **curious** (a) closely observant (*OED a.* 3b, first example), (b) inquisitive **quote** notice (*OED v.* 5b)

30 **beetle . . . blush** Probably a mask with prominent eyebrows and reddened cheeks, although M. P. Tilley argues for a simple black velvet mask ('Two Shakespearian Notes', *MLN* 25 (1910), 262–3).

32 **But** than (Abbott 127) **betake . . . legs** A quibble on (a) run away, (b) dance (Gibbons).

33–7 **torch . . . done** Romeo persists with antitheses and wordplay which began at l. 9. His language has sexual connotations: *wantons* = promiscuous individuals; *light* = sexually immodest; *tickle* = arouse.

33 **wantons** over-indulged or sportive people (*OED sb.* 1, 2a)

34 **Tickle . . . heels** At the most obvious level Romeo says that dancing lightly stirs the insensate rushes, the marsh or waterside plants used until the seventeenth century for strewing on floors, including the stages of theatres. At a secondary level he seems to mock the dancers for engaging in pointless activity; he describes them stimulating the rushes, which not only lack sensation but stand for something without value or significance.

For I am proverbed with a grandsire phrase:
I'll be a candle-holder and look on;
The game was ne'er so fair, and I am done.

MERCUTIO

Tut, dun's the mouse, the constable's own word.
If thou art dun, we'll draw thee from the mire
Or—save your reverence—love, wherein thou stickest
Up to the ears. Come, we burn daylight, ho!

37 done] Q3 (dun); dum Q2; done Q1, F   40 Or] Q2; Of Q1   save your reverence] F; saue you reuerence Q2; this surreuerence Q1

35 **proverbed . . . grandsire phrase** i.e. furnished with proverbs by an old expression (*OED*'s only illustration of *proverb*, v. 2). Bartenschlager proposes that the *grandsire phrase* is 'He that worst may must hold the candle' (Dent C40), and that it provides the reference for ll. 36–7 (423–4). Yet scholars have long maintained that Romeo echoes two other proverbs: 'When play (game, jest) is best it is time to leave' (Dent P399), and 'A good candle-holder proves a good gamester' (Tilley C51). The second is unlikely; Dent finds no evidence of currency at this time. Romeo uses the maxims to rationalize his behaviour; but P399, which refers to making the most of a game of chance through disengagement, proves an ironic statement from a protagonist heading to meet his fate.

37 **game** Spencer finds a pun on (a) gambling, (b) quarry (i.e. Rosaline).

done The wordplay in ll. 37–9 has convinced editors that Q2 'dum' is a minim misreading of 'dun', the spelling restored by Q3. Although Hosley and Williams interpret 'dun' in l. 39 as the adjective, most scholars prefer Q1's past participle *done*. This edition adopts Jowett's reasoning: 'The senses "done" and "dun" are simultaneous in Romeo's speech; as "dun" must be read in Mercutio's reply, we prefer to give Romeo "done" in the modernized text, to emphasize the wordplay'. In Romeo's line *done*/dun = (a) finished (in more than one sense; see proverbs Dent C40 and P399 cited for ll. 36–7), (b) dull (vs. *fair*).

38–9 **Tut, dun's . . . mire** Mercutio matches Romeo's proverbs with three others which play on the *dun/done* quibble. Literally 'dun's the mouse' means 'the mouse is of a dingy brown colour'; punningly it says 'the mouse is finished'; and proverbially it refers to the mouse's invisibility and silence (Dent D644), the reason Mercutio identifies the phrase with a constable's watchword such as 'Be still!' Consequently Mercutio tells Romeo in more than one way (and perhaps with mild impatience) to stop sounding depressed. The proverbial allusions in l. 39 make two points besides the obvious one: they indicate a standstill ('Draw dun (the horse) out of the mire' (D642), 'Dun is in the mire' (D643)); and they allude to a Christmas game in which the players lifted and carried a heavy log (see *OED*, *dun*, *sb.*[1] 5). As he pokes fun at his friend, Mercutio promises to cheer him up.

40 **Or . . . love** Since compositorial slips with the letter *r* could easily account for Q2's phrasing 'Or saue you reuerence loue', most editors adopt F's *your* and quite a few print Q1's 'Of'. The expression *save your reverence*, connected with the term *sir-reverence*, is both apologetic and rude: it means 'with due respect' and excuses itself for offending (*OED*, *reverence*, *sb.* 5a) even while it is a euphemism for excrement which coarsely degrades love (*sir-reverence*, *sb.* 2). Dent cites 'Saving your (Sir) Reverence' (R93).

40–1 **wherein . . . ears** Dent compares 'To be over head and ears (up to the ears) in a thing (love)' (H268).

41–2 **we burn daylight . . . so** Mercutio uses a proverbial phrase meaning 'we waste time' (Dent D123); Romeo takes him literally, as if he had said 'we burn our torches in the daytime', and in his contradiction emphasizes that this scene takes place at night. With these lines the exchange begins to include rhyme, especially couplets, which will continue until Mercutio's description of Queen Mab (l. 51).

ROMEO
Nay, that's not so.

MERCUTIO
I mean, sir, in delay
We waste our lights in vain, light lights by day.
Take our good meaning, for our judgement sits
Five times in that ere once in our five wits.

ROMEO
And we mean well in going to this masque,
But 'tis no wit to go.

MERCUTIO
Why, may one ask?

ROMEO
I dreamt a dream tonight.

MERCUTIO
And so did I.

ROMEO
Well, what was yours?

MERCUTIO
That dreamers often lie.

ROMEO
In bed asleep while they do dream things true.

MERCUTIO
O, then I see Queen Mab hath been with you.
She is the fairies' midwife, and she comes

43 light lights] DANIEL (*conj.* Nicholson); lights lights Q2; like Lampes Q1; like lights JOHNSON; light lamps MUNRO (*conj.* Greg) 45 five] MALONE (*conj.* Wilbraham); fine Q2; right Q1

43 **light lights** Editors differ about the degree of error in Q2's reading 'lights lights', frequently adopting Johnson's emendation 'like lights' (cf. Q1's 'like Lampes' and see Collation). As Williams says, however, the least intrusive remedy for the apparent dittograph is removal of the first *s*.

44–5 **Take . . . wits** *Good meaning* seems to conflate two overlapping definitions: (a) intended sense (i.e. of the proverb), (b) good intention (*OED vbl. sb.*[1] 1). Apparently Mercutio tells Romeo to understand both his real meaning and the purpose behind it, sources of discernment far more often than *our five wits*: either the five bodily senses (which perceive only physical stimuli and literal meaning) or mental faculties in general. Q2's 'fine wits' appears to be a printing error (a minim misreading or foul case), because *five* produces the familiar phrase *five wits* and therefore balances *Five times*. As McKerrow suggests, however, there may be a proverbial reference here, too (cf. 'The finest wits are soonest subject to love' (Dent W576)).

46–7 **mean well . . . go** Romeo's *mean well* plays on Mercutio's *good meaning*, and his *no wit* (*wit* = good judgement, *OED sb.* 6a) on *judgement* and *five wits*.

48 **I . . . dream** Real misgivings surface in this dialogue (cf. ll. 37, 46–7), even while Romeo plays the melancholy lover, and the puns and rhetoric continue. As Wilson–Duthie point out (citing J. C. Maxwell), the Queen Mab speech which follows shortly 'enables Sh. to register the effect of foreboding in Rom.'s dream without telling us what the dream was'.
tonight last night (*OED adv.* 3)

49 **lie** The friends trade obvious puns on three definitions: (a) speak falsely, (b) engage in love-making (see Partridge), (c) recline. According to Dent, Mercutio's response may be proverbial (D587).

51–89 **O . . . bodes** Q1 presents this passage differently from Q2, adding a question

In shape no bigger than an agate stone
On the forefinger of an alderman,
Drawn with a team of little atomi
Over men's noses as they lie asleep.
Her wagon-spokes made of long spinners' legs;
The cover of the wings of grasshoppers;
Her traces of the smallest spider-web;
Her collars of the moonshine's wat'ry beams;
Her whip of cricket's bone, the lash of film;

55 atomi] Q (ottamie Q2, Atomi Q1); atomies Q3

from Benvolio after the equivalent of l. 51 ('Queene Mab whats she?') and attributing to him ll. 52–89. Since Keightley (conj. Hunter) a few editors have considered the question authentic, incorporating it into their texts and giving it to either Benvolio or Romeo. They assign the rest of the speech to Mercutio.

51 **Queen Mab** Although Mercutio's wordplay on this name is clear—*Queen*/Quean = a prostitute, *Mab* = a promiscuous woman (*OED sb.* 1)—the folkloric background remains obscure. K. Briggs suggests that Shakespeare's 'minute Queen Mab . . . probably comes from a Celtic strain and was once much more formidable, the Mabb of Wales, with possibly some connection with the warlike Queen MAEVE of Ireland' (*An Encyclopedia of Fairies* (New York, 1976), p. 275).

52–89 **She is . . . bodes** Q2 prints as prose, but all editors follow Q1 and Pope in arranging as verse: blank verse rhythms are obvious, as is the compression of type to save space on signature C2[r]. In many editions the lineation and commentary for ll. 52–67 result from scholarly attempts to visualize Mercutio's fantastic catalogue in whole or in part. This edition offers no rearrangement and little intervention generally. In its own terms the passage makes sense, demanding suspension of disbelief. It may also preserve authorial revisions (see Pearlman, pp. 119–25).

52 **fairies' midwife** Recent editors frequently quote or adapt Steevens's interpretation: 'This does not mean the midwife *to* the fairies, but that she was the person *among* the fairies whose department it was to deliver the fancies of sleeping men of their dreams, those *children of an idle brain*'. Yet *fairies' midwife* allows Mab both functions, and perhaps that of assisting at human births (see wordplay on *bear* in l. 91). *OED* cites to illustrate *sb.* 1, 'a woman who assists other women in childbirth', rather than 3, 'One who or that which helps to produce or bring anything to birth'.

53 **agate stone** The precious stone often engraved with small figures for seal-rings, a composite image of diminutiveness. There is also a bawdy pun on *stone* (= testicle) in this line and *forefinger* (= penis) in the next (see Partridge).

55 **with** by (Abbott 193)
atomi tiny beings. Q2's 'ottamie' slightly misrepresents *attomie*, plural of the Latin *atomus* = atom. In *little atomi* the adjective emphasizes the minuteness of the team, performing with a noun the kind of function that it usually shares with another adjective (*OED a.* 1e).

57–93 **Her wagon-spokes . . . she—** On the rhetoric of this speech, see Introduction, p. 47.

57 **spinners'** A. S. Cairncross argues that the *OED* definition 'spider' does not apply to Shakespeare's use of *spinner* here (or in *Dream* 2.2.21): the context indicates the 'crane-fly', popularly known as 'daddy-long-legs' ('"Spinner" ("M.N.D.", II.ii.21; "Romeo", I.iv.60)', *N&Q*, NS 22 (1975), 166–7).

60 **Her collars . . . beams** This line plays on individual words (*collars*/colours; *wat'ry* = (a) connected with water (*OED a.* 6), (b) pale); on the idea of the moon controlling the tides; and on the proverbial phrase 'moonshine in the water', an expression of insubstantiality (Dent M1128; cf. *L.L.L.* 5.2.207, *Dream* 2.1.162).

61 **cricket's bone** i.e. the leathery casing of the insect

Her wagoner, a small grey-coated gnat,
Not half so big as a round little worm
Pricked from the lazy finger of a maid.
Her chariot is an empty hazelnut
Made by the joiner squirrel or old grub,
Time out o' mind the fairies' coach-makers.
And in this state she gallops night by night
Through lovers' brains, and then they dream of love;
On courtiers' knees, that dream on curtsies straight;
O'er lawyers' fingers, who straight dream on fees;
O'er ladies' lips, who straight on kisses dream,
Which oft the angry Mab with blisters plagues,
Because their breath with sweetmeats tainted are.

64 maid] Q1; man Q2 70 On] Q2; O're Q1 74 breath] Q2; breathes Q1

61 **film** a very fine thread, as of gossamer. (*OED sb.* 6, first illustration; Q2 prints the unusual disyllabic spelling 'Philome'.)

62 **wagoner** charioteer (*OED sb.*[1] 2)
small . . . gnat i.e. a small specimen of a small insect which is a type of insignificance

64 **maid** All editors change Q2 'man' to Q1 *maid*, offering two kinds of evidence: Nares's reference to the view 'that when maidens were idle, worms bred in their fingers' (quoted in Furness) and Hoppe's suggestion (cited by Hosley) that Q2 misreads 'maie', 'may, maiden'. Gibbons cites H. Keil, who finds evidence in contemporary folklore that Queen Mab and other fairies were concerned with the cleanliness of maids or servant-girls; they punished neglect. Keil identifies the *round little worm* as the mite that causes scabies ('Scabies and the Queen Mab Passage in *Romeo and Juliet*', *Journal of the History of Ideas* 18 (1957), 394–410).

66 **joiner squirrel . . . grub** Mercutio imagines the rodent and the insect or worm as craftsmen who engage in woodwork both lighter and more ornamental than a carpenter's: one gnaws his material and the other bores through it. In view of l. 67 (*Time out o' mind*), *old* probably means 'age-old'.

67 **Time . . . mind** Proverbial (Dent T332.2).
coach-makers Wilson–Duthie, citing *Shakespeare's England* (Oxford, 1916), i. 204–5, make the point that 'coaches were an innovation in Sh.'s day'.

68–93 **in . . . she—** The catalogue elaborates a topos that existed from the time of Lucretius: the somnium animale, or dream which arises from agitation of the waking mind. According to R. K. Presson, Shakespeare produces a new mythology by making Queen Mab the agent for all the dreams ('Two Types of Dreams in the Elizabethan Drama, and their Heritage: Somnium Animale and the Prick of Conscience', *SEL* 7 (1967), 240–6). A. Thompson summarizes the scholarship which traces these lines to Chaucer's *Parlement of Foules* 99–105 (*Shakespeare's Chaucer* (New York, 1978), pp. 78–9).

70 **On courtiers' knees . . . straight** Q2 *On* makes as much sense as Q1 'O're'. Although it does not correspond precisely with the opening prepositions in the next two lines, it enhances the symmetry of its own verse as well as the rhetorical devices of repetition, play on sounds (*courtiers'/curtsies*), and quibbles (*curtsies* = (a) salutations with bended knees, (b) courtesies; *straight* works as adverb and adjective).

72–3 **ladies' lips . . . plagues** N. Brooke finds an image of venereal disease in these lines (p. 94).

74 **breath . . . are** Q2's reading may result from the contiguity of *sweetmeats* and the verb, or from the use of *breath* as a collective noun (cf. *L.L.L.* 5.2.88, *Dream* 3.2.169, *Richard II* 3.2.52). Q1 and most modern editions print 'breaths'.

Sometime she gallops o'er a courtier's nose,
And then dreams he of smelling out a suit;
And sometime comes she with a tithe-pig's tail,
Tickling a parson's nose as a lies asleep—
Then he dreams of another benefice.
Sometime she driveth o'er a soldier's neck,
And then dreams he of cutting foreign throats,
Of breaches, ambuscados, Spanish blades,
Of healths five fathom-deep; and then anon
Drums in his ear, at which he starts and wakes,
And being thus frighted, swears a prayer or two

79 he dreams] Q2; dreames he Q1

75 **courtier's** This second item about courtiers within six lines suggests that the manuscript contained two versions, neither clearly marked for deletion. Some early editions and prompt books have substituted another occupation at this point, e.g. 'a lawyer's' (from Q1 and Pope), producing another repetition, or 'a counsellor's' (Collier 1853). Jowett omits Q2's reference to lawyers and replaces this line with an emended version of Q1's entry about lawyers (conj. Seymour). Like most editions and prompt books, the present edition allows the redundancy to stand. Repetition, which has become part of the literary and theatrical experience of this passage, has not reduced its edge or clarity.

75–6 **nose . . . suit** The *nose* in l. 75 may be a double entendre (= penis) which ll. 77–91 will elaborate. Literally, Mercutio says that the courtier dreams of finding someone who will pay him to represent a petition before a high-ranking figure at court. *OED* quotes Lodge's *Phillis* (1593) to illustrate the obsolete definition of *suit* as 'scent' (*sb.* 5b).

77 **tithe-pig's tail** the *tail* of a *pig* due as *tithe*, i.e. as part of a community's payment—ten per cent of its agricultural produce—to support a religious establishment. Alliteration calls attention to the puns in ll. 77–8 on *tail* (= penis) and *Tickling*, which lead to quibbles on *parson's nose* (see previous note).

78 **a lies** he lies (see 1.3.42 n.)

79 **he dreams** Some editors, following Q1 and Pope, invert this phrase to make it correspond with ll. 76 and 81, and to regularize the metre. This edition follows Q2 for three reasons: the passages about courtier, parson, and soldier are not exactly parallel (e.g. in length and syntax); the metre of l. 78 is irregular; a pause after l. 78 virtually eliminates the metrical awkwardness from l. 79.

79 **another benefice** Pluralism, the holding of more than one benefice at a time by one person, continued through and after the Elizabethan period.

82 **breaches** *Breach* seems to mean 'a gap in a fortification made by a battery' (Johnson), although *OED* cites the first instance of this usage in *2 Henry IV* 2.4.49 (*sb.* 7c). Other appropriate definitions are less specific: 'injurious assault' (4) and 'quarrel' (5b). This word may also have bawdy implications, i.e. female genitals, which give a sexual edge to the following images of ambush and weapons.

ambuscados *OED* calls *ambuscados* 'an affected refashioning of AMBUSCADE' after the Spanish and cites this line as the earliest illustration. E. P. Kuhl counters that the word occurred in a contemporary military work, R. Barret, *The Theorike and Practike of Moderne Warres* (1598); and he finds topical Spanish references in the Q2 line ('*Romeo and Juliet*, I, IV, 84 F.', *PQ* 9 (1930), 307–8).

Spanish blades Spain was well known for its finely tempered sword-blades. Gibbons notes possible wordplay on *blade* = gallant (cf. 2.3.29).

83 **healths five fathom-deep** i.e. toasts drunk very deeply (although *OED*, *fathom*, *sb.* 3d cites Middleton's *Trick to Catch the Old One*, which it dates 1608, as the first example of 'fathoms deep' or *fathom-deep* (6)).

And sleeps again. This is that very Mab
That plaits the manes of horses in the night,
And bakes the elf-locks in foul sluttish hairs,
Which once untangled much misfortune bodes.
This is the hag, when maids lie on their backs,
That presses them and learns them first to bear,
Making them women of good carriage.
This is she—

ROMEO Peace, peace, Mercutio, peace,
Thou talk'st of nothing.

MERCUTIO True, I talk of dreams,
Which are the children of an idle brain,
Begot of nothing but vain fantasy,
Which is as thin of substance as the air,
And more inconstant than the wind who woos
Even now the frozen bosom of the north;

88 elf-locks] Q1 (Elfelocks); Elklocks Q2

87 **plaits** intertwists

88–9 **bakes . . . bodes** The images seem to shift from animal to human hair. Since *foul* and *sluttish* both signify not only physical but moral uncleanliness, the *hairs* in l. 88 function in part as synecdoche for offensive persons, especially females (see Partridge on *foul*, *sluttish*, *hairs*, and *OED*, *sluttish*). Apparently Mab 'hates sluts and sluttery', like the fairies imitated in *Merry Wives* (5.5.45), and forms tangles in their hair (see *bake*, *v.* 4, *elf-lock*). Undoing the tangles, it appears, results in more ill luck.

90 **hag** malicious female sprite (*OED sb.*[1] 1a). In its context this word is especially effective because it also refers to various 'terrors of the night' (1b) and to a light which supposedly appears at night on horses' manes and human hair (4a).

91 **learns** teaches (not a vulgar usage)
to bear Quibbling on (a) childbirth, (b) the weight of a man. In this description of an erotic dream (ll. 90–2), Mercutio delivers a witty, fantastic version of the simple joke told by the Nurse's husband and repeated by the Nurse at 1.3.43 ff. The key phrases all refer to positions for sexual intercourse, from prone bearing of a partner's weight (*lie on their backs*, *bear*, *carriage*) to active stimulation by the partner on top (*presses*).

92 **of good carriage** The wordplay continues on *carriage* (= bearing), adding 'deportment' to the two quibbles in l. 91 and perhaps a last punning allusion to Mab's chariot. In this line *carriage* is trisyllabic. The expression 'To be a woman of good carriage' is proverbial and bawdy (Dent W637.3).

93 **she—** Although Q2 has a full stop after *she*, editors follow F2 in printing a dash to indicate that Mercutio is interrupted. R. O. Evans suggests that the conclusion of the speech may be a deliberate omission or rhetorical ellipsis: traditionally accounts of Mab ended with maidens' visions of their future husbands or lovers (pp. 76–8).

94 **nothing** can refer to male or female parts; a double entendre seems probable.

96 **Begot** Short form of the past participle (Abbott 343).
vain fantasy While *fantasy* means 'delusive imagination' in the first place (*OED sb.* 3a), it also connotes 'phantom' (2), 'whim', and 'desire' (7). With the familiar word *vain* (= idle, worthless, empty), it alludes to several motifs in the Queen Mab speech.

97 **as thin . . . air** Proverbial (Dent A90).

98 **inconstant . . . wind** Proverbial (Dent W412).

And being angered puffs away from thence,
Turning his side to the dew-dropping south.

BENVOLIO

This wind you talk of blows us from ourselves;
Supper is done, and we shall come too late.

ROMEO

I fear too early, for my mind misgives
Some consequence yet hanging in the stars
Shall bitterly begin his fearful date
With this night's revels, and expire the term
Of a despisèd life closed in my breast
By some vile forfeit of untimely death.
But he that hath the steerage of my course
Direct my suit. On, lusty gentlemen.

BENVOLIO

Strike, drum.

101 side] Q2; face Q1 111 Direct] Q2; Directs Q1 suit] Q2; saile Q1

100 **being angered** Curiously, Mercutio associates imagination with anger here and in his description of Mab (l. 73).

101 **Turning his side** (a) moving his body laterally, (b) changing his direction. Pope and some later editors substitute Q1 'face' for Q2 *side*, despite the effectiveness of the Q2 phrase, the proverbial echo ('To turn with (as) the wind', Dent W439), and the unlikelihood of a printing error.

dew-dropping south This expression connects the compass-point with heavenly powers of refreshment and gentle precipitation, completing the antithesis with 'the frozen bosom of the north'.

102 **blows . . . ourselves** i.e. carries us away (with an obvious pun on the literal and figurative senses)

105–10 **Some consequence . . . course** These lines echo the Prologue, not only presaging the tragedy to come but repeating the key words *stars*, *fearful*, *life*/*death* and rephrasing in *course* the idea of 'passage'. *Consequence* implies that whatever is about to happen results from something which has preceded and follows logically.

106 **his** its (Abbott 228)

fearful i.e. causing fear

107–9 **expire . . . death** The legal conceit seems less clear than recent editors infer, because the expressions *term* and *forfeit* admit ambiguities. While *expire* plainly means 'cause to expire' (*OED v.* 7a), *term* denotes two specific kinds of duration as well as the general sense: an appointed time for payment of money due (*sb.* 3a), and interest in and for a certain period; *term* also has astrological implications (2). In the next line the metaphor of life as an enclosed property will suggest that the payment owed is conceived as a mortgage. *Forfeit* may refer to a transgression (*sb.* 1), penalty, or loss, and its agent could be the consequence, death, or Romeo.

110–11 **But he . . . suit** Wilson–Duthie compare a couplet in Brooke (799–800): 'In stormy wind and wave, in danger to be lost, | Thy steerless ship (O Romeus) hath been long while betossed'.

111 **suit** Most modern editors, following Steevens, substitute Q1 'saile' to finish the nautical metaphor. But Williams offers a convincing argument for Q2 based on the spelling and usage of both words, and Gibbons defends *suit* on stylistic grounds. In the full poetic context of this speech *suit* may mean (a) adventure's sequel (Johnson), (b) courtship of Rosaline, (c) legal proceedings; and the pronoun *he* in l. 110 may refer to either the god of love or Providence.

112–13 **drum . . .** [CHIEF] It has been traditional since Steevens to indicate a change of scene here, but the direction does not clear the stage or even specify a

They march about the stage, and Serving-men come forth with napkins

[CHIEF] SERVING-MAN Where's Potpan, that he helps not to take away? He shift a trencher, he scrape a trencher?

FIRST SERVING-MAN When good manners shall lie all in one or two men's hands, and they unwashed too, 'tis a foul thing.

single exit (see 112.1–2 and n.); Q1 has a similar shift of locale. As A. C. Dessen concludes, 'In both quartos . . . the ball comes to the masquers; in neither do the masquers *exeunt* and *re-enter* to a new place' ('Q1 *Romeo and Juliet* and Elizabethan Theatrical Vocabulary', in *Shakespeare's 'Romeo and Juliet'*, ed. Halio, p. 115). In addition, A. Gaw explains how the arrangement here keeps the stage full to create the illusion of numbers at the party ('The Impromptu Mask in Shakspere', *SAB* 11 (1936), 149–60). Two similar transitions occur at 2.1.43–4 and 4.4.26–7. In order to emphasize the original fluidity of staging, this edition omits the usual scene-breaks.

112.1–2 ***They . . . napkins*** In Q2 this direction indicating a transition from outside to inside the Capulet house is flexible, and performances have treated the shift in various ways. (Prompt books which reverse the order of 1.3 and the traditional 1.4 avoid this particular transition.) Many prompt books omit the servants' dialogue (not in Q1); and most have the masquers exit here, re-entering for the ball. By comparison modern editors, trying to preserve the integrity of the Elizabethan play-text, usually give a version of the original direction; they instruct the masquers either to stand aside on the stage or to exit. (The phrase *march about* is ambiguous, because the preposition means both 'round the outside of' and 'across or over'.) Since the Q2 direction allows more than one interpretation, this edition prints it unchanged.

112.2 ***napkins*** At this point Q2 prints '*Enter* Romeo' on a new line. While the instruction appears out of place in its context and somehow erroneous, it too calls attention to the playwright's various ideas about staging this transition. Jowett thinks it may represent a false start or evidence that Shakespeare added the servants' exchange later, originally intending the Serving-men to *march about* in pantomime and Romeo's group to exit before the servants' entry. Along different lines, McKerrow conjectures that Romeo may participate in the domestic event, coming forward to observe the servants clearing away and thereby indicating that his party has arrived in the house. According to this view, the fifteen lines of dialogue which immediately follow would conclude the masquers' episode.

113–257 **[CHIEF] . . . *Exeunt*** All source narratives contain a party-scene where the lovers meet, but this version makes several additions—from details of the servants' preparations to Capulet's prominence and Tybalt's outburst—which give the episode a more complex relationship to the action as a whole. In particular, the preparations anticipate those for marriage with Paris in the fourth act.

113 **[CHIEF] SERVING-MAN** Q2 differentiates the speech-prefix of this servant (*Ser.*) from those of the others (numbers *1*, *2*, *3*), a distinction this edition follows.

113–28 **Where's . . . all** Q2 contains no directions between the entrance of these Serving-men and their *Exeunt* after l. 128, allowing different kinds of business in performance. Modern editors tend to identify Anthony and Potpan with Serving-man 2 and Serving-man 3, sometimes providing them with a separate entrance at l. 121 so that they seem to answer to their names.

114 **trencher** plate or platter of non-precious material, probably wood. The Capulet family also has plate (see l. 119), fashionable with wealthy Elizabethans. From earlier references (1.3.102, 1.4.103), it appears that the Serving-men are clearing up after the supper and preparing for the dance.

115–16 **good manners . . . hands** Gibbons finds wordplay on *manners*: (a) polite behaviour, (b) 'belonging to the hand' (from Latin, *manuārius*; see *OED*, *manner*,

[CHIEF] SERVING-MAN Away with the joint-stools, remove the court-cupboard, look to the plate. Good thou, save me a piece of marchpane, and as thou loves me, let the porter let in Susan Grindstone and Nell, Anthony and Potpan.

SECOND SERVING-MAN Ay boy, ready.

[CHIEF] SERVING-MAN You are looked for and called for, asked for and sought for, in the great chamber.

THIRD SERVING-MAN We cannot be here and there too. Cheerly boys, be brisk a while, and the longer liver take all. *Exeunt*

Enter Capulet, attendants, and all the guests and gentlewomen to the masquers

CAPULET

Welcome, gentlemen. Ladies that have their toes
Unplagued with corns will walk a bout with you.

128.1–2 *Enter . . . masquers*] This edition (*following* Capell); *Enter all the guests and gentlewomen to the Maskers*. Q2 130 walk] Q2; haue Q1 a bout] POPE; about Q

sb.[1] Forms). There is also quibbling allusion to the commonplace 'with unwashed hands' (Dent H125), which means 'at once' (Onions), i.e. without waiting to observe proprieties. The play on *foul* is obvious.

118 **joint-stools** stools crafted of parts fitted together by a joiner (as distinguished from those of rougher workmanship; *OED* 1)

119 **court-cupboard** movable cabinet or sideboard for the display of plate and other domestic utensils (*OED*'s first example)
plate. Good Q2 punctuates with a comma, perhaps indicating that the Chief Serving-man should speak these orders in a run-on sentence.

120 **marchpane** marzipan
loves lovest (see Abbott 340)

120–2 **let the porter . . . Potpan** Some editors assume that the two women will join a party for servants after the main festivities, and that the Chief Serving-man first makes this arrangement with the porter, then calls for Anthony and Potpan. With the names *Grindstone* and *Potpan*, however, the text allows another interpretation: the Chief Serving-man, sending a message to the porter, asks him to admit four more to help.

123 **ready** The second Serving-man is either responding to the instructions just given or announcing his general state of readiness.

126 **THIRD SERVING-MAN** Jowett follows F in assigning this retort to the speaker of ll. 115–17 and thus reducing the number of actors needed for the exchange.
We . . . too Proverbial (Dent H438.1).

127–8 **longer . . . all** Proverbial (Dent L395; cf. A192.1, 'He that wins shall take all').

128.1–2 ***Enter . . . masquers*** Q2 suggests again that Romeo and his party have never left the stage, although theatrical tradition and some editors have them re-enter for the dance (see 112.1–2 n.). Q2's general direction, which does not specify Capulet's family and attendants, gives no indication of when or where the musicians take their places. In performance, however, the opening of this episode is usually choreographed with care, whether the participants enter the stage, a curtain rises to discover them, or both.

129 **gentlemen** Either the masquers or all the male guests.

130 **walk a bout** (a) promenade, (b) dance a round (see Onions *walk*, *v.* 2 and *bout*). This phrase may signal a particular dance, the graceful pavane, 'for the basic

Ah my mistresses, which of you all
Will now deny to dance? She that makes dainty,
She I'll swear hath corns. Am I come near ye now?
Welcome, gentlemen. I have seen the day
That I have worn a visor and could tell
A whispering tale in a fair lady's ear,
Such as would please. 'Tis gone, 'tis gone, 'tis gone.
You are welcome, gentlemen. Come, musicians, play.
Music plays and they dance
A hall, a hall! Give room, and foot it, girls.—
More light, you knaves, and turn the tables up,
And quench the fire, the room is grown too hot.—
Ah sirrah, this unlooked-for sport comes well.—
Nay sit, nay sit, good cousin Capulet,

pavane movement is a sliding, walking step' (A. Brissenden, 'Shakespeare's Use of Dance: *L.L.L.*, *Much Ado* and *Merry Wives*', in *Shakespeare and Some Others*, ed. A. Brissenden (Adelaide, 1976), p. 38; cf. Don Pedro's invitation to Hero to 'walk a bout' with him in *Much Ado* 2.1.78).

131 **mistresses, which** Capulet employs a term of polite address (*OED sb.* 13a); *which* = who (Abbott 265).

132 **deny** refuse (*OED v.* 8)
makes dainty acts coy (*OED sb.* 7)

133 **Am . . . ye** have I touched you on a sensitive point (*OED*, *near*, *adv.*[2] (and *prep.*) 16b; see Abbott 295 for 'be' with the intransitive verb). The expression is proverbial (Dent N56.1).

134 **Welcome, gentlemen** See l. 129 n.
I . . . day Proverbial (Dent D81.1).

136 **whispering** i.e. uttered in a whisper (*OED ppl. a.* 1b, first illustration)

138 **You . . . gentlemen** Capulet extends his hospitality for a third time. Q2 has no punctuation after *gentlemen*, so *come* may be addressed to the guests or the musicians.

138.1 ***they dance*** Dance, which becomes essential to the dramatic action in this scene, also performs an important symbolic role in the tragedy. First, it represents harmony, contrasting with events (particularly the duelling with which it will be linked metaphorically). Second, the allegorical Dance of Death gives it ominous associations with the graveyard, where this play ends. (See A. Brissenden, *Shakespeare and the Dance* (London and Basingstoke, 1981), pp. 63–6, and P. C. McGuire, 'On the Dancing in *Romeo and Juliet*', *Renaissance and Reformation*, NS 5 (1981), repr. in *Critical Essays*, ed. Andrews, pp. 215–28.) J. H. Long considers the kind of dance and music that this episode requires (*Shakespeare's Use of Music: The Histories and Tragedies* (Gainesville, Fla., 1971), pp. 39–41).

139 **A hall, a hall!** An exclamation to clear space for a dance (*OED* 12, first example).

140 **turn . . . up** Capulet orders the Servingmen to disassemble and set aside the trestle-tables (which they had earlier been clearing of trenchers).

141 **quench the fire** If *the fire* does not refer to heat from the kitchen on this July night, it must be an inadvertent recollection of the Christmas feast in Brooke and Painter (see 1.2.20 n.).

142 **sirrah** Either Capulet addresses a servant or young male guest (*sirrah* = a man or boy with whom one assumes authority), or 'he hugs himself' (Wilson–Duthie; *sirrah* = self-address (Onions)). It is less likely that he means his 'cousin Capulet', a relative and contemporary.
unlooked-for sport i.e. the unexpected diversion of the masquers' arrival

143 **Nay sit . . . cousin Capulet** This line calls for at least one seat near Capulet and a bit of stage business. *Cousin* = kinsman (*OED sb.* 1a; probably 'Mine uncle Capulet' from the invitation list, 1.2.70).

For you and I are past our dancing days.
How long is't now since last yourself and I
Were in a mask?

CAPULET'S COUSIN By'r Lady, thirty years.

CAPULET

What man, 'tis not so much, 'tis not so much,
'Tis since the nuptial of Lucentio,
Come Pentecost as quickly as it will,
Some five-and-twenty years, and then we masked.

CAPULET'S COUSIN

'Tis more, 'tis more, his son is elder, sir.
His son is thirty.

CAPULET Will you tell me that?
His son was but a ward two years ago.

ROMEO (*to a Serving-man*)

What lady's that which doth enrich the hand
Of yonder knight?

SERVING-MAN I know not, sir.

ROMEO

O, she doth teach the torches to burn bright!
It seems she hangs upon the cheek of night

153 two years ago.| Q2; three yeares agoe, | Good youths I faith. Oh youth's a iolly thing. Q1
154 (*to a Serving-man*)] CAPELL (*to a Servant.*); *not in* Q

144 **past our dancing days** Dent compares 'My dancing days are done' (D118).

146 **Were . . . mask** (a) wore a mask, (b) attended a masked ball (cf. ll. 135–6)

149–50 **Come Pentecost . . . years** i.e. it will be twenty-five years next spring. Capulet's expression is colloquial (cf. the Nurse's at 1.3.19).

151 **elder** older (*OED a.* 1a)

153 **but a ward** i.e. not yet twenty-one years old (*a ward* = a minor under the control of a guardian)

154–5 **What lady's . . . knight?** Based on Brooke 246: 'With torch in hand a comely knight did fetch her forth to dance'.

156 **I . . . sir** It seems odd that a servant of Capulet's cannot identify Juliet, and prompt books since the mid nineteenth century show that some productions have cut this line (not in Q1) or assigned it to a more credible speaker (e.g. Benvolio, Balthazar, Mercutio's page). Shakespeare may have been trying to dramatize a moment in the novellas when Romeo, overcome with love at first sight, lacks the boldness to ask Juliet's name and goes on to meet her without knowing who she is. The line can be read as either prose or verse.

157–64, 206–9 **O, she . . . hand, If . . . kiss** The early seventeenth-century Crewe manuscript includes these twelve lines and may provide independent authority for some of the readings adopted by this edition and others, such as 'sin' (l. 207) and 'ready stand' (l. 208). (Presently this manuscript is in Meisei University, Tokyo; a set of black-and-white prints is available in the British Library, RP 2031, Manuscript Room. Its provenance has not yet been established.)

157 **torches** Romeus witnesses a torch-dance in Brooke at this point (see ll. 154–5 n.), a detail that may have inspired the image of *torches* if not the choreography of this staged dance.

158–9 **she . . . Ethiop's ear** The image of a jewel shining near a dark face (*Ethiop* = person with black skin) appears also in

As a rich jewel in an Ethiop's ear,
Beauty too rich for use, for earth too dear.
So shows a snowy dove trooping with crows,
As yonder lady o'er her fellows shows.
The measure done, I'll watch her place of stand
And, touching hers, make blessèd my rude hand.
Did my heart love till now? Forswear it, sight,
For I ne'er saw true beauty till this night.

TYBALT

This, by his voice, should be a Montague.
Fetch me my rapier, boy. *Exit Page*
What, dares the slave
Come hither, covered with an antic face,
To fleer and scorn at our solemnity?

168 *Exit Page*] COLLIER 1853 (*Exit Boye.*); *not in* Q

Lyly's *Euphues* 2.89, 'a fair pearl in a Murrian's ear' (cited by Wilson–Duthie), and in Sonnet 27.11–12: 'Which like a jewel hung in ghastly night | Makes black night beauteous and her old face new'. It belongs to a larger body of imagery, jewels shining in the dark, which refers to the Elizabethan belief that precious stones had the power to emit light. In addition, Dent suggests that the line echoes three proverbs (B435, D573.2, C844).

160 **Beauty . . . dear** Mahood analyses the wordplay: 'When we recall that *use* means "employment", "interest" and "wear and tear", that *earth* means both "mortal life" and "the grave", that *dear* can be either "cherished" or "costly" and that there is possibly a play upon *beauty* and *booty* . . ., the line's range of meanings becomes very wide indeed'. In relation to the play's events thus far, Romeo's balanced phrases contrast his estimation of Juliet as priceless with her family's appraisal of her for marriage. In relation to the legendary narrative, they imply a range of ironies: Juliet's beauty will be entombed after the briefest enjoyment and therefore will never diminish; that beauty is not *for earth too dear* because nothing can prevent Juliet's death, and she is too rare for mortal existence (see pp. 62–3). (With this wordplay cf. 1.2.14–15.)

163 **measure** According to A. Brissenden, Romeo uses this term to mean part of a dance consisting of several figures in different rhythms (*Shakespeare and the Dance*, p. 64).

163 **place of stand** Shakespeare deliberately has the older generation sit (l. 143) while the young stand or dance, a visual and dynamic contrast, while Brooke makes no such distinction (cf. 249 ff.).

164 **make blessèd** This line reintroduces the conventional terms which describe amatory as religious devotion (see 1.2.91 n.) and which will become the central conceit of the lovers' first meeting (ll. 206–19).

165 **Forswear it, sight** Romeo renounces his former vows of love (to Rosaline and perhaps others) through a personification of his eyes, a device he had used earlier to express the immutability of his faith (see 1.2.91–6).

167 **by his voice . . . Montague** What identifies a Montague voice is unclear; but the auditory clue seems logical because Romeo, wearing a mask, provides Tybalt with no visual evidence.

168 **What** Usually construed as a 'mere sign of interrogation' (*OED adv.* 21; Evans interprets *What* as 'How'), although Abbott explains that *What* was often used as an exclamation of impatience (73a). Q2 has no comma after *What*.

169 **antic face** Evidently Romeo's mask appears as grotesque as Mercutio's (see l. 30 n.).

170 **fleer and scorn . . . solemnity** grin and jeer at our celebration (*OED*, *fleer*, *v.* 1,

Now by the stock and honour of my kin,
To strike him dead I hold it not a sin.

CAPULET
Why, how now, kinsman, wherefore storm you so?

TYBALT
Uncle, this is a Montague, our foe;
A villain that is hither come in spite
To scorn at our solemnity this night.

CAPULET
Young Romeo is it?

TYBALT 'Tis he, that villain Romeo.

CAPULET
Content thee, gentle coz, let him alone.
A bears him like a portly gentleman;
And, to say truth, Verona brags of him
To be a virtuous and well-governed youth.
I would not for the wealth of all this town
Here in my house do him disparagement.
Therefore be patient, take no note of him:
It is my will, the which if thou respect,
Show a fair presence and put off these frowns,
An ill-beseeming semblance for a feast.

TYBALT
It fits when such a villain is a guest;
I'll not endure him.

CAPULET He shall be endured.

scorn, v. 1); i.e. Tybalt associates the mask with Romeo's audacity. Later Capulet will use *solemnity* for a celebration mocked by death (4.4.87).

171 **stock and honour** honourable stock. An example of hendiadys (Wilson–Duthie), i.e. the expression of an idea by two nouns linked by *and*.

176 **scorn . . . solemnity** Tybalt, like his uncle, repeats himself (cf. l. 170 and see n.).

177 **Young . . . Romeo** Surrounded by heroic couplets and blank verse, these two speeches sound like irregular verse appropriate to tense dialogue; they hover between verse and prose.

178 **coz** A term of fond or familiar address, in this case for a kinsman. Under the circumstances *gentle coz* is an oxymoron (*gentle* = noble + courteous, *OED a.* 1a, 3a), although Capulet uses it to appease Tybalt.

179 **A . . . him** He . . . himself (Abbott 402,223)
portly dignified

183 **do** Sometimes used as a transitive verb with an object (Abbott 303).
disparagement reinforces the language of valuation in l. 182 because it means not only 'dishonour', but 'lowering of value, honour, or estimation', 'depreciation', 'undervaluing'.

186 **Show . . . presence** Capulet implies a comparison with Romeo (cf. l. 179).

187–8 **ill-beseeming . . . fits** Tybalt plays on Capulet's word for 'unfitting'.

187 **semblance** demeanour

What, goodman boy, I say he shall, go to!
Am I the master here or you? Go to!
You'll not endure him, God shall mend my soul,
You'll make a mutiny among my guests!
You will set cock-a-hoop, you'll be the man!

TYBALT
Why, uncle, 'tis a shame.

CAPULET Go to, go to,
You are a saucy boy. Is't so indeed?
This trick may chance to scathe you I know what,
You must contrary me—marry, 'tis time—
(*To the dancers*) Well said, my hearts—(*to Tybalt*) you
are a princox, go,

199, 201 (*To the dancers*)] This edition; *not in* Q

190 **goodman boy** A double-edged insult: *goodman* = a title prefixed to the name of someone ranking below a gentleman (*OED* 3b); *boy* = a slight or an expression of contempt (*sb.*[1] 4). In 3.1 Tybalt will direct the insult *boy* at Romeo (ll. 65, 130).

190, 191, 195 **go to!** An archaic phrase expressing both protest and impatience.

192 **God . . . soul** Capulet delivers an oath among his expostulations (*OED v.* 12b); Dent suggests it was a commonplace (cf. G173.1).

193 **a mutiny** discord (*OED sb.* 2)

194 **set cock-a-hoop** act like a dunghill cock. M. Andrews argues convincingly that Shakespeare uses this colloquial expression to represent 'masculine self-assertiveness and self-display'. Andrews derives the phrase from those inn-signs where the object of the sign was carved and hung within a hoop; he emphasizes the truculence of the birds and the popularity of cock-fighting; and he supports his interpretation by quoting from Cotgrave's definition of *Se mettre aux champs*: 'To brave it in show, to put the better leg before; to set cock a hoop, or himself out to the utmost' (*The Upstart Crow* 12 (1992), 91–5; see *OED* 1b for standard definitions). The expression was proverbial (Dent C493).
be the man i.e. play the man (although you are only 'goodman boy'); another proverbial phrase (Dent I88).

196 **saucy** insolent (another double-edged insult; cf. l. 190 and n.). Onions points out that *saucy* often expressed strong disapproval (see also *OED a.*[1] 2a).

196 **Is't so indeed?** i.e. is it indeed a disgrace? (responding to l. 195). Some editors propose a different reading, on the assumption that Capulet's attention is turning back to the festivities and his other guests: he politely asks someone other than Tybalt, 'Is that indeed so?'

197 **trick** (a) foolish act, (b) characteristic trait
scathe injure. Capulet's threat is vague, but probably refers to his power over Tybalt's status in the family and related financial circumstances (see *OED v.* 1b, 'subject to pecuniary loss').
I know what Elizabethans may have heard either 'let me tell you' (an elliptical phrase used for emphasis, *OED pron.* 8d), or 'I know how much' (Bartenschlager, 424–5).

198–9 **You . . . hearts** Capulet alternates between fulminations against Tybalt, courteous remarks to other guests, and orders to the servants. Since some of his phrases are ambiguous and Q2 punctuates the speech primarily with commas, the direction or meaning of each phrase is not always clear (cf. 1. 196 and n.). *Marry, 'tis time*, set off by commas in Q2, permits several interpretations: Capulet may address it to Tybalt, the company, or himself; it may refer to his rebuking Tybalt at last, Tybalt's showing a sign of compliance, or some matter requiring Capulet's attention as host.

198 **contrary** (a) oppose, (b) contradict (*OED v.* 1a, 2a); accented on second syllable.

199 **Well said, my hearts** Capulet compliments the dancers: *Well said* = Well done

Be quiet, or—(*to Serving-men*) more light, more light—
for shame—
(*To Tybalt*) I'll make you quiet. What! (*To the dancers*)
Cheerly, my hearts!

TYBALT

Patience perforce, with wilful choler meeting,
Makes my flesh tremble in their different greeting.
I will withdraw, but this intrusion shall
Now seeming sweet convert to bitt'rest gall. *Exit*

ROMEO

If I profane with my unworthiest hand
This holy shrine, the gentle sin is this,
My lips, two blushing pilgrims, ready stand
To smooth that rough touch with a tender kiss.

207 sin] Q; fine THEOBALD (*conj.* Warburton); pain WILSON–DUTHIE 208 ready] Q1; did readie Q2

(*OED v.*[2] 4); *hearts* = a term of commendation and endearment.

199 **princox** conceited boy (*OED* a)

200 **for shame** This phrase may be linked with either Capulet's order to the servants or his next threat to Tybalt (Q2 prints no punctuation after *more light, more light* and a comma after *for shame*).

202–3 **Patience . . . greeting** Commentators repeatedly assume that Tybalt sees himself as the personification of patience constrained to deal with Capulet, the embodiment of *wilful choler* or stubborn anger. Read this way, the lines sound blatantly ironic. But G. Monsarrat points out (in correspondence) that Tybalt refers to the emotional conflict producing his visceral reaction: the phrase *Patience perforce* means 'Patience under compulsion' (Dent P111, *OED sb.* 1f); and *wilful* also signifies 'willing, eager' or 'not enforced' (see Onions, who cites this line, and *OED a.*[1] 4a). In Monsarrat's view, 'the conflict is between Tybalt's natural feelings of anger and an enforced, unnatural patience'.

203 **their different greeting** i.e. the confrontation of their differences

205 **seeming sweet . . . bitt'rest gall** Tybalt uses the antithesis which Romeo introduced in the first scene (see 1.1.190 and n.) and which Dent cites as a commonplace (cf. S1040.1, H551.1); staging—Tybalt's exit as the lovers meet—brings it to life. (This edition construes *seeming sweet* as the object of *convert*, but others read it as an adjectival or appositional phrase modifying *intrusion*.)

205 ***Exit*** Q2 gives only the direction for Tybalt, but prompt books indicate that in production business between Romeo and Juliet often occurs before Tybalt's *Exit*. Usually Romeo takes the more active role, joining Juliet, leading her forward to the position where they will exchange their first words. Q2 makes no reference to Paris in this scene, but productions since the early nineteenth century have often introduced him as Juliet's partner in dance or conversation; as the dance ends, Romeo takes Paris's place at Juliet's side.

206–19 **If . . . take** This sonnet, followed by or incorporating a quatrain, elaborates the religious terms which Romeo used earlier and incidentally (see 1.2.91 n. and l. 164 n.). Earl points out that the imagery of religion and pilgrimage has an antecedent in Petrarch's sonnet 16 and, more immediately, in a poem by Henry Constable ('*Romeo and Juliet* and the Elizabethan Sonnets', 114–15). These lines seem also to play on the Italian word *romeo*, which Shakespeare's contemporary Florio would define in his Italian dictionary *A Worlde of Wordes* (1598) as 'a roamer, a wanderer, a palmer for devotion's sake'. The contrivance of the poetry, invented for this exchange, may

JULIET

Good pilgrim, you do wrong your hand too much,
Which mannerly devotion shows in this,
For saints have hands that pilgrims' hands do touch,
And palm to palm is holy palmers' kiss.

ROMEO

Have not saints lips, and holy palmers too?

JULIET

Ay, pilgrim, lips that they must use in prayer.

ROMEO

O then, dear saint, let lips do what hands do;
They pray, grant thou, lest faith turn to despair.

heighten the decorum which the lovers observe at the social gathering. Despite its artifice, the medium is animated by their obvious attraction to each other and by the gestures it requires in performance. According to representative editions and prompt books, however, eighteenth- and nineteenth-century productions made substantive cuts to the speeches, eliminating the sonnet/quatrain format.

207 **This holy shrine** i.e. Juliet's hand
gentle sin Editors have tried to make this phrase logical, producing various emendations: e.g. 'fine' = penalty (Theobald, conj. Warburton; justified by a minim misreading); 'gentler' (conj. Dowden; explained by loss of the comparative *r*). Yet it owes less to logic than to the conventions of amatory verse. It is an oxymoron belonging to the quatrain's larger contradiction between *gentle* and 'rough', the antithesis which Benvolio connected with love in the first scene (ll. 165–6) and which Romeo promptly exploited in a sometimes illogical set of oxymora (ll. 172–7). With *gentle sin* Romeo seems to describe his plan for atonement (the 'tender kiss' of l. 209) as only a mild transgression (cf. ll. 220–23 and 3.3.39).

208 **pilgrims** (because they are prepared to pay homage at the shrine)
ready stand Q2 reads 'did readie stand', producing an awkward sequence of tenses and the only metrically irregular line in the sonnet. This edition assumes a printing error (perhaps an undeleted false start, as Hosley suggests).

210–13 **Good . . . kiss** Juliet defends Romeo's hand from his charges of profanation. As she excuses him for touching her hand, she seems to evade his request for a kiss. Meantime she takes up his conceit, accepts his compliment, and borrows one of his rhymes (*this*/*kiss*).

210 **Good pilgrim** The emphasis on this conceit has led to the suggestion that Romeo wears a pilgrim's costume; but the text gives no clear evidence for this, and Tybalt's description of Romeo's mask (l. 169) seems to argue against it. Prompt books suggest that the idea has not significantly influenced productions, although Romeo sometimes appears in full pilgrim dress or with an item or two of pilgrim's gear (e.g. a staff).

211 **mannerly** seemly (*OED a.* 1).

212 **saints** i.e. representations of saints

213 **palm to palm . . . palmers'** Juliet plays on *palm* (= part of the hand) and *palmer* (= pilgrim returning from the Holy Land with a palm-branch or palm-leaf as a sign of the journey). In Brooke Juliet is more impulsive: 'Then she with tender hand his tender palm hath pressed' (267).

215 **prayer** Metaphor and wordplay allow *prayer* to be understood not only as an act of religious worship, but also as supplication to a person (e.g. courtship of a lady). Despite her inexperience, Juliet encourages this suitor with tact and style.

216 **let lips . . . hands do** Romeo's ardour momentarily undermines his logic, although his general intent remains clear. He seems to accept Juliet's hint, skipping over the rest of what she says to pursue his own less subtle thought about saints and palmers having *lips*. He makes this analogy in his second bid for a kiss.

217 **pray . . . despair** This line picks up the main point of Juliet's 'lips that they must

JULIET
Saints do not move, though grant for prayer's sake.

ROMEO
Then move not while my prayer's effect I take.
He kisses her
Thus from my lips, by thine, my sin is purged.

JULIET
Then have my lips the sin that they have took.

ROMEO
Sin from my lips? O trespass sweetly urged!
Give me my sin again.
He kisses her

JULIET
You kiss by th' book.

NURSE
Madam, your mother craves a word with you.
Juliet moves towards her mother

ROMEO
What is her mother?

NURSE
Marry, bachelor,

219.1 *He kisses her*] ROWE ('*Kissing her.*', *after* l. 220); *not in* Q 223 *He kisses her*] CAPELL (*kissing her again.*); *not in* Q 224.1 *Juliet . . . mother*] JOWETT, MOWAT–WERSTINE; *not in* Q

use in prayer' and connects it with the analogy between lips and hands. The key words—*prayer*, *grant*, *faith*, *despair*—refer to both religious worship and amorous entreaty. Q2 prints *grant thou* in parentheses, where the words are probably a mild imperative, 'grant their prayer'; but Romeo may also mean 'if you consent', or even 'you must admit'.

218–19 **Saints . . . take** Juliet plays on Romeo's metaphor: *saints* = (a) canonized persons, (b) representations of canonized persons. He joins her in punning: *move* = (a) propose, prefer a request (*OED* v. 14a), (b) change position. When she tells him she cannot take the initiative in granting his prayer, he quickly acts to take it himself.

221 **took** This curtailed form of the past participle (Abbott 343) sets up the rhyme for *book* (l. 223), a recurrent motif. Juliet invites a second kiss.

222 **urged** (a) alleged, (b) provoked

223 **You . . . book** Juliet reintroduces her mother's figure of speech. *By the book* means 'formally, in set phrase; also, according to the rules' (*OED*, *sb.* 15). Both definitions suit Romeo's behaviour, as he follows the set phrases of poetic convention and gentlemanly etiquette. Later Mercutio will sarcastically describe Tybalt fighting 'by the book of arithmetic' (3.1.102). (Q2 prints *by th'* as *bith*, indicating monosyllabic pronunciation.)

224 **Nurse** Neither Q2 nor Q1 indicates when the Nurse enters, or why Capulet's Wife speaks through her. In a review of Gibbons's edition, S. Wells suggests three explanations: the Nurse may not be included in the direction at 127.1–2 and therefore enters the scene here; Shakespeare may have imagined Capulet's Wife to have left the stage but omitted the necessary exit; or he may have forgotten that Capulet's Wife was still on the stage ('The bettering of Burby', *TLS*, 20 June 1980).

225 **What** who (Abbott 254)

Marry, bachelor *Marry* shows surprise at the question; *bachelor* (= young gentleman) may have been suggested by Brooke 163, as Gibbons conjectures.

Her mother is the lady of the house,
And a good lady, and a wise and virtuous;
I nursed her daughter that you talked withal.
I tell you, he that can lay hold of her
Shall have the chinks.

ROMEO
Is she a Capulet?
O dear account! My life is my foe's debt.

BENVOLIO
Away, be gone, the sport is at the best.

ROMEO
Ay, so I fear, the more is my unrest.

CAPULET
Nay, gentlemen, prepare not to be gone;
We have a trifling foolish banquet towards.
[*They signal to Capulet that they must leave*]
Is it e'en so? Why then I thank you all.
I thank you, honest gentlemen, good night.
(*To Serving-men*) More torches here—come on—then
let's to bed.

235.1 [*They signal . . . leave*]] This edition; *They whisper in his eare.* Q1; *not in* Q2

228 **withal** with (Abbott 196). See also l. 256.

229 **lay hold** 'grasp' in both the literal and figurative senses

230 **the chinks** ready money (*OED sb.*[1] 3). The expression is also bawdy, as C. Leech points out by comparing the five references to *chink* in *Dream* ('Chinks', *TLS*, 25 December 1970).

231 **dear account** grievous reckoning (*OED a.*[2] 2). At the same time the lovers' poetry and the language of valuation (cf. ll. 154, 182) give *dear* overtones of 'beloved', 'precious', 'costly'.

My life . . . debt i.e. I owe my life to my enemies (because he cannot live without Juliet). Brooke's corresponding line, 'Thus hath his foe in choice to give him life or death' (325), draws attention to Shakespeare's auditory pun on *debt*/death and the resulting antithesis *life*/death.

232 **Away . . . best** Benvolio repeats the proverb to which Romeo alluded earlier in refusing to dance (l. 37): 'When play (game, jest) is best it is time to leave' (Dent P399). Again the maxim has ironic resonance (see l. 35 n.), reinforced in the next line.

235 **trifling . . . banquet towards** Capulet disparages the dessert course just coming—sweetmeats, fruit, wine (*OED sb.*[1] 3)—as silly and without value, probably to enhance the effect of its sumptuous arrival.

235.1 [**They . . . leave**] Q2 does not indicate how the masquers signal their departure to Capulet; Q1 prints '*They whisper in his eare*'. Prompt books stage the moment variously: Benvolio, Mercutio, or the group whispers to Capulet; Mercutio or Benvolio mimes that the gentlemen wish to be excused; the masquers bow a negative; the guests murmur; Capulet's lines are cut and the guests simply depart. (Curiously, many prompt books give no annotations for staging of the polite rebuff, although most of them carefully orchestrate these exits.)

236 **Is . . . all** Capulet's response to whatever signal of departure he has received.

238 **More torches . . . bed** The host calls for light to show his guests out; he gives no further thought to the banquet.

Ah, sirrah, by my fay, it waxes late,
I'll to my rest. *Exeunt all but Juliet and the Nurse*

JULIET
Come hither, Nurse. What is yon gentleman?

NURSE
The son and heir of old Tiberio.

JULIET
What's he that now is going out of door?

NURSE
Marry, that, I think, be young Petruccio.

JULIET
What's he that follows here that would not dance?

NURSE
I know not.

JULIET
Go, ask his name.
The Nurse goes
If he be marrièd,
My grave is like to be my wedding-bed.

NURSE (*returning*)
His name is Romeo, and a Montague,
The only son of your great enemy.

240 *Exeunt . . . Nurse*] Malone; *Exeunt.* Q1; *not in* Q2 247 *The Nurse goes*] JOWETT; *not in* Q
249 (*returning*)] JOWETT; *not in* Q

239 **sirrah** See l. 142 n.
fay faith (*OED sb.*[1] 6b)

240 ***Exeunt all*** As the following dialogue indicates, not all guests leave at this point. The departure begins here.

241–5 **What . . . dance** Juliet's contrivance for guarding her privacy, identifying two other young gentlemen before Romeo, derives from Brooke 341–52 (cf. Painter, 86–7).

242–4 **The son . . . Petruccio** These guests, first mentioned here, were not on Capulet's invitation list at 1.2.65–73. *Petruccio*'s name (pronounced with a soft *ch* sound) will reappear with Tybalt's in the Q2 direction at 3.1.33.1.

243 **What's** who's (Abbott 254)

244 **that . . . be** Abbott describes as 'a confusion of "That, I think, *is*" and "I think that that *be*" ' (411).

245 **What's . . . dance?** This line indicates that Juliet noticed Romeo before he approached 'her place of stand', as he observed the dancers (ll. 154–205).

247–8 **If . . . wedding-bed** As Mahood, p. 57, and Spencer point out, this couplet introduces the tragedy's leitmotiv of death as Juliet's bridegroom, a theme which will recur (3.2.136–7, 3.5.200–1, 4.4.61–5, 5.3.102–8) and which connects the play with the *amour-passion* myth defined by Denis de Rougement (see 'Myth' in the Introduction). (Dent compares 'To be married rather to one's grave' (G426), suggesting that the idea is a commonplace.) Spencer draws attention to Juliet's immediate thought of marriage, a striking contrast with her reaction at 1.3.68 ('It is an honour that I dream not of') and a reminder that this scene has not involved Paris, her intended suitor.

249 **and a Montague** i.e. and he is a Montague, a common type of ellipsis (Abbott 383)

JULIET

My only love sprung from my only hate,
Too early seen unknown and known too late!
Prodigious birth of love it is to me
That I must love a loathèd enemy.

NURSE

What's tis? What's tis?

JULIET A rhyme I learnt even now

Of one I danced withal.

One calls within, 'Juliet!'

NURSE Anon, anon!

Come, let's away, the strangers all are gone.

Exeunt

2.0 *Enter Chorus*

CHORUS

Now old desire doth in his death-bed lie,
And young affection gapes to be his heir;

255 tis . . . tis] Q2; *this . . . that* Q1; this . . . this F
2.0.0.1–14 *Enter Chorus . . .* sweet. *Exit*] Q2 (*but without 'Enter' and 'Exit'* (THEOBALD)); *scene not in* Q1 1 CHORUS] CAMBRIDGE; *not in* Q2

251–2 **My . . . late** This couplet not only declares Juliet's love but emphasizes the elements of contradiction and chance in her meeting with Romeo, as if she were both enacting and narrating events.

253 **Prodigious** (a) ominous (*OED a.* 1), (b) unnatural, monstrous. In Juliet's metaphoric terms, *prodigious birth* results from loving an enemy, the couplet's central antithesis, and expresses her first premonition about her fate. Figures of repetition emphasize *love*, the key word in ll. 253–4.

255 **tis** this. In his edition Williams explains that *tis* is 'a common dialect or subliterary pronunciation of "this"'.

255–6 **A rhyme . . . withal** Juliet evades the Nurse's question by directing her attention away from Romeo (to a gentleman with whom she *danced*) and to the sound (*rhyme*) rather than the substance of her words.

256 **Anon** right away, coming

2.0.1–14 **Now . . . sweet** The second Chorus has been in disfavour since Johnson wrote 'The use of this Chorus is not easily discovered'. Editors debate whether it should end 1.4 or begin 2.1; and Q1, like most stage productions, omits it. But it suits both content and style at this juncture, reprising two-thirds of the ball episode in a quatrain before previewing the next four scenes, so acting as a bridging device and prologue to 2.1; and its verse and rhetoric echo conventions employed repeatedly in the first Chorus and preceding dialogue. Nevertheless, it fails to convey the speed and intensity of unfolding events; it more accurately reproduces that portion of the source narratives where the lovers' secret meetings continue through a month or two of marriage.

1–2 **Now . . . heir** These verses echo the antitheses and very language with which 1.4 closed. Despite this continuity and the description of Romeo's changed state, the deathbed tableau distances the audience from the lovers as personified affection *gapes* (longs eagerly, *OED v.* 4b) for an inheritance from personified desire. At the same time the image of youth anticipating property or rank conveys material themes—inheritance, valuation, ambition, and greed—which sounded in earlier scenes from Capulet's

That fair for which love groaned for and would die,
  With tender Juliet matched is now not fair.
Now Romeo is beloved and loves again,
  Alike bewitchèd by the charm of looks;
But to his foe supposed he must complain,
  And she steal love's sweet bait from fearful hooks.
Being held a foe, he may not have access
  To breathe such vows as lovers use to swear;
And she, as much in love, her means much less
  To meet her new belovèd anywhere.
But passion lends them power, time means, to meet,
Temp'ring extremities with extreme sweet. *Exit*

2.1 *Enter Romeo alone*

ROMEO
  Can I go forward when my heart is here?

4 matched] Q3; match Q2

exchange with Paris to Mercutio's fantasy of Queen Mab.

3 **fair for . . . groaned for** This line, personifying Rosaline as *fair* and Romeo as *love*, allows the next to play rhetorically on *fair*. In *groaned for*, later repeated as 'groaning for' (2.3.83), *for* means (a) because of, (b) in order to have.

5 **again** in return (*OED adv.* 2a)

6 **Alike** i.e. both equally. Brooke supplies the ellipsis: 'But each of them alike did burn in equal flame' (487).
looks (a) appearance, (b) glances (Evans)

7 **to his foe . . . complain** Romeo and Juliet are described as stereotypical lovers: *he must complain* = (a) he must make moan (cf. *groaned* in l. 3), (b) he must compose laments (*OED v.* 3a, 1b); she is *his foe supposed*, the 'dear enemy' of amatory verse.

8 **she . . . hooks** The fish conceit and the antithesis (*sweet/fearful*) are Petrarchan devices, the trope conventionally associated with the unrequited lover. In this configuration, inspired by Brooke 388 ('the poisoned hook is hid, wrapped in the pleasant bait'), they stress the danger of Juliet's attraction to Romeo. (Cf. Dent P456.1.)
fearful i.e. causing fear. The Chorus echoes the Prologue, which introduced this word as a pun (l. 9 n.).

9 **access** (accented on second syllable)

10 **use** are accustomed

11–12 **And . . . anywhere** These lines concentrate figures of repetition but lack an inflected verb.

13–14 **But . . . sweet** The sonnet closes, as it began, with strong sound effects, repeating *means* and *meet*; and the couplet ends with a flourish of rhetoric that includes a key antithesis, *extremities/ sweet*. Here *extremities* means 'extremes', referring both to the lovers' trials and to their intensity of feeling (*OED* 4a). As a result, *Temp'ring extremities* has a paradoxical edge reinforced by *extreme* (accented on first syllable). For a proverbial connection, see Dent D357 (cf. 4.1.69–70 n.).

14 **Exit** The formal Chorus now disappears and the choric function is performed solely by characters of the play. Pearlman, pp. 112–15, elaborates the theory that Shakespeare planned a full set of choruses but changed his mind, establishing a pattern in the style of Elizabethan tragedy and then discarding it.

2.1 This scene makes the invented exchange between Benvolio and Mercutio a prelude to the wooing episode adapted from Brooke 467–564. In the Bodleian First Folio, the lovers' dialogue here is reputedly 'best thumbed of all' (Granville-Barker, p. 51 n. 5).

1–2 **Can . . . out** Dent compares 'The lover is not where he lives but where he loves' (L565), and 'As dull as earth' (E27.1).

Turn back, dull earth, and find thy centre out.
[He turns back, withdrawing.]
Enter Benvolio with Mercutio

BENVOLIO Romeo, my cousin Romeo, Romeo!

MERCUTIO He is wise and, on my life, hath stol'n him home to bed.

BENVOLIO
He ran this way and leapt this orchard wall.
Call, good Mercutio.

2.1.2.1 *[He . . . withdrawing]*] JOWETT (*[He turns back and withdraws.]*); *not in* Q 3 Romeo, Romeo!] Q2; *Romeo.* Q1

2 **dull earth** The implications of this phrase broaden the world of the play momentarily, referring to a larger design and system. By addressing his body as *earth*, Romeo describes its composition in terms familiar from the Bible (Genesis 2: 7, 1 Corinthians 15: 45–50) and from the doctrine of elements: 'Of these four | The earth and water for their mass and weight are sunken lower' (Ovid, *Metamorphoses*, 15.264–5). The epithet *dull* suits these concepts both here and in the similar first line of Sonnet 44: 'the dull substance of my flesh'. According to Booth, *dull* in this context means 'sluggish, inert, heavy, slow of motion'. In addition, Romeo puns on 'melancholy'; and his image of himself as *dull earth* will be further complicated by the next metaphor.

centre This image represents several ideas, like its counterpart in Sonnet 146.1, 'Poor soul, the centre of my sinful earth': (a) the defining point of a circle, (b) 'the centre of attraction, the being which should be served', i.e. Juliet (W. G. Ingram and Theodore Redpath, eds., *Shakespeare's Sonnets* (1964); see also J. D. Rea, 'A Note on *Romeo and Juliet*, II, 1, 1–2', *MP* 18 (1921), 163–4), (c) the location of the soul (see Booth). At the same time it brings cosmic associations to *earth*, regarded as the centre of the Ptolemaic universe. Romeo's metaphor becomes an emblem at once of strength and weakness, power and sluggishness; his body is both a microcosm and a handful of dust. Moreover, since the centre of earth was conceived as one site of hell, the centre which Romeo seeks can lead him potentially not only to self-definition but also to self-destruction.

2.1 **[*He . . . withdrawing*]** Benvolio's first words show that Romeo has disappeared from the view of his friends, but no early text indicates how or where. Capell's direction, '*leaps the wall*', understands Benvolio literally at l. 6. Though Capell ignores other evidence (l. 31) and takes no account of Elizabethan stage practice, his decision influenced almost all editors until Hosley. Gibbons and Evans represent the latest scholarly consensus; they imagine the simplest and most fluid staging, Romeo concealing himself behind a stage-post until l. 43, when he reappears. In productions over the past two centuries three solutions occur: some version of the uncluttered arrangement; introduction of a wall; and omission of Romeo's opening speech or the first forty-three lines. As Romeo's opening lines in 2.1 set this scene, all the action takes place near the Capulet house.

3 **Romeo, Romeo!** Q1 and some editors print only one *Romeo* at the end; the editors produce a pentameter with 'He is wise'. It is not clear, however, that Q2 prints verse at this point; its lines hover between prose and verse. This edition interprets the opening of the dialogue as rhythmic prose and follows the Q2 lineation.

4 **stol'n him** withdrawn himself secretly (*OED v.*[1] 8)

6 **orchard wall** Brooke's line 830, 'he leapt the wall', does not reveal whether this *orchard wall* encloses fruit trees only or other plants as well (*OED*, *orchard*, 1a).

[MERCUTIO] Nay, I'll conjure too.
Romeo! Humours! Madman! Passion! Lover!
Appear thou in the likeness of a sigh;
Speak but one rhyme and I am satisfied.
Cry but 'Ay me', pronounce but 'love' and 'dove';
Speak to my gossip Venus one fair word,
One nickname for her purblind son and heir,
Young Abraham Cupid, he that shot so true

7–8 [MERCUTIO] Nay . . . Romeo!] Q1 (*reading* Call, nay *for* Q2 Nay), Q4; Nay . . . *Mer<cutio>*. *Romeo*, Q2 10 one] Q2 (on), Q1 11 pronounce‸] Q1 (Pronounce); prouaunt, Q2 dove] Q1; day Q2 13 heir] Q1; her Q2 14 Abraham‸Cupid] Q2 (*Abraham:Cupid*); Adam Cupid STEEVENS 1778 (*conj.* Upton) true] Q2; trim Q1

7 [**MERCUTIO**] Q2 prints the speech-prefix at l. 8, but gives 'Nay, I'll conjure too' on a separate line of type. Since Mercutio (not Benvolio) does the conjuring, Q1 and Q4 seem to correct a mechanical error by assigning half of l. 7 to him.
conjure i.e. not just call, but call him to appear by the invocation of names, as one would call a devil or spirit to appear (*OED v.* 5a). For proper conjurations the names invoked are sacred; in Mercutio's parody the names will represent aspects of Romeo's loverlike posturing before the ball in 1.4.

8 **Humours** whims or affectations. Dent compares with 'Love is a madness (lunacy)' (L505.2).

9 **Appear . . . sigh** The imperative is a paradox.

11 **'Ay me'** The lover's sigh just conjured by Mercutio (l. 9), Romeo's words as he entered the play (1.1.157), and Juliet's when she first appears in this scene (l. 68).
pronounce . . . 'dove' Q1's prose version helps to correct Q2's evident misreadings of two words in manuscript: 'prouaunt' for *pronounc* (a minim error and mistaking of *t* for *c*), and 'day' ('daie') for *doue* or *dou*. Unemended, the Q2 line makes little sense: 'provant' = provision (*OED* gives only one illustration for the verb, Nashe's *Lenten Stuff* (1599)); and 'day' spoils the rhyme for which Mercutio has called.

12 **my gossip Venus** Mercutio reduces the goddess of love to a familiar acquaintance who enjoys idle talk.

13 **One nickname** The lover's custom of nicknaming Cupid is illustrated with wit by Biron in *L.L.L.* 3.1.175–81.
purblind totally blind (*OED a.* 1), obtuse

14 **Young Abraham Cupid** Mercutio suggests a nickname for Cupid, 'young patriarch', an oxymoron which corresponds to Biron's 'Signor Junior' and sums up Cupid's position among the gods as boy-elder (see *L.L.L.* 3.1.175 and 5.2.11). The phrase has been much disputed and variously emended. Steevens (conj. Upton) thought *Abraham* a misreading of 'Adam', i.e. the legendary archer Adam Bell (cf. *Much Ado* 1.1.240–2); Jowett adopts 'Adam' on the assumption that Q1 corrupted Q2. (Williams and the following note raise questions about these conclusions.) Other glosses seem to miss the main point: they maintain that *Abraham* = a spelling of 'abram', which misreads 'abron', a spelling of 'auburn'; or that *Abraham* = 'Abraham-man', a ragged beggar who might be blind, almost naked, crippled, wily, or mad (the insanity real or pretended).

14 **true** Q1 has 'trim' (= accurately), quoting the ballad of King Cophetua: 'The blinded boy that shoots so trim'. Following Q1, recent editors impute a minim misreading to Q2; and they emphasize Shakespeare's familiarity with this ballad, mentioned at *L.L.L.* 1.2.104–5, 4.1.64–6, *Richard II* 5.3.78, and *2 Henry IV* 5.3.103. Yet l. 14 is so anomalous that it seems reasonable to preserve the Q2 reading. The first half (to *Cupid*) is identical with Q1 in spelling, punctuation, and typeface; the second half and the next line differ. If the compositor checked Q1 to clarify an illegible phrase, he read only three words of the line. This may be so, but equally Q2 may represent the playwright's slightly different recollection: Shakespeare refers to the ballad several other times, but does not quote it (and see next note for differing versions of the ballad).

When King Cophetua loved the beggar maid.—
He heareth not, he stirreth not, he moveth not:
The ape is dead, and I must conjure him.
I conjure thee by Rosaline's bright eyes,
By her high forehead and her scarlet lip,
By her fine foot, straight leg, and quivering thigh,
And the demesnes that there adjacent lie,
That in thy likeness thou appear to us.

BENVOLIO

An if he hear thee, thou wilt anger him.

MERCUTIO

This cannot anger him. 'Twould anger him
To raise a spirit in his mistress' circle
Of some strange nature, letting it there stand
Till she had laid it and conjured it down:

15 **King Cophetua . . . beggar maid** The earliest extant copy of this ballad, 'A Song of a Beggar and a King', appeared in Richard Johnson's *Crown Garland of Golden Roses* (1612). According to Hibbard's edition of *L.L.L.*, 'the original ballad must have been far more robust than Johnson's decorous version' (1.2.104–5 n.; see also R. David's note to *L.L.L.* 4.1.66–82 in his Arden edition (1951)). More robustness and less decorum would make the allusion even more appropriate for Mercutio.

16 **He . . . moveth not** Mercutio combines rhetoric with wordplay to comic effect: the device of symploce (repetition of words at the beginnings and ends of a series of clauses) frames two bawdy puns (*stirreth* and *moveth*; cf. 1.1.5–6, and n.).

17 **The ape is dead** *Ape* (which meant any kind of monkey) is used as a term of affection even as it signifies 'fool'; *The ape is dead* evidently refers to a trick of performing monkeys who played dead until signalled to revive (see W. Strunk, Jr., 'The Elizabethan Showman's Ape', *MLN* 32 (1917), 215–21).

I . . . conjure him From ll. 16–30 this dialogue gives Mercutio's conjuring a new slant. Although he again calls Romeo to appear, he now entreats him through Rosaline, for whom Romeo had a strong regard; and his emphasis on raising Romeo from immobility and apparent death makes this invocation wittily indecent. Dent connects ll. 17–22 with the expression 'To show oneself in one's own likeness' (L293.1).

18–21 **I conjure . . . lie** Mercutio continues to mock the loverlike Romeo with this version of a literary blazon, a catalogue of the beloved's anatomical charms. From *bright eyes* to *straight leg* Mercutio recites a standard list; with the last two items he shifts to ribaldry.

20–1 **By . . . lie** The first of several couplets in the conversation between Mercutio and Benvolio; alliteration also becomes noticeable.

21 **demesnes** domains (*OED* 6, first illustration of the figurative usage)

22 **in thy likeness** i.e. in your own shape

23 **An if** if (Abbott 105)

25 **raise . . . circle** Mercutio's conjuring jargon is replete with double entendres: *raise* = (a) summon, (b) arouse; *spirit* = (a) incorporeal being, (b) penis (see Partridge, and Booth's note on Sonnet 129.1); *circle* = (a) magic circle (*OED sb.* 3), (b) female genitals (Partridge).

26 **strange** i.e. belonging to someone other than Romeo

stand A continuation of the puns on 'raise a spirit' (see Partridge and cf. 1.1.8 n., 27).

27 **laid . . . down** This line repeats a bawdy pun as the mistress subdues the 'spirit' in both of its capacities (see *lay it* in Partridge, and cf. 1.4.26 and 25–6 n.).

That were some spite. My invocation
Is fair and honest, in his mistress' name;
I conjure only but to raise up him.

BENVOLIO

Come, he hath hid himself among these trees
To be consorted with the humorous night.
Blind is his love, and best befits the dark.

MERCUTIO

If love be blind, love cannot hit the mark.
Now will he sit under a medlar tree
And wish his mistress were that kind of fruit
As maids call medlars when they laugh alone.
O Romeo, that she were, O that she were
An open-arse, or thou a popp'rin' pear.
Romeo, good night. I'll to my truckle-bed;

39 open-arse, or] HOSLEY; open, or Q2; open *Et caetera*, Q1; open-arse and WILSON–DUTHIE

28 **spite** provocation (*OED sb.* 4b)
invocation (five syllables)

28–9 **My . . . name** One line in Q2.

29 **honest** (a) respectable, (b) chaste

30 **I conjure . . . him** The expressions *conjure* and *raise up him* extend the jokes that began with 'I must conjure him' (l. 17) and 'raise a spirit' (l. 25). (See Abbott 130 and 240 for the redundant *but* and transposed pronoun *him*.)

31 **he . . . trees** Benvolio adds foliage to the setting he described at l. 6, his words stressed with alliteration and rhyme.

32 **be consorted** (a) keep company, (b) harmonize
humorous (a) damp, (b) full of humours or moods (*OED a.* 1, 3; *a.* 1, first illustration). Mercutio connected humours with a lover's state of mind and feeling in l. 8, and Montague linked his son's melancholy with both humours and darkness at 1.1.135–7 (see l. 137 n.).

33 **Blind . . . dark** Proverbial (Dent L506). This line continues to echo the romantic commonplaces exchanged by the Montague men in 1.1 and 1.2, an ironic effect in light of Romeo's transformation in 1.4.

34 **If . . . mark** Mercutio inverts Romeo's statement about blind Cupid finding 'pathways to his will' (1.1.168), and repeats Benvolio's bawdy quibbling on *hit* and *mark* (see 1.1.203 n., 204 n.).

35–7 **medlar tree . . . medlars** The bawdiness has become intense and graphic, *medlar* furnishing two more obvious puns: it sounds like 'meddler', one who 'meddles' or has sexual intercourse (*OED v.* 5); and it names a fruit 'resembling a small, brown-skinned apple, with a large cup-shaped "eye" ' (2; see Partridge).

38 **O . . . O** These exclamations may add to the bawdy quibbles, since *O* can be understood (like 'circle', 'eye', and 'ring') as an image of female genitals (Partridge).

39 **open-arse** medlar fruit (repeating the pun from ll. 35–7 even more graphically). Q2 prints 'open, or', the compositor's impression of the form 'openers' (which *OED* cites, e.g., in Chaucer's *Reeve's Prologue* 17). Among editors who follow Q2 here, almost all read 'open-arse and', assuming that 'and' appeared in the original text but was deleted as superfluous. More probably the compositor understood dittography and dropped an *or*. (S. G. Culliford suggests a different misreading, of a contracted form of *Et caetera* (as in Q1), in ' "Romeo and Juliet", 2.1.38', *N&Q*, NS 2 (1955), 475.)
popp'rin' pear i.e. poppering pear, named after the Flemish town of Poperinghe. According to Partridge, the *popp'rin' pear* supplies Mercutio with additional quibbles on both copulation and the male body: it sounds like 'pop 'r in', and it looks like male genitals.

40–1 **truckle-bed . . . field-bed** Mercutio con-

This field-bed is too cold for me to sleep.
Come, shall we go?

BENVOLIO Go then, for 'tis in vain
To seek him here that means not to be found.

Exeunt Benvolio and Mercutio

[*Romeo comes forward, Juliet entering above*]

ROMEO
He jests at scars that never felt a wound—
But soft, what light through yonder window breaks?
It is the east, and Juliet is the sun.
Arise, fair sun, and kill the envious moon,
Who is already sick and pale with grief

43.1 *Exeunt . . . Mercutio*] Q4, F (*Exeunt.*); *Exit.* Q2 43.2 [*Romeo . . . above*]] This edition (*following* Spencer); *not in* Q

trasts an indoor *truckle-bed* (a low bed on castors stored beneath a higher bed when not in use) with an outdoor *field-bed* (portable, for use in the field, or a bed on the ground itself; *OED* 2 cites as its first example, but Brooke introduces the word). Since a *truckle-bed* was used by servants and children, Mercutio says jokingly that right now he would prefer the humblest domestic comfort to remaining in the orchard. The line about the *field-bed* seems to echo the nurse's words to the lovers in Brooke: 'Lo here a field, (she showed a field-bed ready dight) | Where you may, if you list, in arms, revenge yourself to fight' (897–8). With Mercutio's references to love-making and with Romeo in earshot, the image of a *field-bed* may represent the motif of love as war (see Mahood, p. 63 n. 1, and l. 44).

42–3 **Come . . . found** Q2 prints as a blank verse line between a dimeter and a trimeter. This edition makes the adjustment, traditional since Pope, which results in two blank verse lines.

43.1 ***Exeunt . . . Mercutio*** This edition does not make the traditional scene-break, since Q2 gives no evidence that Romeo has exited (see l. 2.1 n.), and there is no change of place. When Romeo steps forward his first line, rhyming with Benvolio's last, suggests that he has been near enough to overhear his friends.

43.2 [***Romeo . . . above***] The Renaissance staging conventions of the wooing episode which follows—the woman above at her window, the man below and outside—are discussed by L. Thomson, 'Window Scenes in Renaissance Plays: A Survey and Some Conclusions', *MARDE* 5 (1991), 225–43. As the woman appears on the upper level, usually with a candle burning in the space representing her window, she gives literal sense to the metaphoric speeches associating her with light and heaven. (On the symbolism of Juliet's walled garden, see Colie, *Shakespeare's 'Living Art'*, p. 145.) In the absence of instructions from the quartos, these staging conventions support the early placement of Juliet's entrance, although editors give the stage direction at various points between ll. 43 and 53.

44 **He jests . . . wound** As Gibbons points out, this line has ironic repercussions in 3.1. More immediately it begins an episode, the second meeting of Romeo and Juliet, which R. Stamm analyses in terms of its stillness, silence, and musical patterning of voices (*Shakespeare's Theatrical Notation: The Early Tragedies* (Bern, 1989), pp. 90–103). J. Colaco explains the use of literary and folk traditions ('The Window Scenes in *Romeo and Juliet* and Folk Songs of the Night Visit', *SP* 83 (1986), 138–57).

46 **the east . . . the sun** The cosmic imagery which has appeared sporadically (e.g. 1.1.114–15, 130–2; 1.2.95–6; 2.1.1–2) now becomes prominent.

48 **sick and pale** Alluding to the pallor of moonlight (cf. 'sick and green' in l. 51).

That thou, her maid, art far more fair than she.
Be not her maid, since she is envious;
Her vestal livery is but sick and green,
And none but fools do wear it. Cast it off.
It is my lady, O it is my love,
O that she knew she were!
She speaks, yet she says nothing. What of that?
Her eye discourses; I will answer it.
I am too bold; 'tis not to me she speaks.
Two of the fairest stars in all the heaven,
Having some business, do entreat her eyes
To twinkle in their spheres till they return.
What if her eyes were there, they in her head?
The brightness of her cheek would shame those stars
As daylight doth a lamp; her eye in heaven
Would through the airy region stream so bright
That birds would sing and think it were not night.

59 do] Q1; to Q2 63 eye] Q2; eyes Q1

49 **thou, her maid** Romeo personifies the moon as Diana, goddess of chastity, and addresses Juliet as a votary. (*Far more fair* combines alliteration with a jingle.)

51 **Her vestal . . . green** Elaborating this conceit, Romeo imagines Juliet in a pale habit signifying devotion to Diana and to chastity. (Evans suggests a quibble on *livery* as 'provision', 'allowance'.) The expression *sick and green* refers in particular to green sickness (or chlorosis), an anaemic disease believed to affect young women at puberty and to turn the complexion pallid. Later Capulet will call Juliet 'you green-sickness carrion' (3.5.155).

52 **fools . . . it** Punning on *fools* as (a) credulous followers of Diana, (b) jesters in parti-coloured garb (i.e. green and pale or white).

53–4 **It . . . were** Q2 prints as one line, leading Greg to notice duplication (*Editorial Problem*, p. 61), and Wilson–Duthie to conjecture that *It is my lady* was a 'first shot'. *O that she knew she were* echoes Mercutio's bawdy 'O that she were' (l. 38) in a different key.

55 **speaks . . . nothing** Romeo may mean that he cannot hear what Juliet says, or that she expresses herself without words. In his question and the next five lines he extends the paradox.

56 **Her eye discourses** The image of the *eye*, a traditional source of love, has already appeared in Romeo's dialogue with Benvolio about Rosaline (e.g. 1.1.209; 1.2.49–50, 91–4). Now Juliet's presence gives the trope a new dimension of reality.

59 **some business** i.e. an errand

60 **twinkle** (a) close and open quickly, blink, (b) shine with quick, intermittent flashes of light

spheres An image from the old or Ptolemaic astronomy, which visualized *spheres* as clear, hollow, concentric globes revolving around the earth and carrying with them the various heavenly bodies.

61–3 **What . . . lamp** This conceit, full of hyperbole, transforms Juliet's face into an extraordinary play of light.

63 **As daylight . . . lamp** Proverbial (Dent S988).

eye Many editors adopt Q1 'eyes' for consistency with l. 61; but Romeo's effusive speech hardly requires such refinement, and McKerrow is surely right to conclude that 'the recognition of the sun as the "eye" of heaven overweighed the impropriety of a monocular Juliet'.

64–5 **Would . . . night** A couplet rhyming on the antithesis *bright/night* and

See how she leans her cheek upon her hand.
O that I were a glove upon that hand,
That I might touch that cheek!

JULIET Ay me.

ROMEO (*aside*) She speaks.
O speak again, bright angel, for thou art
As glorious to this night, being o'er my head,
As is a wingèd messenger of heaven
Unto the white upturnèd wond'ring eyes
Of mortals that fall back to gaze on him
When he bestrides the lazy puffing clouds
And sails upon the bosom of the air.

JULIET
O Romeo, Romeo, wherefore art thou Romeo?
Deny thy father and refuse thy name;
Or if thou wilt not, be but sworn my love,
And I'll no longer be a Capulet.

ROMEO (*aside*)
Shall I hear more, or shall I speak at this?

JULIET
'Tis but thy name that is my enemy;
Thou art thyself, though not a Montague.

68 (*aside*)] WILSON–DUTHIE; *not in* Q 74 puffing] Q2; passing Q1 (pacing) 80 (*aside*)] ROWE; *not in* Q

introducing the topos of *birds* from Petrarchan verse. (Lines 69–70 will repeat the antithesis through internal rhyme.)

66 **See . . . hand** This line, calling for a gesture, must have been inspired by Brooke: 'In window on her leaning arm, her weary head doth rest' (518).

69–75 **O . . . air** Romeo explicates the metaphor of Juliet as *bright angel*, using *messenger* in l. 71 as a synonym for *angel* (*angel* derives from the Greek word for *messenger*).

71–5 **As . . . air** Shaheen suggests the influence of Acts 1 : 9–11 on this simile: 'while they beheld, he was taken up: for a cloud took him up out of their sight. And while they looked steadfastly toward heaven, as he went, behold, two men stood by them in white apparel, which also said, . . . why stand ye gazing into heaven . . . [?]'

72 **white upturnèd** Hyphenated by most editors since Theobald, somewhat limiting Romeo's image. With a hyphen the upturning refers specifically to the *white* (and to the expression 'to turn up the whites of one's eyes'); without a hyphen it makes the same reference and the phrase also describes in a second way the appearance of the *wond'ring eyes*.

74 **puffing** This Q2 reading seems to describe the motion of the *clouds*, floating as puffs or perhaps swaggering across the sky; it probably does not mean 'swelling' (as some annotators gloss it), a definition first illustrated in 1661 (*OED ppl. a.* 3). Despite its appropriateness, many editors consider *puffing* a corruption of Q1 'pacing', a spelling of 'passing' (see *pass*, *v.* Forms); they assume misreading of *ſſ* for *ſſ* and *u* for *a* (see Wilson–Duthie, Gibbons). *OED* also adopts Q1 'pacing' (*bestride*, *v.* 1b).

82 **Thou . . . Montague** i.e. your identity is a constant, whatever your family name

What's Montague? It is nor hand nor foot,
Nor arm nor face, nor any other part
Belonging to a man. O be some other name!
What's in a name? That which we call a rose
By any other word would smell as sweet;
So Romeo would, were he not Romeo called,
Retain that dear perfection which he owes
Without that title. Romeo, doff thy name,
And for thy name, which is no part of thee,
Take all myself.

ROMEO I take thee at thy word.
Call me but love, and I'll be new baptized:
Henceforth I never will be Romeo.

JULIET
What man art thou that, thus bescreened in night,
So stumblest on my counsel?

ROMEO By a name
I know not how to tell thee who I am.
My name, dear saint, is hateful to myself,

84–5 nor any . . . name!] MALONE; ô be some other name‸ | Belonging to a man. Q2; nor any other part. Q1 86 What's‸ in a name?] Q1; Whats‸ in a name‸ Q2; What? in a names‸ F 87 word] Q2; name Q1 88 were] Q1, Q3; wene Q2

84–5 **Nor . . . name!** This well-known crux has become a touchstone for the editor/bibliographer's understanding of the control-text (see Introduction, 'Quarto 1 and Quarto 2: Provenance'). Since copy is unknowable at this point and the verses make sense in an odd way, Hosley's view is sympathetic: 'it is not entirely clear that Q2 is corrupt'. But Q2 is certainly awkward (see Collation). Most modern editors incorporate a phrase from Q1, *nor any other part*. The majority adopt Malone's arrangement, accepted here because it clarifies the text with minimum interference, and because it can be explained sensibly in bibliographical terms (see Duthie, 'The Text of Shakespeare's *Romeo and Juliet*', *SB* 4 (1951–2), 214–15). In all its forms the passage incorporates a blazon.

86 **What's . . . name?** The F version, 'What? in a names', must be a bungled attempt to correct the unpunctuated Q2 'Whats in a name' (Jowett).

86–7 **rose . . . sweet** The sweetness of the *rose* was proverbial (Dent R178), the flower a standard symbol of feminine beauty. Juliet complicates the image.

87 **word** Early editors substituted Q1 'name', making it the familiar reading. Yet Q2 shows no sign of error here, and *word* in this context means 'a name, title, appellation' (see *OED sb.* 12b (a), and cf. ll. 98–100).

89 **dear** (a) cherished, (b) costly. (Cf. the wordplay in Romeo's first description of Juliet at 1.4.160, and see n.)
owes possesses (*OED v.* 1a)

92 **I take . . . word** Playing on *word* as (a) promise, (b) utterance, (c) name (see l. 87 n. and l. 93).

95 **bescreened** hidden (*OED v.*, first illustration)

96 **counsel** private thoughts (*OED sb.* 5b)

98 **dear saint** Romeo echoes a phrase from his first dialogue with Juliet (1.4.216).

Because it is an enemy to thee.
Had I it written, I would tear the word.

JULIET
My ears have yet not drunk a hundred words
Of thy tongue's uttering, yet I know the sound.
Art thou not Romeo, and a Montague?

ROMEO
Neither, fair maid, if either thee dislike.

JULIET
How camest thou hither, tell me, and wherefore?
The orchard walls are high and hard to climb,
And the place death, considering who thou art,
If any of my kinsmen find thee here.

ROMEO
With love's light wings did I o'erperch these walls,
For stony limits cannot hold love out,
And what love can do, that dares love attempt:
Therefore thy kinsmen are no stop to me.

JULIET
If they do see thee, they will murder thee.

ROMEO
Alack, there lies more peril in thine eye
Than twenty of their swords. Look thou but sweet,
And I am proof against their enmity.

JULIET
I would not for the world they saw thee here.

ROMEO
I have night's cloak to hide me from their eyes,
And but thou love me, let them find me here.

108 kinsmen | Q1; kisman Q2 (*a tilde error*)

101–2 **My ears . . . uttering** Evans cites classical precedents (Horace, Ovid, and Propertius) for Juliet's figure of 'Ears drinking words'.

104 **dislike** displease (*OED v.* 1; Abbott 297)

105 **wherefore** (accented on second syllable)

109 **love's light wings** A conventional image of Cupid (cf. 1.4.15–16, 18).
o'erperch fly over (*OED v.*, only illustration). This metaphoric line probably derives from Brooke: 'So light he wox, he leapt the wall' (830), echoed by Benvolio at l. 6.

112 **stop** obstacle (*OED sb.*[2] 7a)

113 **do see** See Abbott 306 for this use of the auxiliary *do*.

114–15 **Alack . . . swords** Evans points out Romeo's unintentional foreshadowing in these lines, as well as conventional hyperbole.

116 **proof** *OED a.* 1a, first instance of *proof* meaning 'impervious'.

118 **night's cloak** Brooke may have inspired this image (and perhaps 3.2.15): 'on earth the night her mantle black hath spread' (457; cf. Painter, 88).

119 **but** unless (Abbott 120)

My life were better ended by their hate
Than death prorogued, wanting of thy love.

JULIET

By whose direction found'st thou out this place?

ROMEO

By love, that first did prompt me to inquire:
He lent me counsel, and I lent him eyes.
I am no pilot, yet wert thou as far
As that vast shore washed with the farthest sea,
I should adventure for such merchandise.

JULIET

Thou knowest the mask of night is on my face,
Else would a maiden blush bepaint my cheek
For that which thou hast heard me speak tonight.
Fain would I dwell on form, fain, fain deny
What I have spoke; but farewell, compliment.
Dost thou love me? I know thou wilt say 'Ay',
And I will take thy word; yet if thou swear'st,
Thou mayst prove false. At lovers' perjuries
They say Jove laughs. O gentle Romeo,
If thou dost love, pronounce it faithfully;

126 washed] Q1; washeth Q2 135 false. . . . perjuries$_\wedge$] Q1 (~: . . . ~$_\wedge$); ~$_\wedge$ . . . ~. Q2

120–1 **My life . . . thy love** Romeo combines the antitheses central to his narrative (*life/death, hate/love*).

121 **proroguèd** deferred (*OED v.* 2a)
wanting of lacking. See Abbott 178 for the construction (participle followed by *of*). *OED pres. pple.* 3b cites as its first example of the phrase, now obsolete. Although Q2 has no punctuation, most editors print a comma between *proroguèd* and *wanting*. However the line is punctuated, the referent for *wanting* is ambiguous.

125–7 **I . . . merchandise** These lines recast the Petrarchan conceit of the unguided ship, a topos of lost identity and confusion which Romeo has already used (1.4.110–11).

126 **vast** (a) immense, (b) desolate (Evans; see *OED, waste, a.* etymology)

127 **I . . . merchandise** The Petrarchan topos gains a new twist: the non-pilot turns into a merchant-adventurer, his distant mistress a precious commodity.

129 **a maiden blush** Proverbial (Dent B479.1).

131 **form** In its context *form* seems slightly indefinite, like Juliet's earlier phrase 'by th' book' (see 1.4.223 and n.). Certainly it means 'decorum'; but it may also connote 'literary style'.

132 **compliment** formality (*OED, complement, sb.* 8b)

134 **I . . . word** Juliet echoes Romeo's quick acceptance of the vow she spoke in monologue (see l. 92 and n.).

135–6 **At lovers' . . . laughs** This proverbial idea (Dent J82) had classical origins: Ovid, *Ars Amatoria* 1.633 and Tibullus 3.6.49–50. J. Bate distinguishes the laugh of complicity in the *Ars Amatoria* from the laugh of superiority in *Romeo*: the Ovidian phrase is reanimated in an antithetical context where it assumes new meaning (*Shakespeare and Ovid* (Oxford, 1993), pp. 178–80).

136 **gentle** The epithet applies to Romeo's birth, manners, and disposition.

Or if thou thinkest I am too quickly won,
I'll frown and be perverse and say thee nay,
So thou wilt woo, but else not for the world.
In truth, fair Montague, I am too fond,
And therefore thou mayst think my behaviour light;
But trust me, gentleman, I'll prove more true
Than those that have the coying to be strange.
I should have been more strange, I must confess,
But that thou overheard'st, ere I was ware,
My true-love passion. Therefore pardon me,
And not impute this yielding to light love,
Which the dark night hath so discoverèd.

ROMEO

Lady, by yonder blessèd moon I vow,
That tips with silver all these fruit-tree tops—

JULIET

O swear not by the moon, th'inconstant moon,

142 behaviour| Q2; hauiour Q1   144 the coying| This edition; coying Q2; more cunning Q1; more coying Q4; more coyning F2; the coyning WILLIAMS   147 true-love| Q2; true loues Q1, F (Loues)

140 **So** provided that (Abbott 133)

141 **fond** infatuated

142 **behaviour** Most editors print Q1 'hauiour', regularizing the metre. As McKerrow points out, however, 'it is difficult to see why Q2–F1 should read "behauior", as "haviour" or "havour" was well recognised [as] an independent word' (see *OED*, *haviour*, Forms). It is also possible that the original of this Q2 line was not perfectly regular metrically.

144 **the coying** Editors have emended to 'more cunning', 'more *coying*', and 'the coining' (see Williams, Gibbons, and Evans for detailed explanations). It is possible to argue convincingly for both *coying* and 'cunning' (a simple tilde error), and for the compositor's omission of an article (although the original line may have been metrically irregular). This edition opts for the Q2 reading and addition of *the*; editors who adopt 'more' from Q1 assume a larger oversight by the printer. While *OED v.* 6 defines the verbal substantive as 'fondling, coaxing, blandishing', definitions of the verb indicate clearly that *coying* also signifies 'coyness', 'affectation of reserve or shyness'. They allow for wordplay with *strange*, which means 'reserved' (*a.* 11b).

146 **ware** aware (*OED a.* 1). There may be a quibble on 'prudent' (5a).

147 **true-love** i.e. faithful love's (see *OED* 5). Most early editors substitute 'true love's' from Q1 or F, but the attributive expression *true-love* also appears in two Shakespeare plays roughly contemporary with *Romeo* (*Richard II* 5.1.10, *Two Gentlemen* 2.7.46).

148 **And not** See Abbott 305 on the omission of 'do' before *not*.

148–9 **light love . . . dark night** Juliet repeats *light* (= immodest) from l. 142, now with a quibble (= not *dark*) as part of antithesis.

149 **Which** i.e. 'this yielding'

150–1 **Lady . . . tops—** Romeo begins a conventional lover's vow, responding to Juliet's play on 'light' with a different version of the moon imagery from his monologue (ll. 47–52). Romeus in Brooke simply 'swore an oath' to seal his pledge of faith (516).

152–9 **O swear not . . . do not swear** Evans cites H. M. Richmond's suggestion that *swear not*, *Do not swear at all*, and *do not*

That monthly changes in her circled orb,
Lest that thy love prove likewise variable.

ROMEO
What shall I swear by?

JULIET
Do not swear at all;
Or if thou wilt, swear by thy gracious self,
Which is the god of my idolatry,
And I'll believe thee.

ROMEO
If my heart's dear love—

JULIET
Well, do not swear. Although I joy in thee,
I have no joy of this contract tonight:
It is too rash, too unadvised, too sudden,
Too like the lightning which doth cease to be
Ere one can say 'It lightens'. Sweet, good night.
This bud of love, by summer's ripening breath,
May prove a beauteous flower when next we meet.
Good night, good night. As sweet repose and rest
Come to thy heart as that within my breast.

153 circled] Q1 (circld); circle Q2

swear echo Matthew 5: 34–6 (*Shakespeare's Sexual Comedy* (Indianapolis and New York, 1971), p. 115); Shaheen gives the same reference ('Swear not at all') as well as the homily 'Against Swearing and Perjury', part 1. If those resonances are heard, they bring to mind the next biblical passage which enjoins plain-speaking among other moral imperatives (Matthew 5: 37); and they deepen, for a moment, not only this romantic exchange but the antisocial acts that account for its secrecy.

152–3 **the moon . . . changes** Juliet interrupts with still another concept of the moon, which had become a type of inconstancy because of its recurring changes (Dent M1111). As she spells out the idea, her lines are emphatic with figures of repetition.

153 **circled orb** i.e. sphere (see l. 60 n.). Q2's compositor probably misread final *d* as *e*.

156 **gracious** This word, associated with divinity, also means (a) courteous, (b) pleasing, (c) attractive (*OED a.* 2b). Shaheen compares ll. 156–7 with Hebrews 6: 13.

160 **contract** Accented on second syllable. In context this word refers to the lovers' vows, but its primary associations with legal agreements and marriage formalities give it an ironic edge.

161 **sudden** lacking in forethought or warning, charged with immediacy and spontaneousness (*OED a.* 2a, 3a, 7)

162–3 **like the lightning . . . 'It lightens'** These rhetorical lines define a flash of *lightning* through polyptoton, complicating Brooke's analogous metaphor of passion as 'sudden kindled fire' (209–10). According to Dent, they may recast 'As swift as lightning' (L279).

164–5 **bud . . . flower** Juliet's qualified but optimistic use of this trope for love contrasts with Montague's application of it earlier to Romeo (see 1.1.146–8 and nn.); it also echoes her mother's description of Paris (1.3.79).

166–7 **repose and rest . . . that** Synonymy (heightened by alliteration) probably explains the singular pronoun *that*, although some editors assume ellipsis (*that* = to that heart).

ROMEO
O wilt thou leave me so unsatisfied?

JULIET
What satisfaction canst thou have tonight?

ROMEO
Th'exchange of thy love's faithful vow for mine.

JULIET
I gave thee mine before thou didst request it;
And yet I would it were to give again.

ROMEO
Wouldst thou withdraw it? For what purpose, love?

JULIET
But to be frank and give it thee again,
And yet I wish but for the thing I have:
My bounty is as boundless as the sea,
My love as deep; the more I give to thee,
The more I have, for both are infinite.
The Nurse calls within
I hear some noise within. Dear love, adieu.—
Anon, good Nurse!—Sweet Montague, be true.
Stay but a little; I will come again. *Exit*

ROMEO
O blessèd, blessèd night! I am afeard,
Being in night, all this is but a dream,
Too flattering sweet to be substantial.
Enter Juliet again

178.1 *The Nurse calls within*] ROWE (*following* F '*Cals within.*' *one line later*); *not in* Q 181 *Exit*] ROWE; *not in* Q 184.1 *Enter Juliet again*] This edition; *not in* Q

168 **O . . . unsatisfied?** Brooke describes Romeo's situation dispassionately: 'favour found he none | That night, at lady Juliet's hand, save pleasant words alone' (563–4). Painter's narrator makes the same observation in prose (90).

174 **frank** (a) bounteous (cf. l. 176), (b) outspoken

176–8 **My bounty . . . infinite** Juliet's expression shares its sea image and hyperbole with Romeo's (ll. 125–6), yet her figures of speech are different (beginning with the play on homophones). Dent hears proverbial allusions (S169.1, S169.3).

178.1 ***Nurse . . . within*** The lines demand sound effects; some form of this direction, which Rowe derived from F, has been adopted in most editions and prompt books.

180 **Anon** right away, coming

181 ***Exit*** The history of this direction is comparable to that of 178.1 (see n.).

184 **flattering** i.e. flatteringly (*OED ppl. a.* 6; its only illustration of *flattering* as a quasi-adverb)

substantial Four syllables. *OED*'s first instance (*a.* 15) of *substantial* meaning 'true, solid, real'.

184.1 ***Enter . . . again*** This invented direction takes its model from Q2 (l. 203.1) rather than F2 '*Enter*' or Rowe's '*Re-enter* Juliet *above*'.

JULIET
Three words, dear Romeo, and good night indeed.
If that thy bent of love be honourable,
Thy purpose marriage, send me word tomorrow,
By one that I'll procure to come to thee,
Where and what time thou wilt perform the rite,
And all my fortunes at thy foot I'll lay,
And follow thee, my lord, throughout the world.
[NURSE] (*within*) Madam!
JULIET
I come, anon!—But if thou meanest not well,
I do beseech thee—
[NURSE] (*within*) Madam!
JULIET By and by, I come!—
To cease thy strife and leave me to my grief.
Tomorrow will I send.
ROMEO So thrive my soul—
JULIET A thousand times good night. *Exit*
ROMEO
A thousand times the worse to want thy light.
Love goes toward love as schoolboys from their books,

189 rite] Q2 (right) 191 lord] Q2 (L.), Q1, F 191–2 world . . . Madam!] CAPELL (*following* F: world. | *Within* : Madam.); world. Madam. Q2 194–6 thee . . . come!] CAPELL (*following* F: theee *Within*: Madam. | (By and by I come)); thee (by and by I come) Madam. Q2 197 strife] Q2; sute Q4 200 *Exit*] F; *not in* Q

186–98 **If . . . send** Juliet makes this case in the sources (e.g. Brooke 535–44; Painter, 89).

186 **If that** *That* may be a redundancy for the sake of metre (see Abbott 287).

bent (a) inclination, (b) object (*OED sb.*[2] 7). Both definitions complement 'Thy purpose marriage'.

188 **procure** arrange or persuade

192, 195 [*Nurse*] (**within**) Capell's speech-prefix and direction have been adopted in most editions and prompt books. In Q2 'Madam.' appears without a speech-prefix in the right-hand margin; in F '*Within*: Madam.' is also justified right.

196 **By and by** right away (*OED advb. phr.* 3)

197 **strife** Recent editors gloss 'striving' or 'endeavour', definitions appearing in Onions and *OED* 4, which gives 1601 as the first instance of this rare usage. At the same time *strife* may carry its more familiar meaning, 'act of antagonism', after Juliet's conditional 'if thou meanest not well'. In this sense *strife* may apply not only to her person, but also to her family and the feud. Wilson–Duthie and others substitute Q4 '*sute*', which corresponds with Brooke's 'To cease your suit' (544). But it is difficult to see how Q2 *strife* could be a misprint (unless it was influenced by *grief*, as McKerrow suggests), and Q4 may have changed the line independently.

199 **soul—** Theobald punctuated with a comma and dash, as if Romeo were interrupted in the middle of another vow. The actor might give this reading or deliver the line with Q2's full stop, as a pledge. The verse can be heard not only as the end of l. 198 but as the beginning of l. 200.

But love from love, toward school with heavy looks.

Enter Juliet again

JULIET

Hist, Romeo, hist! O for a falc'ner's voice
To lure this tassel-gentle back again.
Bondage is hoarse and may not speak aloud,
Else would I tear the cave where Echo lies
And make her airy tongue more hoarse than mine
With repetition of my 'Romeo'.

ROMEO

It is my soul that calls upon my name.
How silver-sweet sound lovers' tongues by night,
Like softest music to attending ears.

JULIET

Romeo!

ROMEO My nyas?

203.1 *Enter Juliet again*] This edition; *not in* Q 208 mine] Q1; *not in* Q2; Fame DANIEL 209 'Romeo'.] Q2 (*Romeo.*); *Romeos* name. | *Romeo?* Q1; Romeo's name. STEEVENS (*following* Q1) 213 My nyas] WILSON–DUTHIE (My niëss); My Neece Q2; Madame Q1; My Deere Q4

204–5 **Hist . . . again** *Hist* calls for attention and silence at the same time (see Onions; *OED int.* 1, first illustration from the seventeenth century). With *falconer* and hawk Juliet not only praises Romeo but imagines controlling him. A *tassel-gentle* or male peregrine falcon was considered a noble bird of prey: 'There is a falcon-gentle, and a tercel-gentle, and these be for a prince' (*The Book of St Albans* (1486), D iii b). To train the falcon, a *falconer* used his voice as well as a lure or bait (see George Turberville, *The Booke of Faulconrie* (1575), p. 147).

206 **Bondage is hoarse** Depersonalizing her immediate situation, Juliet says that one who is subject to a bond (as she is to the Capulet family) must speak in a voice that is low in pitch and harsh.

207–9 **Else . . . 'Romeo'** i.e. Juliet would compete with the mythological figure of Echo, a nymph personifying resonant sound; her voice would rend the air of Echo's dwelling-place (*OED*, *tear*, *v.*[1] 3c, first illustration). In Ovid, Echo's unrequited love for the youth Narcissus led her to pine until she was nothing but a voice: 'ever since she lives alone in dens and hollow caves' (*Metamorphoses* 3.491).

208 **tongue** voice (cf. l. 211 and Q1)
mine Q2 lacks a final word, and most editors follow Q1.

209 **With . . . 'Romeo'.** Although this Q2 line is metrically regular, editors since Steevens, assuming that it lacks a final word (like the previous line), adopt Q1's 'Romeo's name'. Williams was the first to propose that both lines may have been illegible at the bottom edge of a manuscript leaf. Among editors who follow Q1, a few include its extra vocative 'Romeo' (which Williams considers an actor's interpolation); Jowett suggests that Romeo's response in the next line validates the Q1 reading.

211–12 **How silver-sweet . . . ears** These lines are onomatopoeic and proverbial (Dent S458.1, M1319.1); they will be echoed at 4.4.149–62.

213 **nyas** young hawk. Dover Wilson explicates this word in Wilson–Duthie, resolving a textual crux (Q2's spelling 'Neece' misinterprets 'niesse') and showing how the term fits its context: the young hawk about to leave its nest, not yet able to fly, is an image appropriate both to Juliet at her bedroom window and as Romeo's response to 'tassel-gentle'. Wilson also points out that Greene had applied *nyas* to

JULIET What o'clock tomorrow
Shall I send to thee?
ROMEO By the hour of nine.
JULIET
I will not fail; 'tis twenty year till then.
I have forgot why I did call thee back.
ROMEO
Let me stand here till thou remember it.
JULIET
I shall forget, to have thee still stand there,
Rememb'ring how I love thy company.
ROMEO
And I'll still stay to have thee still forget,
Forgetting any other home but this.
JULIET
'Tis almost morning, I would have thee gone;
And yet no farther than a wanton's bird,
That lets it hop a little from his hand,
Like a poor prisoner in his twisted gyves,
And with a silken thread plucks it back again,
So loving-jealous of his liberty.
ROMEO
I would I were thy bird.
JULIET Sweet, so would I,
Yet I should kill thee with much cherishing.

224 his] Q2; her Q1 226 silken] Q2; silke Q1

an inexperienced girl; and he compares Romeo's expression here with Capulet's at 1.2.8.

215 **year** years (see 1.3.2 n.)

218 **still** Juliet means 'yet' or 'forever', while the context suggests 'motionless' and perhaps 'silently' and 'secretly' as well (*OED adv.* 1a, b). When Romeo picks up half of the antithesis about memory in l. 220, the play on *still* continues.

221 **Forgetting . . . this** Dent compares 'The lover is not where he lives but where he loves' (L565), cited also for 1.1.193–4.

223 **wanton's** In this gentle analogy, *wanton's* probably refers to a playful or spoiled child (*OED sb.* 1, 2a). As Williams and others have argued, *wanton's* here could easily mean 'boy's', and there is no reason to follow editors who changed Q2 *his* to 'her' in l. 224.

225 **gyves** fetters

226 **silken** Although Pope and some later editors print Q1 'silke' to regularize the metre, the line scans with Q2 *silken* (cf. l. 142 and n.).

227 **his** its. Abbott 228 explains the relation of these genitives.

229 **kill . . . cherishing** Juliet's paradox, unintentionally ironic, echoes the proverb 'To kill with kindness' (Dent K51). Adding nuance, the word *cherishing* is defined by its proximity to the image of the lovingly protected bird; it probably means not only 'pampering' but 'guarding carefully' (*OED v.* 1, 5).

Good night, good night. Parting is such sweet sorrow,
That I shall say 'good night' till it be morrow. *Exit*

⌈ROMEO⌉
Sleep dwell upon thine eyes, peace in thy breast.
Would I were sleep and peace, so sweet to rest.
Hence will I to my ghostly Friar's close cell,
His help to crave and my dear hap to tell. *Exit*

230–3 Parting . . . ⌈ROMEO⌉ Sleep . . . Would] Q1; Parting . . . *Iu*<*liet*>. Sleep . . . *Ro*<*meo*>. Would Q2; *Ro*<*meo*>. Parting . . . *Iu*<*liet*>. Sleepe . . . *Rom*<*eo*>. Would Q3; *Romeo*. Parting . . . *Juliet*. Sleep . . . Would HOSLEY (*assigning the lines following* Would . . . rest *to Romeo*) 231 *Exit*] POPE; *not in* Q 233 rest.] Q1; rest | The grey eyde morne smiles on the frowning night, | Checkring the Easterne Clouds with streaks of light, | And darknesse fleckted like a drunkard reeles, | From forth daies pathway, made by *Tytans* wheeles. Q2 234 Friar's close] Q2; fathers Q1; sire's close WILSON–DUTHIE (*conj.* Delius)

230 **Good night . . . sorrow** Q2 produces two lines (with a break between *good night* and *Parting*), the first of several printing anomalies as the scene ends (see Hosley and C. Leech on l. 230 in *SQ* 4 (1953), 27–8, and 5 (1954), 94–5, 96–8). Hosley, following Q3, assigns Juliet the farewell and Romeo the proverb with its oxymoron (Dent P82.1); but most editors, following Q1, give a full pentameter line to Juliet. As Williams points out, a divided line in Q2 does not always require two speakers (cf. 3.3.68 and 83), and both parts of this verse suit the characterization of Juliet: 'the speaker who wishes to say goodnight till it be morrow is surely the speaker who has already said it many times in this scene'.

231 **morrow** morning

232–3 **Sleep . . . rest** Q2 erroneously repeats the speech-prefix '*Iu.*' at l. 232 and reintroduces '*Ro.*' at l. 233. Q1 and most editors give both lines to Romeo, a good solution for reasons summarized by Wilson–Duthie: 'each lover has a farewell couplet in parting, while [the two lines] clearly belong to the same speaker'.

233–4 **rest. | Hence** Between these lines in Q2 Romeo speaks two couplets which Friar Laurence will repeat virtually unchanged at the beginning of 2.2 (see Collation). (Scholars identify the two passages as Version A and Version B; Q3 and F1 reprint the duplication.) Clearly Shakespeare had second thoughts, but editors have not agreed what they were: some follow F2 and Rowe, assigning the couplets to Romeo; others follow Q1 and Pope, assigning them to Friar Laurence; a few scholars ascribe A to the Friar or B to Romeo. Lacking evidence, arguments tend to rely on insecure hypotheses about text or literary style (see Jowett's summary, 232 n.). This edition makes its choice on the basis of Q1, which attributes the lines to Friar Laurence.

234 **ghostly** spiritual, devout (*OED a.* 2; see also 1c, 'used *esp.* with reference to what is rendered by a priest to a penitent or one near death'). Q2's *ghostly Friers* introduces Friar Laurence from Romeo's point of view as the holy figure who administers to his spiritual needs. Nevertheless, many editors since Capell have emended the phrase, finding it redundant. Of these, most since Wilson–Duthie substitute 'ghostly sire's': they assume a misreading of *ſ* for *ſ* and intrusion of an *r*, and find support for their emendation in Brooke (559 as well as 595).

close (a) confined, narrow, (b) secret, secluded (cf. Brooke's 'secret cell', 1264)

235 **hap** (a) good fortune (*OED sb.*[1] 3), (b) chance, luck. (Cf. the wordplay on *dear* in 1.4.160.)

2.2 *Enter Friar Laurence, alone with a basket*

FRIAR LAURENCE

The grey-eyed morn smiles on the frowning night,
Checking the eastern clouds with streaks of light;
And fleckled darkness like a drunkard reels
From forth day's path and Titan's burning wheels.
Now ere the sun advance his burning eye,
The day to cheer and night's dank dew to dry,
I must upfill this osier cage of ours
With baleful weeds and precious-juicèd flowers.

2.2.0.1 *Enter . . . basket*] Q2 (*Enter Frier alone with a basket.*); *Enter Frier Francis.* Q1
2 Checking] Q2; Checkring Q1, Q3, Q2 (*Version* A) 4 path and Titan's burning] Q2; path, and *Titans* fierie Q1; pathway, made by *Tytans* Q2 (*Version* A)

2.2 Friar Laurence's opening soliloquy has been invented for this largely derivative scene. Its rhetoric not only indicates his narrative importance, but also strikes his character notes.

1–4 **The grey-eyed . . . wheels** The couplets establish precisely the time of day.

1 **grey-eyed** Both colour and epithet are conventionally associated with early morning (Evans compares Golding's translation of Ovid's *Metamorphoses* 1.69 and 4.774), which is personified as part of the antitheses in this line. According to Dent *grey-eyed morn* is proverbial (M1168.1), though *OED a.* b cites l. 1 as its first example and an illustration from 1670 as its second.

2 **Checking** chequering, variegating with rays of different colours (*OED v.*[2] 2). As McKerrow notes, *Checking* is a much less usual form than 'Check'ring', which appears in Version A of this line (see (2.1.233–4 Collation and n.) as well as Q1. The printer of Q3 and other editors have considered *Checking* an error.

3 **fleckled** dappled (*OED a.*, first illustration)
like a drunkard Shaheen compares Isaiah 24: 20 ('The earth shall reel to and fro like a drunken man'), as well as Psalm 107: 27 ('They are tossed to and fro, and stagger like a drunken man'); Dent suggests that the line is proverbial (M399).

4 **From forth** out of (Abbott 156)
Titan's . . . wheels *Titan* refers to the sun-god, Sol, or to the sun personified (*OED* 1); the *burning wheels* belong to the chariot he drives across the sky in his diurnal track or *path* (cf. Golding's translation of Ovid's *Metamorphoses* 2.172–5 and 3.2.1–4). According to Bate, however, 'It seems to be Phaëthon at the wheel, streaking headlong to disaster' (pp. 176–7). *Burning* may anticipate the next line through the author's oversight or a compositor's error. On the other hand, as the rest of the speech shows, Friar Laurence tends to repeat himself, and the redundancy may be deliberate. Many editors avoid repetition by substituting 'fiery' from Q1.

5 **advance** raise
his . . . eye The sun as an *eye* of heaven or day was a poetical commonplace. Personifying the sun complicates the image.

6 **cheer** 'warm' (*OED v.* 5b), as well as 'comfort', 'gladden', 'animate'
dank This word, which contrasts with both *cheer* and *dry*, hovers between two definitions: (a) damp, with disagreeable connotations, (b) wet (*OED a.* 1a).

7–30 **I must . . . plant** As the Friar collects plants and makes observations about them, he identifies himself not only as a philosopher but also as a chemist. In the latter role he establishes a motif which will play a crucial part in 4.1, when he offers Juliet the sleeping potion, and in 5.1, when the Apothecary sells Romeo poison. T. P. Harrison, Jr., traces the natural philosophy in this speech to contemporary plant lore ('"Hang Up Philosophy"', *SAB* 22 (1947), 203–9).

7 **osier cage** i.e. willow basket

The earth that's nature's mother is her tomb;
What is her burying grave, that is her womb;
And from her womb children of divers kind
We sucking on her natural bosom find;
Many for many virtues excellent,
None but for some, and yet all different.
O mickle is the powerful grace that lies
In plants, herbs, stones, and their true qualities;
For naught so vile that on the earth doth live,
But to the earth some special good doth give;
Nor aught so good but, strained from that fair use,
Revolts from true birth, stumbling on abuse.

16 plants, herbs] Q2; hearbes, plants Q1

9–10 **The earth . . . womb** Rhyme and antimetabole rephrase an old antithesis: Steevens compares Lucretius 5.259 ('Omniparens eadem rerum commune sepulchrum'; see Furness); Dent cites E28.1 and E30.

11–12 **And . . . find** Anadiplosis (*womb*, repeated from the end of one clause at the beginning of the next) and polyptoton (*nature's/natural*) stress key words from the previous couplet. *Kind*, which means not only 'variety', but also 'birth' and 'nature' (*OED sb.* 1a, 3a), fuses the main ideas of the couplets.

13–14 **Many . . . different** This couplet states another antithesis in rhetorical terms (e.g. *Many/many* = antistasis) heightened by assonance; and it plays on *virtues* as 'inherent powers' (medicinal in this case) and 'moral excellences'.

15 **mickle** great

grace In this context Friar Laurence probably means 'beneficent virtue or efficacy' (*OED sb.* 13a), but the word is charged with other senses appropriate to his religious preoccupations ('an individual virtue or excellence, divine in its origin' (11e)) and to the play's continual irony ('hap, luck, or fortune' (10)). Brooke's Friar uses the word 'force' in a corresponding passage (2109–11).

16 **plants, herbs, stones** McKerrow notes that this series is arranged in descending order, conforming to Elizabethan notions of degree. Nevertheless Q1 and some editors have transposed *plants* and *herbs*.

16 **qualities** (a) attributes, (b) natures (*OED sb.* 8a)

17–18 **naught . . . give** Dent compares N327 and N43; Evans cites the opening of Brooke's prose 'To the Reader': 'The God of all glory created universally all creatures to set forth his praise, both those which we esteem profitable in use and pleasure, and also those which we account noisome and loathsome'.

on the earth . . . to the earth A combination of anadiplosis with wordplay: *earth* means (a) ground for cultivation or burial (*OED sb.*[1] 3), (b) dwelling-place of humankind, (c) inhabitants of the world (cf. ll. 9–10).

19–20 **Nor aught . . . abuse** This couplet, connected to the one above by internal rhyme and antistasis, has proverbial and literary precedents: Dent cites N317; Wilson–Duthie compare Brooke 573–4; and Evans quotes Nashe, *Christs Teares over Jerusalem* (1593), 'Nothing doth profit, but perverted may hurt' (ii. 39).

19 **aught** Williams notes that Q2 'ought' may be an obsolete spelling or an *a:o* misreading.

strained . . . fair use The obsolete *strained* means 'applied beyond its province', or beyond its *fair use* (*OED v.*[1] 11d, first illustration).

20 **stumbling on abuse** *Stumbling on*, with its moral implications, may suggest 'tripping over' or 'encountering' *abuse*, which signifies not only improper use but deceit and wrong (*OED sb.* 4, 5).

Virtue itself turns vice, being misapplied,
And vice sometime by action dignified.
Enter Romeo
Within the infant rind of this weak flower
Poison hath residence and medicine power:
For this, being smelt, with that part cheers each part;
Being tasted, stays all senses with the heart.
Two such opposèd kings encamp them still
In man as well as herbs, grace and rude will;
And where the worser is predominant,
Full soon the canker death eats up that plant.

ROMEO

Good morrow, father.

22 sometime] Q2; sometimes Q1 22.1 *Enter Romeo*] Q; *after l.* 30 POPE 26 stays] Q2; slaies Q1; slayes Q3

21–2 **Virtue . . . dignified** This couplet, described by Spencer as 'somewhat casuistical', sums up the preceding two in content and style.

22 **sometime** sometimes. After Capell many editors have read 'sometime's' (from Q1 'sometimes'). This edition follows Q2 and assumes ellipsis of 'is' (Abbott 403).

22.1 ***Enter Romeo*** Except for Q1 (which prints no direction for Romeo's entrance), Q and F introduce Romeo here. Nevertheless, a number of editors since Pope have delayed Romeo's appearance until l. 30; theatrical tradition also favours the late entrance. As Spencer argues, anticipatory directions are not unusual, and the later entrance avoids diverting attention from Friar Laurence's monologue. By now, however, the audience probably has the gist of these antithetical couplets; and other editors have noticed how Romeo's presence gives the Friar's lines an ironic edge. In addition Q2 permits Romeo time to approach Friar Laurence without interrupting him (cf. 1.1.54–5 and n.), and allows the audience to register emblematic connections among the 'weak flower', the play's floral metaphors, and Romeo.

25 **this . . . each part** As Friar Laurence examines the flower (*this*) in rhetorical terms, his play on *part* creates slight ambiguity. In all likelihood *with that part* refers to the blossom's odour, but it may also allude to 'the olfactory nerves, the part that smells' (Malone, in Furness). *Cheers*, the still familiar verb (see l. 6 n.), may carry two rare and obsolete definitions: (a) cures, (b) warms (*OED v.* 3, 5b).

26 **stays** stops. Many editors have followed Q1 (or Q3) in reading 'slays'. Williams adopts this word because he suspects foul case (he cites the 'stay'/'slay' error at 4.1.72), and believes that Friar Laurence is speaking of death rather than 'suspended animation'. But Q2 *stays*, appropriate in context, allows for both interpretations, as Mommsen's paraphrase indicates: 'To bring the heart to a standstill, and with it all the senses' (quoted in Furness).

27–8 **Two . . . will** Wilson–Duthie compare this 'thought' with *Caesar* 2.1.66–9, where the military trope and correspondences between the human body and the state are more explicit.

27 **encamp them** i.e. form themselves into a camp. This reflexive is obsolete (*OED v.* 1b).

28 **grace . . . will** The antithesis sets *grace* in its scriptural and theological senses (cf. l. 15 and n.) against wilfulness and appetite (*OED sb.*[1] 9a, 2).

29 **worser** A common variant of 'worse' in all its applications (see *OED*, *worser*, *a.* and *adv.*).

30 **canker** cankerworm (cf. 1.1.147–49 and see 147 n.)

FRIAR LAURENCE *Benedicite!*
What early tongue so sweet saluteth me?
Young son, it argues a distempered head
So soon to bid good morrow to thy bed.
Care keeps his watch in every old man's eye,
And where care lodges, sleep will never lie;
But where unbruisèd youth with unstuffed brain
Doth couch his limbs, there golden sleep doth reign.
Therefore thy earliness doth me assure
Thou art uproused with some distemp'rature;
Or if not so, then here I hit it right,
Our Romeo hath not been in bed tonight.

ROMEO
That last is true; the sweeter rest was mine.

FRIAR LAURENCE
God pardon sin! Wast thou with Rosaline?

ROMEO
With Rosaline, my ghostly father? No,
I have forgot that name and that name's woe.

FRIAR LAURENCE
That's my good son; but where hast thou been then?

ROMEO
I'll tell thee ere thou ask it me again.
I have been feasting with mine enemy,
Where on a sudden one hath wounded me
That's by me wounded. Both our remedies
Within thy help and holy physic lies.

31 ***Benedicite!*** expresses a wish (Bless you!) as well as surprise (Bless me!).

33 **distempered** disturbed. This word and its cognate 'distemp'rature' in l. 40 both refer to disorder of the bodily 'humours', the sources of mental and physical conditions in human beings (see *OED ppl. a.*[1] 2; *sb.* 2, 3); they extend the concept of imbalance from ll. 27–30.

37 **unbruisèd** As White points out, the epithet has special pertinence for Friar Laurence, who has just called himself a careworn old man and who practises a form of medicine.

40 **with . . . distemp'rature** On *distemp'rature* see l. 33 n.; *with* = by (Abbott 193).

41 **hit it right** Just as Friar Laurence begins to direct his thoughts towards Romeo's infatuation, he echoes a phrase used by Benvolio (1.1.203) and Mercutio (2.1.34) to ridicule that ardour.

44–5 **with Rosaline? | With Rosaline** In this scene Romeo's speech shares both rhyme and rhetoric with the Friar's diction, as his first couplet illustrates with figures of repetition. Q2 punctuates l. 45 with commas after *Rosaline* and *no*, allowing for several readings.

45 **ghostly** spiritual, devout (as in 2.1.234)

50 **one . . . wounded me** Reintroducing the conceit of love as war, Romeo makes quibbles of *enemy* in the previous line, *foe* in l. 54, and *remedies/physic* in ll. 51–2.

52 **physic** (a) healing art, medicine, (b) spiritual remedy (*OED sb.* 5b)

I bear no hatred, blessèd man, for lo,
My intercession likewise steads my foe.

FRIAR LAURENCE

Be plain, good son, and homely in thy drift;
Riddling confession finds but riddling shrift.

ROMEO

Then plainly know my heart's dear love is set
On the fair daughter of rich Capulet.
As mine on hers, so hers is set on mine,
And all combined, save what thou must combine
By holy marriage. When and where and how
We met, we wooed, and made exchange of vow,
I'll tell thee as we pass; but this I pray,
That thou consent to marry us today.

FRIAR LAURENCE

Holy Saint Francis, what a change is here!
Is Rosaline, that thou didst love so dear,
So soon forsaken? Young men's love then lies
Not truly in their hearts, but in their eyes.
Jesu Maria, what a deal of brine
Hath washed thy sallow cheeks for Rosaline!
How much salt water thrown away in waste
To season love, that of it doth not taste.

55 and] Q; rest F

54 **intercession** petition (with religious connotations; see *OED sb.* 1)
steads (a) profits, (b) succours. *OED* cites to illustrate the first definition (*v.* 1a), but the love/war conceit allows for the second as well (1c).

55 **and** See Jowett for consideration of F's unusual 'rest'.
homely Synonymous with *plain*.

56 **shrift** absolution (*OED sb.* 2)

60 **combined** joined in an ideal union (*OED v.* 1b)

63 **as we pass** Romeo anticipates not only his request but expedition in carrying out the marriage arrangements; his hurriedness will become urgency by l. 93. In Brooke the themes of impatience and haste are more pronounced here: the Friar cannot 'warn his friend to stop, amid his race begun, | Whom Cupid with his smarting whip enforceth forth to run' (605–6).

65 **Holy . . . Francis** An oath appropriate to a Franciscan.

67–8 **love . . . eyes** Friar Laurence applies what Booth calls 'the endlessly reiterated Renaissance distinction between true love—from the heart—and mere infatuation—inspired by the sight of beauty' (headnote to Sonnet 46). Dent suggests that the distinction may be proverbial (cf. L501).

69 **brine** (a) salt water, (b) tears (*OED sb.* 3, first illustration)

70 **sallow** i.e. with grief

72 **season** (a) preserve, (b) flavour. With this pun the salt water/tears metaphor turns into a domestic conceit found elsewhere in Shakespeare's poems (*Lucrece* 796, *Complaint* 17–18) and drama (*Twelfth Night* 1.1.28–31, *All's Well* 1.1.44–6). It allows Friar Laurence to say, as the line ends, that Romeo's tears have failed *To season love* in either way.

The sun not yet thy sighs from heaven clears,
Thy old groans yet ringing in mine ancient ears.
Lo, here upon thy cheek the stain doth sit
Of an old tear that is not washed off yet.
If e'er thou wast thyself, and these woes thine,
Thou and these woes were all for Rosaline.
And art thou changed? Pronounce this sentence then:
Women may fall when there's no strength in men.

ROMEO
Thou chid'st me oft for loving Rosaline.

FRIAR LAURENCE
For doting, not for loving, pupil mine.

ROMEO
And bad'st me bury love.

FRIAR LAURENCE
Not in a grave,
To lay one in, another out to have.

ROMEO
I pray thee, chide me not. Her I love now
Doth grace for grace and love for love allow;
The other did not so.

FRIAR LAURENCE
O she knew well
Thy love did read by rote, that could not spell.

74 yet ringing] Q2; yet ring Q4; ring yet Q1

73 **sun . . . clears** A playful and hyperbolic version of the familiar conceit introduced by Montague at 1.1.129.

74 **yet ringing** This edition retains the slightly irregular metre of Q2; most editors since Rowe have followed Q4 or Q1 and made an adjustment.

75 **Lo, here . . . sit** This line calls for a gesture which suggests that Friar Laurence and Romeo are standing still, at least for the moment, despite Romeo's impatience to 'pass'.

76 **yet** Rhyme calls for the common Elizabethan pronunciation 'yit' (Hosley).

79 **sentence** maxim (*OED sb.* 4a)

80 **may fall** The auxiliary verb signifies either possibility or permission. Clearly Friar Laurence conceives of women as the weaker sex in body and spirit; his quibble on *fall* (in relation to male *strength* which fails to be supportive) centres on moral frailty. The 'sentence' echoes the theme of at least two proverbs: Dent W655, 'A woman is the weaker vessel', and W700.1, 'Women are frail'.

81–4 **Thou . . . have** Stichomythia, or alternate lines of verse, propel this dialogue towards resolution.

81 **chid'st** Spencer points out the short vowel in the past tense.

85 **Her** she whom (as in Q1). The Q2 construction, inverting subject and object, omits the relative pronoun between *now* in l. 85 and *Doth* in l. 86 (see Abbott 244).

86 **grace** Romeo means 'favour', but *grace* may retain spiritual and other shades of meaning from Friar Laurence's use earlier in this scene (see l. 15 n., l. 28 n.) and from Romeo's introduction of amatory/religious conceits during the first act (e.g. see 1.4.206–19 n.). Shaheen compares 'grace for grace' (John 1: 16).

88 **Thy love . . . spell** In this new application of the book motif, Friar Laurence personifies Romeo's former *love* as illiterate; *love* recites its text from memory instead of

But come, young waverer, come, go with me;
In one respect I'll thy assistant be:
For this alliance may so happy prove,
To turn your households' rancour to pure love.

ROMEO
O let us hence! I stand on sudden haste.

FRIAR LAURENCE
Wisely and slow; they stumble that run fast.

Exeunt

2.3 *Enter Benvolio and Mercutio*

MERCUTIO Where the devil should this Romeo be? Came he
not home tonight?

BENVOLIO
Not to his father's; I spoke with his man.

MERCUTIO
Why, that same pale hard-hearted wench, that
Rosaline,
Torments him so that he will sure run mad.

recognizing the words by the arrangement of their letters (cf. 1.4.223 and n.). The idea behind the figure was not original: Dent suggests a correspondence with R38, and Evans quotes Sidney, *Astrophil and Stella*, Second Song, 24: 'Who will read must first learn spelling'.

90 **In one respect** for one reason. McKerrow notes that the phrase is properly 'For one respect' (*OED sb.* 14b).

91–2 **For . . . love** echoes Juliet's words in Brooke, equally ironic in context: 'For so perchance this new alliance may procure | Unto our houses such a peace as ever shall endure' (427–8).

92 **To** as to. The second part of the relatival construction *so* (l. 91) . . . *as* has been omitted (Abbott 281).

93 **stand on** (a) practise, (b) urge. *OED v.* 74e quotes to illustrate (a); 74k cites *2 Henry IV* 1.2.36–7 as the first instance of (b). In contrast Onions and most editorial glosses offer 'insist upon', a version of (b). Romeo's sentiment seems to allow both interpretations.

sudden Romeo means *haste* that is 'prompt in action or effect; producing an immediate result' (*OED a.* 6; cf. 3.3.45), but *sudden* also has the now obsolete senses 'immediate, without delay' and 'unpremeditated, done without forethought' (3a, 2a). Friar Laurence responds at once to the third definition.

94 **Wisely . . . fast** Proverbial (Dent cites, e.g., H198, F141, R211.1; cf. 2.5.15).

2.3 This scene creates an interlude; it borrows only the Nurse's errand from the source narrative (Brooke 631–72, Painter, 91). Centring on witty exchange, it displays the concentrated use of rhetorical figures as the discourse of choice among Romeo's friends and as the definition of sociability for Mercutio.

1–7 **Where . . . house** Q2 sets ll. 4–5 as verse. Various editors since Johnson have done the same with the rest of the opening. (Q1 also sets these lines as verse.) As a whole the passage illustrates what J. Barish calls 'indeterminacy' ('Mixed Prose-Verse Scenes in Shakespearean Tragedy', in *Shakespeare and Dramatic Tradition*, ed. W. R. Elton and W. B. Long (Newark, Del., 1989), p. 37): some lines sound like pentameters; others do not; and the exchange leads into prose dialogue. This edition attempts to convey the rhythmic modulations.

1 **should** could. The auxiliary *should* adds emphasis to direct questions relating to the past (Abbott 325).

2 **tonight** last night (*OED adv.* 3)

BENVOLIO
Tybalt, the kinsman to old Capulet,
Hath sent a letter to his father's house.

MERCUTIO
A challenge, on my life.

BENVOLIO Romeo will answer it.

MERCUTIO Any man that can write may answer a letter.

BENVOLIO Nay, he will answer the letter's master, how he dares, being dared.

MERCUTIO Alas, poor Romeo, he is already dead, stabbed with a white wench's black eye, run through the ear with a love-song, the very pin of his heart cleft with the blind bow-boy's butt-shaft; and is he a man to encounter Tybalt?

[BENVOLIO] Why, what is Tybalt?

MERCUTIO More than Prince of Cats. O, he's the courageous captain of compliments. He fights as you sing

2.3.6–8 BENVOLIO Tybalt . . . MERCUTIO A] Q2; *Mer<cutio>: Tybalt* . . . Some Q1 6 kinsman] Q1; kisman Q2 (*a tilde error*) 17 [BENVOLIO]] Q1, F; *Ro<meo>*. Q2 19 He fights] Q2; Catso, he fightes Q1

8 **answer it** i.e. meet the summons to fight, accept the challenge. Mercutio deliberately misconstrues *answer it* as 'answer a letter', deflating the danger of Tybalt's threat and the boldness of the contenders. This bit of dialogue, which makes the transition to rhythmic prose, can be heard as either prose or irregular verse.

10 **how** (a) however, (b) by saying how. Benvolio's phrasing makes his description of Romeo ambiguous.

11 **dares . . . dared** This wording plays rhetorically (and obviously) on two familiar definitions of the verb *dare*: (a) have courage, (b) challenge.

13 **white . . . eye** Biron uses the same striking image to describe his beloved, also Rosaline (*L.L.L.* 3.1.191–2). In both passages *eye*(s) probably has bawdy connotations.

14 **pin** 'a peg, nail, or stud fixed in the centre of a target' (*OED sb.*[1] 1c); the proverbial expression 'hitting the *pin*' (Dent P336) lent itself to bawdy quibbling (cf. Costard's reference to 'cleaving the pin', *L.L.L.* 4.1.135). Mercutio seems to shift here from duelling to archery, a conceit introduced by Romeo and Benvolio at 1.1.201–5.

15 **blind . . . butt-shaft** Cupid's strong, unbarbed arrow for shooting at butts or marks in archery. (See also Armado's version of the metaphor, *L.L.L.* 1.2.167–8.) Mercutio's conceit may also refer to the arrow's repeated use, since these unbarbed missiles easily came unstuck from targets.

17 **what** who (Abbott 254). Spencer reads this line as an expression of contempt (cf. Benvolio's description of Tybalt's fighting skills at 1.1.105–8).

18–25 **More . . . *hay*!** Mercutio satirizes Tybalt as a duellist in the newly fashionable Italian style: contestants used rapiers instead of English swords, and fought according to rules printed in a spate of manuals (e.g. Sir William Segar, *The Book of Honor and Armes* (1590), Giacomo di Grassi, *His True Arte of Defence* (1594), Vincentio Saviolo, *His Practise of the Rapier and Dagger* (1595)). In Mercutio's portrayal Tybalt represents polite violence, a contradiction which repeatedly made such duellists the objects of

prick-song, keeps time, distance, and proportion; he rests his minim rests, one, two, and the third in your bosom—the very butcher of a silk button—a duellist, a duellist, a gentleman of the very first house of the first

ridicule (see, e.g., Jonson's *Every Man in His Humour* (1598), 1.3.171–230, and Porter's *Two Angry Women of Abingdon* (1599), 1329–47 (Malone Society Reprint, ed. W. W. Greg (Oxford, 1912)). Touchstone's burlesque sums up both the type and the absurdity: 'O sir, we quarrel in print, by the book, as you have books for good manners' (*As You Like It* 5.4.88–9).

18 **Prince of Cats** Shakespeare identified 'Tybalt' with 'Tibert' (or 'Tybert'), originally the name of the cat in the moral fable of Reynard the Fox (translated by William Caxton, from a Dutch version, in 1481), then both a name for cats and a noun meaning 'cat' (see *OED*, *Tibert*). In *Have with You to Saffron-walden* (1596), Nashe attaches the phrase 'Prince of Cats' to the name 'Tibault' (iii. 51). Mercutio pursues this wordplay at 3.1.74, 76–8.

19 **captain of compliments** 'a complete master of all the laws of ceremony, the principal man in the doctrine of punctilio' (Johnson, quoted in Furness)

20 **prick-song** (a) written (or 'pricked') vocal music, (b) written descant or counterpoint for a simple melody (*OED* 1, 2), thus a kind of music requiring discipline in performance. (L. P. Elson suggests that Mercutio uses the motion of the singer's hand when counting *prick-song* to picture the motions of the expert fencer (*Shakespeare in Music* (Boston, 1900), p. 90).) Mercutio's wordplay echoes his bawdy quibbling above with the archery metaphor: *prick* = (a) bull's-eye, (b) sharp, piercing implement, (c) penis.

distance, and proportion *Distance* refers specifically to the space between duelling contestants and to musical intervals (*OED*, *sb*. 5b, first illustration; see also 5d). *Proportion* means rhythm in music (*sb*. 10a) as well as balance in general; it may also quibble on the geometric arrangements of the duellists' motions and rapiers (Gibbons).

21 **rests . . . rests** Both the verb and substantive *rests* mean 'pauses'; the verb also means 'places'. *Minim* signifies the note of shortest duration in early music (*OED sb*. 1), as well as minuteness in general. As the metaphor is phrased, Tybalt the duellist takes very brief pauses between feints and before striking; one who sings prick-song takes very brief pauses between notes. The conceit stops rather abruptly with the words *in your bosom*.

22 **butcher . . . button** The hyperbole mocks Tybalt's efforts as it continues to emphasize his precision: he fences so accurately that he can pierce a button on his opponent's garment. Apparently this expression had precedent: Howard Staunton first cited the passage in George Silver's *Paradoxes of Defence* (1599) which records how the earliest fencing-master in London, Signor Rocco, claimed that he could 'hit any Englishman with a thrust upon any button', and 'this was much spoken of' (*Three Elizabethan Fencing Manuals*, pp. 563, 514). Gibbons quotes Lyly, *Sapho and Phao* (1584), 2.3.9–13: 'he that . . . can hit a button with a thrust, and will into the field man to man . . . is a shrewd fellow'; other editors point out later examples.

duellist *OED*'s first illustration, but Evans finds what is probably an earlier instance in Gabriel Harvey, *Pierces Supererogation* (1593), p. 19. Evidently the word was new, derived from French and Italian models, and Mercutio's repetition sets it apart for ridicule.

23 **very first house** (a) best school of fencing, (b) family of highest rank. Again Mercutio plays on the fashionable jargon of duelling. A *house* was and is both a dwelling-place and a college in a university. Signor Rocco, representative of the foreign 'Teachers of Offence', called his establishment in a leased *house* a 'College' because he thought 'a fence-school' was beneath his dignity as 'the only famous master of the art of arms in the whole world' (Silver, in *Three Elizabethan Fencing Manuals*, p. 562). Dent calls the phrase 'a common derisive expression' (cf. G66).

23–4 **first and second cause** two grounds for

and second cause. Ah, the immortal *passado*, the *punto riverso*, the *hay*!

BENVOLIO The what?

MERCUTIO The pox of such antic, lisping, affecting phantasims, these new tuners of accent! 'By Jesu, a very good blade, a very tall man, a very good whore.' Why, is not this a lamentable thing, grandsire, that we should be

25 *hay*] Q (Hay) 27–8 phantasims] WILLIAMS (*conj.* Crow); phantacies Q2; fan- | tasticoes Q1

a duel. The prolific literature of duelling in the 1590s catalogued reasons for issuing a challenge, a convention which Touchstone would parody in *As You Like It* 5.4.49–101. Segar's *Book of Honor and Armes* condensed the list to a pair: 'Wherefore whensoever one man doth accuse another of such a crime as meriteth death, in that case the combat ought be granted. The second cause of combat is honour, because among persons of reputation, honour is preferred before life' (Scholars' Facsimiles and Reprints (Delmar, NY, 1975), $D3^{v}$–$D4^{r}$). In *L.L.L.* Armado uses this expression (1.2.169), and in Q1 Mercutio repeats it in his death-speech.

24–5 **immortal . . . *hay*!** Mercutio lists duelling terms derived from Italian, French or Spanish which elaborate his description in ll. 19–22. As Wilson–Duthie suggest, he probably acts out the passes in naming them. Gibbons hears a pun on *immortal*: (a) famous, (b) fatal.

24 ***passado*** forward thrust with sword, one foot advanced at the same time (*OED* 1; see Saviolo, *Practise*, pp. 243, 281). Armado in *L.L.L.* claims that love does not respect the *passado* (1.2.170), which Bobadil in *Every Man in His Humour* will describe as 'a most desperate thrust' (1.3.211).

24–5 ***punto riverso*** backhanded thrust (*OED*, *punto*[1], 3, and see Saviolo, *Practise*, p. 281)

25 ***hay*** home-thrust (from the Italian *hai*, 'thou hast (it)'). Since *OED sb.*[5] gives this line as its first and only illustration, *hay* must have been a new word (like *duellist*) in the mid-1590s. Benvolio's response indicates that the term is unfamiliar to him.

27 **The pox of** a plague on; a double-edged curse, since *pox* also alludes to venereal disease.

lisping mincing. This insult refers to pronunciation (of foreign words or English with a foreign accent) as well as pretentiousness.

affecting pretentious (though *OED* and Onions cite *Merry Wives* 2.1.133 as the first example)

27–8 **phantasims** fantastic beings. This reading, which agrees with that of Williams and several more recent editors, adopts John Crow's emendation of Q2 'phantacies' ('Editing and Emending', *E&S*, NS 8 (1955), 13–14): Crow posits a tilde error, which occurs elsewhere in Q2 (cf. 'kinsman' in l. 6 and 2.1.108). Apparently a coinage, *phantasim*(s) appears twice with reference to Armado in *L.L.L.* 4.1.98 and 5.1.18, the only two illustrations cited by *OED*. Other editors print Q1 'fantasticoes', used by Nashe in *Saffron-walden* (iii. 31).

28 **tuners of accent** speakers who modulate their pronunciation in affected ways. *OED* 1b cites as the only instance of *tuner* meaning 'One who gives a particular (vocal) tone to something'; Evans illustrates the whole phrase with a quotation from Nashe, *Saffron-walden* (iii. 76).

28–9 **very good blade . . . whore** The unsubtle wordplay and deflation seem to mimic the gallants' hearty terms of appraisal rather than their pronunciation: *blade* = (a) sword, (b) fellow (*OED sb.* 11a, first illustration of (b)); *tall* = (a) brave, (b) of more than average height (see *OED a.* 3 and cf. *Twelfth Night* 1.3.18).

29–31 **Why . . . flies** Mercutio's diction changes briefly, as if he were questioning a grandfather or old man about the excesses of currently fashionable behaviour; his phrasing may caricature the

thus afflicted with these strange flies, these fashion-mongers, these 'pardon-me's', who stand so much on the new form that they cannot sit at ease on the old bench? O their bones, their bones!

Enter Romeo

BENVOLIO Here comes Romeo, here comes Romeo!

MERCUTIO Without his roe, like a dried herring. O flesh, flesh, how art thou fishified! Now is he for the numbers that Petrarch flowed in. Laura to his lady was a kitchen-wench—marry, she had a better love to berhyme her—

32 'pardon-me's'] Q1 (pardonmees), F (pardon-mee's); pardons mees Q2

sometimes earnest Benvolio or distinguish the two of them from the modish Tybalt and his kind.

31 **strange flies** eccentric parasites (*OED* sb.[1] 5c), probably alluding to *fly* as 'a type of something insignificant' (1d), and certainly punning on *strange* as (a) peculiar, (b) foreign.

31–2 **fashion-mongers** This instance precedes *OED*'s first illustration, in Marston's *Scourge of Villanie* (1598).

32 **'pardon-me's'** An expression mocking the formality and affectation of 'fashion-mongers', particularly their ceremonious language of duelling with its foreign inflexions. Because Q2 has 'pardons mees', some editors since Theobald have translated the phrase into French or Italian. Wilson–Duthie propose that the compositor may have read final *e* of 'pardone' as final *s*.

32–4 **stand . . . bench** Quibbles multiply in antitheses at the end of this rhetorical question: *stand on*, in addition to its literal meaning, = (a) practise, (b) carefully observe, (c) insist on (*OED v.* 74a, e, k; see also 2.2.93 and n.); *form* = (a) fashion, or way of behaving (*sb.* 10, 14b), (b) formal procedure, or ceremony (often depreciatively), (c) bench (cf. *L.L.L.* 1.1.202–8). In glossing, Crofts and later editors cite Sir John Harington, *A Treatise on Playe* (*c.*1597), which complains about 'the great plank forms' at court and the 'wainscot stools so hard that, since great breeches were laid aside, men can scant endure to sit on' (*Nugae Antiquae* (1779), ii. 173).

34 **bones** i.e. aching bones (from the uncomfortable 'old bench'), with play on 'bone-ache' or venereal disease (*OED sb.* 17) and on French '*bon*' (see ll. 27–8).

34.1 ***Enter Romeo*** Some early editors delay this Q2 entrance until l. 42, after the word 'purpose'.

36 **Without his roe** (a) without the first syllable of his name (because he has been reduced to a lover's sigh, 'me, O!'), (b) without his milt or sperm (i.e. sexually exhausted, as if he were a fish that had spawned; cited in *OED*, *roe*[2], 1). Mercutio's quibbles on fish echo Gregory's earlier ones in both their sexual and Petrarchan senses (see 1.1.29, 30 and nn.). Although recent editors add a third pun on *roe* (= small deer/dear), the quadruped seems out of place in context. Dent indicates that the herring simile is proverbial (H447).

37–8 **Now . . . in** Alliteration reinforces hyperbole in this speech which mocks poetizing. According to Mercutio, Romeo in his present state is fit only for writing verses in the Petrarchan mode (see Abbott 155 on *for*; cf. the enamoured Armado in *L.L.L.* 1.2.174–6); and Petrarch *flowed in* verses, i.e. (a) wrote them fluently, (b) overflowed with them (*OED v.* 14), (c) composed them tearfully (12). By naming Petrarch, Mercutio identifies a main component of the play's style (see Introduction, 'Tragedy, Comedy, Sonnet').

38–9 **Laura . . . her** Mimicking Romeo's claims, Mercutio compares Rosaline to the idealized beloved of Petrarch's sonnets, Laura de Noves (*to* = in comparison with (Abbott 187)). His qualification is rather vague: either it accounts for Laura's celebrity in terms of Petrarch's verse, or it simply belittles Romeo's poetry.

Dido a dowdy, Cleopatra a gypsy, Helen and Hero hildings and harlots, Thisbe a grey eye or so, but not to the purpose. Signor Romeo, *bonjour*: there's a French salutation to your French slop. You gave us the counterfeit fairly last night.

ROMEO Good morrow to you both. What counterfeit did I give you?

MERCUTIO The slip, sir, the slip—can you not conceive?

ROMEO Pardon, good Mercutio, my business was great, and in such a case as mine a man may strain courtesy.

MERCUTIO That's as much as to say, such a case as yours constrains a man to bow in the hams.

ROMEO Meaning to curtsy.

MERCUTIO Thou hast most kindly hit it.

ROMEO A most courteous exposition.

MERCUTIO Nay, I am the very pink of courtesy.

ROMEO Pink for flower.

MERCUTIO Right.

40–2 **Dido . . . purpose** In addition to Laura, Mercutio compares Rosaline with five classical heroines. These women, both legendary and fictional, were all renowned for beauty, celebrated in verse of different kinds, and engaged in love affairs which ended tragically.

40 **gypsy** originated as an aphetic form of 'Egyptian', and Elizabethans believed that gypsies came from Egypt (*OED*, *gipsy*, *sb.* 1a). With their dark skin and hair, gypsies represented the antithesis of the English Renaissance ideal of beauty: only Theseus's mad lover 'Sees Helen's beauty in a brow of Egypt' (*Dream* 5.1.10–11).

40–1 **hildings** good-for-nothing women (*OED* 2b)

41 **a grey eye** A standard of beauty, whether or not *grey* means blue as Malone thought (*OED a.* 3; cf. *Venus* 140 and *Two Gentlemen* 4.4.189).

43 **slop** wide, baggy trousers (*OED sb.*[1] 4b). Wilson–Duthie quote Crofts's annotation for l. 58: 'Having been up all night, he is still in his masquing-clothes: loose-fitting French slops and dancing-pumps'.
gave . . . counterfeit Mercutio sets up the pun in l. 47, playing on the expression 'to give (one) the slip': *counterfeit* and *slip* both refer to false coins. *OED* cites this quibble on *slip* (*sb.*[3] 8c), and Evans finds a parallel in Nashe's *Unfortunate Traveller* (1594; ii. 258).

47 **conceive** understand

49 **strain courtesy** act with less courtesy than is due (*OED sb.* 1c, first example)

50–1 **case . . . hams** Mercutio gives Romeo's excuse a bawdy twist. In his rendition, *a case* = (a) circumstances, (b) genitals (Partridge); *courtesy* = the action of bowing (*OED sb.* 8); and the joke is that Romeo, sexually exhausted, can hardly stand up straight.

52 **curtsy** A frequent sixteenth-century variant of 'courtesy' produced by elision of the medial short *e* (*OED*, *courtesy*, *sb.* Forms).

53 **kindly hit it** Reintroducing the bawdy pun on hitting the mark (see 2.1.34 and n.), Mercutio plays on at least four senses of *kindly*: (a) characteristically, (b) suitably, (c) readily, (d) exactly (*OED adv.* 1a–d). He encourages Romeo to continue quibbling in an exchange very often cut in productions, especially between ll. 59 and 94.

55–6 **pink** ' "flower", or finest example of excellence' (cf. 2.4.42). *OED sb.*[4] 2a cites as first instance of this figurative usage; *pink* refers literally to a flowering plant.

ROMEO Why, then is my pump well flowered.

MERCUTIO Sure wit, follow me this jest now till thou hast worn out thy pump, that when the single sole of it is worn, the jest may remain, after the wearing, solely singular.

ROMEO O single-soled jest, solely singular for the singleness!

MERCUTIO Come between us, good Benvolio, my wits faints.

ROMEO Switch and spurs, switch and spurs, or I'll cry 'a match!'

MERCUTIO Nay, if our wits run the wild goose chase, I am done; for thou hast more of the wild goose in one of thy wits than I am sure I have in my whole five. Was I with you there for the goose?

ROMEO Thou wast never with me for anything when thou wast not there for the goose.

64–5 wits faints] Q2; wits faile Q1; wits faint Q5; wit faints F2 66 Switch . . . switch] Q (Swits . . . swits)

58 **flowered** (a) decorated with flowers (*OED ppl. a.* 3a, first example), (b) ornamented by perforation (Romeo quibbles on the verb 'pink')

59 **Sure** steadfast (*OED a.* 6a). The epithet implies that Mercutio considers wordplay a test not only of intellection but perhaps of constancy.

me with me, for me (see Abbott 220 on pronouns used as datives)

60 **single** of one thickness (*OED a.* 10). Originally a *pump* was a light shoe, often made of delicate material, for indoor wear (*sb.*[2] a). Mercutio reintroduces a *sole* pun connected with dancing-shoes (cf. 1.4.12–13).

61–2 **solely singular** Mercutio and Romeo, playing with homonyms and rhetorical figures, quibble on both terms in this phrase: *solely* = (a) alone, (b) entirely; *singular* = (a) alone (*OED a.* 1b), (b) single or unique, (c) special or extraordinary.

63 **single-soled** thin, poor (*OED a.* 2; see l. 60 and n.)

singleness *OED sb.* 3a cites as (a) its first illustration for 'the fact of consisting of one in number or kind', (b) a pun on 'simplicity'.

64 **Come between us** Mercutio appeals to Benvolio as his second in a duel, a jest first noticed by Wilson–Duthie.

66 **Switch and spurs** i.e. at full speed (*OED*, *switch*, *sb.* 1a, first illustration of the phrase; see also *spur*, *sb.*[1] 2a); Dent indicates that the expression became commonplace (S1046). Romeo encourages Mercutio to keep up the contest of wit as if he were racing a horse.

66–7 **'a match!'** done! (*OED sb.*[1] 11); i.e. Romeo will declare the competition over.

68–9 **if . . . done** Mercutio immediately takes Romeo's challenge by continuing to play on his words: 'Switch and spurs' prompts *wild goose chase*, which means (a) a horse-race in which the second (or any succeeding) horse had to follow the leader's course with precision and at a specific interval, the effect resembling a flight of wild geese, (b) an erratic course led by one person or thing and followed by another (*OED* 1, 2 *fig.*; first illustration for 2 *fig.*); 'a match!' leads to *I am done*, echoing the puns at 1.4.37–9. According to Dent, *run the wild goose chase* became proverbial (W390).

68 **wild goose** simpleton (*OED* 2a, only instance before the nineteenth century). Geese were known for their witlessness (Dent G348).

70 **my whole five** See 1.4.44–5 n.

70–1 **Was . . . you** i.e. was I even with you

71 **for the goose** Mercutio asks if his wordplay on *goose* has tied the score.

72–3 **Thou . . . goose** Romeo turns virtually

MERCUTIO I will bite thee by the ear for that jest.

ROMEO Nay, good goose, bite not.

MERCUTIO Thy wit is a very bitter-sweeting; it is a most sharp sauce.

ROMEO And is it not then well served into a sweet goose?

MERCUTIO O here's a wit of cheverel, that stretches from an inch narrow to an ell broad.

ROMEO I stretch it out for that word 'broad', which, added to the goose, proves thee far and wide a broad goose.

MERCUTIO Why, is not this better now than groaning for love? Now art thou sociable, now art thou Romeo, now art thou what thou art by art as well as by nature; for this drivelling love is like a great natural that runs lolling up and down to hide his bauble in a hole.

BENVOLIO Stop there, stop there.

every word from Mercutio's last line into a pun, including the prepositions. In his rendering *for the goose* means 'as the fool', and may have a bawdy edge (see Partridge).

74 **bite . . . ear** i.e. as a sign of affection (*OED v.* 16 (a))

75 **good . . . not** Proverbial (Dent G349); quibbling on *bite* as 'nip' and 'speak sharply' (*OED v.* 14).

76 **very bitter-sweeting** Play on two senses of *very* and the oxymoron in *bitter-sweeting*, which refers to the bitter-sweet apple (*OED*'s unique illustration of the obsolete *bitter-sweeting*).

78 **is . . . sweet goose** Retort with another proverb, 'Sweet meat must have sour sauce' (Dent M839).

into i.e. with

79 **cheverel** kid-leather, pliant and easily stretched (*OED sb.*[1] 1, only illustration of figurative usage)

79–80 **stretches . . . ell broad** Mercutio seems to fashion this backhanded compliment from two proverbial expressions (Dent C608, I49), acknowledging the versatility of Romeo's wit while implying that he extends a limited resource. An *ell* = forty-five inches (*OED* 1a), or 1.143 metres.

82 **a broad goose** Punning on *broad* as (a) large, (b) obvious, (c) indecent. Romeo also plays on 'abroad' and possibly on 'brood-goose' (see Evans).

83 **for** (a) because of, (b) in order to have. On *groaning for* in this double sense, see Booth's note for Sonnet 133.1–2 and cf. l. 3 of the second Chorus.

84–5 **Now . . . sociable . . . nature** With a concentrated display of rhetoric—anaphora, antistasis (*art* the verb, *art* the noun), antimetabole—Mercutio defines sociability in rhetorical terms. The *art* which complements *nature* in Romeo may be understood not only as skill but also as rhetoric (*OED sb.* 2a, 3a). Thomas Wilson makes similar connections among rhetoric, *nature*, and sociability at various points in his *Arte of Rhetorique* (1553; rev. 1560).

86 **drivelling** (a) idiotic, (b) slavering

natural fool

87 **bauble . . . hole** Wordplay allows *bauble* several meanings: (a) toy or trinket, (b) fool's baton, (c) penis (Partridge). With the pun on *hole* (cf. 'circle' at 2.1.25 and n.), it begins a series of bawdy quibbles.

88–90 **stop . . . hair** The interruption generates more ribaldry: *stop* = (a) cease, (b) thrust; *tale* = (a) talk (*OED sb.* 1a), (b) penis (Partridge). Mercutio takes 'there' literally (as 'hole'), compounding several puns with the proverbial expression *against the hair* (Dent H18). Here the phrase contains auditory play on *the hair*/there, and means (a) against my inclination, (b) against the pubic hair (Partridge).

MERCUTIO Thou desirest me to stop in my tale against the hair.

BENVOLIO Thou wouldst else have made thy tale large.

MERCUTIO O thou art deceived, I would have made it short; for I was come to the whole depth of my tale and meant indeed to occupy the argument no longer.

ROMEO Here's goodly gear.

Enter the Nurse and her man, Peter

A sail, a sail!

MERCUTIO Two, two, a shirt and a smock.

NURSE Peter!

PETER Anon.

NURSE My fan, Peter.

95.1 *Enter Nurse . . . Peter*] Q2 (*Enter Nurse and her man.*); *after l.* 94 *in* F 96–7 A . . . MERCUTIO Two] Q2; *Mer<cutio>:* A . . . *Ben<uolio>:* Two Q1

91–2 **tale large . . . short** more bawdy quibbling on *tale*/tail: *large* = (a) lengthy (*OED a.* 7a), (b) obscene (13), (c) large in size; *short* = (a) brief, (b) small in size (see Partridge).

93 **was come** See Abbott 295 on this form of the intransitive verb.

whole depth . . . tale Mercutio adds to the puns on *whole*/hole and *tale*/tail a bawdy quibble on *depth*, which refers to the climax of both his story and his sexual fantasy (*OED* 12a cites to illustrate 'the inmost, remotest, or extreme part').

94 **occupy . . . longer** The match ends with a rush of indecent wordplay: *occupy* = (a) carry on, (b) engage with sexually (*OED v.* 6a, 8, and Partridge; cf. *2 Henry IV* (Quarto) 2.4.143–4 on 'the word "occupy"'); *argument* = (a) discussion, (b) vagina (see Booth's note on Sonnet 38.3). Mercutio's *longer* quibbles on Benvolio's 'large'.

95 **goodly gear** An ironical phrase (see *OED a.* 3b), ambiguous in context: *gear* means (a) matter or stuff, in various senses (*sb.* 11), (b) apparel; *goodly gear* may give Romeo's impression of either the bawdy exchange between his friends or the appearance of the Nurse and Peter as they come into view.

95.1 ***Enter . . . Peter*** Some editors follow F and place this direction after l. 92, reducing the ambiguity of 'goodly gear' by making it refer, like 'sail' in l. 96, 'to the Nurse's voluminous garments and ship-like motion' (Wilson–Duthie). As Williams points out, however, Q2 prints entrance directions on a line of dialogue or in the middle of a speech not only here but four other times. Consequently, there is no bibliographical imperative to reposition the direction, or to reproduce Q1 and those editions which assign Romeo's next line to Mercutio and Mercutio's next line to Benvolio. Among others, Williams and Jowett (who gives l. 96 to Benvolio and l. 97 to Mercutio) suggest literary and dramatic reasons for changing the speech-prefixes. Most prompt books at this point follow the editions on which they are based.

96 **A sail** This exclamation, like 'sail ho!', announces the first sighting of an unfamiliar ship at sea, usually by its sails (*OED sb.*[1] 4b). Although some critics think it out of character for Romeo, it echoes his bantering tone in the dialogue just interrupted.

97 **shirt . . . smock** Mercutio identifies a man and a woman by their undergarments: the Nurse's man wears a *shirt* (*OED sb.* 1a); she has on a *smock* or chemise, the word *smock* used typically as a synonym for a woman (*sb.* 1a, c).

99 **Anon** right away, coming

100 **My fan, Peter** The Nurse seems to be affecting the manners of a lady as described, e.g., in *The Serving Man's Comfort* (1598), a pamphlet cited in Furness: 'The mistress must have one to

MERCUTIO Good Peter, to hide her face, for her fan's the fairer face.

NURSE God ye good morrow, gentlemen.

MERCUTIO God ye good e'en, fair gentlewoman.

NURSE Is it good e'en?

MERCUTIO 'Tis no less, I tell ye, for the bawdy hand of the dial is now upon the prick of noon.

NURSE Out upon you! What a man are you?

ROMEO One, gentlewoman, that God hath made, himself to mar.

NURSE By my troth, it is well said. 'For himself to mar', quoth a? Gentlemen, can any of you tell me where I may find the young Romeo?

109 himself] Q2; for himselfe Q1

carry her cloak and hood, another her *fan*' (cf. *L.L.L.* 4.1.143–4). In many productions between the mid nineteenth and early twentieth century this request prompted comic business with the fan later in the scene, usually starting as Mercutio and Benvolio exited at l. 134: they mimicked the Nurse and Peter, Benvolio fanning Mercutio with a hat. At other times—late eighteenth century to early nineteenth, mid nineteenth for a while—Peter engaged in broad comedy with an enormous fan.

101–2 **for . . . face** Some editors cut this phrase or adopt Q1's version, 'the fairer of the two', reducing Q2's comic repetition. (Cf. Q2's phrase with 1.4.28 and n.)

103 **God . . . morrow** God give you good morning (*OED* explains this kind of elliptical expression, *god*, *sb.* 8a).

104 **good e'en** A salutation used any time after noon (cf. 1.2.57), informing the audience that the Nurse has arrived at least three hours late for her appointment with Romeo (see 2.1.213–15, 2.4.1–11).

106 **bawdy** (a) lewd, (b) characteristic of a bawd (*OED a.*[2] 1)

106–7 **hand . . . dial** Partridge (followed by Evans) makes this expression doubly obscene, interpreting *dial* as another image of female genitals (cf. 'circle' at 2.1.25 and n., 'hole' at l. 87) and therefore another indecent term for a woman. J. H. Astington reads Mercutio's bawdy in the context of Hans Sebald Beham's 1529 engraving 'Death and the Lascivious Couple'. Beham offers a particularly ironic version of a general graphic theme which Shakespeare must have known, the triumph of death as it threatens all human relationships ('Three Shakespearean Prints', *SQ* 47 (1996), 182–5).

107 **prick** (a) mark on the dial's circumference (representing *noon*), (b) penis

108 **Out . . . you!** An indignant reproach. **What** what kind of

109–10 **made . . . mar** Romeo plays on two proverbs (Dent M162, M48; cf. Capulet at 1.2.13), and may also be quibbling on *made* as (a) created, (b) caused (Hosley). According to some editors, the phrase should read 'for *himself to mar*': they cite Q1's 'for himselfe' and the Nurse's version of Romeo's wording in l. 111; several think 'for' has dropped out of Q2, either by accident or perhaps deliberately, because the line is tightly justified (see Jowett).

112 **a** he (Abbott 402)

112–13 **Gentlemen . . . Romeo?** The Nurse has already learned Romeo's identity (1.4.249–50), and Spencer considers her question here an authorial oversight. Although her non-recognition may also be explained by the circumstances of the first encounter, such as darkness or Romeo's mask, it nevertheless strikes a note at once ironic and humorous.

ROMEO I can tell you, but young Romeo will be older when you have found him than he was when you sought him. I am the youngest of that name, for fault of a worse.

NURSE You say well.

MERCUTIO Yea, is the worst well? Very well took, i'faith, wisely, wisely.

NURSE If you be he, sir, I desire some confidence with you.

BENVOLIO She will indite him to some supper.

MERCUTIO A bawd, a bawd, a bawd! Soho!

ROMEO What hast thou found?

MERCUTIO No hare, sir, unless a hare, sir, in a Lenten pie, that is something stale and hoar ere it be spent.

He sings

An old hare hoar, and an old hare hoar,

125.1 *He sings*] This edition; *He walkes by them, and sings.* Q1; *not in* Q2

114–16 **I can . . . worse** Romeo's diction, a diluted version of the wordplay and other rhetoric exchanged with his friends, continues to impress the Nurse (l. 117).

116 **for fault of** through want of. Romeo plays on the proverbial phrase 'for fault (want) of a better' (Dent F106).

118 **worst well . . . well** The Nurse gets caught in the verbal crossfire between Mercutio and Romeo, as Mercutio produces antithesis (from Romeo's 'worse' and her 'well') and antistasis (from *well* the adjective and *well* the adverb). McKerrow would punctuate this according to Q2, with a comma instead of a question mark after the first *well*.

took taken (Abbott 343)

120 **confidence** *OED* cites as first illustration for 'the confiding of private or secret matters', adding that 'some take *confidence* as a humorous blunder for *conference*' (*sb.* 6). Benvolio's immediate response, misusing *indite* for 'invite', suggests that he too hears a malapropism (*v.* 5 quotes his line as its first example of catachresis).

122 **bawd** (a) procuress, (b) hare (*OED sb.* 2, first instance of this dialectal usage)

Soho! Hunter's call on discovering or starting a hare, and therefore call to announce a discovery.

123 **found** The question picks up both implications of 'Soho!', *found* meaning 'discovered' not only in the familiar sense but also with specific reference to game or hunting.

124–5 **No hare . . . spent** Bawdy wordplay on *hare*, which signifies both the animal and a prostitute (Partridge); *stale*, which functions as the familiar adjective and the noun for 'prostitute' (*OED sb.*[3] 4); *hoar*, an adjective meaning 'mouldy' (*a.* 5) or 'grey with age', as well as an easy pun on 'whore'; and *spent*, denoting both 'consumed' and 'exhausted', perhaps sexually (see Partridge, and cf. Sonnet 119.14). After emphasizing the Nurse's connection with *hare*/prostitute (*No hare sir, unless*), Mercutio develops the *hare*/game comparison. Since a true Lenten pie contains no meat, he seems to describe a leftover dish going bad during Lent, or possibly a meat pie made surreptitiously at that time from less-than-fresh meat.

125.1 ***He sings*** Q1 prints a direction (see Collation), which most editors reproduce in some form. Few prompt books elaborate the direction here or the refrain at l. 134 with business (such as '*a little dance*' or '*Exits kissing fingers*').

126–9 **An old hare . . . spent** This edition prints Mercutio's continuing ribaldry as Q1 sets it. (Q2 prints the passage uneconomically, as two justified lines of verse taking up four lines of space; most editors set six lines.) In rhyme and metre, the lines roughly approximate a ballad-stanza, suitable for what appears to be an

Is very good meat in Lent;
But a hare that is hoar is too much for a score,
When it hoars ere it be spent.
Romeo, will you come to your father's? We'll to dinner thither.

ROMEO I will follow you.

MERCUTIO Farewell, ancient lady; farewell, lady, (*sings*) 'lady, lady'. *Exeunt Mercutio and Benvolio*

NURSE I pray you, sir, what saucy merchant was this that was so full of his ropery?

ROMEO A gentleman, Nurse, that loves to hear himself talk, and will speak more in a minute than he will stand to in a month.

NURSE An a speak anything against me, I'll take him

133 (*sings*)] EVANS; *not in* Q 134 *Exeunt . . . Benvolio*] Q1 (*Exeunt Benuolio, Mercutio.*), F (*Exit. Mercutio, Benvolio.*); *Exeunt.* Q2 136 ropery] Q2 (roperie); roperipe Q1; Roguery F4

extemporized bit of song. Two popular tunes have been suggested as appropriate settings: 'Up Tails All' (Long, pp. 42–3) and 'The Staines Morris Tune' (Cécile de Banke, *Shakespearean Stage Production* (New York, London, Toronto, 1953), p. 272).

126–7 **old hare hoar . . . Is** Either the repeated pun on *hare hoar* is conceived as a singular subject noun, or the verb is a third person plural in *-s* (Abbott 333).

127 **meat** (a) food of any kind (*OED sb.* 3e), (b) animal flesh, (c) prostitute (Partridge)

128 **too much . . . score** i.e. not worth the price

129 **hoars** grows hoary or old; quibbling on the obsolete verb this time

133 **ancient** (a) aged, (b) hoary (*OED a.* 5a)

134 **'lady, lady'** Mercutio's parting shot at the Nurse comes from the refrain of a ballad, probably amorous. Although editors have adopted Warton's identification of a song in *Twelfth Night*, 'The Goodly and Constant Wife Susanna' (see Furness), Long is probably closer to the mark in citing an older, more popular ballad, 'The Pangs of Love and Lovers' Fires' (1559), for which he gives the tune (pp. 42–4). 'Lady, lady' was a common refrain.

135 **saucy merchant** insolent fellow (see 1.4.196 n. on *saucy*)

136 **ropery** *OED* 2, first illustration of 'roguery'. Gibbons relates the term to 'rope-ripe', which appears in Q1 and means 'One who is ripe for the gallows' (*sb.*). According to his argument, these and other 'rope' words refer to lewd speaking, and the Nurse's *ropery* is a malapropism for 'roguery' prompted by Mercutio's bawdy jests. According to R. Levin, *ropery* was interchangeable with 'rope-ripe' ('Grumio's "Rope-Tricks" and the Nurse's "Ropery"', *SQ* 22 (1971), 82–6). In both cases 'rope' alludes not only to Mercutio's lewdness (it was a common slang term for 'penis'), but also to his rhetoric ('rope-ripe', applied to language, meant self-conscious and over-elaborate). Romeo's answer, with its play on 'stand', replies to both senses.

137 **Nurse** The Nurse may not have recognized Romeo (ll. 112–13), but he remembers her.

137–8 **loves . . . talk** Proverbial (Dent L563).

138–9 **stand to** abide by. Romeo seems to repeat the inevitable pun, which first occurred at 1.1.8 and suits this description of Mercutio (see Partridge).

140, 141 **An a** if he (Abbott 101, 402)

140–1 **take him down** bring him low. Unwittingly the Nurse responds to Romeo's pun with another bawdy quibble introduced by Mercutio at 1.4.26. R. Levin

down, an a were lustier than he is, and twenty such jacks; and if I cannot, I'll find those that shall. Scurvy knave! I am none of his flirt-gills, I am none of his skains mates. (*To Peter*) And thou must stand by too and suffer every knave to use me at his pleasure.

PETER I saw no man use you at his pleasure. If I had, my weapon should quickly have been out. I warrant you, I dare draw as soon as another man, if I see occasion in a good quarrel, and the law on my side.

NURSE Now, afore God, I am so vexed that every part about me quivers. Scurvy knave! (*To Romeo*) Pray you, sir, a word; and as I told you, my young lady bid me inquire you out. What she bid me say I will keep to myself; but

144 (*To Peter*)] Q1 (*She turnes to Peter her man.*); *not in* Q2 151 (*To Romeo*)] JOWETT; *not in* Q

points out that Q1 has a better version of the joke, because it prints 'stand' instead of *speake*; H. F. Brooks adds that the Q2 compositor may have repeated *speake* from l. 138 ('A Good Reading from the Bad Quarto of *Romeo and Juliet*', *RES*, NS 23 (1972), 56–8, 459).

141 **lustier** (a) more arrogant (*OED a.* 6), (b) more vigorous

142 **jacks** rude fellows (*OED sb.*[1] 2a)
and if Q2 *and* may be the conjunction or part of the construction 'an if', i.e. 'even if' (Abbott 105).

143 **flirt-gills** loose women (*OED*'s first illustration). The phrase 'twenty such jacks' may have prompted this expression: *gill* is both a contemptuous term for a woman and a proper name.

143–4 **skains mates** *OED* states 'Origin and exact meaning uncertain', yet several scholars interpret *skains mates* as 'cut-throat companions' because 'skene' means 'knife' or 'dagger'. The Nurse's expression may be more benign, however, and *skain* a dialectal word for 'rascal' (see Furness). Perhaps Cotgrave gives a clue in the early seventeenth century with a phrase based on the word 'knife' ('cousteau'), 'au cousteau avec', which he translates as 'familiar with' or 'a daily companion with'. (Cf. the entries for *skain* in Walter W. Skeat's *Etymological Dictionary of the English Language* (Oxford, 1888).)

144 **(*To Peter*)** In most productions *Peter* spends his time between speeches dozing on a bench or step, against a wing or near a pillar. The Nurse wakes him for his dialogue by striking him with her hand, a cane, or the fan.

145 **use me . . . pleasure** She intends to say 'treat me as he pleases', but the phrase obviously means 'treat me as a sexual partner'. If the bawdy pun escapes her, it seems to engage Peter, who elaborates it with a quibble on *weapon* in his next lines (cf. 1.1.32).

148 **occasion** opportunity of taking offence (*OED sb.*[1] 1a)

149 **the law . . . side** Samson, another Capulet servant, introduced these legal concerns (1.1.36, 44).

150–1 **every part . . . quivers** Again the Nurse inadvertently compromises herself as she echoes Mercutio's conjuration by Rosaline's 'quivering thigh' (2.1.20).

152–3 **as I told you . . . out** No text indicates when this exchange took place, a vagueness which allows various interpretations: e.g. the Nurse and Romeo conversed during Mercutio's song (Spencer), or the Nurse, agitated, only imagines that she has given Romeo this information. Here *inquire* means 'seek'. *OED v.* 6 explains that the obsolete phrase *inquire out* often connotes 'asking'.

first let me tell ye, if ye should lead her in a fool's paradise, as they say, it were a very gross kind of behaviour, as they say. For the gentlewoman is young; and therefore if you should deal double with her, truly it were an ill thing to be offered to any gentlewoman, and very weak dealing.

ROMEO Nurse, commend me to thy lady and mistress. I protest unto thee—

NURSE Good heart and i'faith I will tell her as much. Lord, lord, she will be a joyful woman.

ROMEO What wilt thou tell her, Nurse? Thou dost not mark me.

NURSE I will tell her, sir, that you do protest, which, as I take it, is a gentlemanlike offer.

ROMEO

Bid her devise some means to come to shrift this
    afternoon,
And there she shall at Friar Laurence' cell
Be shrived and married. Here is for thy pains.

NURSE No, truly, sir, not a penny.

ROMEO Go to, I say you shall.

154–9 **first . . . dealing** At the close of this speech there may be a residue of unintentional bawdy innuendo with the echo of Mercutio's fool image (ll. 86–7) and such double-edged words as *gross*, *thing*, and *weak* (see Partridge).

154–5 **lead . . . paradise** Proverbial (Dent F523).

157 **double** deceitfully (*OED adv.* 3, only illustration before the nineteenth century)

158 **weak** Often glossed or emended (since Collier) on the assumption that the Nurse means a stronger term such as 'wicked' or 'contemptible'. The adjective speaks for itself, however, because it has been defined in strong moral terms from the fourteenth century to the present.

161 **protest** declare or vow. The Nurse interrupts Romeo at the end of l. 161 (punctuated here with a dash, as in F2 and later texts); her next lines suggest that she takes his unfinished protest as a formal declaration or vow of love.

168 **Bid . . . afternoon** Most editions print *Bid her devise* as a separate dimeter line, but this one follows Q2 and Hosley in presenting it as part of a fourteener (cf. 2.4.15). The resulting verse resembles the poulter's measure of Brooke's poem, as the play returns to the source narrative after a long departure. (Cf. ll. 168–70 with Brooke 633–4: 'On Saturday, quod he, if Juliet come to shrift, | She shall be shrived and married, how like you nurse this drift?')

170 **Here is for** Romeo's stage-action is meant to supply the ellipsis of 'money' after the verb (see Abbott 382), whereas Brooke's narrative provides the specifics: 'Then he six crowns of gold out of his pocket drew | And gave them her, a slight reward (quod he) and so adieu' (667–8). Productions add comic business to the exchange at ll. 170–2: the Nurse takes the coin or purse conspicuously as she says 'not a penny', with her hand extended or behind her back and with accompanying gestures (e.g. weighing the purse, putting the money in a pocket or satchel).

NURSE
This afternoon, sir, well, she shall be there.

ROMEO
And stay, good Nurse, behind the abbey wall.
Within this hour my man shall be with thee
And bring thee cords, made like a tackled stair,
Which to the high topgallant of my joy
Must be my convoy in the secret night.
Farewell, be trusty, and I'll quit thy pains.
Farewell, commend me to thy mistress.

NURSE
Now God in heaven bless thee! Hark you, sir.

ROMEO What sayst thou, my dear Nurse?

NURSE
Is your man secret? Did you ne'er hear say,
'Two may keep counsel, putting one away'?

ROMEO
Warrant thee, my man's as true as steel.

NURSE
Well, sir, my mistress is the sweetest lady.
Lord, lord, when 'twas a little, prating thing—
O there is a nobleman in town, one Paris,

185 Warrant] Q2; I warrant F2 186–96 Well . . . letter] *verse* (*following* Capell); *prose in* Q2

176 **tackled** made of tackle or rope (*OED a.* 1, only illustration). Brooke describes 'a corden ladder' (813), and Johnson compares 'stairs of rope in the tackle of a ship'. As Wilson–Duthie and Gibbons point out, the device of the rope ladder prompts Romeo to a nautical metaphor: *topgallant* = (a) summit, (b) platform at the head of the topmast (*sb.* 1; *sb.* 3b, first instance of the figurative usage).

178 **convoy** means of conveyance (*OED sb.* 9, first illustration). Other definitions as forms of 'escort' link *convoy*, in Cotgrave's phrase, with 'marriage and burial matters' (6c); it is also connected with war.

179 **quit** repay

180 **mistress** Three syllables (see Abbott 477).

183–4 **Is . . . away?** Q2 prints as one prose sentence, but editors follow Rowe, as well as metre and rhyme, in setting as a couplet.

184 **'Two . . . away'** Proverbial (Dent T257).

185 **Warrant** Many editors adopt F2's more metrical 'I *warrant*', though the dialogue hovers between verse and prose. This edition allows the irregular metre and ellipsis of the first person pronoun (see Abbott 401; cf. 3.5.106).

as true as steel The proverbial phrase (Dent S840) condenses lines from Brooke (809–11).

186–96 **Well . . . letter** Q2 sets as prose, Q1 omits, and Capell versifies the lines. Though Capell's lineation has not been adopted by later editors, the stylistic arguments that support his versification of the Nurse's earlier speech about Juliet (1.3.18–50) apply here as well: e.g. metric irregularities (a short line, hypermetric lines) result from the combination of blank verse rhythms and prosaic diction; line endings tend to coincide with sense-units. This edition follows Capell to em-

That would fain lay knife aboard; but she, good soul,
Had as lief see a toad, a very toad,
As see him. I anger her sometimes,
And tell her that Paris is the properer man;
But I'll warrant you, when I say so she looks
As pale as any clout in the versal world.
Doth not 'rosemary' and 'Romeo' begin
Both with a letter?

ROMEO
Ay, Nurse, what of that? Both with an 'R'.

NURSE Ah, mocker, that's the dog's name. 'R' is for

191 I] Q; I do CAPELL 198 Ah,] Q2 (A$_\wedge$) dog's name.] Q3; dog, name$_\wedge$ Q2

phasize the continuing experimentation that distinguishes the Nurse's voice. (Like the speech in 1.3, this derives from the passage in Brooke centring on 653–4.)

189 **lay knife aboard** 'i.e., establish his claim. The diner at an ordinary brought his own knife with him and used it not only to mark his place but also to secure his helping' (Crofts). There is also a quibble on the nautical term '*lay . . . aboard*', meaning to run alongside a ship, usually to board it (*OED v.*[1] 25d), and a sexual pun on 'boarding' (see Partridge). According to Dent, this is the earliest known example of a proverbial phrase (K157.1).

190 **see . . . very toad** Dent compares 'To hate one like a toad' (T361).

191 **sometimes** At odds with the time-scheme, since the Nurse and Juliet have learned about Paris's suit and met Romeo within the past twenty-four hours. The word may suggest a second, longer time-scheme operating simultaneously with the first, or could represent an authorial lapse (Evans; cf. 3.5.237–9). It might also enhance the characterization of the Nurse in her highly embellished account of Juliet. When Brooke's nurse has the same conversation, the narrator comments: 'And part they say is true, and part they do devise, | Yet boldly do they chat of both when no man checks their lies' (665–6).

194 **pale . . . clout** Proverbial (Dent C446). Gibbons compares the modern equivalent, 'as white as a sheet'.

194 **versal** whole. *OED a.*[2] calls this an 'Illiterate or colloq. abbrev. of UNIVERSAL', citing the Nurse's line as its first example of the term in this sense paired with *world*. The phrase 'In the universal (versal, varsal) world' is proverbial (Dent W876.1).

195 **'rosemary'** An aromatic evergreen shrub symbolizing remembrance, rosemary was used as an emblem at both weddings and funerals (*OED* 2). The Nurse relates it to *Romeo* only because of its sound effect, but *rosemary* has ironic resonance here and becomes a motif in the play (cf. 4.4.105–6; and see P. Williams, 'The Rosemary Theme in *Romeo and Juliet*', *MLN* 68 (1953), 400–3).

196 **a** the same (Abbott 79, 81)

198 **dog's name** Q2's punctuation (omitted in Q1) has resulted in various emendations. The present edition accepts Williams's reasoning that Q2's comma probably derives from misreading final *s*. If the syntax remains puzzling, the meaning seems relatively clear. The Nurse, illiterate, does not connect the first sound in *Romeo* and *rosemary* with the letter *R*. Association of the letter's sound with *the dog's name* was commonplace: *OED v.*[2] *lists* 'arr' as an onomatopoeic word meaning 'to snarl as a dog', and cites Persius calling it '*littera canina*'; illustrations include Nashe, *Summers Last Will and Testament* (1600): 'They arr and bark at night against the moon' (iii. 254). In the Nurse's mind, 'arr' is too coarse to suit the names *Romeo* and *rosemary*.

the—no, I know it begins with some other letter; and she hath the prettiest sententious of it, of you and rosemary, that it would do you good to hear it.

ROMEO Commend me to thy lady.
NURSE Ay, a thousand times. Peter!
PETER Anon.
NURSE Before and apace. *Exeunt*

2.4 *Enter Juliet*

JULIET
The clock struck nine when I did send the Nurse;
In half an hour she promised to return.
Perchance she cannot meet him—that's not so.
O she is lame! Love's heralds should be thoughts,
Which ten times faster glides than the sun's beams,
Driving back shadows over louring hills.
Therefore do nimble-pinioned doves draw Love,
And therefore hath the wind-swift Cupid wings.
Now is the sun upon the highmost hill

205 *Exeunt*] Q1 (*Ex.omnes.*); *Exit.* Q2; *Exit Nurse and Peter.* F
2.4.5 glides] Q2; glide F4

198–9 **'R' . . . the—** P. Williams, Jr., thinks the Nurse just stops herself from saying 'arse' ('"Romeo and Juliet": Littera Canina', *N&Q* 195 (1950), 181–2). In the next line she concludes again that 'Romeo' and 'rosemary' must begin with a more refined letter.

200 **sententious of** i.e. saying(s) about. She seems to confuse *sententious* with 'sentence(s)' (*OED sb.* 4a). See Abbott 174 on her use of the preposition.
you Wilson–Duthie suggest that the Nurse is relating a quibble on *you/yew*, the tree emblematic of sadness and death.

204 **Anon** right away, coming

205 ***Exeunt*** Q2 and Q1 both have a general exit, but many editors place Romeo's departure at l. 202. Editions and prompt books also show variation in the Nurse's last line and stage business, her exit influenced by her parting speech in Q1 ('*Peter*, take my fanne, and goe before'). Many productions since the mid nineteenth century have added 'fan business'.

2.4 The opening corroborates information in 2.3.103–7 about the time-scheme of the action.

4 **heralds** Juliet intends 'messengers', but *heralds* had specific duties which these lines may evoke, carrying messages between hostile parties and arranging funerals.
thoughts The swiftness of thought is still proverbial (Dent T240).

5 **faster . . . beams** Possibly proverbial (Dent S992.1, 995.1).

7 **nimble-pinioned doves . . . Love** *Doves*, emblematic of love and fidelity, were believed sacred to Venus. In the last stanza of *Venus*, the goddess 'yokes her silver doves, by whose swift aid | Their mistress, mounted, through the empty skies | In her light chariot quickly is conveyed' (see also *Venus* 153, *Dream* 1.1.171; and cf. Mercutio's rhyming of '"love" and "dove"' at 2.1.11).

8 **wind-swift** Dent compares 'As swift as the wind' (W411).

9 **highmost** highest (*OED a.*, first illustration). Juliet indicates that it is still midday

Of this day's journey, and from nine till twelve
Is three long hours, yet she is not come.
Had she affections and warm youthful blood,
She would be as swift in motion as a ball;
My words would bandy her to my sweet love,
And his to me; but old folks, many feign as they were
    dead,
Unwieldy, slow, heavy, and pale as lead.

Enter the Nurse and Peter

O God, she comes! O honey Nurse, what news?
Hast thou met with him? Send thy man away.

NURSE Peter, stay at the gate. *Exit Peter*

JULIET
Now, good sweet Nurse—O Lord, why lookest thou sad?
Though news be sad, yet tell them merrily.
If good, thou shamest the music of sweet news
By playing it to me with so sour a face.

11 three| Q3; there Q2   14–15 love, | And| Q4, F; loue. | *M.* And Q2 (*'M.' indented as speech-prefix*)   16.1 *Enter . . . Peter*| THEOBALD; *not in* Q   19 *Exit Peter*| THEOBALD; *not in* Q

in a conceit which Wilson–Duthie link with Golding's Ovid (*Metamorphoses* 2.84–7): 'Now first the morning way | Lies steep upright, so that the steeds . . . | . . . have much ado to climb against the hill'.

11 **hours** (two syllables)

13 **She would** Possibly elided in pronunciation.

14 **bandy** Playing on the senses of (a) toss a ball back and forth, (b) exchange words.

15 **And . . . dead** Most editions print *And his to me* as a separate line; this one follows Q2 and Hosley. Hosley compares l. 15 with 2.3.168, but the verse here does not mark a return to Brooke's poem which might prompt an echo of poulter's measure (see 2.3.168 n.); and Q2 starts l. 15 with an '*M.*', an errant speech-prefix which may represent something omitted (McKerrow) or an interpolation (see Wilson–Duthie).

feign . . . dead (a) make themselves appear insensate, (b) pretend they have died (*OED* v. 9a, *a.* 2b, 1d). The couplet plays on various meanings of *dead*: e.g. pale (*a.* 13a); 'pale as lead' was proverbial (Dent L135; cf. L134).

20–77 **Now . . . farewell** On the stage, traditionally a busy scene. Usually the Nurse sits and rises more than once, and Juliet attempts to mollify her through physical contact: hugging, kneeling by her side, placing her head in the Nurse's lap, and rubbing the Nurse's aching head, ankles, knees, shoulders, and back.

21 **merrily** pleasantly. In early use *merrily* was more subdued (*OED adv.* 1), making the antithesis less extreme than it might at first appear.

22–3 **sweet . . . sour** These lines give an original edge to the commonplace antithesis through the punning connection with music: *sweet* = melodious; *sour* = out of tune (*OED a.* 5b cites *Richard II* 5.5.42–3 as its first example, indicating that Shakespeare may have created the link between *sour* and music).

23 **playing** seems to quibble on performing (a) a piece of music, and (b) a part on stage.

NURSE
I am aweary, give me leave a while.
Fie, how my bones ache. What a jaunce have I!

JULIET
I would thou hadst my bones, and I thy news.
Nay come, I pray thee, speak, good good Nurse, speak.

NURSE
Jesu, what haste! Can you not stay a while?
Do you not see that I am out of breath?

JULIET
How art thou out of breath, when thou hast breath
To say to me that thou art out of breath?
The excuse that thou dost make in this delay
Is longer than the tale thou dost excuse.
Is thy news good or bad? Answer to that,
Say either, and I'll stay the circumstance.
Let me be satisfied, is't good or bad?

NURSE Well, you have made a simple choice; you know not how to choose a man. Romeo? No, not he, though his face be better than any man's, yet his leg excels all men's, and for a hand and a foot and a body, though they be not to be talked on, yet they are past compare.

25 jaunce] Q2; iaunt Q1   have I] Q2; haue I had Q1, Q3; had I DANIEL (*conj.*)

24 **give me leave** allow me to rest (see 1.3.8 n.)

25 **jaunce** wearying journey. Probably a dialect pronunciation rather than the misreading for 'jaunt' that *OED* and many editors have inferred (B. Gaines, 'Another Example of Dialect from the Nurse in *Romeo and Juliet*', *SQ* 32 (1981), 96–7; cf. 1.4.255 and n.).
have I i.e. have I had (see Onions for elliptical uses of *have*)

28 **stay** stop (i.e. Juliet's demands, her impatience, or her speech (*OED v.*¹ 2b))

30–3 **How . . . excuse** Juliet enlists rhetoric—rhetorical question, diacope and epistrophe (*breath*), antistasis (*excuse*)—to win the Nurse's co-operation.

35 **stay the circumstance** i.e. wait for the detailed story (Juliet modifies the Nurse's *stay* at l. 28)

38–43 **though . . . lamb** Brooke's nurse (679–82) praises Romeus in plain terms for his appearance and demeanour; Shakespeare's describes Romeo through non sequiturs which incorporate a blazon. In the poem, the nurse explains why she delays her news about the marriage plan and Juliet suspects her motive: 'Nay, soft, quoth she, I fear your hurt by sudden joy. | I list not play quoth Juliet, although thou list to toy' (685–6). In the play, her motivation remains slightly more obscure.

38–42 **his face . . . courtesy** The Nurse's imagery echoes earlier passages, her anatomical catalogue of Romeo a version of Juliet's at 2.1.83–5 (Gibbons) and *the flower of courtesy* a variant of Mercutio's 'pink of courtesy' at 2.3.55 (Evans). Some editors find a pun on *body*, spelled 'baudie' in Q1 and 'bawdy' in F2. This would generate wordplay in the clause *though they be not to be talked on*.

40 **for** as regards (Abbott 149)

He is not the flower of courtesy, but I'll warrant him as gentle as a lamb. Go thy ways, wench, serve God. What, have you dined at home?

JULIET

No, no. But all this did I know before.
What says he of our marriage, what of that?

NURSE

Lord, how my head aches! What a head have I!
It beats as it would fall in twenty pieces.
My back—a t'other side—ah my back, my back!
Beshrew your heart for sending me about
To catch my death with jauncing up and down.

JULIET

I'faith, I am sorry that thou art not well.
Sweet, sweet, sweet Nurse, tell me, what says my love?

NURSE

Your love says, like an honest gentleman,
And a courteous, and a kind, and a handsome,
And, I warrant, a virtuous—where is your mother?

JULIET

Where is my mother? Why, she is within.
Where should she be? How oddly thou repliest:
'Your love says, like an honest gentleman,
"Where is your mother?"'

NURSE O God's Lady dear,

49 ah] Q2 (a)   55 And] Q2 (An)

43 **gentle . . . lamb** Proverbial (Dent L34).

43–4 **Go . . . home?** The Nurse's diction as she abruptly changes topic may signify annoyance: e.g. *What* as an interjection often conveys impatience (cf. 1.4.168 and n.).

45–6 **But . . . that?** Evans compares Brooke 683–4.

48 **as . . . fall** The 'if' is implied by the subjunctive (Abbott 107).

49 **a t'other** on the other (Abbott 140). In performance Juliet rubs the Nurse's back at this point (see ll. 20–77 n.).

ah my back Q2 prints 'a my backe'; 'a' is probably the interjection, but may carry prepositional force from the beginning of the line.

51 **jauncing** prancing (*OED v.* b infers this definition; cf. *Richard II* 5.5.94, and l. 25 and n.)

54–6 **Your love . . . mother?** Unlike Q2, Q1 and some editors set as prose (Q1 abbreviates this speech). The lines, comparable to ll. 38–43, derive from Brooke 679–82.

54 **honest** (a) respectable (*OED a.* 1a), (b) virtuous (3a), (c) truthful

55 **kind** In context, may mean (a) well-bred (*OED a.* 4a), (b) gentle, (c) loving (6).

57–8 **Where . . . repliest** This edition follows Rowe in normalizing as blank verse; Q2 ends the first line 'wher shuld she be?', making it hypermetrical and the second one short; Q1 gives a different, prose version.

60 **God's Lady** the Virgin Mary

Are you so hot? Marry come up, I trow.
Is this the poultice for my aching bones?
Henceforward do your messages yourself.

JULIET
Here's such a coil! Come, what says Romeo?

NURSE
Have you got leave to go to shrift today?

JULIET I have.

NURSE
Then hie you hence to Friar Laurence' cell;
There stays a husband to make you a wife.
Now comes the wanton blood up in your cheeks;
They'll be in scarlet straight at any news.
Hie you to church; I must another way,
To fetch a ladder by the which your love
Must climb a bird's-nest soon when it is dark.
I am the drudge, and toil in your delight,
But you shall bear the burden soon at night.
Go—I'll to dinner—hie you to the cell.

JULIET
Hie to high fortune! Honest Nurse, farewell. *Exeunt*

67 hie] Q2 (high) 76–2.5.37 Go . . . one.| Q2; Q1 *has a different version of these lines.*

61 **Marry come up** *OED int.* d, first instance for this expression of indignant surprise, 'hoity-toity'. The phrase became proverbial (Dent M699.2).

64 **coil** fuss

65 **Have . . . today?** Derives from Brooke 716: 'And leave for her to go to shrift on Saturday she got'; Q2 not only shortens time but eliminates Juliet's stratagem (cf. Q1's version of the line, and 2.3.168 and n.).

69 **wanton** has sexual connotations, like 'hot' in l. 61, but the Nurse probably intends (a) unrestrained, (b) lively (*OED a.* 3d).

73 **a bird's-nest** i.e. Juliet's bedroom, or perhaps her bed. The metaphor is apt because *bird* could refer to a young, virginal woman (*OED sb.* 1d), and *nest* has still familiar associations with a place of shelter or retreat. Partridge discovers bawdy associations in *bird's-nest*.

75 **bear the burden** (a) work hard, (b) support the weight of a man (Partridge). The phrase may also hint at the pleasures of love (*bear the burden* refers to singing) and their consequences, childbirth (*OED sb.* 4a).

soon at night towards evening (see Onions, *soon*)

76–2.5.37 **Go . . . one** Q1 has a different version of ll. 76–7 and the next scene.

77 **Hie to high . . . farewell** Juliet exits on an ominous pun and good terms with the Nurse (*honest* = an epithet of appreciation).

Hie hasten

2.5 *Enter Friar Laurence and Romeo*

FRIAR LAURENCE

So smile the heavens upon this holy act,
That after-hours with sorrow chide us not.

ROMEO

Amen, amen! But come what sorrow can,
It cannot countervail the exchange of joy
That one short minute gives me in her sight.
Do thou but close our hands with holy words,
Then love-devouring death do what he dare,
It is enough I may but call her mine.

FRIAR LAURENCE

These violent delights have violent ends,
And in their triumph die like fire and powder,
Which as they kiss consume. The sweetest honey
Is loathsome in his own deliciousness,
And in the taste confounds the appetite.
Therefore love moderately: long love doth so;
Too swift arrives as tardy as too slow.

Enter Juliet

2.5.0.1 *Enter . . . Romeo*] Q2 (*Enter Frier and Romeo.*) 15.1 *Enter Juliet*] Q2; *Enter Iuliet somewhat fast, and embraceth Romeo.* Q1

2.5 All the Romeo and Juliet narratives include a marriage-scene. Shakespeare complicates the language of Brooke and Painter, but reduces the number of characters and the intrigue.

1 **smile the heavens** i.e. may the heavens smile (Abbott 364–5)

3 **come . . . can** i.e. let whatever sorrow come that can. In this speech Romeo echoes Friar Laurence's language and striking if unintentional irony. Evans compares ll. 3–8 with the corresponding passage in Brooke, spoken by Juliet (859–62).

4 **countervail** counterbalance

exchange of joy (a) mutual joy, or (b) joy traded for sorrow

6 **close** join

7 **love-devouring death** Dent compares 'Death devours all things' (D138.1).

9 **violent delights . . . violent ends** Friar Laurence begins his short, ominous wedding-sermon by combining two proverbs, 'Such beginning such end' and 'Nothing violent can be permanent' (Dent B262, N321). Typically he emphasizes each point with rhetoric, in particular with figures of repetition and antithesis. Editors have compared l. 9 with *Lucrece* 894 (part of the victim's exclamation against 'opportunity') and with Juliet's verses at 2.1.161–3.

10–11 **triumph die . . . consume** The sexual figures of speech are epitomized in *consume*: (a) perish or burn away, (b) consummate (*OED* v.[2]).

11–13 **sweetest honey . . . appetite** Proverbial, 'Too much honey cloys the stomach' (Dent H560), originally from Proverbs 25: 16 and 27: 7.

13 **confounds** destroys (*OED* v. 1c)

14 **long . . . so** Possibly proverbial. Dent compares 'Love me little love me long' (L559).

15 **Too swift . . . too slow** Dent cites 'The more haste the less (worse) speed' (H198; cf. the Friar's warning at 2.2.94 and n.).

15.1 ***Enter Juliet*** The Q2 direction allows for a strikingly emblematic entrance (cf. 2.2.22.1 and n.). Q1, more specific (see

Here comes the lady. O, so light a foot
Will ne'er wear out the everlasting flint;
A lover may bestride the gossamers
That idles in the wanton summer air,
And yet not fall, so light is vanity.

JULIET

Good even to my ghostly confessor.

FRIAR LAURENCE

Romeo shall thank thee, daughter, for us both.

JULIET

As much to him, else is his thanks too much.

ROMEO

Ah Juliet, if the measure of thy joy
Be heaped like mine, and that thy skill be more
To blazon it, then sweeten with thy breath
This neighbour air, and let rich music tongue

27 music] Q2; musicks Q4, F (musickes)

Collation) and therefore limiting, may represent contemporary stage usage, but not necessarily for all performances. Since the nineteenth century Juliet's entrance has been variously handled: prompt books usually follow the editions on which they are based, adopting the direction from either Q2 or Q1; or they have Romeo exit at l. 15 or 16, and return with Juliet at l. 20.

16–17 **so light . . . everlasting flint** Mahood explains how these lines articulate central paradoxes through ambiguity and wordplay (pp. 65–8).

17 **everlasting flint** Proverbial (Dent S878).

19 **idles** move idly (*OED v.* 1, first instance of a rare usage)
wanton Frequently glossed 'sportive', but also connotes amorousness and lack of restraint.

20 **vanity** i.e. the vanity of all temporal things, as in Ecclesiastes 1: 2 and 2: 1. Friar Laurence creates an exemplum from his conceit of a lover's buoyancy and from wordplay: *vanity* = emptiness (see *OED*, *vanitas*), and *light* = (a) insubstantial, (b) not heavy.

21 **Good even** i.e. good afternoon (see 2.3.104 n.)
ghostly confessor Romeo used the same epithet for the Friar at 2.1.234 (see n.). In *confessor* the first syllable receives the primary accent.

22 **Romeo . . . both** It was customary to kiss a lady on greeting. Friar Laurence permits Romeo to return Juliet's salutation on behalf of them both.

23 **As much . . . too much** 'I must repay him in kind (a kiss) or I shall have been overpaid' (Evans). Juliet's response echoes her first dialogue with Romeo in 1.4. It construes *thanks* as singular (*OED sb.* 4b).

24–5 **measure . . . heaped** a 'heaped measure', 'a dry measure used for certain commodities which are heaped up in a cone above the brim of the measure' (*OED ppl. a.* 2). *Measure* also alludes to the idea of music which becomes more obvious in ll. 26–7 (Mahood, pp. 13–14). P. Edwards discusses the exchange which follows in 'The declaration of love' (*Shakespeare's Styles*, pp. 39–43).

25 **that** if. Lines 24 and 25 vary the phrase 'if *that*' (see Abbott 287).

26 **blazon it** celebrate it in words (*OED v.* 4)

27 **music tongue** Editors change to 'music's tongue' (Q4 and F), but Q2's 'musicke' may be attributive or quasi-adjectival in the sense 'musical' (see *OED sb.* 13c; cf. 'music vows' in *Hamlet* 3.1.159).

Unfold the imagined happiness that both
Receive in either by this dear encounter.

JULIET

Conceit, more rich in matter than in words,
Brags of his substance, not of ornament.
They are but beggars that can count their worth;
But my true love is grown to such excess,
I cannot sum up sum of half my wealth.

FRIAR LAURENCE

Come, come with me, and we will make short work;
For, by your leaves, you shall not stay alone
Till holy church incorporate two in one. *Exeunt*

3.1 *Enter Mercutio, Benvolio, and men*

BENVOLIO

I pray thee, good Mercutio, let's retire.
The day is hot, the Capels are abroad;

34 sum of half my] Q2; some of halfe my Q4, F; sums of half my JOHNSON; half my sum of CAPELL; half of half my JOWETT (*conj.*) 37 *Exeunt*] Q1 (*Exeunt omnes.*); *not in* Q2

3.1.0.1 *Enter . . . men*] Q2; *Enter Benuolio, Mercutio.* Q1 2 Capels are] Q1; *Capels* Q2; *Capulets* Q4, F

28–9 **both . . . either** i.e. we receive in each other (see Onions, *either*, Abbott 12)

29 **dear encounter** may be heard as wordplay or as an oxymoron typical of Renaissance love-poetry. Romeo has used *dear* in multiple and ironic senses with similar naïve ardour (cf. 1.4.160 and n.). He has used *encounter*, too, in its negative sense as a meeting of adversaries (1.1.209); but here he means either a friendly or an amatory meeting.

30 **Conceit** Difficult to define. Interpretation of ll. 30–1 depends on whether it is understood as (a) idea (*OED sb.* 1a), (b) understanding (2a), (c) imagination, (d) device, invention. Juliet clearly rejects Romeo's invitation to verbalize their experience. She also picks up Romeo's 'measure' in its primary sense and turns it into a monetary figure (Mahood, p. 14).

32 **worth** possessions (*OED sb.*[1] 5, the first example of *worth* meaning status with respect to property). The epigram appears earlier in Martial 6.34.8 (Evans) and later in *Antony* 1.1.15.

33 **excess** Juliet intends *excess* in its neutral sense of superabundance, but it has obvious connotations of intemperateness.

34 **sum up sum . . . wealth** The sense is clear: Juliet cannot reckon the totality of her love (*wealth* = (a) happiness (*OED* 1a), (b) possessions). Moreover the wordplay and rhetoric, which fit character, scene, and play, appear not only in other Shakespeare texts but elsewhere (cf. variations on *sum* (*v.*)/*sum* (*sb.*)/some in *Merchant* 3.2.157–8; Sonnets 4.8, 109.12; Sidney's *Astrophil and Stella*, Sonnet 85.10). As a result this edition follows Q2, avoiding editorial changes from Johnson's and Capell's to Jowett's.

37 **Till . . . one** Shaheen hears overtones of the Bible (Genesis 2: 24, Matthew 19: 5–6, Mark 10: 7–8), the Marriage Service, and the homily on Matrimony.

3.1 This scene, centring on Mercutio for over 100 lines, reapportions the traditional narrative of the fight and gives an edge of unfamiliarity to the familiar.

0.1 ***Enter . . . men*** The group includes Mercutio's page, addressed at l. 94.

2–4 **day is hot . . . stirring** As 1.3.15–17 has established, the play takes place in July.

And if we meet we shall not scape a brawl,
For now, these hot days, is the mad blood stirring.

MERCUTIO Thou art like one of these fellows that, when he enters the confines of a tavern, claps me his sword upon the table and says, 'God send me no need of thee'; and, by the operation of the second cup, draws him on the drawer, when indeed there is no need.

BENVOLIO Am I like such a fellow?

MERCUTIO Come, come, thou art as hot a jack in thy mood as any in Italy; and as soon moved to be moody, and as soon moody to be moved.

BENVOLIO And what to?

MERCUTIO Nay, an there were two such, we should have none shortly, for one would kill the other. Thou—why, thou wilt quarrel with a man that hath a hair more or a hair less in his beard than thou hast. Thou wilt quarrel with a man for cracking nuts, having no other reason but because thou hast hazel eyes. What eye but such an eye would spy out such a quarrel? Thy head is as full of quarrels as an egg is full of meat, and yet thy head hath been beaten as addle as an egg for quarrelling. Thou

Sir Thomas Smith's *Commonwealth of England* (1583) provides a gloss on the connection between *hot days* and *mad blood stirring*: 'in the warm time people for the most part be more unruly' (quoted by Reed in Furness).

2 **Capels are** Q2's abbreviated form appears in Brooke (1123; cf. 157), Q1 in the second line of the scene, and other lines in Q2 (5.1.18, 5.3.189.1). It seems that *are* has dropped out by accident.

3–4 **And . . . stirring** Q2 sets as prose and Hosley follows (printing the first four lines as prose). Like the first two verses, however, ll. 3–4 scan. The resulting verse speech makes an effective transition between scenes, as well as a distinct contrast with Mercutio's style (see Leech's note in *SQ* 5 (1954), 94).

3 **And if** Spencer suggests the meaning 'if indeed', i.e. emphatic *if* (Abbott 105).

5–9 **Thou . . . need** Mercutio portrays Benvolio in colloquial terms as a duellist unsubtly provoking a quarrel, a stereotype clearly antithetical to Benvolio's role as peacemaker (cf. Mercutio's description of Tybalt at 2.3.22–4).

8 **by the operation . . . cup** i.e. when his second drink has taken effect

10 **Am I . . . fellow?** With even mild stress on *I*, this response emphasizes the incongruity in Mercutio's speech.

11 **jack** fellow (with insulting connotations of the plebeian or knavery; cf. 2.3.142 and n.)

11–13 **mood . . . moody** anger . . . angry (*OED sb.*[1] 2b, *a.* 3)

12–13 **as soon . . . as soon** at one time . . . at another (*OED adv.* 7c)
moved provoked, incited, aroused (cf. 1.1.5–6 and n.)

15 **an . . . two such** Imagining a bizarre event (*an* = if), Mercutio quibbles on Benvolio's previous line (*two*/to).

20–1 **eye** puns on 'I' (l. 10)

21 **spy out** seek an opportunity in a covert or hostile manner

21–2 **as full . . . meat** Proverbial (Dent K149).

23 **addle** (a) useless (an *addle* egg is inedible), (b) muddled

hast quarrelled with a man for coughing in the street, because he hath wakened thy dog that hath lain asleep in the sun. Didst thou not fall out with a tailor for wearing his new doublet before Easter? With another for tying his new shoes with old ribbon? And yet thou wilt tutor me from quarrelling!

BENVOLIO An I were so apt to quarrel as thou art, any man should buy the fee-simple of my life for an hour and a quarter.

MERCUTIO The fee-simple? O simple!

Enter Tybalt, Petruccio, and others

BENVOLIO By my head, here comes the Capulets.

MERCUTIO By my heel, I care not.

TYBALT (*to his companions*)
Follow me close, for I will speak to them.—
Gentlemen, good e'en, a word with one of you.

MERCUTIO And but one word with one of us? Couple it with something; make it a word and a blow.

28 ribbon] Q2 (ri- | band) 33.1 *Enter . . . others*] Q2; *Enter Tybalt.* Q1 (*after l.* 34) 34 the Capulets] Q2; a *Capolet* Q1 36 (*to his companions*)] MOWAT–WERSTINE; *not in* Q

26–7 **fall out . . . before Easter** Elizabethans wore new clothes for Easter (probably to celebrate the new year, beginning 25 March, as well as the holiday). Laroque quotes 'Poor Robin's Almanac': 'At Easter let your clothes be new | Or else be sure will it rue' (see pp. 108, 337). Mercutio implies that Benvolio has antagonized a tailor by putting on his new garment during Lent.

27 **another** i.e. a shoemaker

28 **ribbon** used for shoe-laces (Wilson–Duthie cite Linthicum, p. 283). It is unclear whether Benvolio or the shoemaker committed this faux pas.

28–9 **tutor me from** warn me against (*OED* v. 2, first instance)

31–2 **buy the fee-simple . . . quarter** i.e. purchase the full value of my life for a fraction of its worth (*fee-simple* = estate belonging to its owner and his heirs for ever). Benvolio also suggests that in a quarrel his life would end in virtually no time.

33 **simple** The pun refers to both Benvolio and his conceit, since *simple* means (a) low (of price or sale) (*OED a.* 7b), (b) slight (of value), (c) slow-witted.

33.1 ***Petruccio*** This name, which the Nurse gave to one of Capulet's guests (1.4.244), here identifies a non-speaking character. Editors speculate that Shakespeare either could not find a particular use for him or intended him to warn 'Away, Tybalt!' at l. 89.

34–5 **By my head . . . not** Benvolio swears mildly by his life; Mercutio curses scornfully, playing on antitheses of *head* and *heel* in various phrases.

37 **good e'en** This salutation, used any time after noon, is repeated and marks each phase during this eventful afternoon (cf. 2.3.104 and n., 2.5.21 and n.).

38 **And** emphasizes Mercutio's provocative question (Abbott 95, 99).

39 **a word . . . blow** Proverbial, '(He is but) a word and a blow' (Dent W763; *OED*, *word*, *sb.* 16, first illustration of the phrase expressing anger or defiance which leads to a fight).

TYBALT You shall find me apt enough to that, sir, an you will give me occasion.

MERCUTIO Could you not take some occasion without giving?

TYBALT Mercutio, thou consortest with Romeo.

MERCUTIO 'Consort'! What, dost thou make us minstrels? An thou make minstrels of us, look to hear nothing but discords. Here's my fiddlestick; here's that shall make you dance. Zounds, 'consort'!

BENVOLIO
We talk here in the public haunt of men.
Either withdraw unto some private place,
Or reason coldly of your grievances,
Or else depart. Here all eyes gaze on us.

MERCUTIO
Men's eyes were made to look, and let them gaze.
I will not budge for no man's pleasure, I.

Enter Romeo

TYBALT
Well, peace be with you, sir, here comes my man.

MERCUTIO
But I'll be hanged, sir, if he wear your livery.

40–1 **an . . . occasion** i.e. if you will give me cause. Tybalt, requiring proper grounds for a fight, corroborates Mercutio's description of him as a duellist in the new Italian style, a 'captain of compliments' and 'a gentleman . . . of the first and second cause' (2.3.19, 23–4). In addition, the fateful narrative gives *occasion* nuances of 'opportunity' and circumstance(s) (*OED sb.*[1] 1a, 7a, b).

42 **take . . . occasion** The phrase effectively reduces Tybalt's *occasion* to the single meaning 'opportunity'.

45 **'Consort'** Punning on (a) associate, (b) play music together (*OED v.* 7), definitions which apply also to the noun meaning (a) fellowship (*sb.*[2] 1a), (b) group of musicians.

minstrels The link between musicians and *minstrels*, professional entertainers classed as menials or vagabonds, allows Mercutio to construe Tybalt's statement as an insult and to provide him with both a challenge and a cause. (At 4.4.137–8 this insult will materialize when Peter calls the First Musician a *minstrel*.)

46–8 **make minstrels . . . dance** A new version of an earlier conceit (cf. 2.3.19–22).

47 **fiddlestick** i.e. sword (a phallic weapon; cf. 1.1.30 and n.). With this line Mercutio may touch, point to, or even draw his sword.

that that which

48 **Zounds** An abbreviated euphemism for 'by God's wounds' (a stronger oath than those at ll. 34–5).

52 **depart** take leave of each other (*OED v.* 5). As an intransitive verb *depart* also meant 'die' (7), allowing an ominous pun.

54 **budge** move, perhaps also 'flinch'. *OED v.*[1] 1b identifies first occurrence later, *Caesar* 4.2.98.

55–6 **my man . . . livery** Wordplay on *man* as 'manservant' changes Tybalt's dismissal to another kind of insult. This instance of *my man* precedes *OED*'s first illustration, from the Bible (1611), *sb.*[1] 4k.

Marry, go before to field, he'll be your follower;
Your worship in that sense may call him 'man'.

TYBALT

Romeo, the love I bear thee can afford
No better term than this: thou art a villain.

ROMEO

Tybalt, the reason that I have to love thee
Doth much excuse the appertaining rage
To such a greeting. Villain am I none.
Therefore farewell; I see thou knowest me not.

TYBALT

Boy, this shall not excuse the injuries
That thou hast done me. Therefore turn and draw.

ROMEO

I do protest I never injuried thee,
But love thee better than thou canst devise
Till thou shalt know the reason of my love.
And so, good Capulet, which name I tender
As dearly as mine own, be satisfied.

59 love] Q2; hate Q1 67 injuried] Q2; iniured Q1, Q3, F (iniur'd)

57 **go** A command or a condition, i.e. if you go (see Abbott 361). The phrase means '(if you) lead the way to (the field of) combat'.
follower Wordplay on 'man' continues with the pun on *follower* as (a) pursuer, (b) imitator, (c) attendant. Cf. Lyly's *Sapho and Phao* 2.3.9–13, quoted in 2.3.22 n.

59 **love** Some editors adopt Q1's 'hate', finding 'love' ironic and therefore inappropriate to the straightforward Tybalt. But he may be choosing his words to appear courteous while starting a fight.

60 **villain** (a) low-born peasant, (b) unprincipled scoundrel. Tybalt's term, on his mind since Capulet's party, demeans Romeo's birth as well as his moral character (cf. 1.4.175, 177).

61–71 **Tybalt . . . be satisfied** In these speeches Painter's Rhomeo (95–6) is closer than Brooke's Romeus (999–1002, 1011–15) to the Shakespearian character (Evans).

62–3 **excuse . . . greeting** *Appertaining* here means 'appropriate'; and Romeo says that love accounts for his lack of due fury in response to Tybalt's insult. Since *excuse* applies to *rage* that is absent or wanting, it anticipates *OED*'s earliest illustration for this sense (*v.* 8) by some fifty years.

65 **Boy . . . injuries** Tybalt uses *Boy* as an expression of contempt (*OED sb.*[1] 4) and *excuse* in a familiar sense different from Romeo's (cf. Brooke 1016–18).

67 **injuried** Most editors follow Q3, Q1, or F, substituting 'injured' for this verb which it would replace *c.*1600 (see *OED*, *injury*, *v.*). Although McKerrow and Jowett both note that *injuried* disturbs the metre, the *r* sound permits elision to regularize the verse (Abbott 464), or 'never' could be pronounced as a monosyllable.

68 **devise** conceive (*OED v.* 10)

70–1 **tender . . . satisfied** *Tender*, denoting 'value' in the sense of 'regard' or even 'cherish' (*OED v.*[2] 3a), may also pick up a nuance of commercial transaction from *dearly* and *satisfied*. Romeo seems to echo his wordplay on 'dear' at 1.4.160, since *dearly* at this point can mean not only

MERCUTIO
O calm, dishonourable, vile submission!
Alla stoccado carries it away.
Tybalt, you rat-catcher, will you walk?

TYBALT What wouldst thou have with me?

MERCUTIO Good king of cats, nothing but one of your nine lives, that I mean to make bold withal, and as you shall use me hereafter, dry-beat the rest of the eight. Will you pluck your sword out of his pilcher by the ears? Make haste, lest mine be about your ears ere it be out.

TYBALT I am for you.

They fight

ROMEO
Gentle Mercutio, put thy rapier up.

73 *stoccado*] Q2 (*stucatho*), Q1 (*stockado*) 74 will you walk?] Q2; come back, come back. Q1; come, will you walk? HANMER 81.1 *They fight*] ROWE (Mer. *and* Tyb. *fight*.); *not in* Q

'fondly' but 'costly'. Slightly more complex, *satisfied* refers to accepting a state of affairs as well as compensation for injury (*v*. 2a) and payment of a debt.

71 **be satisfied** In Brooke Tybalt rejects conciliation and immediately strikes at Romeus with his sword (1016–20). In the play, as Spencer points out, Tybalt says and does nothing until Mercutio taunts him. As a result the dramatic event is ambiguous and suspenseful, allowing for various theatrical interpretations.

73 ***Alla stoccado* . . . away** i.e. the duellist à la mode wins the day (*OED v*. 46e). Mercutio flouts Tybalt by naming him after a thrust mentioned in the Italian fencing manuals.

74 **rat-catcher** Beginning to play on the connection between Tybalt's name and cats, as at 2.3.18 (see ll. 76–8 and 100–1; *OED*, *rat-catcher*, 1a, first illustration).

walk go away (*OED v*.[1] 8a). Mercutio may be inviting Tybalt to withdraw in order to fight a duel, or asking if he intends to leave the scene without a confrontation. Jowett, following Hanmer and influenced by Q1, reads 'come, will you walk?', which clarifies Mercutio's challenge and regularizes the metre; this edition prefers the original indeterminacy and rough-edged verse (about to become prose).

76–8 **nine lives . . . eight** A distinctive rendition of the adage (Dent C154).

77 **make bold withal** take liberties with (*OED a*. 3)

78 **dry-beat** thrash, without drawing blood (*OED v*., *a*. 12; cf. 4.4.146). If Tybalt's behaviour fails to please him *hereafter*, Mercutio will finish off the damage begun today and kill him brutally.

79 **pilcher** scabbard (Q1's reading). *OED*, *pilcher*[2], 2 cites this as the only example of the 'apparently *contemptuous*' usage, and questions whether *pilcher* derives from 'pilch', *sb*. 1, an outer garment made of leather or coarse wool.

ears The *ears* become the hilt of the rapier, and the image 'suggests a reluctant sword' (Wilson–Duthie).

81 **for** i.e. ready for (Abbott 155)

81.1 ***They fight*** Q2 has no directions for this fight; Q1 has a single instruction at the equivalent of l. 88.1. The texts allow a variety of editorial and theatrical decisions about when characters draw their swords (l. 47 at the earliest, l. 81 at the latest), when they begin to fight (usually between ll. 81 and 83), and when Romeo enters the fray (any time between ll. 84 and 88). Prompt books generally choreograph the fights in great detail.

MERCUTIO Come, sir, your *passado*.

ROMEO

Draw, Benvolio, beat down their weapons.
Gentlemen, for shame forbear this outrage.
Tybalt, Mercutio, the Prince expressly hath
Forbid this bandying in Verona streets.
Hold, Tybalt! Good Mercutio!

Tybalt stabs Mercutio under Romeo's arm

[PETRUCCIO] Away, Tybalt!

Exeunt Tybalt and followers

MERCUTIO I am hurt.
A plague a both houses, I am sped.
Is he gone and hath nothing?

BENVOLIO What, art thou hurt?

88.1 *Tybalt . . . arm*] Q1 (*Tibalt vnder Romeos arme thrusts Mercutio, in and flyes.*); *not in* Q2 89 [PETRUCCIO] Away, Tybalt!] WILLIAMS (*conj.* Greg); *Away* Tybalt. Q2 (*as stage direction*); *Exit Tybalt.* F 89.1 *Exeunt . . . followers*] GLOBE *following* Malone (*Tybalt under Romeo's arm stabs Mercutio and flies with his followers.*); *not in* Q 91 both] Q2; both your DYCE; your Q1; both the F 92–108 What . . . houses.] Q2; Q1 *has a different version of these lines*

83 ***passado*** forward thrust with sword, one foot advanced at the same time (see 2.3.24 n.)

85 **outrage** violent action (*OED sb.* 2a), also connoting irrationality and recklessness (1a, b)

87 **Forbid . . . bandying** *OED* cites Romeo's use of *bandying*, which means 'fighting', as its first illustration for the verbal substantive. See Abbott 343 on the abbreviated past participle *Forbid*.

88.1 ***Tybalt . . . arm*** Q1's direction (see Collation), adapted here, clearly indicates the action which Mercutio will describe at l. 103: 'I was hurt under your arm'.

89 [**PETRUCCIO**] **. . . Tybalt!** Q2 prints '*Away* Tybalt.' as a direction, but Williams argues persuasively for Greg's conjecture that it is a line of dialogue (cf. l. 132) probably spoken by Petruccio, Tybalt's only named follower. Shakespeare never substitutes 'Away' for 'Exit' in directions, although he frequently uses the adverb for 'Come away' or 'Go away' in dialogue (see Williams's edition and 'A New Line of Dialogue in *Romeo and Juliet*', *SQ* 11 (1960), 84–7).

91 **plague . . . houses** Many editors follow Dyce, printing 'both your houses' by analogy with the wording in ll. 99–100 and 106. As a result they smooth the metre and emphasize the pronouns. Nevertheless, several editors since Duthie favour Q2, whose various irregularities suit the dialogue of a fight and its aftermath. The present edition reproduces Q2's phrase, including the preposition *a* (= on), which has an entry in *OED* (see also Abbott 140).

91 **sped** dispatched (*OED v.* 9c). This verb's more familiar associations with haste (as well as success) may echo ironically Mercutio's impatient challenge to Tybalt just before the duel (ll. 76–80).

92–108 **What . . . houses** Jowett analyses this passage in Q1, which contains transposed material and additions. Concentrating on the additions, he conjectures that they may be interpolated by the dramatist-editor of Q1 'most plausibly identified as Chettle', although parallels between the lines in Q1 and the rest of Shakespeare's plays point to Shakespeare's authorship. Jowett concludes that Q1 represents a corrupted version of the revised text or a thorough reformulation of the passage. An editor who accepted these lines as Shakespeare's might take them, with certain qualifications, as control-text.

MERCUTIO
Ay, ay, a scratch, a scratch; marry, 'tis enough.
Where is my page? Go, villain, fetch a surgeon.
Exit Page

ROMEO
Courage, man, the hurt cannot be much.

MERCUTIO No, 'tis not so deep as a well, nor so wide as a church-door, but 'tis enough, 'twill serve. Ask for me tomorrow, and you shall find me a grave man. I am peppered, I warrant, for this world. A plague a both your houses! Zounds, a dog, a rat, a mouse, a cat, to scratch a man to death! A braggart, a rogue, a villain, that fights by the book of arithmetic! Why the devil came you between us? I was hurt under your arm.

ROMEO I thought all for the best.

MERCUTIO
Help me into some house, Benvolio,
Or I shall faint. A plague a both your houses!
They have made worms' meat of me—

94.1 *Exit Page*] CAPELL; *not in* Q 100 Zounds] Q2 (sounds)

93 **scratch** Mercutio continues to play on Tybalt's name here and at ll. 100–1; he also describes the Spanish thrust which has wounded him, 'a short stabbing motion rather than a full thrust' (Soens, 126–7).

94 **villain** Term of address for a servant, used by Mercutio without negative implications and perhaps with some affection for his young attendant.

96 **deep . . . well** Proverbial (Dent W260.1).

96–7 **so wide . . . church-door** Mercutio may be thinking of his own funeral (Gibbons). Dent disputes the conventional annotation of this phrase as a proverb.

97–8 **Ask . . . grave man** Shaheen compares Job 7: 21: 'Now must I sleep in the dust, and if thou seekest me tomorrow in the morning, I shall not be' (or 'I shall be gone'). Mercutio's pun occurs, e.g., in Lydgate's elegy on Chaucer ('My master *Chaucer* now is *grave*' (quoted in Furness)). But its context gives it singularity. Mahood describes it as an expression of vitality in the face of death, as well as 'a grim joke, to accompany a dying curse' (p. 69).

98–9 **peppered** ruined (*OED* v. 5b)

100 **Zounds** Mercutio used this oath at l. 48 (see n.).

102 **by the book of arithmetic** according to numerical rules, or by the fencing manual (see 2.3.18–25 and nn.)

104 **all . . . best** Dent compares 'All is for the best' (A136.1).

107–8 **They . . . houses** Evans argues for Dyce's relineation (adding *I have it* to l. 107), because the original metre of l. 107 is deficient for no apparent reason, and because he thinks Q2's pointing of l. 108 may indicate textual corruption. (Of course, changing the metre of l. 107 disrupts that of l. 108.) Whatever produced the short line in Q2, its effect suits this last speech of the fainting and probably breathless character as he exits. Moreover, Q2's punctuation of l. 108, ignored by editors who point according to F3, makes sense under the circumstances: Mercutio's final words conflate two phrases, 'into some house' and 'a both your houses'.

107 **worms' meat** Dent compares 'A man is nothing but worms' meat' (M253).

I have it, and soundly, to your houses.
[*Exit Mercutio with Benvolio*]

ROMEO
This gentleman, the Prince's near ally,
My very friend, hath got this mortal hurt
In my behalf; my reputation stained
With Tybalt's slander—Tybalt, that an hour
Hath been my cousin. O sweet Juliet,
Thy beauty hath made me effeminate,
And in my temper softened valour's steel.
Enter Benvolio

BENVOLIO
O Romeo, Romeo, brave Mercutio is dead.
That gallant spirit hath aspired the clouds,
Which too untimely here did scorn the earth.

ROMEO
This day's black fate on more days doth depend;
This but begins the woe others must end.
Enter Tybalt

108 soundly, to‸| Q2; ~‸~, F3   108.1 [*Exit . . . Benvolio*] | ROWE (*Ex.* Mer. Ben.); *Exit.* Q2; *Exeunt.* Q1   110 this| Q2, Q1; his Q3   120.1 *Enter Tybalt*| Q1, F; *not in* Q2

108 **I have it** *OED* v. 14d, first example of this colloquial expression; Gibbons compares *I have it* with '*hay*' in 2.3.25 (see n.), giving the phrase an ironic edge.

108.1 [***Exit . . . Benvolio***] The original directions do not indicate how many actors leave here. Some recent editors have assumed that all but Romeo exit; various productions since the eighteenth century have left him alone. In a number of twentieth-century performances this ambiguity disappears because Mercutio dies on stage.

109 **ally** relative (*OED sb.*[1] 5)

110 **very** true (*OED a.* 6)

hurt Either the blow (*OED sb.*[1] 1) or the injury it caused.

112 **slander** i.e. ll. 59–60, 65–6

113 **cousin** kinsman (*OED sb.* 1)

115 **temper** (a) temperament (*OED sb.* 4a), (b) degree of hardness given to steel by tempering (cf. 1.1.83 and n.). The pun heightens the impression of oxymoron.

116 **Mercutio is** Some editors (e.g. Wilson–Duthie and Hosley), following F2, print 'Mercutio's' to adjust the metre. As Q2 sets it, however, the line allows more than one vocalization, and it is possible to omit the extra beat through elision.

117 **aspired** mounted up to (*OED v.* 8). Gibbons, like Malone, hears Marlovian echoes: 'And both our souls aspire celestial thrones' (*1 Tamburlaine* 1.2.237).

118 **Which . . . earth** Although Benvolio's meaning is clear, two words complicate this line: *untimely* = (a) prematurely, (b) inopportunely; *scorn* = (a) disdain, (b) mock (*OED v.* 2; cf. 1.4.170, 176).

119–20 **This day's . . . end** As Evans suggests, these lines correspond to Romeo's premonition at 1.4.105–7: the present hangs threateningly (*depend* = impend) over *more days*, i.e. the future. Again the expression is forceful, a heroic couplet and concentrated rhetorical devices from alliteration to antithesis.

119 **more** Q2 'mo' occurs only here in *Romeo*, *more* over sixty times. There seems no basis for the distinction, although the words are historically distinct (*OED* gives 'mo' a separate entry as obsolete).

BENVOLIO

Here comes the furious Tybalt back again.

ROMEO

He gan in triumph and Mercutio slain?
Away to heaven, respective lenity,
And fire-eyed fury be my conduct now.
Now, Tybalt, take the 'villain' back again
That late thou gavest me; for Mercutio's soul
Is but a little way above our heads,
Staying for thine to keep him company.
Either thou or I, or both, must go with him.

TYBALT

Thou wretched boy, that didst consort him here,
Shalt with him hence.

ROMEO This shall determine that.

They fight. Tybalt falls

BENVOLIO

Romeo, away, be gone!
The citizens are up, and Tybalt slain.
Stand not amazed—the Prince will doom thee death
If thou art taken—hence, be gone, away!

122 He gan] Q2; He gon Q3; A liue Q1; Alive POPE; Again CAPELL; He gay HOPPE; He yare WILLIAMS; He gad JOWETT 124 fire-eyed] Q1 (fier eyed); fier end Q2; fier and Q3

122 **He gan** i.e. 'is he gone', or 'he to go'. Since most editors make no sense of Q2, l. 122 has generated much debate. Some substitute Q1 'A liue'; others, assuming a compositor's misreading, emend Q2 (see Collation; Williams and Jowett offer the most thorough notes on this crux). Yet McKerrow thinks 'He gone' perhaps awkward but not impossible; and Jowett explains that Q2 may represent one of two current infinitive forms, but cannot see why either would appear uniquely here (see *OED*, *go*, *v*. 8a, 1a, *gan*). As *OED* and recent commentary indicate, however, *Romeo* employs words uniquely elsewhere. Moreover *gan*, past participle or infinitive, may describe Romeo's view of Tybalt's public style, as well as his exit at l. 89.1: Tybalt 'goes' in *triumph*, revelling in brutal victory.

123 **respective** *OED a*. 2b defines as 'discriminating, partial', giving this as its first illustration. Romeo's behaviour earlier probably brings other meanings into play, such as 'considerate' and 'civil' (1a, 3).

124 **fire-eyed fury** This edition adopts Pope's correction, through Q1, of an apparent misprint: cf. *1 Henry IV* 4.1.115, 'the fire-eyed maid of smoky war'. At the same time it acknowledges Q3's hendiadys as an equally sensible reading. Both versions complete the antithesis with 'heaven' and 'lenity' in l. 123.

conduct guide (*OED sb.*[1] 3; cf. 1.4.110–11 and 5.3.116)

130 **wretched boy . . . consort him** Tybalt repeats his insults: *boy* from l. 65 (see n.), and *consort*, meaning 'accompany' here (*OED v*. 1), from l. 44.

131 **This** i.e. his sword

133 **up** on the move, agitated, and perhaps armed

134 **amazed** confounded (*OED ppl. a*. 2)

135–6 **away . . . stay** As Spencer points out, after the climactic duels and except for Benvolio's account to the Prince,

ROMEO

O, I am fortune's fool!

BENVOLIO

Why dost thou stay?

Exit Romeo

Enter Citizens

CITIZEN

Which way ran he that killed Mercutio?
Tybalt, that murderer, which way ran he?

BENVOLIO

There lies that Tybalt.

CITIZEN

Up, sir, go with me.
I charge thee in the Prince's name obey.

Enter Prince, old Montague, Capulet, their Wives, and all

PRINCE

Where are the vile beginners of this fray?

BENVOLIO

O noble Prince, I can discover all
The unlucky manage of this fatal brawl.
There lies the man, slain by young Romeo,
That slew thy kinsman, brave Mercutio.

CAPULET'S WIFE

Tybalt, my cousin, O my brother's child!

136.1 *Exit Romeo*] Q2; *Exeunt* Q1   140.1–2 *Enter . . . all*] Q2; *Enter Prince, Capolets wife.* Q1
142 all‸] Q1, F; ~: Q2   145, 148 kinsman] Q1; kisman Q2 (*tilde errors*)

rhymed couplets predominate for the rest of this scene.

136 **fortune's fool** This expression became proverbial (Dent F617.1). In context *fool* allows two or more still current definitions: (a) dupe or sport, (b) jester (therefore servant). A number of prompt books cut all or some of the text which follows this line and concludes the scene.

137, 139 **CITIZEN** Q2's abbreviated speech-prefixes ('*Citti.*' and '*Citi.*') fail to distinguish singular from plural or to establish the speaker of ll. 139–40 as a man of authority. This edition assigns the first speech to a single man; it notes that the two pairs of lines may have different speakers, and that the second (possibly the first as well) may be delivered by a member of the watch (Q1 has '*Watch.*' as speech-prefix for both lines).

140.1 ***Capulet, their Wives*** Spencer remarks on the silence of Capulet and Montague's Wife in this scene. In Brooke's narrative the Capulets ask for severe punishment of Romeus, and the Montagues plead for mercy (1040–3).

142 **discover** reveal

143 **unlucky . . . fatal brawl** *Unlucky* still means not only 'characterized by misfortune' but 'ill-omened' or 'inauspicious'; *fatal* signifies both 'deadly' and 'fateful' (cf. Prologue 5 and n.). The line forges a conspicuous link between the *brawl* and destiny.

manage conduct (*OED sb.* 5a)

146 **cousin** kinsman (see l. 113 n.)

146–7 **child . . . spilled** A rhyme according to Elizabethan pronunciation (Wilson–Duthie).

O Prince, O cousin, husband, O, the blood is spilled
Of my dear kinsman! Prince, as thou art true,
For blood of ours shed blood of Montague.
O cousin, cousin!

PRINCE

Benvolio, who began this bloody fray?

BENVOLIO

Tybalt, here slain, whom Romeo's hand did slay—
Romeo, that spoke him fair, bid him bethink
How nice the quarrel was, and urged withal
Your high displeasure. All this, utterèd
With gentle breath, calm look, knees humbly bowed,
Could not take truce with the unruly spleen
Of Tybalt, deaf to peace, but that he tilts
With piercing steel at bold Mercutio's breast,
Who, all as hot, turns deadly point to point,
And, with a martial scorn, with one hand beats
Cold death aside, and with the other sends
It back to Tybalt, whose dexterity
Retorts it. Romeo he cries aloud,

147 cousin,] Q2; *not in* CAPELL 151 bloody] Q2; *not in* Q1, F 154–75 and . . . die] Q2; Q1 *has a different version of these lines.*

147 **cousin** Beginning with Capell many editors have omitted *cousin*, judging it unmetrical and redundant. Some blame the compositor for catching a word from the previous line or not deleting a first thought. Yet Q2 provides the distraught Capulet's Wife with suitably jarring verse: this speech is redundant throughout, concluding with a short line which repeats the word *cousin*. It might also be argued that the presence of Tybalt's body and the insistent references to kinship by Capulet's Wife together form an emblem of the play's many losses.

151 **bloody fray** Jowett, influenced by Q1 and F, deletes *bloody*; he suggests that Shakespeare might have cut the word unclearly in the foul papers or later to avoid repetition of 'blood' from the preceding speech. Repetition, however, characterizes these speeches of discovery.

152–75 **Tybalt, here slain . . . let Benvolio die** In addition to its breathless effect, the speech is notable for its straightforward, often monosyllabic diction; its rhetorical devices, especially repetition; and its inconsistencies in relation to what the audience has just seen (e.g. Benvolio omits Mercutio's provoking of Tybalt and elaborates Romeo's gestures of peaceful intervention).

154 **nice** senseless or trivial (*OED a.* 1b, 10b)

154–75 **and . . . die** Jowett notes that Q1's account is similar in content but generally different in wording.

155 **high** Referring not only to the degree and gravity of the Prince's reaction but also to his rank.

157 **take truce** make peace (*OED sb.* 1a)
spleen hot temper (*OED sb.* 5a, first illustration)

161 **martial** befitting a warrior (*OED a.* 5, first illustration)

161–2 **with one hand . . . with the other** Benvolio describes a fencing-match with sword and dagger: each duellist parries with a dagger held in his left hand and thrusts with a sword in his right.

164 **Retorts it** turns it back (*OED v.*[1] 5a)

'Hold, friends, friends, part!', and swifter than his tongue,
His agile arm beats down their fatal points,
And 'twixt them rushes; underneath whose arm
An envious thrust from Tybalt hit the life
Of stout Mercutio; and then Tybalt fled,
But by and by comes back to Romeo,
Who had but newly entertained revenge,
And to't they go like lightning; for, ere I
Could draw to part them, was stout Tybalt slain,
And, as he fell, did Romeo turn and fly.
This is the truth, or let Benvolio die.

CAPULET'S WIFE

He is a kinsman to the Montague;
Affection makes him false, he speaks not true.
Some twenty of them fought in this black strife,
And all those twenty could but kill one life.
I beg for justice, which thou, Prince, must give:
Romeo slew Tybalt; Romeo must not live.

PRINCE

Romeo slew him, he slew Mercutio.
Who now the price of his dear blood doth owe?

166 agile] Q1; aged Q2; agent JOWETT (*conj.* McKerrow MS) 176 kinsman] Q3; kisman Q2 (*a tilde error*)

165 **'Hold . . . part!'** Cf. Brooke 999: 'Part friends (said he) part friends, help friends to part the fray'.

166 **agile** Q2's 'aged' is a probable misreading; Q1 and most editors have *agile*, which matches Tybalt's 'dexterity' in l. 163. Jowett reads 'agent' (conj. McKerrow) primarily on linguistic grounds: *agile* occurs nowhere else in Shakespeare; 'agent' refers to doing something rather than talking, or works as a Latinism meaning 'effective'; and 'agent' emphasizes the origin of both words and acts in thought, a process known for its speed. As Jowett points out, *OED* records 'agent' as an adjective from 1620 on, but illustrates the substantive as 'the adj. used *absol.*' from 1579.

168 **envious** malicious (*OED a.* 2)

170 **by and by** immediately (*OED adv. phr.* 3)

172 **like lightning** This phrase condenses Brooke's epic simile, 1031–3. Like 2.1.162–3, it echoes 'As swift as lightning' (Dent L279).

177 **Affection** (a) partiality (*OED sb.* 8), (b) goodwill

false . . . not true Johnson concludes: 'The charge of falsehood on Benvolio, though produced at hazard, is very just'. While Benvolio tells no lies, he does skew the truth (see ll. 152–75 n.; cf. his description of the fight at 1.1.102–11).

183 **Who . . . owe** Although Q2 ends with a full stop, the next speech indicates that the Prince asks a question: who will repay Mercutio's death? For the wordplay on *dear*, cf. 1.4.160 and n.

⌈MONTAGUE⌉
Not Romeo, Prince, he was Mercutio's friend;
His fault concludes but what the law should end,
The life of Tybalt.

PRINCE And for that offence
Immediately we do exile him hence.
I have an interest in your hearts' proceeding;
My blood for your rude brawls doth lie a-bleeding.
But I'll amerce you with so strong a fine,
That you shall all repent the loss of mine.
I will be deaf to pleading and excuses;
Nor tears nor prayers shall purchase out abuses.
Therefore use none. Let Romeo hence in haste,
Else, when he is found, that hour is his last.
Bear hence this body, and attend our will;
Mercy but murders, pardoning those that kill.

Exeunt

184 ⌈MONTAGUE⌉] Q4; *Capu<let>*. Q2; *La<dy>*. *Mont<ague>*. THEOBALD 188 hearts'] Q2; hates Q1 192 I] Q1; It Q2 197.1 *Exeunt*] F, Q1 (*Exeunt omnes.*); *Exit*. Q2

184 ⌈**MONTAGUE**⌉ Q2 gives this speech to Capulet, an obvious mistake.

185–6 **His fault . . . offence** The first speaker uses *should* to express contingent futurity, meaning 'would have ended', but the Prince interprets 'ought to' (see Abbott 322, 323). Consequently these lines represent two different attitudes towards Romeo's *fault*, i.e. anticipating the law.

187 **exile** (accent on second syllable)

188 **interest** has legal and financial nuances.
hearts' Many editors substitute Q1 'hates' (Jowett argues sensibly for this). In manuscript the two words are easily mistakable for each other, and at the equivalent of 3.2.73 Q1 clearly makes the same error. Since the line is figurative in either case, *hearts'* seems intelligible if less apparent. Williams supports Q2 with reference to 1.1.80–1.

189 **My blood** i.e. Mercutio, the Prince's kinsman
lie a-bleeding The description makes a proverb literal ('All lies and bleeds (lies a bleeding)', Dent A159) and plays on it rhetorically through polyptoton (*blood/bleeding*).

190 **amerce** punish (*OED v.* 2c, first example of the phrase *amerce with*)

192 **I** Virtually all editors adopt Q1 *I*, less strained than Q2 'It'. As McKerrow notes, however, 'It' might be understood as a reference to 'My blood'. On that assumption Mommsen made a connection with Genesis 4: 10, 'the voice of thy brother's blood crieth unto me from the ground' (see Furness).

193 **purchase out abuses** redeem injuries (*OED sb.* 5); *purchase out*, equivalent to 'buy out', appears nowhere else in Shakespeare. Like 'interest' in l. 188, it has legal (*v.* 4b) as well as financial associations.

194 **use** The Prince may mean not only 'employ' but 'speak' (*OED v.* 16b), effectively silencing the two families.

196 **attend** pay heed to (*OED v.* 2a)

197 **Mercy . . . kill** Hosley glosses with a passage from Machiavelli: '[a prince] must not mind incurring the charge of cruelty for the purpose of keeping his subjects united and faithful; for, with a very few examples, he will be more merciful than those who, from excess of tenderness, allow disorders to arise, from whence

3.2 *Enter Juliet alone*

JULIET

Gallop apace, you fiery-footed steeds,
Towards Phoebus' lodging. Such a wagoner
As Phaëton would whip you to the west,
And bring in cloudy night immediately.
Spread thy close curtain, love-performing night,
That runaways' eyes may wink, and Romeo

3.2.1 JULIET] Q1, F; *not in* Q2 6 runaways'] Q2 (runnawayes); th' Run-away's THEOBALD (*conj.* Warburton); runnaway KITTREDGE (*conj.* Blackstone, *in* Steevens–Reed)

spring bloodshed and rapine' (*The Prince*, trans. Luigi Ricci (New York, 1940), p. 60).

3.2 This scene originates in a highly rhetorical episode in Brooke where Juliet debates her situation first with herself and then with her nurse. The play turns these events into a sequence of discovery which begins, because of its timing, with irony absent from the sources. Although 3.2 seems indispensable, some late nineteenth-century and early twentieth-century performances cut it entirely.

1–31 **Gallop apace . . . wear them** A variation on the epithalamium, a song or poem celebrating a wedding. G. McCown analyses the speech in relation to classical and Renaissance traditions ('"Runnawayes Eyes" and Juliet's Epithalamium', *SQ* 28 (1976), 150–70). As N. Brooke notices, Juliet's key images, from steeds and wagoner to whip and night, have all appeared in Mercutio's Queen Mab speech, 1.4.51–93 (pp. 84–5).

1–4 **Gallop apace . . . immediately** Scholarship has traced these lines to particular sources: Brooke 821–6 and 919–20, where the narrator describes the lovers' responses to the passage of time; Marlowe's *Edward II* 4.3.43–5, beginning 'Gallop apace bright Phoebus through the sky' (Evans also compares Lyly's *Woman in the Moon* 4.1.248–9); and Ovid's story of Phaëton in Golding's translation of the *Metamorphoses* 2.

1 **fiery-footed steeds** Juliet addresses the horses that draw the chariot of the sun-god, Phoebus, from east to west (cf. 2.2.4 and n., and 'fiery-footed horse' in Golding's translation of Ovid's *Metamorphoses* 2.491).

2 **lodging** Specifically, a place for resting at night (*OED vbl. sb.* 3a).

wagoner charioteer (*OED*, *wagoner*[1] 2; cf. 1.4.62). In his translation of *Metamorphoses*, Golding calls Phaëton 'the wagoner' of Phoebus's chariot (2.394).

3–4 **Phaëton . . . immediately** This description of Phaëton may originate in Golding's translation of *Metamorphoses* 2.169–70. A Renaissance type for disaster, Phaëton, son of Phoebus and the mortal Clymene, lost control of the horses while driving his father's chariot. When the fiery chariot began to ignite the earth, Jove destroyed him with lightning 'Which struck his body from the life and threw it over wheel | And so with fire he quenched fire' (2.395–6).

5 **close curtain** *Close* attributes to night's *curtain* both secrecy and darkness (*OED a.* 5), fittingly because a *curtain* encloses beds, regulates light, and hides or covers in a figurative sense.

love-performing characterizes *night* as a time for love.

6 **runaways'** A famous crux because scholars cannot agree about its meaning in the context of l. 6. They have proposed various emendations and numerous interpretations (see, e.g., Furness's Appendix, pp. 367–95). Jowett dismisses the emendations, citing correspondences with *Merchant* 2.6.47 and 36 in defence of Q2. In most recent editions '*runnawayes*' appears as a plural or singular possessive. According to editors and critics its referents vary from the mythical and abstract (Phoebus, Phaëton, 'fiery-footed steeds', Cupid, night) to the human and immediate (Juliet, Romeo, vagabonds). J. O. Holmer makes a strong case on philological grounds for 'fugitives' eyes'

Leap to these arms, untalked of and unseen.
Lovers can see to do their amorous rites
By their own beauties; or, if love be blind,
It best agrees with night. Come, civil night,
Thou sober-suited matron all in black,
And learn me how to lose a winning match,
Played for a pair of stainless maidenhoods.
Hood my unmanned blood, bating in my cheeks,
With thy black mantle, till strange love grow bold,
Think true love acted simple modesty.

9 By] Q4; And by Q2   15 grow] Q2; grown ROWE

(a conjecture offered by Johnson and Delius), her explanation giving the line ironic resonance ('"Runnawayes Eyes": A Fugitive Meaning', *SQ* 33 (1982), 97–9).

6 **wink** (a) close (in sleep) (*OED v.*[1] 1b), (b) pretend not to notice anything

7 **Leap** rush (*OED v.* 1a). Gibbons compares Marlowe's *Tragedy of Dido* 5.1.179–80: 'if thou wilt stay, | Leap in mine arms, mine arms are open wide'.

8–9 **Lovers can see . . . beauties** Several editors have noticed parallels between these lines and Marlowe's *Hero and Leander*, which probably circulated before its publication in 1598: 1.191, '(dark night is *Cupid's* day)'; 2.240–2, beginning 'Rich jewels in the dark are soonest spied'; 2.318–22, beginning 'And from her countenance behold ye might | A kind of twilight break'; and 2.64, 'Some amorous rites or other were neglected'.

9 **By** Q2's 'And by', slightly jarring in the rhythmic and conceptual flow of this verse, may preserve a remnant of the line from an earlier draft. In defence of Q2, however, Sisson maintains that 'And' gives emphasis to a parenthesis between 'Lovers can see' and 'or if love be blind'.

if love be blind Proverbial (Dent L506; cf. 2.1.33).

10 **civil** probably means 'sober in apparel or demeanour' (in view of the next line), although *OED a.* 10 dates first illustration 1606.

11 **sober-suited** (a) modestly dressed, (b) dressed to befit sober-mindedness. Onions defines *suited* as 'clothed, apparelled'; *OED ppl. a.* 2 gives first illustration from Milton's *Il Penseroso* (1632).

12 **learn** teach (not a vulgar usage; cf. 1.4.91)

lose a winning match Paradoxically Juliet gains a victory by surrendering herself (*OED ppl. a.* 2, first illustration).

13 **stainless maidenhoods** Juliet includes Romeo in her assertion of virginity, since *maidenhoods* refers to both sexes (see the *OED* definition and *maiden, sb.* 2b). In its figurative sense, *stainless* appears for the first time here (*a.* 1b).

14 **Hood . . . cheeks** *Hood* refers to blindfolding a hawk not in action pursuing game (Onions); *unmanned* describes a bird untrained or unaccustomed to men; *bating* means 'fluttering impatiently to escape a perch or hand' (*OED*, *unmanned, ppl. a.*[1] 3 and *bate, v.*[1] 2b both cite this line as their first illustrations). Asking the 'sober-suited matron' to hide her blushes (cf. 2.1.128–9), Juliet not only blends metaphors of night and falconry but plays on the words *unmanned* (= without a man) and *bating* (sounds like 'beating'). The concentrated verbal imagery, typical of this speech, conveys restlessness as well as desire.

15 **strange** (a) reserved, (b) inexperienced (cf. 2.1.144 and n.)

grow Some editors prefer Rowe's 'grown'; they assume that misreading has produced an awkward transition between ll. 15 and 16. But, as even Keightley admits, there may be ellipsis of the conjunction 'And' (the rhetorical figure asyndeton), as the excited Juliet speaks '*allo staccato*'.

Come night, come Romeo, come thou day in night;
For thou wilt lie upon the wings of night
Whiter than new snow upon a raven's back.
Come gentle night, come loving black-browed night,
Give me my Romeo; and when I shall die,
Take him and cut him out in little stars,
And he will make the face of heaven so fine,
That all the world will be in love with night,
And pay no worship to the garish sun.
O, I have bought the mansion of a love,
But not possessed it; and though I am sold,
Not yet enjoyed. So tedious is this day
As is the night before some festival
To an impatient child that hath new robes

19 new] Q2; *not in* Q4 upon] Q2; on F2 21 I] Q2; hee Q4

17 **Come . . . in night** Juliet may be playing on *night*/knight in the double imperative with its rhetorical amplification.

18 **wings of night** The metaphor retains traces of earlier lines with images of haste, falconry, and darkness.

19 **Whiter . . . back** Editors uncomfortable with the metre follow either Q4 or F2, which reduce the number of beats (see Collation). Among the former, Wilson–Duthie consider the phrase *new snow* nonsense ('One cannot have *old* snow on a raven's back!') and a false start; but as Gibbons and Evans indicate, *new* emphasizes the freshness of the snow and the starkness of the contrast. Among the latter, Jowett conjectures that *upon* may result from dittography (from l. 18) or an earlier version of the line without *new*. Those who preserve Q2 read the substitution in the first foot as a dactyl rather than a trochee. In any case, the line has proverbial echoes (Dent compares B435, S591, R32.2).

20 **Come . . . black-browed night** Evans compares Lyly's *Woman in the Moon* 4.1.254: 'Come night, come gentle night, for thee I stay'. On *black-browed night* see *Dream* 3.2.388 and *K. John* 5.6.18.

21 **I** Although many recent editors follow Q2, most earlier ones adopt Q4 'hee'. Those who explain their decisions base their arguments on interpretations of ll. 21–5, since evidence related to metre, philology, or printing is beside the point. Consequently this passage has inspired an array of readings, from Juliet's fantasy of shared sexual climax to her premonition of shared death.

21 **die** The common Elizabethan pun on death and orgasm.

22–5 **cut him out . . . sun** Gibbons notes the parallel between Romeo's celestial transformation and Julius Caesar's, the last of Ovid's *Metamorphoses*. Taking his spirit from the dead Caesar, Venus sets it among the stars where it becomes a heavenly body excelling all others in heat and brightness (Golding's translation, 15. 948–59). Gibbons also compares Romeo at 2.1.63–5.

25 **garish** *OED a.*[1] 2b, first instance of *garish* describing light.

26 **mansion** Whether a modest dwelling-place or a manor-house (*OED sb.* 3a, b), *mansion* may connect the dual metaphor of ll. 26–8 with the conceit of Romeo as stars through its astrological definition: one of the twenty-eight divisions of the ecliptic which the moon occupies on successive days (5). Partridge makes explicit the sexual implications in *mansion of a love*, i.e. human body which is a source of sexual pleasure ('possessed', and 'enjoyed' as Juliet's will be, according to the next two lines).

30–1 **impatient . . . wear them** Gibbons notes a correspondence with Lyly's

And may not wear them. O, here comes my Nurse—
Enter the Nurse with cords
And she brings news, and every tongue that speaks
But Romeo's name speaks heavenly eloquence.
Now, Nurse, what news? What hast thou there,
The cords that Romeo bid thee fetch?

NURSE
Ay, ay, the cords.

JULIET
Ay me, what news? Why dost thou wring thy hands?

NURSE
Ah weraday, he's dead, he's dead, he's dead!
We are undone, lady, we are undone.
Alack the day, he's gone, he's killed, he's dead!

JULIET
Can heaven be so envious?

NURSE
Romeo can
Though heaven cannot. O Romeo, Romeo,
Whoever would have thought it Romeo?

JULIET
What devil art thou that dost torment me thus?
This torture should be roared in dismal hell.

31.1 *Enter . . . cords*] Q2; *Enter Nurse wringing her hands, with the ladder of cordes in her lap.* Q1
34–5 there, | The] Q2; ~, the Q1; ~? the HANMER 42 it‸] Q2; ~? CAPELL

Euphues and his England (1580) which applies also to the 'mansion' conceit: 'To love women and never enjoy them, is as much as . . . to be delighted with fair apparel, and never wear it' (2.158).

31.1 ***Enter . . . cords*** i.e. she brings the rope ladder. In Q1 the equivalent direction follows a speech of only four lines (Juliet does not say 'here comes my Nurse') and suggests that the front portion of the Nurse's skirt has been adjusted to carry the rope ladder (see Collation and *OED*, *lap*, *sb.*^{1}, 4b). Q1 may record a performance in which the Nurse was discovered seated on the rear stage (Hosley), or it may conflate her entrance with bits of dialogue elsewhere in the text (Gibbons). However the earliest productions handled this entrance, prompt books make no fuss about it and add little to directions in the editions they follow.

34 **What . . . there,** Q2 punctuation, reproduced here, has led editors to interpret *What* as either an interjection (*What, hast thou there*) or an interrogative (*What hast thou there?*).

34–5 **there, | The cords** Some editors adopt Hanmer's lineation, more similar to Q1 than to Q2 (see Collation).

37 **weraday** An exclamation of sorrow which *OED* lists as a dialectal form of 'welladay'. The Nurse will repeat it at 4.4.41, when Juliet appears dead.

40 **envious** malicious (*OED a.* 2)

42 **it Romeo?** Most editors replace Q2's punctuation with Capell's (see Collation). Dent identifies a proverbial correspondence which fits either reading: 'Who would have thought it?' (W318.2).

43 **devil** (one syllable)

44 **dismal** Associated with woeful sounds and the devil, bad luck and malevolence (*OED sb.*^{2} 1a).

Hath Romeo slain himself? Say thou but 'Ay',
And that bare vowel 'I' shall poison more
Than the death-darting eye of cockatrice.
I am not I if there be such an 'I',
Or those eyes shut that makes thee answer 'Ay'.
If he be slain say 'Ay', or if not, 'No'.
Brief sounds determine of my weal or woe.

NURSE

I saw the wound, I saw it with mine eyes—
God save the mark!—here on his manly breast.
A piteous corse, a bloody piteous corse,
Pale, pale as ashes, all bedaubed in blood,
All in gore blood—I sounded at the sight.

JULIET

O break, my heart, poor bankrupt, break at once!
To prison, eyes, ne'er look on liberty.
Vile earth, to earth resign, end motion here,
And thou and Romeo press one heavy bier.

45–6 'Ay' . . . 'I'| Q2 (I . . . I)   47 darting| Q3; arting Q2   49 shut| Q2 (shot)   51 Brief‸ sounds‸| F4; ~, ~, Q2   of my| F; my Q2   60 one heavy bier| Q2 (on heauie beare)

45–50 **'Ay' . . . 'Ay'** Mahood describes three effects produced by this frenzied series of puns: the sound of high-pitched keening which counterpoints the Nurse's moans 'O Romeo, Romeo'; the sustaining of eye imagery from the epithalamium; and the manifestation of profound psychological disturbance (p. 70). Rhetorical figures of repetition are part of the wordplay and contribute to these effects.

46 **'I'** The Elizabethan spelling of 'ay'.

47 **cockatrice** Fabled serpent, identified with the basilisk and supposedly hatched from a cock's egg, proverbial for killing by its mere glance (Dent C496.2).

48–50 **I am . . . 'No'** Gibbons compares *Richard II* 4.1.191: 'Ay, no; no, ay; for I must nothing be'.

49 **shut** Q2 has '*shot*', a dialectal form of *shut* (*OED v.*) or an easily made compositor's error. Although Hoppe retains '*shot*' and Hankins defends it, Juliet clearly refers to Romeo's eyes closed in death. Capell first printed *shut*, eliminating any confusion.

51 **of my** F regularizes the metre. McKerrow and J. C. Maxwell (cited by Evans) propose 'me my'; Collier's manuscript (cited by Furness) suggests 'or my'; and Jowett's note offers 'determining' as an alternative.

52 **I . . . eyes** Proverbial (Dent E266.1). Juliet's wordplay peters out as the Nurse echoes it.

53 **God . . . mark!** Proverbial (Dent G179.1); an exclamation to apologize for mentioning something offensive (as *OED* specifies, *mark*, *sb.*[1] 18, something 'horrible, disgusting, indecent or profane'). Nevertheless the Nurse describes the scene in graphic detail. She seems to illustrate the wound by pointing to her own breast.

55 **Pale . . . ashes** Proverbial (Dent A339).

56 **in gore blood** covered with blood (*OED* 2a)
sounded swooned (*OED v.*[4])

57–8 **O break . . . liberty** Juliet quibbles on *break* (= become insolvent) and *bankrupt* ('rupt' = 'broken'; see *OED sb.* Forms), puns which lead to the *prison* metaphor.

57 **at once** J. C. Maxwell explains that this phrase means not just 'immediately' but 'once for all' ('"At once" in Shakespeare', *MLR* 49 (1954), 464–6).

59 **Vile earth . . . resign** Gibbons compares Ecclesiastes 12:7, 'And dust return to the

NURSE

O Tybalt, Tybalt, the best friend I had!
O courteous Tybalt, honest gentleman,
That ever I should live to see thee dead!

JULIET

What storm is this that blows so contrary?
Is Romeo slaughtered, and is Tybalt dead,
My dearest cousin and my dearer lord?
Then dreadful trumpet sound the general doom,
For who is living if those two are gone?

NURSE

Tybalt is gone and Romeo banishèd;
Romeo that killed him, he is banishèd.

JULIET

O God, did Romeo's hand shed Tybalt's blood?

[NURSE]

It did, it did, alas the day, it did.

[JULIET]

O serpent heart, hid with a flow'ring face!
Did ever dragon keep so fair a cave?

72–4 [NURSE] It . . . [JULIET] O . . . Did] *speech-prefixes as* Q1; It . . . *Nur<se>*. O . . . *Iu<liet>*. Did Q2

earth as it was'; Shaheen adds Genesis 3: 19, 'thou art dust, and to dust shalt thou return'. According to Dent, the phrase is proverbial (E30; cf. 2.2.9).

59 **motion** evokes obsolete definitions referring to intense emotion (*OED sb.* 4, 9a).

62 **honest** honourable (*OED a.* 1a)

67 **dreadful trumpet . . . doom** Shaheen quotes 1 Corinthians 15: 52, 'At the last trumpet: for the trumpet shall blow', and compares Matthew 24: 31, 'A great sound of a trumpet', as well as Revelation 8–11, the sounding of the seven trumpets at the end of the world.

72, 73 [NURSE], [JULIET] Correcting Q2, all editors take these speech-headings from Q1. Williams explains that the prefixes for the Nurse and Juliet appear one line low in Q2, 'so that "It did . . . " is continued to Juliet, and the questioner thus answers herself'.

73–85 **O serpent heart . . . palace** Coleridge thought these lines expressed 'the mind's audible struggles with itself' (p. 138; cf. Romeo's catalogue of oxymora at 1.1.172–8 and see 172 n.).

73 **serpent heart . . . flow'ring face** Proverbial (Dent S585, F3). Gibbons and other editors cite parallels with *Macbeth* 1.5.64–5, and Wilson–Duthie compare Genesis 3: 1–6, these passages suggesting an allusion to Satan. Corresponding lines in *2 Henry VI* (*Contention*) 3.1.228–30 provide an especially suitable gloss: 'the snake rolled in a flow'ring bank | With shining chequered slough doth sting a child | That for the beauty thinks it excellent'.

flow'ring face i.e. face serving as a floral cover, a metaphor clearly applying to Romeo's youth and beauty (*OED ppl. a.* 2; see also *v.* 4, 3)

74 **dragon . . . cave** The *dragon*, closely linked with the snake in legend and Juliet's mind, supposedly guarded treasure in a cave (see Cirlot).

Beautiful tyrant, fiend angelical,
Dove-feathered raven, wolvish-ravening lamb,
Despisèd substance of divinest show,
Just opposite to what thou justly seem'st,
A damnèd saint, an honourable villain.
O nature, what hadst thou to do in hell
When thou didst bower the spirit of a fiend
In mortal paradise of such sweet flesh?
Was ever book containing such vile matter
So fairly bound? O, that deceit should dwell
In such a gorgeous palace!

NURSE

There's no trust, no faith, no honesty in men;
All perjured, all forsworn, all naught, all dissemblers.

76 Dove-feathered] THEOBALD; Rauenous douefeatherd Q2 79 damnèd] Q4; dimme Q2

75 **tyrant** Juliet may mean not only 'usurper' but 'ruffian' (Gibbons's annotation from *OED sb.* 4b). With its associations of roughness, the latter definition sharpens the oxymoron.
fiend angelical Spencer compares 2 Corinthians 11: 14, 'Satan himself is transformed into an angel of light'.

76 **Dove-feathered raven** Most editors adopt Theobald's emendation and agree that Q2 preserves a rejected first version. At the same time, Wilson–Duthie admit the possibility of a compositor's slip; and McKerrow speculates that the line may have read 'Raven dove-feathered, wolvish-ravening lamb' before the two first words were carelessly transposed. Dent hears proverbial echoes in the emended phrase (e.g. D573.2, R32.2).
wolvish-ravening lamb Shaheen and some editors cite Matthew 7: 15, 'Beware of false prophets, which come to you in sheep's clothing, but inwardly they are ravening wolves'; Dent compares 'A wolf in lamb's (sheep's) skin' (W614).

77 **Despisèd substance . . . divinest show** This antithesis verges on impiety because *substance* means not only 'reality' but also 'essence', especially in a theological sense (*OED* 1), and *divinest* plays on 'sacred' as well as weaker definitions of the adjective. Dent compares 'More show than substance' (S408).

78 **Just . . . justly** A quibble on the two adverbs, since *justly* = (a) exactly, (b) honourably (*OED adv.* 5a, 1).

79 **damnèd** Q2's 'dimme' may have resulted from misreading 'damnd', in particular the minims and final *d*; but mistaking *a* for *i*, as Evans notes, is more difficult to explain graphically.

81–2 **thou didst bower . . . flesh** Shaheen cites 2 Corinthians 11: 14, 'Satan himself is transformed into an angel of light', although these lines clearly owe their imagery to Genesis 2 and 3 (cf. l. 73 and n.).

81 **bower** enclose as in a bower (*OED v.* 1, first illustration)

83–4 **book . . . bound** Juliet echoes her mother's conceit of the book at 1.3.83–94.

86–7 **There's . . . dissemblers** Editors and others have frequently tried to improve the metre of these lines. Most have produced three verses from two: new lines follow *trust* and *perjured* (Capell) or, with a rearrangement of words, follow *trust* and *naught* (Daniel (conj. Fleay), Williams). Two editors have simply adjusted words: Hosley deletes *all naught*; Jowett changes *all dissemblers* to 'dissemblers all' (conj. Gary Taylor). Yet the equivalent of l. 86 in Q1 is also irregular. More important, the Nurse's medium has often hovered between verse and prose; and her verse here, prosaic and consistently inconsistent, contrasts

Ah, where's my man? Give me some aqua-vitae.
These griefs, these woes, these sorrows make me old.
Shame come to Romeo!

JULIET
Blistered be thy tongue
For such a wish! He was not born to shame.
Upon his brow shame is ashamed to sit;
For 'tis a throne where honour may be crowned
Sole monarch of the universal earth.
O, what a beast was I to chide at him!

NURSE
Will you speak well of him that killed your cousin?

JULIET
Shall I speak ill of him that is my husband?
Ah, poor my lord, what tongue shall smooth thy name
When I, thy three-hours wife, have mangled it?
But wherefore, villain, didst thou kill my cousin?
That villain cousin would have killed my husband.
Back, foolish tears, back to your native spring;
Your tributary drops belong to woe,
Which you, mistaking, offer up to joy.
My husband lives, that Tybalt would have slain,
And Tybalt's dead, that would have slain my husband.
All this is comfort. Wherefore weep I then?
Some word there was, worser than Tybalt's death,

effectively with Juliet's. Wilson–Duthie note that she applies the proverb 'There is no faith (trust, honesty) in man' (Dent F34), which she elaborates in this earliest known example, only to the male sex.

86 **trust** i.e. trustworthiness (*OED sb.* 4)
honesty (a) truthfulness, (b) honourable character (*OED* 3a)

87 **perjured** Not only guilty of perjury but characterized by it (*OED ppl. a.* 2).
naught (a) good for nothing, (b) wicked (*OED a.* 2a)

88 **aqua-vitae** strong spirits

90–1 **Blistered . . . wish** Proverbial (Dent R84, '(Report has) a blister on her tongue'). Gibbons compares Brooke 1145–6.

91 **to shame** Either (a) to be shamed, or (b) to feel shame.

94 **universal** whole. *OED a.* 8a describes this usage as common in the sixteenth century (cf. 2.3.194 and n.).

95 **chide at** rebuke (*OED v.* 2a calls this construction obsolete)

98 **poor my lord** i.e. my poor lord (transposed possessive adjective, Abbott 13; cf. 3.5.198, 5.3.124)
smooth *OED v.* 1a cites as first example of the figurative usage. In l. 99 *mangled*, forming another antithesis, applies in particular to the mutilation of spoken or written words. Brooke 1145–54 corresponds with this speech, especially the first two verses: 'Ah cruel murdering tongue, murd'rer of others' fame, | How durst thou once attempt to touch the honour of his name?'

100, 101 **villain** Juliet probably tempers *villain* in the negative sense with its connotation of endearment.

103 **tributary** (a) of tribute, (b) of a stream

104 **joy** i.e. Romeo's survival

108 **worser** See 2.2.29 and n.

That murdered me. I would forget it fain,
But O, it presses to my memory,
Like damnèd guilty deeds to sinners' minds:
'Tybalt is dead and Romeo banishèd'.
That 'banishèd', that one word 'banishèd',
Hath slain ten thousand Tybalts. Tybalt's death
Was woe enough, if it had ended there;
Or, if sour woe delights in fellowship,
And needly will be ranked with other griefs,
Why followed not, when she said 'Tybalt's dead',
'Thy father' or 'thy mother', nay, or both,
Which modern lamentation might have moved?
But with a rearward following Tybalt's death,
'Romeo is banishèd'—to speak that word
Is father, mother, Tybalt, Romeo, Juliet,
All slain, all dead. 'Romeo is banishèd'—
There is no end, no limit, measure, bound,
In that word's death; no words can that woe sound.
Where is my father and my mother, Nurse?

NURSE

Weeping and wailing over Tybalt's corse.
Will you go to them? I will bring you thither.

JULIET

Wash they his wounds with tears? Mine shall be spent,
When theirs are dry, for Romeo's banishment.
Take up those cords. Poor ropes, you are beguiled,

109–11 **I . . . minds** Shaheen cites Psalm 51: 3, Morning and Evening Prayer, 'I do know mine own wickedness, and my sin is alway against me', as well as Psalm 51: 3 and the General Confession, Communion Service.

116 **sour woe . . . fellowship** Proverbial (Dent compares M1012, 'Misfortune (Evil) never (seldom) comes alone').

117 **needly** of necessity (*OED adv.*[2])
ranked *OED v.*[1] 3a, first instance of *rank* meaning 'give a certain position or station'.

120 **modern lamentation** *Modern* = ordinary (*OED a.* 4); *lamentation* is the object of *moved*.

121 **rearward** rear-guard (*OED sb.*[1] 1); Collier 1858 first noticed the quibble 'rear-word' (see Furness). With this line Juliet completes her military conceit linking the Nurse's report of disasters to troops appearing in successive ranks (cf. Sonnet 90.5–6).

126 **that word's death** Editors understand this phrase as a construction with either (a) the contraction 'word is', or (b) the objective genitive 'word's', meaning 'the death inherent in that word' (cf. 3.3.20).
sound (a) express, (b) measure, as by plumbing the depth of water

127 **is** The inflection in *-s* preceding a plural subject is common in Shakespeare (Abbott 335).

130 **tears?** Some editors follow Q3 or F, turning a rhetorical question to the optative or imperative mode.

Both you and I, for Romeo is exiled.
He made you for a highway to my bed,
But I, a maid, die maiden-widowèd.
Come cords, come Nurse, I'll to my wedding-bed,
And death, not Romeo, take my maidenhead.

NURSE

Hie to your chamber. I'll find Romeo
To comfort you; I wot well where he is.
Hark ye, your Romeo will be here at night.
I'll to him; he is hid at Laurence' cell.

JULIET

O find him, give this ring to my true knight,
And bid him come to take his last farewell. *Exeunt*

3.3 *Enter Friar Laurence and Romeo*

FRIAR LAURENCE

Romeo, come forth, come forth, thou fearful man.
Affliction is enamoured of thy parts,
And thou art wedded to calamity.

ROMEO (*advancing*)

Father, what news? What is the Prince's doom?

143 *Exeunt*] Q1; *Exit*. Q2
3.3.0.1 *Enter . . . Romeo*] Q2 (*Enter Frier and* Romeo.); *Enter Frier*. Q1 4 (*advancing*)] This edition; *Enter Romeo*. Q1 (*after l.* 3)

137 **death . . . maidenhead** On this leitmotiv, death as Juliet's bridegroom, see 1.4.247–8 and n. The rhymes in this speech have created an abstract of the lovers' whole narrative.

139 **wot** know

142 **knight** Juliet not only associates Romeo with the chivalric code but echoes the military conceit in ll. 113–21.

3.3 This scene makes a straightforward episode ambivalent. Focusing on Romeo's anguish and Friar Laurence's power to dispel it, 3.3 gives the Friar an extensive speech of disputation. Brooke leaves no doubt that Friar Lawrence's rhetoric has the desired effect; Shakespeare sets an accomplished performance into a context which reduces its persuasiveness, thus calling rhetoric itself into question.

0.1 *Enter . . . Romeo* Most editors and many productions follow Q1: Friar Laurence enters alone, then Romeo appears after the third line. Whereas Q1 gives specific directions, Q2 (followed here) is more open. As McKerrow conjectures, Friar Laurence may enter from one door and call Romeo out from another or, more likely, enter leading him out. In the theatre, Romeo has also been discovered (lying on a cot, sitting on a bench or behind a desk, set under stairs), or he and Friar Laurence have entered at the same time from different directions. Q2 is general enough that it even permits the characters to enter as in Q1.

1 **fearful** (a) frightened (and perhaps wary, *OED a.* 5), (b) causing fear (cf. Prologue 9 and n.)

2 **parts** personal qualities (cf. 3.5.181)

4 **doom** judgement. Repetition may add a nuance of fatefulness.

What sorrow craves acquaintance at my hand
That I yet know not?

FRIAR LAURENCE Too familiar
Is my dear son with such sour company.
I bring thee tidings of the Prince's doom.

ROMEO
What less than doomsday is the Prince's doom?

FRIAR LAURENCE
A gentler judgement vanished from his lips:
Not body's death, but body's banishment.

ROMEO
Ha, banishment? Be merciful, say 'death';
For exile hath more terror in his look,
Much more than death. Do not say 'banishment'.

FRIAR LAURENCE
Here from Verona art thou banishèd.
Be patient, for the world is broad and wide.

ROMEO
There is no world without Verona walls,
But purgatory, torture, hell itself.
Hence banishèd is banished from the world,
And world's exile is death. Then 'banishèd'
Is death mistermed. Calling death 'banishèd',
Thou cutt'st my head off with a golden axe,
And smilest upon the stroke that murders me.

10 vanished] Q; even'd WARBURTON; 'banish'd' DOWDEN (*conj.*); vantaged WILSON (*conj.*)
15 Here] Q2; Hence Q1 19 banished] Q1; blanisht Q2

6 **familiar** (four syllables)

9 **doomsday** death (cf. the proverb 'Death's day is doomsday' (Dent D161), and 5.3.234)

10 **vanished from** escaped from (Onions). Q1 also prints *vanished*, often emended because it seems incongruous; but there is a comparable image of breath vanishing from the lips in *Lucrece*, 1040–2.

15 **Here** Most editors prefer Q1's 'Hence', noting its correspondence with 'Hence banished' in l. 19 of both quartos. Williams, acknowledging the conjecture of minim error in Wilson–Duthie, argues that the manuscript had 'Hēce' and the compositor, failing to notice the tilde, also mistook *c* for *r*. Whatever the reading, any verbal correspondence with l. 19 is inexact. This edition follows Q2 because it makes sense.

16 **world . . . wide** Proverbial (Dent W895, 'The world is (a) wide (parish, place)'). Gibbons compares with Brooke 1443–4 and *Richard II* (Q) 1.3.273–4.

20 **world's exile** i.e. exile from the world (objective genitive; cf. 3.2.126); *exile* is accented on its second syllable here and in l. 139. Evans compares Romeo's speeches from this point to l. 60 with Valentine's lament on being banished from Silvia in *Two Gentlemen* 3.1.170–87.

FRIAR LAURENCE

O deadly sin, O rude unthankfulness!
Thy fault our law calls death; but the kind Prince,
Taking thy part, hath rushed aside the law,
And turned that black word 'death' to 'banishment'.
This is dear mercy, and thou seest it not.

ROMEO

'Tis torture and not mercy. Heaven is here
Where Juliet lives; and every cat and dog
And little mouse, every unworthy thing,
Live here in heaven and may look on her,
But Romeo may not. More validity,
More honourable state, more courtship lives
In carrion-flies than Romeo. They may seize
On the white wonder of dear Juliet's hand,
And steal immortal blessing from her lips,
Who even in pure and vestal modesty
Still blush, as thinking their own kisses sin;
But Romeo may not, he is banishèd.

26 rushed] Q; push'd CAPELL (*conj.*); brush'd COLLIER MS; thrust WILSON–DUTHIE (*conj.*)
40–3 But . . . death?] GLOBE (*conj.* Steevens); This may flyes do, when I from this must flie, | And sayest thou yet, that exile is not death? | But *Romeo* may not, he is banished. | Flies may do this, but I from this must flie: | They are freemen, but I am banished. Q2

24 **deadly . . . unthankfulness** Quibbling on *deadly*, Friar Laurence seems to give his own version of 'Ingratitude comprehends (is the worst of) all faults (vices)' (Dent I66).

26 **rushed** forced (*OED v.*[2] 1b, only example of figurative usage). Like 'vanished', l. 10, *rushed* occurs also in Q1 and seems to many editors an odd choice. McKerrow conjectures influence from 'ruse', which describes a hunted animal's detour to escape from dogs (see *v.*[1] 2). If *aside* is taken as a preposition governing *the law* (i.e. 'by the side of the law'), he suggests, the expression may mean 'evaded the law'.

28 **dear** (a) unusual, (b) kind. *OED a.*[1] 7b singles out this line and questions whether either definition applies. Certainly *dear* must mean 'precious' in some sense (4a, b), strengthening the impression that Friar Laurence says everything more than once for emphasis in these passages (e.g. 'black word "death"' in l. 27 = deadly word death). Q1 reads 'meere mercie', i.e. absolute mercy (*a.*[2] 4).

30–2 **every cat . . . look on her** may echo 'A cat may look on a king' (C141), although Dent finds the parallel unconvincing.

32 **Live** 'Every' often took a plural verb (Abbott 12).

33 **validity** value. Responding to the report of the Prince's merciful justice, Romeo's language in ll. 33–4—*validity*, *state*, *courtship*—has legal and political connotations.

34 **courtship** dignity befitting a courtier (*OED* 2, first instance), with a quibble on 'wooing'

39 **their own kisses** i.e. the way they touch each other when closed

40–3 **But . . . death?** Q2 prints a different version, beginning with a variant of l. 41 (see Collation) and following it with l. 43. Although a few editors reproduce Q2, most argue for emending because of its duplication and illogic. As Williams shows in most detail, the majority favour two solutions: they omit either the variant or l. 41, transposing l. 43 to end the sequence. This edition, cutting the variant, adopts

Flies may do this, but I from this must fly;
They are free men, but I am banishèd.
And sayest thou yet that exile is not death?
Hadst thou no poison mixed, no sharp-ground knife,
No sudden mean of death, though ne'er so mean,
But 'banishèd' to kill me? 'Banishèd'?
O Friar, the damnèd use that word in hell;
Howling attends it. How hast thou the heart,
Being a divine, a ghostly confessor,
A sin-absolver, and my friend professed,
To mangle me with that word 'banishèd'?

FRIAR LAURENCE
Thou fond mad man, hear me a little speak.

ROMEO
O, thou wilt speak again of banishment.

FRIAR LAURENCE
I'll give thee armour to keep off that word,
Adversity's sweet milk, philosophy,
To comfort thee though thou art banishèd.

43 sayest | Q2; saist Q3   52 Thou | Q1; Then Q2

the Globe lineation on the basis of supporting arguments by Hosley ('The Corrupting Influence of the Bad Quarto on the Received Text of *Romeo and Juliet*', *SQ* 4 (1953), 29), Williams, and Jowett: it assumes that l. 41 revises Shakespeare's first thought, and that unclear copy failed to signal deletion of the first thought or placement of the revision (including l. 42) before l. 43. Q1 prints ll. 40–1, corroborating this decision; F preserves the first three lines of Q2 and their illogic.

41 **Flies . . . fly** Mahood compares Romeo's puns with Juliet's in 3.2. Again the wordplay reveals profound psychological distress (pp. 70–1; see 3.2.45–50 and n.).

43 **sayest** Some editors regularize the metre by substituting the Q3/F contraction 'saist', although the slight unevenness seems appropriate to this climactic rhetorical question. (By contrast, editors rarely emend 'smilest' in l. 23.)

45 **mean . . . mean** method . . . base

48 **attends** *OED v.* 10a cites the first example of this usage (= accompanies) as 1615.

49 **ghostly confessor** Juliet employed this phrase at 2.5.21 (see n.). In *confessor* the first syllable again receives the primary accent.

50 **absolver** Q2 has the unusual spelling 'obsoluer', repeated at 3.5.233 (cf. 'ottamie', 1.4.55 n.).
professed (a) self-acknowledged (and perhaps 'alleged'), (b) bound by vow to a religious order

51 **mangle** Used by Juliet in this sense at 3.2.99 (see 3.2.98 n. on *smooth*).

52 **Thou** Almost all editors, recognizing a common printing error, follow Q1; Williams points to 'Thou fond, mad woman', *Richard II* 5.2.95.
fond foolish (with a quibble on 'loving')

55 **Adversity's . . . philosophy** Friar Laurence epitomizes the truism 'He is wise that can be patient in adversity' (Dent A42.1), a thought which appears in Brooke 1393–4, and combines it with the proverbial 'As sweet as milk' (Dent M930.1). In Furness, a passage cited by Malone from Lyly's *Euphues* (1580) specifically recommends philosophy as a

ROMEO

Yet 'banishèd'? Hang up philosophy!
Unless philosophy can make a Juliet,
Displant a town, reverse a prince's doom,
It helps not, it prevails not, talk no more.

FRIAR LAURENCE

O, then I see that mad men have no ears.

ROMEO

How should they, when that wise men have no eyes?

FRIAR LAURENCE

Let me dispute with thee of thy estate.

ROMEO

Thou canst not speak of that thou dost not feel.
Wert thou as young as I, Juliet thy love,
An hour but married, Tybalt murderèd,
Doting like me, and like me banishèd,
Then mightst thou speak, then mightst thou tear thy
hair,
And fall upon the ground as I do now,
Taking the measure of an unmade grave.

Knock within

61 mad men] Q3, Q1 (madmen); mad man Q2 68 Then mightst . . . hair,] Q1; Then mightest . . . speake, | Then . . . hayre, Q2 70.1 *Knock within*] ROWE; *Enter Nurse, and knocke*. Q2; *Nurse knockes*. Q1

comfort for banishment (see 1.313–16). R. Soellner argues persuasively for a different source: Erasmus's model letter of consolation for exile in *De Conscribendis Epistolis*, a popular textbook for epistle-writing in Elizabethan grammar schools ('Shakespeare and the "Consolatio" ', *N&Q* 199 (1954), 108–9).

57 **Hang up** i.e. on the wall, like the armour used as a metaphor by Friar Laurence (l. 54) and becoming obsolete in the late sixteenth century (Wilson–Duthie).

59 **Displant** uproot (Onions). *OED* v. 2 defines 'to undo the settlement or establishment of', citing this as its first illustration.

60 **prevails** avails (*OED* v. 4a)

61–2 **mad men . . . eyes** If this exchange refers to 'Discreet women have neither eyes nor ears' (W683), as some editors think, it completely inverts the sense (see Dent). Evans compares l. 61 with Brooke 1317.

62 **when that** when (Abbott 287)

63 **dispute** debate (*OED* v. 1b)

64 **that** that which (Abbott 244)

68–70 **tear thy hair . . . grave** The actor's cues derive from Brooke 1291–4. In most productions Romeo spends at least thirty lines on the floor, a posture which nineteenth-century male actors considered effeminate and which put them off the part. During this period there were a number of female Romeos. (See Introduction, 'Performance History', pp. 80–1.)

70 **Taking . . . grave** Romeo enacts a morbid version of 'To measure one's length' (Dent MM12; cf. *Dream* 3.3.17).

70.1 ***Knock within*** Since Q2 repeats the direction '*Enter Nurse*' at l. 78, it seems that she remains off stage while she continues to *knock*. Most prompt books place heavy emphasis on the cues for knocking.

FRIAR LAURENCE
Arise, one knocks. Good Romeo, hide thyself.

ROMEO
Not I, unless the breath of heartsick groans
Mist-like enfold me from the search of eyes.
Knock within

FRIAR LAURENCE
Hark, how they knock!—Who's there?—Romeo, arise,
Thou wilt be taken.—Stay a while!—Stand up.
Still knock
Run to my study.—By and by!—God's will,
What simpleness is this?—I come, I come!
Knock
Who knocks so hard? Whence come you? What's your
will?
Enter the Nurse

NURSE
Let me come in, and you shall know my errand.
I come from Lady Juliet.

FRIAR LAURENCE Welcome, then.

NURSE
O holy Friar, O tell me, holy Friar,
Where's my lady's lord? Where's Romeo?

FRIAR LAURENCE
There on the ground, with his own tears made drunk.

73.1 *Knock within*] Q2 (*They knocke.*); *Knocke* F 75.1 *Still knock*] Q2 (*Slud knock.*); *Knocke.* F 82 Where's] Q2; Where is Q1 83 There . . . drunk.] Q1; There . . . ground, | With . . . drunke. Q2

72–3 **the breath . . . eyes** A version of the Petrarchan conceit applied to Romeo earlier by both his father and Friar Laurence (see 1.1.129–36, 2.2.73).

75 **taken** i.e. arrested

75.1 ***Still knock*** McKerrow and H. Jenkins (in Gibbons) independently conjectured this direction from Q2's '*Slud knock.*'; others have read '*Slud*' as a corruption of '*Loud*', an actor's name (such as 'Slye'), or ''Slid' (Jowett speculates that the oath may have been intended for Friar Laurence's next speech).

76 **By and by!** right away! (*OED advb. phr.* 3)

77 **simpleness** foolish behaviour (*OED* 3b)

78.1 ***Enter the Nurse*** See note to 70.1. McKerrow suggests that the Nurse becomes visible to the audience at this point while the Friar takes Romeo into his 'study' (i.e. the inner stage) and returns to welcome her. Q2 also permits the Nurse and Friar to converse as she enters. Although Q1 prints no direction for the Nurse's entrance, the dialogue shows that in this version she speaks off stage before entering. Most prompt books observe the same timing.

82 **Where's** Many editors regularize the metre by expanding Q2 *Wheres* to Q1 'Where is' (Wilson–Duthie propose that *Wheres* anticipates *wheres* later in the line); but unpredictable cadences are typical of the Nurse.

NURSE

O, he is even in my mistress' case,
Just in her case! O woeful sympathy,
Piteous predicament! Even so lies she,
Blubb'ring and weeping, weeping and blubb'ring.—
Stand up, stand up, stand an you be a man;
For Juliet's sake, for her sake, rise and stand.
Why should you fall into so deep an O?

ROMEO (*rising*)

Nurse—

NURSE Ah sir, ah sir, death's the end of all.

ROMEO

Spakest thou of Juliet? How is it with her?
Doth not she think me an old murderer,
Now I have stained the childhood of our joy
With blood removed but little from her own?
Where is she, and how doth she, and what says
My concealed lady to our cancelled love?

NURSE

O she says nothing, sir, but weeps and weeps,

85–6 O . . . Even] Q; *Fri<ar>*. O . . . *Nurse*. Even STEEVENS 1778 (*conj*. Farmer) 91 (*rising*)] Q1 (*He rises*.); *not in* Q2 92 Spakest] Q2; Speak'st F

84, 85 **case** The Nurse means 'plight', yet she seems to repeat unintentional puns: *case* is a bawdy quibble on 'genitals' (Partridge), with associations of hap or chance (*OED sb.*[1] 1a, 2a).

85–6 **O woeful . . . predicament!** Editors have debated whether these interjections belong to the Nurse because *sympathy* and *predicament* seem more appropriate to the Friar. On the other hand exclamations of woe hardly suit him, and Q1 supports Q2 in assigning these phrases to the Nurse.

85 **woeful sympathy** likeness in misery (*OED sb.* 2)

88–90 **Stand up . . . O** The Nurse's unwitting double entendres extend from *Stand* to *O* (see 1.1.8 n., 2.1.38 n., and cf. *Merry Wives* 4.1.45–56 for quibbles on *O* as well as 'case'). When she says *O*, however, she means 'groan', coining a noun from an interjection (*OED int.* as *sb.* 1 cites its first example from 1609).

91 ***(rising)*** Sometime between now and l. 106 Romeo rises into a position where he can try to take his own life. Q2 has no direction for this action; Q1 prints '*He rises.*' immediately before Romeo says 'Nurse'. Most editors follow Q1 or variations on it.

91 **death's . . . all** Proverbial (Dent D142.1).

92 **Spakest** A number of editors smooth the metre by substituting F's 'Speak'st' or the contraction 'Spak'st' (Jowett suggests that Q1, which sets this line with 'Spakest' prominently at the top of a page, may have influenced Q2). Perhaps this spelling indicates monosyllabic or disyllabic pronunciation indifferently (like 'devil'), as also e.g. in ll. 118, 121, 137, etc.; or the irregular metre may help to convey Romeo's agitation.

93 **old** (a) experienced, (b) long-lived

97 **concealed . . . cancelled** *Concealed*, accented on the first syllable, results in auditory wordplay and may contribute to a pun: Romeo's *lady* and *love* are both, in a sense, secret / nullified or ended.

And now falls on her bed, and then starts up,
And Tybalt calls, and then on Romeo cries,
And then down falls again—

ROMEO As if that name,
Shot from the deadly level of a gun,
Did murder her, as that name's cursèd hand
Murdered her kinsman. O tell me, Friar, tell me,
In what vile part of this anatomy
Doth my name lodge? Tell me, that I may sack
The hateful mansion.

[Romeo offers to stab himself]

FRIAR LAURENCE Hold thy desperate hand!
Art thou a man? Thy form cries out thou art.
Thy tears are womanish; thy wild acts denote
The unreasonable fury of a beast.
Unseemly woman in a seeming man,
And ill-beseeming beast in seeming both,
Thou hast amazed me. By my holy order,

101–2 As . . . name, | Shot . . . gun] ROWE; *one line in* Q 107 [*Romeo . . . himself*]] *variant of* Q1 (*He offers to stab himselfe, and Nurse snatches the dagger away.*); *not in* Q2 109 denote] Q1; deuote Q2

100 **on . . . cries** This phrase, ambiguous in context, ranges in meaning from 'calls upon' to 'exclaims against' (*OED v.* 17). As the next lines show, Romeo hears the negative definition.

102 **level** aim (*OED sb.* 9a)

105–6 **In . . . lodge** Gibbons compares 2.1.81–94, Juliet's analysis of Romeo's name and his response, calling the results 'acutely ironic'. The irony continues in l. 107, where *mansion* echoes Juliet's image at 3.2.26 (see n.).

105 **anatomy** *OED* 7 cites as the word's first depreciative application.

107 [***Romeo . . . himself***] Q2 has no direction here, allowing different kinds of business for Romeo's suicide attempt (*offers* = tries) and disarming. In most modern productions Friar Laurence removes a weapon. In many modern editions, however, the Nurse performs this act because the Q1 direction is reprinted (see Collation); and some twentieth-century prompt books follow such editions or direct the Nurse to snatch the dagger. For arguments in favour of the Q1 staging, see A. Brissenden, '*Romeo and Juliet* III.iii.108: The Nurse and the Dagger', *N&Q*, NS 28 (1981), 126–7, and Jowett.

108–12 **Art . . . both** The opening of Friar Laurence's admonition closely parallels Brooke 1353–8, which begin a sermon lasting almost 130 lines. The dramatic version refines and consolidates the original in a speech less than half its length. R. O. Evans gives a thorough explication of the Shakespeare passage as a premier specimen of rhetoric, 'a brilliant example both of argumentation and of the use of figures' (pp. 54–60). The questions which begin here represent epiplexis: they reproach the person addressed rather than asking for information or implying their own answers.

109 **denote** *OED v.* 3a, first instance of the sense 'be the outward sign of'.

111–12 **Unseemly . . . both** *Unseemly woman* allows l. 111 to mean (a) unsuitably womanish for a man, (b) outlandish behaviour, even for a woman, in a man.

113 **amazed** 'astonished', with overtones of 'bewildered' and 'alarmed' (*OED v.* 2, 3)

I thought thy disposition better tempered.
Hast thou slain Tybalt? Wilt thou slay thyself,
And slay thy lady, that in thy life lives,
By doing damnèd hate upon thyself?
Why railest thou on thy birth, the heaven, and earth,
Since birth and heaven and earth, all three do meet
In thee at once, which thou at once wouldst lose?
Fie, fie, thou shamest thy shape, thy love, thy wit,
Which like a usurer aboundst in all
And usest none in that true use indeed
Which should bedeck thy shape, thy love, thy wit.
Thy noble shape is but a form of wax,
Digressing from the valour of a man;
Thy dear love sworn but hollow perjury,
Killing that love which thou hast vowed to cherish;
Thy wit, that ornament to shape and love,
Mis-shapen in the conduct of them both,

116 that . . . lives] F4; that in thy life lies Q2; too, that liues in thee Q1

114 **tempered** balanced (probably with reference to the four humours of pre-modern physiology and with play on temper/*disposition*; see *OED a.* etymology and 1a)

116 **lives** Apparently Q2 omitted a letter; wordplay and Q1 support the F4 reading (cf. Sonnets 18.14, 83.13).

118–20 **Why . . . lose?** As Malone first noted, these lines reflect Brooke 1325–48, where Romeus castigates all the forces governing his life from nature to fortune. The play transforms Brooke in focusing Romeo's complaint on his name and everything it represents. In consequence, any 'railing' against *heaven and earth* occurs fleetingly in Romeo's dismissal of 'dear mercy' along with the world outside Verona.

121, 124 **thy shape . . . wit** Here the striking rhetorical figure is epistrophe, which ends two clauses with the same phrase.

121 **shape** Since *shape* means 'form' in certain biblical expressions and also in the philosophical sense (*OED sb.*[1] 1e), it begins to consolidate Friar Laurence's argument in this line: 'form' (l. 108) was his point of departure for defining manliness.

122 **Which** who (Abbott 265)

122–3 **like a usurer . . . use** The simile quibbles on *use*, as verb and substantive, in the ordinary sense of employment as well as the more specialized definition connected with usury (see Onions).

125 **wax** Dent compares 'Soft wax will take any impression' (W136), a contrast to the Nurse's image at 1.3.78 (see n.). As R. O. Evans points out, play on the word in this line makes it ambiguous: it signifies Romeo's weakness as well as the idea of the soul as a block of wax. Evans also notices the balance and climactic effect of the argument which follows: two lines on injury to *shape*, two on injury to 'love', and four on injury to 'wit' (p. 57).

126 **Digressing . . . man** The phrasing makes this statement emphatic: *Digressing* = deviating (from a standard (*OED v.* 2)), and *valour* = worth in respect of manly qualities (1b).

127–8 **dear love . . . cherish** A paradox results from antithesis, diacope, and reference to the Anglican marriage service (cited by Shaheen); l. 128 echoes 2.1.229.

130 **Mis-shapen** *OED* quotes Johnson's tentative 'ill directed' to explain this term; but definitions meaning 'distorted', particularly in a moral sense, fit as well (*ppl. a.* 4,2). *Mis-shapen* also plays rhetorically on 'shape'.
conduct guidance

Like powder in a skilless soldier's flask,
Is set afire by thine own ignorance,
And thou dismembered with thine own defence.
What, rouse thee, man! Thy Juliet is alive,
For whose dear sake thou wast but lately dead:
There art thou happy. Tybalt would kill thee,
But thou slewest Tybalt: there art thou happy.
The law that threatened death becomes thy friend,
And turns it to exile: there art thou happy.
A pack of blessings light upon thy back,
Happiness courts thee in her best array,
But like a mishavèd and sullen wench,
Thou pouts upon thy fortune and thy love.
Take heed, take heed, for such die miserable.
Go, get thee to thy love, as was decreed;
Ascend her chamber, hence and comfort her.
But look thou stay not till the watch be set;
For then thou canst not pass to Mantua,
Where thou shalt live till we can find a time
To blaze your marriage, reconcile your friends,
Beg pardon of the Prince, and call thee back
With twenty-hundred-thousand times more joy

142 mishavèd] Q2; misbehaude Q1; mishaped F sullen] Q; a sullen F2 143 pouts upon] Q4 (powts vpon); puts vp Q2; frownst vpon Q1; puttest vp F

131–3 **Like powder . . . defence** As Gibbons shows, this conceit alludes to the danger of loading a matchlock gun: an unskilled/ignorant soldier ignites gunpowder in its container, worn at his waist or held in his hand. Similar images occur at 2.5.9–11 and 5.1.63–5.

135 **thou wast . . . dead** Friar Laurence recalls Romeo's sentiments and posture at l. 70.

136 **would** wished to (Abbott 329)

139 **exile** (accented on second syllable, as at l. 20)

140–57 **A pack . . . coming** Rhetoric subsides into a kind of philophronesis or mitigating speech (ll. 140–4) and then into practical arrangements.

142 **mishavèd** misbehaved (see *OED v.*). Williams summarizes the evidence for allowing this Q2 word to stand, citing in particular Crow's analogy with 'haviour' (15–16).

143 **pouts upon** Second person singular in *-ts* (Abbott 340). Q2 prints 'puts vp', an awkward phrase in context because it means 'puts aside' (*OED v.*[1] 56 n. (a)). Consequently most editors adopt the Q4 reading.

145 **decreed** decided (*OED v.* 4)

147 **watch be set** The guard would be posted at Verona's gates during the night (see Brooke 1729–31 and ll. 166–7).

148 **Mantua** On the distance of this town from Verona, see 1.3.30 n.

150 **blaze** make public
friends families

151–3 **call . . . lamentation** Shaheen compares Psalm 126: 6–7 (the Psalter; 126: 5–6 Geneva), but also points out similar phrasing in Brooke 1220, 1447–8, 1676, and 2554.

Than thou went'st forth in lamentation.
Go before, Nurse, commend me to thy lady,
And bid her hasten all the house to bed,
Which heavy sorrow makes them apt unto.
Romeo is coming.

NURSE

O Lord, I could have stayed here all the night
To hear good counsel. O, what learning is!—
My lord, I'll tell my lady you will come.

ROMEO

Do so, and bid my sweet prepare to chide.

NURSE

Here, sir, a ring she bid me give you, sir.
Hie you, make haste, for it grows very late.

ROMEO

How well my comfort is revived by this.

Exit the Nurse

FRIAR LAURENCE

Go hence, good night—and here stands all your state:
Either be gone before the watch be set,
Or by the break of day, disguised from hence,
Sojourn in Mantua. I'll find out your man,
And he shall signify from time to time
Every good hap to you that chances here.
Give me thy hand; 'tis late. Farewell, good night.

162 sir,] Q2; is‸ Q1   164.1 *Exit the Nurse*] Q1; *not in* Q2   167 disguised] Q3; disguise Q2

153 **lamentation** (five syllables)

158–9 **I could . . . learning is** These sentiments may be proverbial (see Dent C684.1, 'Good counsel is good to hear (lere)'); their context makes them deflationary. In Brooke Romeus is persuaded by Friar Lawrence's speech. Here the Nurse responds to the rhetoric and perhaps counteracts the audience's perception of tediousness by (unintentionally) expressing it.

161–2 **chide. . . . NURSE Here** Q1 has a direction which many editors insert in the Q2 text: '*Nurse offers to goe in and turnes againe*'. (Scripts which follow these editions do not elaborate on them.) At this line, however, Q1 differs in more than one way from Q2; Romeo says 'Farwell good Nurse', prompting the stage business.

162 **bid** bade

165 **here . . . state** Friar Laurence introduces his outline of Romeo's entire situation. The first part of the line may be directed at either the Nurse or Romeo.

167 **disguised** Cf. Brooke 1734, where Romeus leaves Verona at dawn 'Clad like a merchant venturer, from top even to the toe'. The play never establishes whether Romeo flees in disguise.

ROMEO

But that a joy past joy calls out on me,
It were a grief so brief to part with thee.
Farewell. *Exeunt*

3.4 *Enter old Capulet, his Wife, and Paris*

CAPULET

Things have fall'n out, sir, so unluckily,
That we have had no time to move our daughter.
Look you, she loved her kinsman Tybalt dearly,
And so did I. Well, we were born to die.
'Tis very late; she'll not come down tonight.
I promise you, but for your company,
I would have been abed an hour ago.

PARIS

These times of woe afford no times to woo.
Madam, good night; commend me to your daughter.

CAPULET'S WIFE

I will, and know her mind early tomorrow;
Tonight she's mewed up to her heaviness.

CAPULET

Sir Paris, I will make a desperate tender
Of my child's love. I think she will be ruled

3.4.13 be] Q1; me Q2

3.4 In the source narratives the parents' wedding plans, initiated by Capulet's Wife, follow Romeo's departure for Mantua. In the play negotiations begun in 1.2 resume while Juliet consummates her marriage. As a result of the dramatic strategy, this brief scene with Paris is strikingly ironic and at times suspenseful.

2 **move** make a proposal to (*OED* v. 12a)

4 **we . . . die** Proverbial (Dent B140.2; cf. 3.3.91 and n.).

8 **These times . . . woo** Many editors have preferred Q1's 'no time' for style or sense, yet Q2 allows Paris not only prophetic wordplay but rhetorical phrasing.

11 **mewed up . . . heaviness** confined with her grief (*OED sb.* e). The expression, from falconry, refers to putting a hawk in a 'mew' or cage at moulting time. (McKerrow remarks the strange use of *to*, but Abbott 187 and 188 indicate the flexibility of this preposition.)

11–12 **heaviness. . . . CAPULET Sir** Q1 has a direction between the speeches, similar to the one at the equivalent of 3.3.161–2 (see n.), which many editors insert in the Q2 text: '*Paris offers to goe in, and Capolet calles him againe*'. Like the earlier instance, however, the dialogue also differs between the two quartos. Q1 omits the lines of Capulet's Wife, and the direction follows immediately on Paris's 'Maddam farwell, commend me to your daughter'.

12 **desperate tender** rash offer. *Desperate* has associations with risk, danger, and hopelessness; and *tender*, used in a general sense here, is a legal term specifically applied to money. This scene brings all the definitions into play.

In all respects by me. Nay, more, I doubt it not.
Wife, go you to her ere you go to bed,
Acquaint her here of my son Paris' love,
And bid her—mark you me?—on Wednesday next—
But soft, what day is this?

PARIS
Monday, my lord.

CAPULET
Monday, ha, ha! Well, Wednesday is too soon;
A Thursday let it be—a Thursday, tell her,
She shall be married to this noble earl.
Will you be ready? Do you like this haste?
We'll keep no great ado, a friend or two;
For, hark you, Tybalt being slain so late,
It may be thought we held him carelessly,
Being our kinsman, if we revel much.
Therefore we'll have some half a dozen friends,
And there an end. But what say you to Thursday?

PARIS
My lord, I would that Thursday were tomorrow.

CAPULET
Well, get you gone. A Thursday be it then.
(*To his Wife*) Go you to Juliet ere you go to bed;
Prepare her, wife, against this wedding day.—

16 here of] Q2; with Q1; there of KEIGHTLEY; yeere of WILSON–DUTHIE 23 We'll] Q1 (Wee'le‸); Well, Q2 31 (*To his Wife*)] ROWE (*To Lady* Capulet.); *not in* Q2

16 **here** Wilson–Duthie print 'ear' on Wilson's assumption of the copy-spelling 'yeere'.

son Capulet now anticipates the marriage, as Paris will at 4.1.2.

19 **ha, ha!** An actor could interpret this phrase as an expression of surprise or a signal of interrupted speech (although *OED int.* 3 cites *Troilus* as its first illustration of the latter).

20 **A . . . a** on . . . on (see the first n. for 3.1.91)

20–1 **tell her . . . earl** The play hurries the wedding preparations which begin in Brooke at 2255, the equivalent of 4.2 and the beginning of 4.4 in the dramatic narrative.

21 **earl** i.e. count (*OED sb.* 3b)

22–8 **Will . . . end** At moments in these lines Capulet may address Paris, his Wife, or himself. Nevertheless editors have argued for directing the whole passage towards either Paris or Capulet's Wife, and their reasoning has sometimes affected their treatment of l. 23. Q2 has 'Well', a reading adopted by Mommsen (see Furness), Duthie, and Evans on the assumption that Capulet responds to his Wife's dismay at *this haste*. On the other hand Williams explains how the manuscript could have misled the compositor to set 'Well' instead of 'Weele'. The emendation, corresponding to Q1, allows Capulet to engage in conversation with either character on stage or to think out loud.

23 **friend** probably means 'relative' (cf. 3.3.150).

32 **against** in anticipation of (Abbott 142)

Farewell, my lord.—Light to my chamber, ho!—
Afore me, it is so very late
That we may call it early by and by.
Good night. *Exeunt*

3.5 *Enter Romeo and Juliet aloft*

JULIET

Wilt thou be gone? It is not yet near day.
It was the nightingale, and not the lark,
That pierced the fearful hollow of thine ear.
Nightly she sings on yon pom'granate tree.
Believe me, love, it was the nightingale.

3.5.0.1 *aloft*] Q2; *at the window* Q1

34–6 **Afore me . . . Good night** Towards the centre of signature H2^{v}, Q2 prints ll. 34 and 35 in one long row of type and l. 36 separately, perhaps (as Wilson–Duthie suggest) because Shakespeare wrote the whole as one line at the foot of a page. At the bottom of G2^{v}, with ample space, Q1 offers this arrangement: 'Afore me it is so very very late, | That we may call it earely by and by'. Many editors follow Theobald or Dyce, who divide the Q2 lines after *we*. Like Q1 and some later editions, this text avoids breaking up the subordinate clause. It places *Good night* on another line as in Q2 and by analogy with the close of 3.3. Whatever the lineation, the blank verse falters slightly as the scene ends.

34 **Afore me** Probably an interjection (*OED pers. pron.* 7a), but possibly a direction to the servant carrying the light (Evans).

3.5 This scene conflates in a morning two events which the fictional narrative had separated chronologically: the lovers' parting and the Capulets' arrangements for Juliet to marry. Conventionally these events received equal attention. In the play the arrangements occupy almost three times as many lines as the parting. As a result of its timing and proportions, the dramatic version reconfigures both the fiction's sequence and its implications.

0.1 ***Enter . . . aloft*** Romeo and Juliet appear together in the space which Juliet had occupied alone in 2.1. Like the verse and imagery in this later episode, the staging modifies conventions in ways that complicate the lovers' parting (see 2.1.43.2 n.). The situation comes from Brooke 1703–20. In early productions this scene was set in a garden. In most performances since the late eighteenth century Romeo and Juliet have been discovered on a balcony, in her chamber, on a couch, or (more recently) in a bed.

1–36 **Wilt . . . woes** This dialogue is a version of the *aubade* or dawn-song, which expresses the regret of two lovers that day has arrived so quickly to part them (Evans compares Donne's 'Break of Day' and Ovid's *Amores* 1.13). A poetic form of the troubadours, the *aubade* lacks a fixed metrical pattern, but its stanzas usually end with reference to day or dawn. It often takes shape as a duet in which the lovers debate whether morning has really begun to intrude. As Colie observes, the *aubade* of Romeo and Juliet shows 'peculiar poignancy and relevance because of the way in which these lovers must part on this particular day' (p. 145). Evans indicates in a long note that scholarship has discovered a few additional sources or analogues for the lines on nightingale and lark. (These birds still sing in mid-July, the time of the dramatic action.) Spencer contextualizes the lovers' dialogue in his study of the dawn-parting theme (see *Eos*, ed. A. T. Hatto (London, The Hague, and Paris, 1965), pp. 505–53).

3 **fearful** apprehensive (cf. 3.3.1 and n.)

4 **Nightly she . . . pom'granate tree** Poetic tradition associates the nightingale with the *pomegranate tree*; and Ovid's tale of Philomel, transformed into a nightingale

ROMEO

It was the lark, the herald of the morn,
No nightingale. Look, love, what envious streaks
Do lace the severing clouds in yonder east.
Night's candles are burnt out, and jocund day
Stands tiptoe on the misty mountain tops.
I must be gone and live, or stay and die.

JULIET

Yon light is not daylight; I know it, I.
It is some meteor that the sun exhaled
To be to thee this night a torch-bearer,
And light thee on thy way to Mantua.
Therefore stay yet; thou needst not to be gone.

ROMEO

Let me be ta'en, let me be put to death;
I am content, so thou wilt have it so.
I'll say yon grey is not the morning's eye:
'Tis but the pale reflex of Cynthia's brow;
Nor that is not the lark whose notes do beat

13 sun exhaled] HOSLEY; Sun exhale Q2; Sunne exhales Q1 19 the] Q1; the the Q2

in the *Metamorphoses*, Book 6, may explain why a female sings here when the male does in nature (Evans). Comparable to the bird, the tree is both reality and symbol: an exotic domesticated in England by the late sixteenth century, and the source of fruit which represents both fecundity and a complex type of unity (Spencer, Cirlot).

7–20 **envious streaks . . . Cynthia's brow** The cosmic imagery which the lovers have used as metaphors now becomes a crucial part of the narrative.

7 **envious** malicious (*OED a.* 2), and perhaps jealous

8 **lace** *OED v.* 6a, first instance of the figurative usage 'To mark as with (gold or silver) lace or embroidery; to diversify with streaks of colour'.
severing This participial adjective plays on the verb 'sever': the clouds separate from one another, and in the process they separate the lovers (*OED*'s first illustration of the modifier *severing*).

9 **Night's candles** First instance of a proverbial expression for stars (Dent C49.1).
jocund According to McKerrow, the synonymous 'jocant' (now obsolete) may have influenced the unusual Q2 spelling '*iocand*'.

10 **Stands tiptoe** A common expression used figuratively (see Dent TT20).

11 **be gone . . . die** At this point Brooke 1713–14 also pairs antitheses.

13 **meteor** luminous vapour (*OED* 2b, first illustration). It was believed that the sun *exhaled* or drew up vapours from the earth to produce *meteors* (*v.*[1] 4a; cf. *L.L.L.* 4.3.66–7).
exhaled Q2 prints 'exhale', apparently through a common misreading of final *d* as *e* (cf. l. 31 and see Hosley, 'The Corrupting Influence', 20 n. 27 for a list of such errors in the text).

16 **to be gone** The infinitive used as an object of the verb (Abbott 355).

19 **grey . . . eye** For this imagery of early morning cf. 2.2.1 and see n.

20 **pale . . . brow** Romeo personified the moon and emphasized its pallor at 2.1.47–52; here he imagines a wan reflection of its light.

21 **Nor** Either *Nor* = And or it is part of a double negative for emphasis (see Abbott 408, 406).

The vaulty heaven so high above our heads.
I have more care to stay than will to go.
Come, death, and welcome! Juliet wills it so.
How is't my soul? Let's talk; it is not day.

JULIET

It is, it is! Hie hence, be gone, away!
It is the lark that sings so out of tune,
Straining harsh discords and unpleasing sharps.
Some say the lark makes sweet division;
This doth not so, for she divideth us.
Some say the lark and loathèd toad changed eyes.
O, now I would they had changed voices too,
Since arm from arm that voice doth us affray,
Hunting thee hence with hunt's-up to the day.
O, now be gone! More light and light it grows.

ROMEO

More light and light, more dark and dark our woes.
Enter the Nurse

31 changed] ROWE 1714; change Q2 36.1 *Enter the Nurse*] ROWE; *Enter Madame and Nurse.* Q2; *Enter Nurse hastely.* Q1 (*at the equivalent of l.* 59.1)

23 **care** inclination

27–30 **out of tune . . . divideth us** Wordplay, mostly obvious, enhances the music imagery.

28 **Straining** Uttering in song (*OED v.*[1] 22b). The verb also has associations of exacerbating constraint and tension. F. W. Sternfeld points out that the tradition of sweet and *harsh* tuning gives an added dimension to Juliet's metaphors (*Music in Shakespearean Tragedy* (London and New York, 1963), p. 237).

29 **makes . . . division** performs a rapid and melodious passage of music (*OED*, *division*, 7a). The phrase *sweet division* is also an oxymoron; Juliet spells out its wordplay in the next line. Here *division* is pronounced as four syllables.

31 **Some say . . . eyes** Both Johnson and Warburton identify the exchange of eyes by lark and toad as a popular saying (see Furness). Certainly the toad represents a type of anything hateful, an idea that seems proverbial (Dent T361; cf. 2.3.190 and n.). As a symbol it is known, like the basilisk, for its fascinating gaze (Cirlot).

changed Q2 prints 'change', probably through a misreading of final *d* as *e* (cf. 'exhaled' and n. at l. 13).

33 **affray** frighten

34 **hunt's-up** The *aubade* ends with ironic reference to another form of early morning song, originally called 'the hunt is up'; *hunt's-up* was played to awaken huntsmen and others, including 'a new-married wife, the day after the marriage' (*OED*, and Cotgrave, *Resveil*). But some versions of *hunt's-up* dealt with the parting of secret lovers (see Colaco 153–6, 139, and 2.1.44 n.). As this dialogue closes, figures of repetition appear in every line.

36 **More light . . . woes** Cf. Brooke 1725, 'Then hath these lovers' day an end, their night begun'.

36.1 ***Enter the Nurse*** In Q2 the direction '*Enter Madame and Nurse.*', clearly an error, must stem from a misreading. Hosley suggests that a marginal direction, '*Enter Nurse.* Madam', became amplified and duplicated in print; McKerrow draws a similar conclusion and compares 2.1.192 and 195 (cf. n.; and see Greg, *Editorial Problem*, p. 61 n. 2, and *First Folio*, p. 230). Although Q1

NURSE Madam.
JULIET Nurse?
NURSE
Your lady mother is coming to your chamber;
The day is broke, be wary, look about. *Exit*
JULIET
Then, window, let day in, and let life out.
ROMEO
Farewell, farewell, one kiss and I'll descend.
He goes down
JULIET
Art thou gone so, love, lord, ay husband, friend?
I must hear from thee every day in the hour,
For in a minute there are many days.
O, by this count I shall be much in years
Ere I again behold my Romeo.
ROMEO Farewell.
I will omit no opportunity
That may convey my greetings, love, to thee.
JULIET
O, think'st thou we shall ever meet again?
ROMEO
I doubt it not; and all these woes shall serve
For sweet discourses in our times to come.

40 *Exit*] THEOBALD (*Exit* Nurse.); *not in* Q 42.1 *He goes down*] Q1; *not in* Q2 43 ay] Q2; my Q1 (my Lord, my Loue, my Frend); ah F2

postpones the Nurse's entrance until the equivalent of l. 59, many editors borrow its direction, '*Enter Nurse hastely*'.

40 **wary** *OED a.* 2a, first instance of *wary* meaning 'on one's guard'.
look about A commonplace (Dent L427.1).

42.1 ***He goes down*** Q2 has no direction here, but l. 42 indicates that Romeo descends from the upper level of the stage to the lower. Presumably he uses the rope ladder, as Rowe's direction first specified. Some early revivals performed this scene without a descent: the action took place on one level, a few lines were altered, and Romeo simply exited. In a few others Romeo mimed a descent on the platform by going through a window or over a balustrade.

43 **ay** Williams summarizes the debate over this word, which makes sense in context as an intensifier but seems anomalous in spelling (*ay* instead of 'I') not only for Shakespeare but for other literature of the period. Dissatisfied with its form, some editors emend *ay* by printing Q1 'my' or F2 'ah'. Jowett argues for such emendation; Williams offers an explanation for the Q2 reading adopted by the present text ('perhaps when it stands before a noun as an intensifier (as it does here uniquely) it takes this form to avoid ambiguity').

43 **friend** lover. Wilson–Duthie point out that this line is a chiasmus, i.e. it takes the A-B-B-A pattern of inversion.

44–5 **day . . . days** Juliet's paradoxes derive from commonplaces like those expressed by Brooke 747 and 821–3.

52–3 **all . . . come** Dent compares R73, 'The remembrance of past sorrow (dangers) is joyful'.

⌈JULIET⌉
O God, I have an ill-divining soul!
Methinks I see thee now, thou art so low,
As one dead in the bottom of a tomb.
Either my eyesight fails, or thou look'st pale.

ROMEO
And trust me, love, in my eye so do you.
Dry sorrow drinks our blood. Adieu, adieu. *Exit*

JULIET
O fortune, fortune, all men call thee fickle.
If thou art fickle, what dost thou with him
That is renowned for faith? Be fickle, fortune,
For then I hope thou wilt not keep him long,
But send him back.

Enter Capulet's Wife ⌈below⌉

CAPULET'S WIFE Ho, daughter, are you up?

JULIET
Who is't that calls? It is my lady mother.
Is she not down so late or up so early?
What unaccustomed cause procures her hither?

⌈She goes down and enters below⌉

54 ⌈JULIET⌉] Q2 (*c.w.*), Q1; *Ro<meo>*. Q2 (*text*) 55 thee now,] Q2; ~, ~‸ POPE (*similarly* Q1, ~‸ ~‸) 64 *Enter . . .* ⌈*below*⌉] EVANS; *Enter Mother.* Q2 67.1 ⌈*She . . . below*⌉] JOWETT; *She goeth downe from the window.* Q1; *not in* Q2

54 ⌈**JULIET**⌉ Q2 assigns this speech to Romeo at the top of signature H3ᵛ, but the catchwords '*Iu.* O' on H3ʳ, the content of the lines, and Q1 all support ascription to Juliet.

55–6 **Methinks . . . tomb** Juliet modifies Petrarchan custom, as Romeo will at the beginning of 5.1: typically the male lover imagines in a dream the death of his female beloved (Whittier, 'The Sonnet's Body', p. 58).

59 **Dry sorrow . . . blood** Proverbial (cf. Dent S656, 'Sorrow is dry'). *Dry* or thirsty grief supposedly made its victims pale by consuming blood, drop by drop, with each sigh (see *3 Henry VI* (*True Tragedy*) 4.5.22, *Dream* 3.2.96–7).

60 **O fortune . . . fickle** Proverbial (Dent compares F606, 'Fortune is fickle'). Lines 60–2 play not only on the maxim but on its alliteration, creating antithesis in the process.

64 ***Enter . . .*** ⌈***below***⌉ Q2 staging becomes conjectural at this point and remains speculative for at least the next several lines. (The gloss for l. 67.1 summarizes the meagre evidence.)

66 **down** *OED adv.* 10 interprets *down* as 'downstairs, *scil.* from one's bedroom' (see l. 67.1 n.), but most editors annotate *not down so late* as 'not yet in bed' (cf. 4.4.38). Perhaps both definitions apply and wordplay combines with the two antitheses.

67 **procures** brings (*OED v.* 6c)

67.1 ⌈***She . . . below***⌉ Q2 gives only one clue to staging this passage, '*Enter Mother.*' at l. 64.1. As Jowett says, Shakespeare may not have completely visualized the scene when he first wrote it. Q1 has '*She goeth downe from the window.*' immediately after the Nurse's warning, a direction for either the Nurse or Juliet and therefore ambiguous. However vague the texts, the situation seems to demand that the ensuing action move to the lower

CAPULET'S WIFE
Why, how now, Juliet?
JULIET Madam, I am not well.
CAPULET'S WIFE
Evermore weeping for your cousin's death?
What, wilt thou wash him from his grave with tears?
An if thou couldst, thou couldst not make him live.
Therefore have done. Some grief shows much of love,
But much of grief shows still some want of wit.
JULIET
Yet let me weep for such a feeling loss.
CAPULET'S WIFE
So shall you feel the loss, but not the friend
Which you weep for.
JULIET Feeling so the loss,
I cannot choose but ever weep the friend.
CAPULET'S WIFE
Well, girl, thou weep'st not so much for his death,
As that the villain lives which slaughtered him.
JULIET
What villain, madam?
CAPULET'S WIFE That same villain Romeo.

platform. Elizabethan staging would have allowed Juliet to descend from upper to main level by an inner staircase after l. 67 or possibly l. 64, the audience imagining a change of scene from bedroom window to chamber itself. (Q2 provides no dialogue or business to cover such a pause.) Editions and performance have offered various arrangements, from setting the whole scene in either garden or chamber on one level to dividing private from public dialogue between two acting spaces.

70–1 **What . . . live** Evans compares Brooke 1211–12, 1797, and Dent suggests that the lines may be proverbial (see D126, 'To lament the dead avails not and to the living it is hurtful').

71 **An if** even if (Abbott 105)

72–3 **Therefore . . . wit** Shaheen cites Ecclesiasticus 38: 17–23, but finds the thought in Brooke (1211–12, 1789–98) as well as in Bandello, Boaistuau, and Painter.

74 **feeling** heartfelt. Juliet responds to her mother with equivocations from here to l. 102; she also matches the rhetoric of Capulet's Wife. Brooke has Juliet confuse her mother with a single enigma (1802–8); Shakespeare creates a new version of this exchange through the figure asteismus: 'the answerer catches a certain word and throws it back to the first speaker with an unexpected twist, an unlooked for meaning. It usually has a mocking or scoffing character' (Sister Miriam Joseph, p. 167). Juliet plays a one-sided game until her mother, oblivious, changes the topic.

75–6 **So . . . for** This statement permits at least two readings: (a) as another version of ll. 70–1 which plays on *feel* as 'experience' and 'touch' (i.e. Juliet will experience grief without bringing her cousin to life so that she can touch him again), (b) as a new insult (i.e. Juliet will experience grief to the extent that she will lose sight of its object in pitying herself). Here *friend* = kinsman (cf. 3.3.150).

76 **Which** whom (Abbott 265; cf. l. 79)

77 **friend** (a) kinsman, (b) lover (cf. l. 43)

JULIET
Villain and he be many miles asunder.
God pardon him—I do with all my heart;
And yet no man like he doth grieve my heart.
CAPULET'S WIFE
That is because the traitor murderer lives.
JULIET
Ay, madam, from the reach of these my hands.
Would none but I might venge my cousin's death.
CAPULET'S WIFE
We will have vengeance for it, fear thou not.
Then weep no more. I'll send to one in Mantua,
Where that same banished runagate doth live,
Shall give him such an unaccustomed dram,
That he shall soon keep Tybalt company;
And then I hope thou wilt be satisfied.
JULIET
Indeed, I never shall be satisfied
With Romeo till I behold him—dead—
Is my poor heart so for a kinsman vexed.
Madam, if you could find out but a man

82 him] Q4; *not in* Q2

81 **Villain . . . asunder** Many editors turn l. 81 into an aside, but this seems unnecessary because Juliet's comment works as an equivocation like her others. If *Villain and he* are understood as synonyms or hendiadys (= Villainous *he*), Juliet seems to adopt her mother's point of view: 'That villainous Romeo is very far away', or 'May that villainous Romeo be very far away' (see *OED adv.* 1). At the same time she wishes no harm to threaten Romeo and defends his integrity. The verb, both indicative and optative, facilitates the wordplay.

82 **pardon him** Most editors follow Q4 in adding *him* to this line, where Q2 already has one misprint ('padon, I').

83 **like he** Editions usually omit Q2's comma after *he*, allowing this line its full measure of ambiguity; Abbott 205–6 explain the use of *he* for 'him'. Nevertheless this particular grammatical construction is unusual in Shakespeare, as Wilson–Duthie note, and Williams argues for placing the comma after *like* to emphasize Romeo rather than *no man*.

83 **grieve** (a) anger, (b) pain (*OED v.* 6a, 5a)

89 **runagate** Holmer finds an ironic connection between this archaic term for a fugitive or vagabond and Juliet's at 3.2.6 (see n.).

90 **Shall** who *shall* (Abbott 244)

93–5 **Indeed . . . vexed** Mahood points out a triple ambiguity 'with one meaning for Juliet, another for her mother and a third for us, the audience: Juliet will never in fact see Romeo again until she wakes and finds him dead beside her' (p. 71). Specifically *dead* connects with both *him* and *heart*, wordplay which most editors since Pope heighten by setting it off with dashes (Q2 has a period after *him*). In addition, as Gibbons demonstrates, Juliet's quibbles on *satisfied* and *kinsman* permit these lines multiple readings.

96 **find out but** i.e. only find out (Abbott 129)

To bear a poison, I would temper it,
That Romeo should, upon receipt thereof,
Soon sleep in quiet. O, how my heart abhors
To hear him named, and cannot come to him
To wreak the love I bore my cousin
Upon his body that hath slaughtered him.

CAPULET'S WIFE
Find thou the means, and I'll find such a man.
But now I'll tell thee joyful tidings, girl.

JULIET
And joy comes well in such a needy time.
What are they, beseech your ladyship?

CAPULET'S WIFE
Well, well, thou hast a careful father, child;
One who, to put thee from thy heaviness,
Hath sorted out a sudden day of joy
That thou expects not, nor I looked not for.

JULIET
Madam, in happy time. What day is that?

CAPULET'S WIFE
Marry, my child, early next Thursday morn
The gallant, young, and noble gentleman,
The County Paris, at Saint Peter's Church,
Shall happily make thee there a joyful bride.

JULIET
Now by Saint Peter's Church, and Peter too,

106 beseech] Q2; I beseech Q4

97 **temper** (a) prepare, (b) modify

100 **To hear . . . him** The syntax joins two constructions (cf. Abbott 411).

101 **wreak** (a) avenge, (b) bestow

106 **beseech** Many editions follow Q4 to regularize the metre (see Collation). As Evans notes, however, adding the pronoun shortens an effective pause after *they*. Shakespeare often omits 'I' before 'pray thee' or '*beseech* thee' (Abbott 401), and other metrically irregular lines occur near this one (e.g. ll. 88, 101; cf. 2.3.185 and n.).

107 **careful** solicitous

108 **heaviness** grief (cf. 3.4.11 and n.)

109 **sorted out** contrived (*OED v.*[1] 14a)
sudden Capulet's Wife means that the day will happen very soon (*OED a.* 9), but the narrative situation implies that the *sudden day* comes without warning, forethought, or provision.

110 **expects** A common form for verbs ending in -*t* (Abbott 340; cf. 'counterfeits' in l. 130).

111 **in happy time** apropos (Onions). Johnson underscores the irony: 'This phrase was interjected, when the hearer was not quite so well pleased as the speaker'.

115 **happily** echoes Juliet's 'happy' (l. 111), probably with a trace of its irony. In light of the play's emphasis on fate, *happily* seems to combine 'with pleasure' and 'by good fortune' (cf. 5.3.169 and n.).

116 **Saint Peter's . . . Peter** Shaheen points out that references to the Apostle Peter

He shall not make me there a joyful bride!
I wonder at this haste, that I must wed
Ere he that should be husband comes to woo.
I pray you tell my lord and father, madam,
I will not marry yet; and when I do, I swear
It shall be Romeo, whom you know I hate,
Rather than Paris. These are news indeed!

CAPULET'S WIFE

Here comes your father; tell him so yourself,
And see how he will take it at your hands.

Enter Capulet and Nurse

CAPULET

When the sun sets, the earth doth drizzle dew;
But for the sunset of my brother's son
It rains downright. How now, a conduit, girl? What,
still in tears?
Evermore show'ring? In one little body
Thou counterfeits a bark, a sea, a wind:

125.1 *and Nurse*] Q2; *not in* Q1   126 earth] Q2; Ayre Q4   128 It . . . tears] Q2; It . . . downright. | How . . . tears Q4, F   129–30 show'ring? . . . body‸ . . . counterfeits‸ a] *Punctuation as* Q1 (*subs.*); ~‸ . . . ~? . . . ~. A Q2

change Brooke's house of worship from 'Saint Francis' church' (2006, etc.); however, Shakespeare's Friar appeals to St Francis (2.2.65, 5.3.121).

122 **whom . . . hate** Part of the equivocation if *know* is read as 'understand' or 'believe'.

126–36 **When the sun sets . . . body** These conceits for intense sorrow or tearfulness are conventional (cf. *Lucrece* 1226–39), and perhaps even satirical, as A. P. Slater suggests in 'Petrarchanism Come True in *Romeo and Juliet*' (*Images of Shakespeare*, ed. W. Habicht, D. J. Palmer, and R. Pringle (Newark, Del., London, and Toronto, 1988), p. 129). Slater identifies ll. 128–33 as a ponderous imitation of Wyatt's 'My galley charged with forgetfulness', translating Petrarch's *Rime* 189; Gibbons compares ll. 129–36 with *Titus* 3.1.220–8 and the *bark* metaphor with Romeo's last image, 'thy sea-sick weary *bark*', at 5.3.118.

126 **earth . . . dew** i.e. *earth* sheds *dew* in drops like a fine spray (*OED v.* 2). Some editors print Q4's 'air' instead of *earth*, rationalizing their decision in terms of meteorology. As Malone noticed, however, this line bears comparison with *Lucrece* 1226: 'But as the earth doth weep, the sun being set'. Poetic licence allows the Q2 reading, and *earth* seems an unlikely misreading for 'air'.

128 **It . . . tears** Editors conventionally follow Q4, F in printing one short, abrupt verse. This edition reproduces the equally irregular long line of Q2, which does not seem especially pressed for space on the page (sig. H4[v]). In this speech the metre, like the rest of the poetry, is awkward and unpredictable. Another long line occurs at l. 132.

conduit fountain, often shaped as a human figure (*OED sb.* 2a, Onions)

129 **show'ring** weeping (*OED v.* 3c, first instance of an absolute usage now obsolete)

130 **counterfeits** On this verb form see l. 110 n.

For still thy eyes, which I may call the sea,
Do ebb and flow with tears; the bark thy body is,
Sailing in this salt flood; the winds, thy sighs,
Who, raging with thy tears, and they with them,
Without a sudden calm will overset
Thy tempest-tossèd body. How now, wife,
Have you delivered to her our decree?

CAPULET'S WIFE

Ay, sir, but she will none, she gives you thanks.
I would the fool were married to her grave!

CAPULET

Soft, take me with you, take me with you, wife.
How, will she none? Doth she not give us thanks?
Is she not proud? Doth she not count her blessed,
Unworthy as she is, that we have wrought
So worthy a gentleman to be her bride?

JULIET

Not proud you have, but thankful that you have.
Proud can I never be of what I hate,
But thankful even for hate that is meant love.

CAPULET

How, how, how, how, chopped-logic? What is this?
'Proud' and 'I thank you', and 'I thank you not',

138 gives] Q3; giue Q2 148 chopped-logic] Q2; chop logicke Q1

134 **Who** which (Abbott 264)

135 **Without** unless

calm seems to pun on the condition opposite to storm and the emotional state (although *OED sb.*[1] 1d cites its first illustration of the latter as 1606).

overset upset, capsize (*OED v.* 3a, first example of a usage now rare)

136 **tempest-tossèd** According to *OED*, this poetical expression made its first appearance here.

137 **delivered . . . decree** Legal terminology deriving from Brooke's character, who reminds his daughter 'How much the Roman youth of parents stood in awe, | And eke what pow'r upon their seed the fathers had by law' (1951–2).

139 **married . . . grave** Dent cites this ominous phrase as a proverb (G426) with an analogue in Sidney's *Arcadia*, *c.*1583 (1590) (cf. 1.4.247–8).

140 **take . . . you** i.e. speak so that I can follow your meaning. *OED v.* 59b gives this first example of an expression for uncertainty now obsolete; but Dent, who cites it as proverbial (T28.1), provides earlier illustrations and notes that context may imply anger rather than lack of comprehension.

143 **wrought** (a) won, (b) persuaded

144 **bride** bridegroom (*OED sb.*[1] 2)

145–7 **Not proud . . . love** Juliet begins to equivocate in rhetorical terms (various figures of repetition, antithesis), as she had with her mother in ll. 74–102; Capulet sabotages these tactics immediately in ll. 148–51.

148 **chopped-logic** (a) a person who chops logic, (b) a misleading argument. The contemptuous phrase seems ambiguous,

And yet 'not proud', mistress minion you?
Thank me no thankings, nor proud me no prouds;
But fettle your fine joints 'gainst Thursday next
To go with Paris to Saint Peter's Church,
Or I will drag thee on a hurdle thither.
Out, you green-sickness carrion! Out, you baggage,
You tallow-face!

CAPULET'S WIFE Fie, fie, what, are you mad?

JULIET (*kneeling*)
Good father, I beseech you on my knees,
Hear me with patience but to speak a word.

CAPULET
Hang thee, young baggage, disobedient wretch!
I tell thee what: get thee to church a Thursday,
Or never after look me in the face.

150 proud', . . . you?] Q2; ~? . . . ~, Q4 155 Out] Q2 (*text*), Q1; You Q2 (*c. w.*). *The catchword anticipates l.* 156. 157 (*kneeling*)] Q1 (*She kneeles downe.*); *not in* Q2

although *OED* 2 cites this line to illustrate (a). Before Williams most editors followed Q1 spelling, 'chop', assuming a printing error because the form *chopped-logic* occurs only in this instance. As Williams points out, however, *OED v.*[2] 8a gives examples of 'chop logic' in verbal senses analogous with Capulet's. Dent compares the expression 'To chop logic' (L412).

150 **mistress minion** This epithet gains force through alliteration, lengthening of *mistress* to three syllables (cf. 2.3.180 and n.), use of *minion* in the sense 'good-for-nothing woman' (*OED sb.*[1] 1e (b)), and interjection of the vocative *you*. In its phrasing the expression holds its own as a disparaging term of address at the close of a long question. Nevertheless, many editors end the question with *proud* and start the next insult with *mistress minion* (as in Q4).

151 **Thank . . . prouds** Cf. *Richard II* 2.3.86–8, where York's plain diction (as he counters Bolingbroke's equivocation) strikingly resembles Capulet's. Dent finds a proverbial model for the construction 'X me no x' (X1.0).

152 **fettle** make ready (*OED v.* 1a). This verb may increase Capulet's sarcasm, since it also refers to grooming a horse and in that sense as well accords with *fine joints*.

153 **Saint Peter's** See l. 116 n.

154 **hurdle** frame or sledge on which traitors were drawn through the streets to their executions, part of their legal punishment (*OED sb.* 1c).

155 **green-sickness carrion** This compound insult, emphasizing Juliet's pallor, refers to the anaemic disease which affects young women at puberty (cf. 2.1.51 and n.) and uses *carrion* as a term of utter contempt in the sense 'no better than *carrion*' (*OED sb.* 4).

156 **tallow-face** a person with a pale, yellowish-white face (*OED*, first illustration). Again Capulet draws attention to Juliet's pallidness, a signifier of her strong emotions.

157–8 **JULIET . . . word** Q2 has no formal direction here; Q1 prints '*She kneeles downe.*' after Juliet's entreaty; modern editors provide a direction after either the speech-prefix or one of the lines. Since Juliet seems to deliver the plea while kneeling, this edition places the direction early. In most prompt books Juliet sinks to her knees at l. 157 and remains on the ground, like Romeo in 3.3, for much of the exchange which follows.

160 **a** on (cf. 3.4.20 and see 3.1.91 n.)

Speak not, reply not, do not answer me.
My fingers itch. Wife, we scarce thought us blessed
That God had lent us but this only child;
But now I see this one is one too much,
And that we have a curse in having her.
Out on her, hilding!

NURSE God in heaven bless her!
You are to blame, my lord, to rate her so.

CAPULET
And why, my lady Wisdom? Hold your tongue,
Good Prudence, smatter with your gossips, go.

NURSE
I speak no treason.

⌈CAPULET⌉ O God 'i' good e'en!

⌈NURSE⌉
May not one speak?

CAPULET Peace, you mumbling fool!
Utter your gravity o'er a gossip's bowl,
For here we need it not.

CAPULET'S WIFE You are too hot.

171 ⌈CAPULET⌉ O] Q1 (*Cap:* Oh); Father, ô Q2 172 ⌈NURSE⌉ May] Q4; May Q2 174 CAPULET'S WIFE] Q2 (*Wi.*), Q1 (*Mo:*), F (*La.*)

163 **fingers itch** Included by Dent in his proverbial index (F237). Originally it signalled an inclination to thrash someone (*OED* v.[1] 2).

164 **only child** The play repeats this fact, e.g. at 1.2.14–15, 1.4.229–30, and 4.4.72–4.

165 **one . . . much** echoes a proverb which Benvolio introduced at 1.1.124 (Dent O62.1).

167 **hilding** good-for-nothing woman. *OED* 2b cites as its first example, although Mercutio made comic use of the word at 2.3.40–1.

168 **to blame** i.e. blameworthy. As *OED* v. 6 explains, in the sixteenth and seventeenth centuries *to* was misinterpreted as 'too' and *blame* taken as an adjective. Illustrating the pattern, Q2 prints *to blame* but F1 has 'too blame' (as does the F1 text of *Henry VIII* (*All is True*) 4.2.102). Cf. *1 Henry IV* 3.1.173.

rate scold (with perhaps a trace of the other meaning, 'assess')

170 **smatter** prate (*OED* v. 2b)

171–2 **I . . . speak?** Q2 prints three short lines (see Collation) as the Nurse's speech; editors, following Q1 and Q4, read 'Father' as a speech-heading and give the middle line to Capulet. This editorial arrangement takes account of the fact that Q2 assigns Capulet the speech-heading '*Fa.*' in this scene from l. 159. McKerrow suggests that 'Father, ô Godigeden' may have been a marginal addition in the manuscript, intended as part of Capulet's preceding or next speech.

171 **God 'i' good e'en** The salutation 'God give you good evening', used at 1.2.58 and 2.3.104, becomes an expression of impatience here.

172 **mumbling** babbling (*OED* v. 1a)

173 **gravity** serious remarks (*OED* 1d). This sarcastic usage predates the first *OED* illustration, from the Quarto Epistle for *Troilus* (1609).

gossip's bowl Puck describes a *gossip's bowl* as a cup of ale in *Dream* 2.1.47–50.

CAPULET
God's bread, it makes me mad!
Day, night, hour, tide, time, work, play,
Alone, in company, still my care hath been
To have her matched; and having now provided
A gentleman of noble parentage,
Of fair demesnes, youthful and nobly ligned,
Stuffed, as they say, with honourable parts,
Proportioned as one's thought would wish a man—
And then to have a wretched puling fool,
A whining maumet, in her fortune's tender,

176–7 Day . . . company] Q2; Day, night, early, late, at home, abroad, | Alone, in company, waking or sleeping Q1 180 ligned] GIBBONS (*conj.* Jenkins); liand Q2; trainde Q1; allied Q3; lined JOWETT (*following* Chambers); limb'd HOSLEY

175–7 **God's . . . been** Editors vary these Q2 lines, primarily to regularize the metre. Recently most have followed Hoppe, who omits *hour, tide, time* as 'first shots' for the *Day, night* opposition and combines ll. 175 and 176 into a pentameter. This attractive emendation makes the passage an uninterrupted catalogue of antitheses in blank verse (Gibbons compares the Folio version of *2 Henry VI* (*Contention*) 1.1.26–7). On the other hand, the metre of Q2 does not settle down until l. 179; and its roughness, along with the disrupted list of oppositions, effectively conveys the impression of an infuriated Capulet threatening to spin out of control. Since Shakespeare's intentions remain elusive, the present edition reproduces Q2.

175 **God's bread** A strong oath by the sacramental bread of communion (*OED sb.*[1] 2f).

mad Capulet seems to reinterpret and answer his wife's question at l. 156: she asks him if he has lost his mind; he replies that circumstances have moved him to extreme anger.

177–82 **still . . . man** Wilson–Duthie call attention to parallels with Brooke 1962 ff.

180 **ligned** Q2 prints 'liand', a verbal form variously interpreted (see Collation). Crow concludes that Paris had noble '*liens de famille*', was '*nobly lien'd*' (14–15). Gibbons argues persuasively for *ligned*: H. Jenkins suggests that the manuscript read 'lind' or 'lignd' (*OED sb.*[2] 24b), past participle (adjective) from the noun 'line', often spelled 'ligne'. *Nobly ligned* would therefore mean that Paris comes from noble lineage, status emphasized by both Brooke and the play. At the same time the audience might hear a pun on 'lined', glossed immediately (as Jowett points out) by the word 'stuffed'.

181 **Stuffed** Capulet means 'filled' (as in *Much Ado* 1.1.54–5), but *Stuffed* also has bawdy implications (see Partridge and cf. *Much Ado* 3.4.59–61). With the phrase *as they say*, which sets the word off for a moment, and the proximity of 'ligned'/ 'lined' and *parts*, which also permit equivocation (see Partridge and cf. *As You Like It* 3.2.103–4), Capulet's praise admits an indelicate subtext. Dent compares the whole line with a proverb, 'To be stuffed with virtues (good parts)' (S945.1).

parts personal qualities (cf. 3.3.2)

183–4 **puling fool . . . whining maumet** Shakespeare's Capulet belittles Juliet's youth and sorrow even more than Brooke's, who says 'thou playest in this case, | The dainty fool, and stubborn girl' (1968–9). *Puling*, onomatopoeic and synonymous with *whining*, refers to crying as a child would; *maumet*, a term of contempt, also means a doll or puppet (3, 2a).

184 **in . . . tender** i.e. as fortune offers her a gift (cf. Brooke 1970, 'Thou dost refuse thy offered weal'). Evans suggests play on the adjective 'tender' and the reading 'in her fortunes tender' (cf. Booth's gloss on Sonnet 83.4).

To answer 'I'll not wed, I cannot love,
I am too young, I pray you pardon me'.
But an you will not wed, I'll pardon you!
Graze where you will, you shall not house with me.
Look to't, think on't; I do not use to jest.
Thursday is near. Lay hand on heart, advise.
An you be mine, I'll give you to my friend;
An you be not, hang, beg, starve, die in the streets!
For, by my soul, I'll ne'er acknowledge thee,
Nor what is mine shall never do thee good.
Trust to't, bethink you; I'll not be forsworn. *Exit*

JULIET

Is there no pity sitting in the clouds
That sees into the bottom of my grief?
O sweet my mother, cast me not away!
Delay this marriage for a month, a week;
Or if you do not, make the bridal bed
In that dim monument where Tybalt lies.

CAPULET'S WIFE

Talk not to me, for I'll not speak a word.
Do as thou wilt, for I have done with thee. *Exit*

JULIET

O God! O Nurse, how shall this be prevented?
My husband is on earth, my faith in heaven.

186 **pardon** (a) forgive, (b) give leave to go (cf. *Two Gentlemen* 3.2.97)

188 **Graze** Onions follows *OED v.*[1] 2b (which cites l. 188), '*humorously* of persons: to feed'; but Capulet states immediately 'I do not use to jest', i.e. I am not accustomed to joking. As he cites a relevant proverb, 'To graze on the plain (common)' (P380), Dent gives an illustration from John Heywood's *Dialogue* (1546) II.x.L3[v] which supports a reading of *Graze* as a threat: 'He turned her out at doors, to graze on the plain'.

189–95 **Look . . . forsworn** The last lines of this irate speech have correspondences with the version in Brooke, 1977–86.

190 **Lay hand on heart** reflect (Onions, *hand*); get a grip on yourself. Capulet seems to combine two expressions: 'lay hand on' (*OED v.*[1] 21c (b)) in the sense 'take hold of', and 'lay to heart' or 'give serious thought' (although *sb.* 42 gives its first illustration as 1602). In the process he creates an image of Juliet making a vow.

190 **advise** consider (*OED v.* 6)

198 **sweet my mother** i.e. my sweet mother (Abbott 13; cf. 3.2.98, 5.3.124)

200–1 **make the bridal bed . . . Tybalt lies** On this leitmotiv, death as Juliet's bridegroom, see 1.4.247–8 and n., and cf. 3.2.136–7.

201 **monument** sepulchre (*OED sb.* 1)

205–8 **My husband . . . earth** Rhetorical devices complicate the verse (which almost forms a quatrain with a pair of identical rhymes); the intricacies of repetition convey the strain as Juliet analyses her impossible situation. Mahood writes, 'Juliet's agony of mind . . . is in part a concern for her marriage vow' (p. 58), i.e. her *faith* (*OED sb.* 8a). Only Romeo's death can release her from that solemn promise.

How shall that faith return again to earth,
Unless that husband send it me from heaven
By leaving earth? Comfort me, counsel me.
Alack, alack, that heaven should practise stratagems
Upon so soft a subject as myself.
What say'st thou? Hast thou not a word of joy?
Some comfort, Nurse.

NURSE Faith, here it is.
Romeo is banishèd, and all the world to nothing
That he dares ne'er come back to challenge you;
Or if he do, it needs must be by stealth.
Then, since the case so stands as now it doth,
I think it best you married with the County.
O, he's a lovely gentleman!
Romeo's a dish-clout to him. An eagle, madam,
Hath not so green, so quick, so fair an eye
As Paris hath. Beshrew my very heart,
I think you are happy in this second match,
For it excels your first; or if it did not,

212–13 is. | Romeo is] F; is, *Romeo* is Q2; 'tis. *Romeo* | Is CAPELL

209–10 **that heaven . . . myself** Evans notes the wordplay on *soft*: (a) gentle, (b) weak. In addition, two other words seem ambiguous: *stratagems* = (a) tricks, (b) deeds of violence (*OED* 3); and *subject* = (a) person towards whom an action is directed (*sb.* 12a, first illustration), (b) one who owes allegiance to a state (l. 205 supports this reading).

212–35 **Some comfort . . . fiend** These lines parallel Brooke 2295–2312 (Evans).

212–13 **Some . . . nothing** This exchange disrupts the blank verse for a moment, whether the Nurse's portion is printed as one line or two (see Collation). Although the lineation may represent a compositor's judgement, the metrical irregularity is consistent with the Nurse's style of speech (cf. ll. 218–19). Williams notes that Q2's spelling *banished* always signals pronunciation as three syllables.

213 **all . . . nothing** i.e. the odds are everything against nothing (cf. *Richard III* 1.2.225). Dent questions whether the phrase had proverbial currency (W865.1).

214 **challenge** lay claim to

215 **by stealth** secretly (its modern neutral sense); also refers to taking or appropriating without permission and to wrongful or forbidden acts (*OED* 5)

216 **case** (a) state of affairs, (b) legal situation

219 **dish-clout** cloth for washing dishes, etc., and term of contempt (*OED* a, c). Dent compares 'Not worth a dish-clout (cloth)' (D380.1).

219–20 **eagle . . . eye** The eagle, king of birds, was proverbial for its keen vision (Dent compares 'The eagle's eye pierces the sun' (E4.1), and cites these lines as his first example of the adage 'To have an eagle's eye' (E6)).

220 **green** Onions claims that a *green* eye was considered 'a point of beauty' (cf. 'thy rare green eye' in *Kinsmen* 5.3.8 and the parodic version in *Dream* 5.1.330); McKerrow notes that the colour probably alludes to youth and vigour.

221 **Beshrew** A mild imprecation here and a stronger one (= a curse on) in l. 227.

Your first is dead, or 'twere as good he were,
As living here and you no use of him.

JULIET
Speak'st thou from thy heart?

NURSE
And from my soul, too, else beshrew them both.

JULIET Amen.

NURSE What?

JULIET
Well, thou hast comforted me marvellous much.
Go in and tell my lady I am gone,
Having displeased my father, to Laurence' cell,
To make confession and to be absolved.

NURSE
Marry, I will, and this is wisely done. *Exit*

JULIET
Ancient damnation! O most wicked fiend!
Is it more sin to wish me thus forsworn,
Or to dispraise my lord with that same tongue
Which she hath praised him with above compare
So many thousand times? Go, counsellor;
Thou and my bosom henceforth shall be twain.

225 here] Q2; hence HANMER 234 *Exit*] Q4; *not in* Q2

225 **here** Although Q2 *here* seems reasonable in context, Williams argues for Hanmer's emendation 'hence' (i.e. 'hēce'), adopted also by Jowett.
you no use The position of *you* makes it chime with *use*, accenting the wordplay on (a) profit, (b) sexual enjoyment (Partridge).

226–7 **Speak'st . . . soul, too** Dent compares 'What the heart thinks the tongue speaks' (H334); Shaheen suggests parallels with Mark 12: 30, 'With all thine heart, and with all thy soul', as well as Matthew 22: 37 and Deuteronomy 6: 5.

228 **Amen** *OED* defines 'as a concluding formula' which means 'Finis' (*int.* or *adv.* 1). Here it seals the Nurse's imprecation 'beshrew'.

230 **marvellous** Adjectives frequently served as adverbs in Elizabethan English (*OED adv.*, Abbott 1).

233 **absolved** Q2 repeats an unusual spelling, 'obsolu'd' (see 3.3.50 n.).

234 ***Exit*** Q2 prints no direction, but Juliet's speech makes it obvious that the Nurse leaves here (as in Q4), and Q1 suggests '*She lookes after Nurse.*'.

235 **Ancient damnation** The phrase in apposition helps to define this epithet: *damnation* means not only perdition itself but also the cause of perdition (see *OED* 2). *Ancient* = (a) aged, (b) hoary; it echoes Mercutio's insult to the Nurse at 2.3.133.

237–9 **dispraise . . . times** Shaheen cites corresponding passages in James 3: 8–10 and Brooke 1145–6. As Spencer notes, Juliet's hyperbole seems at odds with the play's time-scheme (cf. 2.3.191 n.).

240 **Thou . . . twain** This line, reworking Brooke 2288–90, is more concerned with division: *twain* means 'separate' or

I'll to the Friar to know his remedy.
If all else fail, myself have power to die. *Exit*

4.1 *Enter Friar Laurence and the County Paris*

FRIAR LAURENCE
On Thursday, sir? The time is very short.

PARIS
My father Capulet will have it so,
And I am nothing slow to slack his haste.

FRIAR LAURENCE
You say you do not know the lady's mind?
Uneven is the course; I like it not.

PARIS
Immoderately she weeps for Tybalt's death,
And therefore have I little talk of love,
For Venus smiles not in a house of tears.
Now, sir, her father counts it dangerous
That she do give her sorrow so much sway;

4.1.0.1 *Enter . . . Paris*] Q2 (*Enter Frier and Countie* Paris.); *Enter Fryer and Paris.* Q1
7 talk] Q2; talkt Q1 10 do] Q2; doth Q1, Q3

'separated', and calls into play the proverbial notion of 'being at odds', 'being unfriendly' (Dent TT26).

242 **myself** See Abbott 20 on the reflexive pronoun in a nominative position.
Exit Prompt books from the first half of the twentieth century often give Juliet some business with a dagger (taking it from a table, kissing it, placing it under a cloak) before she leaves, evidently in preparation for the next scene.

4.1 The visit to Friar Laurence's cell comes from the source narrative, but the introduction of Paris at the beginning changes the tone and effect of the episode.

1 **sir?** Almost all editors replace Q2's colon with a question mark, perhaps influenced by Q1's 'say ye'.
time . . . short i.e. it is now Tuesday

2 **father** father-in-law (*OED sb.* 1e, first example of the colloquial usage). Paris anticipates the marriage, as Capulet did at 3.4.16.

3 **nothing slow . . . haste** not at all willing to slow his haste (*OED v.* 5a). Early commentators have objected to Paris's wording, which they construe as obscure phraseology or the reverse of his meaning (see Furness); but the concentration to which they object—the antithesis, wordplay (Q1 transposes *slow* and *slack*), alliteration, and effect of a double negative—has distinguished much of the play.

4 **mind** could signify desire (or wish) and, more particularly, one person's disposition towards another (*OED sb.*[1] 10, 15b).

5 **Uneven** irregular (*OED a.* 4a, first illustration of this figurative sense)

7 **talk** Although Q2's *talk* makes sense, most editors adopt Q1's 'talkt'; they assume misreading of final *d* or *t* (see Williams).

8 **Venus . . . tears** Mahood notices the astrological pun, in particular the *house of tears* which represents both the grieving Capulet household and an inauspicious part of the heavens; she compares Spenser's *Faerie Queene* 2.9.52, 'When oblique *Saturn* sat in the house of agonies' (pp. 71–2). In this context Venus is both goddess and planet; her unsmiling aspect neither favours love nor casts a beneficent influence.

9 **dangerous** (a) unsafe (the current sense), (b) hurtful, injurious (*OED a.* 5)

10 **do** Early editions which print *doth* lose the subjunctive effect.

And in his wisdom hastes our marriage
To stop the inundation of her tears,
Which, too much minded by herself alone,
May be put from her by society.
Now do you know the reason of this haste.

FRIAR LAURENCE (*aside*)
I would I knew not why it should be slowed.—
Look, sir, here comes the lady toward my cell.

Enter Juliet

PARIS
Happily met, my lady and my wife.

JULIET
That may be, sir, when I may be a wife.

PARIS
That 'may be' must be, love, on Thursday next.

JULIET
What must be shall be.

FRIAR LAURENCE That's a certain text.

PARIS
Come you to make confession to this father?

JULIET
To answer that, I should confess to you.

PARIS
Do not deny to him that you love me.

JULIET
I will confess to you that I love him.

16 (*aside*) | THEOBALD; *not in* Q

11 **marriage** (three syllables)

13 **Which . . . minded** i.e. towards which she inclines too much. This elliptical phrase omits the preposition.

14 **put from her** dispelled (*OED v.*[1] 10b)
society Shaheen interprets as 'companionship in marriage', citing the Marriage Service: 'Thirdly, for the mutual society, help, and comfort, that the one ought to have of the other'.

15 **of** for (Abbott 174)

18 **Happily** (a) by good fortune, (b) with pleasure (cf. 3.5.115 and n.). This line introduces a stichomythic exchange (rhymed at first) between Paris and Juliet with no precedent in the source narratives. Juliet's rhetoric keeps Paris at a distance. Like the dialogue with her mother in 3.5, this one relies on asteismus, combining it with devices such as sententia, antithesis, and paradox. Again the context turns this form of wordplay into other figures: noema, an obscure or subtle speech; and schematismus, circuitous speech. Paris misses the distinctions.

21 **What . . . shall be** Proverbial and sententious (Dent M1331).
text adage (*OED sb.*[1] 4b)

23 **should confess** would be confessing (Abbott 322)

PARIS
So will ye, I am sure, that you love me.

JULIET
If I do so, it will be of more price,
Being spoke behind your back, than to your face.

PARIS
Poor soul, thy face is much abused with tears.

JULIET
The tears have got small victory by that,
For it was bad enough before their spite.

PARIS
Thou wrong'st it more than tears with that report.

JULIET
That is no slander, sir, which is a truth;
And what I spake, I spake it to my face.

PARIS
Thy face is mine, and thou hast slandered it.

JULIET
It may be so, for it is not mine own.—
Are you at leisure, holy father, now,
Or shall I come to you at evening mass?

FRIAR LAURENCE
My leisure serves me, pensive daughter, now.
My lord, we must entreat the time alone.

26 **ye** A mark of deference (*OED pers. pron.* 2).

27–36 **If . . . own** The third and last phase of stichomythia displays the highest concentration of rhetorical devices: e.g. diacope, anadiplosis (*with tears./The tears*, *my face./Thy face*), polyptoton, epizeuxis or repetition of a phrase with no words between (*I spake, I spake*), antithesis, and alliteration.

27 **price** value

29 **abused** violated (*OED ppl. a.* 2, first instance of the still current usage)

31 **spite** injury (*OED sb.* 1b)

33 **no slander . . . truth** Dent compares 'It may be a slander but it is no lie' (S520).

34 **to my face** (a) openly (playing on l. 28), (b) about my face (*OED prep.* 22)

36 **It . . . own** i.e. I may have misrepresented this face as my own (it belongs, of course, to Romeo)

38 **evening mass** *OED* devotes most of one entry to this anomalistic phrase (*mass*, *sb.*[1] 2c): 'Shakspere's mention of *evening mass* is prob. due to ignorance or forgetfulness of the fact that mass was not (normally) celebrated in the evening. In ecclesiastical antiquities, however, the expression is a literal rendering of L. *missa vespertina*', where *missa* has the more general sense of 'religious service'. (Furness cites evidence of conventional practice; Shaheen argues that the Catholic prohibition against afternoon and evening masses was often ignored; and Evans finds a mass said about six o'clock in London in 1576.) According to convention, Brooke's Juliet makes her way to mass at the appropriate time in the morning, and there is no question of her return (2005–203).

40 **entreat** request (*OED v.* 8, first example from *Tempest* 5.1.120). As Wilson–Duthie note, *OED* misquotes and misreads this line from *Romeo* at 2c.

PARIS

God shield I should disturb devotion!
Juliet, on Thursday early will I rouse ye.
Till then, adieu, and keep this holy kiss. *Exit*

JULIET

O shut the door, and when thou hast done so,
Come weep with me, past hope, past care, past help.

FRIAR LAURENCE

O Juliet, I already know thy grief;
It strains me past the compass of my wits.
I hear thou must, and nothing may prorogue it,
On Thursday next be married to this County.

JULIET

Tell me not, Friar, that thou hearest of this,
Unless thou tell me how I may prevent it.
If in thy wisdom thou canst give no help,
Do thou but call my resolution wise,
And with this knife I'll help it presently.
God joined my heart and Romeo's, thou our hands;
And ere this hand, by thee to Romeo's sealed,
Shall be the label to another deed,

45 care] Q2; cure Q1

41 **shield** forbid (*OED* v. 5)

42 **early . . . rouse ye** Paris introduces the motif from the epithalamium or wedding poem of awakening the bride; this theme will become increasingly prominent and ironic in later scenes.

43 **holy kiss** religious salutation which the New Testament mentions four times (Shaheen). On the stage Paris kisses Juliet on the forehead, a hand, or (sometimes) the cheek.

45 **care** Most editors, following Q1, assume an *a*:*u* misreading and print 'cure' here and at 4.4.91. As Gibbons suggests, however, the definition 'oversight with a view to protection, preservation, or guidance' is possible for *care* (*OED sb.*[1] 4a; see also 1–3a); and the proverb 'Past cure past care' (Dent C921), reversed in *L.L.L.* 5.2.28 (Q, F), indicates a close association between the two words. *Richard II* 4.1.184–8 puns on *care*, showing the word's versatility.

48 **prorogue** postpone (*OED* v. 2a)

50–67 **Tell me . . . remedy** Juliet makes her case in rhetorical terms, particularly figures of repetition which have occurred earlier in the scene. By contrast Q1's version of this speech, lacking the equivalent of ll. 52–60, sounds less formal and more impetuous.

54 **this knife** K. Duncan-Jones has found references to wearing of knives by upper-class girls in the revised version of Sidney's *Arcadia* ('"O happy dagger": The Autonomy of Shakespeare's Juliet', *N&Q*, NS 45 (1998), 314–15). In performance Juliet draws the knife from somewhere on her person (a sheath, her cloak, around her neck).

55–67 **God . . . remedy** As Wilson–Duthie note, these lines follow Brooke 2019–29.

55 **God . . . hands** Shaheen compares the Marriage Service: 'Then shall the priest join their hands together, and say: those whom God hath joined together, let no man put asunder'.

56–7 **this hand . . . deed** The wordplay treats the act of matrimony as a *deed* or legal document: *hand* becomes 'signature'

Or my true heart with treacherous revolt
Turn to another, this shall slay them both.
Therefore, out of thy long-experienced time,
Give me some present counsel; or behold,
'Twixt my extremes and me this bloody knife
Shall play the umpire, arbitrating that
Which the commission of thy years and art
Could to no issue of true honour bring.
Be not so long to speak; I long to die,
If what thou speak'st speak not of remedy.

FRIAR LAURENCE

Hold, daughter, I do spy a kind of hope,
Which craves as desperate an execution
As that is desperate which we would prevent.
If rather than to marry County Paris
Thou hast the strength of will to slay thyself,
Then is it likely thou wilt undertake
A thing like death to chide away this shame,
That cop'st with death himself to scape from it;
And if thou darest, I'll give thee remedy.

72 slay] Q1; stay Q2

(*OED sb.* 17); *sealed* alludes to the impress in wax which guarantees genuineness; *label* means 'codicil' (*sb.*[1] 2).

59 **this . . . them both** i.e. the knife . . . hand and heart

60 **time** lifetime. *Long-experienced time* emphasizes both the Friar's age and his wisdom, because *time* may be understood as both the concept and a personification: (a) your long experience of time, (b) your time's long experience.

61 **present** immediate

62 **extremes** hardships (*OED sb.* 4b)
bloody (a) signifying bloodshed, (b) cruel. Brooke's Juliet imagines a *bloody knife* at 496 and 1915.

63–5 **umpire . . . issue** Resuming the legal figures of speech introduced at ll. 56–7: *umpire* refers to the third person appointed to resolve a matter which arbitrators cannot decide; *arbitrating* appears in its now obvious sense, 'settling by arbitration' (*OED v.* 4, first illustration); *commission* means 'delegated authority to perform judicial functions'; and *issue* is an undecided point in question 'at the conclusion of the pleadings between contending parties in an action' (*sb.* 11a). Non-legal definitions also come into play: e.g. *commission* simply denotes 'authority', and *issue*, 'outcome'.

64 **art** learning

66 **not so** none too (*OED*, *so*, *adv.* 13a); cf. Q1, 'Speake not, be briefe'.

69–70 **Which craves . . . prevent** Dent compares 'A desperate disease must have a desperate cure' (D357), perhaps echoed earlier by the last line of the second Chorus.

72 **slay** The sense makes it clear that Q2's reading is the result of a foul case error (see Collation); cf. 2.2.26 and n.

74 **chide away** drive away with reproof

75 **That cop'st . . . it** i.e. you who would encounter death itself to escape from this shame (the antecedent of *That* is 'thou' (ll. 72–3), and see *OED*, *cope*, *v.*[2] 2)

76 **And if** As Wilson–Duthie note, *And if* may = 'An if', an emphatic 'If' (Abbott 103).

JULIET

O bid me leap, rather than marry Paris,
From off the battlements of any tower,
Or walk in thievish ways; or bid me lurk
Where serpents are. Chain me with roaring bears;
Or hide me nightly in a charnel-house,
O'ercovered quite with dead men's rattling bones,
With reeky shanks and yellow chapless skulls;
Or bid me go into a new-made grave,
And hide me with a dead man in his tomb—
Things that, to hear them told, have made me tremble—
And I will do it without fear or doubt,
To live an unstained wife to my sweet love.

FRIAR LAURENCE

Hold then, go home, be merry, give consent
To marry Paris. Wednesday is tomorrow:
Tomorrow night look that thou lie alone;
Let not the Nurse lie with thee in thy chamber.
Take thou this vial, being then in bed,

78 off] Q2 (of), Q1 83 chapless] Q1; chapels Q2 85 tomb] WILLIAMS (*conj*. Malone; *similarly* Q1); *not in* Q2; shroud Q4; graue F

77–8 **bid me leap . . . tower** For Juliet's image of a suicidal fall, cf. Brooke 1603–4.

78 **off** Q2 has the common spelling variant 'of', reproduced by Q3–4 and F1–2. According to Williams, 'of' may be a misprint, anticipating the preposition later in the line; it occurs only once in Q2 (*off* appears nine times).

79 **thievish** infested by thieves (*OED a.* 1)

81 **charnel-house** A structure or place—building, house, vault—for storing dead bodies or piling up skeletal remains. Whatever structure or place Juliet imagines, this morbid vision (not in Brooke) anticipates her enactment of the Friar's plan in 4.3 and 5.3.

83 **chapless** with the lower jaws missing. Shakespeare may have coined *chapless*; *OED a.* cites this line as its first illustration and *Hamlet* 5.1.87 as its second. Novelty may account for the Q2 misprint 'chapels', which A. Walker gives a bibliographical explanation: the manuscript 'must have had the short spelling "chaples". If the copy had had the long spelling [cf. F *Hamlet*] the error would not have occurred' ('Compositor Determination and Other Problems in Shakespearian Texts', *SB* 7 (1955), 9–10).

85 **tomb** An editor has three options for filling the gap in Q2: 'shroud', 'grave', and *tomb* (see Collation). Although most recent editions follow Q4, this one accepts Williams's argument for Malone's conjecture based on Q1, 'Or lay me in tombe with one new dead'. Williams gives correspondences for his rendering of the line from elsewhere in the text; and he distinguishes between 'grave' and *tomb* in the play (individual burial-place vs. structure above ground), demonstrating that his version does not repeat l. 84. Gibbons makes the best case for 'shroud', particularly on stylistic evidence.

87 **doubt** (a) hesitation, (b) dread (*OED sb.*[1] 3a)

88 **unstained** (stressed on first syllable)

92 **Let not . . . chamber** A recollection of Brooke 2091–3.

93–120 **Take thou . . . acting it** This speech condenses the Friar's advice to Juliet

And this distilling liquor drink thou off;
When presently through all thy veins shall run
A cold and drowsy humour, for no pulse
Shall keep his native progress, but surcease.
No warmth, no breath shall testify thou livest;
The roses in thy lips and cheeks shall fade
To wanny ashes, thy eyes' windows fall
Like death when he shuts up the day of life.
Each part, deprived of supple government,
Shall stiff and stark and cold appear like death;
And in this borrowed likeness of shrunk death
Thou shalt continue two-and-forty hours,

94 distilling] Q2; distilled Q1 98 breath] Q1; breast Q2 100 wanny] HOPPE (*conj.* Kellner); many Q2; paly Q4; mealy F2

from Brooke 2125–72, making redundancy an effective character note and adding metaphor.

94 **distilling** (a) distilled (see Abbott 372 on the instability of active participles), (b) infusing. *Distilling* makes sense in a complicated way; but many early editors have printed Q1's 'distilled'. McKerrow considers *distilling* a possible instance of misread handwriting ('distillīg' for 'distillyd').

95 **presently** immediately

96 **humour** fluid (*OED sb.* 2a, b). Friar Laurence probably means blood (one of the four chief fluids or *humours* of the body), intermingled with the potion, running through the veins to produce *cold and drowsy* sensations.

97 **native** natural

98 **breath** Q2 prints 'breast', a word appearing at this point in Brooke: 'No pulse shall go, ne heart once beat within thy hollow breast' (2156). Among recent editors only Evans attempts to find an applicable definition for 'breast' (*OED sb.* 6, 'place where the lungs are situated; *hence*, breath, voice in singing'), but he decides that context supports *breath*.

100 **wanny** pallid (*OED a.*). As a result of punctuation and spelling ('fade: | Too many ashes'), Q2 fails to make sense at this juncture. Mechanical adjustments ('fade | To many ashes') leave the conceit unfinished: roses were proverbially red, ashes pale (Dent R177, A339, and cf. 3.2.55, Brooke 957, and other illustrations in Dent). Assuming that the standard conceit appeared in the manuscript, this edition follows Hoppe in basing emendation on compositorial misreading of 'wany'. Q4 'paly', an attractive alternative, may be a well-informed guess (Gibbons, McKerrow) or a reflection of stage practice (Spencer, pp. 283–4).

100 **eyes' windows** eyelids (*OED sb.* 4a; cf. *Venus* 482 and *Richard III* 5.5.69 for other examples of this figure, a Shakespearian invention)

102 **supple government** flexible movement (*OED sb.* 2a; *a.* 3c, first illustration)

103 **stiff and stark** This synonymous phrase originated here (*OED*, *stark*, *a.* 4b).

104 **shrunk** reduced. *OED ppl. a.* 1b describes the attributive usage as somewhat rare, and cites this line and *Lucrece* 1455 as its first two instances.

105 **two-and-forty hours** According to time references from 4.2 to 5.3, Juliet's sleep cannot last so long: she takes the potion between 'near night' on Tuesday (4.2.38) and 3 a.m. on Wednesday (4.4.4); she awakes between night and dawn on Thursday, or perhaps Friday (5.3.121, 305–6). The figure of forty-two may derive from Painter, '40 hours at the least' (109; Brooke gives no specific number). The inconsistency makes no real difference to the narrative in performance. A reader may interpret it in more than one way: e.g. the number represents Friar Laurence's concern with details; the discrepancy, his lack of control over events.

And then awake as from a pleasant sleep.
Now, when the bridegroom in the morning comes
To rouse thee from thy bed, there art thou dead.
Then, as the manner of our country is,
In thy best robes, uncovered on the bier,
Thou shall be borne to that same ancient vault
Where all the kindred of the Capulets lie.
In the meantime, against thou shalt awake,
Shall Romeo by my letters know our drift;
And hither shall he come, and he and I
Will watch thy waking, and that very night
Shall Romeo bear thee hence to Mantua.
And this shall free thee from this present shame,
If no inconstant toy nor womanish fear
Abate thy valour in the acting it.

JULIET

Give me, give me! O, tell not me of fear!

FRIAR LAURENCE

Hold, get you gone; be strong and prosperous

110 In] Q3; Is Q2 bier,] HANMER; Beere, | Be borne to buriall in thy kindreds graue: Q2
111 shall] Q2; shalt Q3 115 and] Q2 (an) 116 waking] Q3; walking Q2

106 **pleasant sleep** Brooke emphasizes that the 'sweet and quiet sleep' is a marvellous virtue of the potion (2135–8, 2153).

108 **rouse thee** See l. 42 n.

109–11 **as the manner . . . vault** Cf. Brooke 2523–5.

110–11 **In . . . vault** Q2 prints an additional line between these two (see Collation). Although Friar Laurence repeats himself often in this speech, carefully setting out his plan, editors agree that this obvious redundancy is a first version of ll. 111–12 not clearly deleted in the manuscript and printed by mistake. Williams believes that the extra line contains an error: Juliet could not share a 'grave', an individual burial-place (see l. 85 n.).

110 **uncovered** barefaced (cf. Brooke's 'with open face' (2524), and *Hamlet* 4.5.165)

111 **shall** Evans cites Franz 152 for analogues of this Q2 verb-form.

113 **against** in anticipation of the time when (see Abbott 142)

114 **letters** may mean 'letter', the plural form used with singular effect here and at l. 124 (cf. 5.2.4, 13, 18).

114 **drift** intention or plan of action (*OED sb.* 4a, 5)

116 **waking** Q2's 'walking', an obvious error, recurs at 4.3.48; cf. Brooke, 'when out of thy sleep thou shalt awake again, | Then mayst thou go with him from hence' (2165–6).

119 **toy** whim or aversion (*OED sb.* 4a, b). This line borrows two of Brooke's expressions, 'inconstant toy' (2190) and 'womanish dread' (2145).

womanish fear Dent compares the apparent proverb 'To fear is womanish' (W724.1), citing this as the earliest known instance.

120 **valour** Used to denote manly qualities (*OED* 1b) and still refers especially to courage in battle, making the Friar's stipulation antithetical.

the acting it See Abbott 373 and 93 for this construction omitting 'of'.

122 **prosperous** is positioned for conspicuous irony; it means in the first place 'having continued success or good fortune'.

In this resolve. I'll send a friar with speed
To Mantua with my letters to thy lord.

JULIET
Love give me strength, and strength shall help afford.
Farewell, dear father. *Exeunt*

4.2 *Enter Capulet, his Wife, the Nurse, and two or three Serving-men*

CAPULET (*to a Serving-man*)
So many guests invite as here are writ.
Exit the Serving-man
(*To another Serving-man*)
Sirrah, go hire me twenty cunning cooks.

SERVING-MAN You shall have none ill, sir, for I'll try if they can lick their fingers.

CAPULET How canst thou try them so?

SERVING-MAN Marry, sir, 'tis an ill cook that cannot lick his own fingers; therefore he that cannot lick his fingers goes not with me.

126 *Exeunt*] Q1; *(Exit.* Q2

4.2.0.1–2 *Enter . . . Serving-men*] Q2 (*Enter Father* Capulet, *Mother, Nurse, and Seruing men, two or three.*); *Enter olde Capolet, his Wife, Nurse, and Seruingman.* Q1 1, 1.1 (*to a Serving-man*), *Exit the Serving-man*] CAPELL (*to a Servant; who goes out.*); *not in* Q 1.2 (*To . . . Serving-man*) | JOWETT (*To the other Servingman*); *not in* Q

123 **resolve** According to *OED sb.* 1, the now familiar sense of 'determination or resolution' appears first in this line.

124 **letters** Cf. l. 114 and see n.

126 ***Exeunt*** Both quartos allow the actors to exit separately or together (see Collation). Revivals tend to choose among three options: Friar Laurence and Juliet go in different directions; Friar Laurence stays and Juliet leaves; or the scene ends in a blackout.

4.2 This brief scene turns Juliet's reconciliation with her parents into a kind of domestic interlude. Capulet's wedding preparations frame the event with bustle and housekeeping. A number of prompt books between the late nineteenth century and the early twentieth omit 4.2, reducing the variations in mood which continue to destabilize a familiar narrative.

0.1–2 ***Enter . . . two or three Serving-men*** In Jowett's view the dialogue limits to two the number of serving-men in Q2's permissive stage direction; in Mowat–Werstine's, Capulet's first instruction allows for one or two and the opening of the scene therefore permits two or three. (It is also possible that one or two remain on stage.) Q1 has only one serving-man here and at the equivalent of 4.4.12.2; revivals which perform this part of the scene usually cast two serving-men.

2 **cunning** skilful. Capulet's second instruction, promising lavish preparations like those in Brooke (2258, 2281–7), contradicts his plans for a modest wedding at 3.4.23–8. The discrepancy (similar to others in this characterization) may suggest a range of traits from hospitableness to impetuosity.

6–7 **'tis . . . own fingers** Proverbial for one who lacks confidence in his own skills (Dent C636).

CAPULET

Go, be gone. We shall be much unfurnished for this
time. *Exit the Serving-man*
What, is my daughter gone to Friar Laurence?

NURSE Ay, forsooth.

CAPULET

Well, he may chance to do some good on her;
A peevish self-willed harlotry it is.

Enter Juliet

NURSE

See where she comes from shrift with merry look.

CAPULET

How now, my headstrong, where have you been
gadding?

JULIET

Where I have learned me to repent the sin
Of disobedient opposition
To you and your behests; and am enjoined
By holy Laurence to fall prostrate here (*kneeling*)

9 Go . . . time.] Q2; Go . . . gone. | We . . . time. POPE *Exit the Serving-man*] Q1; *not in* Q2 13 self-willed harlotry] Q1 (selfewild harlotrie); selfwield harlottry Q2 (*most copies*); selfewieldhar lottry Q2 (*other copies*) 19 here (*kneeling*)] Q1 (*'She kneeles downe.' after Juliet's speech*); *not in* Q2

9 **Go . . . time** This edition, breaking with convention, prints Q2's hypermetrical line (see Collation). The Q2 configuration hovers between verse and prose, and it registers Capulet's mind changing course.

unfurnished i.e. with provisions, arrangements, etc.

11 **forsooth** according to Onions (citing Schmidt), expresses 'honest asseveration' from a character of low social status. The Nurse's emphatic response may show her eagerness to restore both Juliet and herself in Capulet's favour.

12 **do . . . good on** prevail upon (Onions, *good, sb.*)

13 **peevish . . . harlotry** reappears in *1 Henry IV* 3.1.194–5, applied to Lady Mortimer: 'a peevish self-willed harlotry, | One that no persuasion can do good upon'. *Peevish* = headstrong, and perhaps foolish (*OED a.* 4, 1); *harlotry*, a pejorative term for a woman, may refer either to feminine stubbornness (see D. Bevington's note in the Oxford edition of *1 Henry IV* 3.1.193) or to a silly girl (Onions).

14 **she comes . . . merry look** Juliet begins to obey Friar Laurence's directions to the letter (cf. 4.1.89).

15 **headstrong** The transformation of adjective into noun was common (Abbott 5).

16 **learned me** i.e. learned, or possibly (if *learned* means 'taught') taught myself. Abbott's explanation for the reflexive use of verbs in Shakespeare's time does not fully account for this instance (see 296).

17 **opposition** a contrary position, both in the general sense and in rhetoric (*OED* 4b); Juliet implies that she will both adopt her father's point of view and stop arguing with him.

18 **enjoined** in early use applied especially to the directions of a spiritual adviser, as here (*OED v.* 2a).

19 **here (*kneeling*)** Q2 provides no direction, but the dialogue requires Juliet to kneel (l. 27 will prompt her to stand); Q1 prints

To beg your pardon. Pardon, I beseech you.
Henceforward I am ever ruled by you.

CAPULET
Send for the County; go tell him of this.
I'll have this knot knit up tomorrow morning.

JULIET
I met the youthful lord at Laurence' cell,
And gave him what becomèd love I might,
Not stepping o'er the bounds of modesty.

CAPULET
Why, I am glad on't, this is well—stand up—
This is as't should be. Let me see the County.
Ay, marry, go, I say, and fetch him hither.
Now, afore God, this reverend holy friar,
All our whole city is much bound to him.

JULIET
Nurse, will you go with me into my closet,
To help me sort such needful ornaments
As you think fit to furnish me tomorrow?

CAPULET'S WIFE
No, not till Thursday; there is time enough.

25 becomèd] Q4, F; becomd Q2; becoming ROWE

'*She kneeles downe.*' after her speech; modern editors give a direction at the end of l. 19, in the middle of l. 20, or at the close of l. 21. Since Juliet could begin to kneel as soon as l. 19, this edition places the direction early (cf. 3.5.157–8 and n.).

22 **Send . . . this** Q2 does not specify who receives the orders here and at l. 29 (Q1 is also vague): Capulet may speak to the household (not noticing that the serving-men seem to have disappeared) or directly to the Nurse (as Jowett supposes and a few recent prompt books direct). In either case, no one obeys him and he will exit from this scene to perform the errand himself.

23 **tomorrow** i.e. Wednesday (cf. 4.1.90). This sudden change of plan originates in the play, as Evans demonstrates in citing relevant passages from Brooke.

25 **becomèd** becoming, suitable. Q2 prints 'becomd' and *OED ppl. a.* gives this line as its only illustration, metrical/linguistic anomalies which lead Jowett to adopt Rowe's 'becoming'. Despite the irregularities, however, most editors follow Q2: participles frequently shifted between forms in Elizabethan English, a process which may have resulted in this coinage (see Abbott 374 on passive participles, and the note on 'distilling', 4.1.94).

27 **on't** of it (Abbott 182)

28 **This . . . be** Proverbial (Dent S398.1).

30–1 **Now . . . him** Brooke's Capilet makes the same point in some of the same words (2249–50).

32–4 **Nurse . . . tomorrow?** In Brooke, Juliet declares slightly earlier in this episode, 'Unto my closet fare I now'; she goes alone and purposely to 'remove all doubt' about her change of heart (2233–6).

32 **closet** private room

33 **sort** choose (*OED v.*[1] 14b)
ornaments attire (*OED sb.* 1a; cf. 1.1.89)

34 **furnish** provide with what is necessary, or adorn (*OED v.* 5a, b give *Merchant* and *Much Ado* as their first examples)

35 **there . . . enough** i.e. that is soon enough (*OED sb.* 36)

CAPULET

Go, Nurse, go with her; we'll to church tomorrow.
Exeunt Juliet and the Nurse

CAPULET'S WIFE

We shall be short in our provision;
'Tis now near night.

CAPULET Tush, I will stir about,
And all things shall be well, I warrant thee, wife.
Go thou to Juliet, help to deck up her.
I'll not to bed tonight—let me alone—
I'll play the housewife for this once. What, ho!
They are all forth. Well, I will walk myself
To County Paris, to prepare up him
Against tomorrow. My heart is wondrous light,
Since this same wayward girl is so reclaimed.
Exeunt

4.3 *Enter Juliet and the Nurse*

JULIET

Ay, those attires are best. But, gentle Nurse,
I pray thee leave me to myself tonight;
For I have need of many orisons
To move the heavens to smile upon my state,
Which, well thou knowest, is cross and full of sin.
Enter Capulet's Wife

36.1 *Exeunt Juliet and Nurse*] Q1 (*Exeunt Nurse and Iuliet.*), F; *Exeunt.* Q2 40 up her] Q2; her up HUDSON (*conj.* Lettsom) 44 up him] Q2; him up F 46.1 *Exeunt*] Q1, F (*Exeunt Father and Mother.*); *Exit.* Q2

38 **now . . . night** Scenes 3.5 to 4.2 have telescoped this eventful Tuesday from Romeo's departure at dawn to the *near night* of Capulet's Wife. Various allusions to time (Juliet's reference to 'evening mass', Friar Laurence's plan for 'tomorrow night', Capulet's wedding preparations for 'tomorrow') enhance the impression of a narrative becoming more and more rushed.

39 **warrant** Often monosyllabic.

40 **deck up** deck out, adorn

42 **housewife** Pronounced 'huz'if'.

43 **They** i.e. the servants

44 **up him** Early editors frequently adopted F's 'him up', but Wilson–Duthie compare Franz 444, l. 40 ('to deck up her'), and *Tempest* 3.3.56 ('to belch up you').

45 **Against** in anticipation of (Abbott 142)

4.3 This scene follows Brooke closely (e.g., cf. ll. 1–5 with 2320–33).

3 **orisons** prayers. The usage may be literary rather than popular (see G. Taylor's note to the Oxford edition of *Henry V* 2.2.52).

4 **state** 'condition' in senses ranging from physical circumstances (still current) to spiritual welfare (now less common, *OED sb.* 1b). Juliet emphasizes the latter.

5 **cross** adverse

CAPULET'S WIFE
What, are you busy, ho? Need you my help?
JULIET
No, madam, we have culled such necessaries
As are behoveful for our state tomorrow.
So please you, let me now be left alone,
And let the Nurse this night sit up with you,
For I am sure you have your hands full all
In this so sudden business.
CAPULET'S WIFE Good night.
Get thee to bed and rest, for thou hast need.
Exeunt Capulet's Wife and the Nurse
JULIET
Farewell.—God knows when we shall meet again.
I have a faint cold fear thrills through my veins
That almost freezes up the heat of life.
I'll call them back again to comfort me.
Nurse!—What should she do here?
My dismal scene I needs must act alone.
Come, vial. What if this mixture do not work at all?

4.3.13.1 *Exeunt . . . Nurse*] CAPELL (*Exeunt* Lady, *and Nurse.*); *Exeunt.* Q2; *Exit.* [*Capulet's Wife*] Q1 ('*Exit.* [*Nurse*]' *after l.* 5) 20 Come . . . all?] Q2; Come, vial. | —What . . . all? HANMER

7–8 **we have culled . . . tomorrow** Spencer hears hidden allusions to the potion and dagger. With this reading the definitions of *state* multiply. Specifically, Juliet seems to mean 'observance of form or ceremony' (although *OED sb.* 18b dates its first illustration 1604); she may also refer to the family's status (15a) or the pomp attending it on such an occasion. At the same time *state* carries the various denotations outlined in l. 4 n. The terms *necessaries* and *behoveful*, both connected with necessity, subtly accent that notion; 'need(s)', substantive and verb, contributes to the effect in ll. 3, 6, 13, 19.

8 **behoveful** required. Common in Elizabethan English (*OED a.*), *behoveful* occurs only here in Shakespeare.

11 **have . . . hands full** Dent associates with a proverb (H114).

12 **business** (three syllables)

15–57 **I have . . . thee** This soliloquy derives from Juliet's complaint in Brooke 2349–402. There she has hidden the potion under a bolster, 'and so unto her bed she hied: | Where divers novel thoughts arise within her head' (2341–3). In the play too she seems to speak near and then on a curtained bed. As Thomson explains, the dramatic monologue not only describes her actions (perhaps difficult to see because of the curtains), but also creates proleptic irony and a vivid image of the tomb in which 5.3 will be set ('*Romeo and Juliet* on the Elizabethan Stage', 239–40). Eighteenth- and nineteenth-century prompt books often give the actress detailed instructions for voice and gesture, but revivals have never limited the major prop to a curtained bed (see l. 57.1 n.).

15 **faint cold fear** i.e. *fear* causing sensations of faintness and cold (cf. Brooke 2387–91)
thrills through *OED v.*[1] 5b, first illustration for 'to pass with a thrill *through*'.

19 **dismal** calamitous (*OED a.* 3, first example of a usage now rare)

20 **Come . . . all?** This edition follows Q2, which prints a single hypermetrical line (on a full page); most editors follow Hanmer.

Shall I be married then tomorrow morning?
No, no! This shall forbid it.—Lie thou there.—
She lays down a knife
What if it be a poison which the Friar
Subtly hath ministered to have me dead,
Lest in this marriage he should be dishonoured,
Because he married me before to Romeo?
I fear it is, and yet methinks it should not,
For he hath still been tried a holy man.
How if, when I am laid into the tomb,
I wake before the time that Romeo
Come to redeem me? There's a fearful point.
Shall I not then be stifled in the vault,
To whose foul mouth no healthsome air breathes in,
And there die strangled ere my Romeo comes?
Or, if I live, is it not very like,
The horrible conceit of death and night,
Together with the terror of the place—
As in a vault, an ancient receptacle,
Where for this many hundred years the bones
Of all my buried ancestors are packed;
Where bloody Tybalt, yet but green in earth,

22.1 *She . . . knife*] JOHNSON (*Laying down a dagger.*); *not in* Q   39 this] Q2; these Q3

22 **This . . . there** Q1's text is explicit: 'Knife, lye thou there'. In both versions Juliet probably uses the dagger she showed Friar Laurence in 4.1 (see l. 54 n.). Again Brooke has no precedent for the knife (cf. 2361–402, and Painter, 111–12).

24 **Subtly . . . ministered** This phrase sounds antithetical: *Subtly* = cunningly, or deceitfully (*OED adv.* 3), and *ministered* = furnished with something helpful or necessary.

28 **tried** proved (*OED v.* 13)

holy man Q1 introduces a line which eliminates Juliet's suspicion: 'I will not entertaine so bad a thought'. Some early editors added this line to their texts (see Furness).

29–53 **How if . . . desp'rate brains?** Spencer notes how these macabre images elaborate the fantasy Juliet expressed to Friar Laurence at 4.1.81–6.

33 **healthsome** wholesome (*OED a.* 2). *Healthsome* forms an antithesis with *foul*, which here connotes the loathsomeness of disease (*a.* 1b).

34 **strangled** suffocated (*OED v.* 2a)

35, 44 **like** likely

36 **conceit** idea, or process of conceiving the idea (*OED sb.* 1b, 3). The word also means 'a (morbid) affection or seizure of the body or mind' (11), a definition which may connect this line with others in the speech about disease and suffocation.

38 **As in** This phrase, variously interpreted by editors, may simply be redundant and mean 'In' (*OED adv.* (*conj.* and *rel. pron.*) 33a).

receptacle (accented on first and third syllables)

41 **green in earth** just buried (*OED a.* 10d, first and only example). As Gibbons suggests, the line may quibble on colour: *green* can also describe complexion (cf. 2.1.51 and n.); and *bloody* may denote 'sanguinary' in more than one sense, as it still does.

Lies fest'ring in his shroud; where, as they say,
At some hours in the night spirits resort—
Alack, alack, is it not like that I,
So early waking—what with loathsome smells,
And shrieks like mandrakes torn out of the earth,
That living mortals hearing them run mad—
O if I wake, shall I not be distraught,
Environèd with all these hideous fears,
And madly play with my forefathers' joints,
And pluck the mangled Tybalt from his shroud,
And in this rage with some great kinsman's bone,
As with a club, dash out my desp'rate brains?
O look! Methinks I see my cousin's ghost
Seeking out Romeo that did spit his body
Upon a rapier's point. Stay, Tybalt, stay!
Romeo, Romeo, Romeo! Here's drink—I drink to thee.
[*She falls upon her bed within the curtains*]

48 O] Q2; Or Q4 wake] Q4; walke Q2 57 Romeo, Romeo, Romeo . . . thee.] Q2; *Romeo I come, this doe I drinke to thee.* Q1; Romeo, Romeo, Romeo, I drink to thee. KNIGHT (*conj.* Dyce); *Romeo, Romeo,* heeres drinke, I drinke to thee. WILLIAMS (*conj.* Nicholson) 57.1 *She . . . curtains*] Q1; *not in* Q2

46 **mandrakes** Plants of the genus *Mandragora*, believed to utter deadly shrieks when pulled from the earth, the sound causing madness or death to the hearer. In the context of these morbid lines other properties of the plant, both real and imagined, might come into play. It has fetid leaves or 'loathsome smells'; it is a narcotic and a poison, like the potion in Juliet's mind; and it seemed an image of the human body (with its fleshy, thick, and forked roots) produced where executed murderers had been buried (*OED* 1a, and see Furness).

48 **wake** Q2 prints 'walke', an error which appeared earlier (see 4.1.116 n.). At this point in Q2 and the corresponding passages in Q1 and Brooke, Juliet voices anxiety about waking too soon, not about moving here and there in the vault (a possibility which Spencer considers).

distraught *OED ppl. a.* 2a, first example of 'driven to madness'.

49 **fears** things to be feared (*OED sb.*[1] 5d; cf. *Dream* 5.1.21)

52 **great kinsman's bone** *Great* may indicate degree of kinship (as in 'great-grandfather'), but may also refer to the eminence of the *kinsman* (see *OED a.* 21) or even the size of the *bone*.

56 **Stay, Tybalt, stay!** Juliet cries out to stop Tybalt's ghost from threatening Romeo (not to prevent it from leaving).

57 **Romeo . . . thee** Q2's hypermetrical line captures intensity in both its rhythm and its repetition. As Williams explains, the irregular verse has led to substitution of the Q1 version (see Collation); omission of one *Romeo* as a dittograph; or cutting *Here's drink* as a direction ('*here drink*') mistakenly included in the text. (Jowett suggests that *Here's drink* may be a false start.) In Brooke Juliet seizes the glass, 'as she had frantic been', and drinks the potion 'withouten farther thought' (2399–400). In the play she seems to toast Romeo's success in the fight, as Gertrude will toast Hamlet's in the last scene of that tragedy (Wilson–Duthie).

57.1 **[*She falls . . . curtains*]** As in Q1; Q2 gives no instruction. Scholars have constructed three possible early stagings: a curtained bed introduced when the scene begins; a bed situated behind curtains in

4.4 *Enter Capulet's Wife and the Nurse*

CAPULET'S WIFE

Hold, take these keys and fetch more spices, Nurse.

NURSE

They call for dates and quinces in the pastry.

Enter Capulet

CAPULET

Come, stir, stir, stir! The second cock hath crowed.
The curfew-bell hath rung; 'tis three o'clock.
Look to the baked meats, good Angelica,
Spare not for cost.

4.4.0.1 *Enter . . . Nurse*] Q2 (*Enter Lady of the house and Nurse.*); *Enter Nurse with hearbs, Mother.* Q1 2.1 *Enter Capulet*] Q2 (*Enter old* Capulet.); *Enter Oldeman.* Q1

the discovery space; or a curtained structure projecting from the tiring-house wall. They have also considered the visual foreshadowing that would result if the tomb in 5.3 were located in the space occupied by the bed in this scene and 4.4. (See Gibbons's note and Evans, p. 33.) In productions after the seventeenth century, however, Juliet has performed not only with a curtained bed, but with a couch, an ottoman, or the sheets on a bed; she has even fallen down steps or on the stage itself. Prompt books give no clear indication of any concern with the symbolic placement of bed and tomb.

4.4 Like 4.2, this scene frames a key episode from the Romeo and Juliet narrative with invented material: it brackets Juliet's apparent death first with domestic activity and finally with the Musicians' exchange. At the centre highly rhetorical lamentations further complicate the irony.

0.1 ***Enter . . . Nurse*** In McKerrow's view, this direction does not indicate a new scene because Juliet has not left the stage. Retiring to her bed, however, Juliet removes herself from the action as effectively as if she had made a conventional exit. (Q1 has a row of printer's ornaments between its two directions (Juliet falling on her bed and Capulet's Wife entering with the Nurse), its means for indicating a break in the action.) Productions generally give the end of 4.3 a sense of closure: usually the stage curtain falls or the actress pulls a drape around the bed; sometimes there is a blackout. If 4.4 opens at l. 26, it often discovers Juliet on her bed or the Nurse in Juliet's chamber. For fifty years from the end of the nineteenth century some performances omitted the scene entirely.

1 **Hold** here (*OED v.* 15b)

2 **pastry** room where pastry—food made with paste or dough—is prepared (*OED* 2)

3 **second cock . . . crowed** i.e. it is 3 a.m. Gibbons quotes Tusser, *Husbandry* (1573), who writes that cocks crow 'At midnight, at three, and an hour ere day'.

4 **curfew-bell** *OED* 1c, first illustration of *curfew* applied 'to the ringing of a bell at a fixed hour in the morning'. Originally it signalled the hour for extinguishing domestic fires (= French *couvre-feu*; see 1a and etymology).

5 **baked meats** pastries, pies (*OED ppl. a.* 4)

good Angelica Assumed to be a Christian name because Q2 capitalizes the word, prints it in italics, and sets off the phrase *good Angelica* in commas. Editors find the name in a single literary source, Ariosto's *Orlando Furioso* (1532), where it belongs to a beautiful princess (see Spencer's gloss); and they debate whether it is addressed to Capulet's Wife, the Nurse (ironically), or even another servant. In a note, L. Ferguson and P. Yachnin argue that the term refers only to the aromatic herb used for culinary purposes; J. Bate cites textual and other evidence to show that *Angelica* is a name in the first place and a pun on the herb in the second (*SQ* 32 (1981), 95–6 and 33 (1982), 336).

6 **Spare . . . cost** The matter of *cost* becomes an issue in Brooke 2258–60, as the wedding preparations begin (cf. 3.4.20–1 n.).

NURSE Go, you cotquean, go,
Get you to bed. Faith, you'll be sick tomorrow
For this night's watching.

CAPULET
No, not a whit. What, I have watched ere now
All night for lesser cause, and ne'er been sick.

CAPULET'S WIFE
Ay, you have been a mouse-hunt in your time,
But I will watch you from such watching now.

Exeunt Capulet's Wife and the Nurse

Enter three or four Serving-men with spits and logs and baskets

CAPULET
A jealous-hood, a jealous-hood!—Now, fellow, what is there?

FIRST SERVING-MAN
Things for the cook, sir, but I know not what.

CAPULET
Make haste, make haste.

Exit the First Serving-man

12.1 *Exeunt . . . Nurse*] Q2 (*Exit Lady and Nurse.*); *not in* Q1 12.2–3 *Enter . . . baskets*] Q2 (*Enter three or foure with spits and logs, and Baskets.*); *Enter Seruingman with Logs & Coales.* Q1 15 *Exit . . . Serving-man*] CAPELL (*Exit* Ser.); *not in* Q

6 **cotquean** man who meddles in housework (*OED* 3, first illustration). Q1, which has the same speech-prefix and diction, supports this portrayal of the Nurse as typically unceremonious.

8 **watching** staying awake, as in ll. 9 and 12, the latter adding wordplay: Capulet's Wife promises that she will supervise her husband to prevent the kind of *watching* he has done in the past (*OED v.* 1b, 9a).

11 **mouse-hunt** pursuer of women; literally 'a creature that hunts mice', but *mouse* plays on a term of endearment used especially for women (*OED*, *mouse-hunt*[1] and *mouse*, *sb.* 3a). Dent compares 'Cat after kind, good mouse hunt' (C136).

12.2–3 ***Enter . . . baskets*** Q2 places after l. 13; most editors follow Cambridge and set between the second 'jealous-hood' and 'Now fellow'. Departing from general practice, this edition has the *Serving-men* enter as the women exit, allowing more time for Capulet to see *three or four* approach. The coming and going could have happened simultaneously through different entries, as Q1 suggests by placing the direction before the equivalent of l. 13. (Q1 prints no direction for the ladies, but the action requires that they leave here.)

13 **jealous-hood** Meaning uncertain. *OED* summarizes three widely accepted readings of the term as it first appears in this line: (a) jealousy (i.e. *jealous* + *hood*, hyphenated as in F4, is a nonce-formation with the suffix *-hood* denoting a state or condition), (b) jealous woman (*hood* = the type of the female head, and *jealous-hood* is analogous to 'madcap'; see also Evans's note), (c) a jealous woman who spies (*hood* = a jealous spy's disguise, and *jealous-hood* is analogous to 'sly-boots').

15 ***Exit . . . Serving-man*** Q2 gives no signals for the exits of the '*three or four*'

Sirrah, fetch drier logs.
Call Peter; he will show thee where they are.

SECOND SERVING-MAN
I have a head, sir, that will find out logs,
And never trouble Peter for the matter.
Exit the Second Serving-man

CAPULET
Mass, and well said! A merry whoreson, ha!
Thou shalt be loggerhead. Good Father, 'tis day.
Play music within
The County will be here with music straight,
For so he said he would. I hear him near.
Nurse! Wife! What ho! What, Nurse, I say!
Enter the Nurse
Go waken Juliet; go and trim her up.
I'll go and chat with Paris. Hie, make haste,

18.1 *Exit . . . Serving-man*| Q1 (*Exit.*); *not in* Q2 20 Father| Q2 (father); faith Q4 20.1 *Play . . . within*| Q2 (*Play Musicke.*)

serving-men. Apparently one leaves now with kitchen supplies, and another will go for logs at l. 18.1 or 20. The remaining one or two may depart at either time, although the wordplay in ll. 17–20 implies that the second takes at least one assistant with him (see ll. 17–20 n.). Q1 introduces only one servant to this scene.

15 **drier logs** Unless intended for the kitchen, they must be an inadvertent recollection of the Christmas feast in Brooke and Painter (like the fire at 1.4.141; see 1.2.20 n.).

16 **Peter** Q1 has the name 'Will' here; Q2 prints '*Enter Will Kemp*' when *Peter* enters at l. 125.2. Both references suggest that Will Kemp played Peter at some time during early productions.

17–20 **I have a head . . . loggerhead** Capulet's hearty response in l. 19 indicates that the Serving-man makes a deliberate pun: (a) I can use my own *head* to locate the wood, (b) my *head* has an affinity to wood. The wordplay provides Capulet with the quibble in l. 20: *loggerhead* = (a) leader of the servants who fetch logs, (b) blockhead.

18.1 ***Exit . . . Serving-man*** Q2 has no direction; Q1 prints one after the equivalent of l. 18; editors place the exit between ll. 18 and 26. With the Q1 option, adopted here, the Serving-man may leave the stage listening to Capulet's pun, or Capulet may remain alone chortling to himself.

20 **Father** Most recent editors adopt Q4's 'faith': they find no other examples of *Good Father* as a mild oath in Shakespeare, or they assume a misreading of 'faith' as 'fath'. But verbal uniqueness rarely constitutes substantive evidence for a Shakespeare text; and *1 Henry IV* 2.5.396 seems to offer a correspondence, 'O the Father, how he holds his countenance!' (noticed but rejected by Wilson–Duthie because it may allude to Falstaff's role-playing as Hal's father, Henry IV).

20.1 ***Play music within*** Long assumes that music sounds continuously from now until l. 91, and he chooses an old ballad-tune, 'The Hunt is Up', as appropriate to the occasion (pp. 45–8). In pointing out that the Musicians play a morning serenade, he draws attention to the theme of waking early which Shakespeare extends from a short reference in Brooke (2403–17) to almost fifty lines of this scene. The motif, introduced by Paris at

Make haste! The bridegroom, he is come already. Make
haste, I say! *Exit*

NURSE

Mistress, what, mistress! Juliet!—Fast, I warrant her,
she.—
Why lamb, why lady! Fie, you slug-abed!
Why love, I say, madam, sweetheart, why bride!
What, not a word? You take your pennyworths now,
Sleep for a week; for the next night, I warrant,
The County Paris hath set up his rest
That you shall rest but little, God forgive me.
Marry and amen!—How sound is she asleep!

26 Make . . . say! | Q2; Make . . . already: | Make . . . say. F *Exit* | ROWE (*Exit* Capulet.); *not in* Q

4.1.42, distinguishes the epithalamium or wedding poem where it signifies harmony, linking the rites of marriage with those of nature. The play, like some epithalamia, sets this motif of harmony in contrast with the dissonance of events (see Dubrow, *A Happier Eden* (Ithaca, NY, and London, 1990), pp. 50–7).

26 **Make . . . say** This edition follows Q2, which prints l. 26 as one hypermetrical verse without full stops; other editors follow F. With either arrangement Capulet's speech ends rhythmically askew, as the Nurse's will begin in the next line. It may also end ironically: Shaheen hears an echo of Matthew 25: 6, 'Behold, the bridegroom cometh: go out to meet him'.

Exit Q2 gives no direction, but most editors since Pope have called for both characters to exit and the Nurse to re-enter, or Capulet to exit alone. In Q1 the Nurse's dialogue makes Capulet's departure explicit ('Goe, get you gone'), and she remains on stage. Both quartos therefore suggest continuous action in original performances; and this edition, like Hosley and Jowett, maintains the continuity. Nevertheless, revivals which preserve the whole scene have tended to divide 4.4 in two.

27–44 **Mistress . . . day!** Shakespeare adapts Brooke 2403–23, where the nurse tries to wake Juliet by raising the volume of her voice.

27 **Fast** i.e. fast asleep (*OED a.* 1d, first illustration)

27 **her, she** This construction occurs even more rarely than the one Capulet has used in l. 26; it ends the line emphatically.

28 **slug-abed** Cited by *OED* as its first illustration.

30 **take . . . pennyworths** sleep soundly (Dent gives this line as the earliest known example of the saying 'To take one's pennyworths of the pillow' (P219.2)). *Pennyworths* (pronounced 'penn'orths') may mean 'small amount', and in this speech may imply taking compensation now for Paris's demands later (see *OED* 3f).

31 **Sleep . . . week** The Nurse rephrases 'take your pennyworths now'; *a week* makes *next night* sound contradictory.

32 **set up his rest** decided. Gibbons summarizes five of the quibbles in this proverbial phrase, some bawdy: the expression, deriving from the card-game primero and meaning 'to stake everything', refers as well to resting, making one's abode, firing a musket, and couching a lance (see also *OED sb.*[2] 6, 7; Partridge, *set up one's rest*; and Dent R86.1). With l. 33 the wordplay turns into a still more obvious joke found also in Nashe's *Terrors of the Night* (1594) (i. 384–5), and *Merchant* 2.2.97–8, 'I have set up my rest to run away'.

33–4 **God . . . amen** The Nurse apologizes for her bawdy joke (cf. 1.3.3–4 and n.), but continues to pun on 'take' in l. 36 (see Partridge) and 'fright' in l. 37

I needs must wake her.—Madam, madam, madam!
Ay, let the County take you in your bed;
He'll fright you up, i'faith.—Will it not be?—
[She draws back the curtains]
What, dressed and in your clothes, and down again?
I must needs wake you. Lady, lady, lady!—
Alas, alas! Help, help! My lady's dead!
O weraday, that ever I was born!
Some aqua-vitae, ho! My lord! My lady!
Enter Capulet's Wife

CAPULET'S WIFE
What noise is here?

NURSE
O lamentable day!

CAPULET'S WIFE
What is the matter?

NURSE
Look, look! O heavy day!

CAPULET'S WIFE
O me, O me, my child, my only life!
Revive, look up, or I will die with thee.—
Help, help! Call help!
Enter Capulet

37.1 *[She . . . curtains]*] CAPELL (*undraws the Curtains.*); *not in* Q   42.1 *Enter . . . Wife*] Q1, F (*Enter Mother.*); *not in* Q2   47.1 *Enter Capulet*] Q2 (*Enter Father.*); *Enter Oldeman.* Q1

(= (a) scare, (b) freight). (According to *OED v.* 2b, l. 37 is the first instance of 'fright' with a complement meaning 'scare'.)

37 **Will . . . be?** Proverbial (Dent B112.2).

37.1 **[*She draws . . . curtains*]** Capell first placed a direction here. The Nurse could begin to draw the curtains earlier.

41 **O weraday . . . born** Proverbial (Dent B140.1). The Nurse used *weraday*, an exclamation of sorrow, when she reported Tybalt's death to Juliet (see 3.2.37 and n.).

42 **aqua-vitae** strong spirits (as in 3.2.88)

43 **O . . . day!** Beginning here figures of pathos become prominent in this scene. With them Shakespeare seems deliberately to have realized the awkwardness latent in Brooke's version of the episode (2421–72), which arises from the same false premise. (The audience remains keenly aware of Juliet's actual condition.) Apostrophe introduces the theme of lamentation, and exergasia (repeating the same thought in many figures) amplifies it; figures of repetition and prosopopoeia personify (and distance) both death and time; asyndeton (omission of conjunctions) gives the lists of adjectives a pronounced sense of rhythm, although synonyms accumulate in no particular order; recurring epizeuxis suggests characters at a loss for words. The Nurse introduces pleonasmus, empty repetition and a vice of language which accentuates stylistic idiosyncrasies in the other speeches. (For a thorough analysis of the episode, see Moisan, 'Rhetoric and the Rehearsal of Death', 389–404.)

45 **life** (a) source of life, (b) dearest (*OED sb.* 5)

CAPULET
For shame, bring Juliet forth; her lord is come.

NURSE
She's dead, deceased, she's dead, alack the day!

CAPULET'S WIFE
Alack the day, she's dead, she's dead, she's dead!

CAPULET
Ha, let me see her. Out alas, she's cold!
Her blood is settled, and her joints are stiff;
Life and these lips have long been separated.
Death lies on her like an untimely frost
Upon the sweetest flower of all the field.

NURSE
O lamentable day!

CAPULET'S WIFE O woeful time!

CAPULET
Death, that hath ta'en her hence to make me wail,
Ties up my tongue and will not let me speak.

Enter Friar Laurence and the County Paris

FRIAR LAURENCE
Come, is the bride ready to go to church?

CAPULET
Ready to go, but never to return.—

58.1 *Enter . . . Paris*] Q2 (*Enter Frier and the Countie.*); *Enter Fryer and Paris.* Q1 59 FRIAR] Q2; *Par<is>:* Q1

49 **alack the day!** *OED int.* b, first example of this archaism.

51 **Out alas** Exclamation of sorrow, with play on 'gone out', 'extinguished' (cf. Sonnet 33.11 and Booth's note).

52 **is settled** has ceased to flow (*OED* v. 22b, first illustration of *settle* in this passive construction)

54–5 **Death . . . field** Capulet brings together the imagery of flower and frost in the tradition of Renaissance love-poetry. As Colie mentions, an analogue might be Petrarch's sonnet 131, 'where the rose blooms against the snow and, after its brief life, cannot be revived' (p. 162). Editors have found a somewhat different parallel, Don Mathias's description of Abigail in Marlowe's *Jew of Malta* (1589) 1.2.378–80. At l. 63 Capulet will vary the flower metaphor.

58 **Ties . . . speak** This sentiment echoes Brooke 2451–4, where the narrator describes how Capilet's intense grief prevents him from shedding tears or speaking. The dramatic speech is a contradiction in terms.

58.1 ***Enter . . . Paris*** Q2 has no direction for the entrance of the Musicians, whose dialogue begins at l. 122. Although recent editors, following Q4, tend to introduce them here, a few, like Q1, keep them off stage until l. 121. (Q2's direction at l. 121 may hint a later entrance; see l. 121.1 n.) This edition adopts Q1's staging. Early productions often brought Friar Laurence and Paris on stage alone; modern ones usually furnish them with music (two or three instrumentalists, an adult or children singing, even a live band). With or without the Musicians, Paris enters dressed as a bridegroom.

O son, the night before thy wedding-day
Hath death lain with thy wife. There she lies,
Flower as she was, deflow'red by him.
Death is my son-in-law, death is my heir;
My daughter he hath wedded. I will die
And leave him all life living, all is death's.

PARIS

Have I thought long to see this morning's face,
And doth it give me such a sight as this?

CAPULET'S WIFE

Accursed, unhappy, wretched, hateful day!
Most miserable hour that e'er time saw
In lasting labour of his pilgrimage!

62 There] Q2; see, where Q1; see there F2 (*following* Capell) 67 long] Q1, Q3; loue Q2 66 all‸ life‸] Q2; ~, ~, Q4; ~; ~, COLLIER

61–5 **the night . . . wedded** On this leitmotiv, death as Juliet's bridegroom, see 1.4.247–8 n., and cf. 3.2.136–7, 3.5.200–1. Whittier explains that these lines construct an epitaph from models in the Renaissance source book *The Greek Anthology* (p. 57).

62 **wife. There** Some editors prefer the F2 reading (similar in Q1) which regularizes the metre. Yet Capulet typically speaks metrically irregular and repetitive verse (cf. 1.2.14–15 n.). Now he initiates a set of laments composed primarily from figures of repetition.

63 **Flower . . . him** Riess and Williams compare this line with *Dream* 5.1.287, part of the correspondence between the seeming deaths of Juliet and Thisbe. For these critics comparison argues the chronological precedence of *Romeo* ('From *Romeo* to *Dream*', p. 103). See Introduction, 'Date (s)'.

66 **all life . . . death's** Q2 has the light punctuation reproduced here, allowing for polyptoton within the phrase *life living*. Since Collier, however, most editors have added a strong stop after the first *all* and a comma after *life* (see Collation). Pointed in this way, the line emphasizes inheritance and plays on *living* as the verbal substantive meaning (a) aliveness, (b) property (*OED* 4a).

67–90 **Have I . . . burièd** These laments, frequently cut or omitted on the stage since the eighteenth century, have often impressed editors and producers as indecorous or unsuitably comic. Q1 has a different version, an additional direction and a speech-prefix indicating simultaneous performance of at least one couplet: '*All at once cry out and wring their hands*' and '*All cry*'. With evidence from Q1, C. B. Lower argues that critical editions should include the direction and in other ways call attention to choral delivery of what he terms 'purposeful comedy' (*SSt* 8 (1975), 177–94). Jowett is the first editor to adopt these suggestions; Mowat–Werstine acknowledge them in a note; and modern theatre, such as Terry Hands's 1973 production for the Royal Shakespeare Company, has endorsed the direction. Evans finds at least three weaknesses in Lower's argument. This edition, like most others and Q2, permits more than one reading.

67 **thought long** been impatient (*OED v.*[2] 10c); the play allows Paris's impatience on Wednesday for a wedding arranged on Monday (see 2.3.191 n.). Q2 has 'thought loue', which makes awkward sense (as a vocative construction) and cannot be disproved. As Williams explains, however, three witnesses independently testify for *long*: Q1, Q3, and Brooke 2274 ('And now his longing heart thinks long for their appointed hour'). Wilson–Duthie propose that Q2 may have miscorrected 'lone', intending to replace an omitted *g*.

71 **lasting** everlasting (*OED ppl. a.* and *a.* 1)

But one, poor one, one poor and loving child,
But one thing to rejoice and solace in,
And cruel death hath catched it from my sight.

NURSE

O woe! O woeful, woeful, woeful day!
Most lamentable day, most woeful day
That ever, ever, I did yet behold!
O day, O day, O day, O hateful day!
Never was seen so black a day as this.
O woeful day, O woeful day!

PARIS

Beguiled, divorcèd, wrongèd, spited, slain!
Most detestable death, by thee beguiled;
By cruel, cruel thee quite overthrown.
O love, O life, not life, but love in death!

CAPULET

Despised, distressèd, hated, martyred, killed!
Uncomfortable time, why cam'st thou now
To murder, murder our solemnity?
O child, O child, my soul and not my child!
Dead art thou, alack, my child is dead;
And with my child my joys are burièd.

FRIAR LAURENCE

Peace, ho, for shame! Confusion's care lives not

77 behold| Q3; bedold Q2; bedole EVANS (*conj.*) 91 care| Q2; cure THEOBALD

73 **solace** delight (*OED* v. 3)

77 **behold** Q2 prints 'bedold'; Evans conjectures 'bedole', a possibility because 'dole' meant 'mourn, bewail' (*OED* v.² 2).

81–7 **Beguiled . . . solemnity?** In these lines the identity of the victim, Juliet or the speaker, is at times unclear.

81 **Beguiled** cheated of hopes (*OED* v. 3) **spited** *OED* v. 2, first illustration of *spite* meaning 'to treat spitefully or maliciously'.

82 **detestable** (accented on first and third syllables)

84 **O love . . . in death!** Paris verbalizes the *Liebestod* motif, already heard in this scene, with rhetoric and wordplay similar to that of Capulet's Wife in l. 72 (see ll. 61–5 n.). According to H. Levin, he may also echo Kyd's *Spanish Tragedy* (1587) 3.2.2: 'O life! no life, but lively form of death' (p. 46). In this line Paris reaches for an oxymoron and misses.

86 **Uncomfortable** *OED* a. 1 cites as its first illustration in the sense 'disquieting'; Onions defines as 'cheerless'.

87 **solemnity** festivity (cf. 1.4.170), celebration of nuptials

88 **O child . . . not my child** Capulet produces a simple antithesis with play on *soul*/sole in a number of familiar senses.

91–2 **Confusion's . . . confusions** *OED* 6c cites these lines as its first illustration of the plural meaning 'disorders, commotions'. The verse probably plays on two senses of *confusion*, which also denotes 'calamity' in l. 91 (1a). For analysis of this speech see R. O. Evans, pp. 162–4, and Moisan, 399–401.

In these confusions. Heaven and yourself
Had part in this fair maid; now heaven hath all,
And all the better is it for the maid.
Your part in her you could not keep from death,
But heaven keeps his part in eternal life.
The most you sought was her promotion,
For 'twas your heaven she should be advanced;
And weep ye now, seeing she is advanced
Above the clouds, as high as heaven itself?
O, in this love you love your child so ill
That you run mad, seeing that she is well.
She's not well married that lives married long,
But she's best married that dies married young.
Dry up your tears, and stick your rosemary
On this fair corse; and as the custom is,
And in her best array, bear her to church.
For though some nature bids us all lament,
Yet nature's tears are reason's merriment.

107 And in] Q2; In all Q1; All in ROWE 108 some] Q2; fond F2

91 **care** Most editors adopt Theobald's 'cure'; but the words were closely related (see 4.1.45 n.), and *care* here could signify 'control'.

92 **yourself** In its plural sense this pronoun is emphatic (see *OED pron.* 1 and Abbott 20).

93–4 **fair maid . . . the maid** Friar Laurence calmly (and deliberately) keeps the marriage a secret (Gibbons).

97–8 **promotion . . . advanced** Pointed references to the Capulets' social ambitions (through marriage) for Juliet.

101 **ill** in addition to its familiar implications, may reflect two other definitions: (a) sinfully (*OED adv.* 1), (b) with hostility.

102 **she is well** Dent compares 'He is well since he is in heaven' (H347). Abbreviating this conventional saying about the dead, Friar Laurence produces a neat antithesis with 'ill' in l. 101. Romeo's man will repeat both adage and opposition at 5.1.17.

103–4 **well married . . . married young** The Friar seems to invent a (rhyming) commonplace. In the scene's context his words sound inappropriate to Juliet; in the play's, they ring ironic.

105 **your rosemary** A symbol of remembrance intended for the wedding but now adapted for the funeral. (At the equivalent of l. 121 Q1 instructs the actors to cast *rosemary* on Juliet as they leave the stage.) *Rosemary* has already been associated with Romeo (see 2.3.195 and n.).

106–7 **as the custom . . . church** Friar Laurence expedites the plan he outlined at 4.1.109–11, again echoing Brooke 2523–5.

108–9 **For though . . . merriment** Dent suggests comparison with 'To lament the dead avails not and to the living it is hurtful' (D126).

108 **some** Most editors accept F2's 'fond', meaning (a) foolish, (b) loving; they consider Q2 *some* nonsense and attribute it to misreading of *f*, final *d*, and a minim in secretary hand. Yet *some* (= part of) produces an antithesis with *all*, a device typical of this speech, concentrated in its last line, and pivotal in Capulet's response.

109 **nature's tears . . . reason's merriment** This line is slightly ambiguous. First, it means that *reason* joys in Juliet's death, the cause of lamentation, because 'Christ *is* to me both in life, and in death, advantage' (Philippians 1: 21, cited by Kit-

CAPULET

All things that we ordainèd festival,
Turn from their office to black funeral:
Our instruments to melancholy bells,
Our wedding cheer to a sad burial feast,
Our solemn hymns to sullen dirges change;
Our bridal flowers serve for a buried corse,
And all things change them to the contrary.

FRIAR LAURENCE

Sir, go you in, and madam, go with him,
And go, Sir Paris. Everyone prepare
To follow this fair corse unto her grave.
The heavens do lour upon you for some ill;
Move them no more by crossing their high will.

Exeunt all but the Nurse

Enter Musicians

[FIRST] MUSICIAN

Faith, we may put up our pipes and be gone.

121.1 *Exeunt . . . Nurse*] Q1 (*They all but the Nurse goe foorth, casting Rosemary on her and shutting the Curtens.*); *Exeunt manet.* Q2; *Exeunt.* F 121.2 *Enter Musicians*] Q1; *not in* Q2 122 [FIRST] MUSICIAN] CAPELL (1. *M.*); *Musi.* Q2; *Mu.* F; *not in* Q1

tredge). Second, it implies that *reason* finds *nature's* inappropriate reaction a source of mirth.

110–16 **All . . . contrary** A passage deriving from Brooke 2507–14.

110 **ordainèd** planned (*OED v.* 5b)

festival (a) befitting a feast, (b) joyful (*OED a.* 1, 2)

111 **Turn** The verbs in this speech are imperative.

office proper function

113 **cheer** i.e. provisions

114 **solemn** (a) ceremonious, or (b) festive (see *OED a.* etymology)

sullen mournful (*OED a.* 3b, first illustration of *sullen* applied to sound)

116 **them** may be reflexive (Abbott 223).

120 **ill** sin (*OED sb.* 2a, b; cf. l. 101 and n.)

121 **Move them** provoke them to anger (*OED v.* 9b)

high Playing on the literal and figurative senses in relation to 'heavens'.

121.1 ***Exeunt . . . Nurse*** Q2 prints the vague instruction '*Exeunt manet.*': the plural directs Capulet and his Wife, Paris, and Friar Laurence; the singular directs the Nurse; and nothing accounts for the Musicians, who may enter here (cf. l. 58.1 n. and see Hosley's note). By contrast Q1 has a specific instruction appropriated in various ways by most editors (see Collation). Early productions which included 4.4 usually ended the scene here, often with a tableau around the bed; and the eighteenth century introduced a dirge/procession which lasted through the nineteenth century and survives in some modern performances as well as in adaptations such as ballet (see Introduction, 'Performance History'). With these alterations among others, prompt books make no fuss about the strewing of flowers.

122 **[FIRST] MUSICIAN** As McKerrow says, 'The Musicians are troublesome'. Q2's inconsistent and sometimes ambiguous speech-prefixes do not clearly identify the characters, establish their number, or indicate whether they are musicians or minstrels (see Collation). More distinctly, Q1 specifies *1.*, *2.*, *3.*, and F differentiates *2.M.* (or *M.2.*) and *3.Mu.* from *Mu.* With only these guidelines editors

NURSE

Honest good fellows, ah, put up, put up,
For well you know this is a pitiful case.

[FIRST] MUSICIAN

Ay, by my troth, the case may be amended.

Exit the Nurse

Enter Peter

PETER Musicians, O musicians, 'Heart's ease', 'Heart's ease'! O, an you will have me live, play 'Heart's ease'.

[FIRST] MUSICIAN Why 'Heart's ease'?

125 [FIRST] MUSICIAN] Q1 (*1.*); *Fid<ler>*. Q2 (*one line earlier*); *Exit omnes.* Q2; *not in* F 128 [FIRST] MUSICIAN] F (*Mu.*); *Fidler.* Q2 by my] Q1; my my Q2 125.1 *Exit the Nurse*] Q1 125.2 *Peter*] Q4, F; *Will Kemp* Q2; *Seruingman* Q1

distinguish three musicians, at least one a fiddler and one a singer; prompt books tend to agree. (The Collation cites evidence for the major distinctions.)

122–5 **Faith . . . amended** These lines seem to form a blank verse transition to prose; Q2 prints the Nurse's speech as poetry, and the other two lines scan.

122 **put up our pipes** (a) put away our instruments, (b) quit, 'shut up' (*OED v.*^{1} 56n. (a), *sb.*^{1} 1e). This phrase seems proverbial (Dent P345); it does not limit the Musicians to wind instruments (see Q2 references to *Fid.*, *Fidler.*, and the names assigned to the Musicians at ll. 151, 154, 157). According to Wilson–Duthie, the expression occurs four times in Nashe, once in connection with 'silver sound' (as in ll. 149–56) and again as a jest in *Summers Last Will and Testament* (written *c.* 1592–3): 'we were as good even put up our pipes, and sing merry, merry, for we shall get no money' (iii. 263, l. 933). In Q2's line the phrase introduces wordplay which becomes more obvious as the episode continues. The Nurse unintentionally heightens the bawdy subtext when she repeats *put up* in her next speech lamenting 'a pitiful case' (cf. 3.3.84, 85 and n.).

125 **the case . . . amended** The First Musician quibbles on *case* in senses deriving from the previous line; he refers also to the protective covering of his instrument. Echoing 'The case is altered' (Dent C111), he says that each *case* may be made good or repaired.

125.1, 2 ***Exit . . . Peter*** Q2 prints two different directions (see Collation), on separate lines at the bottom of K3^{r} and the top of K3^{v}; it provides no exit specifically for the Nurse (who disappears from the play at this time). As Spencer points out, the First Musician's puns on 'case' sound like an exit line: the playwright may have originally intended that the Nurse and Musicians leave the stage now. (The Nurse could also leave by herself at l. 124.) Together the Q2 directions suggest interpolation of ll. 126–66 for the popular comedian Will Kemp, who seems to have played Peter in early performances (see l. 16 n.). Kemp belonged to Shakespeare's company from the mid 1590s; his name will appear in speech-prefixes for Dogberry in Quarto *Much Ado* 4.2.

126–64 **Musicians . . . same** Q2 and the later quartos, the Folios, and Rowe print these lines as verse, setting off irregular numbers of beats with capitalization. (Wilson–Duthie, noting three turnovers, think the compositor followed his copy 'at some pains'.) Although certain lines scan, many do not. The passage, like others in the play, seems to hover between blank verse and prose. Because the balance appears to tip away from verse, this edition prints the lines as prose.

126–8 **'Heart's ease'** A popular song of the early modern era, *'Heart's ease'* survives as a tune only in John Playford's *The English Dancing Master* (1651) and as an allusion in the unattributed play *Misogonus* (*c.* 1570). For reprints of the tune see William Chappell, *The Ballad Literature and Popular Music of the Olden Time*

PETER O musicians, because my heart itself plays 'My heart is full'. O, play me some merry dump to comfort me.

[FIRST] MUSICIAN Not a dump, we. 'Tis no time to play now.

PETER You will not then?

FIRST MUSICIAN No.

PETER I will then give it you soundly.

FIRST MUSICIAN What will you give us?

PETER No money, on my faith, but the gleek. I will give you the minstrel.

FIRST MUSICIAN Then will I give you the serving-creature.

PETER Then will I lay the serving-creature's dagger on your pate. I will carry no crochets; I'll re you, I'll fa you. Do you note me?

FIRST MUSICIAN An you re us and fa us, you note us.

130 full'] Q2; full of woe Q4 131 [FIRST MUSICIAN]] Q1 (*1.*), F (*Mu.*); *Minstrels.* Q2

(repr. New York, 1965), i. 209; Elson, pp. 68–9; Edward W. Naylor, *Shakespeare and Music* (repr. New York, 1965), p. 186; or Sternfeld, p. 102. Evans finds an association of 'heart's ease' with having money in the anonymous play *Wily Beguiled* (*c.*1602) 4–6: 'O this red chink, and silver coin' (Malone Society, ed. W. W. Greg (Oxford, 1912)).

129–30 **'My heart is full'** According to Steevens's conjecture, Peter refers to the burden of the first stanza in 'A pleasant new Ballad of two Lovers': 'Heigh-ho! my heart is full of woe'. (A. Barton printed the ballad in *The Shakespeare Society Papers*, I (1844), 12.) Q4 and many editors reproduce the full line; Wilson–Duthie note, 'Prob. the foul papers gave enough to remind the prompter, or Kemp, what should be quoted'. Nevertheless, emendation still rests on conjecture, since the ballad was printed after the play and scholars can establish no earlier date.

130 **merry dump** A *dump* could refer to any tune, but in the first place it denotes 'a mournful or plaintive melody or song' (*OED sb.*[1] 3), and therefore it contributes to this oxymoron.

135 **give . . . soundly** Since *give it* with the dative = attack with either blows or words, *soundly* puns on 'thoroughly', 'with force', and 'with sound, or music' (see *OED sb.*[3] 1b). The First Musician, missing (or ignoring) the quibble on his profession, understands a simpler and more benign sense with his next response. In its musical wordplay the dialogue which begins here echoes Mercutio's challenging of Tybalt at 3.1.38–48.

137 **gleek** gibe. To give the *gleek* = to mock (*OED sb.*[2] 1a, b).

137–8 **give . . . minstrel** call you a *minstrel*, i.e. a menial or vagabond (cf. 3.1.45, Mercutio's use of *minstrels*, and n.)

139 **serving-creature** serving-man, but *creature* expresses contempt

141 **carry no crotchets** Quibbling on *crotchets* as (a) peculiar notions, (b) musical notes; *carry* still means 'sustain' in more than one way. As a result the expression can signify 'I will not put up with your strange ideas', or 'I will not sing to your tune'.

re . . . fa Notes of the musical scale used as verbs to threaten the First Musician with a beating. Peter may also quibble on 'ray' (= dirty, *OED v.*[2] 5b) and 'fay' (= clean, *v.*[2]), which together in this context imply thorough and rough treatment.

142, 143 **note** *OED v.*[2] 6a quotes these lines to illustrate its definition 'To mark (a book, words, etc.) with a musical score', but wordplay gives *note* a slightly

SECOND MUSICIAN Pray you, put up your dagger and put out your wit. Then have at you with my wit.

PETER I will dry-beat you with an iron wit, and put up my iron dagger. Answer me like men.

When griping griefs the heart doth wound,
Then music with her silver sound—

Why 'silver sound'? Why 'music with her silver sound'? What say you, Simon Catling?

FIRST MUSICIAN Marry, sir, because silver hath a sweet sound.

144–5 SECOND MUSICIAN . . . Then] Q2; *Peter*. Then Q4 148–9 wound, | Then] Q2; wound, | And dolefull dumps the minde oppresse: | Then Q1

different meaning in each case. Clearly Peter asks, 'Are you paying attention to me?', and perhaps, 'Are you trying to disgrace me?' (7c), as he continues to pun on words connected with music. The First Musician, who probably emphasizes subject and object when he states 'you *note* us', seems to apply the musical definition in a figurative way, i.e. 'a beating would mark us up like a musical score'; but he also alludes to the two other senses of *note*.

144–5 **put out** (a) display, (b) do away with

145 **Then . . . wit** Q2 gives this line to the Second Musician, making it part of the challenge; Q4 (followed by many editors) assigns it to Peter, turning it into a response.

146 **dry-beat . . . iron wit** In the first instance Peter says, 'I will thrash you with my strong wit' (cf. 3.1.78 and n.). In the second he undermines himself with a quibble, presumably unintended: *iron wit* = obtuseness (see *OED a.* 3d, 4a and *Richard III* 4.2.29, 'iron-witted fools'). Gibbons suggests another pun on *dry* (= stupid), comparing *As You Like It* 2.7.38–40.

147 **Answer me** (a) fight, or defend yourselves (*OED v.* 26), (b) reply

148–9, 162–3 **When griping griefs . . . redress** These lines come (with slight variation) from the song 'In commendation of Musick' attributed to Richard Edwards in the popular miscellany *The Paradise of Dainty Devices* (1576) (ed. H. E. Rollins (Cambridge, Mass., 1927), p. 63). A contemporary setting is extant; D. Stevens, ed., *The Mulliner Book*, 2nd rev. edn. (1954), pp. 83, 96 provides keyboard music; Naylor, p. 187 and Elson, pp. 70–2 give words and setting.

148–9 **When griping griefs . . . sound** Recent editors, following Q1, interpolate between ll. 148 and 149 a verse rhyming with 'redress' which the song prints as part of the stanza's first line: 'and doleful dumps them oppress'. Like Greg, they assume that Shakespeare 'did not trouble to write more than the first and last lines' (*Editorial Problem*, p. 62 n. 2; cf. ll. 129–30 n.), although the stanza continues for another verse. While Q1 may support this editorial view of the line's performance in early production(s), Q2 offers another interpretation which this edition allows. Q2 may omit the verse deliberately to show Peter muddling the song before he interrupts it. According to Sternfeld, context implies that Peter sings rather than speaks the lines (p. 103).

148 **griping** painful. As Onions points out and Shaheen corroborates, the expressions 'griping grief' and 'gripes of grief' were common in the sixteenth century.

doth Third person plural in *-th* (Abbott 334).

149 **music . . . silver sound** Dent compares 'Music has a silver sound (tongue)' (M1319.1) and 'Silver is sweet' (S458.1); Nashe uses the phrase 'silver-sounding' in *The Unfortunate Traveller* (ii. 222; see l. 122 n. on 'put up our pipes'). The phrase also echoes two of Romeo's speeches in the orchard scene (2.1.151, 211), as Levin first pointed out (p. 52).

151 **Catling** i.e. Catgut for a stringed instrument (*OED* 2, first illustration). Jowett changes this name to Matthew Minikin,

PETER Prates. What say you, Hugh Rebec?

SECOND MUSICIAN I say 'silver sound' because musicians sound for silver.

PETER Prates too. What say you, James Soundpost?

THIRD MUSICIAN Faith, I know not what to say.

PETER O, I cry you mercy, you are the singer. I will say for you. It is 'music with her silver sound' because musicians have no gold for sounding.

Then music with her silver sound
With speedy help doth lend redress. *Exit*

FIRST MUSICIAN What a pestilent knave is this same!

SECOND MUSICIAN Hang him, jack! Come, we'll in here, tarry for the mourners, and stay dinner. *Exeunt*

5.1 *Enter Romeo*

ROMEO

If I may trust the flattering truth of sleep,

154, 157 Prates] Q2; Pret(t)ie Q1 166 *Exeunt*] Q1; *Exit.* Q2
5.1.1 truth] Q2; Eye Q1

the epithet which Q1 assigns to the Second Musician. His argument is based on a single definition of *catling* (a small lute-string, inappropriate as a fiddler's name); it seems to over-refine the word and Q2.

154, 157 **Prates** idle chatter. Peter's clipped expression, verb without pronoun, suits his tone as he becomes more and more surly (see Abbott 402 on the ellipsis). Although some commentators prefer Q1's 'Pret(t)ie', assuming that Q2 misprints 'Pratie', approval or irony seems out of character in this dialogue.

154 **Rebec** An early type of fiddle with three strings. Peter may be quibbling on *Hugh*/you.

157 **Soundpost** *OED* cites the name as its first illustration for 'a small peg of wood fixed beneath the bridge of a violin or similar instrument, serving as a support for the belly and as a connecting part between this and the back'.

159 **cry you mercy** beg your pardon (*OED sb.* 3), a mock-apology for asking the singer to speak

161 **sounding** (a) playing music, (b) jingling

163 **redress** relief (*OED sb.* 2a). In her analysis of this episode, J. Hartwig points out that its musical emphasis and concluding riddle suggest an approved cure for melancholy which could affect audience response to events in 4.4 and 5.1 (*Shakespeare's Analogical Scene* (Lincoln, Nebr., and London, 1983), pp. 84–90). Sternfeld also maintains that the dialogue between Peter and the Musicians has two levels, and that one calls to mind established humanist theories about the elevating powers of music (pp. 100–1).

164 **pestilent** *OED a.* 4, first illustration of 'troublesome'.

165 **jack** rude fellow (cf. 2.3.142 and n., and 3.1.11)

166 **stay** wait for (cf. 2.4.35)

5.1–5.2 The narrative is slightly recast as the play reaches its climax: it centres not only on the accidents which miscarry news of Juliet, but also on Romeo's psychological state before and after he receives the report. In the sources, his expression is highly rhetorical and his preparation for suicide deliberate. In the play, his recollections of a dream and of the Apothecary's shop, and his impetuous decision, create a more complex impression of this protagonist immediately before he dies.

1–9 **If I may . . . emperor** J. W. Hale noticed a parallel with Chaucer's *Troilus and*

My dreams presage some joyful news at hand.
My bosom's lord sits lightly in his throne,
And all this day an unaccustomed spirit
Lifts me above the ground with cheerful thoughts.
I dreamt my lady came and found me dead—
Strange dream that gives a dead man leave to think!—
And breathed such life with kisses in my lips
That I revived and was an emperor.
Ah me, how sweet is love itself possessed,
When but love's shadows are so rich in joy.

Enter Romeo's man Balthazar

News from Verona! How now, Balthazar?
Dost thou not bring me letters from the Friar?
How doth my lady? Is my father well?
How doth my lady Juliet? That I ask again,
For nothing can be ill if she be well.

3 lord] Q2 (L.), Q1   11.1 *Enter . . . Balthazar*] Q2 (*Enter* Romeos man.); *Enter Balthasar his man booted.* Q1   15 doth my lady Juliet] Q2; fares my *Iuliet* Q1

Criseyde 5.1163–9, where Troilus has a delusive dream of good fortune ('Chaucer and Shakespeare', *Quarterly Review*, 134 (1873), 252–3); Earl points out that Petrarch used this topos in *Rime* 33 and again in 279 (111). Like Juliet at 3.5.55–6, Romeo inverts the topos (see n.).

1 **flattering** (a) encouraging with hopeful signs, (b) delusive. The second definition makes *flattering truth* an oxymoron which represents manifestations of dream as both illusive and genuine (cf. Sonnet 87.13–14 or *Shrew* Ind. 1.42). The contradictory views were (and are) widely known; Evans notes two proverbs on illusive dreams and one on the authentic morning variety. In the play 1.4 includes both Romeo's premonitory dream and Mercutio's exposition on 'vain fantasy'.

3 **bosom's lord . . . throne** Either love sits cheerfully in his heart (cf. *Twelfth Night* 1.1.36–8), or his heart sits cheerfully in his body. As Steevens remarks, 5.3.88–90 provides a gloss for this passage. Dent suggests a comparison of ll. 2–5 with 'A lightening (lightning) before death' (L277).

8 **breathed . . . lips** Eighteenth-century commentators discovered a parallel with Marlowe's *Hero and Leander* 2.3, 'He kissed her, and breathed life into her lips'. (See earlier comparison, 3.2.8–9 n.)

10 **possessed** A word with sexual implications, used earlier by Juliet (see 3.2.27 and 26 n.).

11 **shadows** Referring to his dream, also connotes ephemera and reflected or delusory images.

11.1 ***Enter . . . Balthazar*** Q1's direction specifies that Balthazar enters '*booted*', as if he has come from riding; prompt books do not make a special point of the boots.

12 **Balthazar** (accented on first and third syllables)

15 **How . . . again** Most editors emend Q2's hypermetrical line: either they assume that the printer accidentally duplicated *lady* from the previous line and omit that word; or they argue that the compositor's error extends to the verb and substitute Q1's 'How fares my *Iuliet*?' (see Williams and Jowett). Since Romeo deliberately repeats the question, however, the elaboration and extra poetic foot may have manuscript authority to register the intense tone of his voice.

16–17 **nothing . . . ill** Dent compares Balthazar's response with 'He is well

BALTHAZAR
Then she is well, and nothing can be ill.
Her body sleeps in Capels' monument,
And her immortal part with angels lives.
I saw her laid low in her kindred's vault,
And presently took post to tell it you.
O, pardon me for bringing these ill news,
Since you did leave it for my office, sir.

ROMEO
Is it e'en so? Then I deny you stars!—
Thou knowest my lodging. Get me ink and paper,
And hire post-horses. I will hence tonight.

BALTHAZAR
I do beseech you, sir, have patience.
Your looks are pale and wild, and do import
Some misadventure.

ROMEO
Tush, thou art deceived.
Leave me, and do the thing I bid thee do.
Hast thou no letters to me from the Friar?

BALTHAZAR
No, my good lord.

24 e'en] Q2 (in), Q1, Q3 (euen) deny] Q2; defie Q1 you] Q2; my Q1

since he is in heaven' (H347), cited by Friar Laurence at 4.4.102.

18 **Capels' monument** i.e. the Capulet family's sepulchre (*OED sb.* 1). Q2's '*Capels*' could be a singular or plural possessive, or even a proper noun used as an adjective (Abbott 22). On the abbreviated form of the name, see 3.1.2 n.

21 **presently** immediately
took post travelled as quickly as possible by post-horse (*OED sb.*[2] 8i, first illustration; see l. 26 and cf. 5.3.273)

24 **e'en** Q2 has '*in*', a rare spelling which may indicate unstressed Elizabethan pronunciation (Hosley).
deny The familiar reading here is 'defy', adopted from Q1 and supported by lines from Brooke which occur in an earlier context (1328, 1347). Since editors cannot dismiss *deny* as a printer's error, they argue its inappropriateness in terms of theme and tone (see Williams for the most detailed commentary). Only McKerrow and a few others see no reason to abandon Q2. *OED* strengthens the minority position by defining both words as 'repudiate' or 'renounce' (cf. *deny v.* 4a and *defy v.*[1] 1b, 5). D. Atkinson gives additional support for *deny* ('*Romeo and Juliet* V.i.24', *N&Q*, NS 35 (1988), 49–52).

25–6 **ink and paper . . . post-horses** Brooke supplies the same writing materials but only one *post-horse*, i.e. a horse kept at an inn or some other house for the use of travellers (2604, 2612).

27 **patience** (three syllables)

28 **import** portend

32 **No . . . lord** Q2 prints Balthazar's exit after his last line, awkward timing because Romeo continues to address him.

ROMEO No matter. Get thee gone,
And hire those horses. I'll be with thee straight.
Exit Balthazar
Well, Juliet, I will lie with thee tonight.
Let's see for means. O mischief, thou art swift
To enter in the thoughts of desperate men.
I do remember an apothecary,
And hereabouts a dwells, which late I noted,
In tattered weeds, with overwhelming brows,
Culling of simples. Meagre were his looks,
Sharp misery had worn him to the bones;
And in his needy shop a tortoise hung,
An alligator stuffed, and other skins
Of ill-shaped fishes; and about his shelves
A beggarly account of empty boxes,
Green earthen pots, bladders, and musty seeds,
Remnants of packthread, and old cakes of roses
Were thinly scattered to make up a show.
Noting this penury, to myself I said,

33.1 *Exit Balthazar*] Q1; *Exit.* Q2 (*after* 'Lord', *l.* 32); *Exit Man.* F (*as* Q2)

34 **lie with** This expression, referring to the posture of both love and death, reintroduces the leitmotiv of death as Juliet's bridegroom (see 1.4.247–8 n. and cf. 3.2.137, 3.5.200–1, and 4.4.61–5). The closing scenes will finally realize this verbal theme as part of their action.

35 **see for** try to find (*OED v.* 19a)

37–48 **I do . . . show** A speech elaborating Brooke's sketch of the shop (2567–70).

38 **a** he (see 1.3.42 n.)

39 **weeds** clothing

overwhelming prominent. This gloss is based on context, because l. 39 provides the only example of the usage. (*OED ppl. a.* 2 defines *overwhelming* here as 'overhanging'.)

40 **Culling of simples** selecting herbs or other plants used for medical purposes (see Abbott 178 for the grammatical construction, *of* following a verbal noun). As Evans notes, Romeo's image of the Apothecary reflects Friar Laurence to strongly ironic effect.

42–8 **a tortoise . . . show** Evidence from Shakespeare's period and later indicates that the Apothecary attempts to offer a typical *show*. For instance, Malone cites this passage from Nashe's *Have with You to Saffron-walden*: 'the next rat he seized on he made an anatomy of, . . . and after hanged her over his head in his study, instead of an apothecary's crocodile, or dried alligator' (iii. 67). The items on display represent either medicinal use (e.g. the reptile and fish remains) or other non-perishable commodities sold in this kind of shop. They are also twisted versions of Petrarchan conceits.

45 **account** number

46 **Green earthen pots** Halliwell quotes a letter written in 1594 which refers to green clay pots used for drinking (see Furness).

bladders These may come from plants, where they contain seeds, or from animals.

47 **cakes of roses** preparations of rose-petals in the forms of *cakes*, used as perfume, etc. (see *OED*, *rose-cake*, 1). Like the 'musty seeds' in l. 46, they no longer have any purpose.

'An if a man did need a poison now,
Whose sale is present death in Mantua,
Here lives a caitiff wretch would sell it him'.
O, this same thought did but forerun my need,
And this same needy man must sell it me.
As I remember, this should be the house.
Being holy-day, the beggar's shop is shut.
What ho, Apothecary!

Enter the Apothecary

APOTHECARY Who calls so loud?

ROMEO

Come hither, man. I see that thou art poor.
Hold, there is forty ducats. Let me have
A dram of poison, such soon-speeding gear
As will disperse itself through all the veins,

57 *Enter the Apothecary*] Q1, F; *not in* Q2

50–2 **'An if . . . him'** Evans deduces that Romeo has entertained thoughts of suicide during his banishment. *An if* = if indeed (Abbott 105).

51 **present** immediate. Laws on the Continent made it illegal to sell poison (see Furness). In Brooke, too, Mantua's law forbids the Apothecary from trafficking in poison. At the end of the poem, 'Th' apothecary high is hanged by the throat' (2574, 2993).

52 **caitiff** miserable

wretch . . . him This line seems especially concentrated because it omits the nominative 'who' and uses an abbreviated form of the dative (Abbott 399, 220).

56 **Being holy-day . . . shut** Both Q2 and Q1 include this observation, which Shakespeare has added to the narrative without specifying a *holy-day*. Clearly the Apothecary could not sit idly at his door, as he does in Brooke, during Romeo's soliloquy. At the same time the religious detail heightens the unlawfulness of the following exchange.

57 ***Enter the Apothecary*** In addition to a direction, Romeo's line in Q1 calls for the entrance: 'What ho Apothecarie, come forth I say'.

59 **there is** Common before a plural subject in Shakespeare (Abbott 335).

ducats Gold coins of differing values current in most European countries at this time. The line substitutes *forty ducats* for 'fifty crowns of gold' in Brooke (2577) and fifty ducats in Painter (115). Romeo's *forty ducats* seem to represent a considerable sum. Gibbons compares *Errors* 4.3.83, 96, where the Courtesan claims this amount as the value of a diamond ring and says 'forty ducats is too much to lose'; he suggests that Shakespeare remembers *Errors* here, preferring the 'memorable effect' of l. 96 (which ends a couplet and the scene) to the calculations of his sources. (Romeo in Q1 offers only 'twentie duckates'.)

59–61 **Let me . . . veins** Dent suggests a proverbial connection, 'Poison disperses itself into every vein' (P457.1).

60 **A dram** one eighth of a fluid ounce

soon-speeding gear This expression allows more than one interpretation of the quickly acting *gear* or substance (*OED sb.* 10a): *speeding* makes the alliterative phrase very emphatic if it means 'swiftly moving' (cf. Brooke 2585, 'the speeding gear'); it may also signify 'successful' and 'fatal' in grim wordplay (although *OED ppl. a.* 3a and *v.* 9c both cite their first examples for 'fatal' slightly later).

61 **disperse itself** spread (*OED v.* 6b, first example). Gibbons and Evans both compare Daniel's *Rosamond* 603, 'The poison soon dispersed through all my veins'.

That the life-weary taker may fall dead,
And that the trunk may be discharged of breath
As violently as hasty powder fired
Doth hurry from the fatal cannon's womb.

APOTHECARY

Such mortal drugs I have, but Mantua's law
Is death to any he that utters them.

ROMEO

Art thou so bare and full of wretchedness,
And fearest to die? Famine is in thy cheeks,
Need and oppression starveth in thy eyes,
Contempt and beggary hangs upon thy back.
The world is not thy friend, nor the world's law;
The world affords no law to make thee rich.
Then be not poor, but break it and take this.

APOTHECARY

My poverty, but not my will, consents.

ROMEO

I pray thy poverty and not thy will.

70 starveth] Q2; stareth ROWE 1714   76 pray] Q2; pay Q1

62 **That** so that (Abbott 283)

63–5 **trunk . . . womb** This conceit reintroduces imagery from 2.5.9–11 and 3.3.131–3. As Evans notes, *trunk* = (a) body, (b) cylindrical case to discharge explosives (*OED sb.* 11).

67 **he** man (Abbott 224)

utters sells (*OED v.*[1] 1a)

68–71 **Art thou . . . back** With his sketch of the Apothecary, Romeo not only epitomizes misery in general but draws a bleak caricature of the suffering lover in Petrarchan terms: unkempt, pale, lean, and *full of wretchedness*. Together the two figures reflect the conventions of love-poetry in unconventional ways. According to his man, Romeo appears like the typical distraught lover: 'Your looks are pale and wild' (l. 28).

70 **oppression** (a) distress, (b) injustice. Evans reads *Need and oppression* as hendiadys, 'oppressive poverty', citing Franz 673 (c) and comparing 'Contempt and beggary' (= contemptible beggarliness) in l. 71.

starveth Thomas Otway changed *starveth* to 'stareth' in his adaptation, *Caius Marius* (1679); Rowe adopted the emendation. As Malone points out, however, Q1 supports Q2's *starveth*, which has associations of hunger, cold, poverty, and death. The Apothecary's eyes reflect both effects and cause. (See Abbott 334 on the third person plural in *-th*.)

71 **Contempt . . . back** The audience may hear *Contempt and beggary* as two more illustrations of the Apothecary's miserable state or as hendiadys (see l. 70 n. on 'oppression'). The rest of the line alludes to his emblematic 'tattered weeds' (l. 39). (See Abbott 336 on the inflexion in *s* with two singular nouns as subject.)

74 **it** i.e. the law

76 **pray** entreat. Almost all editors adopt Q1's 'pay', assuming a Q2 printing error because *pray* appears to make no sense. As McKerrow notes, however, Q1 may have mistaken *pray* for 'pay', and 'l. 74 is definitely a prayer'. Romeo's previous speech, with the rhetoric and measures of a sermon, seems to end as a petition; his stichomythic exchange with the Apothecary may counterpoint *pray* and 'consents' (cf. 1.4.217, 'They pray, grant thou').

APOTHECARY

Put this in any liquid thing you will
And drink it off; and if you had the strength
Of twenty men, it would dispatch you straight.

ROMEO

There is thy gold, worse poison to men's souls,
Doing more murder in this loathsome world,
Than these poor compounds that thou mayst not sell.
I sell thee poison; thou hast sold me none.
Farewell, buy food, and get thyself in flesh.
Exit Apothecary
Come, cordial and not poison, go with me
To Juliet's grave, for there must I use thee. *Exit*

5.2 *Enter Friar John*

FRIAR JOHN

Holy Franciscan friar, brother, ho!
Enter Friar Laurence

FRIAR LAURENCE

This same should be the voice of Friar John.—
Welcome from Mantua! What says Romeo?
Or if his mind be writ, give me his letter.

84.1–86 *Exit Apothecary . . . Exit*| WILSON–DUTHIE; *Exeunt. (at scene-end)* Q
5.2.0.1 *Enter Friar John*| Q1; *Enter Frier* Iohn *to Frier* Lawrence. Q2 1.1 *Enter Friar Laurence*| Q2 (*Enter* Lawrence.)

77–9 **Put . . . straight** A speech deriving from Brooke 2585–8.

82 **compounds** compounded drugs, i.e. poisons made from the 'simples' mentioned above (see l. 40 and n.; *OED sb.*[1] 2a gives *Cymbeline* as its first illustration)

84 **get . . . flesh** grow plump (*OED sb.* 3)

85 **cordial** substance which invigorates or comforts the heart. The antithesis *cordial/poison* will become more complex and prominent in the last scene (see 5.3.119–20 n.).

84.1–86 ***Exit Apothecary . . . Exit*** Both Q2 and Q1 print *Exeunt* at Romeo's last line, a direction which suggests departure by different routes. Adjusting the text, some editions (like the present one) give the Apothecary an earlier departure after l. 84. The theatre favours the editors' arrangement.

5.2.0.1, 1.1 ***Enter . . . Laurence*** Q2's duplicate directions (see Collation) and the opening dialogue suggest that the friars enter from opposite sides of the stage to meet at the centre. In almost all editions the first direction appears in its shorter Q1 format, '*Enter Frier Iohn*'. (Q1 has no entry for Friar Laurence.) Hosley assumes that a bookkeeper corrected Shakespeare's manuscript by adding the entrance for Friar Laurence, then forgot to cut the last three words of the first direction. In the theatre staging has been variously managed: the actors enter to each other; one or both may speak 'without' before appearing; one may be discovered before the other is heard or seen; they have even performed on different sides of a stage-curtain, one in front and the other pushing his head through the middle.

FRIAR JOHN

Going to find a barefoot brother out,
One of our order to associate me,
Here in this city visiting the sick,
And finding him, the searchers of the town,
Suspecting that we both were in a house
Where the infectious pestilence did reign,
Sealed up the doors and would not let us forth,
So that my speed to Mantua there was stayed.

FRIAR LAURENCE

Who bare my letter then to Romeo?

FRIAR JOHN

I could not send it—here it is again—
Nor get a messenger to bring it thee,
So fearful were they of infection.

FRIAR LAURENCE

Unhappy fortune! By my brotherhood,
The letter was not nice but full of charge,
Of dear import, and the neglecting it
May do much danger. Friar John, go hence;
Get me an iron crow, and bring it straight
Unto my cell.

FRIAR JOHN Brother, I'll go and bring it thee. *Exit*

FRIAR LAURENCE

Now must I to the monument alone;
Within this three hours will fair Juliet wake.

5–8 **Going . . . him** The elliptical syntax, lacking a subject for *going* and *finding*, suggests a speaker in haste to tell his story (see Abbott 401). In Brooke the narrator gives this information at greater length (2485–99).

5 **a barefoot brother** i.e. another Franciscan friar, either literally *barefoot* or sandalled.

6 **associate** accompany (*OED v.* 5a). Friars travelled in pairs as a check on each other's conduct. (Brooke 2488–92 describes what he calls this 'wonted guise'.)

8 **searchers** persons appointed to view dead bodies and report the causes of death (*OED* 2e, first illustration)

9 **house** a private dwelling (where the second friar had been 'visiting the sick' (l. 7)) or a residence for the Franciscan order (where Brooke and Painter locate the infection)

11 **Sealed . . . doors** i.e. to enforce quarantine. By the end of the sixteenth century this practice happened during outbreaks of the plague in London.

12 **my speed . . . stayed** *Speed*, meaning the journey to Mantua, combines familiar denotations of success, rapidity, and promptness; *stayed*, balancing *speed* in antithesis, frustrates all its senses.

18 **nice . . . charge** trivial . . . importance (*OED a.* 10b, first illustration; *sb.* 9a)

19 **dear** precious (*OED a.*[1] 4b, first example of 'precious in import or significance')

20 **danger** harm (*OED sb.* 6)

21 **crow** crowbar

She will beshrew me much that Romeo
Hath had no notice of these accidents;
But I will write again to Mantua,
And keep her at my cell till Romeo come—
Poor living corse, closed in a dead man's tomb. *Exit*

5.3 *Enter Paris and his Page*

PARIS
Give me thy torch, boy—hence and stand aloof—
Yet put it out, for I would not be seen.
Under yon yew trees lay thee all along,
Holding thy ear close to the hollow ground;
So shall no foot upon the churchyard tread,
Being loose, unfirm with digging up of graves,
But thou shalt hear it. Whistle then to me
As signal that thou hearest something approach.
Give me those flowers. Do as I bid thee, go.

PAGE (*aside*)
I am almost afraid to stand alone
Here in the churchyard, yet I will adventure.
He retires

5.3.3 yew trees] Q1 (Ew-tree); young Trees Q2 10 (*aside*) | CAPELL; *not in* Q 11.1 *He retires*] CAPELL (*retires.*); *Exit.* F2; *not in* Q

25 **beshrew me much** lay very great blame on me (*OED v.* 3)

26 **accidents** 'events' (*OED sb.* 1a); but the word also connotes unexpected incidents and unfortunate happenings.

5.3 In this last, long scene of catastrophe and dénouement Paris's role is an invention which the Elizabethan audience could not have predicted in any detail. It has a variety of effects. At the start Paris creates ambience for the scene; with his rituals, challenge, and death he adds a dimension to the tragedy as a whole and to the characterization of Romeo in particular.

0.1 ***Enter . . . Page*** Q2's dialogue will indicate that Paris and his Page carry a torch and flowers (ll. 1, 9); Q1's direction specifies '*flowers and sweete water*' or liquid scent (*OED* 2a; see l. 14). Prompt books call for a torch (sometimes a lantern) and flowers.

1 **aloof** away at some distance. Paris's opening lines fix him in the posture of a lovelorn gallant with flowers, torch, and a penchant for solitude.

3 **yew trees** Q2 has 'young Trees', inappropriate to setting and context: *yew trees*, which symbolize mourning, are still traditionally planted in churchyards. Originally Pope's, the emendation derives from Q1. (The same error and emendation occur at l. 137.) Williams reconstructs the manuscript spelling 'yeug' (cf. *OED* 'yeugh') as the source of the printing error.

lay . . . along stretch at full length (*OED v.*[1] 46a)

8 **hearest** Another place where metre invites elision.

10 **stand** i.e. stay

11.1 ***He retires*** Neither Q2 nor Q1 has a direction to indicate how far the Page withdraws from Paris. F2's '*Exit.*' makes him leave the stage; Capell's '*retires.*' allows several interpretations

PARIS

Sweet flower, with flowers thy bridal bed I strew—
O woe, thy canopy is dust and stones!—
Which with sweet water nightly I will dew,
Or, wanting that, with tears distillèd by moans.
The obsequies that I for thee will keep
Nightly shall be to strew thy grave and weep.
The Page whistles
The boy gives warning, something doth approach.
What cursèd foot wanders this way tonight,
To cross my obsequies and true love's rite?
What, with a torch? Muffle me, night, a while.
He retires.
Enter Romeo and ⌈*Balthazar*⌉

17.1 *Page whistles*] Q2 (*Whistle Boy.*); *Boy whistles and calls.* My Lord. Q1 20 rite] Q2 (right); rites Q1 21.1 *He retires*] CAPELL (*retires.*); *not in* Q 21.2 ⌈*Balthazar*⌉] Q1; *Peter* Q2

(cf. ll. 21.1 and 44.1). In the theatre a character who does not exit from this scene finds a place to retreat on the set: behind a tree, at the gates of the tomb, on steps or a balcony, near a grille or wall.

12–17 **Sweet . . . weep** Paris makes this vow as a sestet woven from Petrarchan topoi that have occurred frequently in the play: he personifies the suffering lover, and his enactment of grief gives material form to the flowers, sweetness, and perhaps the tears of amatory verse. (Q1 has a different version, preferred and adapted by Pope and other early editors: six new lines after the first contain only one end-rhyme and almost no Petrarchan images; the fifth new line rhymes with the original first.)

12 **Sweet . . . strew** Q2 gives no direction at this point, where the dialogue tells the actor what to do. Q1, more explicit, says that '*Paris strewes the Tomb with flowers*'. In both texts Paris begins with the metaphor of a *bridal bed*, reintroducing the leitmotiv of death as Juliet's bridegroom which this scene will finally realize. Staging may reinforce the effect, if the position of the tomb corresponds to that of Juliet's bed in 4.3 and 4.4 (see 5.1.34 n. and 4.3.57.1 n.).

14 **sweet water** liquid scent (see 0.1 n.)

16 **obsequies** rites of remembrance (*OED*, *obsequy*², b)

20 **rite** Q2 has 'right', which *OED sb.*² calls an erroneous spelling of *rite*; Q1 and Pope print *rite(s)*. Although an audience may hear both homonyms, *rite* stands out because of 'obsequies' here and in l. 16.

21 **Muffle . . . a while** Gibbons notes the ironic parallel between Paris concealing himself here and Romeo 'bescreened in night' in 2.1: both situations, focused on Juliet, include a prototypical lover making observations in the dark about another character.

21.1 ***He retires*** No early text provides a direction to indicate how far Paris withdraws. Again Capell's '*retires.*' seems appropriate in its openness (cf. l. 11.1 n. and l. 44.1 n.).

21.2 ⌈***Balthazar***⌉ Although Q2 names *Balthazar* in the dialogue at 5.1.12 and the speech-prefix at 5.3.272, it prints 'Peter' in this direction and the speech-prefixes at 5.3.40 and 43. The inconsistency, not present in Q1, has been traced to two possible sources: either Shakespeare absent-mindedly used the name of Romeo's man from Brooke 2697 (servants called 'Peter' or the equivalent appear throughout the Romeo and Juliet narratives), or the names reflect Kemp's doubling of Peter and *Balthazar*.

ROMEO

Give me that mattock and the wrenching-iron.
Hold, take this letter. Early in the morning
See thou deliver it to my lord and father.
Give me the light. Upon thy life I charge thee,
Whate'er thou hearest or seest, stand all aloof,
And do not interrupt me in my course.
Why I descend into this bed of death
Is partly to behold my lady's face,
But chiefly to take thence from her dead finger
A precious ring, a ring that I must use
In dear employment. Therefore hence, be gone.
But if thou, jealous, dost return to pry
In what I farther shall intend to do,
By heaven, I will tear thee joint by joint,
And strew this hungry churchyard with thy limbs.
The time and my intents are savage-wild,
More fierce amd more inexorable far
Than empty tigers or the roaring sea.

[BALTHAZAR]

I will be gone, sir, and not trouble ye.

25 light.] Q3 (light;); light‸ Q2   40, 43 [BALTHAZAR]] Q1 (*Balt:*); *Pet<er>.* Q2

22 **Give . . . wrenching-iron** Again Q2's dialogue indicates the props required (see also ll. 23, 25); Q1's direction specifies '*a torch, a mattocke, and a crow of yron*'. *OED vbl. sb.* 3 cites the attributive use of *wrenching* as its first illustration (*wrenching-iron* = crowbar).

26 **stand all aloof** Gibbons points out that this wording emphasizes the correspondence with Paris and his Page (see l. 1 and n.).

31–2 **I must use | In dear employment** The ambiguous excuse plays on *dear* as (a) significant or precious in import, (b) costly, and on *employment* as (a) business, or (b) purpose (*OED* 2b). With Romeo's first view of Juliet a similar collocation of terms, 'Beauty too rich for use, for earth too dear', produced an even wider range of meanings (see 1.4.160 n.).

33 **jealous** suspicious (*OED a.* 5a)

33–4 **pry | In** *OED v.*[1] 2a gives the first instance of 'pry into' as 1629, even though this expression and *pry in* appear several times in Shakespeare.

34 **intend** as well as 'purpose', may mean 'direct my course' and 'endeavour' (*OED v.* 6a, 9).

36 **hungry churchyard** A striking contrast to Paris's scattered flowers, Romeo's conceit of scattered limbs in a *hungry churchyard* (elaborated in ll. 45–8) derives from the proverb 'Death devours all things' (Dent D138.1; cf. 2.5.7).

37 **intents** Probably 'frame of mind', although the ambiguous 'intend' three lines above suggests additional readings (see l. 34 n. and *OED sb.* 4, 3, 6a).

savage-wild A Shakespearian coinage (*OED*, *savage a.* 11); the repetition compounds vehemence.

38–9 **More fierce . . . roaring sea** Dent compares the proverbial 'As fierce as tiger(s)' (T287.1), which Romeo intensifies by making the tigers hungry; Gibbons finds parallels in *K. John* 3.1.186 and 2.1.452.

ROMEO

So shalt thou show me friendship. Take thou that.
Live and be prosperous, and farewell, good fellow.

[BALTHAZAR] (*aside*)

For all this same, I'll hide me hereabout;
His looks I fear, and his intents I doubt.

He retires.

[*Romeo opens the tomb*]

ROMEO

Thou detestable maw, thou womb of death,
Gorged with the dearest morsel of the earth,
Thus I enforce thy rotten jaws to open,
And in despite I'll cram thee with more food.

PARIS

This is that banished haughty Montague
That murdered my love's cousin, with which grief

43 (*aside*)] CAPELL; *not in* Q 44.1 *He retires*] HANMER (Balthasar *retires.*); *Exit.* F2; *not in* Q 44.2 [*Romeo . . . tomb*]] Q1; *not in* Q2

41 **friendship** may mean specifically 'a favour' (*OED* 3).
that i.e. money (perhaps in a purse). The farewell echoes Romeo's last exchange with the Apothecary in 5.1.

44 **fear . . . doubt** These verbs, virtually synonymous in context, each express both fear and suspicion (*OED*, *fear*, *v.* 8a, 9 and *doubt*, *v.* 5a, 6b).
intents See l. 37 n.

44.1 ***He retires*** More than once in this scene a character withdraws from the action, and early texts give little or no indication of when, how far, or where (cf. ll. 11.1 n. and 21.1 n.). Hanmer's direction, adopted here, specifies the appropriate timing but leaves distance and placement open to interpretation.

44.2 [***Romeo . . . tomb***] Q2 gives no direction, and the staging raises at least two questions: when does Romeo open the tomb, and what does he open? Editors suggest that he opens or begins to open the tomb at several points between ll. 44 and 83. Theatre historians and others speculate that the tomb was represented by a trap, the rear stage, a structure, or dialogue alone (see Thomson, '*Romeo and Juliet* on the Elizabethan Stage', 230–2). A. C. Dessen analyses the issues in Chapter 9 of *Recovering Shakespeare's Theatrical Vocabulary* (Cambridge, 1995), pp. 176–95. In prompt books timing varies as it has in editions. Usually Romeo forces open a door or gate after striking at it several times with a crowbar. The monument has been complex to various degrees, occupying the entire stage at more than one level in certain productions.

45 **detestable** (accented on first and third syllables)
maw . . . womb This imagery, extending the 'hungry churchyard' of Romeo's threat to Balthazar, refers primarily to organs of digestion (see l. 36 n.): *maw* = gullet or stomach, *womb* = stomach or bowels (*OED sb.* 1b, c). *Maw* could also be synonymous with *womb* in the more familiar sense, the two words making the line an oxymoron (*maw*, *sb.*[1] 2b).

46 **dearest morsel . . . earth** The wordplay echoes that of earlier speeches: *dearest* means both 'most cherished' and 'most costly'; *morsel*, not only a choice dish but a small piece, links Juliet with *earth* in all its contradictory implications (see 1.4.160 and n., 1.2.14–15 and n.).

47 **enforce** forcibly drive (*OED v.* 7a)

48 **despite** expresses malice, contempt, and defiance (*OED sb.* 2b), as Romeo force-feeds the already gorged tomb with himself.

It is supposèd the fair creature died,
And here is come to do some villainous shame
To the dead bodies. I will apprehend him.
He comes forward
Stop thy unhallowed toil, vile Montague!
Can vengeance be pursued further than death?
Condemnèd villain, I do apprehend thee.
Obey and go with me, for thou must die.

ROMEO
I must indeed, and therefore came I hither.
Good gentle youth, tempt not a desp'rate man.
Fly hence and leave me. Think upon these gone;
Let them affright thee. I beseech thee, youth,
Put not another sin upon my head
By urging me to fury. O, be gone!
By heaven, I love thee better than myself,
For I come hither armed against myself.
Stay not, be gone; live, and hereafter say
A madman's mercy bid thee run away.

PARIS
I do defy thy conjuration,
And apprehend thee for a felon here.

53.1 *He comes forward*] CAMBRIDGE (*Comes forward.*); *not in* Q 68 conjuration] CAPELL; commiration Q2; coniurations Q1; commisseration Q3; commination WILLIAMS (*conj.* Mommsen)

52–3 **villainous shame . . . dead bodies** Brooke's watchmen share Paris's distrust of activity near the tomb, suspecting abuse of dead bodies for witchcraft (2795–8; cf. Painter, 119).

53.1 ***He comes forward*** Paris may draw his sword as he advances. Prompt books are rarely specific on this matter.

55 **Can vengeance . . . death?** This challenge may have been suggested by Romeus's questions to the dead Tybalt in Brooke 2663–6 (Evans).

62 **Put . . . head** Shaheen identifies this as a common biblical expression.

68 **defy** (a) reject (*OED v.*[1] 5), (b) challenge
conjuration Q2 prints the unknown 'commiration'. Q3 (and F) have 'commisseration', metrically awkward but sensible; Q1 gives 'coniurations' (= solemn appeals), copied or adapted by most editors since Capell; Mommsen suggested 'commination' (= threatening; see *OED* etymology). Williams supports Mommsen primarily in terms of printing error: 'commiration' is an easy misreading of either 'coniuration' (minims) or 'commination' (*r* for *n*), but the latter seems the easier slip. Williams argues persuasively, pointing out that the word expresses Paris's view of Romeo's speech, but 'commination' had religious associations with divine punishment, strange in this context, that remain current. *Conjuration* better fits Paris's dismissal of Romeo: its necromantic definition, applied opprobriously (3b), picks up his earlier allusions to 'unhallowed' behaviour at ll. 52–4.

69 **felon** in addition to its obvious sense, may have non-legal implications: it meant 'a vile or wicked person' (*OED sb.*[1] 1).

ROMEO

Wilt thou provoke me? Then have at thee, boy!
They fight

[PAGE]

O Lord, they fight! I will go call the watch. *Exit*

PARIS

O, I am slain! If thou be merciful,
Open the tomb, lay me with Juliet. *He dies*

ROMEO

In faith, I will. Let me peruse this face.
Mercutio's kinsman, noble County Paris!
What said my man when my betossèd soul
Did not attend him as we rode? I think
He told me Paris should have married Juliet.
Said he not so? Or did I dream it so?
Or am I mad, hearing him talk of Juliet,
To think it was so? O, give me thy hand,
One writ with me in sour misfortune's book.
I'll bury thee in a triumphant grave.
A grave—O no, a lantern, slaughtered youth;

70.1 *They fight*] Q1; *not in* Q2 71 [PAGE]] Q1 (*Boy:*), Q4; *not in* Q2; *Pet*<*er*>. F *Exit*] CAPELL (*Exit* Page.); *not in* Q 73 *He dies*] THEOBALD (Dyes.); *not in* Q

70.1 ***They fight*** The text corroborates Soens's reconstruction of this encounter without daggers: Friar Laurence will discover only swords at the entrance of the tomb, and Juliet will find Romeo's dagger on his person (ll. 142, 169). Combined with other details of staging, this suggests that the pair fight with rapiers and torches (122 n. 7). In eighteenth-century performances Romeo threatened Paris with the crowbar before engaging in a duel, an 'attitude' which some observers considered ungentlemanly.

71 **O Lord . . . watch** Q2 prints l. 71 in italics, without a speech-prefix, and centred (cf. 3.1.89 and n.); Q1 and F assign it to a speaker (see Collation). According to Greg, a marginal insertion in the manuscript may have produced the Q2 anomaly (*Editorial Problem*, p. 61 n. 2); according to Williams, the line in copy may have lacked a speech-prefix and misled the compositor to read it as a direction of some sort. In Q1 this line follows the stage direction '*They fight*'.

75 **Mercutio's** As Spencer observes, this is the only reference to *Mercutio* after 3.1, the scene of his death.

78 **should** was to (Abbott 324)

80 **him** i.e. Paris (l. 73)

83 **triumphant** glorious (*OED a.* 3); also implies 'victorious' (Evans), as well as 'celebratory' (*a.* 1), 'gained by conquest' (2b), and 'exultant'. But *triumphant grave* is ironic, like 'triumphant prize' in Sonnet 151.10, 'as much the triumphant taker as the triumphantly taken' (Booth).

84 **lantern** (a) structure admitting light at the top of a building through pierced sides and glazed apertures, (b) *lanterne des morts* or tall, narrow construction like a minaret, sometimes lit by candles or torches in an upper room, located centrally in Continental cemeteries (M. Omert, 'Romeo's Lantern', *TLS*, 14–20 July 1989). Both definitions may come into play: the first, elaborated in the next lines, directs Romeo's focus once

For here lies Juliet, and her beauty makes
This vault a feasting presence full of light.
Death, lie thou there, by a dead man interred.
How oft, when men are at the point of death,
Have they been merry, which their keepers call
A light'ning before death. O, how may I
Call this a light'ning? O my love, my wife,
Death, that hath sucked the honey of thy breath,
Hath had no power yet upon thy beauty.
Thou art not conquered; beauty's ensign yet
Is crimson in thy lips and in thy cheeks,
And death's pale flag is not advancèd there.
Tybalt, liest thou there in thy bloody sheet?
O, what more favour can I do to thee
Than, with that hand that cut thy youth in twain,
To sunder his that was thine enemy?

again to Juliet as a radiant source of light ('lanterns of the dead' illuminated the dark only in a limited way, guiding funeral processions at night); the second pays tribute to both Paris and Juliet, viewing their burial-place as more imposing than an ordinary grave.

86 **vault** G. West notes that *vault* creates a bitter pun on 'lantern' in l. 84, enhancing a minor sense it had at the time in French, if not in English: 'the scutcheon, or closure of a timber vault, where the ends of the branches thereof do meet' (Cotgrave) (*ELN* 28 (1990), 33–4).
presence presence-chamber (*OED* 2c)

87 **Death . . . interred** This line gives the actor playing Romeo his cue to mime the conveyance of Paris into the tomb. Even here the character speaks in rhetorical terms, polyptoton: *Death* refers to Paris and *dead man* to Romeo himself, anticipating his suicide.

88–90 **How oft . . . death** Dent compares two proverbs, the first not established as authentic: 'When men are merriest death says "checkmate"' (M599.1), and 'A lightening (lightning) before death' (L277).

89 **keepers** suggests the jailer who looks after a prisoner condemned to die or the nurse who attends a deathbed (*OED sb.* 1e).

90 **A light'ning before death** *OED vbl. sb.*[2] b defines the phrase as 'that exhilaration or revival of the spirits which is supposed to occur in some instances just before death'. Although it gives this line as its first illustration, Dent identifies the proverb in 1584. Audiences also hear 'lightning', the complex metaphor first used by Juliet (see 2.1.162–3 and n.).

90–1 **how may I . . . light'ning?** The ambiguous *may*, probably signifying both 'can' and 'ought' (Abbott 307), allows Romeo to pose two questions in one. He asks rhetorically how he can conceive of this sensation as *A light'ning*, and also seems to consider how he should turn the experience into a metaphor.

92–115 **Death . . . death** Evans has the most detailed notes on this passage, which owes far more to contemporary poetry than to Brooke. Apparently two distinctive features originated in Daniel's *Rosamond*, 603–7 and 668–79 in particular: the irony of Romeo's observations about Juliet's lifelike appearance, and the reintroduced conceit of death as Juliet's lover. There are other correspondences with *Lucrece* 400–6 and Sidney's *Astrophil and Stella*, Sonnet 85.

96 **advancèd** raised

97 **sheet** i.e. winding-sheet (cf. 4.3.41–2)

98 **more** greater (Abbott 17)

Forgive me, cousin. Ah, dear Juliet,
Why art thou yet so fair? Shall I believe
That unsubstantial death is amorous,
And that the lean abhorrèd monster keeps
Thee here in dark to be his paramour?
For fear of that I still will stay with thee,
And never from this pallet of dim night
Depart again. Here, here will I remain
With worms that are thy chambermaids. O, here
Will I set up my everlasting rest,
And shake the yoke of inauspicious stars
From this world-wearied flesh. Eyes, look your last.

102–3 Shall I believe | That] THEOBALD; I will beleeue, | Shall I beleeue that Q2; O I beleeue that Q1 107 pallet] Q2; pallace Q3 108 Depart again. Here] Q4; Depart againe, come lye thou in my arme, | Heer's to thy health, where ere thou tumblest in. | O true Appothecarie! | Thy drugs are quicke. Thus with a kisse I die. | Depart againe, here Q2

101 **Forgive me, cousin** Romeo's address corresponds to Brooke 2660–70, where Romeus also refers to Juliet's *cousin* as his kinsman.

102 **Shall I believe** In Q2 l. 102 ends with the phrase 'I will beleeue', and l. 103, hypermetrical, begins with the phrase 'Shall I beleeue'. (Line 105 concludes with a question mark.) Editors agree that 'I will beleeue' represents a first shot which made its way into print. Q1's 'O I beleeue' either opens the possibility of the other reading as first shot (cf. Pope) or reflects a choice made in preparing an ambiguous part of the manuscript for performance.

103 **unsubstantial** *OED a.* 2a, first example for 'having no bodily or material substance'.

106 **still** always

107 **pallet** Q2 prints 'pallat', a common spelling for *pallet*, but most editors adopt Q3's 'pal(l)ace': they assume a simple misreading of *t* for *c* and prefer an image cluster centring on stately buildings (cf. 'lantern' in l. 84, 'presence' in l. 86); Williams suggests that the phrase 'depart from' seems more appropriate to a palace than to a *pallet*. Countering such views, Hosley argues that the image of a *pallet* 'supports the theme that Juliet's wedding bed is indeed her grave'; and R. L. Smallwood finds additional evidence for *pallet* in *K. John* 3.4.27, 'Arise forth from the couch of lasting night' ('*Romeo and Juliet* V.iii.107–8', *SQ* 26 (1975), 298–9). Both Smallwood and Shaheen notice a correspondence with Job 17: 13, 'Though I hope, *yet* the grave shall be mine house, *and* I shall make my bed in the dark'.

107–8 **night | Depart** Between '*pallat of dym night*' and '*Depart againe*', Q2 includes four lines duplicated and expanded in the rest of the speech. Like other duplications at l. 102, at the close of 2.1, and at the opening of 2.2, the lines seem to represent a first draft. The second line remains baffling, but Gibbons notes that 'tumblest in' may be a source for the shipwreck metaphor in ll. 117–18.

109–10 **With worms . . . rest** Shaheen compares with Job 17: 14 and Brooke 2366–8.

110 **set . . . rest** Romeo, anticipating death as repose, nevertheless echoes the wordplay of gambling and sexuality which this phrase introduced at 4.4.32 (see n.).

111–18 **shake . . . bark** With his last words Romeo attempts to command the three metaphors—stars, law, navigation—which he had used to express his misgivings at 1.4.104–11. Walter Whiter, an eighteenth-century commentator, first noticed that the conceits reappear in the same order (see *A Specimen of a Commentary on Shakespeare*, ed. A. Over and completed by M. Bell (1967), pp. 112–13).

112–20 **Eyes . . . die** Lines 112–16, which have no equivalents in Q1, specify the

Arms, take your last embrace. And lips, O you
The doors of breath, seal with a righteous kiss
A dateless bargain to engrossing death.
Come, bitter conduct, come, unsavoury guide,
Thou desperate pilot, now at once run on
The dashing rocks thy sea-sick weary bark.
Here's to my love!
He drinks the poison
O true Apothecary,
Thy drugs are quick. Thus with a kiss I die. *He falls*
Enter Friar Laurence with lantern, crow, and spade

119 *He . . . poison*] THEOBALD (*Drinks the poison.*); *not in* Q 120 *He falls*] Q1 (*Falls.*); *not in* Q2
120.1 *Enter . . . spade*] Q2 (*Entrer Frier with Lanthorne, Crowe, and Spade.*); *Enter Fryer with a Lanthorne.* Q1

actor's gestures as he prepares to drink the poison; ll. 117–20, which appear virtually the same in both texts, direct the suicide itself.

113–15 **lips . . . death** The legal metaphor is straightforward and the idea behind it commonplace in Shakespeare: *lips* = seal; *kiss* = imprint of the seal on a contract; sealing a *bargain* = confirming an agreement (cf. *Two Gentlemen* 2.2.7, *Venus* 511–12, Sonnet 142.7). The term and second party make this agreement less conventional: *dateless* means 'having no limit'; *engrossing* identifies *death* as a figure that observes legal protocol while monopolizing his trade.

116 **conduct** (a) guide, (b) document ensuring safe passage (*OED sb.*[1] 3, 2)

117–18 **Thou . . . bark** This imagery has parallels in Brooke (first sonnet 'To the Reader', 799–808, 1365–70, 1519–26), and also corresponds with Sidney's *Astrophil and Stella*, Sonnet 85.1–4.

118 **sea-sick** exhausted from travel at sea (*OED a.* 2, only illustration)

119 **Here's . . . love** J. MacIntyre believes that Juliet would have appeared in the festive clothes she wore during 1.4, enhancing the irony (' "One that Hath Two Gowns": Costume Change in Some Elizabethan Plays', *English Studies in Canada* 13 (1987), 15–16).

He . . . poison Neither the early texts nor Theobald's direction specify the drinking-vessel, but shortly Juliet will notice a cup in Romeo's hand (l. 161); Spencer thinks there may be stage business as Romeo transfers the poison from a vial. This toast clearly mirrors Juliet's at 4.3.57.

119–20 **true Apothecary . . . die** '[T]he apothecary's poison both heals and destroys. He is *true* not only because he has spoken the truth to Romeo in describing the poison's potency, but because he has been true to his calling in finding the salve for Romeo's ills. His drugs are not only speedy, but also *quick* in the sense of "life-giving" ' (Mahood, p. 72). Soon Juliet will repeat the sexually charged antithesis *quick/die* in 'die'/'restorative' (l. 166).

120 ***He falls*** Q1's direction allows the performer to decide the appropriate position and gestures for the character's last act. Line 155 suggests that Romeo *falls* across Juliet's body (see n.). In the eighteenth-century theatre David Garrick followed Thomas Otway and Theophilus Cibber by having Juliet awake after Romeo has taken the poison; in twentieth-century productions there have been echoes of this variation in the theatre and film. Garrick created a seventy-five-line dialogue for the lovers which intensified their pathos in productions over the next century. (See Introduction, 'Performance History'.)

120.1 ***crow*** crowbar (requested at 5.2.21)

FRIAR LAURENCE
Saint Francis be my speed! How oft tonight
Have my old feet stumbled at graves. Who's there?
BALTHAZAR
Here's one, a friend, and one that knows you well.
FRIAR LAURENCE
Bliss be upon you. Tell me, good my friend,
What torch is yon that vainly lends his light
To grubs and eyeless skulls? As I discern,
It burneth in the Capels' monument.
BALTHAZAR
It doth so, holy sir, and there's my master,
One that you love.
FRIAR LAURENCE Who is it?
BALTHAZAR Romeo.
FRIAR LAURENCE
How long hath he been there?
BALTHAZAR Full half an hour.
FRIAR LAURENCE
Go with me to the vault.
BALTHAZAR I dare not, sir.
My master knows not but I am gone hence,
And fearfully did menace me with death
If I did stay to look on his intents.
FRIAR LAURENCE
Stay then, I'll go alone. Fear comes upon me.
O, much I fear some ill unthrifty thing.
BALTHAZAR
As I did sleep under this yew tree here,
I dreamt my master and another fought,
And that my master slew him.
Friar Laurence moves towards the tomb

128–9 It . . . love] JOHNSON; *one line in* Q2 136 unthrifty] Q2; vnluckie Q3 137 yew tree] POPE (*following* Q1 *at the equivalent of l.* 3); yong tree Q2 139.1 *Friar . . . tomb*] MOWATT–WERSTINE; *not in* Q

121 **be my speed** help me (*OED sb.* 4b). Dent lists this once commonplace expression, Appendix B, SS17.

122 **stumbled at graves** Friar Laurence reports an evil omen (cf. 3 *Henry VI* (*True Tragedy*) 4.8.11–12, *Richard III* 3.4.84); he also seems to enact his own cautionary proverbs (see 2.2.94, 2.5.15, and nn.).

124 **good my friend** i.e. my good friend

136 **unthrifty** harmful (cf. Spenser's *Faerie Queene* 1.4.35, 'unthrifty scathe')

138–9 **I dreamt . . . him** Spencer, assuming that Balthazar watched Romeo kill Paris,

FRIAR LAURENCE Romeo!
Alack, alack, what blood is this which stains
The stony entrance of this sepulchre?
What mean these masterless and gory swords
To lie discoloured by this place of peace?
Romeo! O, pale! Who else? What, Paris too?
And steeped in blood? Ah, what an unkind hour
Is guilty of this lamentable chance!
Juliet rises
The lady stirs.

JULIET
O comfortable Friar, where is my lord?
I do remember well where I should be,
And there I am. Where is my Romeo?

FRIAR LAURENCE
I hear some noise. Lady, come from that nest
Of death, contagion, and unnatural sleep.
A greater power than we can contradict
Hath thwarted our intents. Come, come away.
Thy husband in thy bosom there lies dead,

146.1 *Juliet rises*] Q1; *not in* Q2 151 noise. Lady,] CAMBRIDGE; noyse Lady, Q2; Lady come foorth, I heare some noise at hand, Q1

suspects prevarication. Yet the staging, with Balthazar at a distance from the vault, implies that he has not seen the event clearly: he may have had a dream, or perhaps a dreamlike impression, of what occurred.

139 **him. . . . Romeo!** Staging is uncertain, since only one direction from Q1 specifies any business: '*Fryer stoops and lookes on the blood and weapons*'. Balthazar may withdraw or exit rather than 'stay': he should not seem to witness the dialogue between Friar Laurence and Juliet. Alternatively, Friar Laurence may advance; his exchange with Balthazar could have taken place near the 'yew trees' on a visibly obscure part of the stage. Garrick eliminated the ambiguity by removing Balthazar from the scene; later prompt books rarely indicate staging.

143 **To lie** i.e. lying (Abbott 356)

145 **unkind** (a) evil, (b) unnaturally cruel (*OED a.* 3c, 5); accented on first syllable

147 **The lady stirs** A cue, in both Q2 and Q1, for motion that signals awakening. Q1 adds the direction immediately after the equivalent of l. 146.

148 **comfortable** comforting (*OED a.* 6)

151 **I . . . noise** Many prompt books emphasize this sound effect through l. 167, usually as 'murmuring' which grows louder and louder.

155 **in thy bosom** Shakespeare seems to follow Brooke, where Romeus has fallen across Juliet's body; she, waking 'much amazed', asks 'where is my Romeus?'; Friar Lawrence 'with his finger showed his corpse outstretched, stiff, and cold' (2681–2, 2706–14). In the play, as Evans points out, the phrase *in thy bosom* places Romeo and implies that Juliet's questions 'where is my lord?', 'Where is my Romeo?' (ll. 148, 150) betray momentary bewilderment as she becomes conscious.

And Paris too. Come, I'll dispose of thee
Among a sisterhood of holy nuns.
Stay not to question, for the watch is coming.
Come, go, good Juliet. I dare no longer stay. *Exit*

JULIET
Go, get thee hence, for I will not away.
What's here? A cup closed in my true love's hand?
Poison, I see, hath been his timeless end.
O churl, drunk all, and left no friendly drop
To help me after? I will kiss thy lips.
Haply some poison yet doth hang on them
To make me die with a restorative.
She kisses him
Thy lips are warm.
Enter the Page and Watchmen

CHIEF WATCHMAN Lead, boy. Which way?

159 Come, go] Q2; come, come Q1 166.1 *She . . . him*] CAPELL (*kisses him.*); *not in* Q 167.1 *Enter . . . Watchmen*] Q2 (*Enter Boy and Watch.*); *Enter watch.* Q1 168 CHIEF WATCHMAN] Q2 (*Watch.*); *similarly at ll.* 172, 195, 199 (*Wat.*)

158–9 **Stay not . . . stay** Q1 has 'come, come', which leads Jowett to explain how Q2's *go* might be an error; *Come, go* makes sense, however, and the rhetorical construction supports Q2. In Brooke the Friar and Romeus's man Peter, who accompanied him to the vault, escape wordlessly in their fear (2762–4).

162 **timeless** untimely. If *timeless* also connotes 'eternal', it corresponds to 'dateless' in Romeo's last speech (l. 115), predating the first illustration for *OED a.* 2a by more than three decades.

163 **churl** Cf. Sonnet 1.12, 'And, tender churl, mak'st waste in niggarding', which also applies the familiar definition 'miser'. Shakespeare invented Juliet's attempt to die by Romeo's poison, not found in Q1.

164 **after** seems to function as both an adverb (= later) and a preposition used elliptically with *help* (= follow you).

165 **hang on** 'cling to', a definition first cited by *OED v.* 14b in 1639

166 **die . . . restorative** Juliet's antithesis echoes Romeo's at l. 120 (see ll. 119–20 n.).

166.1 ***She kisses him*** In Q2 l. 164 gives a cue for this gesture. Capell's direction specifies the timing.

167.1 ***Enter . . . Watchmen*** The early texts have watchmen enter here (Q1 may call for only one), suggesting that an actor appears to deliver the next line; editors who follow Capell omit the entrance and direct the actor to speak '*within*'. Despite its logic the change seems unnecessary: the actors may have appeared at some distance from Juliet. Nevertheless, prompt books since the eighteenth century either specify '*within*' or have the watchmen enter at another level.

168 **CHIEF WATCHMAN** As Jowett shows, speech-prefixes for the watch are inconsistent in the early texts. The speaker of this line in Q2, identified as '*Watch.*' or '*Wat.*' here and elsewhere (ll. 172, 195, 199), seems to become '*Chief. watch.*' at l. 183 and '*Chief watch.*' at l. 187; Q1 makes him '*Cap:*' or '*Capt:*' (for '*Captain*'), and F refers to him as '*Con.*' (for '*Constable*') as well as '*Watch.*'. Editors distinguish him as '*First*', '*Chief*', or '*Captain*'.

JULIET

Yea, noise? Then I'll be brief.
She takes Romeo's dagger
O happy dagger,
This is thy sheath. There rust, and let me die.
She stabs herself and falls

⌈PAGE⌉

This is the place, there where the torch doth burn.

CHIEF WATCHMAN

The ground is bloody. Search about the churchyard.
Go, some of you; whoe'er you find, attach.
Exeunt some Watchmen
Pitiful sight! Here lies the County slain,
And Juliet bleeding, warm and newly dead,
Who here hath lain this two days burièd.
Go, tell the Prince. Run to the Capulets,
Raise up the Montagues. Some others, search.
Exeunt other Watchmen
We see the ground whereon these woes do lie,
But the true ground of all these piteous woes
We cannot without circumstance descry.
Enter Watchmen with Balthazar

169 *She . . . dagger*] CAPELL (*taking* Romeo's.); *not in* Q 170 rust] Q2; Rest Q1 170.1 *She . . . falls*] Q1; *not in* Q2; *Kils herselfe.* F 171 ⌈PAGE⌉] Q4, F (*Boy.*); *Watch boy.* Q2 173.1 *Exeunt . . . Watchmen*] HANMER (*Exeunt some of the Watch.*); *not in* Q 178.1 *Exeunt . . . Watchmen*] CAPELL (*Exeunt other Watch.*); *not in* Q 181.1 *Enter . . . Balthazar*] ROWE (*Enter some of the Watch with* Romeo's *Man.*); *Enter one with Romets Man.* Q1; *Enter Romeo's man.* Q2

169 **happy dagger** *Happy* implies that the *dagger* is not only appropriate for the task at hand but also lucky as an omen and fortuitous in its discovery (*OED a.* 1; cf. 3.5.115 and n.). Yet the *dagger* in its spoken and material forms has most impact as part of the sexual wordplay in Juliet's last lines.

170 **rust** Recent editors favour Q2 *rust*, whereas earlier commentators preferred Q1 'Rest'; both Williams and Gibbons defend the more unusual verb in its context (see also Williams's argument in 'A Note on "Romeo and Juliet" V.iii.170', *N&Q* 207 (1962), 332–3).

170.1 ***She . . . falls*** Typically Q2's dialogue indicates the key gestures for this suicide; Q1's direction also leaves much to the actor's judgement. Juliet may take the dagger and use it while she speaks ll. 169–70 or when she stops speaking. After her death Q1 repeats '*Enter watch.*', indicating that these actors may now come forward. Some acting editions and many productions have ended the tragedy here.

173 **attach** arrest

173.1, 178.1 ***Exeunt . . . Watchmen*** In the early texts dialogue signals the timing. The directions added by Hanmer and Capell, unspecific about numbers, formalize the cues.

176 **this two days** This reference agrees (roughly) with Friar Laurence's time-scheme for the potion, although the end of the play has not always kept his schedule (see 4.1.105 n.).

178 **Raise up** (a) wake (*OED v.*[1] 4a), (b) rouse for action (especially attack or defence)

179–81 **We see . . . descry** A familiar

[SECOND] WATCHMAN
Here's Romeo's man. We found him in the churchyard.
CHIEF WATCHMAN
Hold him in safety till the Prince come hither.
Enter Friar Laurence and another Watchman
THIRD WATCHMAN
Here is a friar that trembles, sighs, and weeps.
We took this mattock and this spade from him
As he was coming from this churchyard's side.
CHIEF WATCHMAN
A great suspicion. Stay the friar too.
Enter the Prince with others
PRINCE
What misadventure is so early up,
That calls our person from our morning rest?
Enter Capulet and his Wife
CAPULET
What should it be that is so shrieked abroad?

182 [SECOND] WATCHMAN] ROWE (*similarly* Q1); *Watch<man>.* Q2 183.1 *Enter ... Watchman*] Q2 (*Enter Frier, and another Watchman.*); *Enter one with the Fryer.* Q1 186 churchyard's] Q2; Church-yard Q3 187 too] F; too too Q2 187.1 *with others*] Q1; *not in* Q2 189.1–202 *Enter Capulet and his Wife. . . .* CAPULET O] Q4, F; *Enter Capels. . . . Enter Capulet and his wife.* | *Ca.* O Q2 190 is so shrieked] DANIEL (*conj.* Cambridge); is so shrike Q2; they so shriek Q3

Shakespearian quibble on *ground* as 'earth' and 'reason' extends to *circumstance*, which refers to physical surroundings as well as attendant conditions or details (*OED sb.* 1a, 9a). According to Johnson, *circumstance* also signifies 'adjuncts of a fact which make it more or less criminal' (3).

181.1 ***Enter . . . Balthazar*** Editors and productions fill out Q2's inadequate direction with some version of Q1's (see Collation).

182 [SECOND] WATCHMAN Q2's sequence of speech-prefixes at ll. 182–4 ('*Watch.*', '*Chief. watch.*', '3. *Watch.*') supports Rowe's numbering. As Jowett explains, Q1 also distinguishes this watchman (as '*1.*') from the Captain, but assigns the same speech-prefix to the watchman who accompanies Friar Laurence.

183 **safety** close custody (*OED* 2)

186 **this churchyard's side** Hoppe interprets as 'this side of the churchyard', treating *this churchyard's side* as a contraction which fits the metre. Until recently quite a few editors followed Q3 (or F).

187 **suspicion** ground of suspicion (*OED sb.* 1c, first illustration)

187.1 ***Enter . . . with others*** Q1's '*with others*' allows for citizens as well as attendants (see Hosley's n.).

189.1 ***Enter Capulet . . . Wife*** Q2 prints '*Enter Capels.*' here and '*Enter Capulet and his wife.*' at l. 201, a duplication interpreted in several ways: the first direction corrects the second, or the second, a bookkeeper's marginal note, clarifies the first; the second indicates that Capulet and his Wife enter the tomb, returning from it at l. 207 (Evans); ll. 189.1–201 may represent a late addition (Jowett). Q1, which condenses this episode, does not repeat the direction. This edition adopts the emendation of Q4 and F.

190 **shrieked** Q2 prints 'shrike', apparently

CAPULET'S WIFE

O, the people in the street cry 'Romeo',
Some 'Juliet', and some 'Paris'; and all run
With open outcry toward our monument.

PRINCE

What fear is this which startles in your ears?

CHIEF WATCHMAN

Sovereign, here lies the County Paris slain,
And Romeo dead, and Juliet, dead before,
Warm and new killed.

PRINCE

Search, seek, and know how this foul murder comes.

CHIEF WATCHMAN

Here is a friar, and slaughtered Romeo's man,
With instruments upon them fit to open
These dead men's tombs.

CAPULET

O heavens! O wife, look how our daughter bleeds!
This dagger hath mista'en, for lo, his house
Is empty on the back of Montague,
And it mis-sheathèd in my daughter's bosom.

CAPULET'S WIFE

O me, this sight of death is as a bell
That warns my old age to a sepulchre.

Enter Montague

PRINCE

Come, Montague, for thou art early up
To see thy son and heir now early down.

194 your] Q2; our CAPELL (*conj.* Heath, Johnson) 199 slaughtered] Q3; Slaughter Q2 205 mis-sheathèd] F; missheathd Q2 209 early] Q1; earling Q2

a misreading of final *t* (rather than final *d*, the more common error noted in various editions after Cambridge).

191 **O** Editors from Pope to Hosley have omitted this interjection for various reasons (e.g. its effect on the metre or as a false start), but it seems appropriate in this distracted speech (cf. ll. 202, 206, 214).

194 **your** Many editors adopt the conjecture 'our', but Q2's *your* makes excellent sense: the Prince asks the cause of the sound which has frightened Capulet's Wife.

198 **comes** The present tense describes a continuing action (Abbott 346).

203 **mista'en** taken the wrong direction (*OED* v. 3)

his house i.e. its sheath

207 **warns** summons (*OED* v.[1] 7a)

209 **now early** Q2 has 'now earling', which

MONTAGUE
Alas, my liege, my wife is dead tonight;
Grief of my son's exile hath stopped her breath.
What further woe conspires against mine age?

PRINCE
Look, and thou shalt see.

MONTAGUE
O thou untaught! What manners is in this,
To press before thy father to a grave?

PRINCE
Seal up the mouth of outrage for a while,
Till we can clear these ambiguities
And know their spring, their head, their true descent;
And then will I be general of your woes,
And lead you even to death. Meantime forbear,

211 Grief . . . breath.] Q2; And yong *Benuolto* is deceased too: Q1

leads Williams to identify 'earling' as a dialect form that means 'giving earnest' or 'betrothing' (*OED* v.[1]). If accepted, this definition allows subtle paronomasia in ll. 208–9, a pun on words which sound nearly but not precisely alike. Even without a pun the Prince's short speech, with antithesis and diacope, is noticeably rhetorical. Jowett enhances this effect with Q1's reading 'more early', the choice of Wilson–Duthie and some previous editors; he points out that Q2's *now* could be a misreading of 'more'.

210 **is dead tonight** died last night (*OED* *a.* 1¶, *adv.* 3)

211 **of** on account of
exile (accented on second syllable)
stopped her breath At this point in Q1 Montague adds that Benvolio has died. Since neither death occurs in Brooke or Painter, each quarto heightens the sense of bereavement in the play's last minutes. Montague's report may also serve a theatrical purpose (with particular thoroughness in Q1). As Spencer notes, it seems to account for the absence of a character or two whose roles must have been doubled with others required by this scene.

214 **untaught** i.e. ignorant of good manners (Onions)
manners may be understood as singular (Abbott 333).

216 **Seal . . . outrage** The opening of this speech makes sense on at least two levels: *outrage* means not only 'outcry' (*OED* *sb.* 2b; cf. 1. 193), but also 'violent action', 'irrationality', and 'recklessness' (see 3.1.85 n.); *mouth* is an image of both the organ of sound and the tomb's entrance (cf. l. 47); *Seal up* may refer to lips (*v.*[1] 6b gives its first example as 1633, but cf. *2 Henry VI* (*Contention*) 1.2.89) and certainly refers to openings such as doors. In effect the line can function as a cue for either silence on the stage or concealment of the tableau within the monument. W. F. McNeir considers not only how but why this line may work as a direction to close the tomb ('The Closing of the Capulet Tomb', *Studia Neophilologica* 28 (1956), 3–8).

217 **ambiguities** uncertainties (*OED* 2)

220 **to death** may mean 'until *death*', 'to the uttermost', 'to *death* as punishment for the guilty', or perhaps 'to the cause of *death*'.

220–1 **forbear . . . patience** This advice seems like a variation on the proverb 'to bear and forbear', cited by *OED* v. 8c.

And let mischance be slave to patience.
Bring forth the parties of suspicion.

FRIAR LAURENCE

I am the greatest, able to do least,
Yet most suspected, as the time and place
Doth make against me, of this direful murder;
And here I stand, both to impeach and purge
Myself condemnèd and myself excused.

PRINCE

Then say at once what thou dost know in this.

FRIAR LAURENCE

I will be brief, for my short date of breath
Is not so long as is a tedious tale.
Romeo, there dead, was husband to that Juliet;
And she, there dead, that's Romeo's faithful wife.
I married them, and their stol'n marriage-day
Was Tybalt's doomsday, whose untimely death
Banished the new-made bridegroom from this city,
For whom, and not for Tybalt, Juliet pined.

232 that's] Q2; that Q1, Q4

222 **of suspicion** who are suspected (*OED sb.* 2e)

223–4 **greatest . . . least . . . most** Friar Laurence begins to explain himself with commonplace antitheses. (The term *greatest* refers to 'parties of suspicion' in l. 222.) By comparison with his other long speeches, however, this narrative one is relatively unadorned.

225 **make against** accuse. The auxiliary *Doth* is a third person plural in *-th* (Abbott 334).

226–7 **both to impeach . . . excused** Rhetoric heightens with the balancing of contradictory legal expressions and other figures (diacope, isocolon). Friar Laurence promises to accuse himself as he is guilty and exonerate himself as he is innocent.

228 **in** about (Abbott 162)

229–69 **I will be brief . . . law** The Friar's explanation, often shortened in performance, condenses an even longer passage in Brooke (2837–964; cf. Painter, 120–3); it appears in both Q2 and Q1, worded differently. As McKerrow points out, Q2 punctuates lightly from l. 246 on, and the cancel leaf of F1 in several places retains the lighter punctuation of Q3; yet the Folios and some editors add quite a few stops. Q2's punctuation allows a hint of breathlessness to relieve the formal proceedings. This edition follows it as closely as possible.

229 **short date of breath** i.e. little time remaining to live and speak. This phrase contributes to the antitheses in ll. 229–30, which Shaheen compares with Psalm 90: 9 and several verses in Brooke.

231–2 **Romeo . . . wife** The narrative begins with anaphora and a form of antimetabole. Enhancing the symmetry, most editors follow Q4 or Q1 and print 'that Romeo's' in l. 232. In the process they remove a verb that creates another kind of balance: *was husband/is . . . wife*.

236 **pined** *OED v.* 6, first example of the definitions 'To be consumed with longing; to languish with intense desire'. Here, *pined* must also mean 'languished' in the general sense.

You, to remove that siege of grief from her,
Betrothed and would have married her perforce
To County Paris. Then comes she to me,
And with wild looks bid me devise some mean
To rid her from this second marriage,
Or in my cell there would she kill herself.
Then gave I her—so tutored by my art—
A sleeping potion, which so took effect
As I intended, for it wrought on her
The form of death. Meantime I writ to Romeo
That he should hither come as this dire night
To help to take her from her borrowed grave,
Being the time the potion's force should cease.
But he which bore my letter, Friar John,
Was stayed by accident, and yesternight
Returned my letter back. Then all alone,
At the prefixèd hour of her waking,
Came I to take her from her kindred's vault,
Meaning to keep her closely at my cell
Till I conveniently could send to Romeo.
But when I came, some minute ere the time
Of her awakening, here untimely lay
The noble Paris and true Romeo dead.
She wakes, and I entreated her come forth
And bear this work of heaven with patience;
But then a noise did scare me from the tomb,
And she, too desperate, would not go with me,
But, as it seems, did violence on herself.

247 as] Q2; at KEIGHTLEY 258 awakening] Q2; awaking Q3

237 **remove** raise (*OED v.* 1b)
240, 282 **bid** bade
241 **rid** deliver
242 **there** The adverb works both as a demonstrative to emphasize place and unemphatically to indicate time (= at that juncture); Abbott 70 notes the interconnection.
243 **art** pharmaceutical skills in particular and learning in general
246 **form** likeness (*OED sb.* 2)
247 **as** 'perhaps means "*as* (he did come)"' (Abbott 114). McKerrow takes *as* for 'on', not uncommon before an adverbial phrase (*OED adv.* 34a; cf. *Caesar* 5.1.71).
250 **which** who (Abbott 265)
251 **accident** unforeseen events and mishap (cf. 5.2.26 and n.). The phrase *by accident* further implicates chance or fortune.
253 **hour** two syllables (Q2 prints 'hower')
255 **closely** secretly (*OED adv.* 3)
261 **bear . . . patience** Shaheen compares with Ecclesiasticus 2: 4, 'Whatsoever cometh unto thee, receive it patiently, and be patient in the change of thine affliction'.

All this I know, and to the marriage
Her Nurse is privy; and if aught in this
Miscarried by my fault, let my old life
Be sacrificed, some hour before his time,
Unto the rigour of severest law.

PRINCE

We still have known thee for a holy man.
Where's Romeo's man? What can he say to this?

BALTHAZAR

I brought my master news of Juliet's death,
And then in post he came from Mantua
To this same place, to this same monument.
This letter he early bid me give his father,
And threatened me with death, going in the vault,
If I departed not, and left him there.

PRINCE

Give me the letter; I will look on it.
Where is the County's page that raised the watch?
Sirrah, what made your master in this place?

PAGE

He came with flowers to strew his lady's grave,
And bid me stand aloof, and so I did.
Anon comes one with light to ope the tomb,
And by and by my master drew on him,
And then I ran away to call the watch.

265–8 All . . . time] *lineation as* POPE; Al . . . priuie: | And . . . fault, | Let . . . time, Q2
274 place, to . . . monument.] F (Gg1); ~. To . . . ~‸ Q2 281 PAGE] Q, F (gg3) (*Boy.*), F (Gg1)

265–8 **All . . . time** Q2 prints three unmetrical lines towards the centre of signature M1v. Because the rest of the speech is metrically regular, this edition (like all others) follows Pope's rearrangement.

266 **aught** Q2 has 'ought' (see 2.2.19 n.).

267 **Miscarried** (a) came to harm, misfortune, (b) went wrong (*OED* v. 1a; 4a cites *Coriolanus* as its first illustration)

268 **his** its (Abbott 228)

270 **still** always

271 **Where's . . . this?** From this line until the end, the dialogue of the early texts gives the actors their cues for stepping forward (cf. ll. 279–80, 291) and other gestures (see ll. 275, 278, 296–7).

273 **in post** in haste (*OED sb.*² 8d (a); cf. 5.1.21 and n. on 'took post')

275 **letter . . . father** The *er* in *letter* softens or disappears before the *h* in *he* (Abbott 465); *early* modifies *give* (see ll. 23–4, Abbott 420–1).

277 **not, . . . there** The ellipsis and Q2 punctuation (followed here) allow for two interpretations: (a) and did not leave him there, (b) and I left him there.

278 **on** at (Abbott 180)

280 **what . . . master** i.e. what was your master doing (*OED* v.¹ 58a)

282 **aloof** away at some distance. The Page quotes Paris verbatim (see l. 1).

284 **by and by** at once (*OED advb. phr.* 3a)

PRINCE

This letter doth make good the Friar's words,
Their course of love, the tidings of her death;
And here he writes that he did buy a poison
Of a poor 'pothecary, and therewithal
Came to this vault to die, and lie with Juliet.
Where be these enemies? Capulet, Montague,
See what a scourge is laid upon your hate,
That heaven finds means to kill your joys with love;
And I, for winking at your discords, too,
Have lost a brace of kinsmen. All are punished.

CAPULET

O brother Montague, give me thy hand.
This is my daughter's jointure, for no more
Can I demand.

MONTAGUE But I can give thee more;
For I will ray her statue in pure gold,
That whiles Verona by that name is known,

299 ray] Q2 (raie); raise Q4, F; erect Q1

289 **therewithal** (a) that being done, or (b) with that (poison) (*OED adv.* 3)

290 **die, and lie** The rhyme makes the play's last pun on love and death.

291 **be** This form of the verb typically follows a question and takes a plural subject (Abbott 299, 300). In l. 291 it heightens the assonance.

292–3 **hate . . . love** The Prince phrases his general conclusion in antithesis and paradox.

293 **kill your joys** As Evans's note indicates, the meaning of this phrase shifts with the literality of its key words between 'put your children to death' and 'destroy your happiness'.

294 **winking . . . discords** adapts 'Wink at small faults' (Dent F123).
too (a) too much, (b) also. The adverb can modify either l. 294 or l. 295 (see Abbott 73 for its various functions).

295 **brace** i.e. Mercutio and Paris (*OED sb.*[2] 15d gives first illustration as 1606)

297 **jointure** The handshake can be interpreted in two ways. If *jointure* means 'dowry' in the conventional sense (*OED sb.* 4c), Capulet makes a gesture of reconciliation on his daughter's behalf. If *jointure* refers to the bridegroom's settlement, which provides for the wife if the husband dies first, Capulet accepts a gesture of reconciliation from the bridegroom's family. The next line favours the second interpretation which, under the circumstances, adds irony to the handshake. (Q1 prints 'There is my daughters dowry: for now no more | Can I bestowe on her'.)

299–304 **I . . . enmity** Bate interprets the gold statues as symbolic of transformation, 'the sort of metamorphic release which Ovid usually gives his characters' (*Shakespeare and Ovid*, p. 178).

299 **ray** Most editors consider Q2 'raie' a misprint and adopt Q4, F 'raise', citing Brooke 3014 ('raise they high') and Q1 ('I will erect'); they define 'raise' as 'cause to be made'. Hosley represents the minority view adopted here, emphasizing that Montague proposes not an upright statue but a figure in high relief on a tomb or sarcophagus (see l. 303); he annotates *ray* as 'array, bedeck (i.e. gild)' (Mowat–Werstine compare Sonnet 55.1, 'gilded monuments'). The emendation is sensible; the original reading, less obvi-

There shall no figure at such rate be set
As that of true and faithful Juliet.

CAPULET

As rich shall Romeo's by his lady's lie,
Poor sacrifices of our enmity.

PRINCE

A glooming peace this morning with it brings;
    The sun for sorrow will not show his head.
Go hence to have more talk of these sad things;
    Some shall be pardoned and some punishèd.
For never was a story of more woe
Than this of Juliet and her Romeo. *Exeunt*

303 Romeo's by his lady's] Q2 (*Romeos* by his Ladies); *Romeo* by his Lady Q1, F (Gg1)
310 *Exeunt*] F (*Exeunt omnes.*); *not in* Q

ous, enhances the shining image connected with the motif of light central to the play.

300 **whiles** as long as (*OED conj.* 4b)

301 **no figure . . . set** Montague, referring to the gilded effigy, means that no other statue will be so highly esteemed (Evans compares Brooke 3017–20). Yet his image and diction (*figure*, *rate be set*) imply a more material kind of valuation.

302 **true and faithful** Collier identified this phrase as a tautology (see Furness); Elizabethans could have heard either the rhetorical figure pleonasmus or hendiadys ('truly faithful').

303–4 **As rich . . . enmity** F. Kermode in the Riverside edition recognizes the ambiguity in l. 304; he annotates *poor sacrifices of* as (a) pitiful victims of, (b) inadequate atonement for. (*OED sb.* 4a quotes this line as its first illustration for a thing of value lost or surrendered to an urgent claim.) As a result of this equivocal phrase, the couplet produces more than one rhetorical effect. Clearly *poor* is a quibble, forming an antithesis with *rich* in l. 303. Since *sacrifices* denotes 'propitiation', the phrase *sacrifices of our enmity* sounds like an oxymoron.

305 **glooming** *OED ppl. a.*[1] 2 defines *glooming* in this line as 'appearing dark' in a figurative sense. If *peace* is understood as a personification, *glooming* may also mean 'sullen' or 'frowning' and contribute to another oxymoron. Evans and Gibbons compare different passages in Spenser's *Faerie Queene* where *glooming* results in contradictory terms: 'Scarcely had *Phoebus* in the glooming east | Yet harnessed his fiery-footed team' (1.12.2), and 'A little glooming light, much like a shade' (1.1.14; *OED ppl. a.*[2] a cites *glooming* in this quotation to illustrate 'gleaming').

306 **sun . . . head** Gibbons cites Golding's Ovid 2.419, 'A day did pass without the sun', which marks the end of Phaëton's story (referred to at 3.2.1–4 and nn.); Evans suggests a link between the Ovidian line and the reference to Phoebus by Spenser (who was also using Ovid) in the quotation cited for the preceding note.

308 **Some . . . punishèd** This balanced line (anaphora, diacope, antithesis, alliteration) sums up twenty verses in Brooke (2985–3004) which mete out specific judgements for Juliet's nurse, Romeus's man, 'th' apothecary', and Friar Lawrence.

309–10 **For never was a story . . . Romeo** The closing couplet reconnects the dramatic narrative with the fictional accounts in which it originated.

310 ***Exeunt*** Q2 and Q1 print '*FINIS.*' after the last line of dialogue; F adds the stage direction.

An Excellent Conceited Tragedy of Romeo and Juliet

The Most Excellent Tragedy of Romeo and Juliet

Prologue *Enter Prologue*

PROLOGUE

Two household friends alike in dignity,
In fair Verona, where we lay our scene,
From civil broils broke into enmity,
Whose civil war makes civil hands unclean.
From forth the fatal loins of these two foes,
A pair of star-crossed lovers took their life,
Whose misadventures, piteous overthrows—
Through the continuing of their fathers' strife
And death-marked passage of their parents' rage—
Is now the two hours' traffic of our stage;
The which if you with patient ears attend,
What here we want, we'll study to amend. *Exit*

1.1 *Enter two Serving-men of the Capulets*

FIRST CAPULET SERVING-MAN Gregory, of my word I'll carry no coals.

SECOND CAPULET SERVING-MAN No, for if you do, you should be a collier.

FIRST CAPULET SERVING-MAN If I be in choler, I'll draw.

SECOND CAPULET SERVING-MAN Ever while you live, draw your neck out of the collar.

FIRST CAPULET SERVING-MAN I strike quickly being moved.

SECOND CAPULET SERVING-MAN Ay, but you are not quickly moved to strike.

FIRST CAPULET SERVING-MAN A dog of the house of the Montagues moves me.

SECOND CAPULET SERVING-MAN To move is to stir, and to be valiant is to stand to it: therefore, of my word, if thou be moved thou't run away.

FIRST CAPULET SERVING-MAN There's not a man of them I meet but I'll take the wall of.

SECOND CAPULET SERVING-MAN That shows thee a weakling, for the weakest goes to the wall.

FIRST CAPULET SERVING-MAN That's true: therefore I'll thrust the men from the wall and thrust the maids to the walls. Nay, thou shalt see I am a tall piece of flesh.

SECOND CAPULET SERVING-MAN 'Tis well thou art not fish; for if thou wert, thou wouldst be but Poor John.

FIRST CAPULET SERVING-MAN I'll play the tyrant: I'll first begin with the maids, and off with their heads.

SECOND CAPULET SERVING-MAN The heads of the maids?

FIRST CAPULET SERVING-MAN Ay, the heads of their maids, or the maidenheads, take it in what sense thou wilt.

SECOND CAPULET SERVING-MAN Nay, let them take it in sense that feel it. But here comes two of the Montagues.

Enter two Serving-men of the Montagues

FIRST CAPULET SERVING-MAN Nay, fear not me, I warrant thee.

SECOND CAPULET SERVING-MAN I fear them no more than thee, but draw.

FIRST CAPULET SERVING-MAN Nay, let us have the law on our side; let them begin first. I'll tell thee what I'll do: as I go by I'll bite my thumb, which is disgrace enough if they suffer it.

SECOND CAPULET SERVING-MAN Content, go thou by and bite thy thumb, and I'll come after and frown.

FIRST MONTAGUE SERVING-MAN Do you bite your thumb at us?

FIRST CAPULET SERVING-MAN I bite my thumb.

SECOND MONTAGUE SERVING-MAN Ay, but is't at us?

FIRST CAPULET SERVING-MAN I bite my thumb. Is the law on our side?

SECOND CAPULET SERVING-MAN No.

FIRST CAPULET SERVING-MAN I bite my thumb.

FIRST MONTAGUE SERVING-MAN Ay, but is't at us?

Enter Benvolio

SECOND CAPULET SERVING-MAN Say 'Ay'—here comes my master's kinsman.

They draw. To them enters Tybalt. They fight. To them the Prince, old Montague and his Wife, old Capulet and his Wife, and other Citizens, and part them

PRINCE

Rebellious subjects, enemies to peace,
On pain of torture, from those bloody hands
Throw your mistempered weapons to the ground.
Three civil brawls bred of an airy word,
By thee old Capulet and Montague,
Have thrice disturbed the quiet of our streets.
If ever you disturb our streets again,
Your lives shall pay the ransom of your fault.

For this time every man depart in peace.
Come, Capulet, come you along with me;
And Montague, come you this afternoon,
To know our farther pleasure in this case,
To old Freetown, our common judgement place.
Once more, on pain of death, each man depart.
Exeunt all but Montague, his Wife, and Benvolio

[MONTAGUE]
Who set this ancient quarrel first abroach?
Speak, nephew, were you by when it began?

BENVOLIO
Here were the servants of your adversaries
And yours, close fighting ere I did approach.

MONTAGUE'S WIFE
Ah, where is Romeo—saw you him today?
Right glad I am he was not at this fray.

BENVOLIO
Madam, an hour before the worshipped sun
Peeped through the golden window of the east,
A troubled thought drew me from company;
Where underneath the grove of sycamore
That westward rooteth from the city's side,
So early walking might I see your son.
I drew towards him, but he was ware of me,
And drew into the thicket of the wood.
I, noting his affections by mine own,
That most are busied when th'are most alone,
Pursued my humour, not pursuing his.

MONTAGUE
Black and portentous must this humour prove,
Unless good counsel do the cause remove.

BENVOLIO
Why tell me, uncle, do you know the cause?
Enter Romeo

MONTAGUE
I neither know it, nor can learn of him.

BENVOLIO
See where he is. But stand you both aside,
I'll know his grievance or be much denied.

MONTAGUE
I would thou wert so happy by thy stay

1.1.64 [MONTAGUE]] Q2; *M:wife* Q1   80, 81 humour] Q2; honor Q1

To hear true shrift. Come, madam, let's away.
Exeunt Montague and his Wife

BENVOLIO
Good morrow, cousin.

ROMEO
Is the day so young?

BENVOLIO
But new struck nine.

ROMEO
Ay me, sad hopes seem long.
Was that my father that went hence so fast?

BENVOLIO
It was. What sorrow lengthens Romeo's hours?

ROMEO
Not having that which, having, makes them short.

BENVOLIO In love.

ROMEO Out.

BENVOLIO Of love.

ROMEO
Out of her favour where I am in love.

BENVOLIO
Alas that love, so gentle in her view,
Should be so tyrannous and rough in proof.

ROMEO
Alas that love, whose view is muffled still,
Should without laws give pathways to our will.
Where shall we dine? Gods me, what fray was here?
Yet tell me not, for I have heard it all:
Here's much to do with hate, but more with love.
Why then, O brawling love, O loving hate,
O anything of nothing first create;
O heavy lightness, serious vanity,
Mis-shapen chaos of best-seeming things,
Feather of lead, bright smoke, cold fire, sick health,
Still-waking sleep that is not what it is:
This love feel I, which feel no love in this.
Dost thou not laugh?

BENVOLIO
No, coz, I rather weep.

ROMEO
Good heart, at what?

BENVOLIO
At thy good heart's oppression.

88.1 *Exeunt . . . Wife*] Q2 (*Exeunt.*); *not in* Q1

1.1.102 **Gods** = God save (*OED*, *god*, 8b)

ROMEO
Why, such is love's transgression.
Griefs of mine own lie heavy at my heart,
Which thou wouldst propagate to have them pressed
With more of thine; this grief that thou hast shown
Doth add more grief to too much of mine own.
Love is a smoke raised with the fume of sighs,
Being purged, a fire sparkling in lovers' eyes,
Being vexed, a sea raging with a lover's tears.
What is it else? A madness most discreet,
A choking gall and a preserving sweet.
Farewell, coz.
BENVOLIO Nay, I'll go along.
An if you hinder me, you do me wrong.
ROMEO
Tut, I have lost myself, I am not here;
This is not Romeo, he's some other where.
BENVOLIO
Tell me in sadness whom she is you love.
ROMEO
What, shall I groan and tell thee?
BENVOLIO
Why no; but sadly tell me who.
ROMEO
Bid a sick man in sadness make his will:
Ah, word ill-urged to one that is so ill.
In sadness, cousin, I do love a woman.
BENVOLIO
I aimed so right whenas you said you loved.
ROMEO
A right good markman, and she's fair I love.
BENVOLIO
A right fair mark, fair coz, is soonest hit.
ROMEO
But in that hit you miss: she'll not be hit
With Cupid's arrow, she hath Diana's wit;
And in strong proof of chastity well armed,
'Gainst Cupid's childish bow she lives unharmed.
She'll not abide the siege of loving terms,
Nor ope her lap to saint-seducing gold.
Ah, she is rich in beauty, only poor,
That when she dies, with beauty dies her store. *Exeunt*

1.2 *Enter the County Paris and old Capulet*

[PARIS]
Of honourable reckoning are you both,
And pity 'tis you live at odds so long.
But leaving that, what say you to my suit?

CAPULET
What should I say more than I said before?
My daughter is a stranger in the world,
She hath not yet attained to fourteen years;
Let two more summers wither in their pride
Before she can be thought fit for a bride.

PARIS
Younger than she are happy mothers made.

CAPULET
But too soon marred are these so early married.
But woo her, gentle Paris, get her heart;
My word to her consent is but a part.
This night I hold an old-accustomed feast,
Whereto I have invited many a guest,
Such as I love; yet you among the store,
One more, most welcome, makes the number more.
At my poor house you shall behold this night
Earth-treading stars that make dark heaven light.
Such comfort as do lusty young men feel
When well-apparelled April on the heel
Of limping winter treads, even such delights
Amongst fresh female buds shall you this night
Inherit at my house. Hear all, all see,
And like her most whose merit most shall be.
Such amongst view, of many, mine being one,
May stand in number though in reckoning none.
Enter a Serving-man
(*To Serving-man*) Where are you, sirrah? Go, trudge about,
Through fair Verona streets, and seek them out
Whose names are written here, and to them say,
My house and welcome at their pleasure stay.
Exeunt Capulet and Paris

SERVING-MAN Seek them out whose names are written here, and yet I know not who are written here. I must to the learned to learn of them. That's as much to say, as the tailor must meddle with his last, the shoemaker with his needle, the painter with

1.2.1, 2 you] Q2; they Q1 21 limping] Q2; lumping Q1

his nets, and the fisher with his pencil, I must to the learned.

Enter Benvolio and Romeo

BENVOLIO

Tut, man, one fire burns out another's burning,
One pain is lessened with another's anguish;
Turn backward and be holp with backward turning;
One desperate grief cures with another's languish.
Take thou some new infection to thy eye,
And the rank poison of the old will die.

ROMEO

Your plantain leaf is excellent for that.

BENVOLIO For what?

ROMEO For your broken shin.

BENVOLIO Why, Romeo, art thou mad?

ROMEO

Not mad, but bound more than a madman is:
Shut up in prison, kept without my food,
Whipped and tormented, and—Good e'en, good fellow.

SERVING-MAN

God gi' good e'en. I pray, sir, can you read?

ROMEO

Ay, mine own fortune in my misery.

SERVING-MAN Perhaps you have learned it without book. But I pray, can you read anything you see?

ROMEO

Ay, if I know the letters and the language.

SERVING-MAN Ye say honestly, rest you merry.

ROMEO Stay, fellow, I can read.

He reads the letter

'Signor Martino and his wife and daughters;
County Anselme and his beauteous sisters;
The lady widow of Utruvio;
Signor Placentio and his lovely nieces;
Mercutio and his brother Valentine;
Mine uncle Capulet, his wife and daughters;
My fair niece Rosaline, and Livia;
Signor Valentio and his cousin Tybalt;
Lucio and the lively Helena.'
A fair assembly. Whither should they come?

SERVING-MAN Up.

ROMEO Whither to supper?

SERVING-MAN To our house.

ROMEO Whose house?

SERVING-MAN My master's.

ROMEO
Indeed, I should have asked thee that before.

SERVING-MAN Now I'll tell you without asking. My master is the great rich Capulet, and if you be not of the house of Montagues, I pray come and crush a cup of wine. Rest you merry.
Exit

BENVOLIO
At this same ancient feast of Capulet's
Sups the fair Rosaline whom thou so loves,
With all the admirèd beauties of Verona.
Go thither, and with unattainted eye
Compare her face with some that I shall show,
And I will make thee think thy swan a crow.

ROMEO
When the devout religion of mine eye
Maintains such falsehood, then turn tears to fire;
And these who, often drowned, could never die,
Transparent heretics be burnt for liars.
One fairer than my love, the all-seeing sun
Ne'er saw her match since first the world begun.

BENVOLIO
Tut, you saw her fair, none else being by,
Herself poised with herself in either eye;
But in that crystal scales let there be weighed
Your lady's love against some other maid
That I will show you shining at this feast,
And she shall scant show well that now seems best.

ROMEO
I'll go along no such sight to be shown,
But to rejoice in splendour of mine own. *Exeunt*

1.3 *Enter Capulet's Wife and the Nurse*

CAPULET'S WIFE
Nurse, where's my daughter? Call her forth to me.

NURSE
Now by my maidenhead at twelve year old,
I bade her come. What lamb, what ladybird,
God forbid! Where's this girl? What Juliet!
Enter Juliet

JULIET How now, who calls?

NURSE Your mother.

JULIET
Madam, I am here, what is your will?

CAPULET'S WIFE
This is the matter.—Nurse, give leave a while,
We must talk in secret.—Nurse, come back again,
I have remembered me, thou's hear our counsel.
Thou knowest my daughter's of a pretty age.

NURSE
Faith, I can tell her age unto an hour.

CAPULET'S WIFE She's not fourteen.

NURSE I'll lay fourteen of my teeth, and yet to my teen be it spoken, I have but four, she's not fourteen. How long is it now to Lammas-tide?

CAPULET'S WIFE A fortnight and odd days.

NURSE
Even or odd, of all days in the year,
Come Lammas Eve at night shall she be fourteen.
Susan and she—God rest all Christian souls—
Were of an age. Well, Susan is with God;
She was too good for me. But as I said,
On Lammas Eve at night shall she be fourteen,
That shall she, marry, I remember it well.
'Tis since the earthquake now eleven years,
And she was weaned—I never shall forget it—
Of all the days of the year upon that day;
For I had then laid wormwood to my dug,
Sitting in the sun under the dovehouse wall.
My lord and you were then at Mantua—
Nay, I do bear a brain. But as I said,
When it did taste the wormwood on the nipple
Of my dug and felt it bitter, pretty fool,
To see it tetchy and fall out with the dug!
'Shake', quoth the dovehouse; 'twas no need, I trow,
To bid me trudge.
And since that time it is eleven year,
For then could Juliet stand high-lone—nay, by the rood,
She could have waddled up and down;
For even the day before she brake her brow,
And then my husband—God be with his soul,
He was a merry man—
'Dost thou fall forward, Juliet?
Thou wilt fall backward when thou hast more wit,
Wilt thou not, Juliet?' And by my holidam,
The pretty fool left crying and said 'Ay'.

1.3.12 an] Q2; a Q1

To see how a jest shall come about!
I warrant you, if I should live a hundred year,
I never should forget it. 'Wilt thou not, Juliet?'
And, by my troth, she stinted and cried 'Ay'.

JULIET
And stint thou too, I prithee, Nurse, say I.

NURSE
Well, go thy ways. God mark thee for his grace,
Thou wert the prettiest babe that ever I nursed.
Might I but live to see thee married once,
I have my wish.

CAPULET'S WIFE
And that same marriage, Nurse, is the theme
I meant to talk of. Tell me, Juliet,
How stand you affected to be married?

JULIET
It is an honour that I dream not of.

NURSE
An honour! Were not I thy only nurse,
I would say thou hadst sucked wisdom from thy teat.

CAPULET'S WIFE
Well, girl, the noble County Paris seeks thee for his wife.

NURSE
A man, young lady, lady, such a man
As all the world—why, he is a man of wax.

CAPULET'S WIFE
Verona's summer hath not such a flower.

NURSE
Nay, he is a flower, in faith, a very flower.

CAPULET'S WIFE
Well, Juliet, how like you of Paris' love?

JULIET
I'll look to like, if looking liking move.
But no more deep will I engage mine eye
Than your consent gives strength to make it fly.

Enter a Serving-man

SERVING-MAN Madam, you are called for, supper is ready, the Nurse cursed in the pantry, all things in extremity. Make haste, for I must be gone to wait. *Exeunt*

70.1 *Serving-man*] Q2; *Clowne* Q1 71 SERVING-MAN] Q2; Clowne Q1

1.4 *Enter Masquers with Romeo and a Page*

ROMEO
What, shall this speech be spoke for our excuse?
Or shall we on without apology?

BENVOLIO
The date is out of such prolixity;
We'll have no Cupid hoodwinked with a scarf,
Bearing a Tartar's painted bow of lath,
Scaring the ladies like a crow-keeper;
Nor no without-book prologue faintly spoke,
After the prompter, for our entrance.
But let them measure us by what they will,
We'll measure them a measure and be gone.

ROMEO
A torch for me, I am not for this ambling;
Being but heavy I will bear the light.

MERCUTIO
Believe me, Romeo, I must have you dance.

ROMEO
Not I, believe me. You have dancing-shoes
With nimble soles; I have a soul of lead
So stakes me to the ground I cannot stir.

MERCUTIO
Give me a case to put my visage in,
A visor for a visor. What care I
What curious eye doth quote deformity?

ROMEO
Give me a torch. Let wantons light of heart
Tickle the senseless rushes with their heels;
For I am proverbed with a grandsire phrase:
I'll be a candle-holder and look on;
The game was ne'er so fair, and I am done.

MERCUTIO
Tut, dun's the mouse, the constable's old word.
If thou beest dun, we'll draw thee from the mire
Of this sir reverence love, wherein thou stick'st.
Leave this talk, we burn daylight here.

ROMEO
Nay, that's not so.

MERCUTIO I mean, sir, in delay
We burn our lights by night, like lamps by day.
Take our good meaning, for our judgement sits
Three times a day ere once in her right wits.

ROMEO
So we mean well by going to this masque,
But 'tis no wit to go.
MERCUTIO Why, Romeo, may one ask?
ROMEO
I dreamt a dream tonight.
MERCUTIO And so did I.
ROMEO
Why, what was yours?
MERCUTIO That dreamers often lie.
ROMEO
In bed asleep while they do dream things true.
MERCUTIO
Ah, then I see Queen Mab hath been with you.
BENVOLIO Queen Mab, what's she?
[MERCUTIO]
She is the fairies' midwife, and doth come
In shape no bigger than an agate stone
On the forefinger of a burgomaster,
Drawn with a team of little atomi
Athwart men's noses when they lie asleep.
Her wagon-spokes are made of spinners' webs;
The cover of the wings of grasshoppers;
The traces are the moonshine-wat'ry beams;
The collars, crickets' bones; the lash of films;
Her wagoner is a small grey-coated fly,
Not half so big as is a little worm
Picked from the lazy finger of a maid.
And in this sort she gallops up and down
Through lovers' brains, and then they dream of love;
O'er courtiers' knees, who straight on curtsies dream;
O'er ladies' lips, who dream on kisses straight,
Which oft the angry Mab with blisters plagues,
Because their breaths with sweetmeats tainted are.
Sometimes she gallops o'er a lawyer's lap,
And then dreams he of smelling out a suit;
And sometime comes she with a tithe-pig's tail,
Tickling a parson's nose that lies asleep,
And then dreams he of another benefice.
Sometime she gallops o'er a soldier's nose,
And then dreams he of cutting foreign throats,
Of breaches, ambuscados, countermines,
Of healths five fathom-deep; and then anon
Drums in his ear, at which he starts and wakes,

And swears a prayer or two, and sleeps again.
This is that Mab that makes maids lie on their backs,
And proves them women of good carriage.
This is the very Mab that plaits the manes of horses in the night,
And plaits the elf-locks in foul sluttish hair,
Which once untangled much misfortune breeds.

ROMEO
Peace, peace, thou talk'st of nothing.

MERCUTIO True, I talk of dreams,
Which are the children of an idle brain,
Begot of nothing but vain fantasy,
Which is as thin a substance as the air,
And more inconstant than the wind
Which woos even now the frozen bowels of the north;
And being angered puffs away in haste,
Turning his face to the dew-dropping south.

BENVOLIO
Come, come, this wind doth blow us from ourselves;
Supper is done, and we shall come too late.

ROMEO
I fear too early, for my mind misgives
Some consequence is hanging in the stars
Which bitterly begins his fearful date
With this night's revels, and expires the term
Of a despisèd life closed in this breast
By some untimely forfeit of vile death.
But he that hath the steerage of my course
Directs my sail. On, lusty gentlemen.

Enter old Capulet with the ladies [*and attendants*]

CAPULET
Welcome gentlemen, welcome gentlemen.
Ladies that have their toes unplagued with corns
Will have a bout with you. Aha, my mistresses,
Which of you all will now refuse to dance?
She that makes dainty, she I'll swear hath corns.
Am I come near you now? Welcome, gentlemen, welcome.—
More lights, you knaves, and turn these tables up,
And quench the fire, the room is grown too hot.—
Ah sirrah, this unlooked-for sport comes well.—
Nay sit, nay sit, good cousin Capulet,
For you and I are past our standing days.
How long is it since you and I were in a mask?

CAPULET'S COUSIN
By Lady, sir, 'tis thirty years at least.

CAPULET
'Tis not so much, 'tis not so much,
'Tis since the marriage of Lucentio,
Come Pentecost as quickly as it will,
Some five-and-twenty years, and then we masked.

CAPULET'S COUSIN
'Tis more, 'tis more, his son is elder far.

CAPULET
Will you tell me that? It cannot be so,
His son was but a ward three years ago.
Good youths, i' faith. O, youth's a jolly thing.

ROMEO
What lady is that that doth enrich the hand
Of yonder knight? O, she doth teach the torches to burn
bright!
It seems she hangs upon the cheek of night
Like a rich jewel in an Ethiop's ear,
Beauty too rich for use, for earth too dear.
So shines a snow-white swan trooping with crows,
As this fair lady over her fellows shows.
The measure done, I'll watch her place of stand
And, touching hers, make happy my rude hand.
Did my heart love till now? Forswear it, sight,
I never saw true beauty till this night.

TYBALT
This, by his voice, should be a Montague.
Fetch me my rapier, boy. *Exit Page*
What, dares the slave
Come hither, covered with an antic face,
To scorn and jeer at our solemnity?
Now by the stock and honour of my kin,
To strike him dead I hold it for no sin.

CAPULET
Why, how now, cousin, wherefore storm you so?

TYBALT
Uncle, this is a Montague, our foe;
A villain that is hither come in spite
To mock at our solemnity this night.

CAPULET
Young Romeo, is it not?

TYBALT
It is that villain Romeo.

CAPULET
Let him alone. He bears him like a portly gentleman;

And, to speak truth, Verona brags of him
As of a virtuous and well-governed youth.
I would not for the wealth of all this town
Here in my house do him disparagement.
Therefore be quiet, take no note of him;
Bear a fair presence and put off these frowns,
An ill-beseeming semblance for a feast.

TYBALT
It fits when such a villain is a guest;
I'll not endure him.

CAPULET
He shall be endured. Go to, I say he shall!
Am I the master of the house or you?
You'll not endure him? God shall mend my soul,
You'll make a mutiny amongst my guests!
You'll set cock-a-hoop, you'll be the man!

TYBALT
Uncle, 'tis a shame.

CAPULET Go to, you are a saucy knave.
This trick will scathe you one day I know what.—
(*To the dancers*) Well said, my hearts.—(*To Tybalt*) Be quiet—
(*To Serving-man*) More light—ye knave—(*to Tybalt*) or I will make you quiet.

TYBALT
Patience perforce, with wilful choler meeting,
Makes my flesh tremble in their different greetings.
I will withdraw, but this intrusion shall
Now seeming sweet convert to bitter gall. *Exit*

ROMEO
If I profane with my unworthy hand
This holy shrine, the gentle sin is this,
My lips, two blushing pilgrims, ready stand
To smooth the rough touch with a gentle kiss.

JULIET
Good pilgrim, you do wrong your hand too much,
Which mannerly devotion shows in this,
For saints have hands which holy palmers touch,
And palm to palm is holy palmers' kiss.

ROMEO
Have not saints lips, and holy palmers too?

JULIET
Yes, pilgrim, lips that they must use in prayer.

1.4.157 *Exit*| Q2; *not in* Q1

ROMEO
Why then, fair saint, let lips do what hands do;
They pray, yield thou, lest faith turn to despair.
JULIET
Saints do not move though, grant nor prayer forsake.
ROMEO
Then move not till my prayer's effect I take.
He kisses her
Thus from my lips, by yours, my sin is purged.
JULIET
Then have my lips the sin that they have took.
ROMEO
Sin from my lips? O trespass sweetly urged!
Give me my sin again.
He kisses her
JULIET You kiss by the book.
NURSE Madam, your mother calls.
Juliet moves towards her mother
ROMEO
What is her mother?
NURSE Marry, bachelor,
Her mother is the lady of the house,
And a good lady, and a wise, and a virtuous;
I nursed her daughter that you talked withal.
I tell you, he that can lay hold of her
Shall have the chinks.
ROMEO Is she a Capulet?
O dear account! My life is my foe's thrall.
CAPULET
Nay, gentlemen, prepare not to be gone;
We have a trifling foolish banquet towards.
They whisper in his ear
I pray you let me entreat you. Is it so?
Well then I thank you, honest gentlemen.
I promise you, but for your company,
I would have been abed an hour ago.
(*To Serving-man*) Light to my chamber, ho!
Exeunt all but Juliet and the Nurse
JULIET
Nurse, what is yonder gentleman?
NURSE
The son and heir of old Tiberio.

182 Capulet] Q2; *Mountague* Q1

JULIET
What's he that now is going out of door?
NURSE
That, as I think, is young Petruccio.
JULIET
What's he that follows there that would not dance?
NURSE I know not.
JULIET
Go, learn his name.
The Nurse goes
If he be marrièd,
My grave is like to be my wedding-bed.
NURSE (*returning*)
His name is Romeo, and a Montague,
The only son of your great enemy.
JULIET
My only love sprung from my only hate,
Too early seen unknown and known too late.
Prodigious birth of love is this to me,
That I should love a loathèd enemy.
NURSE What's this? What's that?
JULIET
Nothing, Nurse, but a rhyme I learnt even now
Of one I danced with.
NURSE Come, your mother stays for you; I'll go along with you.
Exeunt

2.1 *Enter Romeo alone*
ROMEO
Shall I go forward, and my heart is here?
Turn back, dull earth, and find thy centre out.
⌈*He turns back, withdrawing.*⌉
Enter Benvolio with Mercutio
BENVOLIO Romeo, my cousin Romeo!
MERCUTIO Dost thou hear, he is wise. Upon my life, he hath stol'n him home to bed.
BENVOLIO
He came this way and leapt this orchard wall.
Call, good Mercutio.
MERCUTIO Call? Nay, I'll conjure too.
Romeo! Madman! Humours! Passion! Lover!

2.1.8–29 **Romeo! . . . him** Q1 sets both of Mercutio's speeches as prose (on a crowded page), even though most of the lines sound like pentameters. This edition relines the passage to convey the rhythms.

Appear thou in likeness of a sigh;
Speak but one rhyme and I am satisfied.
Cry but 'Ay me', pronounce but 'love' and 'dove';
Speak to my gossip Venus one fair word,
One nickname for her purblind son and heir,
Young Abraham Cupid, he that shot so trim
When young King Cophetua loved the beggar wench.—
He hears me not.
I conjure thee by Rosalind's bright eye,
High forehead and scarlet lip,
Her pretty foot, straight leg, and quivering thigh,
And the demesnes that there adjacent lie,
That in thy likeness thou appear to us.

BENVOLIO

If he do hear thee, thou wilt anger him.

MERCUTIO

Tut, this cannot anger him. Marry, if one
Should raise a spirit in his mistress' circle
Of some strange fashion, making it there to stand
Till she had laid it and conjured it down,
That were some spite. My invocation
Is fair and honest, and in his mistress' name
I conjure only but to raise up him.

BENVOLIO

Well, he hath hid himself among those trees
To be consorted with the humorous night.
Blind is his love, and best befits the dark.

MERCUTIO

If love be blind, love will not hit the mark.
Now will he sit under a medlar tree
And wish his mistress were that kind of fruit
As maids call medlars when they laugh alone.
Ah Romeo, that she were, ah that she were
An open et cetera, thou a popp'rin' pear.
Romeo, good night. I'll to my trundle-bed;
This field-bed is too cold for me.
Come, let's away, for 'tis but vain
To seek him here that means not to be found.

Exeunt Benvolio and Mercutio

[*Romeo comes forward, Juliet entering above*]

ROMEO

He jests at scars that never felt a wound—
But soft, what light forth yonder window breaks?
It is the east, and Juliet is the sun.

Arise, fair sun, and kill the envious moon,
That is already sick and pale with grief
That thou, her maid, art far more fair than she.
Be not her maid, since she is envious;
Her vestal livery is but pale and green,
And none but fools do wear it. Cast it off.
She speaks, but she says nothing. What of that?
Her eye discourseth; I will answer it.
I am too bold; 'tis not to me she speaks.
Two of the fairest stars in all the skies,
Having some business, do entreat her eyes
To twinkle in their spheres till they return.
What if her eyes were there, they in her head?
The brightness of her cheeks would shame those stars
As daylight doth a lamp; her eyes in heaven
Would through the airy region stream so bright
That birds would sing and think it were not night.
O, now she leans her cheeks upon her hand.
I would I were the glove to that same hand,
That I might kiss that cheek.

JULIET Ay me.

ROMEO (*aside*) She speaks.

O speak again, bright angel, for thou art
As glorious to this night, being over my head,
As is a wingèd messenger of heaven
Unto the white upturnèd wond'ring eyes
Of mortals that fall back to gaze on him
When he bestrides the lazy passing clouds
And sails upon the bosom of the air.

JULIET

Ah Romeo, Romeo, wherefore art thou Romeo?
Deny thy father and refuse thy name;
Or if thou wilt not, be but sworn my love,
And I'll no longer be a Capulet.

ROMEO (*aside*)

Shall I hear more, or shall I speak to this?

JULIET

'Tis but thy name that is mine enemy.
What's Montague? It is nor hand nor foot,
Nor arm nor face, nor any other part.
What's in a name? That which we call a rose
By any other name would smell as sweet;
So Romeo would, were he not Romeo called,

Retain the divine perfection he owes
Without that title. Romeo, part thy name,
And for that name which is no part of thee,
Take all I have.

ROMEO I take thee at thy word.
Call me but love, and I'll be new baptized:
Henceforth I never will be Romeo.

JULIET
What man art thou that, thus bescreened in night,
Dost stumble on my counsel?

ROMEO
By a name I know not how to tell thee.
My name, dear saint, is hateful to myself,
Because it is an enemy to thee.
Had I it written, I would tear the word.

JULIET
My ears have not yet drunk a hundred words
Of that tongue's utterance, yet I know the sound.
Art thou not Romeo, and a Montague?

ROMEO
Neither, fair saint, if either thee displease.

JULIET
How cam'st thou hither, tell me, and wherefore?
The orchard walls are high and hard to climb,
And the place death, considering who thou art,
If any of my kinsmen find thee here.

ROMEO
By love's light wings did I o'erperch these walls,
For stony limits cannot hold love out,
And what love can do, that dares love attempt:
Therefore thy kinsmen are no let to me.

JULIET
If they do find thee, they will murder thee.

ROMEO
Alas, there lies more peril in thine eyes
Than twenty of their swords. Look thou but sweet,
And I am proof against their enmity.

JULIET
I would not for the world they should find thee here.

ROMEO
I have night's cloak to hide me from their sight,

2.1.113 me] Q2; thee Q1

107 **let** hindrance

And but thou love me, let them find me here;
For life were better ended by their hate
Than death proroguèd, wanting of thy love.

JULIET
By whose directions found'st thou out this place?

ROMEO
By love, who first did prompt me to inquire:
He gave me counsel, and I lent him eyes.
I am no pilot, yet wert thou as far
As that vast shore washed with the furthest sea,
I would adventure for such merchandise.

JULIET
Thou know'st the mask of night is on my face,
Else would a maiden blush bepaint my cheeks
For that which thou hast heard me speak tonight.
Fain would I dwell on form, fain, fain deny
What I have spoke; but farewell, compliments.
Dost thou love me? Nay, I know thou wilt say 'Ay',
And I will take thy word; but if thou swear'st,
Thou mayst prove false. At lovers' perjuries
They say Jove smiles. Ah gentle Romeo,
If thou love, pronounce it faithfully;
Or if thou think I am too easily won,
I'll frown and say thee nay and be perverse,
So thou wilt woo, but else not for the world.
In truth, fair Montague, I am too fond,
And therefore thou mayst think my haviour light;
But trust me, gentleman, I'll prove more true
Than they that have more cunning to be strange.
I should have been strange, I must confess,
But that thou overheard'st, ere I was ware,
My true love's passion. Therefore pardon me,
And not impute this yielding to light love,
Which the dark night hath so discoverèd.

ROMEO
By yonder blessèd moon I swear,
That tips with silver all these fruit-tree tops—

JULIET
O swear not by the moon, the unconstant moon,
That monthly changeth in her circled orb,

119 He] Q2; I he Q1

137 **haviour** i.e. behaviour

Lest that thy love prove likewise variable.

ROMEO

Now by—

JULIET Nay, do not swear at all;
Or if thou swear, swear by thy glorious self,
Which art the god of my idolatry,
And I'll believe thee.

ROMEO If my true heart's love—

JULIET

Swear not at all. Though I do joy in thee,
I have small joy in this contract tonight:
It is too rash, too sudden, too unadvised,
Too like the lightning that doth cease to be
Ere one can say 'It lightens'.

One calls within

I hear some coming.
Dear love, adieu. Sweet Montague, be true.
Stay but a little, and I'll come again. *Exit*

ROMEO

O blessèd, blessèd night! I fear, being night,
All this is but a dream I hear and see,
Too flattering true to be substantial.

Enter Juliet again

JULIET

Three words, good Romeo, and good night indeed.
If that thy bent of love be honourable,
Thy purpose marriage, send me word tomorrow,
By one that I'll procure to come to thee,
Where and what time thou wilt perform that rite,
And all my fortunes at thy foot I'll lay,
And follow thee, my lord, throughout the world. *Exit*

ROMEO

Love goes toward love like schoolboys from their books,
But love from love, to school with heavy looks.

Enter Juliet again

JULIET

Romeo, Romeo! O for a falc'ner's voice
To lure this tassel-gentle back again.
Bondage is hoarse and may not cry aloud,
Else would I tear the cave where Echo lies
And make her airy voice as hoarse as mine
With repetition of my Romeo's name.
Romeo?

ROMEO
It is my soul that calls upon my name.
How silver-sweet sound lovers' tongues in night.

JULIET Romeo?

ROMEO Madam?

JULIET
At what o'clock tomorrow shall I send?

ROMEO At the hour of nine.

JULIET
I will not fail; 'tis twenty years till then.
Romeo, I have forgot why I did call thee back.

ROMEO
Let me stay here till you remember it.

JULIET
I shall forget to have thee still stay here,
Rememb'ring how I love thy company.

ROMEO
And I'll stay still to have thee still forget,
Forgetting any other home but this.

JULIET
'Tis almost morning, I would have thee gone;
But yet no further than a wanton's bird,
Who lets it hop a little from her hand,
Like a poor prisoner in his twisted gyves,
And with a silk thread pulls it back again,
Too loving-jealous of his liberty.

ROMEO
Would I were thy bird.

JULIET Sweet, so would I,
Yet I should kill thee with much cherishing thee.
Good night, good night. Parting is such sweet sorrow,
That I shall say 'good night' till it be morrow. *Exit*

ROMEO
Sleep dwell upon thine eyes, peace on thy breast.
I would that I were sleep and peace, so sweet to rest.
Now will I to my ghostly father's cell,
His help to crave and my good hap to tell. *Exit*

2.2 *Enter Friar* ⌈*Laurence*⌉

FRIAR LAURENCE
The grey-eyed morn smiles on the frowning night,

204 so] Q2; of Q1 206 *Exit*] Q2; *not in* Q1
2.2.0.1 ⌈*Laurence*⌉] This edition; *Francis* Q1

Check'ring the eastern clouds with streaks of light;
And fleckèd darkness like a drunkard reels
From forth day's path and Titan's fiery wheels.
Now ere the sun advance his burning eye,
The world to cheer and night's dark dew to dry,
We must upfill this osier cage of ours
With baleful weeds and precious-juicèd flowers.
O mickle is the powerful grace that lies
In herbs, plants, stones, and their true qualities;
For naught so vile that vile on earth doth live,
But to the earth some special good doth give;
Nor naught so good but, strained from that fair use,
Revolts to vice and stumbles on abuse.
Virtue itself turns vice, being misapplied,
And vice sometimes by action dignified.

Enter Romeo

Within the infant rind of this small flower
Poison hath residence and medicine power:
For this, being smelt to, with that part cheers each part;
Being tasted, slays all senses with the heart.
Two such opposèd foes encamp them still
In man as well as herbs, grace and rude will;
And where the worser is predominant,
Full soon the canker death eats up that plant.

ROMEO
Good morrow to my ghostly confessor.

FRIAR LAURENCE *Benedicite!*
What early tongue so soon saluteth me?
Young son, it argues a distempered head
So soon to bid good morrow to thy bed.
Care keeps his watch in every old man's eye,
And where care lodgeth, sleep can never lie;
But where unbruisèd youth with unstuffed brains
Doth couch his limbs, there golden sleep remains.
Therefore thy earliness doth me assure
Thou art uproused by some distemperature;
Or if not so, then here I hit it right,
Our Romeo hath not been abed tonight.

ROMEO
The last was true; the sweeter rest was mine.

FRIAR LAURENCE
God pardon sin! Wert thou with Rosaline?

19 each part] Q2; ech hart Q1

ROMEO
With Rosaline, my ghostly father? No,
I have forgot that name and that name's woe.

FRIAR LAURENCE
That's my good son; but where hast thou been then?

ROMEO
I'll tell thee ere thou ask it me again.
I have been feasting with mine enemy,
Where on the sudden one hath wounded me
That's by me wounded. Both our remedies
Within thy help and holy physic lies.
I bear no hatred, blessèd man, for lo,
My intercession likewise steads my foe.

FRIAR LAURENCE
Be plain, my son, and homely in thy drift;
Riddling confession finds but riddling shrift.

ROMEO
Then plainly know my heart's dear love is set
On the fair daughter of rich Capulet.
As mine on hers, so hers likewise on mine,
And all combined, save what thou must combine
By holy marriage. Where and when and how
We met, we wooed, and made exchange of vows,
I'll tell thee as I pass; but this I pray,
That thou consent to marry us today.

FRIAR LAURENCE
Holy Saint Francis, what a change is here!
Is Rosaline, whom thou didst love so dear,
So soon forsook? Lo, young men's love then lies
Not truly in their hearts, but in their eyes.
Jesu Maria, what a deal of brine
Hath washed thy sallow cheeks for Rosaline!
How much salt water cast away in waste
To season love, that of love doth not taste.
The sun not yet thy sighs from heaven clears,
Thy old groans ring yet in my ancient ears;
And lo, upon thy cheek the stain doth sit
Of an old tear that is not washed off yet.
If ever thou wert thus, and these woes thine,
Thou and these woes were all for Rosaline.
And art thou changed? Pronounce this sentence then:
Women may fall when there's no strength in men.

43 I'll] Q2; I Q1

ROMEO
Thou chid'st me oft for loving Rosaline.
FRIAR LAURENCE
For doting, not for loving, pupil mine.
ROMEO
And bad'st me bury love.
FRIAR LAURENCE Not in a grave,
To lay one in, another out to have.
ROMEO
I pray thee, chide not. She whom I love now
Doth grace for grace and love for love allow;
The other did not so.
FRIAR LAURENCE O she knew well
Thy love did read by rote and could not spell.
But come, young waverer, come, go with me;
In one respect I'll thy assistant be:
For this alliance may so happy prove,
To turn your households' rancour to pure love. *Exeunt*

2.3 *Enter Mercutio and Benvolio*

MERCUTIO Why, what's become of Romeo? Came he not home tonight?
BENVOLIO
Not to his father's; I spake with his man.
MERCUTIO
Ah, that same pale hard-hearted wench, that Rosaline,
Torments him so that he will sure run mad.
[BENVOLIO]
Tybalt, the kinsman of old Capulet,
Hath sent a letter to his father's house.
MERCUTIO
Some challenge, on my life.
BENVOLIO Romeo will answer it.
MERCUTIO Ay, any man that can write may answer a letter.
BENVOLIO Nay, he will answer the letter's master, if he be challenged.
MERCUTIO Who, Romeo? Why, he is already dead, stabbed with a white wench's black eye, shot through the ear with a love-song, the very pin of his heart cleft with the blind bow-boy's butt-shaft; and is he a man to encounter Tybalt?
BENVOLIO Why, what is Tybalt?
MERCUTIO More than the Prince of Cats, I can tell you. O, he is the

2.3.6 [BENVOLIO]] Q2; *Mer:* Q1

courageous captain of compliments. Catso, he fights as you sing prick-song, keeps time, distance, and proportion; rests me his minim rest, one, two, and the third in your bosom—the very butcher of a silken button—a duellist, a duellist, a gentleman of the very first house of the first and second cause. Ah, the immortal *passado*, the *punto riverso*, the *hay*!

BENVOLIO The what?

MERCUTIO The pox of such limping, antic, affecting fantasticos, these new tuners of accents! 'By Jesu, a very good blade, a very tall man, a very good whore.' Why, grandsire, is not this a miserable case, that we should be still afflicted with these strange flies, these fashion-mongers, these 'pardon-me's', that stand so much on the new form that they cannot sit at ease on the old bench? O their bones, their bones!

Enter Romeo

BENVOLIO Here comes Romeo.

MERCUTIO Without his roe, like a dried herring. O flesh, flesh, how art thou fishified! Sirrah, now is he for the numbers that Petrarch flowed in. Laura to his lady was but a kitchen-drudge—yet she had a better love to berhyme her—Dido a dowdy, Cleopatra a gypsy, Hero and Helen hildings and harlotries, Thisbe a grey eye or so, but not to the purpose. Signor Romeo, *bonjour*: there is a French curtsy to your French slop. Ye gave us the counterfeit fairly yesternight.

ROMEO What counterfeit, I pray you?

MERCUTIO The slip, the slip—can you not conceive?

ROMEO I cry you mercy, my business was great, and in such a case as mine a man may strain courtesy.

MERCUTIO O, that's as much to say as such a case as yours will constrain a man to bow in the hams.

ROMEO A most courteous exposition.

MERCUTIO Why, I am the very pink of courtesy.

ROMEO Pink for flower.

MERCUTIO Right.

ROMEO Then is my pump well flowered.

MERCUTIO Well said. Follow me now that jest till thou hast worn

30.1 *Enter Romeo*] Q2; *not in* Q1

2.3.17 **Catso** An obsolete slang exclamation deriving from the Italian *cazzo* (penis); it might also mean 'rogue' (*OED*). There is obvious wordplay on 'Cats' and 'prick-song' ('prick' = penis) in the same speech.

24 **fantasticos** 'absurd and irrational person[s]'. *OED* cites this as the first of two illustrations for this obsolete word.

33 **Sirrah** Mercutio seems to be using this archaic term of address to express contempt, reprimand, or authority in a general way.

36–7 **harlotries** i.e. harlots, or prostitutes

out thy pump, that when the single sole of it is worn, the jest may remain, after the wearing, solely singular.

ROMEO O single-soled jest, solely singular for the singleness!

MERCUTIO Come between us, good Benvolio, for my wits fail.

ROMEO Switch and spurs, switch and spurs, or I'll cry 'a match!'

MERCUTIO Nay, if thy wits run the wild goose chase, I have done; for I am sure thou hast more of the goose in one of thy wits than I have in all my five. Was I with you there for the goose?

ROMEO Thou wert never with me for anything when thou wert not with me for the goose.

MERCUTIO I'll bite thee by the ear for that jest.

ROMEO Nay, good goose, bite not.

MERCUTIO Why, they wit is a bitter-sweeting, a most sharp sauce.

ROMEO And was it not well served into a sweet goose?

MERCUTIO O here is a wit of cheverel, that stretcheth from an inch narrow to an ell broad.

ROMEO I stretched it out for the word 'broad', which, added to the goose, proves thee far and wide a broad goose.

MERCUTIO Why, is not this better now than groaning for love? Why, now art thou sociable, now art thou thyself, now art thou what thou art as well by art as nature. This drivelling love is like a great natural that runs up and down to hide his bauble in a hole.

BENVOLIO Stop there.

MERCUTIO Why, thou wouldst have me stop my tale against the hair.

BENVOLIO Thou wouldst have made thy tale too long.

MERCUTIO Tut, man, thou art deceived, I meant to make it short; for I was come to the whole depth of my tale and meant indeed to occupy the argument no longer.

ROMEO Here's goodly gear.

Enter the Nurse and her man, Peter

MERCUTIO A sail, a sail, a sail!

BENVOLIO Two, two, a shirt and a smock.

NURSE Peter, prithee, give me my fan.

MERCUTIO Prithee, do, good Peter, to hide her face, for her fan is the fairer of the two.

NURSE God ye good morrow, gentlemen.

MERCUTIO God ye good e'en, fair gentlewoman.

NURSE Is it 'God ye good e'en', I pray you?

MERCUTIO 'Tis no less, I assure you, for the bawdy hand of the dial is even now upon the prick of noon.

NURSE Fie, what a man is this?

ROMEO A gentleman, Nurse, that God hath made for himself to mar.

NURSE By my troth, well said. 'For himself to mar', quoth he? I pray you, can any of you tell where one may find young Romeo?

ROMEO I can, but young Romeo will be elder when you have found him than he was when you sought him. I am the youngest of that name, for fault of a worse.

NURSE Well said.

MERCUTIO Yea, is the worst well? Mass, well noted, wisely, wisely.

NURSE If you be he, sir, I desire some conference with ye.

BENVOLIO O, belike she means to invite him to supper.

MERCUTIO Soho! A bawd, a bawd, a bawd!

ROMEO Why what hast found, man?

MERCUTIO No hare, sir, unless it be a hare in a Lenten pie, that is somewhat stale and hoar ere it be eaten.

He walks by them and sings

And an old hare hoar, and an old hare hoar,
  Is very good meat in Lent;
But a hare that's hoar is too much for a score,
  If it hoar ere it be spent.

You'll come to your father's to supper?

ROMEO I will.

MERCUTIO Farewell, ancient lady; farewell, sweet lady.

Exeunt Benvolio and Mercutio

NURSE Marry, farewell. Pray, what saucy merchant was this that was so full of his rope-ripe?

ROMEO A gentleman, Nurse, that loves to hear himself talk, and will speak more in an hour than he will stand to in a month.

NURSE If he stand to anything against me, I'll take him down, if he were lustier than he is. If I cannot take him down, I'll find them that shall. I am none of his flirt-gills, I am none of his skains mates.

She turns to Peter, her man

And thou like a knave must stand by and see every jack use me at his pleasure.

PETER I see nobody use you at his pleasure. If I had, I would soon have drawn. You know my tool is as soon out as another's, if I see time and place.

NURSE Now, afore God, he hath so vexed me that every member about me quivers. Scurvy jack! (*To Romeo*) But as I said, my lady bade me seek ye out, and what she bade me tell ye, that I'll keep to myself; but if you should lead her into a fool's paradise, as they say, it were a very gross kind of behaviour, as they say, for the gentlewoman is young. Now, if you should deal doubly with her, it were very weak dealing, and not to be offered to any gentlewoman.

ROMEO Nurse, commend me to thy lady, tell her I protest—

NURSE Good heart, i'faith I'll tell her so. O, she will be a joyful woman.

ROMEO Why, what wilt thou tell her?

NURSE That you do protest, which, as I take it, is a gentlemanlike proffer.

ROMEO

Bid her get leave tomorrow morning
To come to shrift to Friar Laurence' cell;
And stay thou, Nurse, behind the abbey wall.
My man shall come to thee and bring along
The cords, made like a tackled stair,
Which to the high topgallant of my joy
Must be my conduct in the secret night.
Hold, take that for thy pains.

NURSE No, not a penny, truly.

ROMEO I say you shall not choose.

NURSE Well, tomorrow morning, she shall not fail.

ROMEO Farewell, be trusty, and I'll quit thy pain. *Exit*

NURSE Peter, take my fan and go before.

Exeunt the Nurse and Peter

2.4 *Enter Juliet*

JULIET

The clock struck nine when I did send my Nurse;
In half an hour she promised to return.
Perhaps she cannot find him—that's not so.
O she is lazy! Love's heralds should be thoughts,
And run more swift than hasty powder fired
Doth hurry from the fearful cannon's mouth.

Enter the Nurse

O now she comes! Tell me, gentle Nurse,
What says my love?

NURSE

O I am weary, let me rest a while.
Lord, how my bones ache. O,where's my man?
Give me some aqua-vitae.

JULIET
I would thou hadst my bones, and I thy news.

NURSE Fie, what a jaunt have I had! And my back—a t'other side. Lord, Lord, what a case am I in!

JULIET
But tell me, sweet Nurse, what says Romeo?

NURSE Romeo, nay, alas,you cannot choose a man. He's nobody, he is not the flower of courtesy, he is not a proper man; and for a hand and a foot and a body, well, go thy way, wench, thou hast it i'faith. Lord, Lord, how my head beats!

JULIET
What of all this? Tell me, what says he to our marriage?

NURSE
Marry, he says, like an honest gentleman,
And a kind, and, I warrant, a virtuous—
Where's your mother?

JULIET
Lord, Lord, how oddly thou repliest:
'He says, like a kind gentleman,
And an honest, and a virtuous,
"Where's your mother?"'

NURSE
Marry come up, cannot you stay a while?
Is this the poultice for mine aching bones?
Next errand you'll have done, even do't yourself.

JULIET
Nay, stay, sweet Nurse, I do entreat thee now.
What says my love, my lord, my Romeo?

NURSE
Go, hie you straight to Friar Laurence' cell,
And frame a scuse that you must go to shrift;
There stays a bridegroom to make you a bride.
Now comes the wanton blood up in your cheeks.
I must provide a ladder made of cords,
With which your lord must climb a bird's-nest soon.
I must take pains to further your delight,
But you must bear the burden soon at night.
Doth this news please you now?

JULIET
How doth her latter words revive my heart!
Thanks, gentle Nurse, dispatch thy business,
And I'll not fail to meet my Romeo. *Exeunt*

2.4.34 **scuse** Aphetic form of 'excuse' (*OED sb.*).

2.5 *Enter Romeo and Friar Laurence*

ROMEO
Now, Father Laurence, in thy holy grant
Consists the good of me and Juliet.

FRIAR LAURENCE
Without more words I will do all I may
To make you happy, if in me it lie.

ROMEO
This morning here she pointed we should meet
And consummate those never-parting bands,
Witness of our hearts' love, by joining hands,
And come she will.

FRIAR LAURENCE I guess she will indeed;
Youth's love is quick, swifter than swiftest speed.

Enter Juliet, somewhat fast, and she embraces Romeo

See where she comes.
So light of foot ne'er hurts the trodden flower.
Of love and joy, see, see the sovereign power.

JULIET Romeo.

ROMEO
My Juliet, welcome. As do waking eyes,
Closed in night's mists, attend the frolic day,
So Romeo hath expected Juliet,
And thou art come.

JULIET I am, if I be day,
Come to my sun. Shine forth, and make me fair.

ROMEO
All beauteous fairness dwelleth in thine eyes.

JULIET
Romeo, from thine all brightness doth arise.

FRIAR LAURENCE
Come, wantons, come, the stealing hours do pass.
Defer embracements till some fitter time;
Part for a while, you shall not be alone
Till holy church have joined ye both in one.

ROMEO
Lead, holy father, all delay seems long.

JULIET
Make haste, make haste, this ling'ring doth us wrong.

FRIAR LAURENCE
O, soft and fair makes sweetest work, they say.
Haste is a common hind'rer in cross' way. *Exeunt*

2.5.5 **pointed** Aphetic form of 'appointed', i.e. determined or agreed (*OED* v.[2]).

27–8 **soft . . . way** This couplet seems to combine two proverbs, 'Soft and

3.1 *Enter Benvolio, Mercutio, and Mercutio's page*

BENVOLIO
I prithee, good Mercutio, let's retire;
The day is hot, the Capels are abroad.

MERCUTIO Thou art like one of those that, when he comes into the confines of a tavern, claps me his rapier on the board and says, 'God send me no need of thee'; and, by the operation of the next cup of wine, he draws it on the drawer, when indeed there is no need.

BENVOLIO Am I like such a one?

MERCUTIO Go to, thou art as hot a jack, being moved, and as soon moved to be moody, and as soon moody to be moved.

BENVOLIO And what to?

MERCUTIO Nay, an there were two such, we should have none shortly. Didst not thou fall out with a man for cracking nuts, having no other reason but because thou hadst hazel eyes? What eye but such an eye would have picked out such a quarrel? With another for coughing, because he waked thy dog that lay asleep in the sun? With a tailor for wearing his new doublet before Easter, and with another for tying his new shoes with old ribbons? And yet thou wilt forbid me of quarrelling!

BENVOLIO By my head, here comes a Capulet.

Enter Tybalt

MERCUTIO By my heel, I care not.

TYBALT Gentlemen, a word with one of you.

MERCUTIO But one word with one of us? You had best couple it with somewhat, and make it a word and a blow.

TYBALT I am apt enough to that if I have occasion.

MERCUTIO Could you not take occasion?

TYBALT Mercutio, thou consorts with Romeo.

MERCUTIO 'Consort'! Zounds, 'consort'! The slave will make fiddlers of us. If you do, sirrah, look for nothing but discord, for here's my fiddlestick.

Enter Romeo

TYBALT
Well, peace be with you, here comes my man.

MERCUTIO But I'll be hanged if he wear your livery. Marry, go before into the field, and he may be your follower; so in that sense your worship may call him 'man'.

fair (goes far)' and 'The more haste the less (worse) speed' (Dent S601, H198).

3.1.31–75 **Well . . . houses!** Q1 sets this whole passage as prose. This edition relines those speeches which can be scanned as blank verse.

TYBALT
Romeo, the hate I bear to thee can afford
No better words than these: thou art a villain.

ROMEO
Tybalt, the love I bear to thee
Doth excuse the appertaining rage
To such a word. Villain am I none.
Therefore I well perceive thou knowst me not.

TYBALT Base boy, this cannot serve thy turn, and therefore draw.

ROMEO
I do protest I never injured thee,
But love thee better than thou canst devise
Till thou shalt know the reason of my love.

MERCUTIO
O dishonourable, vile submission!
Alla stoccado carries it away.
You rat-catcher, come back, come back.

TYBALT What wouldst with me?

MERCUTIO Nothing, king of cats, but borrow one of your nine lives. Therefore come draw your rapier out of your scabbard, lest mine be about your ears ere you be aware.

ROMEO Stay, Tybalt! Hold, Mercutio! Benvolio, beat down their weapons.

Tybalt stabs Mercutio under Romeo's arm and flies

MERCUTIO Is he gone? Hath he nothing? A pox on your houses!

ROMEO
What, art thou hurt, man? The wound is not deep.

MERCUTIO No, not so deep as a well, not so wide as a barn-door, but it will serve, I warrant. What meant you to come between us? I was hurt under your arm.

ROMEO I did all for the best.

MERCUTIO A pox of your houses, I am fairly dressed.
Sirrah, go fetch me a surgeon.

PAGE I go, my lord. *Exit*

MERCUTIO I am peppered for this world, I am sped i'faith. He hath made worms' meat of me. An ye ask for me tomorrow, you shall find me a grave man. A pox of your houses! I shall be fairly mounted upon four men's shoulders—for your house of the Montagues and the Capulets—and then some peasantly rogue, some sexton, some base slave shall write my epitaph:

60 **dressed** prepared (for death). This line anticipates Mercutio's next speech, which completes the wordplay and the metaphor: he is like food seasoned (*dressed*, 'peppered') for cooking.

That Tybalt came and broke the Prince's laws,
And Mercutio was slain for the first and second cause.
Where's the surgeon?

PAGE (*returning*) He's come, sir.

MERCUTIO Now he'll keep a-mumbling in my guts—on the other side—come, Benvolio, lend me thy hand. A pox of your houses! ⌈*Exit Mercutio with Benvolio*⌉

ROMEO
This gentleman, the Prince's near ally,
My very friend, hath ta'en this mortal wound
In my behalf; my reputation stained
With Tybalt's slander—Tybalt, that an hour
Hath been my kinsman. Ah Juliet,
Thy beauty makes me thus effeminate,
And in my temper softens valour's steel.

Enter Benvolio

BENVOLIO
Ah Romeo, Romeo, brave Mercutio is dead.
That gallant spirit hath aspired the clouds,
Which too untimely scorned the lowly earth.

ROMEO
This day's black fate on more days doth depend;
This but begins what other days must end.

Enter Tybalt

BENVOLIO
Here comes the furious Tybalt back again.

ROMEO
Alive in triumph and Mercutio slain?
Away to heaven, respective lenity,
And fire-eyed fury be my conduct now.
Now, Tybalt, take the 'villain' back again
Which late thou gav'st me; for Mercutio's soul
Is but a little way above the clouds
And stays for thine to bear him company.
Or thou or I, or both, shall follow him.

They fight. Tybalt falls

BENVOLIO
Romeo, away! Thou seest that Tybalt's slain.
The citizens approach—away, be gone!—
Thou wilt be taken.

ROMEO Ah, I am fortune's slave. *Exit Romeo*

Enter Citizens

WATCHMAN Where's he that slew Mercutio, Tybalt, that villain?

BENVOLIO
There is that Tybalt.

[WATCHMAN] Up, sirrah, go with us.

Enter the Prince and Capulet's Wife

PRINCE
Where be the vile beginners of this fray?

BENVOLIO
Ah noble Prince, I can discover all
The most unlucky manage of this brawl.
Here lies the man, slain by young Romeo,
That slew thy kinsman, brave Mercutio.

CAPULET'S WIFE
Tybalt, Tybalt, O my brother's child,
Unhappy sight! Ah, the blood is spilled
Of my dear kinsman! Prince, as thou art true,
For blood of ours shed blood of Montague.

PRINCE
Speak, Benvolio, who began this fray?

BENVOLIO
Tybalt, here slain, whom Romeo's hand did slay—
Romeo, who spake him fair, bid him bethink
How nice the quarrel was.
But Tybalt, still persisting in his wrong,
The stout Mercutio drew to calm the storm,
Which Romeo, seeing, called 'Stay, gentlemen!',
And on me cried, who drew to part their strife;
And with his agile arm young Romeo,
As fast as tongue cried 'Peace!', sought peace to make.
While they were interchanging thrusts and blows,
Under young Romeo's labouring arm to part,
The furious Tybalt cast an envious thrust
That rid the life of stout Mercutio.
With that he fled, but presently returned,
And with his rapier bravèd Romeo,
That had but newly entertained revenge;
And ere I could draw forth my rapier
To part their fury, down did Tybalt fall,
And this way Romeo fled.

CAPULET'S WIFE
He is a Montague and speaks partial.

3.1.101 [WATCHMAN]] This edition; *not in* Q1

Some twenty of them fought in this black strife,
And all those twenty could but kill one life.
I do entreat, sweet Prince, thou'lt justice give:
Romeo slew Tybalt; Romeo may not live.

PRINCE

And for that offence
Immediately we do exile him hence.
I have an interest in your hate's proceeding;
My blood for your rude brawls doth lie a-bleeding.
But I'll amerce you with so large a fine,
That you shall all repent the loss of mine.
I will be deaf to pleading and excuses;
Nor tears nor prayers shall purchase for abuses.
Pity shall dwell and govern with us still;
Mercy to all but murd'rers, pardoning none that kill.

Exeunt

3.2 *Enter Juliet*

JULIET

Gallop apace, you fiery-footed steeds,
To Phoebus' mansion. Such a wagoner
As Phaëton would quickly bring you thither,
And send in cloudy night immediately.

Enter the Nurse, wringing her hands, with the ladder of cords in her lap

But how now, Nurse? O Lord, why look'st thou sad?
What hast thou there, the cords?

NURSE

Ay, ay, the cords.
Alack, we are undone, we are undone;
Lady, we are undone.

JULIET

What devil art thou that torments me thus?

NURSE

Alack the day, he's dead, he's dead, he's dead!

JULIET

This torture should be roared in dismal hell.
Can heavens be so envious?

NURSE

Romeo can if heavens cannot.
I saw the wound, I saw it with mine eyes—
God save the sample—on his manly breast.

143 **purchase** provide (*OED* v. 3b)

3.2.14 **sample** mark. See 3.2.53 n. in the edition of Q2 for an explanation of the phrase 'God save the mark!'

A bloody corse, a piteous bloody corse,
All pale as ashes—I swounded at the sight.

JULIET
Ah Romeo, Romeo, what disaster hap
Hath severed thee from thy true Juliet?
Ah, why should heaven so much conspire with woe,
Or fate envy our happy marriage,
So soon to sunder us by timeless death?

NURSE
O Tybalt, Tybalt, the best friend I had!
O honest Tybalt, courteous gentleman!

JULIET
What storm is this that blows so contrary?
Is Tybalt dead and Romeo murderèd,
My dear-loved cousin and my dearest lord?
Then let the trumpet sound a general doom;
These two being dead, then living is there none.

NURSE
Tybalt is dead and Romeo banishèd;
Romeo that murdered him is banishèd.

JULIET
Ah heavens, did Romeo's hand shed Tybalt's blood?

NURSE
It did, it did, alack the day, it did.

JULIET
O serpent's hate, hid with a flow'ring face!
O painted sepulchre, including filth!
Was never book containing so foul matter
So fairly bound. Ah, what meant Romeo?

NURSE
There is no truth, no faith, no honesty in men;
All false, all faithless, perjured, all forsworn.
Shame come to Romeo!

JULIET
A blister on that tongue! He was not born to shame.
Upon his face shame is ashamed to sit.
But wherefore, villain, didst thou kill my cousin?
That villain cousin would have killed my husband.
All this is comfort. But there yet remains
Worse than his death, which fain I would forget;
But ah, it presseth to my memory:
'Romeo is banishèd'. Ah, that word 'banishèd'

17 **disaster** disastrous

Is worse than death. 'Romeo is banishèd'
Is father, mother, Tybalt, Juliet,
All killed, all slain, all dead, all banishèd.
Where are my father and my mother, Nurse?

NURSE
Weeping and wailing over Tybalt's corse.
Will you go to them?

JULIET Ay, ay, when theirs are spent,
Mine shall be shed for Romeo's banishment.

NURSE
Lady, your Romeo will be here tonight.
I'll to him; he is hid at Laurence' cell.

JULIET
Do so, and bear this ring to my true knight,
And bid him come to take his last farewell. *Exeunt*

3.3 *Enter Friar Laurence*

FRIAR LAURENCE
Romeo, come forth, come forth, thou fearful man.
Affliction is enamoured on thy parts,
And thou art wedded to calamity.
Enter Romeo

ROMEO
Father, what news? What is the Prince's doom?
What sorrow craves acquaintance at our hands
Which yet we know not?

FRIAR LAURENCE Too familiar
Is my young son with such sour company.
I bring thee tidings of the Prince's doom.

ROMEO
What less than doomsday is the Prince's doom?

FRIAR LAURENCE
A gentler judgement vanished from his lips:
Not body's death, but body's banishment.

ROMEO
Ha, banishèd? Be merciful, say 'death';
For exile hath more terror in his looks
Than death itself. Do not say 'banishment'.

FRIAR LAURENCE
Hence from Verona art thou banishèd.
Be patient, for the world is broad and wide.

ROMEO
There is no world without Verona walls,

But purgatory, torture, hell itself.
Hence banishèd is banished from the world,
And world exiled is death. Calling death 'banishment',
Thou cutt'st my head off with a golden axe,
And smilest upon the stroke that murders me.

FRIAR LAURENCE

O monstrous sin, O rude unthankfulness!
Thy fault our law calls death; but the mild Prince,
Taking thy part, hath rushed aside the law,
And turned that black word 'death' to 'banishment'.
This is mere mercy, and thou seest it not.

ROMEO

'Tis torture and not mercy. Heaven is here
Where Juliet lives; and every cat and dog
And little mouse, every unworthy thing
Live here in heaven and may look on her,
But Romeo may not. More validity,
More honourable state, more courtship lives
In carrion-flies than Romeo. They may seize
On the white wonder of fair Juliet's skin,
And steal immortal kisses from her lips;
But Romeo may not, he is banishèd.
Flies may do this, but I from this must fly.
O father, hadst thou no strong poison mixed,
No sharp-ground knife, no present mean of death,
Though ne'er so mean, but 'banishment'
To torture me withal? Ah, 'banishèd'.
O Friar, the damnèd use that word in hell;
Howling attends it. How hadst thou the heart,
Being a divine, a ghostly confessor,
A sin-absolver, and my friend professed,
To mangle me with that word 'banishment'?

FRIAR LAURENCE

Thou fond mad man, hear me but speak a word.

ROMEO

O, thou wilt talk again of banishment.

FRIAR LAURENCE

I'll give thee armour to bear off this word,
Adversity's sweet milk, philosophy,
To comfort thee though thou be banishèd.

ROMEO

Yet 'banishèd'? Hang up philosophy!

3.3.27 **mere** pure (*OED a.*[2] 1c)

50 **bear** ward (*OED v.*[1] 34)

Unless philosophy can make a Juliet,
Displant a town, reverse a prince's doom,
It helps not, it prevails not, talk no more.

FRIAR LAURENCE
O, now I see that mad men have no ears.

ROMEO
How should they, when that wise men have no eyes?

FRIAR LAURENCE
Let me dispute with thee of thy estate.

ROMEO
Thou canst not speak of what thou dost not feel.
Wert thou as young as I, Juliet thy love,
An hour but married, Tybalt murderèd,
Doting like me, and like me banishèd,
Then mightst thou speak, then mightst thou tear thy hair,
And fall upon the ground as I do now,
Taking the measure of an unmade grave.
The Nurse knocks

FRIAR LAURENCE
Romeo, arise, stand up, thou wilt be taken—
I hear one knock—arise and get thee gone.

NURSE (*within*)
Ho, Friar!

FRIAR LAURENCE God's will, what wilfulness is this?
The Nurse knocks again

NURSE (*within*) Ho, Friar, open the door.

FRIAR LAURENCE By and by, I come. Who is there?

NURSE (*within*)
One from Lady Juliet.

FRIAR LAURENCE (*opening the door*) Then come near.
Enter the Nurse

NURSE
O holy Friar, tell me, O holy Friar,
Where is my lady's lord? Where's Romeo?

FRIAR LAURENCE
There on the ground, with his own tears made drunk.

NURSE
O, he is even in my mistress' case,
Just in her case! O woeful sympathy,
Piteous predicament! Even so lies she,
Weeping and blubb'ring, blubb'ring and weeping.—
Stand up, stand up, stand an you be a man;
For Juliet's sake, for her sake, rise and stand.

Why should you fall into so deep an O?
Romeo rises

ROMEO
Nurse—

NURSE Ah sir, ah sir, well, death's the end of all.

ROMEO
Spakest thou of Juliet? How is it with her?
Doth she not think me an old murderer,
Now I have stained the childhood of her joy
With blood removed but little from her own?
Where is she, and how doth she, and what says
My concealed lady to our cancelled love?

NURSE
O she saith nothing, but weeps and pules,
And now falls on her bed, now on the ground,
And 'Tybalt' cries, and then on Romeo calls.

ROMEO
As if that name, shot from the deadly level of a gun,
Did murder her, as that name's cursèd hand
Murdered her kinsman. Ah tell me, holy Friar,
In what vile part of this anatomy
Doth my name lie? Tell me, that I may sack
The hateful mansion.
Romeo offers to stab himself, and the Nurse snatches the dagger away

NURSE Ah!

FRIAR LAURENCE
Hold, stay thy hand! Art thou a man? Thy form
Cries out thou art, but thy wild acts denote
The unreasonable furies of a beast.
Unseemly woman in a seeming man,
Or ill-beseeming beast in seeming both,
Thou hast amazed me. By my holy order,
I thought thy disposition better tempered.
Hast thou slain Tybalt? Wilt thou slay thyself,
And slay thy lady, too, that lives in thee?
Rouse up thy spirits. Thy lady Juliet lives,
For whose sweet sake thou wert but lately dead:
There art thou happy. Tybalt would kill thee,
But thou slewest Tybalt: there art thou happy, too.
A pack of blessings lights upon thy back,
Happiness courts thee in his best array,
But like a misbehaved and sullen wench,

Thou frown'st upon thy fate that smiles on thee.
Take heed, take heed, for such die miserable.
Go, get thee to thy love, as was decreed;
Ascend her chamber-window, hence and comfort her.
But look thou stay not till the watch be set;
For then thou canst not pass to Mantua.
Nurse, provide all things in a readiness:
Comfort thy mistress, haste the house to bed,
Which heavy sorrow makes them apt unto.

NURSE
Good Lord, what a thing learning is!
I could have stayed here all this night
To hear good counsel. Well, sir,
I'll tell my lady that you will come.

ROMEO
Do so, and bid my sweet prepare to chide.
Farewell, good Nurse.
The Nurse offers to go in and turns again

NURSE
Here is a ring, sir, that she bade me give you.

ROMEO
How well my comfort is revived by this. *Exit the Nurse*

FRIAR LAURENCE
Sojourn in Mantua. I'll find out your man,
And he shall signify from time to time
Every good hap that doth befall thee here.
Farewell.

ROMEO
But that a joy past joy cries out on me,
It were a grief so brief to part with thee. *Exeunt*

3.4 *Enter old Capulet and his Wife with the County Paris*

CAPULET
Things have fallen out, sir, so unluckily,
That we have had no time to move my daughter.
Look ye, sir, she loved her kinsman dearly,
And so did I. Well, we were born to die.
Wife, where's your daughter? Is she in her chamber?
I think she means not to come down tonight.

PARIS
These times of woe afford no time to woo.
Madam, farewell; commend me to your daughter.
Paris offers to go in, and Capulet calls him again

CAPULET
Sir Paris, I'll make a desperate tender of my child.
I think she will be ruled in all respects by me.
But soft, what day is this?
PARIS Monday, my lord.
CAPULET O, then Wednesday is too soon;
On Thursday, let it be, you shall be married.
We'll make no great ado, a friend or two or so;
For, look ye, sir, Tybalt being slain so lately,
It will be thought we held him carelessly
If we should revel much. Therefore we will have
Some half a dozen friends and make no more ado.
But what say you to Thursday?
PARIS
My lord, I wish that Thursday were tomorrow.
CAPULET
Wife, go you to your daughter ere you go to bed;
Acquaint her with the County Paris' love.—
Farewell, my lord, till Thursday next.—
Wife, get you to your daughter.—Light to my chamber!—
Afore me, it is so very very late
That we may call it early by and by. *Exeunt*

3.5 *Enter Romeo and Juliet at the window*

JULIET
Wilt thou be gone? It is not yet near day.
It was the nightingale, and not the lark,
That pierced the fearful hollow of thine ear.
Nightly she sings on yon pomegranate tree.
Believe me, love, it was the nightingale.
ROMEO
It was the lark, the herald of the morn,
And not the nightingale. See, love, what envious streaks
Do lace the severing clouds in yonder east.
Night's candles are burnt out, and jocund day
Stands tiptoes on the misty mountain tops.
I must be gone and live, or stay and die.
JULIET
Yon light is not daylight; I know it, I.
It is some meteor that the sun exhales
To be this night to thee a torch-bearer,

3.4.27 *Exeunt*] Q2; *not in* Q1

And light thee on thy way to Mantua.
Then stay a while; thou shalt not go soon.

ROMEO
Let me stay here, let me be ta'en and die;
If thou wilt have it so, I am content.
I'll say yon grey is not the morning's eye:
It is the pale reflex of Cynthia's brow.
I'll say it is the nightingale that beats
The vaulty heaven so high above our heads,
And not the lark, the messenger of morn.
Come, death, and welcome! Juliet wills it so.
What says my love? Let's talk; 'tis not yet day.

JULIET
It is, it is! Be gone, fly hence, away!
It is the lark that sings so out of tune,
Straining harsh discords and unpleasing sharps.
Some say the lark makes sweet division;
This doth not so, for this divideth us.
Some say the lark and loathèd toad changed eyes.
I would that now they had changed voices too,
Since arm from arm her voice doth us affray,
Hunting thee hence with hunt's-up to the day.
So now, be gone! More light and light it grows.

ROMEO
More light and light, more dark and dark our woes.
Farewell, my love, one kiss and I'll descend.
He goes down

JULIET
Art thou gone so, my lord, my love, my friend?
I must hear from thee every day in the hour,
For in an hour there are many minutes;
Minutes are days, so will I number them.
O, by this count I shall be much in years
Ere I see thee again.

ROMEO Farewell.
I will omit no opportunity
That may convey my greetings, love, to thee.

JULIET
O, think'st thou we shall ever meet again?

ROMEO
No doubt, no doubt, and all this woe shall serve
For sweet discourses in the time to come.

3.5.31 changed] ROWE 1714; change Q1

JULIET
O God, I have an ill-divining soul!
Methinks I see thee, now thou art below,
Like one dead in the bottom of a tomb.
Either mine eyesight fails, or thou look'st pale.

ROMEO
And trust me, love, in my eye so do you.
Dry sorrow drinks our blood. Adieu, adieu. *Exit*

Enter the Nurse hastily

NURSE
Madam, beware, take heed, the day is broke;
Your mother's coming to your chamber, make all sure.

She goes down from the window.

Enter Capulet's Wife and the Nurse

CAPULET'S WIFE Where are you, daughter?

NURSE What lady, lamb, what Juliet!

JULIET How now, who calls?

NURSE It is your mother.

CAPULET'S WIFE Why, how now, Juliet?

JULIET Madam, I am not well.

CAPULET'S WIFE
What, evermore weeping for your cousin's death?
I think thou'lt wash him from his grave with tears.

JULIET
I cannot choose, having so great a loss.

CAPULET'S WIFE I cannot blame thee.
But it grieves thee more that villain lives.

JULIET
What villain, madam?

CAPULET'S WIFE That villain Romeo.

JULIET
Villain and he are many miles asunder.

CAPULET'S WIFE
Content thee, girl. If I could find a man,
I soon would send to Mantua, where he is,
That should bestow on him so sure a draught,
As he should soon bear Tybalt company.

JULIET
Find you the means, and I'll find such a man;
For whilst he lives my heart shall ne'er be light
Till I behold him—dead—is my poor heart
Thus for a kinsman vexed.

CAPULET'S WIFE
Well, let that pass. I come to bring thee joyful news.
JULIET
And joy comes well in such a needful time.
CAPULET'S WIFE
Well, then, thou hast a careful father, girl;
And one who, pitying thy needful state,
Hath found thee out a happy day of joy.
JULIET
What day is that, I pray you?
CAPULET'S WIFE Marry, my child,
The gallant, young, and youthful gentleman,
The County Paris, at Saint Peter's Church,
Early next Thursday morning must provide
To make you there a glad and joyful bride.
JULIET
Now by Saint Peter's Church, and Peter too,
He shall not there make me a joyful bride!
Are these the news you had to tell me of?
Marry, here are news indeed! Madam, I will not marry yet;
And when I do, it shall be rather Romeo, whom I hate,
Than County Paris, that I cannot love.
Enter old Capulet
CAPULET'S WIFE
Here comes your father; you may tell him so.
CAPULET
Why, how now, evermore show'ring? In one little body
Thou resemblest a sea, a bark, a storm:
For this thy body, which I term a bark,
Still floating in thy ever-falling tears,
And tossed with sighs arising from thy heart,
Will without succour shipwreck presently.
But hear you, wife, what, have you sounded her?
What says she to it?
CAPULET'S WIFE
I have, but she will none, she thanks ye.
Would God that she were married to her grave!
CAPULET
What, will she not? Doth she not thank us?
Doth she not wax proud?

3.5.96–103 **Why . . . it?** Like the corresponding passage in Q2, this speech is metrically irregular. Here ll. 96–7 and 102–3 are relined, because two of the original verses are particularly long. Ll. 106–7 have also been redistributed, in this case from one long line set as prose.

JULIET
Not proud ye have, but thankful that ye have.
Proud can I never be of that I hate,
But thankful even for hate that is meant love.

CAPULET
'Proud' and 'I thank you', and 'I thank you not',
And yet 'not proud'? What's here, chop-logic?
Proud me no prouds, nor thank me no thanks;
But fettle your fine joints on Thursday next
To go with Paris to Saint Peter's Church,
Or I will drag you on a hurdle thither.
Out, you green-sickness baggage! Out, you tallow-face!

JULIET Good father, hear me speak.
She kneels down

CAPULET
I tell thee what: either resolve on Thursday next
To go with Paris to Saint Peter's Church,
Or henceforth never look me in the face.
Speak not, reply not, for my fingers itch.
Why, wife, we thought that we were scarcely blessed
That God had sent us but this only child;
But now I see this one is one too much,
And that we have a cross in having her.

NURSE
Marry, God in heaven bless her, my lord!
You are to blame to rate her so.

CAPULET
And why, my lady Wisdom? Hold your tongue,
Good Prudence, smatter with your gossips, go.

NURSE
Why, my lord, I speak no treason.

CAPULET O God 'i' good e'en!
Utter your gravity over a gossip's bowl,
For here we need it not.

CAPULET'S WIFE My lord, ye are too hot.

CAPULET
God's blessèd mother, wife, it mads me!
Day, night, early, late, at home, abroad,
Alone, in company, waking or sleeping,
Still my care hath been to see her matched;
And having now found out a gentleman
Of princely parentage, youthful and nobly trained,

134 **mads** maddens or infuriates (*OED* v. 1)

Stuffed, as they say, with honourable parts,
Proportioned as one's heart could wish a man—
And then to have a wretched whining fool,
A puling maumet, in her fortune's tender,
To say 'I cannot love, I am too young,
I pray you pardon me'.
But if you cannot wed, I'll pardon you!
Graze where you will, you shall not house with me.
Look to it, think on't; I do not use to jest.
I tell ye what, Thursday is near.
Lay hand on heart, advise, bethink yourself.
If you be mine, I'll give you to my friend;
If not, hang, drown, starve, beg, die in the streets!
For, by my soul, I'll ne'er more acknowledge thee,
Nor what I have shall ever do thee good.
Think on't, look to't; I do not use to jest. *Exit*

JULIET

Is there no pity hanging in the clouds
That looks into the bottom of my woes?
(*To her mother*) I do beseech you, madam, cast me not away!
Defer this marriage for a day or two;
Or if you cannot, make my marriage bed
In that dim monument where Tybalt lies.

CAPULET'S WIFE

Nay, be assured, I will not speak a word.
Do what thou wilt, for I have done with thee. *Exit*

JULIET

Ah Nurse, what comfort? What counsel canst thou give me?

NURSE

Now trust me, madam, I know not what to say.
Your Romeo, he is banished, and all the world to nothing
He never dares return to challenge you.
Now I think good you marry with this County.
O, he is a gallant gentleman!
Romeo is but a dish-clout in respect of him.
I promise you,
I think you happy in this second match.
As for your husband, he is dead,
Or 'twere as good he were, for you have no use of him.

144–53 **To say . . . thee** In this metrically irregular speech ll. 144–5 reline one long verse as two and ll. 152–3 reline three short verses as two pentameters.

169–71 **O . . . you** This awkward passage has been relined from an even more awkward set of mismatched verses, one very long.

JULIET
Speak'st thou this from thy heart?
NURSE
Ay, and from my soul, or else beshrew them both.
JULIET Amen.
NURSE What say you, madam?
JULIET
Well, thou hast comforted me wondrous much.
I pray thee, go thy ways unto my mother.
Tell her I am gone, having displeased my father,
To Friar Laurence' cell, to confess me
And to be absolved.
NURSE I will, and this is wisely done. *Exit*
Juliet looks after the Nurse
JULIET
Ancient damnation! O most cursèd fiend!
Is it more sin to wish me thus forsworn,
Or to dispraise him with the selfsame tongue
That thou hast praised him with above compare
So many thousand times? Go, counsellor;
Thou and my bosom henceforth shall be twain.
I'll to the Friar to know his remedy.
If all fail else, I have the power to die. *Exit*

4.1 *Enter Friar Laurence and the County Paris*
FRIAR LAURENCE
On Thursday, say ye? The time is very short.
PARIS
My father Capulet will have it so,
And I am nothing slack to slow his haste.
FRIAR LAURENCE
You say you do not know the lady's mind?
Uneven is the course; I like it not.
PARIS
Immoderately she weeps for Tybalt's death,
And therefore have I little talked of love,
For Venus smiles not in a house of tears.
Now, sir, her father thinks it dangerous
That she doth give her sorrow so much sway;
And in his wisdom hastes our marriage
To stop the inundation of her tears,
Which, too much minded by herself alone,

183 *Exit*] Q4; *not in* Q1

May be put from her by society.
Now do ye know the reason of this haste.

FRIAR LAURENCE (*aside*)
I would I knew not why it should be slowed.

Enter ⌈*Juliet*⌉

Here comes the lady to my cell.

PARIS
Welcome my love, my lady and my wife.

JULIET
That may be, sir, when I may be a wife.

PARIS
That 'may be' must be, love, on Thursday next.

JULIET
What must be shall be.

FRIAR LAURENCE That's a certain text.

PARIS
What, come ye to confession to this Friar?

JULIET
To tell you that were to confess to you.

PARIS
Do not deny to him that you love me.

JULIET
I will confess to you that I love him.

PARIS
So I am sure you will that you love me.

JULIET
An if I do, it will be of more price,
Being spoke behind your back, than to your face.

PARIS
Poor soul, thy face is much abused with tears.

JULIET
The tears have got small victory by that,
For it was bad enough before their spite.

PARIS
Thou wrong'st it more than tears by that report.

JULIET
That is no wrong, sir, that is a truth;
And what I spake, I spake it to my face.

PARIS
Thy face is mine, and thou hast slandered it.

JULIET
It may be so, for it is not mine own.—

4.1.16.1 ⌈*Juliet*⌉ | Q2; *Paris* Q1

Are you at leisure, holy father, now,
Or shall I come to you at evening mass?

FRIAR LAURENCE
My leisure serves me, pensive daughter, now.
My lord, we must entreat the time alone.

PARIS
God shield I should disturb devotion!
Juliet, farewell, and keep this holy kiss. *Exit*

JULIET
Go shut the door, and when thou hast done so,
Come weep with me that am past cure, past help.

FRIAR LAURENCE
Ah Juliet, I already know thy grief;
I hear thou must, and nothing may prorogue it,
On Thursday next be married to the County.

JULIET
Tell me not, Friar, that thou hear'st of it,
Unless thou tell me how we may prevent it.
Give me some sudden counsel; else behold,
'Twixt my extremes and me this bloody knife
Shall play the umpire, arbitrating that
Which the commission of thy years and art
Could to no issue of true honour bring.
Speak not, be brief; for I desire to die,
If what thou speak'st speak not of remedy.

FRIAR LAURENCE
Stay, Juliet, I do spy a kind of hope,
Which craves as desperate an execution
As that is desperate we would prevent.
If rather than to marry County Paris
Thou hast the strength of will to slay thyself,
'Tis not unlike that thou wilt undertake
A thing like death to chide away this shame,
That cop'st with death itself to fly from blame;
And if thou dost, I'll give thee remedy.

JULIET
O bid me leap, rather than marry Paris,
From off the battlements of yonder tower;
Or chain me to some steepy mountain's top,
Where roaring bears and savage lions are;
Or shut me nightly in a charnel-house,

61 of] Q2; or Q1

4.1.50 **sudden** immediate (*OED a.* 3a)

With reeky shanks and yellow chapless skulls;
Or lay me in tomb with one new dead—
Things that, to hear them named, have made me tremble—
And I will do it without fear or doubt,
To keep myself a faithful unstained wife
To my dear lord, my dearest Romeo.

FRIAR LAURENCE

Hold, Juliet, hie thee home, get thee to bed,
Let not thy Nurse lie with thee in thy chamber;
And when thou art alone, take thou this vial,
And this distillèd liquor drink thou off;
When presently through all thy veins shall run
A dull and heavy slumber which shall seize
Each vital spirit, for no pulse shall keep
His natural progress, but surcease to beat.
No sign of breath shall testify thou liv'st;
And in this borrowed likeness of shrunk death
Thou shalt remain full two-and-forty hours;
And when thou art laid in thy kindred's vault,
I'll send in haste to Mantua to thy lord,
And he shall come and take thee from thy grave.

JULIET

Friar, I go. Be sure thou send for my dear Romeo. *Exeunt*

4.2 *Enter old Capulet, his Wife, the Nurse, and a Serving-man*

CAPULET Where are you, sirrah?

SERVING-MAN Here, forsooth.

CAPULET Go, provide me twenty cunning cooks.

SERVING-MAN I warrant you, sir, let me alone for that; I'll know them by licking their fingers.

CAPULET How canst thou know them so?

SERVING-MAN Ah, sir, 'tis an ill cook cannot lick his own fingers.

CAPULET Well, get you gone. *Exit the Serving-man*
But where's this headstrong?

CAPULET'S WIFE

She's gone, my lord, to Friar Laurence' cell
To be confessed.

CAPULET

Ah, he may hap to do some good of her;
A headstrong self-willed harlotry it is.

Enter Juliet

CAPULET'S WIFE

See, here she cometh from confession.

CAPULET
How now, my headstrong, where have you been gadding?

JULIET
Where I have learnèd to repent the sin
Of froward wilful opposition
'Gainst you and your behests; and am enjoined
By holy Laurence to fall prostrate here
And crave remission of so foul a fact.
She kneels down

CAPULET'S WIFE Why, that's well said.

CAPULET
Now, before God, this holy reverend Friar,
All our whole city is much bound unto.
Go, tell the County presently of this,
For I will have this knot knit up tomorrow.

JULIET (*rising*)
Nurse, will you go with me to my closet,
To sort such things as shall be requisite
Against tomorrow?

CAPULET'S WIFE
I prithee do, good Nurse, go in with her;
Help her to sort tires, rebatos, chains,
And I will come unto you presently.

NURSE
Come, sweetheart, shall we go?

JULIET
Ah, prithee, let us.
Exeunt Juliet and the Nurse

CAPULET'S WIFE
Methinks on Thursday would be time enough.

CAPULET
I say I will have this dispatched tomorrow.
Go, one, and certify the Count thereof.

CAPULET'S WIFE
I pray, my lord, let it be Thursday.

CAPULET
I say tomorrow, while she's in the mood.

CAPULET'S WIFE
We shall be short in our provision.

CAPULET
Let me alone for that; go, get you in.

4.2.20 fact deed (*OED sb.* 1a)
30 **tires** attire; perhaps, specifically, head-dresses
30 **rebatos** Stiff collars worn by both men and women from *c.*1590 to 1630 (*OED* a).

Now, before God, my heart is passing light,
To see her thus conformèd to our will. *Exeunt*

4.3 *Enter the Nurse and Juliet*

NURSE
Come, come, what need you anything else?

JULIET
Nothing, good Nurse, but leave me to myself;
For I do mean to lie alone tonight.

NURSE
Well, there's a clean smock under your pillow,
And so good night. *Exit*

Enter Capulet's Wife

CAPULET'S WIFE
What, are you busy? Do you need my help?

JULIET
No, madam, I desire to lie alone,
For I have many things to think upon.

CAPULET'S WIFE
Well then, good night. Be stirring, Juliet,
The County will be early here tomorrow. *Exit*

JULIET
Farewell.—God knows when we shall meet again.
Ah, I do take a fearful thing in hand.
What if this potion should not work at all?
Must I of force be married to the County?
This shall forbid it.—Knife, lie thou there.—
What if the Friar should give me this drink
To poison me, for fear I should disclose
Our former marriage? Ah, I wrong him much,
He is a holy and religious man;
I will not entertain so bad a thought.
What if I should be stifled in the tomb?
Awake an hour before the appointed time?
Ah, then I fear I shall be lunatic,
And playing with my dead forefathers' bones,
Dash out my frantic brains. Methinks I see
My cousin Tybalt welt'ring in his blood,
Seeking for Romeo. Stay, Tybalt, stay!
Romeo, I come! This do I drink to thee.

She falls upon her bed within the curtains

4.3.14 **of force** by compulsion (*OED sb.*[1] 5b)

4.4 *Enter the Nurse, with herbs, and Capulet's Wife*

CAPULET'S WIFE
That's well said, Nurse, set all in readiness;
The County will be here immediately.
Enter Capulet

CAPULET
Make haste, make haste, for it is almost day.
The curfew-bell hath rung; 'tis four o'clock.
Look to your baked meats, good Angelica.

NURSE Go, get you to bed, you cotquean. I'faith, you will be sick anon.

CAPULET I warrant thee, Nurse, I have ere now watched all night, and have taken no harm at all.

CAPULET'S WIFE
Ay, you have been a mouse-hunt in your time.
Enter a Serving-man with logs and coals

CAPULET
A jealous-hood, a jealous-hood!—How now, sirrah?
What have you there?

SERVING-MAN Forsooth, logs.

CAPULET Go, go, choose drier. Will will tell thee where thou shalt fetch them.

SERVING-MAN Nay, I warrant, let me alone. I have a head, I trow, to choose a log. *Exit*

CAPULET
Well, go thy way, thou shalt be loggerhead.
(*To his Wife*) Come, come, make haste, call up your daughter.
The County will be here with music straight.
Gods me, he's come. Nurse, call up my daughter.

NURSE Go, get you gone. *Exeunt Capulet and his Wife*
What lamb, what ladybird!—Fast, I warrant.—
What Juliet! Well, let the County take you in your bed.
Ye sleep for a week now, but the next night
The County Paris hath set up his rest
That you shall rest but little. What lamb, I say!—
Fast still.—What lady, love, what bride, what Juliet!—
Gods me, how sound she sleeps.—Nay, then I see
I must wake you indeed. What's here,
Laid on your bed, dressed in your clothes, and down?—
Ah me, alack the day! Some aqua-vitae, ho!
Enter Capulet's Wife

4.4.23–32 **What lamb . . . ho!** These lines, which Q1 sets as prose, have been relined as verse (Q2 prints them as verse) to make their rhythm audible.

CAPULET'S WIFE How now, what's the matter?

NURSE
Alack the day, she's dead, she's dead, she's dead!

CAPULET'S WIFE
Accursed, unhappy, miserable time!

Enter Capulet

CAPULET Come, come, make haste! Where's my daughter?

CAPULET'S WIFE Ah she's dead, she's dead.

CAPULET Stay, let me see—all pale and wan.
Accursèd time, unfortunate old man.

Enter Friar Laurence and the County Paris

PARIS
What, is the bride ready to go to church?

CAPULET
Ready to go, but never to return.
O son, the night before thy wedding-day
Hath death lain with thy bride. Flower as she is,
Deflowered by him, see where she lies.
Death is my son-in-law. To him I give all that I have.

PARIS
Have I thought long to see this morning's face,
And doth it now present such prodigies?
Accursed, unhappy, miserable man;
Forlorn, forsaken, destitute I am;
Born to the world to be a slave in it;
Distressed, remediless, and unfortunate.
O heavens, O nature, wherefore did you make me
To live so vile, so wretched as I shall?

CAPULET
O here she lies that was our hope, our joy,
And being dead, dead sorrow nips us all.

All at once cry out and wring their hands

ALL
And all our joy, and all our hope is dead;
Dead, lost, undone, absented, wholly fled.

CAPULET
Cruel, unjust, impartial destinies,
Why to this day have you preserved my life,
To see my hope, my stay, my joy, my life,
Deprived of sense, of life, of all by death,
Cruel, unjust, impartial destinies?
O sad-faced sorrow, map of misery,
Why this sad time have I desired to see,

This day, this unjust, this impartial day,
Wherein I hoped to see my comfort full,
To be deprived by sudden destiny?

CAPULET'S WIFE

O woe, alack, distressed, why should I live
To see this day, this miserable day?
Alack the time that ever I was born
To be partaker of this destiny!
Alack the day, alack and welladay!

FRIAR LAURENCE

O peace, for shame, if not for charity!
Your daughter lives in peace and happiness,
And it is vain to wish it otherwise.
Come, stick your rosemary in this dead corse;
And as the custom of our country is,
In all her best and sumptuous ornaments,
Convey her where her ancestors lie tombed.

CAPULET

Let it be so. Come, woeful sorrow-mates,
Let us together taste this bitter fate.

They all but the Nurse go forth, casting rosemary on Juliet and shutting the curtains.

Enter Musicians

NURSE

Put up, put up, this is a woeful case. *Exit*

FIRST MUSICIAN Ay, by my troth, mistress, is it; it had need be mended.

Enter a Serving-man

SERVING-MAN Alack, alack, what shall I do? Come, fiddlers, play me some merry dump.

FIRST MUSICIAN Ah, sir, this is no time to play.

SERVING-MAN You will not then?

FIRST MUSICIAN No, marry, will we.

SERVING-MAN Then will I give it you, and soundly too.

FIRST MUSICIAN What will you give us?

SERVING-MAN The fiddler—I'll re you, I'll fa you, I'll sol you.

FIRST MUSICIAN If you re us and fa us, we will note you.

SERVING-MAN I will put up my iron dagger and beat you with my wooden wit. Come, Simon Soundpost, I'll pose you.

FIRST MUSICIAN Let's hear.

SERVING-MAN

When griping grief the heart doth wound,

65 **impartial** *OED a.* 3 cites this as the first example of *impartial* misused for 'partial'.

And doleful dumps the mind oppress,
Then music with her silver sound—
Why 'silver sound'? Why 'silver sound'?

FIRST MUSICIAN I think because music hath a sweet sound.

SERVING-MAN Pretty. What say you, Matthew Minikin?

SECOND MUSICIAN I think because musicians sound for silver.

SERVING-MAN Pretty too. Come, what say you?

THIRD MUSICIAN I say nothing.

SERVING-MAN I think so. I'll speak for you because you are the singer. I say 'silver sound' because such fellows as you have seldom gold for sounding. Farewell, fiddlers, farewell.

Exit

FIRST MUSICIAN Farewell and be hanged! Come, let's go.

Exeunt

5.1 *Enter Romeo*

ROMEO

If I may trust the flattering eye of sleep,
My dream presaged some good event to come.
My bosom-lord sits cheerful in his throne,
And I am comforted with pleasing dreams.
Methought I was this night already dead—
Strange dreams that give a dead man leave to think—
And that my lady Juliet came to me,
And breathed such life with kisses in my lips
That I revived and was an emperor.

Enter Romeo's man Balthazar, booted

News from Verona! How now, Balthazar?
How doth my lady? Is my father well?
How fares my Juliet? That I ask again.
If she be well, then nothing can be ill.

BALTHAZAR

Then nothing can be ill, for she is well.
Her body sleeps in Capels' monument,
And her immortal parts with angels dwell.
Pardon me, sir, that am the messenger
Of such bad tidings.

ROMEO

Is it even so? Then I defy my stars!
Go, get me ink and paper, hire post-horse.

102 **Minikin** 'A thin string of gut used for the treble string of the lute or viol' (*OED* *sb.* 2a).

5.1.17–18 **Pardon . . . tidings** Q1 prints these lines as one long verse.

20 **post-horse** i.e. post-horses (*horse* was used as a plural form until the seventeenth century (*OED* *sb.* 1b)). For a

I will not stay in Mantua tonight.

BALTHAZAR

Pardon me, sir, I will not leave you thus;
Your looks are dangerous and full of fear.
I dare not, nor I will not leave you yet.

ROMEO

Do as I bid thee; get me ink and paper,
And hire those horse. Stay not, I say. *Exit Balthazar*
Well, Juliet, I will lie with thee tonight.
Let's see for means. As I do remember,
Here dwells a 'pothecary whom oft I noted
As I passed by, whose needy shop is stuffed
With beggarly accounts of empty boxes;
And in the same an alligator hangs,
Old ends of packthread, and cakes of roses
Are thinly strewèd to make up a show.
Him as I noted, thus with myself I thought:
'An if a man should need a poison now,
Whose present sale is death in Mantua,
Here he might buy it'. This thought of mine
Did but forerun my need; and hereabout he dwells.
Being holiday, the beggar's shop is shut.
What ho, Apothecary, come forth I say!

Enter Apothecary

APOTHECARY

Who calls? What would you, sir?

ROMEO

Here's twenty ducats.
Give me a dram of some such speeding gear
As will dispatch the weary taker's life
As suddenly as powder being fired
From forth a cannon's mouth.

APOTHECARY

Such drugs I have, I must of force confess,
But yet the law is death to those that sell them.

ROMEO

Art thou so bare and full of poverty,
And dost thou fear to violate the law?
The law is not thy friend, nor the law's friend,
And therefore make no conscience of the law.

definition of *post-horse*, see 5.1.25–6n. in the edition of Q2.

47 **of force** perforce, necessarily

51 **nor the** There may be an ellipsis of the nominative 'thou' between these words (Abbott 399).

52 **make no conscience** have no scruples about (*OED*, *conscience*, 11)

Upon thy back hangs ragged misery,
And starvèd famine dwelleth in thy cheeks.

APOTHECARY
My poverty, but not my will, consents.

ROMEO
I pay thy poverty, but not thy will.

APOTHECARY Hold, take you this,
And put it in any liquid thing you will;
And it will serve, had you the lives of twenty men.

ROMEO
Hold, take this gold, worse poison to men's souls
Than this which thou hast given me. Go, hie thee hence;
Go, buy thee clothes, and get thee into flesh.

Exit Apothecary

Come, cordial and not poison, go with me
To Juliet's grave, for there must I use thee. *Exit*

5.2 *Enter Friar John*

FRIAR JOHN
What, Friar Laurence, brother, ho!

Enter Friar Laurence

FRIAR LAURENCE
This same should be the voice of Friar John.—
What news from Mantua? What, will Romeo come?

FRIAR JOHN
Going to seek a barefoot brother out,
One of our order to associate me,
Here in this city visiting the sick,
Whereas the infectious pestilence remained,
And being by the searchers of the town
Found and examined, we were both shut up.

FRIAR LAURENCE
Who bare my letters then to Romeo?

FRIAR JOHN
I have them still, and here they are.

FRIAR LAURENCE Now by my holy order,
The letters were not nice but of great weight.
Go, get thee hence, and get me presently
A spade and mattock.

FRIAR JOHN
Well, I will presently go fetch thee them. *Exit*

57–9 **Hold . . . men** Q1 prints these lines as prose in what is otherwise a verse passage; they sound metrically irregular even when relined.

FRIAR LAURENCE

Now must I to the monument alone,
Lest that the lady should, before I come,
Be waked from sleep. I will hie
To free her from that tomb of misery. *Exit*

5.3 *Enter the County Paris and his Page, with flowers and sweet water*

PARIS

Put out the torch, and lie thee all along
Under this yew tree,
Keeping thine ear close to the hollow ground;
And if thou hear one tread within this churchyard,
Straight give me notice.

PAGE I will, my lord.

He retires.

Paris strews the tomb with flowers

PARIS

Sweet flower, with flowers I strew thy bridal bed,
Sweet tomb that in thy circuit dost contain
The perfect model of eternity;
Fair Juliet, that with angels dost remain,
Accept this latest favour at my hands,
That living honoured thee, and being dead,
With funeral praises do adorn thy tomb.

The Page whistles and calls

PAGE My lord!

Enter Romeo and Balthazar, with a torch, a mattock, and a crow of iron

PARIS

The boy gives warning, something doth approach.
What cursèd foot wanders this way tonight,
To stay my obsequies and true love's rites?
What, with a torch? Muffle me, night, a while.

He retires

ROMEO

Give me this mattock and this wrenching-iron;
And take these letters early in the morning,
See thou deliver them to my lord and father.
So get thee gone and trouble me no more.
Why I descend into this bed of death
Is partly to behold my lady's face,

5.3.2–3 **Under . . . ground** Q1 prints these lines as one long verse.

But chiefly to take from her dead finger
A precious ring which I must use
In dear employment. But if thou wilt stay,
Further to pry in what I undertake,
By heaven, I'll tear thee joint by joint,
And strew this hungry churchyard with thy limbs.
The time and my intents are savage-wild.

BALTHAZAR
Well, I'll be gone and not trouble you.

ROMEO
So shalt thou win my favour. Take thou this.
Commend me to my father. Farewell, good fellow.

BALTHAZAR
Yet, for all this, will I not part from hence.
He retires.
Romeo opens the tomb

ROMEO
Thou detestable maw, thou womb of death,
Gorged with the dearest morsel of the earth,
Thus I enforce thy rotten jaws to ope.

PARIS
This is that banished haughty Montague
That murdered my love's cousin. I will apprehend him.
He comes forward
Stop thy unhallowed toil, vile Montague!
Can vengeance be pursued further than death?
I do attach thee as a felon here.
The law condemns thee; therefore thou must die.

ROMEO
I must indeed, and therefore came I hither.
Good youth, be gone, tempt not a desperate man.
Heap not another sin upon my head
By shedding of thy blood. I do protest,
I love thee better than I love myself,
For I come hither armed against myself.

PARIS
I do defy thy conjurations,
And do attach thee as a felon here.

ROMEO
What, dost thou tempt me? Then have at thee, boy!
They fight

PAGE
O Lord, they fight! I will go call the watch. *Exit*

PARIS

Ah, I am slain! If thou be merciful,
Open the tomb, lay me with Juliet. *He dies*

ROMEO

I'faith, I will. Let me peruse this face.
Mercutio's kinsman, noble County Paris!
What said my man when my betossèd soul
Did not regard him as we passed along?
Did he not say Paris should have married Juliet?
Either he said so, or I dreamed it so.—
But I will satisfy thy last request,
For thou hast prized thy love above thy life.
Death, lie thou there, by a dead man interred.—
How oft have many, at the hour of death,
Been blithe and pleasant, which their keepers call
A light'ning before death. But how may I
Call this a light'ning? Ah dear Juliet,
How well thy beauty doth become this grave.
O, I believe that unsubstantial death
Is amorous, and doth court my love.
Therefore will I, O here, O ever here,
Set up my everlasting rest
With worms that are thy chambermaids.
Come, desperate pilot, now at once run on
The dashing rocks thy sea-sick weary barge.
Here's to my love!

He drinks the poison

O true Apothecary,
Thy drugs are swift. Thus with a kiss I die. *He falls*

Enter Friar Laurence with a lantern

FRIAR LAURENCE

How oft tonight have these my aged feet
Stumbled at graves as I did pass along.
Who's there?

BALTHAZAR A friend, and one that knows you well.

FRIAR LAURENCE

Who is it that consorts so late the dead?
What light is yon? If I be not deceived,
Methinks it burns in Capels' monument.

BALTHAZAR

It doth so, holy sir, and there is one
That loves you dearly.

76 **barge** bark (*OED sb.*[1] 1a)

FRIAR LAURENCE Who is it?
BALTHAZAR Romeo.
FRIAR LAURENCE How long hath he been there?
BALTHAZAR Full half an hour and more.
FRIAR LAURENCE Go with me thither.
BALTHAZAR
I dare not, sir; he knows not I am here.
On pain of death he charged me to be gone,
And not for to disturb him in his enterprise.
FRIAR LAURENCE
Then must I go. My mind presageth ill.
Friar Laurence moves towards the tomb, stoops, and looks on the blood and weapons
What blood is this that stains the entrance
Of this marble stony monument?
What means these masterless and gory weapons?
Ah me, I doubt. Who's here? What, Romeo dead?
Who—and Paris too? What unlucky hour
Is accessory to so foul a sin?
Juliet rises
The lady stirs.
JULIET Ah, comfortable Friar,
I do remember well where I should be,
And what we talked of; but yet I cannot see
Him for whose sake I undertook this hazard.
FRIAR LAURENCE
Lady, come forth. I hear some noise at hand.
We shall be taken. Paris, he is slain,
And Romeo dead; and if we here be ta'en,
We shall be thought to be as accessory.
I will provide for you in some close nunnery.
JULIET
Ah leave me, leave me, I will not from hence.
FRIAR LAURENCE
I hear some noise, I dare not stay. Come, come.
JULIET Go, get thee gone.
What's here? A cup closed in my lover's hands?
Ah churl, drink all, and leave no drop for me?
Enter Watchmen
CHIEF WATCHMAN This way, this way.

5.3.114, 118, 123, 124, 126 CHIEF WATCHMAN] Q2 (*Watch.*); *Cap;* or *Capt:* Q1

92 **for to** to (Abbott 152)

94 **entrance** (pronounced as three syllables)

JULIET
Ay, noise? Then must I be resolute.
O happy dagger, thou shalt end my fear;
Rest in my bosom. Thus I come to thee.
She stabs herself and falls

CHIEF WATCHMAN (*coming forward*)
Come, look about, what weapons have we here?
See, friends, where Juliet, two days burièd,
New bleeding, wounded—search and see who's near;
Attach and bring them to us presently.
Enter a Watchman with Friar Laurence

[SECOND] WATCHMAN
Captain, here's a friar with tools about him
Fit to ope a tomb.

CHIEF WATCHMAN A great suspicion. Keep him safe.
Enter a Watchman with Balthazar

[THIRD] WATCHMAN
Here's Romeo's man.

CHIEF WATCHMAN Keep him to be examined.
Enter the Prince with others

PRINCE
What early mischief calls us up so soon?

CHIEF WATCHMAN O noble Prince, see here,
Where Juliet, that hath lain entombed two days,
Warm and fresh bleeding, Romeo and County Paris
Likewise newly slain.

PRINCE
Search, seek about, to find the murderers.
Enter old Capulet and his Wife

CAPULET
What rumour's this that is so early up?

CAPULET'S WIFE
The people in the streets cry 'Romeo',
And some on 'Juliet', as if they alone
Had been the cause of such a mutiny.

CAPULET
See, wife, this dagger hath mistook,
For lo, the back is empty of young Montague,
And it is sheathèd in our daughter's breast.
Enter old Montague

124 [THIRD] WATCHMAN] This edition; 1. Q1

127–9 **Where . . . slain** There may be an ellipsis of at least one verb in these lines, probably a form or forms of 'to be', which accounts for *Juliet*, *Romeo*, and *Paris* being in the tomb (Abbott 382).

PRINCE

Come, Montague, for thou art early up
To see thy son and heir more early down.

MONTAGUE

Dread sovereign, my wife is dead tonight,
And young Benvolio is deceasèd too.
What further mischief can there yet be found?

PRINCE

First come and see, then speak.

MONTAGUE

O thou untaught! What manners is in this,
To press before thy father to a grave?

PRINCE

Come, seal your mouths of outrage for a while,
And let us seek to find the authors out
Of such a heinous and seldseen mischance.
Bring forth the parties in suspicion.

FRIAR LAURENCE

I am the greatest, able to do least.
Most worthy Prince, hear me but speak the truth,
And I'll inform you how these things fell out.
Juliet, here slain, was married to that Romeo
Without her father's or her mother's grant.
The Nurse was privy to the marriage.
The baleful day of this unhappy marriage
Was Tybalt's doomsday, for which Romeo
Was banishèd from hence to Mantua.
He gone, her father sought by foul constraint
To marry her to Paris. But her soul,
Loathing a second contract, did refuse
To give consent; and therefore did she urge me,
Either to find a means she might avoid
What so her father sought to force her to,
Or else all desperately she threatened,
Even in my presence, to dispatch herself.
Then did I give her—tutored by mine art—
A potion that should make her seem as dead;
And told her that I would with all post-speed
Send hence to Mantua for her Romeo,
That he might come and take her from the tomb.

148 **seldseen** seldom to be seen

154 **grant** permission (*OED sb.*[1] 1a; cf. 2.5.1)

155 **marriage** (pronounced as three syllables)

169 **post-speed** the speed of a courier or a post-horse (*OED*, *post*, *sb.*[2] 12f)

But he that had my letters, Friar John,
Seeking a brother to associate him,
Whereas the sick infection remained,
Was stayèd by the searchers of the town.
But Romeo, understanding by his man
That Juliet was deceased, returned in post
Unto Verona for to see his love.
What after happened, touching Paris' death
Or Romeo's, is to me unknown at all.
But when I came to take the lady hence,
I found them dead, and she awaked from sleep,
Whom fain I would have taken from the tomb,
Which she refusèd, seeing Romeo dead.
Anon I heard the watch, and then I fled.
What after happened I am ignorant of.
And if in this aught have miscarrièd
By me or by my means, let my old life
Be sacrificed some hour before his time
To the most strictest rigour of the law.

PRINCE
We still have known thee for a holy man.
Where's Romeo's man? What can he say in this?

BALTHAZAR
I brought my master word that she was dead,
And then he posted straight from Mantua
Unto this tomb. These letters he delivered me,
Charging me early give them to his father.

PRINCE
Let's see the letters; I will read them over.
Where is the County's boy that called the watch?

PAGE
I brought my master unto Juliet's grave,
But one approaching, straight I called my master.
At last they fought, I ran to call the watch;
And this is all that I can say or know.

PRINCE
These letters do make good the Friar's words.
Come, Capulet, and come, old Montague.
Where are these enemies? See what hate hath done.

CAPULET
Come, brother Montague, give me thy hand.

174 **infection** (pronounced as four syllables)
177 **post** haste (*OED sb.*[2] 8d)
190 **most strictest rigour** See Abbott 11 on the double superlative.

There is my daughter's dowry, for now no more
Can I bestow on her. That's all I have.

MONTAGUE

But I will give them more; I will erect
Her statue of pure gold,
That while Verona by that name is known,
There shall no statue of such price be set
As that of Romeo's lovèd Juliet.

CAPULET

As rich shall Romeo by his lady lie,
Poor sacrifices to our enmity.

PRINCE

A gloomy peace this day doth with it bring.
Come, let us hence to have more talk of these sad things;
Some shall be pardoned and some punishèd.
For ne'er was heard a story of more woe
Than this of Juliet and her Romeo. *Exeunt*

217 **Come . . . things** This line combines two short verses printed in Q1.

INDEX

This is a selective guide to points in the Introduction and Commentary of more than routine note. Biblical allusions are grouped together; proverbs and proverbial allusions (over 200 noted in the Commentary) are not indexed. Asterisks identify entries which supplement the *Oxford English Dictionary*. Obliques and/or square brackets identify puns.

A SELECTION OF **OXFORD WORLD'S CLASSICS**

	Oriental Tales
William Beckford	**Vathek**
James Boswell	**Boswell's Life of Johnson**
Frances Burney	**Camilla** **Cecilia** **Evelina** **The Wanderer**
Lord Chesterfield	**Lord Chesterfield's Letters**
John Cleland	**Memoirs of a Woman of Pleasure**
Daniel Defoe	**Captain Singleton** **A Journal of the Plague Year** **Memoirs of a Cavalier** **Moll Flanders** **Robinson Crusoe** **Roxana**
Henry Fielding	**Joseph Andrews and Shamela** **A Journey from This World to the Next and The Journal of a Voyage to Lisbon** **Tom Jones** **The Adventures of David Simple**
William Godwin	**Caleb Williams** **St Leon**
Oliver Goldsmith	**The Vicar of Wakefield**
Mary Hays	**Memoirs of Emma Courtney**
Elizabeth Haywood	**The History of Miss Betsy Thoughtless**
Elizabeth Inchbald	**A Simple Story**
Samuel Johnson	**The History of Rasselas**
Charlotte Lennox	**The Female Quixote**
Matthew Lewis	**The Monk**

A SELECTION OF **OXFORD WORLD'S CLASSICS**

Ann Radcliffe	**The Castles of Athlin and Dunbayne** **The Italian** **The Mysteries of Udolpho** **The Romance of the Forest** **A Sicilian Romance**
Frances Sheridan	**Memoirs of Miss Sidney Bidulph**
Tobias Smollett	**The Adventures of Roderick Random** **The Expedition of Humphry Clinker** **Travels through France and Italy**
Laurence Sterne	**The Life and Opinions of Tristram Shandy, Gentleman** **A Sentimental Journey**
Jonathan Swift	**Gulliver's Travels** **A Tale of a Tub and Other Works**
Horace Walpole	**The Castle of Otranto**
Gilbert White	**The Natural History of Selborne**
Mary Wollstonecraft	**Mary and The Wrongs of Woman**